1 MONTH OF
FREE
READING

at

www.ForgottenBooks.com

By purchasing this book you are eligible for one month membership to ForgottenBooks.com, giving you unlimited access to our entire collection of over 1,000,000 titles via our web site and mobile apps.

To claim your free month visit:

www.forgottenbooks.com/free928247

ISBN 978-0-260-10438-0
PIBN 10928247

AS YOU LIKE IT.

ACT I. SCENE I.

An Orchard, near Oliver's *House.*

Enter ORLANDO *and* ADAM.

ORL. As I remember, Adam, it was upon this fashion bequeathed me: By will, but a poor thousand crowns; and, as thou say'st, charged my brother, on his blessing, to breed me well:[2] and there begins my sadness. My brother Jaques he keeps

---

[2] *As I remember, Adam, it was upon this* fashion *bequeathed me: By will, but a poor thousand crowns;* &c.] The grammar, as well as sense, suffers cruelly by this reading. There are two nominatives to the verb *bequeathed*, and not so much as one to the verb *charged*: and yet, to the nominative there wanted, [*his blessing*] refers. So that the whole sentence is confused and obscure. A very small alteration in the reading and pointing sets all right.—*As I remember, Adam, it was upon this* my father *bequeathed me*, &c. The grammar is now rectified, and the sense also; which is this. Orlando and Adam were discoursing together on the cause why the younger brother had but a thousand crowns left him. They agree upon it; and Orlando opens the scene in this manner, *As I remember, it was upon this*, i. e. for the reason we have been talking of, that my father left me but a thousand crowns; however, to make amends for this scanty provision, he charged my brother on his blessing to breed me well. WARBURTON.

There is, in my opinion, nothing but a point misplaced, and an omission of a word which every hearer can supply, and which therefore an abrupt and eager dialogue naturally excludes.

I read thus: *As I remember, Adam, it was on this fashion bequeathed me. By will, but a poor thousand crowns; and, as thou sayest, charged my brother, on his blessing, to breed me well.* What is there in this difficult or obscure? The nominative *my father* is certainly left out, but so left out that the auditor inserts it, in spite of himself. JOHNSON.

at school, and report speaks goldenly of his profit: for my part, he keeps me rustically at home, or, to speak more properly, stays me here at home un-kept: ³ For call you that keeping for a gentleman of my birth, that differs not from the stalling of an ox? His horses are bred better; for, besides that they are fair with their feeding, they are taught their manage, and to that end riders dearly hired: but I, his brother, gain nothing under him but growth; for the which his animals on his dung-hills are as much bound to him as I. Besides this nothing that he so plentifully gives me, the some-thing that nature gave me, his countenance seems to take from me: ⁴ he lets me feed with his hinds,

---

—— *it was on this fashion bequeathed me,* as Dr. Johnson reads, is but aukward English. I would read: *As I remember, Adam, it was on this fashion.*—He *bequeathed me by will,* &c. Orlando and Adam enter abruptly in the midst of a conversation on this topick; and Orlando is correcting some misapprehension of the other. As *I* remember (says he) it was thus. He left me a thousand crowns; and, *as thou sayest,* charged my brother, &c.
BLACKSTONE.

Omission being of all the errors of the press the most common, I have adopted the emendation proposed by Sir W. Blackstone.
MALONE.

Being satisfied with Dr. Johnson's explanation of the passage as it stands in the old copy, I have followed it. STEEVENS.

³ Stays *me here at home unkept:*] We should read *stys,* i. e. keeps me like a brute. The following words—*for call you that keeping— that differs not from the stalling of an ox?* confirms this emendation. So Caliban says,

　　" And here you *sty* me
　　" In this hard rock." WARBURTON.

Sties is better than *stays,* and more likely to be Shakspeare's.
JOHNSON.

So, in *Noah's Flood,* by Drayton:
　　" And *sty* themselves up in a little room." STEEVENS.

⁴ —— *his countenance seems to take from me:*] We should cer-tainly read—*his* discountenance. WARBURTON.

There is no need of change; a countenance is either good or bad. JOHNSON.

bars me the place of a brother, and, as much as in him lies, mines my gentility with my education. This is it, Adam, that grieves me; and the ſpirit of my father, which I think is within me, begins to mutiny againſt this ſervitude: I will no longer endure it, though yet I know no wiſe remedy how to avoid it.

Enter OLIVER.

ADAM. Yonder comes my maſter, your brother.

ORL. Go apart, Adam, and thou ſhalt hear how he will ſhake me up.

OLI. Now, ſir! what make you here?[5]

ORL. Nothing: I am not taught to make any thing.

OLI. What mar you then, ſir?

ORL. Marry, ſir, I am helping you to mar that which God made, a poor unworthy brother of yours, with idleneſs.

OLI. Marry, ſir, be better employ'd, and be naught awhile.[6]

---

[5] —— *what* make you *here?*] i. e. what do you here? So, in *Hamlet :*

" What *make you* at Elſinour?" STEEVENS.

[6] —— *be better employ'd, and* be naught a while.] Mr. Theobald has here a very critical note; which, though his modeſty ſuffered him to withdraw it from his ſecond edition, deſerves to be perpetuated, i. e. (ſays he) *be better employed, in my opinion, in being and doing nothing. Your idleneſs, as you call it, may be an exerciſe by which you make a figure, and endear yourſelf to the world: and I had rather you were a contemptible cypher. The poet ſeems to me to have that trite proverbial ſentiment in his eye, quoted from Attilius, by the younger Pliny and others;* ſatius eſt otioſum eſſe quàm nihil agere. *But Oliver, in the perverſeneſs of his diſpoſition, would reverſe the doctrine of the proverb.* Does the reader know what all this means? But 'tis no matter. I will aſſure him—*be nought a*

ORL. Shall I keep your hogs, and eat hufks with them? What prodigal portion have I fpent, that I fhould come to fuch penury?

while is only a north-country proverbial curfe equivalent to, *a mifchief on you.* So, the old poet Skelton:

"" Correct firft thy felfe, walk and *be nought,*
"" Deeme what thou lift, thou knoweft not my thought."

But what the Oxford editor could not explain, he would amend, and reads:

——— *and do aught a while.* WARBURTON.

If *be nought awhile* has the fignification here given it, the reading may certainly ftand; but till I learned its meaning from this note, I read:

Be better employed, and be naught *a while,*

In the fame fenfe as we fay,——*It is better to do mifchief, than to do nothing.* JOHNSON.

Notwithftanding Dr. Warburton's far-fetched explanation, I believe that the words *be naught awhile,* mean no more than this: "" Be content to be a *cypher,* till I fhall think fit to elevate you into confequence."

This was certainly a proverbial faying, I find it in *The Storie of King Darius,* an interlude, 1565:

"" Come away, *and be nought a whyle,*
"" Or furely I will you both defyle."

Again, in *King Henry IV.* P. II. Falftaff fays to Piftol: "" Nay, if he do nothing but fpeak nothing, *he fhall be nothing* here."

STEEVENS.

Naught and *nought* are frequently confounded in old Englifh books. I once thought that the latter was here intended, in the fenfe affixed to it by Mr. Steevens: "" Be content to be a *cypher,* till I fhall elevate you into confequence." But the following paffage in *Swetnam,* a comedy, 1620, induces me to think that the reading of the old copy (*naught*) and Dr. Johnfon's explanation are right:

"" ——— get you both in, and be *naught a while.*"

The fpeaker is a chamber-maid, and fhe addreffes herfelf to her miftrefs and her lover. MALONE.

Malone fays that *nought* (meaning *nothing*) was formerly fpelled with an *a,* *naught;* which is clearly the manner in which it ought ftill to be fpelled, as the word *aught* (any thing) from whence it is derived, is fpelled fo.

A fimilar expreffion occurs in *Bartholomew Fair,* where Urfula fays to Mooncalf: "" Leave the bottle behind you, and *be curs'd awhile;*" which feems to confirm Warburton's explanation. M. MASON.

OLI. Know you where you are, fir?

ORL. O, fir, very well: here in your orchard.

OLI. Know you before whom, fir?

ORL. Ay, better than he I am before knows me.[1] I know, you are my eldeft brother; and, in the gentle condition of blood, you fhould fo know me: The courtefy of nations allows you my better, in that you are the firft-born; but the fame tradition takes not away my blood, were there twenty bro- thers betwixt us: I have as much of my father in me, as you; albeit, I confefs, your coming before me is nearer to his reverence.[2]

OLI. What, boy!

ORL. Come, come, elder brother, you are too young in this.

---

[1] *Ay, better than* he *I am before knows me.*] The firft folio reads—*better than* him—. But, little refpect is due to the anomalies of the play-houfe editors; and of this comedy there is no quarto edition. STEEVENS.

Mr. Pope and the fubfequent editors read—*he* I am before; more correctly, but without authority. Our author is equally irregular in *The Winter's Tale:*
      " I am appointed *him* to murder you." MALONE.

Of *The Winter's Tale* alfo there is none but the play-houfe copy. STEEVENS.

[2] ——*albeit, I confefs, your coming before me is nearer to his* reverence.] This is fenfe indeed, and may be thus underftood.—The reverence due to my father is, in fome degree, derived to you, as the firft born. But I am perfuaded that Orlando did not here mean to compliment his brother, or condemn himfelf; fomething of both which there is in that fenfe. I rather think he intended a fatirical reflection on his brother, who by *letting him feed with his hinds,* treated him as one not fo nearly related to old Sir Rowland as himfelf was. I imagine therefore Shakfpeare might write,—*Albeit your coming before me is nearer his* revenue, i. e. though you are no nearer in blood, yet it muft be owned, indeed, you are nearer in eftate. WARBURTON.

This, I apprehend, refers to the courtefy of diftinguifhing the *eldeft fon* of a knight, by the title of efquire. HENLEY.

Oli. Wilt thou lay hands on me, villain?

Orl. I am no villain:[9] I am the youngeſt ſon of ſir Rowland de Bois; he was my father; and he is thrice a villain, that ſays, ſuch a father begot villains: Wert thou not my brother, I would not take this hand from thy throat, till this other had pulled out thy tongue for ſaying ſo; thou haſt railed on thyſelf.

Adam. Sweet maſters, be patient; for your father's remembrance, be at accord.

Oli. Let me go, I ſay.

Orl. I will not, till I pleaſe: you ſhall hear me. My father charged you in his will to give me good education: you have trained me like a peaſant, obſcuring and hiding from me all gentleman-like qualities: the ſpirit of my father grows ſtrong in me, and I will no longer endure it: therefore allow me ſuch exerciſes as may become a gentleman, or give me the poor allottery my father left me by teſtament; with that I will go buy my fortunes.

Oli. And what wilt thou do? beg, when that is ſpent? Well, ſir, get you in: I will not long be troubled with you: you ſhall have ſome part of your will: I pray you, leave me.

Orl. I will no further offend you than becomes me for my good.

Oli. Get you with him, you old dog.

Adam. Is old dog my reward? Moſt true, I have loſt my teeth in your ſervice.—God be with my old maſter! he would not have ſpoke ſuch a word.

[*Exeunt* ORLANDO *and* ADAM.

---

9 *I am no* villain:] The word *villain* is uſed by the elder brother, in its preſent meaning, for a *worthleſs, wicked,* or *bloody man*; by Orlando in its original ſignification, for a *fellow of baſe extraction.*
JOHNSON.

OLI. Is it even fo? begin you to grow upon me? I will phyfick your ranknefs, and yet give no thoufand crowns neither. Hola, Dennis!

Enter DENNIS.

DEN. Calls your worfhip?

OLI. Was not Charles, the duke's wreftler, here to fpeak with me?

DEN. So pleafe you, he is here at the door, and importunes accefs to you.

OLI. Call him in. [*Exit* DENNIS.]—'Twill be a good way; and to-morrow the wreftling is.

Enter CHARLES.

CHA. Good morrow to your worfhip.

OLI. Good monfieur Charles!—what's the new news at the new court?

CHA. There's no news at the court, fir, but the old news: that is, the old duke is banifhed by his younger brother the new duke; and three or four loving lords have put themfelves into voluntary exile with him, whofe lands and revenues enrich the new duke; therefore he gives them good leave² to wander.

OLI. Can you tell, if Rofalind, the duke's daughter,³ be banifhed with her father.

---

² ——*good leave* —] As often as this phrafe occurs, it means a *ready affent.* So, in *King John:*
   " *Baft.* James Gurney, wilt thou give us leave awhile?
   " *Gur. Good leave,* good Philip." STEEVENS.

³ ——*the duke's daughter,*] The words *old* and *new* [inferted by Sir T. Hanmer] feem neceffary to the perfpicuity of the dialogue. JOHNSON.

Cha. O, no; for the duke's daughter,[1] her cou-fin, fo loves her,—being ever from their cradles bred together,—that fhe would have followed her exile, or have died to ftay behind her. She is at the court, and no lefs beloved of her uncle than his own daughter; and never two ladies loved as they do.

Oli. Where will the old duke live?

Cha. They fay, he is already in the foreft of Ar-den,[4] and a many merry men with him; and there they live like the old Robin Hood of England: they fay, many young gentlemen flock to him every day; and fleet the time carelefsly, as they did in the golden world.

Oli. What, you wreftle to-morrow before the new duke?

Cha. Marry, do I, fir; and I came to acquaint you with a matter. I am given, fir, fecretly to un-

———

——*the duke's daughter,*] i. e. the *banifhed* duke's daughter.
MALONE.

The author of *The Revifal* is of opinion, that the fubfequent words,—*her coufin,* fufficiently diftinguifh the perfon intended.
STEEVENS.

[3] ——*for the duke's daughter,*] i. e. the *ufurping* duke's daughter. Sir T. Hanmer reads here—the *new* duke's; and in the preceding fpeech—the *old* duke's daughter; but in my opinion unneceffarily. The ambiguous ufe of the word *duke* in thefe paffages is much in our author's manner. MALONE.

[4] ——*in the foreft of* Arden,] *Ardenne* is a foreft of confiderable extent in French Flanders, lying near the Meufe, and between Charlemont and Rocroy. It is mentioned by Spenfer, in his *Colin Clout's come home again,* 1595:

"Into a foreft wide and wafte he came,
"Where ftore he heard to be of favage prey;
"So wide a foreft, and fo wafte as this,
"Not famous *Ardeyn,* nor foul Arlo is."

But our author was furnifhed with the fcene of his play by Lodge's Novel. MALONE.

derftand, that your younger brother, Orlando, hath a difpofition to come in difguis'd againſt me to try a fall: To-morrow, fir, I wreſtle for my credit; and he that efcapes me without fome broken limb, ſhall acquit him well. Your brother is but young, and tender; and, for your love, I would be loth to foil him, as I muſt, for my own honour, if he come in: therefore, out of my love to you, I came hither to acquaint you withal; that either you might ſtay him from his intendment, or brook fuch difgrace well as he ſhall run into; in that it is a thing of his own fearch, and altogether againſt my will.

OLI. Charles, I thank thee for thy love to me, which thou ſhalt find I will moſt kindly requite. I had myfelf notice of my brother's purpofe herein, and have by underhand means laboured to diffuade him from it; but he is refolute. I'll tell thee, Charles, —it is the ſtubborneſt young fellow of France; full of ambition, an envious emulator of every man's good parts, a fecret and villainous contriver againſt me his natural brother; therefore ufe thy difcre‐ tion; I had as lief thou didſt break his neck as his finger: And thou wert beſt look to't; for if thou doſt him any ſlight difgrace, or if he do not mightily grace himfelf on thee, he will practife againſt thee by poifon, entrap thee by fome trea‐ cherous device, and never leave thee till he hath ta'en thy life by fome indirect means or other: for, I affure thee, and almoſt with tears I fpeak it, there is not one fo young and fo villainous this day living. I fpeak but brotherly of him; but ſhould I anatomize him to thee as he is, I muſt bluſh and weep, and thou muſt look pale and wonder.

CHA. I am heartily glad I came hither to you: If he come to-morrow, I'll give him his payment:

If ever he go alone again, I'll never wreftle for prize more : And fo, God keep your worfhip!

                           [*Exit.*

Oli. Farewell good Charles.—Now will I ftir this gamefter ? I hope, I fhall fee an end of him ; for my foul, yet I know not why, hates nothing more than he. Yet he's gentle; never fchool'd, and yet learned; full of noble device; of all forts [4] enchantingly beloved; and, indeed, fo much in the heart of the world, and efpecially of my own people, who beft know him, that I am altogether mifprifed : but it fhall not be fo long; this wreft-ler fhall clear all : nothing remains, but that I kin-dle the boy thither, [5] which now I'll go about.

                           [*Exit.*

SCENE II.

A Lawn before the Duke's *Palace.*

Enter ROSALIND *and* CELIA

Cel. I pray thee, Rofalind, fweet my coz, be merry.

Ros. Dear Celia, I fhow more mirth than I am miftrefs of; and would you yet I were merrier? [6]

---

[3] ——*this* gamefter:] *Gamefter,* in the prefent inftance, and fome others, does not fignify a man vicioufly addicted to games of chance, but a frolickfome perfon. Thus, in *King Henry VIII:*
   " You are a merry *gamefter,* my lord Sands." STEEVENS.

[4] ——*of all* forts—] *Sorts* in this place means ranks and degrees of men. RITSON.

[5] ——kindle *the boy thither,*] A fimilar phrafe occurs in *Macbeth,* Act I. fc. iii:
   " ——*enkindle* you unto the crown." STEEVENS.

[6] —— I *were merrier?*] *I* which was inadvertently omitted in the old copy, was inferted by Mr. Pope. MALONE.

I

Unlefs you could teach me to forget a banifhed fa_ther, you muft not learn me how to remember any extraordinary pleafure.

CEL. Herein, I fee, thou loveft me not with the full weight that I love thee: if my uncle, thy ba_nifhed father, had banifhed thy uncle, the duke my father, fo thou hadft been ftill with me, I could have taught my love to take thy father for mine; fo would'ft thou, if the truth of thy love to me were fo righteoufly temper'd as mine is to thee.

Ros. Well, I will forget the condition of my eftate, to rejoice in yours.

CEL. You know, my father hath no child but I, nor none is like to have; and, truly, when he dies, thou fhalt be his heir: for what he hath taken away from thy father perforce, I will render thee again in affeƈtion; by mine honour, I will; and when I break that oath, let me turn monfter: therefore, my fweet Rofe, my dear Rofe, be merry.

Ros. From henceforth I will, coz, and devife fports: let me fee; What think you of falling in love?

CEL. Marry, I pry'thee, do, to make fport withal: but love no man in good earneft; nor no further in fport neither, than with fafety of a pure blufh thou may'ft in honour come off again.

Ros. What fhall be our fport then?

CEL. Let us fit and mock the good houfewife, Fortune, from her wheel,[7] that her gifts may hence-forth be beftowed equally.

---

[7] ——*mock the good houfewife, Fortune, from her wheel,*] The wheel of Fortune is not the *wheel* of a *houfewife.* Shakfpeare has confounded Fortune, whofe wheel only figures uncertainty and

Ros. I would, we could do fo; for her benefits are mightily mifplaced: and the bountiful blind woman doth moft miftake in her gifts to women.·

Cel. 'Tis true: for thofe, that fhe makes fair, fhe fcarce makes honeft; and thofe, that fhe makes honeft, fhe makes very ill-favour'dly.

Ros. Nay, now thou goeft from fortune's office to nature's: fortune reigns in gifts of the world, not in the lineaments of nature.

Enter Touchstone.

Cel. No? When nature hath made a fair crea- ture, may fhe not by fortune fall into the fire?— Though nature hath given us wit to flout at fortune, hath not fortune fent in this fool to cut off the ar- gument?

Ros. Indeed, there is fortune too hard for na- ture; when fortune makes nature's natural the cut- ter off of nature's wit.

Cel. Peradventure, this is not fortune's work neither, but nature's; who perceiving our natural wits too dull to reafon of fuch goddeffes, hath fent this natural for our whetftone: for always the dul- nefs of the fool is the whetftone of the wits.—How now, wit? whither wander you?

---

viciffitude, with the deftiny that fpins the thread of life, though not indeed with a wheel. Johnson.

Shakfpeare is very fond of this idea. He has the fame in *Antony and Cleopatra*:

" —— and rail fo high,
" That the falfe houfewife, Fortune, break her wheel."

Steevens.

⁸ —— *who perceiving our natural wits too dull to reafon of fuch goddeffes, hath fent,* &c.] The old copy reads—" *perceiveth* —." Mr. Malone retains the old reading, but adds—" *and* hath fent," &c. Steevens.

Touch. Miſtreſs, you muſt come away to your father.

Cel. Were you made the meſſenger?

Touch. No, by mine honour; but I was bid to come for you.

Ros. Where learned you that oath, fool?

Touch. Of a certain knight, that ſwore by his honour they were good pancakes, and ſwore by his honou. the muſtard was naught: now, I'll ſtand to it, the pancakes were naught, and the muſtard was good; and yet was not the knight forſworn.

Cel. How prove you that, in the great heap of your knowledge?

Ros. Ay, marry; now unmuzzle your wiſdom.

Touch. Stand you both forth now: ſtroke your chins, and ſwear by your beards that I am a knave.

Cel. By our beards, if we had them, thou art.

Touch. By my knavery, if I had it, then I were: but if you ſwear by that that is not, you are not forſworn: no more was this knight, ſwearing by his honour, for he never had any; or if he had, he had ſworn it away, before ever he ſaw thoſe pan_cakes or that muſtard.

Cel. Pr'ythee, who is't that thou mean'ſt?

Touch. One that old Frederick, your father, loves.

Cel. My father's love is enough to honour him.[9]

9 Touch. *One that old* Frederick, *your father, loves.*
    Roſ. *My father's love is enough to honour him.*] This reply to the Clown is in all the books placed to Roſalind; but Frederick was not her father, but Celia's: I have therefore ventured to prefix the name of Celia. There is no countenance from any paſſage in the play, or from the *Dramatis Perſonæ*, to imagine, that both the Brother-Dukes were nameſakes; and one called the Old, and the other the Younger-Frederick; and without ſome ſuch authority, it would make confuſion to ſuppoſe it. THEOBALD.

Enough! fpeak no more of him; you'll be whip'd for taxation,[2] one of thefe days.

Touch. The more pity, that fools may not fpeak wifely, what wife men do foolifhly.

Cel. By my troth, thou fay'ft true: for fince the little wit, that fools have, was filenced,[3] the

Mr. Theobald feems not to know that the *Dramatis Perfonæ* were firft enumerated by Rowe. JOHNSON.

Frederick is here clearly a miftake, as appears by the anfwer of Rofalind, to whom Touchftone addreffes himfelf, though the queftion was put to him by Celia. I fuppofe fome abbreviation was ufed in the MS. for the name of the rightful, or *old* duke, as he is called, [perhaps *Fer.* for *Ferdinand,*] which the tranfcriber or printer converted into Frederick. *Fernardyne* is one of the perfons introduced in the novel on which this comedy is founded. Mr. Theobald folves the difficulty by giving the next fpeech to Celia, inftead of Rofalind; but there is too much of filial warmth in it for Celia:—befides, why fhould her father be called *old* Frederick? It appears from the laft fcene of this play that this was the name of the *younger* brother. MALONE.

Mr. Malone's remark may be juft; and yet I think the fpeech which is ftill left in the mouth of Celia, exhibits as much tender-nefs for the fool, as refpect for her own father. She ftops Touch-ftone, who might otherwife have proceeded to fay what fhe could not hear without inflicting punifhment on the fpeaker.—*Old* is an unmeaning term of familiarity. It is ftill in ufe, and has no refer-ence to age. The Duke in *Meafure for Meafure* is called by Lucio " the *old* fantaftical Duke," &c. STEEVENS.

[2] —— *you'll be* whip'd *for* taxation,] This was the difcipline ufually inflicted upon fools. Brantome informs us that Legat, fool to Elizabeth of France, having offended her with fome indelicate fpeech, " *fut bien fouetté à la cuifine pour ces paroles.*" A reprefenta-tion of this ceremony may be feen in a cut prefixed to B. II. ch. c. of the German Petrarch already mentioned in Vol. V. p. 44. DOUCE.

Taxation is cenfure, or fatire. So, in *Much ado about Nothing:* " Niece, you *tax* Signior Benedick too much; but he'll be meet with you." Again, in the play before us: " —— my *taxing* like a wildgoofe flies——." MALONE.

[3] —— *fince the little wit, that fools have, was filenced,*] Shak-fpeare probably alludes to the ufe of *fools* or *jefters,* who for fome ages had been allowed in all courts an unbridled liberty of cen-fure and mockery, and about this time began to be lefs tolerated.

                                                                JOHNSON.

little foolery, that wife men have, makes a great fhow. Here comes Monfieur Le Beau.

Enter LE BEAU.

Ros. With his mouth full of news.

CEL. Which he will put on us, as pigeons feed their young.

Ros. Then fhall we be news-cramm'd.

CEL. All the better; we fhall be the more market-able. *Bon jour*, Monfieur le Beau: What's the news?

LE BEAU. Fair princefs, you have loft much good fport.

CEL. Sport? Of what colour?

LE BEAU. What colour, madam? How fhall I anfwer you?

Ros. As wit and fortune will.

TOUCH. Or as the deftinies decree.

CEL. Well faid; that was laid on with a trowel.[4]

TOUCH. Nay, if I keep not my rank,——

Ros. Thou lofeft thy old fmell.

LE BEAU. You amaze me, ladies:[5] I would have

---

[4] —— *laid on with a trowel.*] I fuppofe the meaning is, that there is too heavy a mafs of big words laid upon a flight fubject. JOHNSON.

This is a proverbial expreffion, which is generally ufed to fignify a *glaring falfhood.* See Ray's *Proverbs.* STEEVENS.

It means a good round hit, thrown in without judgment or defign. RITSON.

To lay on with a trowel is, to do any thing ftrongly and without delicacy. If a man flatters grofsly, it is a common expreffion to fay, that he *lays it on with a trowel.* M. MASON.

[5] *You* amaze *me, ladies:*] To *amaze,* here, is not to aftonifh or ftrike with wonder, but to perplex; to confufe, fo as to put out of the intended narrative. JOHNSON.

So, in *Cymbeline,* Act IV. fc. iii:

" I am *amazed* with matter." STEEVENS.

told you of good wreftling, which you have loft the fight of.

Ros. Yet tell us the manner of the wreftling.

Le Beau. I will tell you the beginning, and, if it pleafe your ladyfhips, you may fee the end ; for the beft is yet to do; and here, where you are, they are coming to perform it.

Cel. Well,—the beginning, that is dead and buried.

Le Beau. There comes an old man, and his three fons,——

Cel. I could match this beginning with an old tale.

Le Beau. Three proper young men, of excellent growth and prefence ;——

Ros. With bills on their necks,—*Be it known unto all men by thefe prefents,* [6]——

---

[6] *With* bills *on their necks,—Be it known unto all men by thefe prefents,*] The *ladies* and the *fool,* according to the mode of wit at that time, are at a kind of *crofs purpofes.* Where the words of one fpeaker are wrefted by another, in a repartee, to a different meaning. As where the Clown fays juft before—*Nay, if I keep not my rank.* Rofalind replies—*Thou lofeft thy old fmell.* So here when Rofalind had faid—*With bills on their necks,* the Clown, to be quits with her, puts in—*Know all men by thefe prefents.* She fpoke of an inftrument of war, and he turns it to an inftrument of law of the fame name, beginning with thefe words: So that they muft be given to him. WARBURTON.

This conjecture is ingenious. Where meaning is fo very thin, as in this vein of jocularity, it is hard to catch, and therefore I know not well what to determine; but I cannot fee why Rofalind fhould fuppofe, that the competitors in a wreftling match carried *bills* on their fhoulders, and I believe the whole conceit is in the poor refemblance of *prefence* and *prefents.* JOHNSON.

With bills *on their necks,* fhould be the conclufion of Le Beau's fpeech. Mr. Edwards ridicules Dr. Warburton, " As if people carried fuch inftruments of war, as *bills* and *guns* on *their necks,* not *on their fhoulders!*" But unluckily the ridicule falls upon himfelf. Laffels, in his *Voyage of Italy,* fays of tutors, " Some perfuade their pupils, that it is fine carrying a *gun upon their necks.*"

Le Beau. The eldeſt of the three wreſtled with Charles, the duke's wreſtler; which Charles in a moment threw him, and broke three of his ribs, that there is little hope of life in him: ſo he ſerved the ſecond, and ſo the third: Yonder they lie; the poor old man, their father, making ſuch pitiful dole over them, that all the beholders take his part with weeping.

Ros. Alas!

Touch. But what is the ſport, monſieur, that the ladies have loſt?

Le Beau. Why, this that I ſpeak of.

Touch. Thus men may grow wiſer every day! it is the firſt time that ever I heard, breaking of ribs was ſport for ladies.

But what is ſtill more, the expreſſion is taken immediately from Lodge, who furniſhed our author with his plot. "Ganimede on a day ſitting with Aliena, (the aſſumed names, as in the play,) caſt up her eye, and ſaw where Roſader came pacing towards them with his *foreſt-bill on his necke.*" FARMER.

The quibble may be countenanced by the following paſſage in *Woman's a Weathercock,* 1612:
"Good-morrow, taylor, I abhor *bills* in a morning—
"But thou may'ſt watch at night with *bill* in hand."
Again, in Sidney's *Arcadia,* Book I:
"——with a ſword by his ſide, a foreſt-*bille on his necke,*" &c.
Again, in Rowley's *When you ſee me you know me,* 1621:
"Enter King, and Compton, with *bills on his back.*"
Again, in *The Pinner of Wakefield,* 1599:
"And each of you a good bat *on his neck.*"
Again,
"——are you not big enough to bear
"Your bats *upon your necks?*" STEEVENS.

I don't think that by *bill* is meant either an inſtrument of war, or one of law, but merely a label or advertiſement—as we ſay a *play-bill,* a *hand-bill*; unleſs Farmer's ingenious amendment be admitted, and theſe words become part of Le Beau's ſpeech; in which caſe the word *bill* would be uſed by him to denote a weapon, and by Roſalind perverted to mean a *label.* M. MASON.

CEL. Or I, I promiſe thee.

Ros. But is there any elſe longs to ſee this broken muſick in his ſides?[1] is there yet another dotes upon rib-breaking?—Shall we ſee this wreſtling, couſin?

LE BEAU. You muſt, if you ſtay here; for here is the place appointed for the wreſtling, and they are ready to perform it.

CEL. Yonder, ſure, they are coming: Let us now ſtay and ſee it.

Flouriſh. Enter Duke FREDERICK, *Lords,* ORLANDO, CHARLES, *and Attendants.*

DUKE F. Come on; ſince the youth will not be entreated, his own peril on his forwardneſs.

Ros. Is yonder the man?

---

[1] —— *is there any elſe longs to* ſee *this broken muſick in his ſides?*] A ſtupid error in the copies. They are talking here of ſome who had their ribs broke in wreſtling: and the pleaſantry of Roſalind's repartee muſt conſiſt in the alluſion ſhe makes to *compoſing* in *muſick.* It neceſſarily follows therefore, that the poet wrote—SET *this* broken muſick *in his ſides.* WARBURTON.

If any change were neceſſary, I ſhould write, *feel this broken* muſick, for ſee. But ſee is the colloquial term for perception or experiment. So we ſay every day, ſee if the water be hot; I will ſee which is the beſt time; ſhe has tried, and ſees that ſhe cannot lift it. In this ſenſe ſee may be here uſed. The ſufferer can, with no propriety, be ſaid to ſet the muſick; neither is the alluſion to the act of tuning an inſtrument, or pricking a tune, one of which muſt be meant by ſetting muſick. Roſalind hints at a whimſical ſimilitude between the ſeries of ribs gradually ſhortening, and ſome muſical inſtruments, and therefore calls *broken ribs, broken muſick.* JOHNSON.

This probably alludes to the pipe of Pan, which conſiſting of reeds of unequal length, and gradually leſſening, bore ſome reſemblance to the ribs of a man. M. MASON.

Broken muſick either means the noiſe which the breaking of ribs would occaſion, or the hollow ſound which proceeds from a perſon's receiving a violent fall. DOUCE.

Le Beau. Even he, madam.

Cel. Alas, he is too young: yet he looks fuccefsfully.

Duke F. How now, daughter, and coufin? are
you crept hither to fee the wreftling?

Ros. Ay, my liege; fo pleafe you give us leave.

Duke F. You will take little delight in it, I can
tell you, there is fuch odds in the men:[8] In pity
of the challenger's youth, I would fain diffuade
him, but he will not be entreated: Speak to him,
ladies; fee if you can move him.

Cel. Call him hither, good Monfieur Le Beau.

Duke F. Do fo; I'll not be by.

[*Duke goes apart.*

Le Beau. Monfieur the challenger, the princeffes
call for you.[9]

Orl. I attend them, with all refpect and duty.

Ros. Young man, have you challenged Charles
the wreftler?[2]

Orl. No, fair princefs; he is the general challenger: I come but in, as others do, to try with
him the ftrength of my youth.

Cel. Young gentleman, your fpirits are too bold
for your years: You have feen cruel proof of this
man's ftrength: if you faw yourfelf with your
eyes, or knew yourfelf with your judgment,[3] the

---

[8] ——*odds in the* men:] Sir T. Hanmer. In the old editions,
the *man.* JOHNSON.

[9] ——*the* princeffes call *for you.*] The old copy reads—the
princeffe calls. Corrected by Mr. Theobald. MALONE.

[2] —— *have you challenged Charles the wreftler?*] This wreftling match is minutely defcribed in Lodge's *Rofalynde,* 1592.
MALONE.

[3] ——*if you faw yourfelf with* your *eyes, or knew yourfelf with*
your *judgment,*] Abfurd! The fenfe requires that we fhould read,

C 4

fear of your adventure would counſel you to a more equal enterprife. We pray you, for your own fake, to embrace your own fafety, and give over this attempt.

Roſ. Do, young fir; your reputation ſhall not therefore be mifpriſed: we will make it our fuit to the duke, that the wreſtling might not go forward.

Orl. I befeech you, puniſh me not with your hard thoughts; wherein I confefs me much guilty, to deny fo fair and excellent ladies any thing.[4] But let your fair eyes, and gentle wiſhes, go with me

—our *eyes,* and—our *judgment.* The argument is, *Your ſpirits are too bold, and therefore your judgment deceives you; but did you ſee and know yourſelf with our more impartial judgment, you would forbear.* Warburton.

I cannot find the abfurdity of the prefent reading. *If you were not blinded and intoxicated,* fays the princefs, *with the ſpirit of enterprife, if you could uſe* your own eyes to *ſee,* or your own judgment to know *yourſelf, the fear of your adventure would counſel you.*
Johnson.

[4] *I befeech you, puniſh me not,* &c.] I ſhould wiſh to read, *I befeech you, puniſh me not with your hard thoughts. Therein I confefs myſelf much guilty to deny ſo fair and excellent ladies any thing.*
Johnson.

As the word *wherein* muſt always refer to ſomething preceding, I have no doubt but there is an error in this paſſage, and that we ought to read *herein,* inſtead of *wherein.* The hard thoughts that he complains of are the apprehenſions expreſſed by the ladies of his not being able to contend with the wreſtler. He befeeches that they will not puniſh him with them; and then adds, " Herein I confefs me much guilty to deny ſo fair and excellent ladies any thing. But let your fair eyes and gentle wiſhes go with me to my trial." M. Mason.

The meaning I think is, " puniſh me not with your unfavourable opinion (of my abilities); *which, however, I confefs, I deſerve to incur,* for denying fuch fair ladies any requeſt." The expreſſion is licentious, but our author's plays furniſh many fuch.
Malone.

to my trial:⁵ wherein if I be foiled, there is but one shamed that was never gracious; if killed, but one dead that is willing to be so: I shall do my friends no wrong, for I have none to lament me; the world no injury, for in it I have nothing; only in the world I fill up a place, which may be better supplied when I have made it empty.

Ros. The little strength that I have, I would it were with you.

Cel. And mine, to eke out hers.

Ros. Fare you well. Pray heaven, I be deceived in you!

Cel. Your heart's desires be with you!

Cha. Come, where is this young gallant, that is so desirous to lie with his mother earth?

Orl. Ready, sir; but his will hath in it a more modest working.

Duke F. You shall try but one fall.

Cha. No, I warrant your grace; you shall not entreat him to a second, that have so mightily persuaded him from a first.

Orl. You mean to mock. me after; you should not have mocked me before: but come your ways.

Ros. Now, Hercules be thy speed, young man!

Cel. I would I were invisible, to catch the strong fellow by the leg. [Charles *and* Orlando *wrestle.*

Ros. O excellent young man!

---

⁵ —— *let your gentle wishes, go with me to my trial:*] Addison might have had this passage in his memory, when he put the following words into Juba's mouth:

" —— Marcia, may I hope
" That thy kind wishes follow me to battle?"

STEEVENS.

Cel. If I had a thunderbolt in mine eye, I can tell who fhould down. [CHARLES *is thrown. Shout.*

Duke F. No more, no more.

Orl. Yes, I befeech your grace; I am not yet well breathed.

Duke F. How doft thou, Charles?

Le Beau. He cannot fpeak, my lord.

Duke F. Bear him away. [CHARLES *is borne out.*] What is thy name, young man?

Orl. Orlando, my liege; the youngeft fon of fir Rowland de Bois.

Duke F. I would, thou hadft been fon to fome
        man elfe.
The world efteem'd thy father honourable,
But I did find him ftill mine enemy:
Thou fhouldft have better pleas'd me with this deed,
Hadft thou defcended from another houfe.
But fare thee well; thou art a gallant youth;
I would, thou hadft told me of another father.
      [*Exeunt Duke* FRED. *Train, and* LE BEAU.

Cel. Were I my father, coz, would I do this?

Orl. I am more proud to be fir Rowland's fon,
His youngeft fon;[3]—and would not change that
        calling,[4]
To be adopted heir to Frederick.

Ros. My father lov'd fir Rowland as his foul,
And all the world was of my father's mind:
Had I before known this young man his fon,

---

[3] *His youngeft fon;*] The words "than to be defcended from any other houfe, however high," muft be underftood. Orlando is replying to the duke, who is juft gone out, and had faid,
    "Thou fhould'ft have better pleas'd me with this deed,
    "Hadft thou defcended from another houfe." MALONE.

[4] —— *that* calling,] i. e. appellation; a very unufual, if not unprecedented fenfe of the word. STEEVENS.

I fhould have given him tears unto entreaties,
Ere he fhould thus have ventur'd.

CEL.   Gentle coufin,
Let us go thank him, and encourage him:
My father's rough and envious difpofition
Sticks me at heart.—Sir, you have well deferv'd:
If you do keep your promifes in love,
But juftly, as you have exceeded promife,[5]
Your miftrefs fhall be happy.

Ros.   Gentleman,
    [*Giving him a chain from her neck.*
Wear this for me; one out of fuits with fortune;[6]
That could give more, but that her hand lacks
    means.—
Shall we go, coz?

CEL.   Ay:—Fare you well, fair gentleman.

ORL. Can I not fay, I thank you? My better parts
Are all thrown down; and that which here ftands up,
Is but a quintain, a mere lifelefs block.[7]

---

[5] —— *as you have exceeded promife,*] The old copy, without regard to the meafure, reads—*all* promife. STEEVENS.

[6] —— *one out of fuits with fortune ;*] This feems an allufion to
cards, where he that has no more cards to play of any particular
fort, is *out of fuit.* JOHNSON.

Out of fuits with fortune, I believe means, turned out of her fervice, and ftripped of her livery. STEEVENS.

So afterwards Celia fays, " — but turning thefe jefts *out of fervice,* let us talk in good earneft." MALONE.

[7] *Is but a* quintain, *a mere lifelefs block.*] A *quintain* was a
poft or *butt* fet up for feveral kinds of martial exercifes, againft
which they threw their darts and exercifed their arms. The allufion is beautiful. *I am,* fays Orlando, *only a* quintain, *a lifelefs
block on which love only exercifes his arms in jeft* ; *the great difparity of condition between Rofalind and me, not fuffering me to hope
that love will ever make a ferious matter of it.* The famous fatirift
Regnier, who lived about the time of our authour, ufes the
fame metaphor, on the fame fubject, though the thought be different :

Ros. He calls us back: My pride fell with my
    fortunes:
I'll afk him what he would:—Did you call, fir?—
Sir, you have wreftled well, and overthrown
More than your enemies.

Cel.   Will you go, coz?

Ros. Have with you:—Fare you well.
     [*Exeunt* Rosalind *and* Celia.

Orl. What paffion hangs thefe weights upon my
    tongue?
I cannot fpeak to her, yet fhe urg'd conference.

   " *Et qui depuis dix ans jufqu'en fes derniers jours,*
   " *A foutenu le prix en l' efcrime d' amours;*
   " *Laffe en fin de fervir au peuple de* quintaine,
   " *Elle*" &c. Warburton.

This is but an imperfeft (to call it no worfe) explanation of a
beautiful paffage. The *quintain* was not the objeft of the darts
and arms: it was a ftake driven into a field, upon which were hung
a fhield and other trophies of war, at which they fhot, darted, or
rode, with a lance. When the fhield and the trophies were all
thrown down, the quintain remained. Without this information
how could the reader underftand the allufion of
  —————— *My better parts*
Are all thrown down? Guthrie.

Mr. Malone has difputed the propriety of Mr. Guthrie's animad-
verfions; and Mr. Douce is equally diffatisfied with thofe of Mr.
Malone.
  The phalanx of our auxiliaries, as well as their circumftantiality,
is fo much increafed, that we are often led (as Hamlet obferves) to
   " ————— fight for a fpot
   " Whereon the numbers cannot try the caufe."
  The prefent ftriftures therefore of Mr. Malone and Mr. Douce,
(which are too valuable to be omitted, and too ample to find their
place under the text of our author,) muft appear at the conclufion
of the play. Steevens.
  For a more particular defcription of a *quintain,* fee a note on a
paffage in Jonfon's *Underwoods,* Whalley's edit. Vol. VII. p. 55.
             M. Mason.
  A humourous defcription of this amufement may alfo be read in
Laneham's Letter from " Killingworth Caftle." Henley.

Re-enter LE BEAU.

O poor Orlando! thou art overthrown;
Or Charles, or fomething weaker, mafters thee.

LE BEAU. Good fir, I do in friendfhip counfel you
To leave this place: Albeit you have deferv'd
High commendation, true applaufe, and love;
Yet fuch is now the duke's condition,[8]
That he mifconftrues all that you have done.
The duke is humorous; what he is, indeed,
More fuits you to conceive, than me to fpeak of.[9]

ORL. I thank you, fir: and, pray you, tell me this;
Which of the two was daughter of the duke
That here was at the wreftling?

LE BEAU. Neither his daughter, if we judge by
              manners;
But yet, indeed, the fhorter[2] is his daughter:

---

[8] —— *the duke's* condition,] The word *condition* means character, temper, difpofition. So Antonio, the merchant of Venice,
is called by his friend the *beft condition'd man*. JOHNSON.

[9] —— *than me to fpeak of.*] The old copy has—than *I*. Corrected by Mr. Rowe. MALONE.

[2] —— *the* fhorter—] Thus Mr. Pope. The old copy reads—
the *taller*. Mr. Malone—the *fmaller*. STEEVENS.

Some change is abfolutely neceffary, for Rofalind, in a fubfequent fcene, exprefsly fays that *fhe* is " more than common *tall*,"
and affigns that as a reafon for her affuming the drefs of a man,
while her coufin Celia retained her female apparel. Again, in
Act IV. fc. iii. Celia is defcribed by thefe words—" the woman
low, and browner than her brother;" i. e. Rofalind. Mr. Pope
reads—" the *fhorter* is his daughter;" which has been admitted in
all the fubfequent editions: but furely *fhorter* and *taller* could
never have been confounded by either the eye or the ear. The
prefent emendation, it is hoped, has a preferable claim to a place in
the text, as being much nearer to the corrupted reading. MALONE.

Shakfpeare fometimes fpeaks of *little* women, but I do not recollect that he, or any other writer, has mentioned *fmall* ones.
Otherwife, Mr. Malone's conjecture fhould have found a place in
our text. STEEVENS.

The other is daughter to the banifh'd duke,
And here detain'd by her ufurping uncle,
To keep his daughter company; whofe loves
Are dearer than the natural bond of fifters.
But I can tell you, that of late this duke
Hath ta'en difpleafure 'gainft his gentle niece;
Grounded upon no other argument,
But that the people praife her for her virtues,
And pity her for her good father's fake;
And, on my life, his malice 'gainft the lady
Will fuddenly break forth.—Sir, fare you well;
Hereafter, in a better world than this,[2]
I fhall defire more love and knowledge of you.

   Orl. I reft much bounden to you: fare you well!
                               [Exit Le Beau.
Thus muft I from the fmoke into the fmother;
From tyrant duke, unto a tyrant brother:—
But heavenly Rofalind!   *[Exit.*

SCENE III.

A Room in the Palace.

Enter Celia *and* Rosalind.

   Cel. Why, coufin; why, Rofalind;—Cupid have
mercy!—Not a word?

   Ros. Not one to throw at a dog.

   Cel. No, thy words are too precious to be caft
away upon curs, throw fome of them at me; come,
lame me with reafons.

   Ros. Then there were two coufins laid up; when
the one fhould be lamed with reafons, and the other
mad without any.

---

   [2] *—— in a better world than this,*] So, in *Coriolanus*, Act III.
fc. iii:—" There is a world elfewhere." Steevens.

Cel. But is all this for your father?

Ros. No, fome of it is for my child's father:[3] O, how full of briars is this working-day world!

Cel. They are but burs, coufin, thrown upon thee in holyday foolery; if we walk not in the trodden paths, our very petticoats will catch them.

Ros. I could fhake them off my coat; thefe burs are in my heart.

Cel. Hem them away.

Ros. I would try; if I could cry hem, and have him.

Cel. Come, come, wreftle with thy affections.

Ros. O, they take the part of a better wreftler than myfelf.

Cel. O, a good wifh upon you! you will try in time, in defpite of a fall.—But, turning thefe jefts out of fervice, let us talk in good earneft: Is it poffible, on fuch a fudden, you fhould fall into fo ftrong a liking with old fir Rowland's youngeft fon?

Ros. The duke my father lov'd his father dearly.

Cel. Doth it therefore enfue, that you fhould love his fon dearly? By this kind of chafe,[4] I fhould hate him, for my father hated his father dearly; yet I hate not Orlando.

Ros. No 'faith, hate him not, for my fake.

Cel. Why fhould I not? doth he not deferve well?[5]

---

[3] ——*for my child's father :*] i. e. for him whom I hope to marry, and have children by. THEOBALD.

[4] *By this kind of* chafe,] That is, by this way of *following* the argument. *Dear* is ufed by Shakfpeare in a double fenfe for *beloved*, and for *hurtful, hated, baleful.* Both fenfes are authorifed, and both drawn from etymology; but properly, *beloved* is *dear*, and *hateful* is *dere.* Rofalind ufes *dearly* in the good, and Celia in the bad fenfe. JOHNSON.

[5] *Why fhould I not? doth he not deferve well?*] Celia anfwers Rofalind, (who had defired her " *not to hate* Orlando, for her

Ros. Let me love him for that; and do you love him, becaufe I do:—Look, here comes the duke.

Cel. With his eyes full of anger.

Enter Duke FREDERICK, *with Lords.*

Duke F. Miftrefs, defpatch you with your fafeft hafte,
And get you from our court.

Ros.　　　　　　　　　　Me uncle?

Duke F.　　　　　　　　　　You, coufin:
Within thefe ten days if that thou be'ft found
So near our publick court as twenty miles,
Thou dieft for it.

Ros.　　　　I do befeech your grace,
Let me the knowledge of my fault bear with me:
If with myfelf I hold intelligence,
Or have acquaintance with mine own defires;
If that I do not dream, or be not frantick,
(As I do truft I am not,) then, dear uncle,
Never, fo much as in a thought unborn,
Did I offend your highnefs.

Duke F.　　　　　Thus do all traitors;
If their purgation did confift in words,
They are as innocent as grace itfelf:—
Let it fuffice thee, that I truft thee not.

Ros. Yet your miftruft cannot make me a traitor:
Tell me, whereon the likelihood depends.

fake,") as if fhe had faid—" *love* him, for my fake:" to which the former replies, " Why fhould I *not* [i. e. love him]? So, in the following paffage, in *King Henry VIII:*
　　" ——— Which of the peers
　　" Have uncontemn'd gone by him, or at leaft
　　" Strangely neglected?"
Uncontemn'd muft be underftood as if the author had written—*not* contemn'd; otherwife the fubfequent words would convey a meaning directly contrary to what the fpeaker intends. MALONE.

Duke F. Thou art thy father's daughter, there's
enough.

Ros. So was I, when your highnefs took his
dukedom ;
So was I, when your highnefs banifh'd him :
Treafon is not inherited, my lord ;
Or, if we did derive it from our friends,
What's that to me ? my father was no traitor :
Then, good my liege, miftake me not fo much,
To think my poverty is treacherous.

Cel. Dear fovereign, hear me fpeak.

Duke F. Ay, Celia ; we ftay'd her for your fake,
Elfe had fhe with her father rang'd along.

Cel. I did not then entreat to have her ftay,
It was your pleafure, and your own remorfe ;[6]
I was too young that time to value her,
But now I know her : if fhe be a traitor,
Why fo am I ; we ftill have flept together,
Rofe at an inftant, learn'd, play'd, eat together ;[7]
And wherefoe'er we went, like Juno's fwans,
Still we went coupled, and infeparable.

Duke F. She is too fubtle for thee ; and her
fmoothnefs,
Her very filence, and her patience,
Speak to the people, and they pity her.
Thou art a fool : fhe robs thee of thy name ;

---

[6] —— *remorfe* ;] i. e. *compaffion.* So, in *Macbeth* :
" Stop the accefs and paffage to *remorfe.*" STEEVENS.

[7] —— *we ftill have flept together,*
Rofe at an inftant, learn'd, play'd, eat together ;] Youthful
friendfhip is defcribed in nearly the fame terms in a book publifhed
the year in which this play firft appeared in print. " They ever went
together, *plaid* together, *eate* together, and ufually *flept* together, out
of the great love that was between them." *Life of Guzman de
Alfarache*, folio, printed by Edward Blount, 1623, P. I. B. I.
c. viii. p. 75. REED.

And thou wilt fhow more bright, and feem more
    virtuous,[6]
When fhe is gone: then open not thy lips;
Firm and irrevocable is my doom
Which I have pafs'd upon her; fhe is banifh'd.

 CEL. Pronounce that fentence then on me, my
    liege;
I cannot live out of her company.

 DUKE F. You are a fool:—You, niece, provide
    yourfelf;
If you out-ftay the time, upon mine honour,
And in the greatnefs of my word, you die.
    [Exeunt Duke FREDERICK and Lords.

 CEL. O my poor Rofalind! whither wilt thou go?
Wilt thou change fathers? I will give thee mine.
I charge thee, be not thou more griev'd than I am.

 Ros. I have more caufe.

 CEL.   Thou haft not, coufin;[7]
Pr'ythee, be cheerful: know'ft thou not, the duke
Hath banifh'd me his daughter?

 Ros.   That he hath not.

 CEL. No? hath not? Rofalind lacks then the love
Which teacheth thee that thou and I am one:[8]

<hr/>

 [6] *And thou wilt fhow more bright, and* feem *more virtuous,*] When
fhe was feen alone, fhe would be more noted. JOHNSON.

 [7] *Thou haft not, coufin;*] Some word is wanting to the metre.
Perhaps our author wrote:
  Indeed *thou haft not, coufin.* STEEVENS.

 [8] —— *Rofalind lacks then the love*
 Which teacheth thee that thou and I am one:] The poet certainly wrote—*which teacheth* me. For if Rofalind had learnt to
think Celia one part of herfelf, fhe could not *lack* that love which
Celia complains fhe does. WARBURTON.

 Either reading may ftand. The fenfe of the eftablifhed text is
not remote or obfcure. Where would be the abfurdity of faying,
You know not the law which teaches you to do right? JOHNSON.

 I

Shall we be funder'd? fhall we part, fweet girl?
No; let my father feek another heir.
Therefore devife with me, how we may fly,
Whither to go, and what to bear with us:
And do not feek to take your change upon you,[9]
To bear your griefs yourfelf, and leave me out;
For, by this heaven, now at our forrows pale,
Say what thou canft, I'll go along with thee.

Ros. Why, whither fhall we go?

Cel. To feek my uncle.[1]

Ros. Alas, what danger will it be to us,
Maids as we are, to travel forth fo far?
Beauty provoketh thieves fooner than gold.

Cel. I'll put myfelf in poor and mean attire,
And with a kind of umber fmirch my face;[3]
The like do you; fo fhall we pafs along,
And never ftir affailants.

Ros. Were it not better,
Becaufe that I am more than common tall,
That I did fuit me all points like a man?
A gallant curtle-ax[4] upon my thigh,

---

[9] —— *to take your* change *upon you,*] i. e. to take your *change* or *reverfe of fortune* upon yourfelf, without any aid or participation. MALONE.

I have inferted this note, but without implicit confidence in the reading it explains. The fecond folio has—*charge.* STEEVENS.

[1] *To feek my uncle.*] Here the old copy adds—*in the foreft of Arden.* But thefe words are an evident interpolation, without ufe, and injurious to the meafure:
Why, whither fhall we go?—To feek my uncle.
being a complete verfe. Befides, we have been already informed by Charles the wreftler, that the banifhed Duke's refidence was *in the foreft of Arden.* STEEVENS.

[3] *And with a kind of* umber *fmirch my face;*] *Umber* is a dufky yellow-coloured earth, brought from Umbria in Italy. See a note on. " the *umber'd* fires," in *King Henry V.* Act III. MALONE.

[4] —— *curtle-ax* —] or *cutlace,* a broad fword. JOHNSON.

A boar-fpear in my hand; and (in my heart
Lie there what hidden woman's fear there will,)
We'll have a fwafhing⁵ and a martial outfide;
As many other mannifh cowards have,
That do outface it with their femblances.

 Cel. What fhall I call thee, when thou art a man?

 Ros. I'll have no worfe a name than Jove's own
   page,
And therefore look you call me, Ganymede.
But what will you be call'd?

 Cel. Something that hath a reference to my ftate;
No longer Celia, but Aliena.

 Ros. But, coufin, what if we affay'd to fteal
The clownifh fool out of your father's court?
Would he not be a comfort to our travel?

 Cel. He'll go along o'er the wide world with
   me;
Leave me alone to woo him: Let's away,
And get our jewels and our wealth together;
Devife the fitteft time, and fafeft way
To hide us from purfuit that will be made
After my flight: Now go we in content,⁶
To liberty, and not to banifhment.   [*Exeunt.*

---

⁵ We'll *have a fwafhing*, &c.] A *fwafhing* outfide is an appearance of noify, bullying valour. *Swafhing blow* is mentioned in
Romeo and Juliet; and, in *King Henry V.* the Boy fays :—" As
young as I am, I have obferved thefe three *fwafhers*;" meaning
Nym, Piftol, and Bardolph. STEEVENS.

⁶ —— *Now go* we in *content*,] The old copy reads—Now go
in we content. Corrected by the editor of the fecond folio. I am
not fure that the tranfpofition is neceffary. Our authour might
have ufed *content* as an adjective. MALONE.

ACT II.   SCENE I.

The Foreſt of Arden.

Enter Duke *ſenior,* AMIENS, *and other Lords, in the dreſs of Foreſters.*

DUKE S. Now, my co-mates, and brothers in
   exile,
Hath not old cuſtom made this life more ſweet
Than that of painted pomp? Are not theſe woods
More free from peril than the envious court?
Here feel we but the penalty of Adam,[7]
The ſeaſons' difference; as, the icy fang,
And churliſh chiding of the winter's wind;
Which when it bites and blows upon my body,
Even till I ſhrink with cold, I ſmile, and ſay,—
This is no flattery: theſe are counſellors
That feelingly perſuade me what I am.
Sweet are the uſes of adverſity;
Which, like the toad, ugly and venomous,
Wears yet a precious jewel in his head:[8]

---

[7] *Here feel we* but *the penalty of Adam,*] The old copy reads—
" not *the penalty*"—. STEEVENS.

What was the penalty of Adam, hinted at by our poet? The
being ſenſible of the difference of the ſeaſons. The Duke ſays, the
cold and effects of the winter feelingly perſuade him what he
is. How does he *not* then feel the penalty? Doubtleſs, the text
muſt be reſtored as I have corrected it: and it is obvious in the
courſe of theſe notes, how often *not* and *but* by miſtake have changed
place in our author's former editions. THEOBALD.

As *not* has here taken the place of *but,* ſo, in *Coriolanus,* Act II.
ſc. iii. *but* is printed inſtead of *not:*
  " *Cor.* Ay, *but* mine own deſire.
  " 1 *Cit.* How! *not* your own deſire." MALONE.

[8] *Which, like the toad, ugly and venomous,*
  Wears yet a precious jewel in his head:] It was the current
opinion in Shakſpeare's time, that in the head of an old toad was

And this our life, exempt from publick haunt,
Finds tongues in trees, books in the running brooks,[9]
Sermons in ſtones, and good in every thing.

Ami. I would not change it:[2] Happy is your grace,
That can tranſlate the ſtubbornneſs of fortune
Into ſo quiet and ſo ſweet a ſtyle.

to be found a ſtone, or pearl, to which great virtues were aſcribed.
This ſtone has been often ſought, but nothing has been found more
than accidental or perhaps morbid indurations of the ſkull.
                                                              JOHNSON.

In a book called *A Green Foreſt, or a Natural Hiſtory*, &c. by
John Maplett, 1567, is the following account of this imaginary
gem: " In this ſtone is apparently ſeene verie often the verie forme
of a tode, with deſpotted and coloured feete, but thoſe uglye and
defuſedly. It is available againſt envenoming."
Again, in Beaumont and Fletcher's *Monſieur Thomas*, 1639:
          " —— in moſt phyſicians' heads,
          " There is a kind of *toadſtone* bred."——
Again, in *Adraſta*, or *The Woman's Spleen*, 1635:
          " Do not then forget the *ſtone*
          " In the *toad*, nor ſerpent's bone," &c.
Pliny, in the 32d book of his *Natural Hiſtory*, aſcribes many
wonderful qualities to a *bone* found in the right ſide of a *toad*, but
makes no mention of any gem in its head. This deficiency however is abundantly ſupplied by Edward Fenton, in his *Secrete
Wonders of Nature*, 4to. bl. l. 1569, who ſays, " That there is
founde in the *heades* of old and great *toades*, a *ſtone* which they call
Borax or Stelon: it is moſt commonly founde in the *head* of a
hee *toad*, of power to repulſe poyſons, and that it is a moſt
ſoveraigne medicine for the ſtone."
Thomas Lupton, in his *Firſt Booke of Notable Things*, 4to. bl. l.
bears repeated teſtimony to the virtues of the " *Tode-ſtone*, called
Crapaudina." In his *Seventh Booke* he inſtructs us how to procure
it; and afterwards tells us—" You ſhall knowe whether the *Tode-
ſtone* be the ryght and perfect ſtone or not. Holde the ſtone before
a Tode, ſo that he may ſee it; and if it be a ryght and true ſtone, the
Tode will leape towarde it, and make as though he would ſnatch it :
He envieth ſo much that man ſhould have that ſtone." STEEVENS.

9 *Finds tongues in trees*, &c.] So, in Sidney's *Arcadia*, Book I:
     " Thus both *trees* and *each thing elſe, be the bookes to a fancie*."
                                                              STEEVENS.

2 *I would not change it :*] Mr. Upton, not without probability,
gives theſe words to the Duke, and makes Amiens begin—*Happy
is your grace*. JOHNSON.

Duke S. Come, fhall we go and kill us venifon?
And yet it irks me, the poor dappled fools,—
Being native burghers of this defert city,[3]—
Should, in their own confines, with forked heads [4]
Have their round haunches gor'd.

1 *Lord.*   Indeed, my lord,
The melancholy Jaques grieves at that;
And, in that kind, fwears you do more ufurp
Than doth your brother that hath banifh'd you.
To-day, my lord of Amiens, and myfelf,
Did fteal behind him, as he lay along
Under an oak, whofe antique root peeps out
Upon the brook that brawls along this wood:[5]
To the which place a poor fequefter'd ftag,
That from the hunters' aim had ta'en a hurt,
Did come to languifh; and, indeed, my lord,
The wretched animal heav'd forth fuch groans,

[3] *Native* burghers *of this defert city,*] In Sidney's *Arcadia,* the deer are called " the wild *burgeffes* of the foreft." Again, in the 18th Song of Drayton's *Polyolbion:*
      " Where, fearlefs of the hunt, the hart fecurely ftood,
      " And every where walk'd free, a *burgefs* of the wood."
                                    STEEVENS.
A kindred expreffion is found in Lodge's *Rofalynde,* 1592:
      " About her wond'ring ftood
      " The *citizens* o' the wood."
Our author afterwards ufes this very phrafe:
      " Sweep on, you fat and greafy *citizens.*" MALONE.

[4] ——*with* forked heads—] i. e. with *arrows,* the points of which were *barbed.* So, in *A Mad World my Mafters:*
      " While the broad arrow with the *forked head*
      " Miffes," &c. STEEVENS.

[5] ——*as he lay along*
  Under an oak, &c.]
      " There at the foot of yonder nodding beech
      " That wreathes its old fantaftic roots fo high,
      " His liftlefs length at noon-tide would he ftretch,
      " And pore upon the brook that babbles by." *Gray's Elegy.*
                                    STEEVENS.

That their difcharge did ftretch his leathern coat
Almoft to burfting; and the big round tears
Cours'd one another down his innocent nofe
In piteous chafe:[6] and thus the hairy fool,
Much marked of the melancholy Jaques,
Stood on the extremeft verge of the fwift brook,
Augmenting it with tears.

DUKE S.   But what faid Jaques?
Did he not moralize this fpectacle?

1 LORD. O, yes, into a thoufand fimiles.
Firft, for his weeping in the needlefs ftream;[7]
Poor deer, quoth he, *thou mak'ft a teftament*
As worldlings do, giving thy fum of more
To that which had too much:[8] Then, being alone,[9]
Left and abandon'd of his velvet friends;
'*Tis right*, quoth he; *thus mifery doth part*
The flux of company: Anon, a carelefs herd,
Full of the pafture, jumps along by him,

---

[6] —— *the big round tears*, &c.] It is faid in one of the marginal notes to a fimilar paffage in the 13th Song of Drayton's *Polyolbion*, that " the harte weepeth at his dying: his tears are held to be precious in medicine." STEEVENS.

[7] —— in *the* needlefs *ftream*;] The ftream that wanted not fuch a fupply of moifture. The old copy has *into*, caught probably by the compofitor's eye from the line above. The correction was made by Mr. Pope. MALONE.

[8] *To that which had too* much:] Old copy—too *muft*. Corrected by the editor of the fecond folio. MALONE.

Shakfpeare has almoft the fame thought in his *Lover's Complaint:*

" ———— in a river ——
" Upon whofe weeping margin fhe was fet,
" Like ufury, applying wet to wet."

Again, in *K. Henry VI.* P. III. Act V. fc. iv:

" With tearful eyes add water to the fea,
" And give more ftrength *to that which hath too much*."
STEEVENS.

[9] —— *Then, being alone,*] The old copy redundantly reads—
Then being there *alone*. STEEVENS.

And never ſtays to greet him; *Ay*, quoth Jaques,
Sweep on, you fat and greaſy citizens;
'Tis juſt the faſhion: Wherefore do you look
Upon that poor and broken bankrupt there?
Thus moſt invectively he pierceth through
The body of the country,[2] city, court,
Yea, and of this our life: ſwearing, that we
Are mere uſurpers, tyrants, and what's worſe,
To fright the animals, and to kill them up,
In their aſſign'd and native dwelling place.

DUKE *S.* And did you leave him in this contem_
plation?

2 LORD. We did, my lord, weeping and commenting
Upon the ſobbing deer.

DUKE *S.* Show me the place;
I love to cope him[3] in theſe ſullen fits,
For then he's full of matter.

2 LORD. I'll bring you to him ſtraight. [*Exeunt.*

---

[2] *The body of* the *country*,] The oldeſt copy omits—*the*; but it
is ſupplied by the ſecond folio, which has many advantages over
the firſt. Mr. Malone is of a different opinion; but let him ſpeak
for himſelf. STEEVENS.

Country is here uſed as a triſyllable. So again, in *Twelfth
Night:*
"The like of him. Know'ſt thou this *country?*"
The editor of the ſecond folio, who appears to have been utterly
ignorant of our author's phraſeology and metre, reads—*The body of*
the *country*, &c. which has been followed by all the ſubſequent
editors. MALONE.

Is not *country* uſed elſewhere alſo as a diſſyllable? See *Coriolanus*, Act I. ſc. vi:
"And that his *country's* dearer than himſelf."
Beſides, by reading *country* as a triſyllable, in the middle of a
verſe, it would become rough and diſſonant. STEEVENS.

[3] —— *to cope him* —] To encounter him; to engage with him.
JOHNSON.

SCENE II.

A Room in the Palace.

Enter Duke FREDERICK, *Lords, and Attendants.*

DUKE F. Can it be poſſible, that no man ſaw
    them?
It cannot be : ſome villains of my court
Are of conſent and ſufferance in this.

    1 *LORD.* I cannot hear of any that did ſee her.
The ladies, her attendants of her chamber,
Saw her a-bed; and, in the morning early,
They found the bed untreaſur'd of their miſtreſs.

    2 *LORD.* My lord, the royniſh clown,[4] at whom
    ſo oft
Your grace was wont to laugh, is alſo miſſing.
Heſperia, the princeſs' gentlewoman,
Confeſſes, that ſhe ſecretly o'er-heard
Your daughter and her couſin much commend
The parts and graces of the wreſtler[5]
That did but lately foil the ſinewy Charles;

---

[4] *——the* royniſh *clown,*] *Royniſh* from *rogneux,* Fr. mangy,
ſcurvy. The word is uſed by Chaucer, in *The Remaunt of the
Roſe,* 988:
    " That knottie was and all *roinous.*"
Again, by Dr. Gabriel Harvey, in his *Pierce's Supererogation,*
4to. 1593. Speaking of Long Meg of Weſtminſter, he ſays—
" Although ſhe were a luſty bouncing rampe, ſomewhat like
Gallemetta or maid Marian, yet was ſhe not ſuch a *roiniſh* rannel,
ſuch a diſſolute gillian-flirt," &c.
    We are not to ſuppoſe the word is literally employed by Shak-
ſpeare, but in the ſame ſenſe that the French ſtill uſe *carogne,* a
term of which Moliere is not very ſparing in ſome of his pieces.
                          STEEVENS,

[5] *——of the* wreſtler —] *Wreſtler,* (as Mr. Tyrwhitt has
obſerved in a note on *The Two Gentlemen of Verona,*) is here to be
founded as a triſyllable. STEEVENS.

And fhe believes, wherever they are gone,
That youth is furely in their company.

Duke F. Send to his brother;[6] fetch that gallant
  hither;
If he be abfent, bring his brother to me,
I'll make him find him: do this fuddenly;
And let not fearch and inquifition quail[7]
To bring again thefe foolifh runaways. [*Exeunt.*

SCENE III.

Before Oliver's *Houfe.*

Enter ORLANDO *and* ADAM, *meeting.*

Orl. Who's there?

Adam. What! my young mafter?—O, my gentle
  mafter,
O, my fweet mafter, O you memory[8]
Of old fir Rowland! why, what make you here?
Why are you virtuous? Why do people love you?
And wherefore are you gentle, ftrong, and valiant?

---

[6] *Send to his* brother;] I believe we fhould read—*brother's.*
For when the Duke fays in the following words: " Fetch that
gallant hither;" he certainly means Orlando. M. MASON.

[7] ———*quail*—] To *quail* is to *faint,* to fink into dejeftion.
So, in *Cymbeline:*
  " ——which my falfe fpirits
  " *Quail* to remember." STEEVENS.

[8] ———*O you* memory—] Shakfpeare often ufes *memory* for
memorial: and Beaumont and Fletcher fometimes. So, in the
Humorous Lieutenant:
  " I knew then how to feek your *memories.*"
Again, in *The Atheift's Tragedy,* by C. Turner, 1611:
  " And with his body place that *memory*
  " Of noble Charlemont."
Again, in *Byron's Tragedy:*
  " That ftatue will I prize paft all the jewels
  " Within the cabinet of Beatrice,
  " The *memory* of my grandame." STEEVENS.

Why would you be fo fond[8] to overcome
The bony prifer[9] of the humorous duke?
Your praife is come too fwiftly home before you.
Know you not, mafter, to fome kind of men[2]
Their graces ferve them but as enemies?
No more do yours; your virtues, gentle mafter,
Are fanctified and holy traitors to you.
O, what a world is this, when what is comely
Envenoms him that bears it!

ORL. Why, what's the matter?

ADAM.   O unhappy youth,
Come not within thefe doors; within this roof
The enemy of all your graces lives:
Your brother—(no, no brother; yet the fon—
Yet not the fon;—I will not call him fon—
Of him I was about to call his father,)—
Hath heard your praifes; and this night he means
To burn the lodging where you ufe to lie,

---

[8] —— fo fond—] i. e. fo indifcreet, fo inconfiderate. So, in
The Merchant of Venice:
  "———— I do wonder,
  " Thou naughty gaoler, that thou art fo fond
  " To come abroad with him ——." STEEVENS.

[9] The bony prifer—] In the former editions—The bonny prifer.
We fhould read—bony prifer. For this wreftler is characterifed
for his ftrength and bulk, not for his gaiety or good humour.
                                        WARBURTON.
So, Milton: " Giants of mighty bone." JOHNSON.
So, in the Romance of Syr Degore, bl. l. no date:
  " This is a man all for the nones,
  " For he is a man of great bones."
Bonny, however, may be the true reading. So, in K. Henry VI.
P. II. Act. V:
  " Even of the bonny beaft he lov'd fo well." STEEVENS.

The word bonny occurs more than once in the novel from which
this play of As you Like it is taken. It is likewife much ufed by the
common people in the northern counties. I believe, however, bony
to be the true reading. MALONE.

[2] —— to fome kind of men—] Old copy—feeme kind. Corrected by the editor of the fecond folio. MALONE.

And you within it: if he fail of that,
He will have other means to cut you off;
I overheard him, and his practices.
This is no place,[3] this house is but a butchery;
Abhor it, fear it, do not enter it.

    ORL. Why, whither, Adam, wouldst thou have
        me go?

    ADAM. No matter whither, so you come not here.

    ORL. What, wouldst thou have me go and beg
        my food?
Or, with a base and boisterous sword, enforce
A thievish living on the common road?
This I must do, or know not what to do:
Yet this I will not do, do how I can;
I rather will subject me to the malice
Of a diverted blood,[4] and bloody brother.

    ADAM. But do not so: I have five hundred crowns,
The thrifty hire I sav'd under your father,
Which I did store, to be my foster-nurse,
When service should in my old limbs lie lame,

---

³ *This is no* place,] *Place* here signifies a *seat*, a *mansion*, a re-
sidence. So, in the first Book of *Samuel:* " Saul set him up a *place*,
and is gone down to Gilgal." We still use the word in compound
with another, as—St. James's *place*, Rathbone *place*; and Crosby
place in *K. Richard III.* &c. STEEVENS.

  Our author uses this word again in the same sense in his *Lover's
Complaint:*
    " Love lack'd a dwelling, and made him her *place*."
Plas, in the Welch language, signifies a mansion-house. MALONE.

  Steevens's explanation of this passage is too refined. Adam
means merely to say—" This is no *place* for you." M. MASON.

⁴ ——diverted *blood*,] Blood turned out of the course of nature.
                                   JOHNSON.

  So, in our author's *Lover's Complaint:*
    " Sometimes *diverted*, their poor balls are tied
    " To the orbed earth"——. MALONE.

  To *divert* a water-course, that is, to *change its course*, was a common legal phrase, and an object of litigation in Westminster Hall
in our author's time, as it is at present. REED,

And unregarded age in corners thrown;
Take that: and He that doth the ravens feed,
Yea, providently caters for the fparrow,[4]
Be comfort to my age! Here is the gold;
All this I give you: Let me be your fervant;
Though I look old, yet I am ftrong and lufty:
For in my youth I never did apply
Hot and rebellious liquors in my blood;[5]
Nor did not with unbafhful forehead woo
The means of weaknefs and debility;
Therefore my age is as a lufty winter,
Frofty, but kindly: let me go with you;
I'll do the fervice of a younger man
In all your bufinefs and neceffities.

ORL. O good old man; how well in thee appears
The conftant fervice of the antique world,
When fervice fweat for duty, not for meed!
Thou art not for the fafhion of thefe times,
Where none will fweat, but for promotion;
And having that, do choke their fervice up
Even with the having:[6] it is not fo with thee.
But, poor old man, thou prun'ft a rotten tree,
That cannot fo much as a bloffom yield,
In lieu of all thy pains and hufbandry:
But come thy ways, we'll go along together;

---

[4] —— *and He that doth the* ravens *feed,*
Yea, providently caters for the fparrow, *&c.*] See Saint
Luke, xii. 6. and 24. Douce.

[5] —— rebellious *liquors in my blood*;] That is, liquors which
inflame the blood or fenfual paffions, and incite them to rebel againft
Reafon. So, in *Othello:*
　　" For there's a young and fweating devil here,
　　" That commonly *rebels.*" Malone.

Perhaps he only means liquors that *rebel* againft the conftitution.
　　　　　　　　　　　　　　　　　　　　Steevens.

[6] *Even with the* having:] Even with the *promotion* gained by
fervice is fervice extinguifhed. Johnson.

And ere we have thy youthful wages spent,
We'll light upon some settled low content.

ADAM. Master, go on; and I will follow thee,
To the last gasp, with truth and loyalty.—
From seventeen years' till now almost fourscore
Here lived I, but now live here no more.
At seventeen years many their fortunes seek;
But at fourscore, it is too late a week:
Yet fortune cannot recompence me better,
Than to die well, and not my master's debtor.

[*Exeunt.*

SCENE IV.

The Forest of Arden.

Enter ROSALIND *in boy's clothes,* CELIA *drest like a
Shepherdess, and* TOUCHSTONE.

Ros. O Jupiter! how weary are my spirits! [8]

⁷ *From* seventeen *years*—] The old copy reads—*seventy.* The
correction, which is fully supported by the context, was made by
Mr. Rowe. MALONE.

⁸ *O Jupiter! how* weary *are my spirits!*] The old copy reads—
how merry, &c. STEEVENS.

And yet, within the space of one intervening line, she says,
she could find in her heart to disgrace her man's apparel, and *cry
like a woman.* Sure, this is but a very bad symptom of the
briskness of spirits: rather a direct proof of the contrary disposition.
Mr. Warburton and I, concurred in conjecturing it should be, as I
have reformed in the text:—*how* weary *are my spirits!* And the
Clown's reply makes this reading certain. THEOBALD.

She invokes Jupiter, because he was supposed to be always in
good spirits. A *Jovial* man was a common phrase in our author s
time. One of Randolph's plays is called ARISTIPPUS, *or the
Jovial Philosopher;* and a comedy of Broome's, *The Jovial Crew,
or, the* Merry Beggars.

In the original copy of *Othello,* 4to. 1622, nearly the same
mistake has happened; for there we find—

    " Let us be *merry,* let us hide our joys,"
instead of—Let us be *wary.* MALONE.

Touch. I care not for my fpirits, if my legs were not weary.

Ros. I could find in my heart to difgrace my man's apparel, and to cry like a woman: but I muft comfort the weaker veffel, as doublet and hofe ought to fhow itfelf courageous to petticoat: therefore, courage, good Aliena.

Cel. I pray you, bear with me; I cannot go no further.

Touch. For my part, I had rather bear with you, than bear you:[9] yet I fhould bear no crofs,[1] if I did bear you; for, I think, you have no money in your purfe.

Ros. Well, this is the foreft of Arden.

Touch. Ay, now am I in Arden: the more fool I; when I was at home, I was in a better place; but travellers muft be content.

Ros. Ay, be fo, good Touchftone:—Look you, who comes here; a young man, and an old, in fo-lemn talk.

Enter CORIN *and* SILVIUS.

Cor. That is the way to make her fcorn you ftill.

Sil. O Corin, that thou knew'ft how I do love her!

Cor. I partly guefs; for I have lov'd ere now.

Sil. No, Corin, being old, thou canft not guefs;
Though in thy youth thou waft as true a lover
As ever figh'd upon a midnight pillow:

---

9 —— *I had rather* bear with *you, than* bear *you:*] This jingle is repeated in *K. Richard III:*
   "You mean to *bear* me, not to *bear with* me."
                                             STEEVENS.

1 ——*yet I fhould bear no* crofs,] A *crofs* was a piece of money ftamped with a *crofs.* On this our author is perpetually quibbling.
                                             STEEVENS.

But if thy love were ever like to mine,
(As sure I think did never man love so,)
How many actions most ridiculous
Haft thou been drawn to by thy fantasy!

'Cor.- Into a thousand that I have forgotten.

Sil. O, thou didst then ne'er love so heartily:
If thou remember'st not the slightest folly[3]
That ever love did make thee run into,
Thou haft not lov'd:
Or if thou haft not sat as I do now,
Wearying thy hearer[4] in thy mistress' praise,
Thou haft not lov'd:
Or if thou haft not broke from company,
Abruptly, as my passion now makes me,
Thou haft not lov'd:—O Phebe, Phebe, Phebe!

                      [*Exit* Silvius.

Ros. Alas, poor shepherd! searching of thy
               wound,[5]
I have by hard adventure found mine own.

Touch. And I mine: I remember, when I was in
love, I broke my sword upon a stone, and bid him

---

[3] *If thou remember'st not the slightest folly*—] I am inclined to
believe that from this passage *Suckling* took the hint of his song:

      "Honest lover, whosoever,
      "If in all thy love there ever
    "Was one wav'ring thought, if thy flame
    "Were not still even, still the same.
      "Know this, ·
      "Thou lov'st amiss,
    "And to love true,
    "Thou must begin again, and love anew," &c. Johnson.

[4] **Wearying** *thy bearer*—] The old copy has—*wearing.* Corrected by the editor of the second folio. I am not sure that the
emendation is necessary, though it has been adopted by all the
editors. Malone.

[5] ——*of thy wound,*] The old copy has—*they would.* The
latter word was corrected by the editor of the second folio, the
other by Mr. Rowe. Malone.

take that for coming anight [5] to Jane Smile: and I
remember the kiffing of her batlet,[6] and the cow's
dugs that her pretty chop'd hands had milk'd: and
I remember the wooing of a peafcod inftead of her;
from whom I took two cods,[7] and, giving her them
again, faid with weeping tears,[8] *Wear thefe for my*

[5] —— *anight*—] Thus the old copy. *Anight*, is *in the night.*
The word is ufed by Chaucer in *The Legende of Good Women.* Our
modern editors read, *o'nights*, or *o'night.* STEEVENS.

[6] —— *batlet*,] The inftrument with which wafhers beat their
coarfe cloaths. JOHNSON.

Old copy—*batler.* Corrected in the fecond folio. MALONE.

[7] —— *two* cods,] For *cods* it would be more like fenfe to
read—*peas*, which having the fhape of pearls, refembled the common prefents of lovers. JOHNSON.

In a fchedule of jewels in the 15th Vol. of *Rymer's Fœdera*, we
find, " Item, two *peafcoddes* of gold with 17 pearles." FARMER.

Peafcods was the ancient term for *peas* as they are brought to
market. So, in Greene's *Groundwork of Cony-catching*, 1592:
" —— went twice in the week to London, either with fruit or
pefcods," &c. Again, in *The Shepherd's Slumber*, a fong publifhed
in *England's Helicon*, 1600:
" In *pefcod time* when hound to horne
" Gives ear till buck be kill'd," &c.
Again, in *The Honeft Man's Fortune*, by Beaumont and Fletcher:
" Shall feed on delicates, the firft *peafcods*, ftrawberries."
STEEVENS.

In the following paffage, however, Touchftone's prefent certainly
fignifies not the *pea* but the *pod*, and fo, I believe, the word is
ufed here. " He [Richard II.] alfo ufed a *peafcod* branch with
the *cods* open, but the *peas* out, as it is upon his robe in his monument at Weftminfter." Camden's Remains 1614. Here we fee
the *cods* and not the *peas* were worn. Why Shakfpeare ufed the
former word rather than *pods*, which appears to have had the fame
meaning, is obvious. MALONE.

The *peafcod* certainly means the whole of the pea as it hangs
upon the ftalk. It was formerly ufed as an ornament in drefs, and
was reprefented with the fhell open exhibiting the peas. The paffage
cited from Rymer by Dr. Farmer, fhows that the peas were fometimes made of pearls, and rather overturns Dr. johnfon's conjecture,
who probably imagined that Touchftone took the *cods* from the
peafcods, and not from his miftrefs. DOUCE.

[8] —— *weeping tears*,] A ridiculous expreffion from a fonnet in

fake. We, that are true lovers, run into ftrange capers; but as all is mortal in nature, fo is all nature in love mortal in folly.[9]

Ros. Thou fpeak'ft wifer, than thou art 'ware of,

Touch. Nay, I fhall ne'er be 'ware of mine own wit, till I break my fhins againft it.

Ros. Jove! Jove! this fhepherd's paffion
Is much upon my fafhion.

Touch. And mine; but it grows fomething ftale with me.

Cel. I pray you, one of you queftion yond man, If he for gold will give us any food;
I faint almoft to death.

Touch. Holla; you, clown!

Ros.   Peace, fool; he's not thy kinfman.

Cor. Who calls?

Touch. Your betters, fir.

Cor. Elfe are they very wretched.

Ros.   Peace, I fay:—.
Good even to you, friend.[2]

Cor. And to you, gentle fir, and to you all.

Lodge's *Rofalynd*, the novel on which this comedy is founded. It likewife occurs in the old anonymous play of *The Victories of K. Henry V.* in Peele's *Jefts*, &c. STEEVENS.

The fame expreffion occurs alfo in Lodge's *Doraftus and Fawnia*, on which *The Winter's Tale* is founded. MALONE.

[9] ——*fo is all nature in love* mortal *in folly*.] This expreffion I do not well underftand. In the middle counties, *mortal*, from *mort*, a great quantity, is ufed as a particle of amplification; as *mortal tall*, *mortal little*. Of this fenfe I believe Shakfpeare takes advantage to produce one of his darling equivocations. Thus the meaning will be, *fo is all nature in love* abounding *in folly*.

JOHNSON.

[2] ——*to you, friend*.] The old copy reads—to *your* friend. Corrected by the editor of the fecond folio. MALONE.

E 2

Ros. I pr'ythee, fhepherd, if that love, or gold,
Can in this defert place buy entertainment,
Bring us where we may reft ourfelves, and feed:
Here's a young maid with travel much opprefs'd,
And faints for fuccour.

Cor.   Fair fir, I pity her,
And wifh for her fake, more than for mine own,
My fortunes were more able to relieve her:
But I am fhepherd to another man,
And do not fheer the fleeces that I graze;
My mafter is of churlifh difpofition,
And little recks [2] to find the way to heaven
By doing deeds of hofpitality:
Befides, his cote, his flocks, and bounds of feed,
Are now on fale, and at our fheepcote now,
By reafon of his abfence, there is nothing
That you will feed on; but what is, come fee,
And in my voice moft welcome fhall you be.[3]

Ros. What is he that fhall buy his flock and paf-
        ture?

Cor. That young fwain that you faw here but
        erewhile,
That little cares for buying any thing.

Ros. I pray thee, if it ftand with honefty,
Buy thou the cottage, pafture, and the flock,
And thou fhalt have to pay for it of us.

Cel. And we will mend thy wages: I like this
        place,
And willingly could wafte my time in it.

Cor. Affuredly, the thing is to be fold:

---

[2] *And little* recks—] i. e. heeds, cares for. So, in *Hamlet:*
    " And *recks* not his own rede." STEEVENS.

[3] *And in my voice moft welcome fhall you be.*] *In my voice,* as far
as I have a voice or vote, as far as I have power to bid you welcome. JOHNSON.

Go with me; if you like, upon report,
The foil, the profit, and this kind of life,
I will your very faithful feeder be,
And buy it with your gold right suddenly.

[*Exeunt.*

SCENE V.

The same.

Enter AMIENS, JAQUES, *and Others.*

SONG.

AMI. *Under the greenwood tree,*
Who loves to lie with me,
And tune [4] *his merry note*
Unto the sweet bird's throat,
Come hither, come hither, come hither;
Here shall be see
No enemy,
But winter and rough weather.

JAQ. More, more, I pr'ythee, more.

AMI. It will make you melancholy, monsieur
Jaques.

JAQ. I thank it. More, I pr'ythee, more. I
can suck melancholy out of a song, as a weazel
sucks eggs: More, I pr'ythee, more.

---

[4] *And* tune—] The old copy has *turne.* Corrected by Mr.
Pope. So, in *The Two Gentlemen of Verona:*
    " And *to* the nightingale's complaining *note*
    " *Tune* my distresses, and record my woes." MALONE.

The old copy may be right, though Mr. Pope, &c. read *tune.*
To *turn* a *tune* or a *note,* is still a current phrase among vulgar
musicians. STEEVENS.

E 3

Ami. My voice is **ragged**;[5] I know, I cannot please you.

Jaq. I do not desire you to please me, I do desire you to sing: Come, more; another stanza; Call you them stanzas?

Ami. What you will, monsieur Jaques.

Jaq. Nay, I care not for their names; they owe me nothing: Will you sing?

Ami. More at your request, than to please myself.

Jaq. Well then, if ever I thank any man, I'll thank you: but that they call compliment, is like the encounter of two dog-apes; and when a man thanks me heartily, methinks, I have given him a penny, and he renders me the beggarly thanks. Come, sing; and you that will not, hold your tongues.

Ami. Well, I'll end the song.—Sirs, cover the while; the duke will drink under this tree:—he hath been all this day to look you.

Jaq. And I have been all this day to avoid him. He is too disputable[6] for my company: I think of as many matters as he; but I give heaven thanks, and make no boast of them. Come, warble, come.

---

[5] —— *ragged*;] Our modern editors (Mr. Malone excepted) read *rugged*; but *ragged* had anciently the same meaning. So, in Nash's *Apologie of Pierce Pennilesse*, 4to. 1593: " I would not trot a false gallop through the rest of his *ragged* verses," &c.
        STEEVENS.

[6] —— *disputable*—] for *disputatious*. MALONE.

S O N G.

Who doth ambition shun,   [All together here]
And loves to live i' the sun,[7]
Seeking the food he eats,
And pleas'd with what he gets,
Come hither, come hither, come hither;
    Here shall he see
    No enemy,
But winter and rough weather.

Jaq. I'll give you a verse to this note, that I made yesterday in despite of my invention.

Ami. And I'll sing it.

Jaq. Thus it goes:

    If it do come to pass,
    That any man turn ass,
    Leaving his wealth and ease,
    A stubborn will to please,
Ducdàme, ducdàme, ducdàme;[8]
    Here shall he see,
    Gross fools as he,
An if he will come to Ami.

[7] —— *to* live *i' the sun,*] Modern editions, *to lie.* JOHNSON.

To live i' the sun, is to labour and "sweat in the eye of Phœbus," or, *vitam agere sub dio*; for by *lying* in the sun, how could they get the food they eat? TOLLET.

[8] —*ducdàme;*] For *ducdàme,* Sir Thomas Hanmer, very acutely and judiciously, reads *duc ad me,* that is, *bring him to me.*
JOHNSON.

If *duc ad me* were right, Amiens would not have asked its meaning, and been put off with "a *Greek invocation.*" It is evidently a word coined *for the nonce.* We have here, as Butler says, "One for *sense,* and one for *rhyme.*"—Indeed we must have a *double rhyme*; or this stanza cannot well be sung to the same tune with the former. I read thus:

E 4

Ami. What's that *ducdàme?*

Jaq. 'Tis a Greek invocation, to call fools into a circle. I'll go ſleep if I can; if I cannot, I'll rail againſt all the firſt-born of Egypt.[9]

> " *Ducdàme, Ducdàme, Ducdàme,*
>> " Here ſhall he ſee
>> " Groſs fools as he,
> " An' if he will come to *Ami.*"

That is, to Amiens. Jaques did not mean to ridicule himſelf.

FARMER.

Duc ad me has hitherto been received as an alluſion to the burthen of Amiens's ſong,

> *Come hither, come hither, come hither.*

That Amiens, who is a courtier, ſhould not underſtand Latin, or be perſuaded it was Greek, is no great matter for wonder. An anonymous correſpondent propoſes to read—*Huc ad me.*

In confirmation of the old reading, however, Dr. Farmer obſerves to me, that, being at a houſe not far from Cambridge, when news was brought that the hen-rooſt was robbed, a facetious old ſquire who was preſent, immediately ſung the following ſtanza, which has an odd coincidence with the ditty of Jaques:

> " *Damè,* what makes your ducks to die?
> " *duck, duck, duck.——*
> " *Damè,* what makes your chicks to cry?
> " *chuck, chuck, chuck.——*"

I have placed Dr. Farmer's emendation in the text. *Ducdàme* is a triſſyllable. STEEVENS.

> *If it do come to paſs,*
> *That any man turn aſs,*
> *Leaving his wealth and eaſe,*
> *A ſtubborn will to pleaſe,*
> Duc ad me, duc ad me, duc ad me;
> *Here ſhall he ſee*
> *Groſs fools as he, &c.*] See Hor. Serm. L. II. ſat. iii:
>> " Audire atque togam jubeo componere, quiſquis
>> " Ambitione mala aut argenti pallet amore;
>> " Quiſquis luxuria triſtive ſuperſtitione,
>> " Aut alio mentis morbo calet: Huc proprius me,
>> " Dum doceo inſanire omnes, vos ordine adite." MALONE.

9 —— *the firſt-born of Egypt.*] A proverbial expreſſion for high-born perſons. JOHNSON.

The phraſe is ſcriptural, as well as proverbial. So, in *Exodus,* xii. 29: " And the Lord ſmote *all the firſt-born in Egypt.*" STEEVENS.

Ami. And I'll go feek the duke; his banquet is prepar'd.   [*Exeunt feverally.*

SCENE VI.

The fame.

Enter ORLANDO *and* ADAM.

Adam. Dear mafter, I can go no further: O, I die for food! Here lie I down, and meafure out my grave.[2] Farewell, kind mafter.

Orl. Why, how now, Adam! no greater heart in thee? Live a little; comfort a little; cheer thy-felf a little: If this uncouth foreft yield any thing favage, I will either be food for it, or bring it for food to thee. Thy conceit is nearer death than thy powers For my fake, be comfortable; hold death awhile at the arm's end: I will here be with thee prefently; and if I bring thee not fomething to eat, I'll give thee leave to die: but if thou dieft before I come, thou art a mocker of my labour. Well faid! thou look'ft cheerly: and I'll be with thee quickly.—Yet thou lieft in the bleak air: Come, I will bear thee to fome fhelter; and thou fhalt not die for lack of a dinner, if there live any thing in this defert. Cheerly, good Adam!   [*Exeunt.*

---

[2] *Here lie I down, and meafure out my grave.*] So, in *Romeo and Juliet* :

    " —— fall upon the ground, as I do now,
    " Taking the meafure of an unmade grave."
                             STEEVENS.

SCENE VII.

The fame.

A table fet out. Enter Duke *Senior*, AMIENS, *Lords,
and Others.*

DUKE S. I think he be transform'd into a beaſt;
For I can no where find him like a man.

1 LORD. My lord, he is but even now **gone**
          hence;
Here was he merry, hearing of a fong.

DUKE S. If he, compact of jars,[2] grow muſical,
We ſhall have ſhortly diſcord in the ſpheres:—
Go, ſeek him; tell him, I would ſpeak with him.

Enter JAQUES.

1 LORD. He faves my labour by his own ap-
          proach.

DUKE S. Why, how now, monſieur! what a life
          is this,
That your poor friends muſt woo your company?
What! you look merrily.

JAQ. A fool, a fool!——I met a fool i' the foreſt,
A motley fool;—a miſerable world![3]—

---

[2] ——*compact of jars,*] i. e. made up of diſcords. In *The
Comedy of Errors* we have "*compact of credit,*" for *made up of cre-
dulity.* Again, in *Woman is a Weathercock,* 1612:
    "——— like gilded tombs
    "*Compacted* of jet pillars."
The ſame expreſſion occurs alſo in *Tamburlane,* 1590:
    "*Compact* of rapine, piracy, and ſpoil."
                                        STEEVENS.
[3] *A motley fool;—a miſerable world!*] What! becauſe he met a

As I do live by food, I met a fool;
Who laid him down and bafk'd him in the fun,
And rail'd on lady Fortune in good terms,
In good fet terms,—and yet a motley fool.
Good-morrow, fool, quoth I : *No, fir,* quoth he,
Call me not fool, till heaven hath fent me fortune :[4]
And then he drew a dial from his poke;
And looking on it with lack-luftre eye,
Says, very wifely, *It is ten o'clock :*
Thus may we fee, quoth he, *how the world wags;*
'Tis but an hour ago, fince it was nine;
And after one hour more, 'twill be eleven;
And fo, from hour to hour, we ripe and ripe,
And then, from hour to hour, we rot, and rot,
And thereby hangs a tale. When I did hear
The motley fool thus moral on the time,

motley fool, was it therefore *a miferable world?* This is fadly blundered; we fhould read :

——————— *a miferable* varlet.

His head is altogether running on this fool, both before and after thefe words, and here he calls him *a miferable varlet,* notwithftanding he *railed on lady Fortune in good terms,* &c. Nor is the change we may make, fo great as appears at firft fight.

WARBURTON.

I fee no need of changing *world* to *varlet,* nor, if a change were neceffary, can I guefs how it fhould certainly be known that *varlet* is the true word. *A miferable world* is a parenthetical exclamation, frequent among melancholy men, and natural to Jaques at the fight of a fool, or at the hearing of reflections on the fragility of life. JOHNSON.

[4] *Call me not fool, till heaven hath fent me fortune :*] *Fortuna favet fatuis,* is, as Mr. Upton obferves, the faying here alluded to; or, as in Publius Syrus :

"*Fortuna, nimium quem fovet, ftultum facit.*"

So, in the prologue to *The Alchemift* :

" Fortune, that favours fooles, thefe two fhort houres
" We wifh away."

Again, in *Every Man out of his Humour,* Act I. fc. iii :

" *Sog.* Why, who am I, fir?
" *Mac.* One of thofe that fortune favours.
" *Car.* The periphrafis of a foole." REED.

My lungs began to crow like chanticleer,
That fools fhould be fo deep-contemplative;
And I did laugh, fans intermiffion,
An hour by his dial.—O noble fool!
A worthy fool! Motley's the only wear.'

Duke S. What fool is this?

Jaq. O worthy fool!—One that hath been a
   courtier;
And fays, if ladies be but young, and fair,
They have the gift to know it: and in his brain,—
Which is as dry as the remainder bifket
After a voyage,—he hath ftrange places cramm'd
With obfervation, the which he vents
In mangled forms:—O, that I were a fool!
I am ambitious for a motley coat.

Duke S. Thou fhalt have one.

Jaq.   It is my only fuit;'
Provided, that you weed your better judgments
Of all opinion that grows rank in them,
That I am wife. I muft have liberty
Withal, as large a charter as the wind,'

 ' —— Motley's *the only wear.*] It would have been unneceffary to repeat that a *motley*, or *party-coloured coat* was anciently the
drefs of a fool, had not the editor of Ben Jonfon's works been
miftaken in his comment on the 53d *Epigram:*
   " —————— where, out of *motley,'s* he
   " Could fave that line to dedicate to thee?"
Motley, fays Mr. Whalley, is the man who *out of any* odd mixture,
or old fcraps, could fave, &c. whereas it means only, *Who but a
fool*, i. e. *one in a fuit of motley*, &c.
 See Fig. XII. in the plate at the end of the firft part of *King
Henry IV.* with Mr. Tollet's explanation. STEEVENS.

 ⁶ —*only* fuit;] *Suit* means *petition*, I believe, not *drefs.* JOHNSON.
 The poet meant a quibble. So Act V: " Not out of your
apparel, but out of your *fuit*." STEEVENS.

 ⁷ —— *as large a charter as the wind*,] So, in *K. Henry V:*
   " The *wind*, that *charter'd* libertine, is ftill." MALONE.

I

To blow on whom I pleafe; for fo fools have:
And they that are moft galled with my folly,
They moft muft laugh: And why, fir, muft they fo?
The *why* is plain as way to parifh church:
He, that a fool doth very wifely hit,
Doth very foolifhly, although he fmart,
Not to feem fenfelefs of the bob:[8] if not,
The wife man's folly is anatomiz'd
Even by the fquandring glances of the fool.[9]
Inveft me in my motley; give me leave
To fpeak my mind, and I will through and through
Cleanfe the foul body of the infected world,[2]
If they will patiently receive my medicine.

 Duke S. Fie on thee! I can tell what thou wouldft
  do.

 Jaq. What, for a counter,[3] would I do, but good?

***

[8] Not to *feem fenfelefs of the bob :*] The old copies read only—
Seem fenfelefs, &c. *Not to* were fupplied by Mr. Theobald. See
the following note. STEEVENS.

 Befides that the third verfe is defective one whole *foot* in meafure, the tenour of what Jaques continues to fay, and the reafoning
of the paffage, fhow it no lefs defective in the fenfe. There is no
doubt, but the two little monofyllables, which I have fupplied,
were either by accident wanting in the manufcript, or by inadver-
tence were left out. THEOBALD.

 [9] ——*if not,* &c.] Unlefs men have the prudence not to appear
touched with the farcafms of a jefter, they fubject themfelves to.
his power; and the wife man will have his folly *anatomifed,* that is,
diffected and *laid open,* by the *fquandring glances* or *random fhots* of
a fool. JOHNSON.

 [2] *Cleanfe the foul body of the infected world,*] So, in *Macbeth:*
   " Cleanfe the ftuff'd bofom of that perilous ftuff."
               DOUCE.

 [3] ——*for a* counter,] Dr. Farmer obferves to me, that about
the time when this play was written, the French *counters* (i. e. pieces
of falfe money ufed as a means of reckoning) were brought into ufe
in England. They are again mentioned in *Troilus and Creffida:*
   " ——will you with *counters* fum
   " The paft proportion of his infinite?" STEEVENS.

Duke S. Moſt miſchievous foul ſin, in chiding ſin:
For thou thyſelf haſt been a libertine,
As ſenſual as the brutiſh ſting[1] itſelf;
And all the emboſſed ſores, and headed evils,
That thou with licence of free foot haſt caught,
Wouldſt thou diſgorge into the general world.

Jaq. Why, who cries out on pride,
That can therein tax any private party?
Doth it not flow as hugely as the ſea,
Till that the very very means do ebb?[4]
What woman in the city do I name,
When that I ſay, The city-woman bears
The coſt of princes on unworthy ſhoulders?
Who can come in, and ſay, that I mean her,
When ſuch a one as ſhe, ſuch is her neighbour?
Or what is he of baſeſt function,
That ſays, his bravery[5] is not on my coſt,
(Thinking that I mean him,) but therein ſuits
His folly to the mettle of my ſpeech?
There then; How, what then?[6] Let me ſee wherein

[1] *As ſenſual as the* brutiſh ſting—] Though the *brutiſh ſting* is capable of a ſenſe not inconvenient in this paſſage, yet as it is a harſh and unuſual mode of ſpeech, I ſhould read the *brutiſh fly.* JOHNSON.

I believe the old reading is the true one. So, in Spenſer's *Faery Queen,* B. I. c. viii:
    " A heard of bulls whom kindly rage doth *ſting.*"
Again, B. II. c. xii:
    " As if that hunger's point, or Venus' *ſting,*
    " Had them enrag'd."
Again, in *Othello:*
    " ——our carnal *ſtings,* our unbitted luſts." STEEVENS.

[4] *Till that the* very *very*—] The old copy reads—*weary* very. Corrected by Mr. Pope. MALONE.

[5] —— *his* bravery—] i. e. his fine clothes. So, in *The Taming of the Shrew:*
    " With ſcarfs and fans, and double change of *bravery.*"
                                        STEEVENS.

[6] *There then; How, what then?* &c.] The old copy reads, very redundantly—
    There then; How then? *What then?* &c. STEEVENS.

My tongue hath wrong'd him: if it do him right,
Then he hath wrong'd himfelf; if he be free,
Why then, my taxing like a wild goofe flies,
Unclaim'd of any man.—But who comes here?

Enter ORLANDO, *with his fword drawn.*

ORL. Forbear, and eat no more.

JAQ.   Why, I have eat none yet.

ORL. Nor fhalt not, till neceffity be ferv'd.

JAQ. Of what kind fhould this cock come of?

DUKE S. Art thou thus bolden'd, man, by thy
         diftrefs;
Or elfe a rude defpifer of good manners,
That in civility thou feem'ft fo empty?

ORL. You touch'd my vein at firft; the thorny
         point
Of bare diftrefs hath ta'en from me the fhow
Of fmooth civility:[7] yet am I inland bred,[8]
And know fome nurture:[9] But forbear, I fay;
He dies, that touches any of this fruit,
Till I and my affairs are anfwered.

I believe we fhould read—*Where* then? So, in *Othello:*
   " What then? How then? *Where's* fatisfaction?" MALONE.

  [7] —— *the thorny point*
     Of bare diftrefs hath ta'en *from me the fhow*
     Of fmooth civility:] We might read *torn* with more elegance,
but elegance alone will not juftify alteration. JOHNSON.

  [8] —— inland *bred,*] *Inland* here, and elfewhere in this play, is
the oppofite to *outland,* or *upland.* Orlando means to fay, that he
had not been *bred among clowns.* HOLT WHITE.

  [9] *And know fome* nurture:] *Nurture* is *education,* breeding, manners. So, in Greene's *Never too Late,* 1616:
     " He fhew'd himfelf as full of *nurture* as of nature."
Again, as Mr. Holt White obferves to me, Barret fays in his
Alvearie, 1580: " It is a point of *nurture,* or *good manners,* to
falute them that you meete. *Urbanitatis eft falutare obvios.*"
                              STEEVENS.

Jaq. An you will not be anſwered with reaſon,
I muſt die.

Duke S. What would you have? Your gentleneſs ſhall force,
More than your force move us to gentleneſs.

Orl. I almoſt die for food, and let me have it.

Duke S. Sit down and feed, and welcome to our
   table.

Orl. Speak you ſo gently? Pardon me, I pray you:
I thought, that all things had been ſavage here;
And therefore put I on the countenance
Of ſtern commandment: But whate'er you are,
That in this deſert inacceſſible,[9]
Under the ſhade of melancholy boughs,
Loſe and neglect the creeping hours of time;
If ever you have look'd on better days;
If ever been where bells have knoll'd to church;
If ever ſat at any good man's feaſt;
If ever from your eye-lids wip'd a tear,
And know what 'tis to pity, and be pitied;
Let gentleneſs my ſtrong enforcement be:
In the which hope, I bluſh, and hide my ſword.

Duke S. True is it that we have ſeen better days;
And have with holy bell been knoll'd to church;
And ſat at good men's feaſts; and wip'd our eyes
Of drops that ſacred pity hath engender'd:
And therefore ſit you down in gentleneſs,
And take upon command what help we have,[2]
That to your wanting may be miniſtred.

---

[9] —— *deſert inacceſſible*,] This expreſſion I find in *The Adventures of Simonides*, by Barn. Riche, 1580: " —— and onely
acquainted himſelfe with the ſolitarineſſe of this *unacceſſible deſert.*"
          HENDERSON.

[2] *And take* upon command *what help we have*,] *Upon command,*
is at your own command. STEEVENS.

Orl. Then, but forbear your food a little while,
Whiles, like a doe, I go to find my fawn,
And give it food.[3]   There is an old poor man,
Who after me hath many a weary ſtep
Limp'd in pure love; till he be firſt ſuffic'd,—
Oppreſs'd with two weak evils, age and hunger,—
I will not touch a bit.

Duke S.   Go find him out,
And we will nothing waſte till you return.

Orl. I thank ye; and be bleſs'd for your good
            comfort!   [*Exit.*

Duke S. Thou ſeeſt, we are not all alone un-
            happy:
This wide and univerſal theatre
Preſents more woeful pageants than the ſcene
Wherein we play in.[4]

---

³ *Whiles, like a* doe, *I go to find my* fawn,
  And give it food.] So, in *Venus and Adonis:*
      " Like a milch *dee,* whoſe ſwelling dugs do ake,
      " Haſting to *feed her fawn.*"   MALONE.

⁴ *Wherein we play* in.] Thus the old copy.   Mr. Pope more
correctly reads:
      Wherein we play.
I believe with Mr. Pope, that we ſhould only read—
      Wherein we play.
and add a word at the beginning of the next ſpeech, to complete
the meaſure; viz.
      " *Why,* all the world's a ſtage."
Thus, in *Hamlet:*
      " *Hor.* So Roſencrantz and Guildenſtern go to't.
      " *Ham. Why,* man, they did make love to their employment."
Again, in *Meaſure for Meaſure:*
      " *Why,* all the ſouls that were, were forfeit once."
Again, *ibid:*
      " *Why,* every fault's condemn'd, ere it be done."
   In twenty other inſtances we find the ſame adverb introductorily
uſed.   STEEVENS.

Jaq.   All the world's a stage,⁴ :
And all the men and women merely players:
They have their exits, and their entrances;
And one man in his time plays many parts,
His acts being seven ages.⁵   At first, the infant,

⁴ *All the world's a stage*, &c.] This obfervation occurs in one
of the fragments of Petronius: " Non duco contentionis finem,
dum conftet inter nos, quod fere *totus mundus exerceat biftrioniam*."
                                                     STEEVENS.

This obfervation had been made in an Englifh drama before the
time of Shakfpeare. See *Damon and Pythias*, 1582:
    " Pythagoras faid, that *this world was like a ftage*,
    " *Whereon many play their parts*."
In *The Legend of Orpheus and Eurydice*, 1597, we find thefe lines:
    " Unhappy man——
    " Whofe life a fad continual tragedie,
    " Himfelf the *actor, in the world, the ftage*,
    " *While as the acts are meafur'd by his age*." MALONE.

⁵ *His acts being feven* ages.] Dr. Warburton obferves, that this was
" *no unufual* divifion of a play before our author's time;" but forbears
to offer any one example in fupport of his affertion. I have carefully perufed almoft every dramatick piece antecedent to Shakfpeare, or contemporary with him; but fo far from being divided
into acts, they are almoft all printed in an onbroken continuity of
fcenes. I fhould add, that there is one play of fix acts to be met
with, and another of twenty-one; but the fecond of thefe is a
tranflation from the Spanifh, and never could have been defigned
for the ftage. In *God's Promifes*, 1577, " A Tragedie or Enterlude,"
(or rather a *Myftery*) by John Bale, feven acts may indeed be
found. STEEVENS.

Dr. Warburton boldly afferts that this was " *no unufual* divifion
of a play before our author's time." One of Chapman's plays
(*Two Wife Men and all the reft Fools*) is indeed in feven acts.
This, however, is the only dramatick piece that I have found
fo divided. But furely it is not neceffary to fuppofe that our
author alluded here to any fuch precife divifion of the drama.
His comparifons feldom run on four feet. It was fufficient for
him that a play was diftributed into *feveral* acts, and that human
life, long before his time, had been divided into *feven* periods.
In *the Treafury of Ancient and Modern Times*, 1613, Proclus, a
Greek author, is faid to have divided the life-time of man into
SEVEN AGES; over each of which one of the feven planets was
fuppofed to rule. " The FIRST AGE is called *Infancy*, containing

Mewling and puking in the nurfe's arms;
And then,[6] the whining fchool-boy, with his fatchel,
And fhining morning face, creeping like fnail
Unwillingly to fchool: And then, the lover;
Sighing like furnace,[7] with a woeful ballad

the fpace of foure yeares.—The SECOND AGE continueth ten years, untill he attaine to the yeares of fourteene: this age is called *Childhood.*—The THIRD AGE confifteth of eight yeares, being named by our auncients *Adolefcencie* or *Youthhood*; and it lafteth from fourteene, till two and twenty yeares be fully compleate.— The FOURTH AGE paceth on, till a man have accomplifhed two and fortie yeares, and is tearmed *Young Manhood.*—The FIFTH AGE, named *Mature Manhood,* hath (according to the faid authour) fifteene yeares of continuance, and therefore makes his progrefs fo far as fix and fifty yeares.—Afterwards in adding twelve to fifty-fixe, you fhall make up fixty-eight yeares, which reach to the end of the SIXT AGE, and is called *Old Age.*—The SEAVENTH and laft of thefe feven ages is limited from fixty-eight yeares, fo far as four-fcore and eight, being called weak, declining, and *Decrepite Age.*—If any man chance to goe beyond this age, (which is more admired than noted in many,) you fhall evidently perceive that he will returne to his firft condition of Infancy againe."

Hippocrates likewife divided the life of man into feven ages, but differs from Proclus in the number of years allotted to each period. See Brown's *Vulgar Errors,* folio, 1686, p. 173.

MALONE.

I have feen, more than once, an old print entitled, *The ftage of Man's Life,* divided into feven ages. As emblematical reprefentations of this fort were formerly ftuck up, both for ornament and inftruction, in the generality of houfes, it is more probable that Shakfpeare took his hint from thence, than from Hippocrates or Proclus. HENLEY.

One of the reprefentations to which Mr. Henley alludes, was formerly in my poffeffion; and confidering the ufe it is of in explaining the paffage before us, " I could have better fpared a better *print.*" I well remember that it exhibited the fchool-boy *with bis fatchel* hanging over his fhoulders. STEEVENS.

[6] And *then,*] *And,* which is wanting in the old copy, was fupplied, for the fake of metre, by Mr. Pope. STEEVENS.

[7] *Sighing like furnace,*] So, in *Cymbeline:* " — he *furnaceth* the thick *fighs* from him—." MALONE.

Made to his miſtreſs' eye-brow : Then, a ſoldier;
Full of ſtrange oaths, and bearded like the pard,'¹
Jealous in honour, ſudden and quick⁴ in quarrel,
Seeking the bubble reputation
Even in the cannon's mouth : And then, the juſtice;
In fair round belly, with good capon lin'd,
With eyes ſevere, and beard of formal cut,
Full of wiſe ſaws and modern inſtances,ᵛ
And ſo he plays his part : The ſixth age ſhifts
Into the lean and ſlipper'd pantaloon ;ᵃ

¹ ——a ſoldier;
Full of ſtrange oaths, and bearded like the pard,] So, in
Cynthia's Revels, by Ben Jonſon:
" —— Your ſoldiers face—the grace of this face conſiſteth
much in a beard." STEEVENS.

Beards of different cut were appropriated in our author's time to
different characters and profeſſions. The ſoldier had one faſhion,
the judge another, the biſhop different from both, &c. See a
note on K. Henry V. Act III. ſc. vi: " And what a beard of the
general's cut," &c. MALONE.

⁴ —— ſudden and quick—] Left it ſhould be ſuppoſed that theſe
epithets are ſynonymous, it is neceſſary to be obſerved that one
of the ancient ſenſes of ſudden, is violent. Thus, in Macbeth:
" —— I grant him ſudden,
" Malicious," &c. STEEVENS.

ᵛ Full of wiſe ſaws and modern inſtances,] It is remarkable that
Shakſpeare uſes modern in the double ſenſe that the Greeks uſed
καινὸς, both for recens and abſurdus. WARBURTON.

I am in doubt whether modern is in this place uſed for abſurd:
the meaning ſeems to be, that the juſtice is full of old ſayings and
late examples. JOHNSON.

Modern means trite, common. So, in K. John:
" And ſcorns a modern invocation."
Again, in this play, Act IV. ſc. i: " —— betray themſelves to
modern cenſure." STEEVENS.

Again, in another of our author's plays: " ——to make
modern and familiar things ſupernatural and cauſeleſs." MALONE.

ᵃ —— The ſixth age ſhifts
Into the lean and ſlipper'd pantaloon;] There is a greater
beauty than appears at firſt ſight in this image. He is here com-

With fpectacles on nofe, and pouch on fide;
His youthful hofe well fav'd, a world too wide
For his fhrunk fhank; and his big manly voice,
Turning again toward childifh treble, pipes
And whiftles in his found: Laft fcene of all,
That ends this ftrange eventful hiftory,
Is fecond childifhnefs, and mere oblivion;
Sans teeth, fans eyes, fans tafte, fans every thing.

Re-enter ORLANDO, *with* ADAM.

DUKE S. Welcome: Set down your venerable.
    burden,[3]
And let him feed.

ORL.   I thank you moft for him.

paring human life to a *ftage play* of feven acts, (which is no unufual
divifion before our author's time.) The fixth he calls the *lean
and flipper'd pantaloon*, alluding to that general character in the
Italian comedy, called *Il Pantalóne*; who is a thin emaciated old
man in *flippers*; and well defigned, in that epithet, becaufe *Pantalóne* is the only character that acts in flippers. WARBURTON.

In *The Travels of the three Englifh Brothers*, a comedy, 1606,
an Italian Harlequin is introduced, who offers to perform a play
at a Lord's houfe, in which among other characters he mentions
" a jealous coxcomb, and an old *Pantaloune.*" But this is feven
years later than the date of the play before us: nor do I know
from whence our author could learn the circumftance mentioned
by Dr. Warburton, that " *Pantalóne* is the only character in the
Italian comedy that acts in flippers." In Florio's Italian Dictionary,
1598, the word is not found. In *The Taming of the Shrew*, one
of the characters, if I remember right, is called " an old *Pantaloon,*" but there is no farther defcription of him. MALONE.

[3] —— *Set down your venerable burden,*] Is it not likely that
Shakfpeare had in his mind this line of the *Metamorphofes?* XIII. 125.
  " —— *Patremque*
  " *Fert humeris,* venerabile onus, *Cythereius heros.*"
         JOHNSON.
 A. Golding, p. 169, b. edit. 1587, tranflates it thus:
  " —— upon his backe
  " His aged father and his gods, an *honorable packe.*"
         STEEVENS.

Adam. So had you need;
I scarce can speak to thank you for myself.

Duke S. Welcome, fall to: I will not trouble you
As yet, to question you about your fortunes :—
Give us some musick ; and, good cousin, sing.

AMIENS *sings.*

S O N G.

I.

Blow, blow, thou winter wind,
Thou art not so unkind
  As man's ingratitude ; [3]
Thy tooth is not so keen,
Because thou art not seen, [4]
  Although thy breath be rude.
Heigh, ho ! sing, heigh, ho ! unto the green holly :
Most friendship is feigning, most loving mere folly :
  Then, heigh, ho, the holly !
  This life is most jolly.

[3] *Thou art not so* unkind, &c.] That is, thy action is not so contrary to thy *kind,* or to human nature, as the ingratitude of man. So, in our author's *Venus and Adonis,* 1593:

  " O had thy mother borne so bad a mind,
  " She had not brought forth thee, but dy'd *unkind.*" MALONE.

[4] *Thy tooth is not so keen,*
  Because thou art not seen,] This song is designed to suit the Duke's exiled condition, who had been ruined by *ungrateful flatterers.* Now the *winter wind,* the song says, is to be preferred to *man's ingratitude.* But why? *Because it is not* seen. But this was not only an aggravation of the injury, as it was done in secret, *not seen,* but was the very circumstance that made the keenness of the ingratitude of his faithless courtiers. Without doubt, Shakspeare wrote the line thus :

  Because thou art not sheen,
i. e. smiling, shining, like an ungrateful court-servant, who flatters while he wounds, which was a very good reason for giving

I

II.

Freeze, freeze, thou bitter sky,
That doſt not bite ſo nigh
As benefits forgot :
Though thou the waters warp,[5]
Thy ſting is not ſo ſharp
As friend remember'd not.[6]
Heigh, ho! ſing, heigh, ho! &c.

the *winter wind* the preference. So, in *The Midſummer Night's Dream :*

" Spangled ſtar-light *ſheen.*"

And ſeveral other places. Chaucer uſes it in this ſenſe :

" Your bliſsful ſiſter Lucina the *ſhene.*

And Fairfax :

" The ſacred angel took his target *ſhene,*
" And by the Chriſtian champion ſtood unſeen."

The Oxford editor, who had this emendation communicated to him, takes occaſion from hence to alter the whole line thus :

Thou cauſeſt not that teen.

But, in his rage of correction, he forgot to leave the reaſon, which is now wanting, Why the *winter wind* was to be preferred to *man's ingratitude.* WARBURTON.

I am afraid that no reader is ſatisfied with Dr. Warburton's emendation, however vigorouſly enforced ; and it is indeed enforced with more art than truth. *Sheen,* i. e. *ſmiling, ſhining.* That *ſheen* ſignifies *ſhining,* is eaſily proved, but when or where did it ſignify *ſmiling?* yet *ſmiling* gives the ſenſe neceſſary in this place. Sir T. Hanmer's change is leſs uncouth, but too remote from the preſent text. For my part, I queſtion whether the original line is not loſt, and this ſubſtituted merely to fill up the meaſure and the rhyme. Yet even out of this line, by ſtrong agitation may ſenſe be elicited, and ſenſe not unſuitable to the occaſion. *Thou winter wind,* ſays Amiens, *thy rudeneſs gives the leſs pain,* as thou art not ſeen, *as thou art an enemy that doſt not brave us with thy preſence, and whoſe unkindueſs is therefore not aggravated by inſult.*

JOHNSON.

Though the old text may be tortured into a meaning, perhaps it would be as well to read :

Becauſe the heart's not ſeen.

ẏ *harts,* according to the ancient mode of writing, was eaſily corrupted. FARMER.

F 4

Duke S. If that you were the good fir **Rowland's**
　　fon,——
As you have whifper'd faithfully, you were;

So, in the Sonnet introduced into *Love's Labour's Loft*:
　" Through the velvet leaves the *wind*
　" All *unfeen* 'gan paffage find." STEEVENS.
Again, in *Meafure for Meafure*:
　" To be imprifon'd in the *viewlefs* winds." MALONE.

⁵ *Though thou the waters* warp,] The furfaee of *waters*, fo long
as they remain unfrozen, is apparently a perfeét plane; whereas,
when they are, this furface deviates from its exaét flatnefs, or
warps. This is remarkable in fmall ponds, the furface of which
when frozen, forms a regular concave; the ice on the fides rifing
higher than that in the middle. KENRICK.

To *warp* was probably in Shakfpeare's time, a colloquial word,
which conveyed no diftant allufion to any thing elfe, phyfical
or mechanical. To *warp* is to *turn*, and to *turn* is to *change*:
when milk is *changed* by curdling, we now fay it is *turned*: when
water is *changed* or *turned* by froft, Shakfpeare fays, it is *curdled*.
To be *warp'd* is only to be changed from its natural ftate.
　　　　　　　　　　　　　　　　　JOHNSON.

Dr. Johnfon is certainly right. So, in *Cynthia's Revels*, of
Ben Jonfon. " I know not, he's grown out of his garb a-late,
he's *warp'd*.—And fo, methinks too, he *is* much *converted.*"
Thus the *mole* is called the mould-*warp*, becaufe it changes the
appearance of the furface of the earth. Again, in *The Winter's
Tale*, Aét I:
　" My favour here begins to *warp*."
Dr. Farmer fuppofes *warp'd* to mean the fame as *curdled*, and
adds that a fimilar idea occurs in *Timon*:
　" ——the icicle
　" That *curdled* by the froft," &c. STEEVENS.

Among a colleétion of Saxon adages in *Hickes's Thefaurus*,
Vol. I. p. 221, the fucceeding appears: pinꞇeꞃ ꞃceal zeþeoꞃpan
peþeꞃ, *winter fhall warp water*. So that Shakfpeare's expreffion
was anciently proverbial. It fhould be remarked, that among the
numerous examples in *Manning's* excellent edition of *Lye's Dictionary*, there is no inftance of þeoꞃpan or zeþeoꞃpan, implying to
freeze, *bend*, *turn*, or *curdle*, though it is a verb of very extenfive
fignification.

Probably this word ftill retains a fimilar fenfe in the Northern part of the Ifland, for in a Scottifh parody on Dr. Percy's
elegant ballad, beginning, " O Nancy, wilt thou go with me,"

And as mine eye doth his effigies witnefs
Moft truly limn'd, and living in your face,—
Be truly welcome hither: I am the duke,
That lov'd your father: The refidue of your for-
tune,
Go to my cave and tell me.—Good old man,
Thou art right welcome as thy mafter is:[7]—
Support him by the arm.—Give me your hand,
And let me all your fortunes underftand.

[*Exeunt.*

I find the verfe " Nor fhrink before the *wintry wind*," is altered to
" Nor fhrink before the *warping wind*." HOLT WHITE.

The meaning is this: Though the very waters, by thy agency,
are forced, againft the law of their nature, to *bend* from their
ftated level, yet thy fting occafions lefs anguifh to man, than
the ingratitude of thofe he befriended. HENLEY.

Wood is faid to *warp* when its furface, from being level, becomes
bent and uneven; from *warpan*, Sax. to caft. So, in this play,
Act III. fc. iii: " —— then one of you will prove a fhrunk
pannel, and, like green timber, *warp, warp*." I doubt whether
the poet here alludes to any operation of froft. The meaning may
be only, Thou bitter wintry fky, though thou *curleft* the waters,
thy fting, &c. *Thou* in the line before us refers only to—*bitter fky*.
The influence of the winter's fky or feafon may, with fufficient
propriety, be faid to *warp* the furface of the ocean, by agitation
of its waves alone.

That this paffage refers to the turbulence of the fky, and the
confequent agitation of the ocean, and not to the operation of
froft, may be collected from our author's having in *King John*
defcribed ice as uncommonly fmooth :
" To throw a perfume on the violet,
" *To fmooth the ice*," &c. MALONE.

[6] *As friend* remember'd *not*.] *Remember'd* for *remembering*. So,
afterwards, Act III. fc. laft:
" And now I am *remember'd*"——.
i. e. and now that I *bethink* me, &c. MALONE.

[7] —— *as thy* mafter *is :*] The old copy has—*mafters*. Corrected
by the editor of the fecond folio. MALONE.

ACT III.　SCENE I.

A Room in the Palace.

Enter Duke FREDERICK, OLIVER, *Lords, and*
Attendants.

DUKE F. Not fee him fince? Sir, fir, that can-
　　　not be:
But were I not the better part made mercy,
I fhould not feek an abfent argument[8]
Of my revenge, thou prefent: But look to it;
Find out thy brother, wherefoe'er he is;
Seek him with candle;[9] bring him dead or living,
Within this twelvemonth, or turn thou no more
To feek a living in our territory.
Thy lands, and all things that thou doft call
　　　thine,
Worth feizure, do we feize into our hands;
Till thou canft quit thee by thy brother's mouth,
Of what we think againft thee.

　　OLI. O, that your highnefs knew my heart in
　　　this!
I never lov'd my brother in my life.

　　DUKE F. More villain thou.—Well, pufh him out
　　　of doors;

---

[8] —— *an abfent* argument —] An *argument* is ufed for the
contents of a book, thence Shakfpeare confidered it as meaning the
fubject, and then ufed it for *fubject* in yet another fenfe.
　　　　　　　　　　　　　　　　　　　JOHNSON.

[9] Seek *him with* candle;] Alluding, probably, to *St. Luke's*
Gofpel, ch. xv. v. 8: " If fhe lofe one piece, doth fhe not light a
candle—and *feek* diligently till fhe find it?" STEEVENS.

And let my officers of such a nature
Make an extent upon his house and lands: [9]
Do this expediently, [2] and turn him going.

[*Exeunt.*

SCENE II.

The Forest.

Enter ORLANDO, *with a Paper.*

ORL. Hang there, my verse, in witness of my love:
And, thou, thrice-crowned queen of night, [3] sur_
vey
With thy chaste eye, from thy pale sphere above,
Thy huntress' name, that my full life doth sway. [4]

[9] *And let my officers of such a nature*
Make an extent *upon his house and lands:*] "To make an *extent* of lands," is a legal phrase, from the words of a writ, (*extendi facias*) whereby the sheriff is directed to cause certain lands to be appraised to their full extended value, before he delivers them to the person entitled under a recognizance, &c. in order that it may be certainly known how soon the debt will be paid.
MALONE.

[2] —— *expediently,*] That is, *expeditiously.* JOHNSON.

Expedient, throughout our author's plays, signifies—*expeditious.*
So, in *King John:*
"His marches are *expedient* to this town."
Again, in *King Richard II:*
"Are making hither with all due *expedience.*" STEEVENS.

[3] —— *thrice-crowned queen of night,*] Alluding to the triple character of Proserpine, Cynthia, and Diana, given by some mythologists to the same goddess, and comprised in these memorial lines:

Terret, lustrat, agit, Proserpina, Luna, Diana,
Ima, superna, feras, sceptro, fulgore, sagittis.
JOHNSON.

[4] —— *that my full life doth sway.*] So, in *Twelfth Night:*
"M. O. A. I. *doth sway my life.*" STEEVENS.

O Rofalind! thefe trees fhall be my books,
 And in their barks my thoughts I'll character;
That every eye, which in this foreft looks,
 Shall fee thy virtue witnefs'd every where.
Run, run, Orlando; carve, on every tree,
The fair, the chafte, and unexpreffive⁵ fhe. [*Exit.*

   Enter CORIN *and* TOUCHSTONE.

 Cor. And how like you this fhepherd's life, mafter Touchftone?

 Touch. Truly, fhepherd, in refpect of itfelf, it
is a good life; but in refpect that it is a fhepherd's
life, it is naught. In refpect that it is folitary, I
like it very well; but in refpect that it is private,
it is a very vile life. Now in refpect it is in the
fields, it pleafeth me well; but in refpect it is not
in the court, it is tedious. As it is a fparc life,
look you, it fits my humour well; but as there
is no more plenty in it, it goes much againft
my ftomach. Haft any philofophy in thee, fhepherd?

 Cor. No more, but that I know, the more one
fickens, the worfe at eafe he is; and that he that
wants money, means, and content, is without three
good friends:—That the property of rain is to wet,
and fire to burn: That good pafture makes fat
fheep; and that a great caufe of the night, is lack
of the fun: That he, that hath learned no wit by

---

4 ——— *unexpreffive*—] For *inexpreffible*. JOHNSON.

 Milton alfo, in his *Hymn on the Nativity*, ufes *unexpreffive* for
inexpreffible:
  " Harping with loud and folemn quire,
  " With *unexpreffive* notes to heaven's new-born heir."
           MALONE.

nature nor art, may complain of good breeding, or comes of a very dull kindred.[5]

TOUCH. Such a one is a natural philosopher.[6] Waſt ever in court, ſhepherd?

COR. No, truly,

TOUCH. Then thou art damn'd.

COR. Nay, I hope,——

TOUCH. Truly, thou art damn'd; like an ill-roaſted egg,[7] all on one ſide.

[5] —— he, that hath learned no wit by nature nor art, may complain of good breeding, or comes of a very dull kindred.] I am in doubt whether the cuſtom of the language in Shakſpeare's time did not authoriſe this mode of ſpeech, and make complain of good breeding the ſame with complain of the want of good breeding. In the laſt line of The Merchant of Venice we find that to fear the keeping is to fear the not keeping. JOHNSON.

I think, he means rather—may complain of a good education, for being ſo inefficient, of ſo little uſe to him. MALONE.

[6] Such a one is a natural philoſopher.] The ſhepherd had ſaid all the philoſophy he knew was the property of things, that rain wetted, fire burnt, &c. And the Clown's reply, in a ſatire on phyſicks or natural philoſophy, though introduced with a quibble, is extremely juſt. For the natural philoſopher is indeed as ignorant (notwithſtanding all his parade of knowledge) of the efficient cauſe of things, as the ruſtic. It appears, from a thouſand inſtances, that our poet was well acquainted with the phyſics of his time; and his great penetration enabled him to ſee this remedileſs defect of it. WARBURTON.

Shakſpeare is reſponſible for the quibble only, let the commentator anſwer for the refinement. STEEVENS.

The Clown calls Corin a natural philoſopher, becauſe he reaſons from his obſervations on nature. M. MASON.

A natural being a common term for a fool, Touchſtone, perhaps, means to quibble on the word. He may however only mean, that Corin is a ſelf-taught philoſopher; the diſciple of nature.
MALONE.

[7] —— like an ill-roaſted egg,] Of this jeſt I do not fully comprehend the meaning. JOHNSON.

There is a proverb, that a fool is the beſt roaſter of an egg, becauſe he is always turning it. This will explain how an egg may

Cor. For not being at court? Your reaſon.

Touch. Why, if thou never waſt at court, thou never ſaw'ſt good manners; if thou never ſaw'ſt good manners, then thy manners muſt be wicked; and wickedneſs is ſin, and ſin is damnation: Thou art in a parlous ſtate, ſhepherd.

Cor. Not a whit, Touchſtone: thoſe, that are good manners at the court, are as ridiculous in the country, as the behaviour of the country is moſt mockable at the court. You told me, you ſalute not at the court, but you kiſs your hands: that courteſy would be uncleanly, if courtiers were ſhepherds.

Touch. Inſtance, briefly; come, inſtance.

Cor. Why, we are ſtill handling our ewes; and their fells, you know, are greaſy.

Touch. Why, do not your courtier's hands ſweat? and is not the greaſe of a mutton as wholeſome as the ſweat of a man? Shallow, ſhallow: A better inſtance, I ſay; come.

Cor. Beſides, our hands are hard.

Touch. Your lips will feel them the ſooner. Shallow, again: A more ſounder inſtance, come.

___

be *damn'd all on one ſide*; but will not ſufficiently ſhow how Touchſtone applies his ſimile with propriety; unleſs he means that he who has not been at court is but *half* educated. STEEVENS.

I believe there was nothing intended in the correſponding part of the ſimile, to anſwer to the words, " all on one ſide." Shakſpeare's ſimiles (as has been already obſerved) hardly ever run on four feet. Touchſtone, I apprehend, only means to ſay, that Corin is completely damned; as irretrievably deſtroyed as an egg that is utterly ſpoiled in the roaſting, by being done all on one ſide only. So, in a ſubſequent ſcene, " and both in a tune, like two gypſies on a horſe." Here the poet certainly meant that the ſpeaker and his companion ſhould ſing in uniſon, and thus *reſemble each other* as perfectly as two gypſies on a horſe;—not that two gypſies on a horſe ſing *both in a tune.* MALONE.

Cor. And they are often tarr'd over with the fur-gery of our sheep; And would you have us kifs tar? The courtier's hands are perfumed with civet.

Touch. Moft shallow man! Thou worms-meat, in refpect of a good piece of flesh: Indeed!—Learn of the wife, and perpend: Civet is of a bafer birth than tar; the very uncleanly flux of a cat. Mend the inftance, shepherd.

Cor. You have too courtly a wit for me; I'll reft.

Touch. Wilt thou reft damn'd? God help thee, shallow man! God make incifion in thee![8] thou art raw.[9]

---

[8] ——make incifion *in thee!*] *To make incifion* was a proverbial expreffion then in vogue for, to make to underftand. So, in Beaumont and Fletcher's *Humorous Lieutenant:*

     " ——O excellent king,
     " Thus he begins, thou life and light of creatures,
     " Angel-ey'd king, vouchfafe at length thy favour;
     " And fo proceeds to *incifion*"——.

i. e. to make him underftand what he would be at.
WARBURTON.

Till I read Dr. Warburton's note, I thought the allufion had been to that common expreffion, of *cutting fuch a one for the fimples;* and I muft own, after confulting the paffage in the *Humorous Lieutenant,* I have no reafon to alter my fuppofition. The editors of Beaumont and Fletcher declare the phrafe to be unintelligible in that as well as in another play where it is introduced.

I find the fame expreffion in *Monfieur Thomas:*

     " We'll bear the burthen: proceed to *incifion*, fidler."
STEEVENS.

I believe that Steevens has explained this paffage juftly, and am certain that Warburton has entirely miftaken the meaning of that which he has quoted from *The Humourous Lieutenant,* which plainly alludes to the practice of the young gallants of the time, who ufed to cut themfelves in fuch a manner as to make their blood flow, in order to fhow 'their paffion for their miftreffes, by drinking their healths, or writing verfes to them in blood. For a more full explanation of this cuftom, fee a note on *Love's Labour's Loft,* Act IV. fc. iii: M. MASON.

[9] ——*thou art raw.*] i. e. thou art ignorant; unexperienced.

Cor. Sir, I am a true labourer: I earn that I eat, get that I wear, owe no man hate, envy no man's happiness, glad of other men's good, content with my harm: and the greatest of my pride is, to see my ewes graze, and my lambs suck.

Touch. That is another simple sin in you; to bring the ewes and the rams together, and to offer to get your living by the copulation of cattle: to be bawd to a bell-wether,[2] and to betray a she-lamb of a twelvemonth, to a crooked-pated, old, cuckoldly ram, out of all reasonable match. If thou be'st not damn'd for this, the devil himself will have no shepherds; I cannot see else how thou shouldst 'scape.

Cor. Here comes young master Ganymede, my new mistress's brother.

Enter ROSALIND, *reading a paper*.

Ros. From the east to western Ind,
No jewel is like Rosalind.[1]
Her worth, being mounted on the wind,
Through all the world bears Rosalind.
All the pictures, fairest lin'd,[3]
Are but black to Rosalind.
Let no face be kept in mind,
But the fair of Rosalind.[4]

So, in *Hamlet*: " ―― and yet but *raw* neither, in respect of his quick sail." MALONE.

[2] ―― bawd to a bell-wether;] *Wether* and *ram* had anciently the same meaning. JOHNSON.

[3] ―― *fairest* lin'd,] i. e. most fairly *delineated*. Modern editors read—*limn'd*, but without authority, from the ancient copies.
STEEVENS.

[4] *But the* fair *of Rosalind*.] Thus the old copy. *Fair* is beauty, complexion. See the notes on a passage in *The Midsummer Night's Dream*, Act I. sc. i. and *The Comedy of Errors*, Act II. sc. i. The

Touch. I'll rhime you so, eight years together; dinners, and suppers, and sleeping hours excepted: it is the right butter-woman's rate to market.[4]

Ros. Out, fool!

Touch. For a taste:——

> *If a hart do lack a hind,*
> *Let him seek out Rosalind.*
> *If the cat will after kind,*
> *So, be sure, will Rosalind.*

modern editors read—*the* face *of Rosalind.* Lodge's *Novel* will likewise support the ancient reading:

"Then muse not, nymphes, though I bemone
"The absence of fair Rosalynde,
"Since for her *faire* there is fairer none," &c.

Again,

"And hers the *faire* which all men do respect." STEEVENS.

Face was introduced by Mr. Pope. MALONE.

[4] ——rate *to market.*] So, Sir T. Hanmer. In the former editions—rank *to market.* JOHNSON.

Dr. Grey, as plausibly, proposes to read—*rant.* Gyll brawled like a *butter-whore,* is a line in an ancient medley. The sense designed, however, might have been—" it is such wretched rhime as the butter-woman sings as she is *riding to* market." So, in Churchyard's *Charge,* 1580, p. 7:

"And use a kinde of *ridynge rime*"——.

Ratt-ryme, however, in Scotch, signifies some verse *repeated by rote.* See Ruddiman's Glossary to G. Douglas's *Virgil.* STEEVENS.

The Clown is here speaking in reference to the ambling pace of the metre, which, after giving a specimen of, to prove his assertion, he affirms to be " the very false gallop of verses."

HENLEY.

I am now persuaded that Sir T. Hanmer's emendation is right. The *hobbling* metre of these verses, (says Touchstone,) is like the *ambling, shuffling* pace of a butter-woman's *horse,* going to market. The same kind of imagery is found in *K. Henry IV.* P. I:

"And that would set my teeth nothing on edge,
"Nothing so much, as *mincing poetry;*
"'Tis like the forc'd gait of a shuffling nag." MALONE.

Winter-garments muſt be lin'd,
So muſt ſlender Roſalind.
They that reap, muſt ſheaf and bind;
Then to cart with Roſalind.
Sweeteſt nut hath ſowreſt rind,
Such a nut is Roſalind.
He that ſweeteſt roſe will find,
Muſt find love's prick, and Roſalind.

This is the very falſe gallop of verſes;[5] Why do you infect yourſelf with them?

Ros. Peace, you dull fool; I found them on a tree.

Touch. Truly, the tree yields bad fruit.

Ros. I'll graff it with you, and then I ſhall graff it with a medlar: then it will be the earlieſt fruit[6] in the country; for you'll be rotten ere you be half ripe, and that's the right virtue of the medlar.

Touch. You have ſaid; but whether wiſely or no, let the foreſt judge.

Enter CELIA, *reading a paper.*

Ros. Peace!
Here comes my ſiſter, reading; ſtand aſide.

CEL. *Why ſhould this deſert ſilent be?[7]*
For it is unpeopled? No;

---

[5] *This is the very* falſe gallop of verſes;] So, in Naſhe's *Apologie of Pierce Pennileſſe,* 4to. 1593: "I would trot a *falſe gallop* through the reſt of his ragged *verſes,* but that if I ſhould retort the rime doggrell aright, I muſt make my verſes (as he doth his) run *bobbling,* like a brewer's cart upon the ſtones, and obſerve no meaſure in their feet." MALONE.

[6] —— *the* earlieſt *fruit* —] Shakſpeare ſeems to have had little knowledge in gardening. The *medlar* is one of the *lateſt* fruits, being uneatable till the end of November. STEEVENS.

[7] *Why ſhould this deſert* ſilent *be?*] This is commonly printed:
Why ſhould this a deſert be?

Tongues I'll hang on every tree,
 That ſhall civil ſayings ſhow. [8]
Some, how brief the life of man
 Runs his erring pilgrimage ;
That the ſtretching of a ſpan
 Buckles in his ſum of age.
Some, of violated vows
 'Twixt the ſouls of friend and friend :
But upon the faireſt boughs,
 Or at every ſentence' end,
Will I Roſalinda write ;
 Teaching all that read, to know
The quinteſſence of every ſprite
 Heaven would in little ſhow. [9]

but although the metre may be aſſiſted by this correction, the ſenſe ſtill is defective ; for how will the *hanging of tongues on every tree,* make it leſs a deſert? I am perſuaded we ought to read :
 Why ſhould this deſert ſilent *be?* TYRWHITT.

The notice which this emendation deſerves, I have paid to it, by inſerting it in the text. STEEVENS.

[8] *That ſhall* civil *ſayings ſhow.*] *Civil* is here uſed in the ſame ſenſe as when we ſay *civil* wiſdom or *civil* life, in oppoſition to a ſolitary ſtate, or to the ſtate of nature. This deſert ſhall not appear *unpeopled,* for every tree ſhall teach the maxims or incidents of ſocial life. JOHNSON.

Civil, I believe, is not deſignedly oppoſed to *ſolitary.* It means only *grave,* or *ſolemn.* So, in *Twelfth Night,* Act III. ſc. iv :
 " Where is Malvolio? he is *ſad* and *civil.*"
i. e. *grave* and *demure.*
 Again, in *A Woman's Prize,* by Beaumont and Fletcher :
  " That fourteen yards of ſatin give my woman ;
  " I do not like the colour ; 'tis too *civil.*"
            STEEVENS.

[9] ——*in* little *ſhow.*] The alluſion is to a miniature-portrait. The current phraſe in our author's time was—" painted in *little.*"
            MALONE.

So, in *Hamlet :* " — a hundred ducats a-piece, for his *picture in little.*" STEEVENS.

> *Therefore heaven nature charg'd*[1]
> *That one body should be fill'd*
> *With all graces wide enlarg'd:*
> *Nature presently distill'd*
> *Helen's cheek, but not her heart;*
> *Cleopatra's majesty;*
> *Atalanta's better part;*[2]
> *Sad*[4] *Lucretia's modesty.*

[1] *Therefore heaven nature charg'd——*] From the picture of Apelles, or the accomplishments of Pandora.

Πανδίρη, ὅτι πάντια Ὀλύμπια δώματ' ἐχόντες
Δῶρον ἰδώρησαν.————

So, before:
" —— But thou
" So perfect, and so peerless, art created
" Of every creature's best." *Tempest.*
Perhaps from this passage Swift had his hint of Biddy Floyd.

JOHNSON.

[2] *Atalanta's* better part;] I know not well what could be the *better part* of Atalanta here ascribed to Rosalind. Of the Atalanta most celebrated, and who therefore must be intended here where she has no epithet of discrimination, the *better part* seems to have been her heels, and the worse part was so bad that Rosalind would not thank her lover for the comparison. There is a more obscure Atalanta, a huntress and a heroine, but of her nothing bad is recorded, and therefore I know not which was her better part. Shakspeare was no despicable mythologist, yet he seems here to have mistaken some other character for that of Atalanta.

JOHNSON.

Perhaps the poet means her beauty and graceful elegance of shape, which he would prefer to her swiftness. Thus *Ovid:*

———— *nec dicere posses,*
Laude pedum, formæne bono præstantior esset.
Ut faciem, et posito corpus velamine *vidit,*
Obstupuit——.

But cannot Atalanta's *better part* mean her virtue or virgin chastity, with which nature had graced Rosalind, together with Helen's beauty without her heart or lewdness, with Cleopatra's dignity of behaviour, and with Lucretia's modesty, that scorned to survive the loss of honour? Pliny's *Natural History,* B. XXXV. c. iii. mentions the portraits of *Atalanta* and *Helen, utraque excellentissima forma, sed altera ut virgo;* that is, " both of them for beauty, incomparable, and yet a man may discerne the one [Atalanta] of

Thus Rosalind of many parts
By heavenly synod was devis'd;
Of many faces, eyes, and hearts,
To have the touches dearest priz'd.

them to be a *maiden*, for her modeft and chafte countenance," as
Dr. P. Holland tranflated the paffage; of which probably our poet
had taken notice, for furely he had judgement in painting. TOLLET.

I fuppofe Atalanta's *better part* is her *wit*, i. e. the *fwiftnefs of*
her mind. FARMER.

Shakfpeare might have taken part of this enumeration of diftinguifhed females from John Grange's *Golden Aphroditū*, 1577:
" —— who feemeft in my fight faire *Helen* of Troy, Polixene,
Calliope, yea *Atalanta* hir felfe in beauty to furpaffe, Pandora in
qualities, Penelope and *Lucretia* in chaftenefle to deface."
Again, *ibid:*

" Polixene fayre, Caliop, and
" Penelop may give place;
" *Atlanta* and dame *Lucres* fayre
" She doth them both deface."

Again, *ibid:* " *Atalanta* who fometyme bore the bell of beauties
price in that hyr native foyle."

It may be obferved, that Statius alfo in his fixth Thebaid, has
confounded *Atalanta* the wife of Hippomenes, and daughter of
Sicoricus, with *Atalanta* the daughter of Œnomaus, and wife of
Pelops. See v. 564. STEEVENS.

Dr. Farmer's explanation may derive fome fupport from a fubfequent paffage: " —— as fwift a *wit* as Atalanta's heels."
MALONE.

I think this ftanza was formed on an old tetraftick epitaph,
which, as I have done, Mr. Steevens may poffibly have read in a
country church-yard:

" She who is dead and fleepeth in this tomb,
" Had Rachel's comely face, and Leah's fruitful womb:
" Sarah's obedience, Lydia's open *heart*,
" And Martha's care, and Mary's *better part*." WHALLEY.

The following paffage in Marfton's *Infatiate Counteffe*, 1613,
might lead one to fuppofe that Atalanta's *better part* was her *lips:*

" —— That eye was Juno's;
" Thofe *lips* were her's that *won the golden ball*;
" That virgin blufh Diana's."

Be this as it may, thefe lines fhow that Atalanta was confidered as
uncommonly beautiful, and therefore may ferve to fupport Mr.
Tollet's firft interpretation.

Heaven would that she these gifts should have,
And I to live and die her slave.

Ros. O most gentle Jupiter!—what tedious ho-
mily of love have you wearied your parishioners
withal, and never cry'd, *Have patience, good people!*

Cel. How now! back friends?—Shepherd, go off
a little:—Go with him, sirrah.

Touch. Come, shepherd, let us make an honourable retreat; though not with bag and baggage,
yet with scrip and scrippage.
       [*Exeunt* Corin *and* Touchstone.

It is observable that the story of Atalanta in the Tenth Book of
Ovid's *Metamorphoses* is interwoven with that of *Venus* and *Adonis*,
which our author had undoubtedly read.   The lines most material
to the present point run thus in Golding's Translation, 1567:
       " She overcame them out of doubt; and hard it is to tell
       " Thee, whether she did in footemanshippe or *beautie* more
          excell."
          " — he did condemne the young men's love.   But when
       " He saw her face and body bare, (for why, the lady then
       " *Did strip her to her naked skin,*) the which was like to mine,
       " Or rather, if that thou wast made a woman, like to thine,
       " He was amaz'd."
              " —— And though that she
       " Did flie as swift as arrow from a Turkie bow, yet hee
       " More wondered at her *beautie,* then at swiftnesse of her pace;
       " Her running greatly did augment her beautie and her
          grace."   Malone.
The passage quoted by Mr. Malone from Marston's *Insatiate*
Countess, has no reference to the *ball of* Atalanta, but to the *golden*
apple which was adjudged to Venus by Paris, on Mount Ida.
   After all, I believe, that " Atalanta's *better part*" means only—
the best part about her, such as was most commended. Steevens.

   4 *Sad—*] Is *grave, sober,* not *light.* Johnson.

So, in *Much ado about Nothing:*—" She is never *sad* but when
she sleeps." Steevens.

   5 —— *the touches—*] The features; *les traits.* Johnson.

So, in *King Richard III:*
       " Madam, I have a *touch* of your condition." Steevens.

                           I

CEL. Didſt thou hear theſe verſes?

Ros. O, yes, I heard them all, and more too; for ſome of them had in them more feet than the verſes would bear.

CEL. That's no matter; the feet might bear the verſes.

Ros. Ay, but the feet were lame, and could not bear themſelves without the verſe, and therefore ſtood lamely in the verſe.

CEL. But didſt thou hear, without wondering how thy name ſhould be hang'd and carved upon theſe trees?

Ros. I was ſeven of the nine days out of the wonder, before you came; for look here what I found on a palm-tree:[6] I was never ſo be-rhimed ſince Pythagoras' time, that I was an Iriſh rat,[7] which I can hardly remember.

[6] ——*a* palm-tree:] A *palm-tree*, in the foreſt of *Arden* is as much out of its place, as the *lioneſs* in a ſubſequent ſcene. STEEVENS.

[7] —— *I was never ſo be-rhimed ſince Pythagoras' time, that I was an* Iriſh *rat,*] Roſalind is a very learned lady. She alludes to the Pythagorean doctrine, which teaches that ſouls tranſmigrate from one animal to another, and relates that in his time ſhe was an *Iriſh rat*, and by ſome metrical charm was rhymed to death. The power of killing rats with rhymes Donne mentions in his *Satires*, and Temple in his *Treatiſes.* Dr. Grey has produced a ſimilar paſſage from *Randolph:*

" ——— My poets
" Shall with a ſatire, ſteep'd in gall and vinegar,
" Rhyme them to death as they do *rats in Ireland.*"
                                                    JOHNSON.

So, in an addreſs to the reader, at the concluſion of Ben Jonſon's *Poetaſter:*

" Rhime them to death, as they do *Iriſh rats*
" In drumming tunes." STEEVENS.

So, in *The Defence of Poeſie* by our author's contemporary, Sir Philip Sidney: " Though I will not wiſh unto you—to be driven by a poet's verſes, as Rubonax was, to hang yourſelf, nor to be rimed to death, as is ſaid to be done in *Ireland*"—. MALONE.

Cel. Trow you, who hath done this?

Ros. Is it a man?

Cel. And a chain, that you once wore, about his neck: Change you colour?

Ros. I pr'ythee, who?

Cel. O lord, lord! it is a hard matter for friends to meet;[7] but mountains may be removed with earthquakes, and so encounter.[8]

Ros. Nay, but who is it?

Cel. Is it possible?

Ros. Nay, I pray thee now, with most petitionary vehemence, tell me who it is.

Cel. O wonderful, wonderful, and most wonderful wonderful, and yet again wonderful, and after that out of all whooping![9]

---

[7] ——*friends to meet*;] Alluding ironically to the proverb:

" Friends may meet, but mountains never greet."

See *Ray's Collection.* STEEVENS.

[8] —— *but* mountains *may be removed with earthquakes, and so* encounter.] " Montes duo inter se concurrerunt," &c. says Pliny, *Hist. Nat.* Lib. II. c. lxxxiii. or in Holland's translation: " Two bills (removed by an earthquake) *encountered* together, charging as it were, and with violence assaulting one another, and retyring again with a most mighty noise." TOLLET.

[9] ——*out of all* whooping!] i. e. out of all measure, or reckoning. So, in the Old Ballad of *Yorke, Yorke for my money, &c.* 1584:

" And then was shooting, *out of cry,*

" The skantling at a handful nie."

Again, in the old bl. l. comedy called *Common Conditions:*

" I have beraed myself *out of cry.*" STEEVENS.

This appears to have been a phrase of the same import as another formerly in use, " out of all *cry.*" The latter seems to allude to the custom of giving notice by a crier of things to be sold. So, in *A Chaste Maide of Cheapside,* a comedy by T. Middleton, 1630: " I'll sell all at an *outcry.*" MALONE.

An *outcry* is still a provincial term for an *auction.*

STEEVENS.

Ros. Good my complexion![2] doſt thou think, though I am caparifon'd like a man, I have a doub_let and hoſe in my difpofition? One inch of delay more is a South-fea-off difcovery.[3] I pr'ythee, tell

[2] *Good my complexion!*] This is a mode of expreſſion, Mr. Theobald ſays, which he cannot reconcile to common ſenſe. Like enough: and ſo too the Oxford editor. But the meaning is—*Hold good my complexion*, i. e. let me not bluſh. WARBURTON.

Good my complexion!] My native character, my female inquifitive difpofition, can't thou endure this!—For thus characterizing the moſt beautiful part of the creation, let our author anſwer. MALONE.

Good my complexion! is a little unmeaning exclamatory addreſs to her beauty; in the nature of a ſmall oath. RITSON.

[3] *One inch of delay more is a South-fea-off difcovery.*] The old copy reads—*is a South-fea of difcoverie.* STEEVENS.

This is ſtark nonfenfe; we muſt read—*off* difcovery, i. e. *from* difcovery. " If you delay me one inch of time longer, I ſhall think this fecret as far from difcovery as the *South-fea* is." WARBURTON.

This fentence is rightly noted by the commentator as nonfenfe, but not ſo happily reſtored to fenfe. I read thus: *One inch of delay more is a South-fea.* Difcover, *I pr'ythee; tell me who is it quickly!*—When the tranfcriber had once made *difcovery* from *difcover I*, he eafily put an article after South-fea. But it may be read with ſtill leſs change, and with equal probability—*Every inch of delay more is a* South-fea difcovery: *Every delay* however ſhort, is to me tedious and irkfome as the longeſt voyage, as a voyage of *difcovery* on the *South-fea*. How much voyages to the South-fea on which the Englifh had then firſt ventured, engaged the converfation of that time, may be eafily imagined. JOHNSON.

Of for *off*, is frequent in the elder writers. A *South-fea of difcovery* is a *difcovery a South-fea off*—as far as the South-fea. FARMER.

Warburton's fophiſtication ought to have been reprobated, and the old, which is the only reading that can preferve the fenfe of Rofalind, reſtored. A *South-fea of difcovery*, is not a difcovery, *as* FAR OFF, but as COMPREHENSIVE as the South-fea; which, being the largeſt in the world, affords the wideſt fcope for exercifing curiofity. HENLEY.

On a further confideration of this paffage I am ſtrongly inclined to think, with Dr. Johnfon, that we fhould read—*a South-fea difcovery.* " Delay, however ſhort, is to me tedious and irkfome as

me, who is it? quickly, and speak apace: I would
thou couldst stammer, that thou might'st pour this
concealed man out of thy mouth, as wine comes
out of a narrow-mouth'd bottle; either too much
at once, or none at all.   I pry'thee take the cork
out of thy mouth, that I may drink thy tidings.

Cel. So you may put a man in your belly.

Ros. Is he of God's making? What manner of man?
Is his head worth a hat, or his chin worth a beard?

Cel. Nay, he hath but a little beard.

Ros. Why, God will send more, if the man will
be thankful: let me stay the growth of his beard, if
thou delay me not the knowledge of his chin.

Cel. It is young Orlando; that tripp'd up the
wrestler's heels, and your heart, both in an instant.

Ros. Nay, but the devil take mocking; speak
sad brow, and true maid.[4]

Cel. I'faith, coz, 'tis he.

Ros. Orlando?

Cel. Orlando.

Ros. Alas the day! what shall I do with my
doublet and hose?—What did he, when thou saw'st
him? What said he? How look'd he? Wherein
went he?[5]   What makes he here? Did he ask for
me? Where remains he? How parted he with
thee? and when shalt thou see him again? Answer
me in one word.

the longest voyage, as a voyage of discovery on the South-Sea."
The word *of*, which had occurred just before, might have been
inadvertently repeated by the compositor.   MALONE.

   [4] ——*speak sad brow, and true maid.*] i. e. speak with a grave
countenance, and as truly as thou art a virgin; speak seriously and
honestly.   RITSON.

   [5] *Wherein went he?*] In what manner was he clothed? How
did he go dressed?   HEATH.

Cel. You muſt borrow me Garagantua's mouth [6] firſt: 'tis a word too great for any mouth of this age's ſize: To ſay, ay, and no, to theſe particulars, is more than to anſwer in a catechiſm.

Ros. But doth he know that I am in this foreſt, and in man's apparel? Looks he as freſhly as he did the day he wreſtled?

Cel. It is as eaſy to count atomies, [7] as to reſolve the propoſitions of a lover:—but take a taſte of my finding him, and reliſh it with a good obſervance. I found him under a tree, like a dropp'd acorn.

Ros. It may well be call'd Jove's tree, when it drops forth ſuch fruit. [8]

<hr>

[6] —— *Garagantua's mouth*—] Roſalind requires nine queſtions to be anſwered in *one word.* Celia tells her that a word of ſuch magnitude is too big for any mouth but that of Garagantua the giant of Rabelais. JOHNSON.

Garagantua ſwallowed five pilgrims, their ſtaves and all, in a ſallad. It appears from the books of the Stationers' Company, that in 1592 was publiſhed, " *Garagantua* his Prophecie." And in 1594, " A booke entitled, The Hiſtory of *Garagantua.*" The book of *Garagantua* is likewiſe mentioned in Laneham's *Narrative of 2. Elizabeth's Entertainment at Kenelworth-Caſtle, in* 1575. Some tranſlator of one of theſe pieces is cenſured by Hall, in his Second Book of *Satires:*

    " But who conjur'd, &c.
    " Or wicked *Rablais* dronken revellings
    " To grace the miſrule of our tavernings?" STEEVENS.

[7] —— *to count* atomies,] *Atomies* are thoſe minute particles diſcernible in a ſtream of ſunſhine that breaks into a darkened room. HENLEY.

" An *atomie* (ſays Bullokar in his *Engliſh Expoſitor,* 1616) is a *mote* flying in the ſunne. Any thing ſo ſmall that it cannot be made leſſe." MALONE.

[8] —— *when it drops forth* ſuch *fruit.*] The old copy reads— *when it drops forth fruit.* The word *ſuch* was ſupplied by the editor of the ſecond folio. I once ſuſpected the phraſe, " when it drops forth," to be corrupt; but it is certainly our author's; for it occurs again in this play:

Cel. Give me audience, good madam.

Ros. Proceed.

Cel. There lay he, stretch'd along, like a wounded knight.

Ros. Though it be pity to see such a sight, it well becomes the ground.

Cel. Cry, holla! to thy tongue, I pr'ythee, it curvets very unseasonably. He was furnish'd like a hunter.

Ros. O ominous! he comes to kill my heart.

Cel. I would, sing my song without a burden: thou bring'st me out of tune.

Ros. Do you not know I am a woman? when I think, I must speak. Sweet, say on.

    " —————— woman's gentle brain

    " Could not *drop forth such* giant-rude invention."

This passage serves likewise to support the emendation that has been made. MALONE.

9 ————*such a fight, it well becomes the ground.*] So, In *Hamlet:*

    " ————Such a fight as this

    " Becomes the field,"———— STEEVENS.

1 *Cry, holla! to thy tongue.*] The old copy has ——the tongue, Corrected by Mr. Rowe. *Holla* was a term of the manege, by which the rider restrained and *stopp'd* his horse. So, in our author's *Venus and Adonis:*

    " What recketh he his rider's angry stir,

    " His flattering *holla,* or his *stand I say?*"

The word is again used in *Othello,* in the same sense as here:

    " *Holla!* stand there." MALONE.

1 ——*to kill my heart.*] A quibble between *heart* and *hart.* STEEVENS.

Our author has the same expression in many other places. So, in *Love's Labour's Lost:*

    " Why, that contempt will *kill* the speaker's *heart.*"

Again, in his *Venus and Adonis:*

    " ————they have *murder'd* this poor *heart* of mine."

But the preceding word, *hunter,* shows that a quibble was here intended between *heart* and *hart.* In our author's time the latter word was often written instead of *heart,* as it is in the present instance, in the old copy of this play. MALONE.

Enter ORLANDO *and* JAQUES.

CEL. You bring me out:—Soft! comes he not here?

Ros. 'Tis he; Slink by, and note him.

[CELIA *and* ROSALIND *retire.*

JAQ. I thank you for your company; but, good faith, I had as lief have been myself alone.

ORL. And so had I; but yet, for fashion sake, I thank you too for your society.

JAQ. God be with you; let's meet as little as we can.

ORL. I do desire we may be better strangers.

JAQ. I pray you, mar no more trees with writing love-songs in their barks.

ORL. I pray you, mar no more of my verses with reading them ill-favouredly.

JAQ. Rosalind is your love's name?

ORL. Yes, just.

JAQ. I do not like her name.

ORL. There was no thought of pleasing you, when she was christen'd.

JAQ. What stature is she of?

ORL. Just as high as my heart.

JAQ. You are full of pretty answers: Have you not been acquainted with goldsmiths' wives, and conn'd them out of rings?

ORL. Not so; but I answer you right painted cloth,[4] from whence you have studied your questions.

---

[4] —— *but I answer you right* painted cloth,] This alludes to the fashion in old tapestry hangings, of mottoes and moral sentences from the mouths of the figures worked or painted in them. The poet again hints at this custom in his poem, called, *Tarquin and Lucrece:*

"Who fears a sentence, or an old man's saw,
" Shall by a *painted cloth* be kept in awe." THEOBALD.

Jaq. You have a nimble wit; I think it was made of Atalanta's heels. Will you sit down with

So, in Barnaby Riche's *Soldier's Wyſhe to Britons welfare, or Captaine Skill and Captaine Pill*, &c. 1604, p. 1: " It is enough for him that can but robbe a *painted cloth* of a hiſtorie, a booke of a diſcourſe, a foole of a faſhion," &c.

The ſame alluſion is common to many of our old plays. So, in *The Two Angry Women of Abington*, 1599: " Now will I ſee if my memory will ſerve for ſome *proverbs*. O, a *painted cloth* were as well worth a ſhilling, as a thief is worth a halter."
Again, in *A Match at Midnight*, 1633:
" There's a witty poſy for you.
" —No, no; I'll have one ſhall favour of a ſaw.—
" Why then 'twill ſmell of the *painted cloth*."
Again, in *The Muſes' Looking Glaſs*, by Randolph, 1638:
" ——I have ſeen in *Mother Redcap's* hall
" In *painted cloth*, the ſtory of the prodigal."
From this laſt quotation we may ſuppoſe that the rooms in publick houſes were uſually hung with what Falſtaff calls *water-work*. On theſe hangings perhaps moral ſentences were depicted as iſſuing from the mouths of the different characters repreſented.
Again, in Sir Thomas More's *Engliſh Works*, printed by Raſtell, 1557: " Mayſter Thomas More in hys youth devyſed in hys father's houſe in London, a goodly hangyng of fyne *paynted clothe*, with nine pageauntes, and verſes over every of thoſe pageauntes; which verſes expreſſed and declared what the ymages in thoſe pageauntes repreſented: and alſo in thoſe pageauntes were paynted the thynges that the verſes over them dyd (in effecte) declare."
Of the preſent phraſeology there is an inſtance in *King John:*
" He *ſpeaks plain cannon-fire*, and bounce, and ſmoke."
                                                                    STEEVENS.
I anſwer you right painted cloth, may mean, I give you a true painted cloth anſwer; as we ſay, ſhe talks *right Billingſgate*: that is, exactly ſuch language as is uſed at Billingſgate. JOHNSON.

This ſingular phraſe may be juſtified by another of the ſame kind in *K. Henry V:*
" I ſpeak to thee *plain ſoldier*."
Again, in *Twelfth Night:*
" He *ſpeaks* nothing but *madman*."
There is no need of Sir T. Hanmer's alteration: " I anſwer you right *in the ſtile of* painted cloth." We had before in this play, " It is the *right* butter-woman's rate to market." So, in Golding's tranſlation of *Ovid*, 1567:
" ——the look of it was *right* a maiden's look."

me? and we two will rail againſt our miſtreſs the world, and all our miſery.

ORL. I will chide no breather in the world,[5] but myſelf; againſt whom I know moſt faults.

JAQ. The worſt fault you have, is to be in love.

ORL. 'Tis a fault I will not change for your beſt virtue. I am weary of you.

JAQ. By my troth, I was ſeeking for a fool, when I found you.

ORL. He is drown'd in the brook; look but in, and you ſhall ſee him.

JAQ. There I ſhall ſee mine own figure.

ORL. Which I take to be either a fool, or a cypher.

JAQ. I'll tarry no longer with you: farewell, good ſignior love.

I ſuppoſe Orlando means to ſay, that Jaques's queſtions have no more of novelty or ſhrewdneſs in them than the trite maxims of the painted cloth. The following lines which are found in a book with this fantaſtick title,—*No whipping nor tripping, but a kind friendly ſnipping,* octavo, 1601, may ſerve as a ſpecimen of painted cloth language:

"Read what is written on the *painted cloth*:

"Do no man wrong; be good unto the poor;

"Beware the mouſe, the maggot and the moth,

"And ever have an eye unto the door;

"Truſt not a fool, a villain, nor a whore;

"Go neat, not gay, and ſpend but as you ſpare;

"And turn the colt to paſture with the mare;" &c.

That moral ſentences were wrought in theſe painted cloths, is aſcertained by the following paſſage in *A Dialogue both pleaſaunt and pitifull,* &c. by Dr. Willyam Bulleyne, 1564, (ſignat. H 5.) which has been already quoted: "This is a comelie parlour,—and faire *clothes,* with pleaſaunte borders aboute the ſame, with many *wiſe ſayings* painted upon them." MALONE.

5 —*no breather in the world,*] So, in our author's 81ſt Sonnet:

"When all the *breathers of this world* are dead."

Again, in *Antony and Cleopatra:*

"She ſhows a body, rather than a life;

"A ſtatue, than a *breather.*" MALONE.

Heaven would that fhe thefe gifts fhould have,
And I to live and die her flave.

Ros. O moft gentle Jupiter!—what tedious ho-
mily of love have you wearied your parifhioners
withal, and never cry'd, *Have patience, good people!*

Cel. How now! back friends?—Shepherd, go off
a little:—Go with him, firrah.

Touch. Come, fhepherd, let us make an honourable retreat; though not with bag and baggage,
yet with fcrip and fcrippage.
                    [*Exeunt* Corin *and* Touchstone.

It is obfervable that the ftory of Atalanta in the Tenth Book of
Ovid's *Metamorphofes* is interwoven with that of *Venus* and *Adonis,*
which our author had undoubtedly read. The lines moft material
to the prefent point run thus in Golding's Tranflation, 1567:
    " She overcame them out of doubt; and hard it is to tell
    " Thee, whether fhe did in footemanfhippe or *beautie* more
        excell."
        " — he did condemne the young men's love. But when
    " He faw her face and body bare, (for why, the lady then
    " *Did ftrip her to her naked fkin,*) the which was like to mine,
    " Or rather, if that thou waft made a woman, like to thine,
    " He was amaz'd."
            " —— And though that fhe
    " Did flie as fwift as arrow from a Turkie bow, yet hee
    " More wondered at her *beautie,* then at fwiftneffe of her pace;
    " Her running greatly did augment her beautie and her
        grace."   Malone.
The paffage quoted by Mr. Malone from Marfton's *Infatiate
Countefs,* has no reference to the *ball of* Atalanta, but to the *golden
apple* which was adjudged to Venus by Paris, on Mount Ida.
    After all, I believe, that " Atalanta's *better part*" means only—
the beft part about her, fuch as was moft commended. Steevens.

⁴ *Sad*—] Is *grave, fober,* not *light.* Johnson.

So, in *Much ado about Nothing:*—" She is never *fad* but when
fhe fleeps." Steevens.

⁵ —— *the touches*—] The features; *les traits.* Johnson.

So, in *King Richard III:*
    " Madam, I have a *touch* of your condition." Steevens.

I

Cel. Didſt thou hear theſe verſes?

Ros. O, yes, I heard them all, and more too; for ſome of them had in them more feet than the verſes would bear.

Cel. That's no matter; the feet might bear the verſes.

Ros. Ay, but the feet were lame, and could not bear themſelves without the verſe, and therefore ſtood lamely in the verſe.

Cel. But didſt thou hear, without wondering how thy name ſhould be hang'd and carved upon theſe trees?

Ros. I was ſeven of the nine days out of the wonder, before you came; for look here what I found on a palm-tree:[6] I was never ſo be-rhimed ſince Pythagoras' time, that I was an Iriſh rat,[7] which I can hardly remember.

---

[6] ——*a* palm-tree:] A *palm-tree*, in the foreſt of *Arden* is as much out of its place, as the *lioneſs* in a ſubſequent ſcene. STEEVENS.

[7] —— *I was never ſo be-rhimed ſince Pythagoras' time, that I was an* Iriſh rat,] Roſalind is a very learned lady. She alludes to the Pythagorean doctrine, which teaches that ſouls tranſmigrate from one animal to another, and relates that in his time ſhe was an *Iriſh rat*, and by ſome metrical charm was rhymed to death. The power of killing rats with rhymes Donne mentions in his *Satires*, and Temple in his *Treatiſes*. Dr. Grey has produced a ſimilar paſſage from *Randolph*:

" ———— My poets
" Shall with a ſatire, ſteep'd in gall and vinegar,
" Rhyme them to death as they do *rats in Ireland*."

JOHNSON.

So, in an addreſs to the reader, at the concluſion of Ben Jonſon's *Poetaſter*:

" Rhime them to death, as they do *Iriſh rats*
" In drumming tunes." STEEVENS.

So, in *The Defence of Poeſie* by our author's contemporary, Sir Philip Sidney: " Though I will not wiſh unto you—to be driven by a poet's verſes, as Rubonax was, to hang yourſelf, nor to be rimed to death, as is ſaid to be done in *Ireland*"—. MALONE.

G 4

Cel. Trow you, who hath done this?

Ros. Is it a man?

Cel. And a chain, that you once wore, about his neck: Change you colour?

Ros. I pr'ythee, who?

Cel. O lord, lord! it is a hard matter for friends to meet;[7] but mountains may be removed with earthquakes, and so encounter.[8]

Ros. Nay, but who is it?

Cel. Is it possible?

Ros. Nay, I pray thee now, with most petitionary vehemence, tell me who it is.

Cel. O wonderful, wonderful, and most wonderful wonderful, and yet again wonderful, and after that out of all whooping![9]

---

[7] ——*friends to meet*;] Alluding ironically to the proverb: " Friends may meet, but mountains never greet."
See *Ray's Collection.* STEEVENS.

[8] ——*but* mountains *may be removed with earthquakes, and so* encounter.] " Montes duo inter se concurrerunt," &c. says Pliny, *Hist. Nat.* Lib. II. c. lxxxiii. or in Holland's translation: " Two *bills* (removed by an earthquake) *encountered* together, charging as it were, and with violence assaulting one another, and retyring again with a most mighty noise." TOLLET.

[9] ——*out of all* whooping!] i. e. out of all measure, or reckoning. So, in the Old Ballad of *Yorke, Yorke for my money,* &c. 1584:
" And then was shooting, *out of cry,*
" The skantling at a handful nie."
Again, in the old bl. l. comedy called *Common Conditions:*
" I have beraed myself *out of cry.*" STEEVENS.

This appears to have been a phrase of the same import as another formerly in use, " out of all *cry.*" The latter seems to allude to the custom of giving notice by a crier of things to be sold. So, in *A Chaste Maide of Cheapside,* a comedy by T. Middleton, 1630: " I'll sell all at an *outcry.*" MALONE.

An *outcry* is still a provincial term for an *auction.*
STEEVENS.

Ros. Good my complexion![2] doſt thou think, though I am capariſon'd like a man, I have a doub_let and hoſe in my diſpoſition? One inch of delay more is a South-ſea-off diſcovery.[3] I pr'ythee, tell

[2] *Good my complexion!*] This is a mode of expreſſion, Mr. Theobald ſays, which he cannot reconcile to common ſenſe. Like enough: and ſo too the Oxford editor. But the meaning is—*Hold good my complexion*, i. e. let me not bluſh. WARBURTON.

Good my complexion!] My native character, my female inquiſitive diſpoſition, can'ſt thou endure this!—For thus characterizing the moſt beautiful part of the creation, let our author anſwer. MALONE.

Good my complexion! is a little unmeaning exclamatory addreſs to her beauty; in the nature of a ſmall oath. RITSON.

[3] *One inch of delay more is a South-ſea-off diſcovery.*] The old copy reads—*is a South-ſea of diſcoverie.* STEEVENS.

This is ſtark nonſenſe; we muſt read—*off* diſcovery, i. e. *from* diſcovery. "If you delay me one inch of time longer, I ſhall think this ſecret as far from diſcovery as the *South-ſea* is." WARBURTON.

This ſentence is rightly noted by the commentator as nonſenſe, but not ſo happily reſtored to ſenſe. I read thus: *One inch of delay more is a South-ſea. Diſcover, I pr'ythee; tell me who is it quickly!*—When the tranſcriber had once made *diſcovery* from *diſcover I*, he eaſily put an article after South-ſea. But it may be read with ſtill leſs change, and with equal probability—*Every inch of delay more is a* South-ſea diſcovery: *Every delay*, however ſhort, is to me tedious and irkſome as the longeſt voyage, as a voyage of *diſcovery* on the *South-ſea.* How much voyages to the South-ſea on which the Engliſh had then firſt ventured, engaged the converſation of that time, may be eaſily imagined. JOHNSON.

Of for *off,* is frequent in the elder writers. A *South-ſea of diſcovery* is a *diſcovery a South-ſea off*—as far as the South-ſea. FARMER.

Warburton's ſophiſtication ought to have been reprobated, and the old, which is the only reading that can preſerve the ſenſe of Roſalind, reſtored. A *South-ſea* of *diſcovery*, is not a diſcovery, *as* FAR OFF, but as COMPREHENSIVE as the South-ſea; which, being the largeſt in the world, affords the wideſt ſcope for exerciſing curioſity. HENLEY.

On a further conſideration of this paſſage I am ſtrongly inclined to think, with Dr. Johnſon, that we ſhould read—*a South-ſea diſcovery.* "Delay, however ſhort, is to me tedious and irkſome as

me, who is it? quickly, and ſpeak apace: I would thou couldſt ſtammer, that thou might'ſt pour this concealed man out of thy mouth, as wine comes out of a narrow-mouth'd bottle; either too much at once, or none at all. I pry'thee take the cork out of thy mouth, that I may drink thy tidings.

Cel. So you may put a man in your belly,

Ros. Is he of God's making? What manner of man? Is his head worth a hat, or his chin worth a beard?

Cel. Nay, he hath but a little beard.

Ros. Why, God will ſend more, if the man will be thankful: let me ſtay the growth of his beard, if thou delay me not the knowledge of his chin.

Cel. It is young Orlando; that tripp'd up the wreſtler's heels, and your heart, both in an inſtant.

Ros. Nay, but the devil take mocking; ſpeak ſad brow, and true maid.⁴

Cel. I'faith, coz, 'tis he.

Ros. Orlando?

Cel. Orlando.

Ros. Alas the day! what ſhall I do with my doublet and hoſe?—What did he, when thou ſaw'ſt him? What ſaid he? How look'd he? Wherein went he?⁵ What makes he here? Did he aſk for me? Where remains he? How parted he with thee? and when ſhalt thou ſee him again? Anſwer me in one word.

---

the longeſt voyage, as a voyage of diſcovery on the South-Sea." The word *of*, which had occurred juſt before, might have been inadvertently repeated by the compoſitor. Malone.

⁴ *——ſpeak ſad brow, and true maid.*] i. e. ſpeak with a grave countenance, and as truly as thou art a virgin; ſpeak ſeriouſly and honeſtly. Ritson.

⁵ *Wherein went he?*] In what manner was he clothed? How did he go dreſſed? Heath.

Cel. You muſt borrow me Garagantua's mouth[6] firſt: 'tis a word too great for any mouth of this age's ſize: To ſay, ay, and no, to theſe particulars, is more than to anſwer in a catechiſm.

Ros. But doth he know that I am in this foreſt, and in man's apparel? Looks he as freſhly as he did the day he wreſtled?

Cel. It is as eaſy to count atomies,[7] as to reſolve the propoſitions of a lover:—but take a taſte of my finding him, and reliſh it with a good obſervance. I found him under a tree, like a dropp'd acorn.

Ros. It may well be call'd Jove's tree, when it drops forth ſuch fruit.[8]

---

[6] —— *Garagantua's mouth*—] Roſalind requires nine queſtions to be anſwered in *one word*. Celia tells her that a word of ſuch magnitude is too big for any mouth but that of Garagantua the giant of Rabelais. JOHNSON.

Garagantua ſwallowed five pilgrims, their ſtaves and all, in a ſallad. It appears from the books of the Stationers' Company, that in 1592 was publiſhed, " *Garagantua* his Prophecie." And in 1594, " A booke entitled, The Hiſtory of *Garagantua.*" The book of *Garagantua* is likewiſe mentioned in Laneham's *Narrative of Q. Elizabeth's Entertainment at Kenelworth-Caſtle, in* 1575. Some tranſlator of one of theſe pieces is cenſured by Hall, in his Second Book of *Satires:*

" But who conjur'd, &c.
" Or wicked *Rablais* dronken revellings
" To grace the miſrule of our tavernings?" STEEVENS.

[7] —— *to count* atomies,] *Atomies* are thoſe minute particles diſcernible in a ſtream of ſunſhine that breaks into a darkened room. HENLEY.

" An *atomie* (ſays Bullokar in his *Engliſh Expoſitor,* 1616) is a *mote* flying in the ſunne. Any thing ſo ſmall that it cannot be made leſſe." MALONE.

[8] —— *when it drops forth* ſuch *fruit.*] The old copy reads— *when it drops forth fruit.* The word *ſuch* was ſupplied by the editor of the ſecond folio. I once ſuſpected the phraſe, " when it drops *forth,*" to be corrupt; but it is certainly our author's; for it occurs again in this play:

Cel. Give me audience, good madam.

Ros. Proceed.

Cel. There lay he, ſtretch'd along, like a wounded knight.

Ros. Though it be pity to ſee ſuch a ſight, it well becomes the ground.⁹

Cel. Cry, holla! to thy tongue,² I pr'ythee, it curvets very unſeaſonably. He was furniſh'd like a hunter.

Ros. O ominous! he comes to kill my heart.³

Cel. I would ſing my ſong without a burden: thou bring'ſt me out of tune,

Ros. Do you not know I am a woman? when I think, I muſt ſpeak. Sweet, ſay on.

"————— woman's gentle brain
"Could not *drop forth ſuch* giant-rude invention."
This paſſage ſerves likewiſe to ſupport the emendation that ha
been made. MALONE.

9 ——*ſuch a fight, it well becomes the ground.*] So, in *Hamlet:*
"——Such a fight as this
"Becomes the field,"—— STEEVENS.

² *Cry,* holla! *to thy tongue.*] The old copy has—*the tongue.*
Corrected by Mr. Rowe. *Holla* was a term of the manege, by
which the rider reſtrained and *ſtopp'd* his horſe. So, in our author's
Venus and Adonis:
"What recketh he his rider's angry ſtir,
"His flattering *holla,* or his *ſtand I ſay?*"
The word is again uſed in *Othello,* in the ſame ſenſe as here:
"*Holla!* ſtand there." MALONE.

³ ——*to* kill *my* heart.] A quibble between *heart* and *hart.* STEEVENS.

Our author has the ſame expreſſion in many other places. So, in
Love's Labour's Loſt:
"Why, that contempt will *kill* the ſpeaker's *heart.*"
Again, in his *Venus and Adonis:*
"——they have *murder'd* this poor *heart* of mine."
But the preceding word, *hunter,* ſhows that a quibble was here
intended between *heart* and *hart.* In our author's time the latter
word was often written inſtead of *heart,* as it is in the preſent
inſtance, in the old copy of this play. MALONE.

Enter ORLANDO *and* JAQUES.

Cel. You bring me out:—Soft! comes he not here?

Ros. 'Tis he; Slink by, and note him.

[CELIA *and* ROSALIND *retire.*

Jaq. I thank you for your company; but, good faith, I had as lief have been myfelf alone.

Orl. And fo had I; but yet, for fafhion fake, I thank you too for your fociety.

Jaq. God be with you; let's meet as little as we can.

Orl. I do defire we may be better ftrangers.

Jaq. I pray you, mar no more trees with writing love-fongs in their barks.

Orl. I pray you, mar no more of my verfes with reading them ill-favouredly.

Jaq. Rofalind is your love's name?

Orl. Yes, juft.

Jaq. I do not like her name.

Orl. There was no thought of pleafing you, when fhe was chriften'd.

Jaq. What ftature is fhe of?

Orl. Juft as high as my heart.

Jaq. You are full of pretty anfwers: Have you not been acquainted with goldfmiths' wives, and conn'd them out of rings?

Orl. Not fo; but I anfwer you right painted cloth,[4] from whence you have ftudied your queftions.

---

4 ———— *but I anfwer you right* painted cloth,] This alludes to the fafhion in old tapeftry hangings, of mottoes and moral fentences from the mouths of the figures worked or painted in them. The poet again hints at this cuftom in his poem, called, *Tarquin and Lucrece*:

"Who fears a fentence, or an old man's faw,

" Shall by a *painted cloth* be kept in awe." THEOBALD.

Jaq. You have a nimble wit; I think it was made of Atalanta's heels. Will you fit down with

---

So, in Barnaby Riche's *Soldier's Wiſbe to Britons welfare, or Captaine Skill and Captaine Pill*, &c. 1604, p. 1 : " It is enough for him that can but robbe a *painted cloth* of a hiſtorie, a booke of a diſcourſe, a foole of a faſhion," &c.

The ſame alluſion is common to many of our old plays. So, in *The Two Angry Women of Abington*, 1599 : " Now will I ſee if my memory will ſerve for ſome *proverbs*. O, a *painted cloth* were as well worth a ſhilling, as a thief is worth a halter."

Again, in *A Match at Midnight*, 1633 :

     " There's a witty poſy for you.
     " —No, no; I'll have one ſhall ſavour of a ſaw.—
     " Why then 'twill ſmell of the *painted cloth*."

Again, in *The Muſes' Looking Glaſs*, by Randolph, 1638 :

     " ——I have ſeen in *Mother Redcap's* hall
     " In *painted cloth*, the ſtory of the prodigal."

From this laſt quotation we may ſuppoſe that the rooms in publick houſes were uſually hung with what Falſtaff calls *water-work*. On theſe hangings perhaps moral ſentences were depicted as iſſuing from the mouths of the different characters repreſented.

Again, in Sir Thomas More's *Engliſh Works*, printed by Raſtell, 1557 : " Mayſter Thomas More in hys youth devyſed in hys father's houſe in London, a goodly hangyng of fyne *paynted clothe*, with nine pageauntes, and verſes over every of thoſe pageauntes; which verſes expreſſed and declared what the ymages in thoſe pageauntes repreſented : and alſo in thoſe pageauntes were paynted the thynges that the verſes over them dyd (in effecte) declare."

Of the preſent phraſeology there is an inſtance in *King John:*
     " He *ſpeaks plain cannon-fire,* and bounce, and ſmoke."
                              STEEVENS.

I anſwer you right painted cloth, may mean, I give you a true painted cloth anſwer; as we ſay, ſhe talks *right Billingſgate:* that is, exactly ſuch language as is uſed at Billingſgate. JOHNSON.

This ſingular phraſe may be juſtified by another of the ſame kind in *K. Henry V:*
     " I ſpeak to thee *plain ſoldier.*"
Again, in *Twelfth Night:*
     " He *ſpeaks* nothing but *madman.*"
There is no need of Sir T. Hanmer's alteration : " I anſwer you right *in the ſtile of* painted cloth." We had before in this play, " It is the *right* butter-woman's rate to market." So, in Golding's tranſlation of *Ovid*, 1567 :
     " ——the look of it was *right* a maiden's look."

me? and we two will rail againſt our miſtreſs the world, and all our miſery.

*O*RL. I will chide no breather in the world,[5] but myſelf; againſt whom I know moſt faults.

*J*AQ. The worſt fault you have, is to be in love.

*O*RL. 'Tis a fault I will not change for your beſt virtue. I am weary of you.

*J*AQ. By my troth, I was ſeeking for a fool, when I found you.

*O*RL. He is drown'd in the brook; look but in, and you ſhall ſee him.

*J*AQ. There I ſhall ſee mine own figure.

*O*RL. Which I take to be either a fool, or a cypher.

*J*AQ. I'll tarry no longer with you: farewell, good ſignior love.

I ſuppoſe Orlando means to ſay, that Jaques's queſtions have no more of novelty or ſhrewdneſs in them than the trite maxims of the painted cloth. The following lines which are found in a book with this fantaſtick title,—*No whipping nor tripping, but a kind friendly ſnipping*, octavo, 1601, may ſerve as a ſpecimen of painted cloth language:

"Read what is written on the *painted cloth*:
" Do no man wrong; be good unto the poor;
" Beware the mouſe, the maggot and the moth,
" And ever have an eye unto the door;
" Truſt not a fool, a villain, nor a whore;
" Go neat, not gay, and ſpend but as you ſpare;
" And turn the colt to paſture with the mare;" &c.

That moral ſentences were wrought in theſe painted cloths, is aſcertained by the following paſſage in *A Dialogue both pleaſaunt and pitifull*, &c. by Dr. Willyam Bulleyne, 1564, (ſignat. H 5.) which has been already quoted: " This is a comelie parlour,— and faire *clothes*, with pleaſaunte borders aboute the ſame, with many *wiſe ſayings* painted upon them." MALONE.

  5 —*no* breather in the world,] So, in our author's 81ſt Sonnet:
  " When all the *breathers of this world* are dead."
Again, in *Antony and Cleopatra*:
  " She ſhows a body, rather than a life;
  " A ſtatue, than a *breather*." MALONE.

Orl. I am glad of your departure; adieu, good monfieur melancholy.

[*Exit* Jaques.—Celia *and* Rosalind *come forward.*

Ros. I will fpeak to him like a faucy lacquey, and under that habit play the knave with him.— Do you hear, forefter?

Orl. Very well; What would you?

Ros. I pray you, what is't a clock?

Orl. You fhould afk me, what time o'day; there's no clock in the foreft.

Ros. Then there is no true lover in the foreft; elfe fighing every minute, and groaning every hour, would detect the lazy foot of time, as well as a clock.

Orl. And why not the fwift foot of time? had not that been as proper?

Ros. By no means, fir: Time travels in divers paces with divers perfons: I'll tell you who time ambles withal, who time trots withal, who time gallops withal, and who he ftands ftill withal.

Orl. I pr'ythee, who doth he trot withal?

Ros. Marry, he trots hard with a young maid, between the contract of her marriage,[6] and the day it is folemnized: if the interim be but a fe'nnight, time's pace is fo hard that it feems the length of feven years.

Orl. Who ambles time withal?

Ros. With a prieft that lacks Latin, and a rich man that hath not the gout: for the one fleeps

---

[6] *Marry, he trots hard with a young maid, between the contract,* &c.] And yet in *Much ado about Nothing,* our author tells us, " *Time* goes on *crutches,* till love have all his rites." In both paffages, however, the interim is equally reprefented as tedious.

MALONE.

eafily, becaufe he cannot ftudy ; and the other lives merrily, becaufe he feels no pain : the one lacking the burden of lean and wafteful learning ; the other knowing no burden of heavy tedious penury : Thefe time ambles withal.

Orl. Who doth he gallop withal ?

Ros. With a thief to the gallows : for though he go as foftly as foot can fall, he thinks himfelf too foon there.

Orl. Who ftays it ftill withal ?

Ros. With lawyers in the vacation : for they fleep between term and term, and then they perceive not how time moves.

Orl. Where dwell you, pretty youth ?

Ros. With this fhepherdefs, my fifter ; here in the fkirts of the foreft, like fringe upon a petticoat.

Orl. Are you native of this place ?

Ros. As the coney, that you fee dwell where fhe is kindled.

Orl. Your accent is fomething finer than you could purchafe in fo removed [4] a dwelling.

Ros. I have been told fo of many : but, indeed, an old religious uncle of mine taught me to fpeak, who was in his youth an in-land man ;[5] one that

---

4 ——*removed*—] i. e. remote, fequeftered. REED.
So, in *A Midfummer Night's Dream*, folio, 1623:
"From Athens is her houfe *remov'd* feven leagues."
STEEVENS.

5 ——in-land *man*;] Is ufed in this play for one *civilifed*, in oppofition to the *ruftick* of the prieft. So, Orlando before—
"Yet am I *inland* bred, and know fome nurture." JOHNSON.

See Marlowe's *Hero and Leander*, 1598:
"His prefence made the *rudeft* peafant melt,
"That in the vaft *uplandifh* countrie dwelt."

knew courtſhip too well, for there he fell in love.
I have heard him read many lectures againſt it; and
I thank God, I am not a woman, to be touch'd
with ſo many giddy offences as he hath generally
tax'd their whole ſex withal.

ORL. Can you remember any of the principal
evils, that he laid to the charge of women?

Ros. There were none principal; they were all
like one another, as half-pence are: every one fault
ſeeming monſtrous, till his fellow fault came to
match it.

ORL. I pr'ythee, recount ſome of them.

Ros. No; I will not caſt away my phyſick, but
on thoſe that are ſick. There is a man haunts the
foreſt, that abuſes our young plants with carving
Roſalind on their barks; hangs odes upon haw-
thorns, and elegies on brambles; all, forſooth, deify-
ing the name of Roſalind: if I could meet that
fancy-monger, I would give him ſome good counſel,
for he ſeems to have the quotidian of love upon him.

ORL. I am he that is ſo love-ſhaked; I pray you,
tell me your remedy.

Ros. There is none of my uncle's marks upon
you: he taught me how to know a man in love; in
which cage of ruſhes, I am ſure, you are not pri-
ſoner.

· ORL. What were his marks?

Ros. A lean cheek; which you have not: a blue
eye,[6] and ſunken; which you have not: an unqueſ-

Again, in Puttenham's *Arte of Poeſie,* 4to. 1589, fol. 120;
" —or finally in any *uplandiſh* village or corner of a realm,
where is no reſort but of poor ruſticall or uncivill people."

MALONE.

[6] —*a blue eye,*] i. e. a blueneſs about the eyes.

STEEVENS.

tionable fpirit;[7] which you have not: a beard neglected; which you have not:—but I pardon you
for that; for, fimply, your having[8] in beard is a
younger brother's revenue:—Then your hofe fhould
be ungarter'd,[9] your bonnet unbanded, your fleeve
unbuttoned, your fhoe untied, and every thing about
you demonftrating a carelefs defolation. But you

[7] —— *an* unqueftionable *fpirit*;] That is, a fpirit not *inquifitive*,
a mind indifferent to common objects, and negligent of common
occurrences. Here Shakfpeare has ufed a paffive for an active
mode of fpeech: fo in a former fcene, "The Duke is too *difputable*
for me, *that is, too* difputatious." JOHNSON.

May it not mean, *unwilling to be converfed with?* CHAMIER.

Mr. Chamier is right in fuppofing that it means a fpirit averfe
to converfation.
So, in *The Midfummer Night's Dream*, Demetrius fays to Helena—
"I will not ftay your *queftion*."
And in *The Merchant of Venice*, Antonio fays—
"I pray you, think you *queftion* with the Jew."
In the very next fcene, Rofalind fays—"I met the Duke yefterday,
and had much *queftion* with him." And in the laft fcene, Jaques
de Bois fays—"The Duke was converted after fome *queftion* with
a religious man." In all which places, *queftion* means *difcourfe* or
converfation. M. MASON.

[8] ——*your* having——] Having is poffeffion, eftate. So, in
The Merry Wives of Windfor: "The gentleman is of no *having*."
STEEVENS.

[9] —— *Then your hofe fhould be* ungarter'd, &c.] Thefe feem to
have been the eftablifhed and characteriftical marks by which the
votaries of love were denoted in the time of Shakfpeare. So, in
The Fair Maid of the Exchange, by Heywood, 1637: "Shall I
that have jefted at love's fighs, now raife whirlwinds! Shall I,
that have flouted *ah me's* once a quarter, now practife *ah me's* every
minute? *Shall I defy bat-bands, and tread garters and fhoe-ftrings*
under my feet? Shall I fall to falling bands, and be a ruffian no
longer? I muft; I am now liegeman to Cupid, and have read all
thefe informations in the book of his ftatutes." Again, in *A
pleafant Comedy how to chufe a good Wife from a bad*, 1602:
"—— I was once like thee
"A figher, melancholy humorift,
"Croffer of arms, a goer *without garters*,
"A *bat-band hater*, and a bufk-point wearer." MALONE.

H 2

are no fuch man; you are rather point-device[9] in your accoutrements; as loving yourfelf, than feeming the lover of any other.

ORL. Fair youth, I would I could make thee believe I love.

Ros. Me believe it? you may as foon make her that you love believe it; which, I warrant, fhe is apter to do, than to confefs fhe does: that is one of the points in the which women ftill give the lie to their confciences. But, in good footh, are you he that hangs the verfes on the trees, wherein Rofalind is fo admired?

ORL. I fwear to thee, youth, by the white hand of Rofalind, I am that he, that unfortunate he.

Ros. But are you fo much in love as your rhimes fpeak?

ORL. Neither rhime nor reafon can exprefs how much.

Ros. Love is merely a madnefs; and, I tell you, deferves as well a dark houfe and a whip, as madmen do: and the reafon why they are not fo punifhed and cured, is, that the lunacy is fo ordinary, that the whippers are in love too: Yet I profefs curing it by counfel.

ORL. Did you ever cure any fo?

Ros. Yes, one; and in this manner. He was to imagine me his love, his miftrefs; and I fet him every day to woo me: At which time would I, being but a moonifh youth,[2] grieve, be effeminate, changeable, longing, and liking; proud, fantaftical, apifh,

---

9 ——*point-device*—] i. e. exact, dreft with finical nicety. So, in *Love's Labour's Loft:* "I hate fuch infociable and *point-device.* companions." STEEVENS.

2 ——*a* moonifh youth,] i. e. variable. So, in *Romeo and Juliet:* "O fwear not by the *moon,* th' *inconftant moon.*" STEEVENS.

I

fhallow, inconftant, full of tears, full of fmiles; for
every paffion fomething, and for no paffion truly
any thing, as boys and women are for the moft part
cattle of this colour: would now like him, now
loath him; then entertain him, then forfwear him;
now weep for him, then fpit at him; that I drave
my fuitor from his mad humour of love, to a living
humour of madnefs;[3] which was, to forfwear the
full ftream of the world, and to live in a nook
merely monaftick: And thus I cured him; and this
way will I take upon me to wafh your liver as clean
as a found fheep's heart,[3] that there fhall not be one
fpot of love in't.

Orl. I would not be cured, youth.

Ros. I would cure you, if you would but call me

---

[2] —— *to a* living *humour of madnefs*;] If this be the true reading
we muft by *living* underftand *lafting*, or *permanent*, but I cannot
forbear to think that fome antithefis was intended which is now
loft; perhaps the paffage ftood thus——*I drove my fuitor from a*
dying *humour of love to a living humour of madnefs.* Or rather
thus——*From a mad humour of love to a* loving *humour of madnefs*,
that is, " from a *madnefs* that was *love*, to a *love* that was *madnefs*."
This feems fomewhat harfh and ftrained, but fuch modes of fpeech
are not unufual in our poet: and this harfhnefs was probably the
caufe of the corruption. JOHNSON.

Perhaps we fhould read——*to a humour of* loving *madnefs*. FARMER.

Both the emendations appear to me inconfiftent with the tenour
of Rofalind's argument. Rofalind by her fantaftick tricks did not
drive her fuitor either into a *loving* humour of madnefs, or a
humour of *loving* madnefs; (in which he was originally without her
aid ;) but fhe drove him *from* love into a fequefter'd and melancholy
retirement. *A living humour of madnefs* is, I conceive, in our author's
licentious language, a humour of *living madnefs*, a mad humour that
operates on *the mode of living*; or, in other words, and more ac-
curately, *a mad humour of life*; " —to forfwear the world, and
to *live* in a nook merely monaftick." MALONE.

[3] —— *as clean as a found fheep's heart*,] This is no very delicate
comparifon, though produced by Rofalind in her affumed character
of a fhepherd. *A fheep's heart*, before it is dreft, is always fplit
and wafhed, that the blood within it may be diflodged. STEEVENS.

H 3

Rosalind, and come every day to my cote, and woo me.

ORL. Now, by the faith of my love, I will; tell me where it is.

Ros. Go with me to it, and I'll show it you: and, by the way, you shall tell me where in the forest you live: Will you go?

ORL. With all my heart, good youth.

Ros. Nay, you must call me Rosalind:—Come, sister, will you go? [*Exeunt.*

SCENE III.

Enter TOUCHSTONE *and* AUDREY;[2] JAQUES *at a distance, observing them.*

TOUCH. Come apace, good Audrey; I will fetch up your goats, Audrey: And how, Audrey? am I the man yet? Doth my simple feature content you?[3]

---

[2] ——*Audrey*;] Is a corruption of *Etheldreda.* The saint of that name is so styled in ancient calendars. STEEVENS.

[3] *Doth my simple* feature *content you?*] says the Clown to Audrey. " Your *features!* (replies the wench,) Lord warrant us! what *features?*" I doubt not, this should be—your *feature!* Lord warrant us! *what's feature?* FARMER.

Feat and *feature,* perhaps had anciently the same meaning. The Clown asks, if the *features of his* face content her, she takes the word in another sense, i. e. *feats, deeds,* and in her reply seems to mean, what *feats,* i. e. what have we done yet? The courtship of Audrey and her gallant had not proceeded further, as Sir Wilful Witwoud says, than a little mouth-glue; but she supposes him to be talking of something which as yet he had not performed. Or the jest may turn only on the Clown's pronunciation. In some parts, *features* might be pronounced, *faitors,* which signify *rascals, low wretches.* Pistol uses the word in the second Part of *King Henry IV.* and Spenser very frequently. STEEVENS.

In Daniel's *Cleopatra,* 1594, is the following couplet:
" I see then, *artless feature can content,*
" And that true beauty needs no ornament."

Aud. Your features! Lord warrant us! what features?

Touch. I am here with thee and thy goats, as the moft capricious poet, honeft Ovid, was among the Goths.[4]

Jaq. O knowledge ill-inhabited![5] worfe than Jove in a thatch'd houfe! [*Afide.*

Touch. When a man's verfes cannot be under-ftood, nor a man's good wit feconded with the for-ward child, underftanding, it ftrikes a man more dead than a great reckoning in a little room:[6]— Truly, I would the gods had made thee poetical.

Again, in *The Spanifh Tragedy:*
    " It is my fault, not fhe, that merits blame;
     " My *feature* is not to *content* her fight;
     " My words are rude, and work her no delight."
Feature appears to have formerly fignified the whole countenance. So, in *K. Henry VI. P. I:*
    " Her peerlefs *feature*, joined with her birth,
     " Approves her fit for none but for a king." MALONE.

[4] *——as the moft capricious poet, honeft Ovid, was among the Goths.*] *Capricious* is not here humourfome, fantaftical, &c. but *lafcivious.* HOR. Epod. 10. Libidinofus immolabitur *caper.* The Goths are the Getæ. Ovid. Trift. V. 7. The *thatch'd houfe* is that of Baucis and Philemon, Ovid. Met. VIII. 630. *Stipulis et canna teĉta paluftri.* UPTON.

Mr. Upton is perhaps too refined in his interpretation of *ca-pricious.* Our author remembered that *caper* was the Latin for a goat, and thence chofe this epithet. This, I believe, is the whole. There is a poor quibble between *goats* and *Goths.* MALONE.

[5] *——ill-inhabited!*] i. e. ill-lodged. An unufual fenfe of the word. STEEVENS.

[6] *——it ftrikes a man more dead than a great* reckoning *in a little room:*] Nothing was ever wrote in higher humour than this fimile. A great reckoning, in a little room, implies that the en-tertainment was mean, and the bill extravagant. The poet here alluded to the French proverbial phrafe *of the quarter of an hour of Rabelais:* who faid, there was only one quarter of an hour in human life paffed ill, and that was between the calling for the

Aud. I do not know what poetical is: Is it honeſt in deed, and word? Is it a true thing?

Touch. No, truly; for the trueſt poetry is the moſt feigning; and lovers are given to poetr ; and what they ſwear in poetry, may be ſaid, as lovers, they do feign.[6]

Aud. Do you wiſh then, that the gods had made me poetical?

Touch. I do, truly: for thou ſwear'ſt to me, thou art honeſt; now, if thou wert a poet, I might have ſome hope thou didſt feign.

Aud. Would you not have me honeſt?

Touch. No truly, unleſs thou wert hard-favour'd: for honeſty coupled to beauty, is to have honey a ſauce to ſugar.

Jaq. A material fool![7]   [*Aſide.*

Aud. Well, I am not fair; and therefore I pray the gods make me honeſt!

Touch. Truly, and to caſt away honeſty upon a

---

reckoning and paying it. Yet the delicacy of our Oxford editor would correct this into—*It ſtrikes a man more dead than a great reeking in a little room.* This is amending with a vengeance. When men are joking together in a merry humour, all are diſpoſed to laugh. One of the company ſays a good thing: the jeſt is not taken; all are ſilent, and he who ſaid it, quite confounded. This is compared to a tavern jollity interrupted by the coming in of a *great reckoning.* Had not Shakſpeare reaſon now in this caſe to apply his ſimile to his own caſe, againſt his critical editor? Who, it is plain, taking the phraſe to *ſtrike dead,* in a literal ſenſe, concluded, from his knowledge in philoſophy, that it could not be ſo effectually done by a *reckoning* as by a *reeking.* WARBURTON.

[6] *—— and what they ſwear in poetry,* &c.] This ſentence ſeems perplexed and inconſequent: perhaps it were better read thus—*What they ſwear as lovers, they may be ſaid to feign as poets.*
                              JOHNSON.

     I would read—*It may be ſaid, as lovers they do feign.* M. MASON.

[7] *A* material *fool!*] A fool with *matter* in him; a fool ſtocked with notions. JOHNSON.

foul slut, were to put good meat into an unclean dish.

Aud. I am not a slut, though I thank the gods I am foul.[8]

Touch. Well, praised be the gods for thy foul-ness! sluttishnefs may come hereafter. But be it as it may be, I will marry thee: and to that end, I have been with Sir Oliver Mar-text, the vicar of the next village; who hath promised to meet me in this place of the forest, and to couple us.

Jaq. I would fain see this meeting. [*Aside.*

Aud. Well, the gods give us joy!

---

[8] ——*I am* foul.] By *foul* is meant *coy* or *frowning*.
HANMER.

I rather believe *foul* to be put for the rustick pronunciation of *full*. Audrey, supposing the Clown to have spoken of her as *a foul slut*, says, naturally enough, *I am not a slut, though, I thank the gods, I am* foul, i. e. full. She was more likely to *thank the gods* for a belly-full, than for her being *coy* or *frowning*.
TYRWHITT.

In confirmation of Mr. Tyrwhitt's conjecture, it may be observed, that in the song at the end of *Love's Labour's Lost*, instead of—" and ways be *foul*," we have in the first quarto, 1598, " —and ways be *full*." In that and other of our author's plays many words seem to have been spelled by the ear. MALONE.

Audrey says, she is not *fair*, i. e. *handsome*, and therefore prays the gods to make her *honest*. The Clown tells her that to cast *honesty* away upon a *foul slut*, (i. e. an ill *favoured dirty creature*) is to put meat in an unclean dish. She replies, she is no *slut* (no dirty *drab*) though in her great simplicity, she thanks the gods for her *foulness* (homelyness) i. e. for being as she is. "Well, (adds he) praised be the gods for thy *foulness*, sluttishness may come here-after." RITSON.

I think that, by *foul*, Audrey means, *not fair*, or what we call *homely*. Audrey is neither coy or ill-humoured; but she thanks God for her homeliness, as it rendered her less exposed to tempta-tion. So, in the next scene but one, Rosalind says to Phebe—
" *Foul* is most *foul*, being *foul*, to be a scoffer."
M. MASON.

Touch. Amen. A man may, if he were of a fearful heart, ftagger in this attempt; for here we have no temple but the wood, no affembly but horn-beafts. But what though?[8] Courage! As horns are odious, they are neceffary. It is faid,—Many a man knows no end of his goods: right; many a man has good horns, and knows no end of them. Well, that is the dowry of his wife; 'tis none of his own getting. Horns? Even fo:—— Poor men alone?——No, no; the nobleft deer hath them as huge as the rafcal. Is the fingle man therefore bleffed? No: as a wall'd town is more worthier than a village,'fo is the forehead of a married man more honourable than the bare brow of a bachelor: and by how much defence[9] is better than no fkill, by fo much is a horn more precious than to want.

Enter Sir OLIVER MAR-TEXT.

Here comes fir Oliver:[2]—Sir Oliver Mar-text, you are well met: Will you defpatch us here under this tree, or fhall we go with you to your chapel?

---

[8] ——*what though?*] What then? JOHNSON.

[9] —*defence*—] *Defence*, as here oppofed to " no fkill," fignifies the *art of fencing.* Thus, in *Hamlet:* " ——and gave you fuch a mafterly report, for arts and exercife in your *defence.*" STEEVENS.

[2] ——*fir Oliver:*] He that has taken his firft degree at the univerfity, is in the academical ftyle called *Dominus*, and in common language was heretofore termed *Sir.* This was not always a word of contempt; the graduates affumed it in their own writings; fo Trevifa the hiftorian writes himfelf *Syr* John de Trevifa.
JOHNSON.

We find the fame title beftowed on many divines in our old comedies. So, in *Wily Beguiled:*

" ——Sir *John* cannot tend to it at evening prayer; for there comes a company of players to town on Sunday in the afternoon, and Sir *John* is fo good a fellow, that I know he'll fcarce leave their company, to fay evening prayer."

Sir Oli. Is there none here to give the woman?

Touch. I will not take her on gift of any man.

Sir Oli. Truly, she must be given, or the marriage is not lawful.

Jaq. [*Discovering himself.*] Proceed, proceed; I'll give her.

Touch. Good even, good master *What ye call't*: How do you, sir? You are very well met: God'ild you [3] for your last company: I am very glad to see you:—Even a toy in hand here, sir:—Nay; pray, be cover'd.

Jaq. Will you be married, motley?

Touch. As the ox hath his bow,[4] sir, the horse his curb, and the faulcon her bells, so man hath his desires; and as pigeons bill, so wedlock would be nibbling.

Jaq. And will you, being a man of your breeding, be married under a bush, like a beggar? Get you to church, and have a good priest that can tell you what marriage is: this fellow will but join you

Again, " We'll all go to church together, and so save *Sir John* a labour." See notes on *The Merry Wives of Windsor*, Act I. sc. i. STEEVENS.

Degrees were at this time considered as the highest dignities; and it may not be improper to observe, that a clergyman, who hath not been educated at the Universities, is still distinguished in some parts of North Wales, by the appellation of *Sir John, Sir William,* &c. Hence the Sir Hugh Evans of Shakspeare is not a Welsh knight who hath taken orders, but only a Welsh clergyman without any regular degree from either of the Universities. See Barrington's *History of the Guedir Family.* NICHOLS.

[3] —— *God'ild you* —] i. e. God *yield* you, God reward you. So, in *Antony and Cleopatra:*
　" And the gods *yield* you for't!"
See notes on *Macbeth*, Act I. sc. vi. STEEVENS.

[4] —— *his* bow,] i. e. his *yoke.* The ancient *yoke* in form resembled a *bow.* See note on *The Merry Wives of Windsor*, Act V. Vol. III. p. 493. STEEVENS.

together as they join wainſcot; then one of you will prove a ſhrunk pannel, and, like green timber, warp, warp.

Touch. I am not in the mind but I were better to be married of him than of another: for he is not like to marry me well; and not being well married, it will be a good excuſe for me hereafter to leave my wife. [*Aſide.*

Jaq. Go thou with me, and let me counſel thee.

Touch. Come, ſweet Audrey;
We muſt be married, or we muſt live in bawdry.
Farewell, good maſter Oliver!

    Not—O ſweet Oliver,
      O brave Oliver,[5]
   Leave me not behi' thee;
     But—Wind away,
     Begone, I ſay,
  I will not to wedding wi' thee.

[*Exeunt* JAQUES, TOUCHSTONE, *and* AUDREY.

Sir Oli. 'Tis no matter; ne'er a fantaſtical knave of them all ſhall flout me out of my calling. [*Exit.*

---

[5] *Not—O ſweet Oliver,*
   O brave, &c.] Some words of an old ballad.
                                 WARBURTON.
Of this ſpeech as it now appears, I can make nothing, and think nothing can be made. In the ſame breath he calls his miſtreſs to be married, and ſends away the man that ſhould marry them. Dr. Warburton has very happily obſerved, that *O ſweet Oliver* is a quotation from an old ſong; I believe there are two quotations put in oppoſition to each other. For *wind* I read *wend,* the old word for *go.* Perhaps the whole paſſage may be regulated thus:
   Clo. I am not in the mind, but it were better for me to be married of him than of another, for he is not like to marry me well, and not being well married, it will be a good excuſe for me hereafter to leave my wife.—Come, ſweet Audrey; we muſt be married, or we muſt live in bawdry.

SCENE IV.

The same. Before a Cottage.

Enter ROSALIND *and* CELIA.

Ros. Never talk to me, I will weep.

Cel. Do, I pr'ythee; but yet have the grace to confider, that tears do not become a man.

Jaq. Go thou with me, and let me counfel thee. [They whifper.
Clo. *Farewel, good fir Oliver, not* O fweet Oliver, O brave Oliver, leave me not behind thee,———*but*
   Wend away,
   Begone, I fay,
  I will not to wedding with thee to-day.
Of this conjecture the reader may take as much as fhall appear neceffary to the fenfe, or conduci.e to the humour. I have received all but the additional words. The fong feems to be complete with-out them. JOHNSON.

The Clown difmiffes fir Oliver only becaufe Jaques had alarmed his pride, and raifed his doubts, concerning the validity of a mar-riage folemnized by one who appears only in the character of an itinerant preacher. He intends afterwards to have recourfe to fome other of more dignity in the fame profeffion. Dr. Johnfon's opinion, that the latter part of the Clown's fpeech is only a re-petition from fome other ballad, or perhaps a different part of the fame, is, I believe, juft.

O brave Oliver, leave me not behind you, is a quotation at the beginning of one of N. Breton's Letters, in his *Packet,* &c. 1600.
            STEEVENS.

That Touchftone is influenced by the counfel of Jaques, may be inferred from the fubfequent dialogue between the former and Au-drey, Act V. fc. i:
Touch. We fhall find a time, Audrey; patience, gentle Audrey.
Aud. 'Faith, *the prieft was good enough, for all the old gentleman's faying.* MALONE.

O fweet Oliver. The epithet of *fweet* feems to have been pecu-liarly appropriated to *Oliver,* for which perhaps he was originally obliged to the old fong before us. No more of it, however, than

Ros. But have I not caufe to weep?

Cel. As good caufe as one would defire; there-fore weep.

Ros. His very hair is of the diffembling colour.

Cel. Something browner than Judas's:[6] marry, his kiffes are Judas's own children.

---

thefe two lines has as yet been produced.   See Ben Jonfon's *Underwood:*
  " All the *mad* Rolands and *fweet* Olivers."
And, in *Every man in his Humour*, p. 88, is the fame allufion:
  " Do not ftink, *fweet* Oliver."   Tyrwhitt.

 In the books of the Stationers' Company, Aug. 6, 1584, was entered by Richard Jones, the ballad of,
  " O *fweete Olyver*
  " Leave me not behinde thee."
Again, " The anfwere of *O fweete Olyver."*
Again, in 1586: " *O fweete Olyver* altered to the Scriptures."
         Steevens.

 I often find a part of this fong applied to Cromwell.   In a paper called, *A Man in the Moon, difcovering a World of Knavery under the Sun,* " the *juncto* will go near to give us the *bagge,* if *O brave Oliver* come not fuddenly to relieve them."   The fame allufion is met with in *Cleaveland.   Wind away,* and *wind off* are ftill ufed *provincially:* and, I believe, nothing but the *provincial* pronuncia-tion is wanting to join the parts together.   I read:
  Not—O fweet Oliver!
   O brave Oliver!
  Leave me not behi' thee——
    But—wind away,
    Begone, I fay,
  I will not to wedding wi' thee.   Farmer.

 To produce the neceffary rhyme, and conform to the pronun-ciation of Shakfpeare's native county, I have followed Dr. Farmer's direction.

 Wind is ufed for *wend* in *Cæfar and Pompey,* 1607:
  " *Winde* we then, Antony, with this royal queen."
         Steevens.

 6 *Something browner than* Judas's:] See Mr. Tollet's note and mine, on a paffage in the fourth fcene of the firft Act of *The Merry Wives of Windfor,* from both which it appears that *Judas* was con-

Ros. I'faith, his hair is of a good colour.[7]

Cel. An excellent colour: your chefnut was ever the only colour.

Ros. And his kiffing is as full of fanctity as the touch of holy bread.[8]

Cel. He hath bought a pair of caft lips of Diana:[9] a nun of winter's fifterhood[2] kiffes not more religioufly; the very ice of chaftity is in them.

---

ftantly reprefented in ancient painting or tapeftry, with *red hair* and *beard.*

So, in *The Infatiate Countefs,* 1613: " I ever thought by his *red beard* he would prove a *Judas.*" STEEVENS.

[7] *I'faith, his hair is of a good colour.*] There is much of nature in this petty perverfenefs of Rofalind; fhe finds faults in her lover, in hope to be contradicted, and when Celia in fportive malice too readily feconds her accufations, fhe contradicts herfelf rather than fuffer her favourite to want a vindication. JOHNSON.

[8] —— *as the touch of holy* bread.] We fhould read *beard,* that is, as the kifs of an holy faint or hermit, called the *kifs of charity.* This makes the comparifon juft and decent; the other impious and abfurd. WARBURTON.

[9] —— *a pair of* caft *lips of Diana:*] i. e. a pair left off by Diana. THEOBALD.

[2] —— *a nun of* winter's fifterhood——] This is finely expreffed. But Mr. Theobald fays, *the words give him no ideas.* And it is certain, that words will never give men what nature has denied them. However, to mend the matter, he fubftitutes *Winifred's fifterhood.* And after fo happy a thought, it was to no purpofe to tell him there was no religious order of that denomination. The plain truth is, Shakfpeare meant *an unfruitful fifterhood,* which had devoted itfelf to chaftity. For as thofe who were of the fifterhood of the fpring, were the votaries of Venus; thofe of fummer, the votaries of Ceres; thofe of autumn of Pomona: fo thefe of the *fifterhood of winter* were the votaries of Diana; called, *of winter,* becaufe that quarter is not, like the other three, productive of fruit or increafe. On this account it is, that when the poet fpeaks of what is moft *poor,* he inftances it in *winter,* in thefe fine lines of *Othello:*

" But riches finelefs is *as poor as winter*
" To him that ever fears he fhall be poor."

Ros. But why did he fwear he would come this morning, and comes not?

Cel. Nay certainly, there is no truth in him.

Ros. Do you think fo?

Cel. Yes: I think he is not a pick-purfe, nor a horfe-ftealer; but for his verity in love, I do think him as concave as a cover'd goblet,[3] or a worm-eaten nut.

Ros. Not true in love?

Cel. Yes, when he is in; but, I think he is not in.

Ros. You have heard him fwear downright, he was.

Cel. *Was* is not *is*: befides, the oath of a lover is no ftronger than the word of a tapfter; they are both the confirmers of falfe reckonings: He attends here in the foreft on the duke your father.

The other property of winter that made him term them of its fifterhood, is its coldnefs. So, in *The Midfummer Night's Dream*:

" To be a *barren fifter* all your life,
" Chanting faint hymns to the *cold fruitlefs* moon."
WARBURTON.

There is certainly no need of Theobald's conjecture, as Dr. Warburton has moft effectually fupported the old reading. In one circumftance, however, he is miftaken. The *Golden Legend*, p. ccci, &c. gives a full account of *St. Winifred* and her fifterhood. Edit. by *Wynkyn de Worde*, 1527. STEEVENS.

[3] —— *as concave as a* cover'd *goblet*,] Why a *cover'd?* Becaufe a goblet is never kept *cover'd* but when *empty*. Shakfpeare never throws out his expreffions at random. WARBURTON.

Warburton afks, " Why a cover'd goblet?"—and anfwers, " Becaufe a goblet is never covered but when empty." If that be the cafe, the cover is of little ufe; for when empty, it may as well be uncovered. But it is the idea of hollownefs, not that of emptinefs, that Shakfpeare wifhes to convey; and a goblet is more completely hollow when covered, than when it is not. M. MASON.

Ros. I met the duke yefterday, and had much queftion[4] with him: He afked me, of what parentage I was; I told him, of as good as he; fo he laugh'd, and let me go. But what talk we of fathers, when there is fuch a man as Orlando?

Cel. O, that's a brave man! he writes brave verfes, fpeaks brave words, fwears brave oaths, and breaks them bravely, quite traverfe, athwart[5] the

---

[4] *—— much* queftion—] i. e. converfation. So, in *The Merchant of Venice*:
" You may as well ufe *queftion* with the wolf." STEEVENS.

[5] *—— quite traverfe, athwart,* &c.] An unexperienced lover is here compared to a *puny tilter*, to whom it was a difgrace to have his lance broken acrofs, as it was a mark either of want of courage or addrefs. This happened when the horfe flew on one fide, in the career: and hence, I fuppofe, arofe the jocular proverbial phrafe *of fpurring the horfe only on one fide.* Now as breaking the lance againft his adverfary's breaft, in a direct line, was honourable, fo the breaking it *acrofs* againft his breaft was, for the reafon above, difhonourable: hence it is, that Sidney, in his *Arcadia,* fpeaking of the mock-combat of Clinias and Dametas fays, " *The wind took fuch hold of his ftaff that it* croft quite over his breaft," &c.—— And to *break acrofs* was the ufual phrafe, as appears from fome wretched verfes of the fame author, fpeaking of an unfkilful tilter:
" Methought fome ftaves he mift: if fo, not much amifs:
" For when he moft did hit, he ever yet did mifs.
" One faid he *brake acrofs,* full well it fo might be," &c.
This is the allufion. So that Orlando, a young gallant, affecting the fafhion, (for *brave* is here ufed, as in other places, for fafhionable,) is reprefented either *unfkilful* in courtfhip, or *timorous.* The lover's meeting or appointment correfponds to the tilter's career; and as the one breaks ftaves, the other breaks oaths. The bufinefs is only meeting fairly, and doing both with addrefs: and 'tis for the want of this, that Orlando is blamed. WARBURTON.

So, in *Northward Hoe,* 1607: " ——melancholick like a *tilter,* that had *broke his ftaves foul* before his miftrefs."
STEEVENS.
A puny tilter, that breaks his ftaff like a noble *goofe:*] Sir Thomas Hanmer altered this to a *nofe-quill'd* goofe, but no one feems to have regarded the alteration. Certainly *nofe-quill'd* is an epithet likely to be corrupted: it gives the image wanted, and may in a

heart of his lover;[1] as a puny tilter, that spurs his
horse but on one side, breaks his staff like a noble
goose: but all's brave, that youth mounts, and folly
guides:—Who comes here?

Enter CORIN.

COR. Mistress, and master, you have oft enquired
After the shepherd that complain'd of love;
Who you saw sitting by me on the turf,
Praising the proud disdainful shepherdess
That was his mistress.

CEL.   Well, and what of him?

COR. If you will see a pageant truly play'd,
Between the pale complexion of true love
And the red glow of scorn and proud disdain,
Go hence a little, and I shall conduct you,
If you will mark it.

ROS.   O, come, let us remove;
The sight of lovers feedeth those in love:—
Bring us unto this sight, and you shall say
I'll prove a busy actor in their play.   [*Exeunt.*

great measure be supported by a quotation from Turberville's
Falconrie: " Take with you a *ducke*, and slip one of her *wing
feathers*, and having thrust it through her *nares*, throw her out
unto your hawke." FARMER.

Again, in *Philaster*, by Beaumont and Fletcher:
        " He shall for this time only be seel'd up
        " With *a feather through his nose*, that he may only
        " See heaven," &c.

Again, in the *Booke of Hawkyng, Huntyng, and Fishing*, &c. bl. L
no date: " —and with a pen put it in the haukes *nares* once or
twice," &c. STEEVENS.

    [1] —*of his lover*;] i. e. of his mistress. See Vol. IV. p. 241,
note 3. MALONE.

SCENE V.

Another part of the Foreſt.

Enter SILVIUS *and* PHEBE.

SIL. Sweet Phebe, do not ſcorn me; do not,
     Phebe:
Say, that you love me not; but ſay not ſo
In bitterneſs: The common executioner,
Whoſe heart the accuſtom'd ſight of death makes
     hard,
Falls not the axe upon the humbled neck,
But firſt begs pardon; Will you ſterner be
Than he that dies and lives by bloody drops?[5]

---

[6] ———— *Will you ſterner be*
   Than he that dies *and* and lives by *bloody drops ?*] This is ſpoken
of the executioner. He *lives* indeed by bloody drops, if you will:
but how does he *die* by bloody drops? The poet muſt certainly
have wrote:
   ———— *that* deals *and lives*, &c.
i. e. that gets his bread by, and makes a trade of cutting off heads;
but the Oxford editor makes it plainer. He reads:
   Than he that lives *and* thrives *by bloody drops.*
                      WARBURTON.
   Either Dr. Warburton's emendation, except that the word *deals,*
wants its proper conſtruction, or that of Sir Tho. Hanmer, may
ſerve the purpoſe; but I believe they have fixed corruption upon
the wrong word, and ſhould rather read:
   Than he that dies his lips *by bloody drops ?*
Will you ſpeak with more ſternneſs than the executioner, whoſe
lips are uſed to be *ſprinkled* with blood? The mention of *drops*
implies ſome part that muſt be ſprinkled rather than dipped.
                      JOHNSON.
   I am afraid our bard is at his quibbles again. To *die,* means
as well *to dip a thing in a colour foreign to its own,* as to *expire.* In
this ſenſe, contemptible as it is, the executioner may be ſaid to *die*
as well as *live* by *bloody drops.* Shakſpeare is fond of oppoſing
theſe terms to each other.

I 2

Enter ROSALIND, CELIA, *and* CORIN, *at a diftance.*

PHE. I would not be thy executioner;
I fly thee, for I would not injure thee.

In *King John* is a play on words not unlike this:
   " ————— all with purple hands
   " *Dy'd* in the *dying* flaughter of their foes."
Camden has preferved an epitaph on a dyer, which has the fame
turn :
   " He that *dyed* fo oft in fport,
   " *Dyed* at laft, no colour for't."
So, Heywood, in his *Epigrams,* 1562 :
   " Is thy hufband a *dyer,* woman ? alack,
   " Had he no colour to *dye* thee on but black ?
   " *Duth* he oft ? yea too oft when cuftomers call ;
   " But I would have him one day *die* once for all.
   " Were he gone, *dyer* never more would I wed,
   " *Dyers* be ever *dying,* but never dead."
Again, Puttenham, in his *Art of Poetry,* 1589 :
   " We once fported upon a country fellow, who came to run for
the beft game, and was by his occupation a *dyer,* and had very big
fwelling legs.
   " He is but *coarfe* to run a *courfe,*
    " Whofe fhanks are bigger than his thigh ;
   " Yet is his luck a little worfe
    " That often *dyes* before he *die.*"
" Where ye fee the words *courfe* and *die* ufed in divers fenfes, one
giving the *rebound* to the other." STEEVENS.

   J. Davies of Hereford, in his *Scourge of Folly,* printed about
1611, has the fame conceit, and ufes almoft our authour's words :
OF A PROUD LYING DYER.
   " Turbine, the *dyer,* ftalks before his dore,
    " Like Cæfar, that by *dying* oft did thrive ;
   " And though the beggar be as proud as poore,
    " Yet (like the mortifide) he *dyes* to *live.*"
Again, *On the fame :*
   " Who lives well, dies well :—not by and by ;
   " For this man *lives* proudly, yet well doth *die.*" MALONE.

   He that lives and dies, i. e. he who to the very end of his life
continues a common executioner. So, in the fecond fcene of the
fifth Act of this play, " *live* and *die* a fhepherd." TOLLET.

   To *die and live* by a thing is to be conftant to it, to perfevere in

Thou tell'ſt me, there is murder in mine eye:
'Tis pretty, ſure, and very probable,[7]
That eyes,—that are the frail'ſt and ſofteſt things,
Who ſhut their coward gates on atomies,—
Should be call'd tyrants, butchers, murderers!
Now I do frown on thee with all my heart;
And, if mine eyes can wound, now let them kill
        thee;
Now counterfeit to ſwoon; why now fall down;
Or, if thou canſt not, O, for ſhame, for ſhame,
Lie not, to ſay mine eyes are murderers.
Now ſhow the wound mine eye hath made in thee:
Scratch thee but with a pin, and there remains
Some ſcar of it; lean but upon a ruſh,[8]
The cicatrice and capable impreſſure[9]
Thy palm ſome moment keeps: but now mine eyes,
Which I have darted at thee, hurt thee not;
Nor, I am ſure, there is no force in eyes
That can do hurt.

    Sil.   O dear Phebe,
If ever, (as that ever may be near,)

---

it to the end. *Lives* therefore does not ſignify *is maintained*, but the two verbs taken together mean, *who is all his life converſant with bloody drops,* MUSGRAVE.

  [7] *'Tis pretty,* ſure, *and very probable,*] *Sure* for *ſurely.* DOUCE.

  [8] —— *lean* but *upon a ruſh,*] *But,* which is not in the old copy, was added for the ſake of the metre, by the editor of the ſecond folio. MALONE.

  [9] *The cicatrice and capable impreſſure—*] *Cicatrice* is here not very properly uſed; it is the ſcar of a wound. *Capable impreſſure, hollow mark.* JOHNSON.

  Capable, I believe, means here—*perceptible.* Our author often uſes the word for *intelligent;* (See a note on *Hamlet,*—
    " His form and cauſe conjoin'd, preaching to ſtones,
    " Would make them *capable.*")
hence, with his uſual licence, for *intelligible,* and then for *perceptible.* MALONE.

                I 3

You meet in some fresh cheek the power of fancy,
Then shall you know the wounds invisible
That love's keen arrows make.

Phe.   But, till that time,
Come not thou near me: and, when that time comes,
Afflict me with thy mocks, pity me not;
As, till that time, I shall not pity thee.

Ros. And why, I pray you? [*Advancing*] Who
    might be your mother,
That you insult, exult, and all at once,
Over the wretched? What though you have more
    beauty,

---

² *—— power of* fancy,] *Fancy* is here used for *love*, as before
in *The Midsummer Night's Dream.* JOHNSON.

³ *—— Who might be your mother,*] It is common for the poets
to express cruelty by saying, of those who commit it, that they
were born of rocks, or suckled by tigresses. JOHNSON.

⁴ *That you insult, exult, and all at once,*] If the speaker intended to accuse the person spoken to only for *insulting* and ex-
ulting; then, instead of—*all at once,* it ought to have been, *both
at once.* But by examining the crime of the person accused, we
shall discover that the line is to be read thus:
    That you insult, exult, and rail *at once.*
For these three things Phebe was guilty of. But the Oxford editor
improves it, and, for *rail at once,* reads *domineer.* WARBURTON.

I see no need of emendation. The speaker may mean thus:
*Who might be your mother, that you insult, exult, and that too all in
a breath?* Such is perhaps the meaning of *all at once.* STEEVENS.

⁵ *—— What though you have* more *beauty,*] The old copy reads:
    —— What though you have no *beauty.* STEEVENS.

Though all the printed copies agree in this reading, it is very accu-
rately observed to me by an ingenious unknown correspondent, who
signs himself L. H. (and to whom I can only here make my acknow-
ledgement) that the *negative* ought to be left out. THEOBALD.

That *no* is a misprint, appears clearly from the passage in Lodge's
Rosalynde, which Shakspeare has here imitated: " Sometimes have I
seen high disdaine turned to hot desires.—Because *thou art beautiful,*
be not *so* coy; as there is nothing more faire, so there is nothing
more fading."—Mr. Theobald corrected the error, by expunging
the word *no;* in which he was copied by the subsequent editors;

I

(As, by my faith, I fee no more in you
Than without candle may go dark to bed,)
Muſt you be therefore proud and pitileſs?
Why, what means this? Why do you look on me?
I fee no more in you, than in the ordinary
Of nature's ſale-work:[6]—Od's my little life!

but omiſſion (as I have often obſerved) is of all the modes of
emendation the moſt exceptionable.   *No* was, I believe, a miſprint
for *mo*, a word often uſed by our author and his contemporaries for
more.   So, in a former ſcene in this play: " I pray you, mar no
mo of my verſes with reading them ill-favour'dly."   Again, in
Much ado about Nothing: " Sing no more ditties, ſing no *mo*."
Again, in *The Tempeſt:* " *Mo* widows of this buſineſs making—"
Many other inſtances might be added.   The word is found in
almoſt every book of that age.   As *mo* is here printed inſtead of
mo, ſo in *Romeo and Juliet*, Act V. we find in the folio, 1623,
Mo matter, for *No* matter.   This correction being leſs violent than
Mr. Theobald's, I have inſerted it in the text.   " What though I
ſhould allow you had *more* beauty than he, (ſays Roſalind,) *though*
by my faith," &c. (for ſuch is the force of *As* in the next line)
" muſt you therefore treat him with diſdain?"   In *Antony and
Cleopatra* we meet with a paſſage conſtructed nearly in the ſame
manner:
    "————— Say, this becomes him,
    " (As his compoſure muſt be rare indeed
    " Whom theſe things *cannot* blemiſh,) yet," &c.
Again, in *Love's Labour's Loſt:*
    " But ſay that he or we, (*as neither have*,)
    " Receiv'd that ſum," &c.
Again, more appoſitely, in Camden's *Remaines*, p. 190, edit. 1605:
" I force not of ſuch fooleries; but if *I have any* ſkill in ſooth-
ſaying (*as* in ſooth I have *none*) it doth prognoſticate that I ſhall
change copie from a duke to a king."   MALONE.

   As *mo* (unleſs rhyme demands it) is but an indolent abbreviation
of *more*, I have adopted Mr. Malone's conjecture, without his
manner of ſpelling the word in queſtion.   If *mo* were right, how
happens it that *more* ſhould occur twice afterwards in the ſame
ſpeech?   STEEVENS.

   [6] *Of nature's* ſale-work:] Thoſe works that nature makes up
careleſsly and without exactneſs.   The alluſion is to the practice
of mechanicks, whoſe *work* beſpoke is more elaborate than that
which is made up for chance-cuſtomers, or to ſell in quantities
to retailers, which is called *ſale-work*.   WARBURTON.

I 4

I think, she means to tangle my eyes too:——
No, 'faith, proud mistress, hope not after it;
'Tis not your inky brows, your black-silk hair,
Your bugle eye-balls, nor your cheek of cream,
That can entame my spirits to your worship.[7]——
You foolish shepherd, wherefore do you follow her,
Like foggy south, puffing with wind and rain?
You are a thousand times a properer man,
Than she a woman: 'Tis such fools as you,
That make the world full of ill-favour'd children:
'Tis not her glass, but you, that flatters her;
And out of you she sees herself more proper,
Than any of her lineaments can show her.——
But, mistress, know yourself; down on your knees,
And thank heaven, fasting, for a good man's love:
For I must tell you friendly in your ear,——
Sell when you can; you are not for all markets:
Cry the man mercy; love him; take his offer;
Foul is most foul, being foul to be a scoffer.[8]
So, take her to thee, shepherd;——fare you well.

Phe. Sweet youth, I pray you chide a year together;
I had rather hear you chide, than this man woo.

Ros. He's fallen in love with her foulness,[9] and
she'll fall in love with my anger: If it be so, as fast
as she answers thee with frowning looks, I'll sauce
her with bitter words.——Why look you so upon me?

Phe. For no ill will I bear you.

Ros. I pray you, do not fall in love with me,
For I am falser than vows made in wine:
Besides, I like you not: If you will know my house,

---

[7] *That can* entame *my spirits to your worship.*] So, in *Much ado about Nothing*:

"*Taming* my wild heart to thy loving hand." Steevens.

[8] *Foul is most foul, being foul to be a scoffer.*] The sense is, *The ugly seem most ugly, when, though ugly, they are scoffers.* Johnson.

[9] —— *with her foulness,*] So, Sir Tho. Hanmer; the other editions—*your* foulness. Johnson.

'Tis at the tuft of olives, here hard by:—
Will you go, fifter?—Shepherd, ply her hard:—
Come, fifter:—Shepherdefs, look on him better,
And be not proud: though all the world could fee,
None could be fo abus'd in fight as he.[2]
Come, to our flock.

[*Exeunt* ROSALIND, CELIA, *and* CORIN.

PHE. Dead fhepherd! now I find thy faw of might;
Who ever lov'd, that lov'd not at firſt fight?[3]

SIL. Sweet Phebe,—

PHE.   Ha! what fay'ſt thou, Silvius?

SIL. Sweet Phebe, pity me.

PHE. Why, I am forry for thee, gentle Silvius,

SIL. Wherever forrow is, relief would be:
If you do forrow at my grief in love,
By giving love, your forrow and my grief
Were both extermin'd.

---

[2] —— *though all the world could fee,*
None could be fo abus'd in fight as he.] Though all mankind
could look on you, none could be fo *deceived* as to think you
beautiful but he. JOHNSON.

[3] *Dead fhepherd! now I find thy faw of might ;*
Who ever lov'd, that lov'd not at firſt fight?] The fecond
of thefe lines is from Marlowe's *Hero and Leander*, 1637, fig. B b.
where it ſtands thus:
" Where both deliberate, the love is flight:
" *Who ever lov'd, that lov'd not at firſt fight?*"
This line is likewife quoted in *Belvidere, or the Garden of the
Mufes*, 1610, p. 29, and in *England's Parnaffus*, printed in 1600,
p. 261. STEEVENS.

This poem of Marlowe's was fo popular, (as appears from many
of the contemporary writers,) that a quotation from it muſt have
been known at once, at leaſt by the more enlightened part of the
audience. Our author has again alluded to it in the *Two Gentlemen
of Verona*.—The " dead fhepherd," Marlowe, was killed in a
brothel in 1593. Two editions of *Hero and Leander*, I believe,
had been publifhed before the year 1600; it being entered in the
Stationers' Books, Sept. 28, 1593, and again in 1597. MALONE.

Phe. Thou haft my love; Is not that neighbourly?

Sil. I would have you.

Phe.   Why, that were covetoufnefs.
Silvius, the time was, that I hated thee;
And yet it is not, that I bear thee love:
But fince that thou canft talk of love fo well,
Thy company, which erft was irkfome to me,
I will endure; and I'll employ thee too:
But do not look for further recompenfe,
Than thine own gladnefs that thou art employ'd.

Sil. So holy, and fo perfect is my love,
And I in fuch a poverty of grace,
That I fhall think it a moft plenteous crop
To glean the broken ears after the man
That the main harveft reaps: loofe now and then
A fcatter'd fmile, and that I'll live upon.

Phe. Know'ft thou the youth that fpoke to me
                ere while?

Sil. Not very well, but I have met him oft;
And he hath bought the cottage, and the bounds,
That the old carlot once was mafter of.

Phe. Think not I love him, though I afk for him;
'Tis but a peevifh boy: —yet he talks well;—
But what care I for words? yet words do well,
When he that fpeaks them pleafes thofe that hear.
It is a pretty youth:—not very pretty:—

---

³ *To glean the broken ears after the man*
   That the main harveft reaps: loofe *now and then*
   A fcatter'd fmile,] Perhaps Shakfpeare owed this image to the
fecond chapter of the book of *Ruth* :—" *Let fall* fome handfuls
of purpofe for her, and leave them that fhe may *glean* them."
                                        STEEVENS.

⁴ *That the old* carlot *once was mafter of.*] i. e. *peafant*, from *carl*
or *churl*; probably a word of Shakfpeare's coinage.   DOUCE.

⁵ —— *a* peevifh *boy*:] *Peevifh*, in ancient language, fignifies
weak, filly. So, in *King Richard III*:
   " When Richmond was a little *peevifh* boy." STEEVENS.

But, fure, he's proud; and yet his pride becomes him:
He'll make a proper man: The beft thing in him
Is his complexion; and fafter than his tongue
Did make offence, his eye did heal it up.
He is not tall; yet for his years he's tall: [6]
His leg is but fo fo; and yet 'tis well:
There was a pretty rednefs in his lip;
A little riper and more lufty red
Than that mix'd in his cheek; 'twas juft the difference
Betwixt the conftant red, and mingled damafk. [7]
There be fome women, Silvius, had they mark'd him
In parcels as I did, would have gone near
To fall in love with him: but, for my part,
I love him not, nor hate him not; and yet
I have more caufe [8] to hate him than to love him:
For what had he to do to chide at me?
He faid, mine eyes were black, and my hair black;
And, now I am remember'd, fcorn'd at me:
I marvel, why I anfwer'd not again:
But that's all one; omittance is no quittance.
I'll write to him a very taunting letter,
And thou fhalt bear it; Wilt thou, Silvius?

SIL. Phebe, with all my heart.

PHE.   I'll write it ftraight;
The matter's in my head, and in my heart:
I will be bitter with him, and paffing fbort:
Go with me, Silvius.   [*Exeunt.*

---

[6] *He is not tall; yet for bis years he's tall:*] The old copy reads:
    He is not very *tall, &c.*
For the fake of metre, I have omitted the ufelefs adverb—*very.*
                                                STEEVENS.

[7] —— *the* conftant *red, and* mingled *damafk.*] "Conftant red"
is *uniform* red. "*Mingled* damafk" is the filk of that name, in
which, by a various direction of the threads, many lighter fhades
of the fame colour are exhibited. STEEVENS.

[8] *I have more caufe*—] *I,* which feems to have been inadvertently omitted in the old copy, was inferted by the editor of the
fecond folio. MALONE.

ACT IV. SCENE I.

The same.

Enter ROSALIND, CELIA, *and* JAQUES.

Jaq. I pr'ythee, pretty youth, let me be better[7] acquainted with thee.

Ros. They say, you are a melancholy fellow.

Jaq. I am so; I do love it better than laughing.

Ros. Those, that are in extremity of either, are abominable fellows; and betray themselves to every modern censure, worse than drunkards.

Jaq. Why, 'tis good to be sad and say nothing.

Ros. Why then, 'tis good to be a post.

Jaq. I have neither the scholar's melancholy, which is emulation; nor the musician's, which is fantastical; nor the courtier's, which is proud; nor the soldier's, which is ambitious; nor the lawyer's, which is politick; nor the lady's, which is nice;[8] nor the lover's, which is all these: but it is a melancholy of mine own, compounded of many simples, extracted from many objects: and, indeed, the sundry contemplation of my travels, in which my often rumination wraps me, is a most humorous sadness.[9]

Ros. A traveller! By my faith, you have great reason to be sad: I fear, you have sold your own

---

[7] —— *let me* be *better*—] *Be*, which is wanting in the old copy, was added by the editor of the second folio. MALONE.

[8] —— *which is* nice;] i. e. silly, trifling. So, in *K. Richard III*:
   " But the respects thereof are *nice* and trivial."
See note on *Romeo and Juliet*, Act V. sc. ii:

[9] —— my *often rumination wraps me, is a most humorous sadness.*] The old copy reads—*in* a most, &c. STEEVENS.

   The old copy has—*by* often. Corrected by the editor of the second folio. Perhaps we should rather read " *and* which, by often rumination, wraps me in a most humorous sadness." MALONE.

lands, to fee other men's; then, to have feen much, and to have nothing, is to have rich eyes and poor hands.

Jaq. Yes, I have gain'd my experience.

Enter ORLANDO.

Ros. And your experience makes you fad: I had rather have a fool to make me merry, than experience to make me fad; and to travel for it too.

Orl. Good day, and happinefs, dear Rofalind!

Jaq. Nay then, God be wi' you, an you talk in blank verfe. [*Exit.*

Ros. Farewel, monfieur traveller: Look, you lifp, and wear ftrange fuits; difable⁹ all the benefits of your own country; be out of love with your nativity, and almoft chide God for making you that countenance you are; or I will fcarce think you have fwam in a gondola.²—Why, how now, Orlando! where have you been all this while? You a lover?—An you ferve me fuch another trick, never come in my fight more.

As this fpeech concludes with a fentence at once ungrammatical and obfcure, I have changed a fingle letter in it; and inftead of " is a moft humorous fadnefs," have ventured to read—" is a moft humorous fadnefs." Jaques firft informs Rofalind what his melancholy was *not*; and naturally concludes by telling her what the quality of it *is*. To obtain a clear meaning, a lefs degree of violence cannot be employed. STEEVENS.

⁹ —— *difable*—] i. e. undervalue. So afterwards :—" he *difabled* my judgement." STEEVENS.

² ——*fwam in a gondola.*] That is, *been at* Venice, the feat at that time of all licentioufnefs, where the young Englifh gentlemen wafted their fortunes, debafed their morals, and fometimes loft their religion.

The fafhion of travelling, which prevailed very much in our author's time, was confidered by the wifer men as one of the principal caufes of corrupt manners. It was therefore gravely cenfured by Afcham in his *Schoolmafter*, and by bifhop Hall in his *Quo Vadis*; and is here, and in other paffages, ridiculed by Shakfpeare. JOHNSON.

Orl. My fair Rofalind, I come within an hour of my promife.

Ros. Break an hour's promife in love? He that will divide a minute into a thoufand parts, and break but a part of the thoufandth part of a minute in the affairs of love, it may be faid of him, that Cupid hath clap'd him o' the fhoulder, but I warrant him heart-whole.

Orl. Pardon me, dear Rofalind.

Ros. Nay, an you be fo tardy, come no more in my fight; I had as lief be woo'd of a fnail.

Orl. Of a fnail?

Ros. Ay, of a fnail; for though he comes flowly, he carries his houfe on his head; a better jointure, I think, than you can make a woman:[3] Befides, he brings his deftiny with him.

Orl. What's that?

Ros. Why, horns; which fuch as you are fain to be beholden to your wives for: but he comes armed in his fortune, and prevents the flander of his wife.

Orl. Virtue is no horn-maker; and my Rofalind is virtuous.

Ros. And I am your Rofalind.

Cel. It pleafes him to call you fo; but he hath a Rofalind of a better leer than you.[4]

---

[3] —— *than you* can *make a woman:*] Old copy—you make a woman. Correcfted by Sir T. Hanmer. MALONE.

[4] —— *a Rofalind of a better* leer *than you.*] i. e. of a better feature, complexion, or colour, than you. So, in P. Holland's *Pliny,* B. XXXI. c. ii. p. 403: " In fome places there is no other thing bred or growing, but brown and dufkifh, infomuch as not only the cattel is all of that *lere,* but alfo the corn on the ground," &c. The word feems to be derived from the Saxon *Hleare,* facies, frons, vultus. So it is ufed in *Titus Andronicus,* Aft IV. fc. ii:

" Here's a young lad fram'd of another *lere.*" TOLLET.

Ros. Come, woo me, woo me; for now I am in a holiday humour, and like enough to confent:—What would you fay to me now, an I were your very very Rofalind?

Orl. I would kifs, before I fpoke.

Ros. Nay, you were better fpeak firft; and when you were gravell'd for lack of matter, you might take occafion to kifs. Very good orators, when they are out, they will fpit; and for lovers, lacking (God warn us!') matter, the cleanlieft fhift is to kifs.

Orl. How if the kifs be denied?

Ros. Then fhe puts you to entreaty, and there begins new matter.

Orl. Who could be out, being before his beloved miftrefs?

Ros. Marry, that fhould you, if I were your miftrefs; or I fhould think my honefty ranker than my wit.

Orl. What, of my fuit?

Ros. Not out of your apparel, and yet out of your fuit. Am not I your Rofalind?

Orl. I take fome joy to fay you are, becaufe I would be talking of her.

Ros. Well, in her perfon, I fay—I will not have you.

In the notes on the *Canterbury Tales* of Chaucer, Vol. IV. p. 320, *lere* is fuppofed to mean fkin. So, in *Ifumbras* MSS. *Cott. Cal.* II. fol. 129:

"His lady is white as whales bone,
"Here *lere* bryghte to fe upon,
"So fair as blofme on tre." STEEVENS.

⁵ —— *(God warn us!)*] If this exclamation (which occurs again in the quarto copies of *A Midfummer Night's Dream*) is not a corruption of—" God *ward* us," i. e. *defend* us, it muft mean, "*fummon* us to himfelf." So, in *King Richard III*:

"And fent to *warn* them to his royal prefence."
STEEVENS.

Orl. Then, in mine own perſon, I die.

Roſ. No, faith, die by attorney. The poor world is almoſt ſix thouſand years old, and in all this time there was not any man died in his own perſon, *vide-licet*, in a love-cauſe. Troilus had his brains daſh'd out with a Grecian club; yet he did what he could to die before; and he is one of the patterns of love. Leander, he would have lived many a fair year, though Hero had turn'd nun, if it had not been for a hot midſummer night : for, good youth, he went but forth to waſh him in the Helleſpont, and, being taken with the cramp, was drown'd; and the fooliſh chroniclers of that age[5] found it was—Hero of Seſtos. But theſe are all lies; men have died from time to time, and worms have eaten them, but not for love.

Orl. I would not have my right Roſalind of this mind; for, I proteſt, her frown might kill me.

Roſ. By this hand, it will not kill a fly: But come, now I will be your Roſalind in a more coming-on diſpoſition; and aſk me what you will, I will grant it.

Orl. Then love me, Roſalind.

[5] —— chroniclers *of that age*—] Sir T. Hanmer reads—*coroners*, by the advice, as Dr. Warburton hints, of ſome anony-mous critick. JOHNSON.

Mr. Edwards propoſes the ſame emendation, and ſupports it by a paſſage in *Hamlet*: "The *coroner* hath ſat on her, and *finds it Chriſtian burial.*" I believe, however, the old copy is right; though *found* is undoubtedly uſed in its forenſick ſenſe. MALONE.

I am ſurprized that Sir Thomas Hanmer's juſt and ingenious amendment ſhould not be adopted as ſoon as ſuggeſted. The alluſion is evidently to a coroner's inqueſt, which Roſalind ſuppoſes to have ſat upon the body of Leander, who was drowned in croſſ-ing the Helleſpont, and that their verdict was, that Hero of Seſtos was the cauſe of his death. The word *found* is the legal term on ſuch occaſions. We ſay, that a jury *found* it lunacy, or *found* it manſlaughter; and the verdict is called the *finding* of the jury.

M. MASON.

Ros. Yes, faith will I, fridays, and faturdays, and all.

Orl. And wilt thou have me?

Ros. Ay, and twenty fuch.

Orl. What fay'ft thou?

Ros. Are you not good?

Orl. I hope fo.

Ros. Why then, can one defire too much of a good thing?—Come, fifter, you fhall be the prieft, and marry us.—Give me your hand, Orlando:— What do you fay, fifter?

Orl. Pray thee, marry us.

Cel. I cannot fay the words.

Ros. You muft begin,——*Will you, Orlando,*——

Cel. Go to:——Will you, Orlando, have to wife this Rofalind?

Orl. I will.

Ros. Ay, but when?

Orl. Why now; as faft as fhe can marry us.

Ros. Then you muft fay,—*I take thee, Rofalind, for wife.*

Orl. I take thee, Rofalind, for wife.

Ros. I might afk you for your commiffion; but,—I do take thee, Orlando, for my hufband: There a girl goes before the prieft; [6] and, certainly, a woman's thought runs before her actions.

Orl. So do all thoughts; they are wing'd.

---

[6] —— There *a girl goes before the prieft*;] The old copy reads— " There's a girl," &c. The emendation in the text was propofed to me long ago by Dr. Farmer. STEEVENS.

Ros: Now tell me, how long you would have her, after you have poffefs'd her.

Orl. For ever, and a day.

Ros. Say a day, without the ever: No, no, Orlando; men are April when they woo, December when they wed: maids are May when they are maids, but the fky changes when they are wives, I will be more jealous of thee than a Barbary cock-pigeon over his hen; more clamorous than a parrot againft rain; more new-fangled than an ape; more giddy in my defires than a monkey: I will weep for nothing, like Diana in the fountain,' and I will do that when you are difpos'd to be merry; I will laugh like a hyen,' and that when thou art inclined to fleep.

---

7 ―――― *I will weep for nothing, like* Diana *in the fountain,*] The allufion is to the crofs in Cheapfide; the religious images with which it was ornamented, being defaced, (as we learn from Stowe,) in 1596, "There was then fet up, a curious wrought tabernacle of gray marble, and in the fame an alabafter image of *Diana,* and water conveyed from the Thames, prilling from her naked breaft." *Stowe, in Cheap Ward.*

* Statues, and particularly that of *Diana,* with water conveyed through them to give them the appearance of weeping figures, were anciently a frequent ornament of fountains. So, in *The City Match,* Act III. fc. iii:

"―――― Now could I cry
" Like any image in a fountain, which
" Runs lamentations."

And again in *Rofamond's Epiftle to Henry II.* by Drayton:

" Here in the garden, wrought by curious hands,
" Naked *Diana* in the fountain ftands." WHALLEY.

* ―――― *I will laugh like a* hyen,] The bark of the hyena was anciently fuppofed to refemble a loud laugh.
So, in Webfter's *Duchefs of Malfy,* 1623:

" ―――― Methinks I fee her *laughing,*
" Excellent *Hyena!*"

Again, in *The Cobler's Prophecy,* 1594:

" You *laugh* hyena-like, weep like a crocodile."
STEEVENS.

Orl. But will my Rosalind do so?

Ros. By my life, she will do as I do.

Orl. O, but she is wise.

Ros. Or else she could not have the wit to do this: the wiser, the waywarder: Make the doors[9] upon a woman's wit, and it will out at the casement; shut that, and 'twill out at the key-hole; stop that, 'twill fly with the smoke out at the chimney.

Orl. A man that had a wife with such a wit, he might say,—*Wit, whither wilt?*[1]

Ros. Nay, you might keep that check for it, till you met your wife's wit going to your neighbour's bed.

Orl. And what wit could wit have to excuse that?

---

[9] —— Make *the doors*—] This is an expression used in several of the midland counties, instead of *bar the doors*. So, in *The Comedy of Errors* :

"The doors are *made* against you." STEEVENS.

[1] —— *Wit, whither wilt?*] This must be some allusion to a story well known at that time, though now perhaps irretrievable.

JOHNSON.

This was an exclamation much in use, when any one was either talking nonsense, or usurping a greater share in conversation than justly belonged to him. So, in Decker's *Satiromastix*, 1602 : " My sweet, *Wit whither wilt thou*, my delicate poetical fury," &c.

Again, in Heywood's *Royal King*, 1637 :

" Wit :—is the word strange to you ? *Wit?*—

" *Whither wilt thou ?*"

Again, in the Preface to *Greene's Groatsworth of Wit*, 1621 :

" *Wit whither wilt thou?* woe is me,

" Thou hast brought me to this miserie."

The same expression occurs more than once in Taylor the water-poet, and seems to have been the title of some ludicrous performance. STEEVENS.

If I remember right, these are the first words of an old madrigal.

MALONE.

Ros. Marry, to fay,—fhe came to feek you there. You fhall never take her without her anfwer,[3] unlefs you take her without her tongue. O, that woman that cannot make her fault her hufband's occafion,[4] let her never nurfe her child herfelf, for fhe will breed it like a fool.

Orl. For thefe two hours Rofalind, I will leave thee.

Ros. Alas, dear love, I cannot lack thee two hours.

Orl. I muft attend the duke at dinner; by two ó'clock I will be with thee again.

Ros. Ay, go your ways, go your ways;—I knew what you would prove; my friends told me as much, and I thought no lefs:—that flattering tongue of yours won me:—'tis but one caft away, and fo,— come, death.—Two o'clock is your hour?

Orl. Ay, fweet Rofalind.

Ros. By my troth, and in good earneft, and fo God mend me, and by all pretty oaths that are not dangerous, if you break one jot of your promife,

---

[3] *You fhall never take her without her anfwer,*] See Chaucer's *Marchantes Tale*, ver. 10,138—10,149:

" Ye, fire, quod Proferpine, and wol ye fo?
" Now by my modre Ceres foule I fwere,
" That I fhall yeve hire fuffifant anfwere,
" And alle women after for hire fake;
" That though they ben in any gilt ytake,
" With face bold they fhul hemfelve excufe,
" And bere hem doun that wolden hem accufe.
" For lack of anfwere, non of us fhall dien.
" Al had ye feen a thing with bothe youre eyen,
" Yet fhul we fo vifage it hardely,
" And wepe and fwere and chiden fubtilly,
" That ye fhul ben as lewed as ben gees."
                                        TYRWHITT.

[4] ——*make her fault her hufband's occafion,*] That is, reprefent her fault as occafioned by her hufband. Sir T. Hanmer reads, *her hufband's* accufation. JOHNSON.

or come one minute behind your hour, I will think you the moſt pathetical break-promiſe,[5] and the moſt hollow lover, and the moſt unworthy of her you call Roſalind, that may be choſen out of the groſs band of the unfaithful: therefore beware my cenſure, and keep your promiſe.

*O*RL. With no leſs religion, than if thou wert indeed my Roſalind: So, adieu.

Ros. Well, time is the old juſtice that examines all ſuch offenders, and let time try:[6] Adieu!

[*Exit* ORLANDO.

*C*EL. You have ſimply miſus'd our ſex in your love-prate: we muſt have your doublet and hoſe pluck'd over your head, and ſhow the world what the bird hath done to her own neſt.[7]

Ros. O coz, coz, coz, my pretty little coz, that thou didſt know how many fathom deep I am in love! But it cannot be founded; my affection hath an unknown bottom, like the bay of Portugal.

*C*EL. Or rather, bottomleſs; that as faſt as you pour affection in, it runs out.

---

[5] —— *I will think you the moſt* pathetical *break-promiſe,*] The ſame epithet occurs again in *Love's Labour's Loſt,* and with as littl℮ apparent meaning:

" —————— moſt *pathetical* nit." STEEVENS.

I believe, by *pathetical* break-promiſe, Roſalind means a lover whoſe falſehood would moſt *deeply affect* his miſtreſs.

MALONE.

[6] —— time *is the* old juſtice *that examines all ſuch offenders, and let* time *try:*] So, in *Troilus and Creſſida:*

" And that *old common arbitrator, Time,*
" Will one day end it." STEEVENS.

[7] —— *to her own neſt.*] So, in Lodge's *Roſalynde:* And " I pray you (quoth Aliena) if your own robes were off, what mettal are you made of, that you are ſo ſatyricall againſt women ? Is it not a foule bird defiles her owne neſt ?" STEEVENS.

Ros. No, that fame wicked baſtard of Venus, that was begot of thought,[7] conceiv'd of ſpleen, and born of madneſs; that blind raſcally boy, that abuſes every one's eyes, becauſe his own are out, let him be judge, how deep I am in love:—I'll tell thee, Aliena, I cannot be out of the ſight of Or-lando: I'll go find a ſhadow, and ſigh till he come.[8]

Cel. And I'll ſleep.   [*Exeunt.*

SCENE II.

Another part of the Foreſt.

Enter JAQUES *and* Lords, *in the habit of Foreſters.*

Jaq. Which is he that kill'd the deer?

1 *Lord.* Sir, it was I.

Jaq. Let's preſent him to the duke, like a Ro-man conqueror; and it would do well to ſet the deer's horns upon his head, for a branch of victory:— Have you no ſong, foreſter, for this purpoſe?

2 *Lord.* Yes, ſir.

Jaq. Sing it; 'tis no matter how it be in tune, ſo it make noiſe enough.

---

[7] —— *begot of* thought,] i. e. of melancholy. So, in *Julius Cæfar:*

"——take *thought*, and die for Cæſar." STEEVENS.

[8] —— *I'll go find a ſhadow, and ſigh till he come.*] So, in *Macbeth:*

" Let us *ſeek out* ſome deſolate *ſhade*, and there

" Weep our ſad boſoms empty." STEEVENS.

SONG.

1. *What shall he have, that kill'd the deer?*
2. *His leather skin, and horns to wear.*[8]
   1. *Then sing him home:*
Take thou no scorn, to wear the horn;[9] } The rest shall
It was a crest ere thou wast born.   } bear this bur-
   1. *Thy father's father wore it;* } den.
   2. *And thy father bore it:*
All. *The horn, the horn, the lusty horn,*
Is not a thing to laugh to scorn.   [Exeunt.

---

[8] *His leather skin, and horns to wear.*] Shakspeare seems to have formed this song on a hint afforded by the novel which furnished him with the plot of his play. " What news, Forrester? Hast thou wounded some deere, and lost him in the fall? Care not, man, for so small a losse; thy fees was but the *skinne*, the shoulders, and the *horns.*" *Lodge's Rosalynde, or Euphues's Golden Legacie,* 1592. For this quotation the reader is indebted to Mr. Malone.

So likewise in an ancient MS. entitled *The Boke of Huntyng, that is cleped Mayster of Game:* " And as of fees, it is to wite that what man that *smyte a dere atte his tree with a dethes stroke,* and he be recouered by sonne going doune, he shall haue the *skyn,* &c."
                    STEEVENS.

[9] *Take thou no scorn, to wear the horn;*] In *King John* in two parts, 1591, a play which our authour had without doubt attentively read, we find these lines:
    " But let the foolish Frenchman *take no scorn,*
    " If Philip front him with an English *horn.*" MALONE.

To *take scorn* is a phrase that occurs again in *King Henry VI.* P. I. Act IV. sc. iv:
    " And *take* foul *scorn,* to fawn on him by sending."
                    STEEVENS.

SCENE III.[1]

The Foreſt.

Enter ROSALIND *and* CELIA.

Ros. How ſay you now? Is it not paſt two
o'clock? and here much Orlando![3]

Cel. I warrant you, with pure love, and troubled
brain, he hath ta'en his bow and arrows, and is gone
forth—to ſleep: Look, who comes here.

Enter SILVIUS.

Sil. My errand is to you, fair youth;—

---

[1] The foregoing noiſy ſcene was introduced only to fill up an
interval, which is to repreſent two hours. This contraction of
the time we might impute to poor Roſalind's impatience, but
that a few minutes after we find Orlando ſending his excuſe. I
do not ſee that by any probable diviſion of the acts this abſurdity
can be obviated. JOHNSON.

[3] —— *and here much Orlando!*] Thus the old copy. Some
of the modern editors read, but without the leaſt authority:
I wonder much, Orlando is not here. STEEVENS.

The word *much* ſhould be explained. It is an expreſſion of
latitude, and taken in various ſenſes. Here's *much* Orlando—i. e.
Here is no Orlando, or we may look for him. We have ſtill
this uſe of it, as when we ſay, ſpeaking of a perſon who we
ſuſpect will not keep his appointment, " Ay, you will be ſure
to ſee him there *much!*" WHALLEY.

So the vulgar yet ſay, " I ſhall get *much* by that no doubt,"
meaning that they ſhall get nothing. MALONE.

Here much Orlando! is ſpoken ironically on Roſalind perceiving
that Orlando had failed in his engagement. HOLT WHITE.

Much, in our author's time, was an expreſſion denoting admira-
tion. So, in *King Henry IV.* P. II. Act II. ſc. iv:
" What, with two points on your ſhoulder? *much!*"
Again, in *The Taming of the Shrew:*
" 'Tis *much!*—Servant, leave me and her alone." MALONE.

Much! was more frequently uſed to indicate diſdain. See notes
on the firſt of the two paſſages quoted by Mr. Malone. STEEVENS.

My gentle Phebe bid me⁴ give you this:

[Giving a letter.

I know not the contents; but, as I guefs,
By the ftern brow, and wafpifh action
Which fhe did ufe as fhe was writing of it,
It bears an angry tenour: pardon me,
I am but as a guiltlefs meffenger.

Ros. Patience herfelf would ftartle at this letter,
And play the fwaggerer;⁵ bear this, bear all:
She fays, I am not fair; that I lack manners;
She calls me proud; and, that fhe could not love me
Were man as rare as phœnix; Od's my will!
Her love is not the hare that I do hunt:
Why writes fhe fo to me?—Well, fhepherd, well,
This is a letter of your own device.

SIL. No, I proteft, I know not the contents;
Phebe did write it.

Ros.   Come, come, you are a fool,
And turn'd into the extremity of love.
I faw her hand: fhe has a leathern hand,
A freeftone-colour'd hand;⁶ I verily did think
That her old gloves were on, but 'twas her hands;
She has a hufwife's hand: but that's no matter:

---

⁴ —— *bid me* —] The old copy redundantly reads—*did* bid me.
                                                    STEEVENS.

⁵ *Patience herfelf would ftartle at this letter,*
   And play the fwaggerer;] So, in *Meafure for Meafure*:
   " This would make mercy fwear, *and play the tyrant.*"
                                                    STEEVENS.

⁶ *Phebe did write it.*
     Rof. *Come, come, you are a fool,*——
   I faw her hand: fhe has a leathern hand,
   A freeftone-colour'd hand;] As this paffage now ftands, the
metre of the firft line is imperfect, and the fenfe of the whole; for
why fhould Rofalind dwell fo much upon Phebe's hands, unlefs
Silvius had faid fomething about them?—I have no doubt but the
line originally ran thus:
     Phebe did write it with her own fair hand.
And then Rofalind's reply will naturally follow. M. MASON,

I fay, fhe never did invent this letter;
This is a man's invention, and his hand.

SIL. Sure, it is hers.

Ros. Why, 'tis a boifterous and a cruel ftile,
A ftile for challengers; why, fhe defies me,
Like Turk to Chriftian: woman's gentle brain [3]
Could not drop forth fuch giant-rude invention,
Such Ethiop words, blacker in their effect
Than in their countenance:—Will you hear the
   letter?

SIL. So pleafe you, for I never heard it yet;
Yet heard too much of Phebe's cruelty.

Ros. She Phebes me: Mark how the tyrant writes.

  Art thou god to fhepherd turn'd,   [Reads.
  That a maiden's heart hath burn'd?—

Can a woman rail thus?

SIL. Call you this railing?

Ros. *Why, thy godhead laid apart,*
  Warr'ft thou with a woman's heart?

Did you ever hear fuch railing?—

  Whiles the eye of man did woo me,
  That could do no vengeance [4] to me.—

Meaning me a beaft.—

  If the fcorn of your bright eyne
  Have power to raife fuch love in mine,
  Alack, in me what ftrange effect
  Would they work in mild afpect?
  Whiles you chid me, I did love;
  How then might your prayers move?

—— woman's *gentle brain*—] Old copy—*women's.* Corrected by Mr. Rowe. MALONE.

—— *vengeance* —] is ufed for *mifchief.* JOHNSON.

He, that brings this love to thee,
Little knows this love in me:
And by him seal up thy mind;
Whether that thy youth and kind [5]
Will the faithful offer take
Of me, and all that I can make; [6]
Or else by him my love deny,
And then I'll study how to die.

SIL. Call you this chiding?

CEL. Alas, poor shepherd!

ROS. Do you pity him? no, he deserves no pity.—
Wilt thou love such a woman?—What, to make
thee an instrument, and play false strains upon thee!
not to be endured!—Well, go your way to her, (for,
I see, love hath made thee a tame snake,) [7] and say this
to her;—That if she love me, I charge her to love
thee: if she will not, I will never have her, unless
thou entreat for her.—If you be a true lover, hence,
and not a word; for here comes more company.

[*Exit* SILVIUS.

Enter OLIVER.

OLI. Good-morrow, fair ones: Pray you, if you
know

---

[5] —— *youth and* kind——] *Kind* is the old word for *nature.*
JOHNSON.
So, in *Antony and Cleopatra:* "You must think this, look you,
that the worm will do his *kind.*" STEEVENS.

[6] —— *all that I can* make;] i. e. raise as profit from any thing.
So, in *Measure for Measure:* "He's in for a commodity of brown
paper; of which he *made* five marks ready money." STEEVENS.

[7] —— *I see, love hath made thee a tame* snake,] This term was,
in our author's time, frequently used to express a poor contemptible fellow. So, in *Sir John Oldcastle,* 1600: "—— and you,
poor *snakes,* come seldom to a booty."
Again, in *Lord Cromwell,* 1602:
"———— the poorest *snake,*
"That feeds on lemons, pilchards——." MALONE.

I

Where, in the purlieus [6] of this foreſt, ſtands
A ſheep-cote, fenc'd about with olive-trees?

CEL. Weſt of this place, down in the neighbour
        bottom,
The rank of oſiers, by the murmuring ſtream,
Left on your right hand, [7] brings you to the place:
But at this hour the houſe doth keep itſelf,
There's none within.

OLI. If that an eye may profit by a tongue,
Then I ſhould know you by deſcription;
Such garments, and ſuch years: *The boy is fair,*
Of female favour, and beſtows himſelf
Like a ripe ſiſter: [8] *but the woman low,* [9]
And browner than her brother. Are not you
The owner of the houſe I did enquire for?

CEL. It is no boaſt, being aſk'd, to ſay, we are.

OLI. Orlando doth commend him to you both;

---

[6] —— purlieus *of this foreſt,*] *Purlieu,* ſays Manwood's *Treatiſe on the Foreſt Laws,* c. xx. " Is a certaine territorie of ground adjoyning unto the foreſt, meared and bounded with unmoveable marks, meeres, and boundaries: which territories of ground was alſo foreſt, and afterwards diſaforeſted againe by the perambulations made for the ſevering of the new foreſt from the old." REED.

Bullokar, in his *Expoſitor,* 1616, deſcribes a *parlieu* as " a place neere joining to a foreſt, where it is lawful for the owner of the ground to hunt, if he can diſpend fortie ſhillings by the yeere, of freeland." MALONE.

[7] *Left on your right hand,*] i. e. paſſing by the rank of oziers, and *leaving* them on your right hand, you will reach the place.
MALONE.

[8] —————— beſtows *himſelf*
Like a ripe ſiſter :] Of this quaint phraſeology there is an example in *King Henry IV.* P. II: " How might we ſee Falſtaff *beſtow* himſelf to-night in his true colours?" STEEVENS.

[9] —— but *the woman low,*] *But,* which is not in the old copy, was added by the editor of the ſecond folio, to ſupply the metre. I ſuſpect it is not the word omitted, but have nothing better to propoſe. MALONE.

And to that youth, he calls his Rofalind,
He fends this bloody napkin;[9] Are you he?

Ros. I am: What muft we underftand by this?

Oli. Some of my fhame; if you will know of me
What man I am, and how, and why, and where
This handkerchief was ftain'd.

Cel.   I pray you, tell it.

Oli. When laft the young Orlando parted from you,
He left a promife to return again
Within an hour;[2] and, pacing through the foreft,
Chewing the food of fweet and bitter fancy,[3]
Lo, what befel! he threw his eye afide,
And, mark, what object did prefent itfelf!
Under an oak,[4] whofe boughs were mofs'd with age,
And high top bald with dry antiquity,[5]

---

[9] —— *napkin*;] i. e. *handkerchief*. Ray fays, that a pocket
handkerchief is fo called about Sheffield in Yorkfhire. So, in
Greene's *Never too Late*, 1616: " I can wet one of my new lock-
ram *napkins* with weeping."

Napery, indeed, fignifies linen in general. So, in Decker's *Honeft
Whore*, 1635:
       " —— pr'ythee put me into wholefome *napery*."
Again, in Chapman's *May-Day*, 1611: " Befides your munition
of manchet *napery* plates." *Naperia*, Ital. STEEVENS.

[2] *Within an hour*;] We muft read—*within two hours*. JOHNSON.
    May not *within an hour* fignify *within a certain time?*
                                                    TYRWHITT.

[3] —— *of fweet and bitter* fancy,] i. e. *love*, which is always
thus defcribed by our old poets, as compofed of contraries. See
a note on *Romeo and Juliet*, Act I. fc. ii.
    So, in Lodge's *Rofalynde*, 1590: " I have noted the variable
difpofition of *fancy*,——a *bitter* pleafure wrapt in *fweet* prejudice."
                                                    MALONE.

[4] *Under an oak*,] The ancient copy reads—Under an *old* oak;
but as this epithet hurts the meafure, without improvement of the
fenfe, (for we are told in the fame line that its " boughs were mofs'd
with *age*," and afterwards, that its top was " bald with dry *antiquity*,") I have omitted *old*, as an unqueftionable interpolation.
                                                    STEEVENS,

[5] *Under on oak*, &c.] The paffage ftands thus in Lodge's no-

A wretched ragged man, o'ergrown with hair,
Lay fleeping on his back : about his neck
A green and gilded fnake had wreath'd itfelf,
Who with her head, nimble in threats, approach'd
The opening of his mouth ; but fuddenly
Seeing Orlando, it unlink'd itfelf,
And with indented glides did flip away
Into a bufh : under which bufh's fhade
A lionefs, with udders all drawn dry,⁵
Lay couching, head on ground, with catlike watch,
When that the fleeping man fhould ftir ; for 'tis
The royal difpofition of that beaft,
To prey on nothing that doth feem as dead :

vel : " Saladyne, wearie with wandring up and downe, and hungry with long fafting, finding a little cave by the fide of a thicket,
eating fuch fruite as the forreft did affoord, and contenting himfelf with fuch drinke as nature had provided, and thirft made
delicate, after his repaft he fell into a dead fleepe. As thus he
lay, a hungry lyon came hunting downe the edge of the grove
for pray, and efpying Saladyne, began to ceaze upon him : but
feeing he lay ftill without any motion, he left to touch him, for
that lyons hate to pray on dead carkaffes : and yet defirous to
have fome foode, the lyon lay downe and watcht to fee if he
would ftirre. While thus Saladyne flept fecure, fortune that was
careful of her champion, began to fmile, and brought it fo to
paffe, that Rofader (having ftricken a deere that but lightly hurt
fled through the thicket) came pacing downe by the grove with a
boare-fpeare in his hande in great hafte, he fpyed where a man
lay afleepe, and a lyon faft by him : amazed at this fight, as he
ftood gazing, his nofe on the fodaine bledde, which made him
conjecture it was fome friend of his. Whereupon drawing more
nigh, he might eafily difcerne his vifage, and perceived by his
phifnomie that it was his brother Saladyne, which drave Rofader
into a deepe paffion, as a man perplexed, &c.——But the prefent
time craved no fuch doubting ambages : for he muft eyther refolve
to hazard his life for his reliefe, or elfe fteale away and leave him
to the crueltie of the lyon. In which doubt hee thus briefly
debated," &c. STEEVENS.

⁵ *A lionefs, with udders all drawn dry,*] So, in *Arden of Fever-
fham,* 1592 :
        "——— the ftarven *lionefs*
        " When fhe is *dry-fucks* of her eager young." STEEVENS.

This ſeen, Orlando did approach the man,
And found it was his brother, his elder brother.

CEL. O, I have heard him ſpeak of that ſame
    brother;
And he did render him[6] the moſt unnatural
That liv'd 'mongſt men.

OLI.   And well he might ſo do,
For well I know he was unnatural.

ROS. But, to Orlando;—Did he leave him there,
Food to the ſuck'd and hungry lioneſs?

OLI. Twice did he turn his back, and purpos'd ſo:
But kindneſs, nobler ever than revenge,
And nature, ſtronger than his juſt occaſion,
Made him give battle to the lioneſs,
Who quickly fell before him; in which hurtling[7]
From miſerable ſlumber I awak'd.

CEL. Are you his brother?

ROS.   Was it you he reſcu'd?

CEL. Was't you that did ſo oft contrive to kill
    him?

OLI. 'Twas I; but 'tis not I: I do not ſhame
To tell you what I was, ſince my converſion
So ſweetly taſtes, being the thing I am.

ROS. But, for the bloody napkin?—

---

[6] *And he did* render *him*—] i. e. deſcribe him. MALONE.
So, in *Cymbeline* :
  " May drive us to a *render* where we have liv'd."
             STEEVENS.

[7] —— *in which* hurtling—] To *hurtle* is to move with impe-
tuoſity and tumult. So, in *Julius Cæſar* :
  " A noiſe of battle *hurtled* in the air."
Again, in Naſh's *Lenten Stuff*, &c. 1591 : " — hearing of the
gangs of good fellows that *hurtled* and buſtled thither," &c.
  Again, in Spenſer's *Faerie Queen*, B. I. c. iv :
  " All *hurtlen* forth, and ſhe with princely pace," &c.
Again, B. I. c. viii :
  " Came *hurtling* in full fierce, and forc'd the knight retire."
             STEEVENS.

OLI.　　　　　　　　　　　　　　　By, and by.

When from the firſt to laſt, betwixt us two,
Tears our recountments had moſt kindly bath'd,
As, how I came into that deſert place; [*]——
In brief, he led me to the gentle duke,
Who gave me freſh array, and entertainment,
Committing me unto my brother's love;
Who led me inſtantly unto his cave,
There ſtripp'd himſelf, and here upon his arm
The lioneſs had torn ſome fleſh away,
Which all this while had bled; and now he fainted,
And cry'd, in fainting, upon Roſalind.
Brief, I recover'd him; bound up his wound;
And, after ſome ſmall ſpace, being ſtrong at heart,
He ſent me hither, ſtranger as I am,
To tell this ſtory, that you might excuſe
His broken promiſe, and to give this napkin,
Dy'd in this blood; [v] unto the ſhepherd youth
That he in ſport doth call his Roſalind.

　　CEL. Why, how now, Ganymede? ſweet Gany-
　　　　mede?　　　　　　　　[ROSALIND faints.

　　OLI. Many will ſwoon when they do look on
　　　　blood.

　　[*] _As, how I came into that deſert place_;] I believe, a line following this has been loſt. MALONE.

　　_As_, in this place, ſignifies—_as for inſtance_. So, in _Hamlet_:
　　　" _As_, ſtars with trains of fire," &c.
I ſuſpect no omiſſion. STEEVENS.

　　[v] _Dy'd in this blood_;] Thus the old copy. The editor of the
ſecond folio changed _this_ blood unneceſſarily to—_his_ blood. Oliver
points to the handkerchief, when he preſents it; and Roſalind
could not doubt whoſe blood it was after the account that had been
before given. MALONE.

　　Perhaps the change of _this_ into _his_, is imputable only to the
compoſitor, who caſually omitted the _t_. Either reading may ſerve;
and certainly that of the ſecond folio is not the worſt, becauſe it
prevents the diſguſting repetition of the pronoun _this_, with which
the preſent ſpeech is infeſted. STEEVENS.

Cel. There is more in it:—Coufin—Ganymede![a]

Oli. Look, he recovers.

Ros.   I would, I were at home.

Cel. We'll lead you thither:—
I pray you, will you take him by the arm?

Oli. Be of good cheer, youth:—You a man?—
You lack a man's heart.

Ros. I do fo, I confefs it. Ah, fir,[b] a body would
think this was well counterfeited: I pray you, tell
your brother how well I counterfeited.—Heigh
ho!—

Oli. This was not counterfeit; there is too great
teftimony in your complexion, that it was a paffion
of earneft.

Ros. Counterfeit, I affure you.

Oli. Well then, take a good heart, and counterfeit to be a man.

Ros. So I do: but, i'faith I fhould have been a
woman by right.

Cel. Come, you look paler and paler; pray you,
draw homewards:—Good fir, go with us.

Oli. That will I, for I muft bear anfwer back
How you excufe my brother, Rofalind.

Ros. I fhall devife fomething: But, I pray you,
commend my counterfeiting to him:—Will you go?
                            [*Exeunt.*

---

[a] —— *Coufin—Ganymede!*] Celia in her firft fright forgets
Rofalind's charaffer and difguife, and calls out *coufin*, then recollects herfelf, and fays, Ganymede. johnson.

[b] *Ah, fir,*] The old copy reads—Ah, *firra*, &c. Correffed
by the editor of the fecond folio. malone.

ACT V.   SCENE I.

The same.

Enter TOUCHSTONE *and* AUDREY.

Touch. We shall find a time, Audrey; patience, gentle Audrey.

Aud. 'Faith, the priest was good enough, for all the old gentleman's saying.

Touch. A most wicked sir Oliver, Audrey, a most vile Mar-text.   But, Audrey, there is a youth here in the forest lays claim to you.

Aud. Ay, I know who 'tis; he hath no interest in me in the world: here comes the man you mean.

Enter WILLIAM.

Touch. It is meat and drink to me to see a clown: By my troth, we that have good wits, have much to answer for; we shall be flouting; we cannot hold.

Will. Good even, Audrey.

Aud. God ye good even, William.

Will. And good even to you, sir.

Touch. Good even, gentle friend: Cover thy head, cover thy head; nay, pr'ythee, be cover'd. How old are you, friend?

Will. Five and twenty, sir.

Touch. A ripe age: Is thy name, William?

Will. William, sir.

Touch. A fair name: Wast born i'the forest here?

WILL. Ay, fir, I thank God.

TOUCH. Thank God;—a good anfwer: Art rich?

WILL. 'Faith, fir, fo, fo.

TOUCH. So, fo, is good, very good, very excellent good:—and yet it is not; it is but fo fo. Art thou wife?

WILL. Ay, fir, I have a pretty wit.

TOUCH. Why, thou fay'ft well. I do now re-member a faying; *The fool doth think he is wife, but the wife man knows himfelf to be a fool.* The heathen philofopher, when he had a defire to eat a grape, would open his lips when he put it into his mouth; [4] meaning thereby, that grapes were made to eat, and lips to open. You do love this maid? [5]

WILL. I do, fir.

TOUCH. Give me your hand: Art thou learned?

WILL. No, fir.

TOUCH. Then learn this of me; To have, is to have: For it is a figure in rhetorick, that drink, being pour'd out of a cup into a glafs, by filling

---

[4] *The heathen philofopher, when he had a defire to eat a grape, &c.*] This was defigned as a fneer on the feveral trifling and infignificant fayings and actions, recorded of the ancient philofophers, by the writers of their·lives, fuch as Diogenes Laertius, Philoftratus, Eunapius, &c. as appears from its being introduced by one of their *wife fayings.* WARBURTON.

A book called *The Dictes and Sayings of the Philofophers,* was printed by Caxton in 1477. It was tranflated out of French into Englifh by Lord Rivers. From this performance, or fome re-publication of it, Shakfpeare's knowledge of thefe philofophical trifles might be derived. STEEVENS.

[5] —— *meaning thereby, that* grapes *were made to eat, and* lips *to open.* You do love this maid?] Part of this dialogue feems to have grown out of the novel on which the play is formed: " Phebe is no latice for your *lips,* and her *grapes* hang fo hie, that gaze at them you may, but touch them you cannot." MALONE.

L 2

the one doth empty the other: For all your writers
do confent, that *ipſe* is he; now you are not *ipſe,*
for I am he.

WILL. Which he, ſir?

Touch. He, ſir, that muſt marry this woman:
Therefore, you clown, abandon,—which is in the
vulgar, leave,—the ſociety,—which in the booriſh
is, company,—of this female,—which in the common is,—woman, which together is, abandon the
ſociety of this female; or, clown thou periſheſt; or,
to thy better underſtanding, dieſt; to wit, I kill
thee,⁵ make thee away, tranſlate thy life into death,
thy liberty into bondage: I will deal in poiſon with
thee, or in baſtinàdo, or in ſteel; I will bandy with
thee in faction; I will o'er-run thee with policy;
I will kill thee a hundred and fifty ways; therefore
tremble, and depart.

Aud. Do, good William.

WILL. God reſt you merry, ſir.   [*Exit.*

Enter CORIN.

Cor. Our maſter and miſtreſs ſeek you; come,
away, away.

Touch. Trip, Audrey, trip, Audrey;—I attend,
I attend.   [*Exeunt.*

⁵ ——*to wit, I kill thee,*] The old copy reads—" *or,* to wit, I
kill thee." I have omitted the impertinent conjunction *or,* by the
advice of Dr. Farmer. STEEVENS.

SCENE II.

The same.

Enter ORLANDO *and* OLIVER.

ORL. Is't poſſible,[6] that on ſo little acquaintance you ſhould like her? that, but ſeeing, you ſhould love her? and, loving, woo? and, wooing, ſhe ſhould grant? And will you perſéver to enjoy her?

OLI. Neither call the giddineſs of it in queſtion, the poverty of her, the ſmall acquaintance, my ſudden wooing, nor her ſudden conſenting;[7] but ſay with me, I love Aliena; ſay with her, that ſhe loves me; conſent with both, that we may enjoy each other: it ſhall be to your good; for my father's houſe, and all the revenue that was old ſir Rowland's, will I eſtate upon you, and here live and die a ſhepherd.

Enter ROSALIND.

ORL. You have my conſent. Let your wedding be to-morrow: thither will I invite the duke, and

---

[6] *Is't poſſible,* &c.] Shakſpeare, by putting this queſtion into the mouth of Orlando, ſeems to have been aware of the impropriety which he had been guilty of by deſerting his original. In Lodge's novel, the elder brother is inſtrumental in ſaving Aliena from a band of ruffians, who " thought to ſteal her away, and to give her to the king for a preſent, hoping, becauſe the king was a great leacher, by ſuch a gift to purchaſe all their pardons." Without the intervention of this circumſtance, the paſſion of Aliena appears to be very haſty indeed. STEEVENS.

[7] —— *nor* her *ſudden conſenting*;] Old copy—nor ſudden. Corrected by Mr. Rowe. MALONE.

all his contented followers: Go you, and prepare
Aliena; for, look you, here comes my Rosalind.

Ros. God save you, brother.

Oli. And you, fair sister.[8]

Ros. O, my dear Orlando, how it grieves me to
see thee wear thy heart in a scarf.

Orl. It is my arm.

Ros. I thought, thy heart had been wounded with
the claws of a lion.

Orl. Wounded it is, but with the eyes of a lady.

Ros. Did your brother tell you how I counterfeited to swoon, when he show'd me your handkerchief?

Orl. Ay, and greater wonders than that.

Ros. O, I know where you are:—Nay, 'tis true:
there was never any thing so sudden, but the fight
of two rams,[9] and Cæsar's thrasonical brag of—*I
came, saw,* and *overcame:* For your brother and my
sister no sooner met, but they look'd; no sooner
look'd, but they lov'd; no sooner lov'd, but they
sigh'd; no sooner sigh'd, but they ask'd one another
the reason; no sooner knew the reason, but they
sought the remedy: and in these degrees have they
made a pair of stairs to marriage, which they will
climb incontinent, or else be incontinent before

---

[8] *And you, fair sister.*] I know not why Oliver should call Rosalind sister. He takes her yet to be a man. I suppose we should
read—*And you,* and your *fair sister.* JOHNSON.

Oliver speaks to her in the character she had assumed, of a woman courted by Orlando his brother. CHAMIER.

[9] —— *never any thing so sudden, but* the fight of two rams,]
So, in Laneham's *Account of Queen Elizabeth's Entertainment at
Kennelworth Castle,* 1575: " —ootrageous in their racez az rams
at their rut." STEEVENS.

marriage: they are in the very wrath of love, and they will together; clubs cannot part them.[1]

Orl. They shall be married to-morrow; and I will bid the duke to the nuptial. But, O, how bitter a thing it is to look into happiness through another man's eyes! By so much the more shall I to-morrow be at the height of heart-heaviness, by how much I shall think my brother happy, in having what he wishes for.

Ros. Why then, to-morrow I cannot serve your turn for Rosalind?

Orl. I can live no longer by thinking.

Ros. I will weary you then no longer with idle talking. Know of me then, (for now I speak to some purpose,) that I know you are a gentleman of good conceit: I speak not this, that you should bear a good opinion of my knowledge, insomuch, I say, I know you are; neither do I labour for a greater esteem than may in some little measure draw a belief from you, to do yourself good, and not to grace me. Believe then, if you please, that I can do strange things: I have, since I was three years old,

---

[1] —— clubs *cannot* part *them.*] It appears from many of our old dramas, that, in our author's time, it was a common custom, on the breaking out of a fray, to call out " *Clubs—Clubs,*" to part the combatants.

So, in *Titus Andronicus:*

" ! *Clubs, clubs*; these lovers will not *keep the peace.*"

The preceding words—" they are in the very *wrath* of love," show that our author had this in contemplation. MALONE.

So, in the First Part of *K. Henry VI.* when the Mayor of London is endeavouring to put a stop to the combat between the partisans of Glocester and Winchester, he says,

" I'll call for *clubs*, if you will not away."

And in *Henry VIII.* the Porter says, " I missed the meteor once, and hit that woman, who cried out *Clubs!* when I might see from far some forty truncheoneers draw to her succour." M. MASON.

L 4

converſed with a magician, moſt profound in his art, and yet not damnable. If you do love Roſalind ſo near the heart as your geſture cries it out, when your brother marries Aliena, you ſhall marry her: I know into what ſtraits of fortune ſhe is driven; and it is not impoſſible to me, if it appear not inconvenient to you, to ſet her before your eyes to-morrow, human as ſhe is,[3] and without any danger.

ORL. Speak'ſt thou in ſober meanings?

Ros. By my life, I do; which I tender dearly, though I ſay I am a magician:[4] Therefore, put you in your beſt array, bid your friends;[5] for if you will be married to-morrow, you ſhall; and to Roſalind, if you will.

Enter SILVIUS and PHEBE.

Look, here comes a lover of mine, and a lover of hers.

PHE. Youth, you have done me much ungentle-
　　　neſs,
To ſhow the letter that I writ to you.

---

[3] —— *human as ſhe is,*] That is, not a phantom, but the real Roſalind, without any of the danger generally conceived to attend the rites of incantation. JOHNSON.

[4] —— *which I tender dearly,* though I ſay I am a magician :] *Though I pretend to be a magician,* and therefore might be ſuppoſed able to elude death. MALONE.

This explanation cannot be right, as no magician was ever ſuppoſed to poſſeſs the art of *eluding death.* Dr. Warburton properly remarks, that this play " was written in King James's time, when there was a ſevere inquiſition after witches and magicians." It was natural therefore for one who called herſelf a magician, to allude to the danger, in which her avowal, had it been a ſerious one, would have involved her. STEEVENS.

[5] —— bid *your friends* ;] i. e. *invite* your friends. REED.

So, in *Titus Andronicus :*
　　" I am not *bid* to wait upon this bride." STEEVENS.

Ros. nI care not, if I have: it is my ftudy,
To feem defpiteful and ungentle to you:
You are there-follow'd by a faithful fhepherd;
Look upon him, love him; he worfhips you.

Phe. Good fhepherd, tell this youth what 'tis to love.

Sil. It is to be all made of fighs and tears;—
And fo am I for Phebe.

Phe. And I for Ganymede.

Orl. And I for Rofalind.

Ros. And I for no woman.

Sil. It is to be all made of faith and fervice;—
And fo am I for Phebe.

Phe. And I for Ganymede.

Orl. And I for Rofalind.

Ros. And I for no woman.

Sil. It is to be all made of fantafy,
All made of paffion, and all made of wifhes;
All adoration, duty and obfervance,
All humblenefs, all patience, and impatience,
All purity, all trial, all obfervance;[6]—
And fo am I for Phebe.

Phe. And fo am I for Ganymede.

Orl. And fo am I for Rofalind.

Ros. And fo am I for no woman.

Phe. If this be fo, why blame you me to love you?
[*To* Rosalind.

[6] —— *all trial, all* obfervance;] I fufpect our author wrote—
all *obedience.* It is highly probable that the compofitor caught
obfervance from the line above; and very unlikely that the fame
word fhould have been fet down twice by Shakfpeare fo clofe to
each other. Malone.

Read—*obeifance.* The word *obfervance* is evidently repeated by
an error of the prefs. Ritson.

Sil. If this be fo, why blame you me to love you?
[*To* Phebe.

Orl. If this be fo, why blame you me to love you?

Ros. Who do you fpeak to,[6] *why blame you me to love you?*

Orl. To her, that is not here, nor doth not hear.

Ros. Pray you, no more of this; 'tis like the howling of Irifh wolves againft the moon.[7]—I will help you, [*To* Silvius] if I can:—I would love you, [*To* Phebe] if I could.—To-morrow meet me all together.—I will marry you, [*To* Phebe] if ever I marry woman, and I'll be married to-morrow:—I will fatisfy you, [*To* Orlando] if ever I fatisfy'd man, and you fhall be married to-morrow:—I will content you, [*To* Silvius] if what pleafes you contents you, and you fhall be married to-morrow.—As you [*To* Orlando] love Rofalind, meet;—as you, [*To* Silvius] love Phebe, meet;—And as I love no woman, I'll meet.—So, fare you well; I have left you commands.

Sil. I'll not fail, if I live.

Phe.   Nor I.

Orl.   Nor I.
[*Exeunt.*

---

[6] Who *do you fpeak to,*] Old copy—*Why* do you fpeak *too.* Corrected by Mr. Rowe. Malone.

[7] —— *'tis like the howling of Irifh wolves againft the moon.*] This is borrowed from Lodge's *Rofalynde,* 1592: " I tell thee, Montanus, in courting Phœbe, thou barkeft with the *wolves* of Syria, *againft the moone."* Malone.

SCENE III.

The same.

Enter TOUCHSTONE *and* AUDREY.

TOUCH. To-morrow is the joyful day, Audrey; to-morrow will we be married.

AUD. I do defire it with all my heart: and I hope it is no difhoneft defire, to defire to be a woman of the world.[8] Here come two of the banifh'd duke's pages.

Enter two Pages.

1 *PAGE.* Well met, honeft gentleman.

TOUCH. By my troth, well met: Come, fit, fit, and a fong.

2 *PAGE.* We are for you: fit i'the middle.

1 *PAGE.* Shall we clap into't roundly, without hawking, or fpitting, or faying we are hoarfe; which are the only prologues to a bad voice?

2 *PAGE.* I'faith, i'faith; and both in a tune, like two gypfies on a horfe.

---

[8] —— *a woman of the world.*] To *go to the world,* is to be married. So, in *Much ado about Nothing:* " Thus (fays Beatrice) every one *goes to the world,* but I."

An anonymous writer fuppofes, that in this phrafe there is an allufion to Saint *Luke's* Gofpel, xx. 34: " The children of this *world marry,* and are given in marriage." STEEVENS,

S O N G.[9]

I.

It was a lover, and his lass,
*   With a hey, and a ho, and a hey nonino,*
That o'er the green corn-field did pass
*   In the spring time, the only pretty rank time,[2]*
When birds do sing, hey ding a ding, ding;
Sweet lovers love the spring.

II.

Between the acres of the rye,
*   With a hey, and a ho, and a hey nonino,*
These pretty country folks would lie,
*   In spring time, &c.*

---

[9] The stanzas of this song are in all the editions evidently transposed: as I have regulated them, that which in the former copies was the second stanza is now the last.

The same transposition of these stanzas is made by Dr. Thirlby, in a copy containing some notes on the margin, which I have perused by the favour of Sir Edward Walpole. JOHNSON.

[2] ——*the only pretty* rank *time,*] Thus the modern editors. The old copy reads:
    In the spring time, the onely pretty rang *time.*
I think we should read:
    In the spring time, the only pretty ring *time.*
i. e. the aptest season for marriage; or, the word *only,* for the sake of equality of metre, may be omitted. STEEVENS.

The old copy reads—*rang* time. The emendation was made by Dr. Johnson. Mr. Pope and the three subsequent editors read—the pretty *spring* time. Mr. Steevens proposes—" ring time, i. e. the aptest season for marriage." The passage does not deserve much consideration. MALONE.

In confirmation of Mr. Steevens's reading, it appears from the old calendars that the spring was the season of marriage.
                                                                DOUCE.[a]

III.

This carol they began that hour,
With a hey, and a ho, and a hey nonino,
How that a life was but a flower
In spring time, &c.

IV.

And therefore take the present time,
With a hey, and a ho, and a hey nonino;
For love is crowned with the prime
In spring time, &c.

TOUCH. Truly, young gentlemen, though there was no great matter in the ditty, yet the note was very untuneable.[4]

1 PAGE. You are deceiv'd, sir; we kept time, we lost not our time.

TOUCH. By my troth, yes; I count it but time lost to hear such a foolish song. God be with you; and God mend your voices!—Come, Audrey. [*Exeunt.*

---

[4] *Truly, young gentlemen, though there was no great matter in the ditty, yet the note was very* untuneable.] Though it is thus in all the printed copies, it is evident from the sequel of the dialogue, that the poet wrote as I have reform'd in my text, *untimeable.*—*Time* and *tune,* are frequently misprinted for one another in the old editions of Shakspeare. THEOBALD.

This emendation is received, I think very undeservedly, by Dr. Warburton. JOHNSON.

The reply of the Page proves to me, beyond any possibility of doubt, that we ought to read *untimeable,* instead of *untuneable,* notwithstanding Johnson rejects the amendment as unnecessary. A mistake of a similar nature occurs in *Twelfth Night.* M. MASON.

The sense of the old reading seems to be—*Though the words of the song were trifling, the music was not (as might have been expected) good enough to compensate their defect.* STEEVENS.

SCENE IV.

Another part of the Foreſt.

Enter Duke *ſenior,* AMIENS, JAQUES, ORLANDO, OLIVER, *and* CELIA.

DUKE S. Doſt thou believe, Orlando, that the boy
Can do all this that he hath promiſed?

ORL. I ſometimes do believe, and ſometimes do
not;
As thoſe that fear they hope, and know they fear.[5]

---

[5] *As thoſe that fear* they hope, *and know* they *fear.*] This ſtrange nonſenſe ſhould be read thus:

As thoſe that fear their hap, *and know* their *ſtar.*

i. e. As thoſe that fear the iſſue of a thing when they know their fear to be well grounded. WARBURTON.

The depravation of this line is evident, but I do not think the learned commentator's emendation very happy. I read thus:

As thoſe that fear with hope, *and hope* with *fear.*

Or thus, with leſs alteration:

As thoſe that fear, they hope, *and now* they *fear.*
JOHNSON.

The author of *The Reviſal* would read:

As thoſe that fear their hope, *and know* their *fear.*
STEEVENS.

Perhaps we might read:

As thoſe that feign they hope, *and know* they *fear.*
BLACKSTONE.

I would read:

As thoſe that fear, then hope; *and know,* then *fear.*
MUSGRAVE.

I have little doubt but it ſhould run thus:

As thoſe who fearing hope, *and* hoping *fear.*

This ſtrongly expreſſes the ſtate of mind which Orlando was in at that time; and if the words *fearing* and *hoping* were contracted in the original copy, and written thus:—*fear*'—*hop*' (a practice not unuſual at this day) the *g* might eaſily have been miſtaken for *y,* a common abbreviation of *they.* M. MASON.

Enter ROSALIND, SILVIUS, *and* PHEBE.

Ros. Patience once more, whiles our compáct is
urg'd:——

You fay, if I bring in your Rofalind, [*To the* DUKE.
You will beftow her on Orlando here?

DUKE S. That would I, had I kingdoms to give
with her.

Ros. And you fay, you will have her, when I
bring her? [*To* ORLANDO.

ORL. That would I, were I of all kingdoms king.

Ros. You fay, you'll marry me, if I be willing?
[*To* PHEBE.

PHE. That will I, fhould I die the hour after.

Ros. But, if you do refufe to marry me,
You'll give yourfelf to this moft faithful fhepherd?

PHE. So is the bargain.

Ros. You fay, that you'll have Phebe, if fhe will?
[*To* SILVIUS.

SIL. Though to have her and death were both
one thing.

Ros. I have promis'd to make all this matter even.
Keep you your word, O duke, to give your daughter;—
You yours, Orlando, to receive his daughter:——
Keep your word, Phebe,[6] that you'll marry me;

I believe this line requires no other alteration than the addition
of a femi-colon:

As thofe that fear; they hope, and know they fear. HENLEY.

The meaning, I think, is, *As thofe who fear,—they*, even thofe
very perfons, entertain *hopes*, that their fears will not be realized;
and yet at the fame time they well *know* that there is reafon for
their fears. MALONE.

[6] *Keep* your *word, Phebe,*] The old copy reads—Keep *you* your
word; the compofitor's eye having probably glanced on the line
next but one above. Corrected by Mr. Pope. MALONE.

Or elfe, refufing me, to wed this fhepherd:—
Keep your word, Silvius, that you'll marry her,
If fhe refufe me:—and from hence I go,
To make thefe doubts all even.[5]

[*Exeunt* ROSALIND *and* CELIA.

DUKE S. I do remember in this fhepherd-boy
Some lively touches of my daughter's favour.

ORL. My lord, the firft time that I ever faw him,
Methought he was a brother to your daughter:
But, my good lord, this boy is foreft-born;
And hath been tutor'd in the rudiments
Of many defperate ftudies by his uncle,
Whom he reports to be a great magician,
Obfcured in the circle of this foreft.

Enter TOUCHSTONE *and* AUDREY.

JAQ. There is, fure, another flood toward, and
thefe couples are coming to the ark! Here comes
a pair of very ftrange beafts, which in all tongues
are call'd fools.[6]

TOUCH. Salutation and greeting to you all!

JAQ. Good my lord, bid him welcome: This
is the motley-minded gentleman, that I have fo
often met in the foreft: he hath been a courtier, he
fwears.

---

[5] *To* make thefe *doubts* all even.] Thus, in *Meafure for Meafure:*
    " ——————— yet death we fear,
    " That *makes thefe* odds *all even.*" STEEVENS.

[6] *Here comes a pair of* very ftrange *beafts*, &c.] What *ftrange beafts?* and yet fuch as have a name in all languages? Noah's ark is here alluded to; into which the *clean* beafts entered by *fevens*, and the unclean by *two*, male and female. It is plain then that Shakfpeare wrote, *here come a pair of* unclean *beafts*, which is highly humorous. WARBURTON.

Strange beafts are only what we call *odd* animals. There is no need of any alteration. JOHNSON.

Touch. If any man doubt that, let him put me to my purgation. I have trod a meafure;[4] I have flatter'd a lady; I have been politick with my friend, fmooth with mine enemy; I have undone three tailors; I have had four quarrels, and like to have fought one.

Jaq. And how was that ta'en up?

Touch. 'Faith, we met, and found the quarrel was upon the feventh caufe.[5]

Jaq. How feventh caufe?—Good my lord, like this fellow.

Duke S. I like him very well.

Touch. God'ild you, fir;[6] I defire you of the like.[7] I prefs in here, fir, amongft the reft of the

---

[4] —— *trod a meafure;*] So, in *Love's Labour's Loft*, Act V. fc. ii:
"To *tread a meafure* with you on this grafs."
See note on this paffage. REED.

Touchftone to prove that he has been a courtier, particularly mentions a *meafure*, becaufe it was a very ftately folemn dance. So, in *Much ado about Nothing:* "—the wedding mannerly modeft, as a *meafure* full of ftate and ancientry." MALONE.

[5] —— *and found the quarrel was upon the* feventh caufe.] So all the copies; but it is apparent from the fequel that we muft read—*the quarrel was* not *upon the feventh caufe.* JOHNSON.

By the *feventh caufe,* Touchftone, I apprehend, means the lie *feven times removed*; i. e. the *retort courteous*, which is *removed* feven times (counting backwards) from the *lie direct*, the laft and moft aggravated fpecies of lie. See the fubfequent note on the words "—a lie feven times removed." MALONE.

[6] *God'ild you,* fir;] i. e. *God yield* you, reward you. So, in the *Collation of Chefter Myfteries* Mercer's play, p. 74, b. MS. Harl. Brit. Muf. 2013:
"The high father of heaven, I pray,
"To *yelde* you your good deed to day."
See note on *Macbeth*, Act I. fc. vi. STEEVENS.

[7] —— *I defire you of the like.*] We fhould read—*I defire of you the like.* On the Duke's faying, *I like him very well,* he replies, I defire you will give me caufe, that I may like you too.
WARBURTON.

country copulatives, to fwear, and to forfwear; according as marriage binds, and blood breaks:[8]—
A poor virgin, fir, an ill-favour'd thing, fir, but mine own; a poor humour of mine, fir, to take that that no man elfe will: Rich honefty dwells like a mifer, fir, in a poor houfe; as your pearl, in your foul oyfter.

Duke S. By my faith, he is very fwift and fententious.

Touch. According to the fool's bolt, fir, and fuch dulcet difeafes.[9]

I have not admitted the alteration, becaufe there are other examples of this mode of expreffion. JOHNSON.

See a note on the firft fcene of the third Act of *A Midfummer Night's Dream*, where many examples of this phrafeology are given. So alfo, in Spenfer's *Faery Queen*, B. II. c. ix:
" If it be I, *of* pardon I you pray."
Again, B. IV. c. viii:
" She dear befought the prince *of* remedy." STEEVENS.

[8] —— *according as marriage binds, and blood breaks:*] *To fwear according as marriage binds,* is to take the oath enjoined in the ceremonial of marriage. JOHNSON.

—— *to* fwear, *and to* forfwear; *according as* marriage binds, *and* blood breaks:] A man by the marriage ceremony SWEARS that *he will keep only to his wife*; when therefore, to *gratify his luft*, he *leaves her for another*, BLOOD BREAKS his *matrimonial obligation*, and he is FORSWORN. HENLEY.

[9] —— *dulcet difeafes.*] This I do not underftand. For *difeafes* it is eafy to read *difcourfes*: but, perhaps, the fault may lie deeper. JOHNSON.

Perhaps he calls a proverb a *difeafe*. Proverbial fayings may appear to him as the *furfeiting difeafes* of converfation. They are often the plague of commentators.

Dr. Farmer would read—*in* fuch dulcet difeafes; i. e. in the fweet uneafineffes of love, a time when people ufually talk nonfenfe. STEEVENS.

Without ftaying to examine how far the pofition laft advanced is founded in truth, I fhall only add, that I believe the text is right, and that this word is *capriciously* ufed for *fayings*, though neither in its primary or figurative fenfe it has any relation to that word. In *The Merchant of Venice* the Clown talks in the fame ftyle, but more

Jaq. But, for the feventh caufe; how did you find the quarrel on the feventh caufe?

Touch. Upon a lie feven times removed;[2]— Bear your body more feeming,[3] Audrey:—as thus,

intelligibly:—"the young gentleman (*according* to the fates and deftinies, and *fuch* odd *fayings*, the fifters three, and *fuch* branches of learning) is indeed deceafed." MALONE.

[2] *Upon a lie feven times* removed;] Touchftone here enumerates feven kinds of lies, from the *Retort courteous* to the *feventh* and moft aggravated fpecies of lie, which he calls the *lie direct*. The courtier's anfwer to his intended affront, he exprefsly tells us, was the *Retort courteous*, the *firft* fpecies of lie. When therefore he fays, that they *found the quarrel* was *on the lie feven times* REMOVED, we muft underftand by the latter word, the lie removed feven times, counting backwards, (as the word *removed* feems to intimate,) from the laft and moft aggravated fpecies of lie, namely, the *lie direct*. So, in *All's well that ends well*:

" Who hath fome four or five *removes* come fhort
" To tender it herfelf."

Again, in the play before us : " Your accent is fomething finer than you could purchafe in fo *removed* a dwelling," i. e. fo *diftant* from the haunts of men.

When Touchftone and the courtier met, they found their quarrel *originated* on the *feventh caufe*, i. e. on *the Retort courteous*, or the lie *feven times removed*. In the courfe of their altercation, *after* their meeting, Touchftone did not dare to go farther than the fixth fpecies, (counting in regular progreffion from the firft to the laft,) the *lie circumftantial*; and the courtier was afraid to give him the *lie direct*; fo they parted. In a fubfequent enumeration of the degrees of a lie, Touchftone exprefsly names the *Retort courteous*, as the *firft*; calling it therefore here " the *feventh* caufe," and " the lie *feven* times removed," he muft mean, *diftant* feven times from the moft offenfive lie, the *lie direct*. There is certainly therefore no need of reading with Dr. Johnfon in a former paffage—" We found the quarrel was *not* on the feventh caufe."

The mifapprehenfion of that moft judicious critick relative to thefe paffages muft apologize for my having employed fo many words in explaining them. MALONE.

[3] ——*feeming*,] i. e. feemly. *Seeming* is often ufed by Shakfpeare for becoming, or fairnefs of appearance. So, in *The Winter's Tale*:

" ———— thefe keep
" *Seeming* and favour all the winter long." STEEVENS.

fir. I did diſlike the cut of a certain courtier's beard;[3] he ſent me word, if I ſaid his beard was not cut well, he was in the mind it was: This is called the *Retort courteous*. If I ſent him word again, it was not well cut, he would ſend me word, he cut it to pleaſe himſelf: This is called the *Quip modeſt*. If again, it was not well cut, he diſabled my judgement: This is call'd the *Reply churliſh*. If again, it was not well cut, he would anſwer, I ſpake not true: This is call'd the *Reproof valiant*. If again, it was not well cut, he would ſay, I lie: This is called the *Countercheck quarrelſome*: and ſo to the *Lie circumſtantial*, and the *Lie direct*.

Jaq. And how oft did you ſay, his beard was not well cut?

Touch. I durſt go no further than the *Lie circumſtantial*, nor he durſt not give me the *Lie direct*; and ſo we meaſured ſwords, and parted.

Jaq. Can you nominate in order now the degrees of the lie?

Touch. O ſir, we quarrel in print, by the book;[4]

---

[3] ——— *as thus, ſir. I did diſlike the cut of a certain courtier's beard*;] This folly is touched upon with high humour by Fletcher, in his *Queen of Corinth* :

      " ——— Has he familiarly
      " Diſlik'd your yellow ſtarch, or ſaid your doublet
      " Was not exactly frenchified ?——
      " ——— or drawn your ſword,
      " Cry'd, 'twas ill mounted ? Has he given the *lie*
      " In *circle*, or *oblique*, or *ſemicircle*,
      " Or *direct parallel*? you muſt challenge him."
                          WARBURTON.

[4] *O ſir, we quarrel in print, by the book*;] The poet has, in this ſcene, rallied the mode of formal duelling, then ſo prevalent, with the higheſt humour and addreſs : nor could he have treated it with a happier contempt, than by making his Clown ſo knowing in the forms and preliminaries of it. The particular book here alluded to is a very ridiculous treatiſe of one Vincentio Saviolo,

as you have books for good manners:⁵ I will name you the degrees. The firſt, the Retort courteous; the ſecond, the Quip modeſt; the third the Reply

intitled, *Of Honour and honourable Quarrels*, in quarto, printed by Wolf, 1594. The firſt part of this tract he entitles, *A diſcourſe moſt neceſſary for all gentlemen that have in regard their honours, touching the giving and receiving the lie, whereupon the* Duello *and the* Combat *in divers forms doth enſue; and many other inconveniences for lack only of true knowledge of honour, and the* right underſtanding of words, *which here is ſet down.* The contents of the ſeveral chapters are as follow. I. *What the reaſon is that the party unto whom the lie is given ought to become challenger, and of the nature of lies.* II. *Of the manner and diverſity of lies.* III. *Of lies certain,* [or direct.] IV. *Of conditional lies,* [or the lie circumſtantial.] V. *Of the lie in general.* VI. *Of the lie in particular.* VII. *Of fooliſh lies.* VIII. *A concluſion touching the wreſting or returning back of the lie,* [or the countercheck quarrelſome.] In the chapter of *conditional lies,* ſpeaking of the particle *if,* he ſays, "—*Conditional lies be ſuch as are given conditionally, as if a man ſhould ſay or write theſe wordes:—if thou haſt ſaid that I have offered my lord abuſe, thou lieſt; or if thou ſayeſt ſo hereafter, thou ſhalt lie. Of theſe kind of lies, given in this manner, often ariſe much contention in wordes,—whereof no ſure concluſion can ariſe.*" By which he means, they cannot proceed to cut one another's throat, while there is an *if* between. Which is the reaſon of Shakſpeare making the Clown ſay, "*I knew when ſeven juſtices could not make up a quarrel: but when the parties were met themſelves, one of them thought but of an if; as, if you ſaid ſo, then I ſaid ſo, and they ſhook hands, and ſwore brothers. Your if is the only peace-maker; much virtue in if.*" Caranza was another of theſe authentick authors upon the Duello. Fletcher, in his laſt Act of *Love's Pilgrimage,* ridicules him with much humour. WARBURTON.

The words which I have included within crotchets are Dr. Warburton's. They have been hitherto printed in ſuch a manner as might lead the reader to ſuppoſe that they made a part of Saviolo's work. The paſſage was very inaccurately printed by Dr. Warburton in other reſpects, but has here been corrected by the original. MALONE.

⁵ —— *books for good manners:*] One of theſe books I have. It is entitled *The Boke of Nurture, or Schole of good Manners, for Men, Servants, and Children,* with *ſtans puer ad menſam;* 12mo. black letter, without date. It was written by Hugh Rhodes, a gentleman, or muſician, of the Chapel Royal; and was firſt publiſhed in 4to. in the reign of King Edward VI. STEEVENS.

churlifh; the fourth, the Reproof valiant; the fifth, the Countercheck quarrelfome; the fixth, the Lie with circumftance; the feventh, the Lie direct. All thefe you may avoid, but the Lie direct; and you may avoid that too, with an *If.* I knew when feven juftices could not take up a quarrel; but when the parties were met themfelves, one of them thought but of an *If,* as, *If you faid fo, then I faid fo*; and they fhook hands, and fwore brothers. Your *If* is the only peace-maker; much virtue in *If.*

Jaq. Is not this a rare fellow, my lord? he's as good at any thing, and yet a fool.

Duke S. He ufes his folly like a ftalking-horfe,[6] and under the prefentation of that, he fhoots his wit.

Enter HYMEN,[7] *leading* ROSALIND *in woman's clothes; and* CELIA.

Still Mufick.

HYM. *Then is there mirth in heaven,*
     When earthly things made even
          Alone together.
     Good duke, receive thy daughter,
     Hymen from heaven brought her,
          Yea, brought her hither;
     That thou might'ft join her hand with his,
     Whofe heart within her bofom is.[8]

Another is, *Galateo of Maifter John Cafa, Archbifhop of Benevento; or rather, a Treatife of the Manners and Behaviours it behoveth a Man to ufe and efchewe in his familiar Converfation. A Work very neceffary and profitable for all Gentlemen or other;* tranflated from the Italian by Robert Peterfon of Lincoln's Inn, 4to. 1576. REED.

6 —— *like a ftalking-horfe,*] See my note on *Much ado about Nothing,* Act II. fc. iii. STEEVENS.

7 *Enter* Hymen,] Rofalind is imagined by the reft of the com-

I

Ros. To you I give myfelf, for I am yours.

[*To* DUKE S.

To you I give myfelf, for I am yours.

[*To* ORLANDO.

pany to be brought by enchantment, and is therefore introduced by a fuppofed aerial being in the character of Hymen. JOHNSON.

In all the allegorical fhows exhibited at ancient weddings, *Hymen* was a conftant perfonage. Ben Jonfon, in his " *Hymenæi*, or the Solemnities of Mafque and Barriers, at a Marriage," has left us inftructions how to drefs this favourite character. " On the other hand entered *Hymen*, the god of marriage, in a *faffron-coloured* robe, his under veftures white, his fockes yellow, a yellow veile of filke on his left arme, his head crowned with rofes and marjoram, in his right hand a *torch*." STEEVENS.

[8] *That thou might'ft join* her *hand with his,*

 Whofe heart within her *bofom is.*] The old copy, inftead of *her*, reads *his* in both lines. Mr. Rowe corrected the firft, and I once thought that emendation fufficient, and that *Whofe* might have referred not to the laft antecedent *his*, but to *her*, i. e. Rofalind. Our author frequently takes fuch licences. But on further confideration it appears to me probable, that the fame abbreviation was ufed in both lines, and that as *his* was *certainly* a mifprint in the firft line for *her*, fo it alfo was in the fecond, the conftruction being fo much more eafy in that way than the other. " That thou might'ft join her hand with the hand of him whofe heart is lodged in her bofom " i. e. whofe affection fhe already poffeffes. So, in *Love's Labour's Loft*, the King fays to the Princefs:

" Hence ever then *my heart is in thy breaft.*"

Again, in our author's *Venus and Adonis:*

" Bids him farewell, and look well to her *heart*,

" The which, by Cupid's bow fhe doth proteft,

" He carried thence *incaged in his breaft.*"

Again, in *King Richard III:*

" Even fo thy breaft inclofeth my poor heart."

Again, in *Romeus and Juliet*, 1562:

" Thy heart thou leav'ft with her, when thou doft hence depart,

" And in thy breaft inclofed bear'ft her tender friendly heart."

In the fame play we meet with the error that has happened here. The Princefs addreffing the *ladies* who attend her, fays:

" But while 'tis fpoke, each turn away *his* face."

Again, in a former fcene of the play before us:

" Helen's cheek, but not *his* heart." MALONE.

M 4

Duke S. If there be truth in fight, you are my
            daughter.

Orl. If there be truth in fight,[9] you are my Ro-
        falind.

Phe. If fight and fhape be true,
Why then,—my love adieu!

Ros. I'll have no father, if you be not he :—
                        [*To* Duke S.
I'll have no hufband, if you be not he :—
                        [*To* Orlando.
Nor ne'er wed woman, if you be not fhe. [*To* Phebe.

Hym. Peace, ho! I bar confufion :
        'Tis I muft make conclufion
            Of thefe moft ftrange events :
            Here's eight that muft take hands,
            To join in Hymen's bands,
                If truth holds true contents.[2]
        You and you no crofs fhall part ;
                [*To* Orlando *and* Rosalind.
        You and you are heart in heart :
                [*To* Oliver *and* Celia.
        You [*To* Phebe] to his love muft accord,
        Or have a woman to your lord :—
        You and you are fure together,
                [*To* Touchstone *and* Audrey.
        As the winter to foul weather.
        Whiles a wedlock-hymn we fing,
        Feed yourfelves with queftioning ;[3]

---

[9] *If there be truth in fight,*] The anfwer of Phebe makes it probable that Orlando fays :
        If there be truth in fhape :——
that is, *if a form may be trufted* ; if one cannot ufurp the form of
another. Johnson.

[2] *If truth holds true contents.*] That is, if there be *truth in truth*,
unlefs truth fails of veracity. Johnson.

[3] ——*with* queftioning ;] Though Shakfpeare frequently ufes

That reason wonder may diminish,
How thus we met, and thefe things finish.

S O N G.

Wedding is great Juno's crown; [4]
  O bleffed bond of board and bed!
'Tis Hymen peoples every town;
  High wedlock then be honoured:
Honour, high honour and renown,
To Hymen, god of every town!

Duke S. O my dear niece, welcome thou art to
      me;
Even daughter, welcome in no lefs degree.

Phe. I will not eat my word, now thou art mine;
Thy faith my fancy to thee doth combine. [5]

                              [*To* Silvius.

Enter Jaques de Bois.

Jaq. de B. Let me have audience for a word, or
      two;
I am the fecond fon of old fir Rowland,
That bring thefe tidings to this fair affembly:—

queftion for *converfation*, in the prefent inftance *queftioning* may have
its common and obvious fignification. Steevens.

⁴ *Wedding is,* &c.] Catullus, addreffing himfelf to Hymen, has
this ftanza:

  Quæ tuis careat facris,
    Non queat dare præfides
  Terra finibus: at queat
  Te volente. Quis huic deo
  Compararier aufit? Johnson.

⁵ —— *combine.*] Shakfpeare is licentious in his ufe of this verb,
which here, as in *Meafure for Meafure,* only fignifies to *bind:*

    " I am *combined* by a facred vow,
    " And fhall be abfent." Steevens.

Duke Frederick,[5] hearing how that every day
Men of great worth reforted to this foreft,
Addrefs'd a mighty power; which were on foot,
In his own conduct, purpofely to take
His brother here, and put him to the fword:
And to the fkirts of this wild wood he came;
Where, meeting with an old religious man,
After fome queftion with him, was converted
Both from his enterprize, and from the world:
His crown bequeathing to his banifh'd brother,
And all their lands reftor'd to them again
That were with him exil'd: This to be true,
I do engage my life.
    Duke S.   Welcome, young man;
Thou offer'ft fairly to thy brothers' wedding:
To one, his lands with-held; and to the other,
A land itfelf at large, a potent dukedom.
Firft, in this foreft, let us do thofe ends
That here were well begun, and well begot:
And after, every of this happy number,
That have endur'd fhrewd days and nights with us,
Shall fhare the good of our returned fortune,
According to the meafure of their ftates.
Meantime, forget this new-fall'n dignity,
And fall into our ruftick revelry:—
Play, mufick;—and you brides and bridegrooms all,
With meafure heap'd in joy, to the meafures fall.

    Jaq. Sir, by your patience:—If I heard you
        rightly,
The duke hath put on a religious life,
And thrown into neglect the pompous court?

----

[5] *Duke Frederick, &c.*] In Lodge's novel the ufurping Duke is
not diverted from his purpofe by the pious counfels of a hermit,
but is fubdued and killed by the twelve peers of France, who were
brought by the third brother of *Rofader* (the *Orlando* of this play)
to affift him in the recovery of his right, STEEVENS.

JAQ. DE B. He hath.

JAQ. To him will I: out of thefe convertites
There is much matter to be heard and learn'd.——
You to your former honour I bequeath;

[*To* DUKE S.

Your patience, and your virtue, well deferves it:——
You [*To* ORLANDO] to a love, that your true faith
doth merit :——
You [*To* OLIVER] to your land, and love, and great
allies :——
You [*To* SILVIUS] to a long and well deferved bed;——
And you [*To* TOUCHSTONE] to wrangling; for thy
loving voyage
Is but for two months victual'd :——So to your plea-
fures;
I am for other than for dancing meafures.

. *DUKE S.* Stay, Jaques, ftay.

JAQ. To fee no paftime, I :——what you would have
I'll ftay to know at your abandon'd cave.[6] [*Exit.*

DUKE S. Proceed, proceed: we will begin thefe
rites,
As we do truft they'll end, in true delights.

[*A dance.*

[6] *To fee no paftime, I :——what you would have*
I'll ftay to know at your abandon'd cave.] Amidft this general
feftivity, the reader may be forry to take his leave of Jaques, who
appears to have no fhare in it, and remains behind unreconciled to
fociety. He has, however, filled with a gloomy fenfibility the
fpace allotted to him in the play, and to the laft preferves that refpect which is due to him as a confiftent character, and an amiable
though folitary moralift.

It may be obferved, with fcarce lefs concern, that Shakfpeare
has on this occafion forgot old Adam, the fervant of Orlando,
whofe fidelity fhould have entitled him to notice at the end of the
piece, as well as to that happinefs which he would naturally have
found, in the return of fortune to his mafter. STEEVENS.

It is the more remarkable, that old Adam is forgotten; fince
at the end of the novel, Lodge makes him *captaine of the king's*
guard. FARMER.

EPILOGUE.

Ros. It is not the fashion to see the lady the epilogue: but it is no more unhandsome, than to see
the lord the prologue. If it be true, that *good wine
needs no bush,*[7] 'tis true, that a good play needs no
epilogue: Yet to good wine they do use good bushes;
and good plays prove the better by the help of good
epilogues. What a case am I in then,[8] that am
neither a good epilogue, nor cannot insinuate with
you in the behalf of a good play? I am not furnish'd like a beggar,[9] therefore to beg will not become me: my way is, to conjure you; and I'll be-

---

[7] —— *no bush,*] It appears formerly to have been the custom
to hang a *tuft of ivy* at the door of a vintner. I suppose *ivy* was
rather chosen than any other plant, as it has relation to Bacchus.
So, in Gascoigne's *Glass of Government,* 1575:
    " Now a days the good wyne needeth none *Ivye Garland.*"
Again, in *The Rival Friends,* 1632:
    " 'Tis like the *ivy-bush* unto a tavern."
Again, in *Summer's last Will and Testament,* 1600:
    " Green *ivy-bushes* at the vintners' doors." STEEVENS.

The practice is still observed in Warwickshire and the adjoining
counties, at statute-hirings, wakes, &c. by people who sell ale at
no other time. And hence, I suppose, the *Bush* tavern at Bristol,
and other places. RITSON.

[8] *What a case am I in then, &c.*] Here seems to be a chasm, or
some other depravation, which destroys the sentiment here intended.
The reasoning probably stood thus: *Good wine needs no bush, good
plays need no epilogue;* but bad wine requires a good bush, and a
bad play a good epilogue. *What case am I in then?* To restore
the words is impossible; all that can be done without copies is, to
note the fault. JOHNSON.

Johnson mistakes the meaning of this passage. Rosalind says,
that good plays need no epilogue; yet even good plays do prove
the better for a good one. What a case then was she in, who had
neither presented them with a good play, nor had a good epilogue
to prejudice them in favour of a bad one? M. MASON.

[9] —— furnish'd *like a beggar,*] That is, *dressed:* so before, he
was *furnished* like a huntsman. JOHNSON.

gin with the women. I charge you, O women, for the love you bear to men, to like as much of this play as pleafe them: and fo I charge you, O men, for the love you bear to women, (as I perceive by your fimpering, none of you hate them,) that between you and the women, the play may pleafe.[2]

[2] —— *I charge you, O women, for the love you bear to men, to like as much of this play as pleafe* them: *and fo I charge you,* &c.] The old copy reads—*I charge you, O women, for the love you bear to men, to like as much of this play as pleafe* you: *and I charge you, O men, for the love you bear to women,* ——*that between you and the women,* &c. STEEVENS.

This paffage fhould be read thus: *I charge you, O women, for the love you bear to men, to like as much of this play as pleafes* them; *and I charge you, O men, for the love you bear to women,* ——to like as much as pleafes them, *that between you and the women,* &c. Without the alteration of *You* into *Them*, the invocation is nonfenfe; and without the addition of the words, *to like as much as pleafes them*, the inference of, *that between you and the women the play may pafs*, would be unfupported by any precedent premifes. The words feem to have been ftruck out by fome fenfelefs player, as a vicious redundancy. WARBURTON.

The words *you* and *y^m* written as was the cuftom in that time, were in manufcript fcarcely diftinguifhable. The emendation is very judicious and probable. JOHNSON.

Mr. Heath obferves, that if Dr. Warburton's interpolation be admitted [" to like as much, &c."] " the men are to like only juft as much as pleafed the women, and the women only juft as much as pleafed the men; neither are to like any thing from their own tafte: and if both of them difliked the whole, they would each of them equally fulfil what the poet defires of them.—But Shakfpeare did not write fo nonfenfically; he defires the women to like as much as pleafed the men, and the men to *fet the ladies a good example*; which exhortation to the men is evidently enough implied in thefe words, ' that between you and the women the play may pleafe."

Mr. Heath, though he objects (I think very properly) to the interpolated fentence, admits by his interpretation the change of " —pleafes *you*" to " —pleafes *them*;" which has been adopted by the late editors. I by no means think it neceffary; nor is Mr. Heath's expofition in my opinion correct. The text is fufficiently clear, without any alteration. Rofalind's addrefs appears to me fimply this: " I charge you, O women, for the love you

If I were a woman,[1] I would kiſs as many of you as
had beards that pleas'd me, complexions that lik'd
me,[4] and breaths that I defy'd not:[5] and, I am ſure,
as many as have good beards, or good faces, or ſweet

bear to men, to approve of as much of this play as affords you
entertainment; and I charge you, O men, for the love you bear
to women, [not to *ſet an example to,* but] to *follow* or *agree in
opinion* with the ladies; that between you both the play may be
ſucceſsful." The words "to follow, or agree in opinion with,
the ladies" are not indeed expreſſed, but plainly implied in thoſe
ſubſequent; "that, between you and the women, the play may
pleaſe." In the epilogue to *King Henry IV.* P. II. the addreſs to the
audience proceeds in the ſame order: "All the gentlewomen here
have forgiven [i. e. are favourable to] me; if the gentlemen will
not, then the gentlemen do not *agree with* the gentlewomen, which
was never ſeen before in ſuch an aſſembly."

The old copy reads—as *pleaſe* you. The correction was made
by Mr. Rowe.

Like all my predeceſſors, I had here adopted an alteration made
by Mr. Rowe, of which the reader was apprized in the note; but
the old copy is certainly right, and ſuch was the phraſeology of
Shakſpeare's age. So, in *K. Richard III:*

"Where every horſe bears his commanding rein,
"And may direct his courſe, as *pleaſe* himſelf."

Again, in *Hamlet:*

"——a pipe for fortune's finger,
"To ſound what ſtop ſhe *pleaſe.*"

Again, in *K. Henry VIII:*

"All men's honours
"Lie like one lump before him, to be faſhion'd
"Into what pitch he *pleaſe.*" MALONE.

I read—"and *ſo* I charge you, O men," &c. This trivial
addition, (as Dr. Farmer joins with me in thinking,) clears the
whole paſſage. STEEVENS.

[1] *If I were a woman,*] Note, that in this author's time, the
parts of women were always performed by men or boys.
HANMER.

[4] ——*complexions that* liked *me,*] i. e. that I liked. So again
in *Hamlet:* "This *likes* me well." STEEVENS.

[5] ——*breaths that I defy'd not:*] This paſſage ſerves to mani-
feſt the indelicacy of the time in which the plays of Shakſpeare

breaths, will, for my kind offer, when I make curt'fy,
bid me farewell.   [*Exeunt.*[6]

were written. Such an idea, ftarted by a modern dramatift, and
put into the mouth of a female charaƈter, would be hooted with
indignation from the ftage. STEEVENS.

[6] Of this play the fable is wild and pleafing. I know not how
the ladies will approve the facility with which both Rofalind and
Celia give away their hearts, To Celia much may be forgiven
for the heroifm of her friendfhip. The charaƈter of Jaques is
natural and well preferved. The comick dialogue is very fprightly,
with lefs mixture of low buffoonery than in fome other plays;
and the graver part is elegant and harmonious. By haftening to
the end of his work, Shakfpeare fuppreffed the dialogue between
the ufurper and the hermit, and loft an opportunity of exhibiting
a moral leffon in which he might have found matter worthy of his
higheft powers. JOHNSON.

See p. 28. *It but a* quintaine, *&c.*] Dr. Warburton's explanation would, I think, have been lefs exceptionable, had it been
more fimple: yet he is here charged with a fault of which he is
feldom guilty, want of refinement. "This (fays Mr. Guthrie) is
but an imperfeƈt (to call it no worfe) explanation of a beautiful
paffage. The *quintaine* was not the objeƈt of the darts and arms; it
was a ftake, driven into a field, upon which were hung a fhield and
trophies of war, at which they fhot, darted, or rode with a lance.
When the fhield and trophies were all thrown down, the quintaine
remained. Without this information, how could the reader underftand the allufion of—

———— *my better parts*
Are all thrown down.——"

In the prefent edition I have avoided as much as poffible all kind
of controverfy; but in thofe cafes where errors by having been
long adopted are become inveterate, it becomes in fome meafure
neceffary to the enforcement of truth.

It is a common but a very dangerous miftake, to fuppofe, that
the interpretation which gives moft fpirit to a paffage is the true
one. In confequence of this notion two paffages of our author,
one in *Macbeth*, and another in *Othello*, have been refined, as I
conceive, into a meaning that I believe was not in his thoughts.
If the moft fpirited interpretation that can be imagined, happens to be inconfiftent with his general manner, and the phrafeology
both of him and his contemporaries, or to be founded on a cuftom

which did not exift in his age, moft affuredly it is a falfe interpretation. Of the latter kind is Mr. Guthrie's explanation of the
paffage before us.

The military exercife of the *quintaine* is as ancient as the time of
the Romans; and we find from Matthew Paris, that it fubfifted in
England in the thirteenth century. *Tentoria variis ornamentorum
generibus venuftantur; terræ infixis fudibus fcuta apponuntur, quibus
in craftinum* quintanæ *ludus, fcilicet equeftris, exerceretur.* M. Paris,
ad ann. 1253. Thefe probably were the very words that Mr.
Guthrie had in contemplation. But Matthew Paris made no part
of Shakfpeare's library; nor is it at all material to our prefent
point what were the cuftoms of any century preceding that in
which he lived. In his time, without any doubt, the *quintaine* was
not a military exercife of tilting, but a mere ruftic fport. So
Minfheu, in his Dict. 1617: "A *quintaine* or quintelle, a game
in requeft at marriages, when Jac and Tom, Dic, Hob and Will,
ftrive for the gay garland." So alfo, Randolph at fomewhat a
later period [Poems, 1642]:

"   Foot-ball with us may be with them [the Spaniards] bal-
        loone;
"   As they at *tilts*, fo we at *quintaine* runne;
"   And thofe old paftimes relifh beft with me,
"   That have leaft art, and moft fimplicitie."

But old Stowe has put this matter beyond a doubt; for in his
Survey of London, printed only two years before this play
appeared, he has given us the figure of a quintaine, as reprefented
in the margin.

"   I have feen (fays he) a *quinten* fet up on
Cornehill, by the Leaden Hall, where the
attendants on the lords of merry difports
have runne, and made greate paftime; for
hee that hit not the broad end of the quinten was of all men laughed to fcorne; and
hee that hit it full, if he rid not the fafter,
had a found blow in his necke with a bagge
full of fand hanged on the other end." Here
we fee were no fhields hung, no trophies of war to be thrown
down. "The great defign of the fport, (fays Dr. Plott in his
Hiftory of Oxfordfhire) is to try both man and horfe, and to *break
the board*; which whoever does, is for the time *Princeps juventutis.*"
—Shakfpeare's fimiles feldom correfpond on both fides. " My
better parts being all thrown down, *my youthful fpirit being fubdued
by the power of beauty*, I am now (fays Orlando) as inanimate as a
wooden quintaine is (not when its better parts are thrown down,
but as that lifelefs block is at all times)." Such, perhaps, is the
meaning. If however the words " better parts," are to be applied

to the quintaine, as well as to the speaker, the *board* above-mentioned, and not any *shield* or *trophy*, must have been alluded to.

Our author has in *Macbeth* used " my better part of man" for *manly spirit :*

    " Accursed be the tongue that tells me so,
    " For it has cow'd *my better part* of man." MALONE.

The explanations of this passage, as well as the accounts of the *quintain*, are by no means satisfactory ; nor have the labours of the critic or the antiquary been exhausted. The whole of Orlando's speech should seem to refer to the quintain, but not to such a one as has been described in any of the preceding notes. Mr. Guthrie is accused of having borrowed *his* account from Matthew Paris, an author with whom, as it has been already observed, Shakspeare was undoubtedly not acquainted; but this charge is erroneous, for no such passage as that above cited is to be found in M. Paris. This writer does indeed speak of the quintain under the year 1253, but in very different words. *Eodem tempore juvenes Londinenses statuto pavone pro bravio ad stadium quod* quintena *vulgariter dicitur, vires proprias & equorum cursus sunt experti.* He then proceeds to state that some of the King's pages, and others belonging to the houshold, being offended at these sports, abused the Londoners with foul language, calling them scurvy clowns and greasy rascals, and ventured to dispute the prize with them; the consequence of which was, that the Londoners received them very briskly, and so belaboured their backs with the broken lances, that they were either put to flight, or tumbled from their horses and most terribly bruised. They afterwards went before the King, the tears still trickling from their eyes, and complained of their treatment, beseeching that he would not suffer so great an offence to remain unpunished; and the King, with his usual spirit of revenge, extorted from the citizens a very large fine. So far M. Paris; but Mr. Malone has through some mistake cited Robertus Monachus, who wrote before M. Paris, and has left an extremely curious account of the Crusades. He is describing the arrival of some messengers from Babylon, who, upon entering the Christian camp, find to their great astonishment (for they had heard that the Christians were perishing with fear and hunger) the tents curiously ornamented, and the young men practising themselves and their horses in tilting against shields hung upon poles. In the oldest edition of this writer, instead of " *quintanæ ludus,*" it is " *ludus equestris.*" However, this is certainly not the quintain that is here wanted, and therefore Mr. Malone has substituted another, copied indeed from a contemporary writer, but still not illustrative of the passage in question. I shall beg leave then to present the reader with fome others, from which it will appear, that the quintain was a military exercife in Shakfpeare's time, and not a mere ruftic fport, as Mr. Malone imagines.

No. 1: is copied from an initial letter in an Italian book, printed in 1560. Here is the figure of a man placed upon the trunk of a tree, holding in one hand a fhield, in the other a bag of fand. No. 2. is the *Saracen* quintain from *Pluvinel' inftruction du Roi Louis XIII. dans l'exercife de monter à cheval.* This fort of quintain, according to Meneftrier, was invented by the Germans, who, from their frequent wars with the Turks, accuftomed their foldiers to point their lances againft the figure of their enemy. The fkill confifted in fhivering the lance to pieces, by ftriking it againft the head of the man, for if it touched the fhield, the figure turned round and generally ftruck the horfeman a violent blow with his fword. No. 3. is the Flemifh quintain, copied from a print after Wouvermans; it is called *La bague Flamande,* from the ring which the figure holds in his right hand; and here the object was to take away the ring with the point of the lance, for if it ftruck any other part, the man turned round and hit the rider with his fand-bag. This is a mixture of the quintain and running at the ring, which two fports have been fome how or other in like manner confounded by the Italians, who fometimes exprefs the running

at the ring by *correre alla quintana*. The principle of all these was the same, viz. to avoid the blow of the sword or sand-bag, by striking the quintain in a particular place.

It might have been expected that some instance had been given of the use of these quintains in England; and for want of it an objection may be taken to this method of illustrating the present subject: but let it be remembered, that Shakspeare has indiscriminately blended the usages of all nations; that he has oftentimes availed himself of hearsay evidence; and again, that as our manners and customs have at all times been borrowed from the French and other nations, there is every reason to infer that this species of the quintain had found its way into England. It is hardly needful to add, that a knowledge of very many of our ancient sports and domestic employments is not now to be attained. Historians have contented themselves to record the vices of kings and princes, and the minutiæ of battles and sieges; and, with very few exceptions, they have considered the discussion of private manners (a theme perhaps equally interesting to posterity,) as beneath their notice and of little or no importance.

As a military sport or exercise, the use of the quintain is very ancient, and may be traced even among the Romans. It is mentioned in Justinian's Code, Lib. III. Tit. 43; and its most probable etymology is from " *Quintus,*" the name of its inventor. In the days of chivalry it was the substitute or rehearsal of tilts and tournaments, and was at length adopted, though in a ruder way, by the common people, becoming amongst them a very favourite amusement. Many instances occur of its use in several parts of France, particularly as a seignorial right exacted from millers, watermen, new-married men, and others; when the party was obliged, under some penalty, to run at the quintain upon Whitsunday and other particular times, at the lord's castle for his diversion. Sometimes it was practised upon the water, and then the quintain was either placed in a boat, or erected in the middle of the river. Something of this kind is described from Fitzstephen by Stowe in his *Survey*, p. 143, edit. 1618, 4to. and still continues to be practised upon the Seine at Paris. Froissart mentions, that the shield quintain was used in Ireland in the reign of Richard II. In Wales it is still practised at weddings, and at the village of Offham, near Town Malling in Kent, there is now standing a quintain, resembling that copied from Stowe, opposite the dwelling-house of a family that is obliged under some tenure to support it, but I do not find that any use has been ever made of it within the recollection of the inhabitants.

Shakspeare then has most probably alluded to that sort of quintain which resembled the human figure; and if this be the case, the fpeech of Orlando may be thus explained : " I am unable to thank you ; for, furprized and fubdued by love, my intellectual powers, which are my better parts, fail me ; and I refemble the quintain, whofe human or active part being thrown down, there remains nothing but the lifelefs trunk or block which once up-held it."

Or, if *better parts* do *not* refer to the quintain, " that which here ftands up" means the *human part* of the quintain, which may be alfo not unaptly called a lifelefs block.   DOUCE.

A L L' S W E L L

T H A T

E N D S W E L L.*

* ALL's WELL THAT ENDS WELL.] The ftory of *All's Well that ends Well*, or, as I fuppofe it to have been fometimes called, *Love's Labour Wonne*, is originally indeed the property of Boccace, but it came immediately to Shakfpeare from Painter's *Giletta of Narbon*, in the Firft Vol. of the *Palace of Pleafure*, 4to. 1566, p. 88. FARMER.

Shakfpeare is indebted to the novel only for a few leading circumftances in the graver parts of the piece. The comic bufinefs appears to be entirely of his own formation. STEEVENS.

This comedy, I imagine, was written in 1598. See *An Attempt to afcertain the Order of Shakfpeare's Plays*, Vol. I. MALONE.

PERSONS reprefented.[1]

King of France.
Duke of Florence.
Bertram, Count of Roufillon.
Lafeu,[2] an old Lord.
Parolles,[3] a follower of Bertram.
Several young French Lords, that ferve with Bertram
     in the Florentine war.

Steward, ⎫
Clown,   ⎬ Servants to the Countefs of Roufillon.
     ⎭
A Page.

Countefs of Roufillon, mother to Bertram.
Helena, a gentlewoman protected by the Countefs.
An old widow of Florence.
Diana, daughter to the widow.
Violenta,[4] ⎫
     ⎬ Neighbours and friends to the widow.
Mariana, ⎭

Lords, attending on the King; Officers, Soldiers, &c.
    French and Florentine.

SCENE, partly in France, and partly in Tufcany.

---

 [1] The perfons were firft enumerated by Mr. Rowe.

 [2] Lafeu,] We fhould read—Lefeu. STEEVENS.

 [3] Parolles,] I fuppofe we fhould write this name—Paroles, i. e.
a creature made up of empty words. STEEVENS.

 [4] Violenta only enters once, and then fhe neither fpeaks, nor is
fpoken to. This name appears to be borrowed from an old metrical hiftory, entitled Didaco and Violenta, 1576. STEEVENS.

A L L'S W E L L

T H A T

E N D S W E L L.

ACT I. SCENE I.

Roufillon. *A Room in the* Counfefs's *Palace.*

Enter BERTRAM, *the Countefs of* Roufillon, HELENA, *and* LAFEU, *in mourning.*

COUNT. In delivering my fon from me, I bury a fecond hufband.

BER. And I, in going, madam, weep o'er my father's death anew: but I muft attend his majefty's command, to whom I am now in ward,[2] evermore in fubjection.

---

[2] — *in* ward,] Under his particular care, as my guardian, till I come to age. It is now almoft forgotten in England, that the heirs of great fortunes were the King's *wards*. Whether the fame practice prevailed in France, it is of no great ufe to enquire, for Shakfpeare gives to all nations the manners of England.

JOHNSON.

Howell's fifteenth letter acquaints us that the province of Normandy was fubject to wardfhips, and no other part of France befides; but the fuppofition of the contrary furnifhed Shakfpeare with a reafon why the King compelled Roufillon to marry Helen.

TOLLET.

Laf. You shall find of the king a husband, madam;—you, sir, a father: He that so generally is at all times good, must of necessity hold his virtue to you; whose worthiness would stir it up where it wanted, rather than lack it where there is such abundance.

Count. What hope is there of his majesty's amendment?

Laf. He hath abandon'd his physicians, madam; under whose practices he hath persecuted time with hope; and finds no other advantage in the process, but only the losing of hope by time.

Count. This young gentlewoman had a father, (O, that *had!* how sad a passage 'tis!*) whose skill

---

The prerogative of a *wardship* is a branch of the feudal law, and may as well be suppofed to be incorporated with the constitution of France, as it was with that of England, till the reign of Charles II. Sir J. Hawkins.

3 —— *O, that* had! *how sad a* passage 'tis!] Imitated from the *Heautontimorumenos* of Terence, (then translated,) where Menedemus says:

" —— Filium unicum adolefcentulum
" *Habeo.* Ah, quid dixi? *habere* me? imo
" —— *habui,* Chreme,
" Nunc *habeam* necne incertum est." Blackstone.

So, in Spenfer's *Shepheard's Calender:*
" Shee, while she was, (that *was* a woeful word to faine,)
" For beauties praife and pleafaunce had no peere."
Again, in *Wily Beguil'd,* 1606:
" She is not mine, I have no daughter now;
" That I should say *I had,* thence comes my grief."
Malone.

Paffage is *any thing that paffes.* So we now say, a *paffage* of an *author,* and we faid about a century ago, the *paffages* of a *reign.* When the *countefs* mentions Helena's lofs of a father, she recollects her own lofs of a hufband, and stops to obferve how heavily that word *had* paffes through her mind. Johnson.

Thus Shakfpeare himfelf. See *The Comedy of Errors,* Act III. fc. i:
" Now in the ftirring *paffage* of the day."

was almoſt as great as his honeſty; had it ſtretch'd ſo far, would have made nature immortal, and death ſhould have play for lack of work. 'Would, for the king's ſake, he were living! I think, it would be the death of the king's diſeaſe.

Laf. How call'd you the man you ſpeak of, madam?

Count. He was famous, ſir, in his profeſſion, and it was his great right to be ſo: Gerard de Narbon.

Laf. He was excellent, indeed, madam; the king very lately ſpoke of him, admiringly, and mourningly: he was ſkilful enough to have liv'd ſtill, if knowledge could be ſet up againſt mortality.

Ber. What is it, my good lord, the king languiſhes of?

Laf. A fiſtula, my lord.[4]

So, in *The Gameſter*, by Shirley, 1637 : " I'll not be witneſs of your *paſſages* myſelf :" i. e. of what paſſes between you.
Again, in *A Woman's a Weathercock*, 1612 :
     " —— never lov'd theſe prying liſtening men
     " That aſk of others' ſtates and *paſſages*."
Again:
     " I knew the *paſſages* 'twixt her and Scudamore."
Again, in *The Dumb Knight*, 1633 :
     " ———— have beheld
     " Your vile and moſt laſcivious *paſſages*."
Again, in *The Engliſh Intelligencer*, a tragi-comedy, 1641 : " —two philoſophers that jeer and weep at the *paſſages* of the world."
STEEVENS.

[4] *A fiſtula, my lord.*] Perhaps Shakſpeare was induced by a paſſage in Puttenham's *Arte of Engliſh Poeſie*, 1589, p. 251, to afflict the *King of France* with this inelegant diſorder. Speaking of the neceſſity which princes occaſionally find to counterfeit maladies, our author has the following remark :—" And in diſſembling of diſeaſes, which I pray you? for I have obſerued it in the *Court of Fraunce*, not a burning feuer, or a pluriſie, or a palſie, or the hydropick and ſwelling gowte, &c.——But it muſt be either a dry dropſie, or a megrim or letarge, or a *fiſtule in ano*, or ſome ſuch

Ber. I heard not of it before.

Laf. I would, it were not notorious.—Was this gentlewoman the daughter of Gerard de Narbon?

Count. His fole child, my lord; and bequeathed to my overlooking. I have thofe hopes of her good, that her education promifes: her difpofitions fhe inherits, which make fair gifts fairer; for where an unclean mind carries virtuous qualities,[5] there commendations go with pity, they are virtues and traitors too; in her they are the better for their fimplenefs;[6] fhe derives her honefty, and achieves her goodnefs.

other fecret difeafe as the common conuerfant can hardly difcouer, and the phyfitian either *not fpeedily beale*, or not honeftly bewray."
                                                STEEVENS.

[5] —— *virtuous qualities*,] By *virtuous qualities* are meant qualities of good breeding and erudition; in the fame fenfe that the Italians fay, *qualità virtuofa*; and not *moral* ones. On this account it is, fhe fays, that, in *an ill mind*, thefe *virtuous qualities are virtues and traitors too*: i. e. the advantages of education enable an ill mind to go further in wickednefs than it could have done without them. WARBURTON.

Virtue, and *virtuous*, as I am told, ftill keep this fignification in the north, and mean *ingenuity* and *ingenious*. Of this fenfe perhaps an inftance occurs in the Eighth Book of Chapman's *Verfion of the Iliad:*

  " Then will I to Olympus' top our *virtuous* engine bind,
  " And by it every thing fhall hang," &c.
Again, in Marlowe's *Tamburlaine*, p. 1, 1590:
  " If thefe had made one poem's period,
  " And all combin'd in beauties worthyneffe,
  " Yet fhould there hover in their reftleffe heads
  " One thought, one grace, one wonder at the leaft,
  " Which into words no *vertue* can digeft." STEEVENS.

[6] —— *they are virtues and traitors too; in her they are the better for their fimplenefs*;] Her *virtues are the better for their fimplenefs*, that is, her excellencies are the better becaufe they are artlefs and open, without fraud, without defign. The learned commentator has well explained *virtues*, but has not, I think, reached the force of the word *traitors*, and therefore has not fhown the full extent

Laf. Your commendations, madam, get from her tears.

Count. 'Tis the beft brine a maiden can feafon her praife in.[7] The remembrance of her father never approaches her heart, but the tyranny of her forrows takes all livelihood[8] from her cheek. No more of this, Helena, go to, no more; left it be rather thought you affect a forrow, than to have.[9]

Hel. I do affect a forrow, indeed, but I have it too.[2]

---

of Shakfpeare's mafterly obfervation. *Virtues in an unclean mind are virtues and traitors too.* Eftimable and ufeful qualities, joined with an evil difpofition, give that evil difpofition power over others, who, by admiring the virtue, are betrayed to the malevolence. The *Tatler*, mentioning the fharpers of his time, obferves, that fome of them are men of fuch elegance and knowledge, that *a young man who falls into their way, is betrayed as much by his judgement as his paffions.* JOHNSON.

In *As you Like it*, *virtues* are called *traitors* on a very different ground :

    " ———— to fome kind of men
    " Their graces ferve them but as enemies ;
    " No more do yours ; your *virtues*, gentle mafter,
    " Are fanctified and holy *traitors* to you.
    " O what a world is this, when what is comely
    " Envenoms him that bears it !" MALONE.

[7] ———— *can* feafon *her praife in.*] To *feafon* has here a culinary fenfe ; *to preferve by falting.* A paffage in *Twelfth Night* will beft explain its meaning :

    " ———— all this to *feafon*
    " A brother's dead love, which fhe would keep *frefh*,
    " And *lafting* in her remembrance." MALONE.

[8] ———— *all livelihood* —] i. e. all appearance of life. STEEVENS.

[9] ———— *left it be rather thought you affect a forrow, than to have.*] Our author fometimes is guilty of fuch flight inaccuracies ; and concludes a fentence as if the former part of it had been conftructed differently.—Thus, in the prefent inftance, he feems to have meant—left *you* be rather thought *to* affect a forrow, than *to have.* MALONE.

[2] *I do affect a forrow, indeed, but I have it too.*] Helena has, I believe, a meaning here, that fhe does not wifh fhould be under-

LAF. Moderate lamentation is the right of the dead, exceſſive grief the enemy to the living.

COUNT. If the living be enemy to the grief, the exceſs makes it ſoon mortal.[3]

BER. Madam, I deſire your holy wiſhes.

LAF. How underſtand we that?

COUNT. Be thou bleſt, Bertram! and ſucceed thy
      father

ſtood by the counteſs. Her *affeɛted* ſorrow was for the death of her father; her *real* grief for the lowneſs of her ſituation, which ſhe feared would for ever be a bar to her union with her beloved Bertram. Her own words afterwards fully ſupport this inter-pretation:

" —————— I think not on my father;——
" —————— What was he like?
" I have forgot him; my imagination
" Carries no favour in it but Bertram's:
" I am undone." MALONE.

The ſorrow that Helen affeɛted, was for her father; that which ſhe really felt, was for Bertram's departure. This line ſhould be particularly attended to, as it tends to explain ſome ſubſequent paſſages which have hitherto been miſunderſtood. M. MASON.

[3] *If the living be enemy to the grief, the exceſs makes it ſoon mortal.*] *Lafeu* ſays, *exceſſive grief is the enemy of the living:* the counteſs replies, *If the living be an enemy to grief, the exceſs ſoon makes it mortal:* that is, *If the living do not indulge grief, grief deſtroys itſelf by its own exceſs.* By the word *mortal* I underſtand *that which dies;* and Dr. Warburton [who reads—*be* not *enemy*—] *that which deſtroys.* I think that my interpretation gives a ſen-tence more acute and more refined. Let the reader judge.
JOHNSON.

A paſſage in *The Winter's Tale*, in which our author again ſpeaks of grief deſtroying itſelf by its own exceſs, adds ſupport to Dr. Johnſon's interpretation:

" —————— ſcarce any joy
" Did ever live ſo long; *no ſorrow,*
" *But kill'd itſelf much ſooner.*"
In *Romeo and Juliet* we meet with a kindred thought:
" Theſe violent delights have violent ends,
" And *in their triumph die.*" MALONE.

In manners, as in fhape! thy blood, and virtue,
Contend for empire in thee; and thy goodnefs
Share with thy birth-right! Love all, truft a few,
Do wrong to none: be able for thine enemy
Rather in power, than ufe; and keep thy friend
Under thy own life's key: be check'd for filence,
But never tax'd for fpeech. What heaven more
    will,
That thee may furnifh,[4] and my prayers pluck
    down,
Fall on thy head! Farewell.—My lord,
'Tis an unfeafon'd courtier; good my lord,
Advife him.

 Laf. He cannot want the beft
That fhall attend his love.

 Count. Heaven blefs him!—Farewell, Bertram.
       [*Exit* Countefs.

 Ber. The beft wifhes, that can be forged in your
thoughts, [*To* Helena.] be fervants to you![5] Be
comfortable to my mother, your miftrefs, and make
much of her.

 Laf. Farewell, pretty lady: You muft hold the
credit of your father.
     [*Exeunt* Bertram *and* Lafeu.

 Hel. O, were that all!—I think not on my father;[6]

---

 [4] *That thee may furnifh,*] That may help thee with more and
better qualifications. Johnson.

 [5] *The beft* wifhes, &c.] That is, may you be miftrefs of your
wifhes, and have power to bring them to effect. Johnson.

 [6] Laf. *Farewell, pretty lady: You muft* hold *the credit of your
father.*
 Hel. *O, were that all!—I think not on my father;*] This paffage
has been paffed over in filence by all the commentators, yet it is
evidently defective. The only meaning that the fpeech of Lafeu
will bear, as it now ftands, is this:—" That Helena, who was a

And thefe great tears grace his remembrance more,
Than thofe I fhed for him. What was he like?
I have forgot him: my imagination
Carries no favour in it; but Bertram's.

young girl, begins to keep up the credit which her father had
eftablifhed, who was the beft phyfician of the age; and fhe by her
anfwer, *O, were that all!* feems to admit that it would be no
difficult matter for her to do fo. The abfurdity of this is evident,
and the words will admit of no other interpretation. Some alteration therefore is neceffary; and that which I propofe is, to read
uphold, inftead of *muft hold,* and then the meaning will be this;
" Lafeu, obferving that Helena had fhed a torrent of tears, which
he and the Countefs both afcribe to her grief for her father, fays
that fhe *upholds* the credit of her father, on this principle, that the
fureft proof that can be given of the merit of a perfon deceafed,
are the lamentations of thofe who furvive him. But Helena, who
knows her own heart, wifhes that fhe had no other caufe of grief,
except the lofs of her father, whom fhe thinks no more of."

M. Mason.

O, were that all! &c.] Would that the attention to maintain the
credit of my father, (or, not to act unbecoming the daughter of
fuch a father,—for, fuch perhaps is the meaning,) were my only
folicitude! I think not of him. My cares are all for Bertram.

Malone.

⁷ —— *thefe great tears*—] The tears which the King and
Countefs fhed for him. Johnson.

And thefe great tears *grace his remembrance more,*
Than thofe I fhed for him.] Johnfon fuppofes that, by *thefe great*
tears, Helena means the tears which the King and the Countefs
fhed for her father; but it does not appear that either of thofe
great perfons had fhed tears for him, though they fpoke of him
with regret. By *thefe great tears,* Helena does not mean the tears
of great people, but the big and copious tears fhe then fhed herfelf,
which were caufed in reality by Bertram's departure, though attributed by Lafeu and the Countefs, to the lofs of her father; and
from this mifapprehenfion of theirs, graced his remembrance more
than thofe fhe actually fhed for him. What fhe calls *gracing his*
remembrance, is what Lafeu had ftyled before, *upholding his credit,*
the two paffages tending to explain each other.—It is fcarcely
neceffary to make this grammatical obfervation—That if Helena
had alluded to any tears fuppofed to have been fhed by the King,
fhe would have faid *thofe* tears; not *thefe,* as the latter pronoun
muft neceffarily refer to fomething prefent at the time.

M. Mason.

I am undone; there is no living, none,
If Bertram be away. It were all one,
That I fhould love a bright part cular ftar,
And think to wed it, he is fo above me:
In his bright radiance and collateral light
Muft I be comforted, not in his fphere.[8]
The ambition in my love thus plagues itfelf:
The hind, that would be mated by the lion,
Muft die for love. 'Twas pretty, though a plague,
To fee him every hour; to fit and draw
His arched brows, his hawking eye, his curls, χ
In our heart's table;[9] heart, too capable
Of every line and trick of his fweet favour:[2]

[8] *In his bright* radiance, &c.] I cannot be united with him and move in the fame *fphere*, but *muft be comforted* at a diftance by the *radiance* that fhoots *on all fides* from him. JOHNSON.

So, in Milton's *Paradife Loft*, B. X:
" —— from his *radiant* feat he rofe
" Of high *collateral* glory." STEEVENS.

[9] ——*'Twas pretty, though a plague,*
To fee him every hour, to fit and draw
His arched brows, his hawking eye, his curls,
In our heart's table;] So, in our author's 24th Sonnet:
" Mine eye hath play'd the *painter*, and hath fteel'd
" Thy beauty's form in *table of my heart.*"
A *table* was in our author's time a term for a *picture*, in which fenfe it is ufed here. *Tableau*, Fr. So, on a picture painted in the time of Queen Elizabeth, in the poffeffion of the Hon. Horace Walpole:
" The Queen to Walfingham this *table* fent,
" Mark of her people's and her own content." MALONE.

Table here only fignifies the *board* on which any picture was painted. So, in Mr. Walpole's *Anecdotes of Painting in England*, Vol. I. p. 58: " Item, one *table* with the *picture* of the Duchefs of Milan." " Item, one *table*, with the *pictures* of the King's Majefty and Queen Jane:" &c. Helena would not have talked of drawing Bertram's *picture* in her *heart's picture*; but confiders her heart as the *tablet* or furface on which his refemblance was to be pourtrayed. STEEVENS.

[2] —— trick *of his fweet favour:*] So, in *King John:* " he hath

But now he's gone, and my idolatrous fancy
Muſt ſanctify his relicks. Who comes here?

Enter PAROLLES.

One that goes with him: I love him for his ſake;
And yet I know him a notorious liar,
Think him a great way fool, ſolely a coward;
Yet theſe fix'd evils ſit ſo fit in him,
That they take place, when virtue's ſteely bones
Look bleak in the cold wind: withal, full oft we ſee
Cold wiſdom waiting on ſuperfluous folly.[3]

   Par. Save you, fair queen.
   Hel. And you, monárch.[4]
   Par. No.
   Hel. And no.[5]
   Par. Are you meditating on virginity?

a *trick* of Cœur de Lion's face." *Trick* ſeems to be ſome peculiarity or feature. JOHNSON.

   Trick is an expreſſion taken from *drawing*, and is ſo explained
in *King John*, Act I. ſc. i. The preſent inſtance explains itſelf:
     —— *to fit and draw*
     His arched brows, &c.
     —— *and* trick *of his ſweet favour.*
Trick, however, on the preſent occaſion, may mean neither *tracing*
nor *outline*, but *peculiarity*. STEEVENS.

   Tricking is uſed by heralds for the delineation and colouring of
arms, &c. MALONE.

   [3] Cold *wiſdom waiting on* ſuperfluous *folly.*] *Cold* for naked;
as *ſuperfluous* for over-cloathed. This makes the propriety of the
antitheſis. WARBURTON.

   [4] *And you,* monárch.] Perhaps here is ſome alluſion deſigned to
Monarcho, a ridiculous fantaſtical character of the age of Shakſpeare.
Concerning this perſon, ſee the notes on *Love's Labour's Loſt,*
Act IV. ſc. i. STEEVENS.

   [5] *And no.*] I am no more a queen than you are a monarch, or
Monarcho. MALONE.

Hel. Ay. You have fome ftain of foldier[6] in you; let me afk you a queftion: Man is enemy to virginity; how may we barricado it againft him?

Par. Keep him out.

Hel. But he affails; and our virginity, though valiant in the defence, yet is weak: unfold to us fome warlike refiftance.

Par. There is none; man, fitting down before you, will undermine you, and blow you up.

Hel. Blefs our poor virginity from underminers, and blowers up!—Is there no military policy, how virgins might blow up men?

Par. Virginity being blown down, man will quicklier be blown up: marry, in blowing him down again, with the breach yourfelves made, you lofe your city.[7] It is not politick in the common-

---

[6] ——ftain *of foldier*—] *Stain* for colour. *Parolles* was in red, as appears from his being afterwards called *red-tail'd humble-bee*.
                                                WARBURTON.
It does not appear from either of thefe expreffions, that Parolles was entirely dreft in red. Shakfpeare writes only *fome ftain of foldier*, meaning in one fenfe, that he had *red breeches on*, (which is fufficiently evident from calling him afterwards *red-tail'd humble-bee*,) and in another, that he was *a difgrace to foldiery*. *Stain* is ufed in an adverfe fenfe by Shakfpeare, in *Troilus and Creffida:*
" ——nor any man an attaint, but he carries *fome ftain* of it."
Mr. M. Mafon obferves on this occafion that " though a *red* coat is now the mark of a foldier in the Britifh fervice, it was not fo in the days of Shakfpeare, when we had no ftanding army, and the ufe of armour ftill prevailed." To this I reply, that the colour *red* has always been annexed to foldierfhip. Chaucer, in his *Knight's Tale*, v. 1749, has " *Mars* the *rede*," and Boccace has given *Mars* the fame epithet in the opening of his Thefeida:
" ——O *rubicondo* Marte." STEEVENS.

Stain rather for what we now fay *tincture*, fome qualities, at leaft fuperficial, of a foldier. JOHNSON.

[7] ——*with the breach yourfelves made, you lofe your city.*] So, in our author's *Lover's Complaint:*

O 2

wealth of nature, to preferve virginity. Lofe of virginity is rational increafe;[8] and there was never virgin got, till virginity was firft loft. That, you were made of, is metal to make virgins. Virginity, by being once loft, may be ten times found : by being ever kept, it is ever loft : 'tis too cold a companion ; away with it.

HEL. I will ftand for't a little, though therefore I die a virgin.

PAR. There's little can be faid in't ; 'tis againft the rule of nature. To fpeak on the part of virginity, is to accufe your mothers ; which is moft infallible difobedience. He, that hangs himfelf, is a virgin : virginity murders itfelf ;[9] and fhould be buried in highways, out of all fanctified limit, as a defperate offendrefs againft nature. Virginity breeds mites, much like a cheefe ; confumes itfelf to the very paring, and fo dies with feeding his own ftomach. Befides, virginity is peevifh, proud, idle, made of felf-love, which is the moft inhibited fin[4] in the canon. Keep it not ; you cannot choofe but lofe by't : Out with't : within ten years it will

" And long upon thefe terms I held my *city,*
" Till thus he 'gan befiege me."
Again, in *The Rape of Lucrece :*
" This makes in him more rage, and leffer pity,
" To make the breach, and enter this fweet *city.*" MALONE.

[8] *Lofs of virginity is* rational *increafe* ;] I believe we fhould read, *national.* TYRWHITT.

Rational increafe may mean the regular increafe by which rational beings are propagated. STEEVENS.

[9] *He, that hangs himfelf, is a virgin : virginity murders itfelf* ;]. i. e. he that hangs himfelf, and a virgin, are in this circumftance alike ; they are both *felf-deftroyers.* MALONE.

[4] —— inhibited *fin* —] i. e. forbidden. So, in *Othello :*
" —————— a practifer
" Of arts *inhibited* and out of warrant." STEEVENS.

make itfelf ten,³ which is a goodly increafe; and the
principal itfelf not much the worfe: Away with't.

³ —— *within ten years, it will make itfelf* ten,] The old copy
reads—" within ten years it will make itfelf *two*." The emendation was made by Sir T. Hanmer. It was alfo fuggefted by Mr.
Steevens, who likewife propofed to read—" within *two* years it
will make itfelf *two*." Mr. Tollet would read—" within ten
years it will make itfelf *twelve*."

I formerly propofed to read—" Out with it: within ten *months*
it will make itfelf two." Part with it, and within ten months'
time it will double itfelf; i. e. it will produce a child.

I now mention this conjecture (in which I once had fome confidence) only for the purpofe of acknowledging my error. I had
not fufficiently attended to a former paffage in this fcene,—
" Virginity, by being once loft, may be *ten* times found," i. e.
may produce *ten* virgins. Thofe words likewife are fpoken by
Parolles, and add fuch decifive fupport to Sir Thomas Hanmer's
emendation, that I have not hefitated to adopt it. The text, as
exhibited in the old copy, is undoubtedly corrupt. It has already
been obferved, that many paffages in thefe plays, in which numbers
are introduced, are printed incorrectly. Our author's fixth Sonnet
fully fupports the emendation here made:
　" That *ufe* is not forbidden ufury,
　" Which happies thofe that pay the willing loan;
　" That's for thyfelf, to breed another thee,
　" Or *ten times* happier, be it *ten* for one.
　" Ten times thyfelf were happier than thou art,
　" *If ten of thine ten times refigur'd thee.*"
　" *Out* with it," is ufed equivocally.—Applied to virginity, it
means, give it away; part with it: confidered in another light,
it fignifies, put it out to intereft. In *The Tempeft* we have—" Each
putter out on five for one," &c. MALONE.

There is no reafon for altering the text. A well-known obfervation of the noble earl, to whom the horfes of the prefent
generation owe the length of their tails, contains the true explanation of this paffage. HENLEY.

I cannot help repeating on this occafion, Juftice Shallow's
remark: " Give me pardon, fir:—if you come with news, I take
it there is but two ways;—*either to utter them, or to conceal them.*"
With this noble earl's notorious remark, I am quite unacquainted.
But perhaps the critick (with a flippancy in which he has fometimes
indulged himfelf at my expence) will reply, like Piftol, " Why
then lament therefore;" or obferve, like Hamlet, that " a knavifh
fpeech fleeps in a foolifh ear." STEEVENS.

HEL. How might one do, fir, to lose it to her own liking?

PAR. Let me fee: Marry, ill, to like him that ne'er it likes.[4] 'Tis a commodity will lose the glofs with lying; the longer kept, the lefs worth: off with't, while 'tis vendible: anfwer the time of requeft. Virginity, like an old courtier, wears her cap out of fafhion; richly fuited, but unfuitable: juft like the brooch and tooth-pick, which wear not now:[5] Your date is better[6] in your pye and your porridge, than in your cheek: And your virginity, your old virginity, is like one of our French wither'd pears; it looks ill, it eats dryly; marry, 'tis a wither'd pear; it was formerly better; marry, yet, 'tis a wither'd pear: Will you any thing with it?

HEL. Not my virginity yet.[8]

---

[4] ——*Marry, ill, to like him that ne'er it likes.*] Parolles, in anfwer to the queftion, " How one fhall lofe virginity to her own liking?" plays upon the word *liking*, and fays, *fhe muft do ill, for virginity, to be fo loft, muft like him that likes not* virginity.
                                                                JOHNSON.

[5] ——*which* wear *not now:*] Thus the old copy, and rightly. Shakfpeare often ufes the active for the paffive. The modern editors read, " which *we* wear not now." TYRWHITT.

The old copy has *were*. Mr. Rowe corrected it.
                                                                MALONE.

[6] ——*Your* date *is better*—] Here is a quibble on the word *date*, which means both age, and a candied *fruit* much ufed in our author's time. So, in *Romeo* and *Juliet:*
    " They call for *dates* and quinces in the paftry."
The fame quibble occurs in *Troilus and Creffida:* " ——and then to be bak'd with no *date* in the pye, for then the man's *date* is out." STEEVENS.

[8] *Not my virginity yet.*] This whole fpeech is abrupt, unconnected, and obfcure. Dr. Warburton thinks much of it fuppofititious. I would be glad to think fo of the whole, for a commentator naturally wifhes to reject what he cannot underftand. Something, which fhould connect Helena's words with thofe of

I

There fhall your mafter have a thoufand loves,
A mother, and a miftrefs, and a friend,

Parolles, feems to be wanting. Hanmer has made a fair attempt
by reading:

    Not my virginity yet.—You're for the court,
    There fhall your mafter, &c.

Some fuch claufe has, I think, dropped out, but ftill the firft
words want connection. Perhaps Parolles, going away after his
harangue, faid, *will you any thing with me?* to which Helen
may reply.——I know not what to do with the paffage.

JOHNSON.

    I do not perceive fo great a want of connection as my predecef-
fors have apprehended; nor is that connection always to be fought
for, in fo carelefs a writer as ours, from the thought immediately
preceding the reply of the fpeaker. Parolles has been laughing
at the unprofitablenefs of virginity, efpecially when it grows
ancient, and compares it to withered fruit. Helena properly
enough replies, that hers is not yet in that ftate; but that in the
enjoyment of her, his mafter fhould find the gratification of all his
moft romantic wifhes. What Dr. Warburton fays afterwards is
faid at random, as all pofitive declarations of the fame kind muft
of neceffity be. Were I to propofe any change, I would read
fhould inftead of *fhall*. It does not however appear that this rap-
turous effufion of Helena was defigned to be intelligible to Parolles.
Its obfcurity, therefore, may be its merit. It fufficiently explains
what is paffing in the mind of the fpeaker, to every one but him
to whom fhe does not mean to explain it. STEEVENS.

    Perhaps we fhould read: " Will you any thing with *us?*" i. e.
will you fend any thing with us to court? to which Helena's anfwer
would be proper enough—

    " Not my virginity yet."

A fimilar phrafe occurs in *Twelfth Night*, Act III. fc. i;

    " *You'll nothing*, madam, to my lord by me?"

TYRWHITT.

    Perhaps fomething has been omitted in Parolles's fpeech. " *I
am now bound for the court*; will you any thing with it [i. e.
with the court]?" So, in *The Winter's Tale:*

    " Tell me what you have to the king."

I do not agree with Mr. Steevens in the latter part of his note;
" —— that in the enjoyment of her," &c. MALONE.

    I am fatisfied the paffage is as Shakfpeare left it. Parolles, after
having cried down with all his eloquence, *old virginity*, in reference
to what he had before faid,—" That *virginity* is a commodity the

O 4

A phœnix, captain, and an enemy;
A guide, a goddess, and a sovereign;
A counſellor, a traitreſs, and a dear;

longer kept, the leſs worth: off with't, while 'tis vendible.
Anſwer the time of Requeſt. aſks Helena. "Will you
any thing with it?"—to which ſhe replied—"Not my virginity
yet."

9 *A phœnix*, &c.] The eight lines following *friend*, I am perſuaded, is the nonſenſe of ſome fooliſh conceited player. What
put it into his head was Helen's ſaying, as it ſhould be read for the
future:

> *There ſhall your maſter have a thouſand lovers;*
> " *A mother, and a miſtreſs, and a* friend,
> *I know not what he ſhall—God ſend him well.*

Where the fellow, finding a *thouſand* loves ſpoken of, and only
three reckoned up, namely, a *mother's*, a *miſtreſs's*, and a *friend's*,
(which, by the way, were all a judicious writer could mention;
for there are but theſe three ſpecies of love in nature) he would
help out the number, by the intermediate nonſenſe: and, becauſe
they were yet too few, he pieces out his *loves* with *enmities*, and
makes of the whole ſuch finiſhed nonſenſe, as is never heard out of
Bedlam. WARBURTON.

3 ——*captain*,] Our author often uſes this word for a head or
chief. So, in one of his Sonnets:

> " Or *captain* jewels in the carkanet."

Again, in *Timon of Athens*: " — the aſs more *captain* than the lion."
Again more appoſitely, in *Othello*, where it is applied to Deſ-
demona:

> " ——our great captain's *captain*."

We find ſome of theſe terms of endearment again uſed in *The
Winter's Tale*. Leontes ſays to the young Mamillius,

> " Come, *captain*, we muſt be neat," &c.

Again, in the ſame ſcene, Polixenes, ſpeaking of his ſon, ſays,

> " He's all my exerciſe, my mirth, my matter;
> " Now my ſworn *friend*, and then mine *enemy*;
> " My paraſite, my ſoldier, ſtateſman, all." MALONE.

3 ——*a traitreſs*,] It ſeems that *traitreſs* was in that age a term
of endearment, for when Lafeu introduces Helena to the king, he
ſays,—" You are like a *traytor*, but ſuch *traytors* his majeſty does
not much fear." JOHNSON.

I cannot conceive that *traitreſs* (ſpoken ſeriouſly) was in any
age *a term of endearment*. From the preſent paſſage, we might as
well ſuppoſe *enemy* (in the laſt line but one) to be *a term of en-*

His humble ambition, proud humility,   A
His jarring concord, and his discord dulcet,   A
His faith, his sweet disaster; with a world   A.
Of pretty, fond, adoptious christendoms,[4]

dearment._ In the other passage quoted, Lafeu is plainly speaking
ironically. TYRWHITT.

Traditora, a traitress, in the Italian language, is generally used
as a term of endearment. The meaning of Helen is, that she shall
prove _every thing_ to Bertram. Our ancient writers delighted in
catalogues, and always characterize love by contrarieties.
STEEVENS.

Falstaff, in _The Merry Wives of Windsor,_ says to Mrs. Ford:
" Thou art a _traitor_ to say so." In his interview with her, he
certainly meant to use the language of love.

Helena however, I think, does not mean to say that she shall
prove every thing to Bertram, but to express her apprehension that
he will find at the court some lady or ladies who shall prove every
thing to him; (" a phœnix, captain, counsellor, traitress; &c.")
to whom he will give all the fond names that " blinking Cupid
gossips." MALONE.

- I believe it would not be difficult to find in the love poetry of
those times an authority for most, if not for every one, of these
whimsical titles. At least I can affirm it from knowledge, that
far the greater part of them are to be found in the Italian lyrick
poetry, which was the model from which our poets chiefly copied.
HEATH.

4 ——_christendoms,_] This word, which signifies the collective
body of christianity, every place where the christian religion is
embraced, is surely used with much licence on the present occasion.
STEEVENS.

It is used by another ancient writer in the same sense; so that the
word probably bore, in our author's time, the signification which
he has affixed to it. So, in _A Royal Arbor of Loyal Poesie,_ by
Thomas Jordan, no date, but printed about 1661 :
    " She is baptiz'd in _Christendom,_
    [i. e. by a christian name,]
    " The Jew cries out he's undone —."

These lines are found in a ballad formed on part of the story of
The Merchant of Venice, in which it is remarkable that it is the
Jew's daughter, and not Portia, that saves the Merchant's life by
pleading his cause. There should seem therefore to have been
some novel on this subject that has hitherto escaped the researches
of the commentators. In the same book are ballads founded on
the fables of _Much ado about Nothing,_ and _The Winter's Tale._ MALONE.

That blinking Cupid goffips. Now fhall he——
I know not what he fhall:—God fend him well!—
The court's a learning-place;—and he is one——

Par. What one, i'faith?

Hel. That I wifh well.—'Tis pity——

Par. What's pity?

Hel. That wifhing well had not a body in't,
Which might be felt: that we, the poorer born,
Whofe bafer ftars do fhut us up in wifhes,
Might with effects of them follow our friends,
And fhow what we alone muft think;[5] which never
Returns us thanks.

Enter a Page.

Page. Monfieur Parolles, my lord calls for you.
                                        [*Exit* Page.

Par. Little Helen, farewell: if I can remember
thee, I will think of thee at court.

Hel. Monfieur Parolles, you were born under a
charitable ftar.

Par. Under Mars, I.

Hel. I efpecially think, under Mars.

Par. Why under Mars?

Hel. The wars have fo kept you under, that you
muft needs be born under Mars.

Par. When he was predominant.

Hel. When he was retrograde, I think, rather.

Par. Why think you fo?

Hel. You go fo much backward, when you fight.

---

[5] *And fhow what we alone muft think;*] And fhow by realities
what we now *muft only think.* JOHNSON.

Par. That's for advantage.

Hel. So is running away, when fear propofes the fafety: But the compofition, that your valour and fear makes in you, is a virtue of a good wing,[6] and I like the wear well.

Par. I am fo full of bufineffes, I cannot anfwer thee acutely: I will return perfect courtier; in the which, my inftruction fhall ferve to naturalize thee,

---

[6] —— *is a virtue of a* good wing,] Mr. Edwards is of opinion, that a *virtue of a good wing* refers to his nimblenefs or fleetnefs in running away. The phrafe, however, is taken from falconry, as may appear from the following paffage in Marfton's *Fawne*, 1606: " —— I love my horfe after a journeying eafinefs, as he is eafy in journeying; my hawk, for the *goodnefs of his wing*, &c." Or it may be taken from drefs: So, in *Every Man out of his Humour:* " I would have mine fuch a fuit without a difference; fuch ftuff, fuch a *wing*, fuch a fleeve," &c. Mr. Toilet obferves, that a *good wing* fignifies a *ftrong wing* in Lord Bacon's *Natural Hiftory*, experiment 866: " Certainly many birds of a *good wing* (as kites and the like) would bear up a good weight as they fly."

STEEVENS.

The reading of the old copy (which Dr. Warburton changed to *ming*,) is fupported by a paffage in *King Henry V.* in which we meet with a fimilar expreffion: " Though his affections are higher mounted than ours, yet when they ftoop, they ftoop with the *like wing.*"
Again, in *K. Henry* IV. P. I:
" Yet let me wonder Harry,
" At thy affections, which do hold a *wing*,
" Quite from the flight of all thy anceftors." MALONE.

The meaning of this paffage appears to be this: " If your valour will fuffer you to go backward for advantage, and your fear for the fame reafon will make you run away, the compofition that your valour and fear make in you, muft be a virtue that will fly far and fwiftly."—A bird of a good wing, is a bird of fwift and ftrong flight.
Though the latter part of this fentence is fenfe as it ftands, I cannot help thinking that there is an error in it, and that we ought to read—" And *is* like *to* wear well."—Inftead of " *I* like *the* wear well." M. MASON.

so thou wilt be capable of a courtier's counsel, and understand what advice shall thrust upon thee; else thou diest in thine unthankfulness, and thine ignorance makes thee away: farewell. When thou hast leisure, say thy prayers; when thou hast none, remember thy friends: get thee a good husband, and use him as he uses thee: so farewell. [*Exit.*

HEL. Our remedies oft in ourselves do lie,
Which we ascribe to heaven: the fated sky
Gives us free scope; only, doth backward pull
Our slow designs, when we ourselves are dull.
What power is it, which mounts my love so high;
That makes me see, and cannot feed mine eye?[8]
The mightiest space in fortune nature brings
To join like likes, and kiss like native things.[9]
Impossible be strange attempts, to those
That weigh their pains in sense; and do suppose,
What hath been[2] cannot be: Who ever strove
To show her merit, that did miss her love?

[7] ——*so thou wilt be* capable *of a* '*courtier's counsel,*] i. e. thou wilt comprehend it. See a note in *Hamlet* on the words—
  " Whose form and cause conjoin'd, preaching to stones,
  " Would make them *capable.*" MALONE.

[8] *What power is it, which mounts my love so high;*
  That makes me see, and cannot feed mine eye?] She means, by what influence is my love directed to a person so much above me? why am I made to discern excellence, and left to long after it, without the food of hope? JOHNSON.

[9] ——*native things.*] Things formed by nature for each other.
  M. MASON.

[2] *The mightiest space in fortune nature brings*
  To join like likes, and kiss like native things.
  Impossible be strange attempts, to those
  That weigh their pains in sense; and do suppose,
  What hath been, &c.] All these four lines are obscure, and, I believe, corrupt; I shall propose an emendation, which those who can explain the present reading, are at liberty to reject:
  Through *mightiest space in fortune nature brings*
  Likes to join likes, *and kiss like native things.*

The king's difeafe—my project may deceive me,
But my intents are fix'd, and will not leave me.

[Exit.

That is, *nature* brings *like qualities* and difpofitions *to meet* through any *diftance that fortune* may fet between them; fhe *joins* them and makes them *kifs like things born together.*

The next lines I read with Sir T. Hanmer:

Impoffible be ftrange attempts to thofe
That weigh their pains in fenfe, and do fuppofe
What ha'n't *been, cannot be.*

New attempts feem impoffible to thofe who eftimate their *labour* or *enterprifes* by fenfe, and believe that nothing can be but what they fee before them. JOHNSON.

I underftand the meaning to be this—*The affections given us by nature often unite perfons between whom fortune or accident has placed the greateft diftance or difparity; and caufe them to join, like likes,* (inftar parium) *like perfons in the fame fituation or rank of life.* Thus (as Mr. Steevens has obferved) in *Timon of Athens*:

" Thou foldereft clofe *impoffibilities,*
" And mak'ft them *kifs.*"

This interpretation is ftrongly confirmed by a fubfequent fpeech of the counteffes fteward, who is fuppofed to have over-heard this foliloquy of Helena: " *Fortune,* fhe faid, was no goddefs, that had put fuch *difference* betwixt their two eftates."

The mightieft fpace in fortune, for *perfons the moft widely feparated by fortune,* is certainly a licentious expreffion; but it is fuch a licence as Shakfpeare often takes. Thus in *Cymbeline, the diminution of fpace* is ufed for the diminution, of which fpace, or *diftance,* is the caufe.

If he had written *fpaces* (as in *Troilus and Creffida,*

" ——her whom we know well
" The world's large *fpaces* cannot parallel,)"

the paffage would have been more clear; but he was confined by the metre. We might, however, read—

The mightieft fpace in nature fortune brings
To join, &c.

i. e. accident fometimes unites thofe whom inequality of rank has feparated. But I believe the text is right. MALONE.

SCENE II.

Paris. *A Room in the King's Palace.*

Flourish of cornets. Enter the King of France, *with letters;* Lords *and others attending.*

KING. The Florentines and Senoys [3] are by the ears;
Have fought with equal fortune, and continue
A braving war.

   1 *LORD.*   So 'tis reported, fir.

KING. Nay, 'tis moft credible; we here receive it
A certainty, vouch'd from our coufin Auftria,
With caution, that the Florentine will move us
For fpeedy aid; wherein our deareft friend
Prejudicates the bufinefs, and would feem
To have us make denial.

   1 *LORD.*   His love and wifdom,
Approv'd fo to your majefty, may plead
For ampleft credence.

   KING.   He hath arm'd our anfwer,
And Florence is denied before he comes:
Yet, for our gentlemen, that mean to fee
The Tufcan fervice, freely have they leave
To ftand on either part.

   2 *LORD.*   It may well ferve
A nurfery to our gentry, who are fick
For breathing and exploit.

   KING.   What's he comes here?

---

[3] *——Senoys——*] The *Sanefi*, as they are termed by Boccace. Painter, who tranflates him, calls them *Senois*. They were the people of a fmall republick, of which the capital was *Sienna*. The Florentines were at perpetual variance with them.
                  STEEVENS.

Enter BERTRAM, LAFEU, *and* PAROLLES.

1 LORD. It is the count Roufillon,[4] my good lord,
Young Bertram.

KING.   Youth, thou bear'ft thy father's face;
Frank nature, rather curious than in hafte,
Hath well compos'd thee. Thy father's moral parts
May'ft thou inherit too! Welcome to Paris.

BER. My thanks and duty are your majefty's.

KING. I would I had that corporal foundnefs now,
As when thy father, and myfelf, in friendfhip
Firft try'd our foldierfhip! He did look far
Into the fervice of the time, and was
Difcipled of the braveft: he lafted long;
But on us both did haggifh age fteal on,
And wore us out of act. It much repairs me
To talk of your good father:[5] In his youth
He had the wit, which I can well obferve
To-day in our young lords; but they may jeft,
Till their own fcorn return to them unnoted,
Ere they can hide their levity in honour.[6]

---

4 ——*Roufillon,*] The old copy reads *Rofignoll.* STEEVENS.

5 ——*It much* repairs *me*
To talk of your good father:] To *repair,* in thefe plays, generally fignifies, to *renovate.* So, in *Cymbeline:*
    " ——O difloyal thing,
    " That fhould'ft *repair* my youth!" MALONE.

6 *He had the wit, which I can well obferve*
  To-day in our young lords; but they may jeft,
  Till their own fcorn return to them unnoted,
  Ere they can hide their levity in honour.] I believe *honour* is not
dignity of birth or rank, but *acquired reputation:*—Your father, fays
the king, *had the fame airy flights of fatirical wit with the young
lords of the prefent time, but they do not what he did,* hide their
unnoted *levity,* in honour, *cover petty faults with great merit.*
  This is an excellent obfervation. Jocofe follies, and flight
offences, are only allowed by mankind in him that over-powers
them by great qualities. JOHNSON.

So like a courtier, contempt nor bitterness
Were in his pride or sharpness; if they were,
His equal had awak'd them, and his honour,
Clock to itself, knew the true minute when
Exception bid him speak, and, at this time,
His tongue obey'd his hand: who were below him
He us'd as creatures of another place;

Point thus:
He had the wit, which I can well observe,
To-day in our young lords: but they may jest,
Till their own scorn returns to them, un-noted,
Ere they can hide their levity in honour,
So like a courtier. Contempt, &c. BLACKSTONE.

The punctuation recommended by Sir William Blackstone, is,
I believe, the true one, at least it is such as deserves the reader's
consideration. STEEVENS.

So like a courtier, contempt nor bitterness
Were in his pride or sharpness; if they were,
His equal had awak'd them;] Nor was used, without reduplication. So, in *Measure for Measure:*
" More *nor* less to others paying,
" Than by self-offences weighing."
The old text needs to be explained. He was so like a courtier,
that there was in *his dignity of manner nothing contemptuous, and in his*
keenness of wit nothing bitter. If *bitterness or contemptuousness* ever
appeared, they had been *awakened* by some injury, not of a man
below him, but of his *equal.* This is the complete image of a
well-bred man, and somewhat like this Voltaire has exhibited his
hero Lewis XIV. JOHNSON.

His tongue obey'd his hand:] We should read—*His tongue*
obey'd the hand. That is, *the hand of his honour's clock,* showing
the true minute when exceptions bad him speak. JOHNSON.

His is put for *its.* So, in *Othello:*
" —————— her motion
" Blush'd at *herself,"*—instead of *itself.* STEEVENS.

He us'd as creatures of another place;] i. e. he made allowances
for their conduct, and bore from them what he would not from
one of his own rank. The Oxford editor, not understanding the
sense, has altered *another place,* to a *brother-race.* WARBURTON.

I doubt whether this was our author's meaning. I rather incline
to think that he meant only, that the father of Bertram treated those
below him with becoming condescension, as creatures not indeed

And bow'd his eminent top to their low ranks,
Making them proud of his humility,
In their poor praise he humbles: Such a man
Might be a copy to these younger times;
Which, follow'd well, would demonstrate them now
But goers backward.

BER.   His good remembrance, sir,
Lies richer in your thoughts, than on his tomb;
So in approof lives not his epitaph,
As in your royal speech.

in so *high* a place as *himself*, but yet holding a certain place; as *one* of the links, though not the largest, of the great chain of society.

In *The Winter's Tale*, *place* is again used for *rank* or situation in life:

"   ———O thou thing,
" Which I'll not call a *creature of thy place.*" MALONE.

² *Making them proud of his humility,*
  In their poor praise he humbled:] But why were they proud of his humility? It should be read and pointed thus:

Making them proud; and his humility,
In their poor praise, he humbled——

i. e. by condescending to stoop to his inferiors, he exalted them and made them *proud*; and, in the gracious receiving their *poor praise*, he humbled even his *humility*. The sentiment is fine.
                                                    WARBURTON.

Every man has seen the *mean* too often *proud* of the *humility* of the great, and perhaps the great may sometimes be *humbled in the praises* of the mean, of those who commend them without conviction or discernment: this, however, is not so common; the *mean* are found more frequently than the *great*. JOHNSON.

I think the meaning is,—Making them proud of receiving such marks of condescension and affability from a person in so elevated a situation, and at the same time lowering or humbling himself, by stooping to accept of the encomiums of mean persons for that humility.—The construction seems to be, " he *being* humbled in their poor praise." MALONE.

Giving them a better opinion of their own importance, by his condescending manner of behaving to them. M. MASON.

³ *So in approof lives not his epitaph,*
  As in your royal speech.] *Epitaph* for character.
                                                    WARBURTON.

KING. 'Would, I were with him! He would al-
    ways say,
(Methinks, I hear him now; his plauſive words,
He ſcatter'd not in ears, but grafted them,
To grow there, and to bear,)—*Let me not live,*——
Thus [3] his good melancholy oft began,
On the cataſtrophe and heel of paſtime,
When it was out,—*let me not live,* quoth he,

I ſhould wiſh to read—
 Approof ſo lives not *in his* epitaph,
 As in your royal ſpeech.
Approof is *approbation.* If I ſhould allow Dr. Warburton's inter-
pretation of *epitaph,* which is more than can be reaſonably ex-
pected, I can yet find no ſenſe in the preſent reading.
            JOHNSON.

We might, by a ſlight tranſpoſition, read—
 So his approof lives not in epitaph.
Approof certainly means *approbation.* So, in *Cynthia's Revenge:*
 " A man ſo abſolute in my *approof,*
 " That nature hath reſerv'd ſmall dignity
 " That he enjoys not."
Again, in *Meaſure for Meaſure:*
 " Either of condemnation or *approof.*" STEEVENS.

 Perhaps the meaning is this:—*His epitaph or inſcription on his
tomb is not ſo much in approbation or commendation of him, as is your
royal ſpeech.* TOLLET.

 There can be no doubt but the word *approof* is frequently uſed
in the ſenſe of *approbation,* but that is not always the caſe; and in
this place it ſignifies *proof* or *confirmation.* The meaning of the
paſſage appears to be this: " The truth of his epitaph is in no way
ſo fully *proved,* as by your royal ſpeech." It is needleſs to remark,
that epitaphs generally contain the character and praiſes of the de-
ceaſed. *Approof* is uſed in the ſame ſenſe by Bertram, in the ſecond Act:
 " *Laf.* But I hope your lordſhip thinks him not a ſoldier.
 " *Ber.* Yes, my lord, and of very valiant *approof.*"
            M. MASON.

 Mr. Heath ſuppoſes the meaning to be this: " His epitaph, or
the character he left behind him, is not ſo well eſtabliſhed by *the
ſpecimens he exhibited of his worth,* as by your royal report in his
favour." The paſſage above quoted from Act II. ſupports this
interpretation. MALONE.

 [3] *Thus* —] Old copy—*This.* Corrected by Mr. Pope. MALONE.

After my flame lacks oil, to be the snuff
Of younger spirits, whose apprehensive senses
All but new things disdain; whose judgements are
Mere fathers of their garments; [4] *whose constancies*
Expire before their fashions:——This he wish'd:
I, after him, do after him wish too,
Since I nor wax, nor honey, can bring home,
I quickly were dissolved from my hive,
To give some labourers room.

2 LORD.   You are lov'd, sir;
They, that least lend it you, shall lack you first.

KING. I fill a place, I know't.—How long is't,
        count,
Since the physician at your father's died?
He was much fam'd.

BER.   Some six months since, my lord.

[4] —— *whose judgements are*
Mere fathers *of their garments*;] Who have no other use of
their faculties, than to invent new modes of dress. JOHNSON.

I have a suspicion that Shakspeare wrote—*meer* feathers *of their*
garments; i. e. whose judgements are meerly *parts* (and insignificant
parts) *of their dress*, worn and laid aside, as *feathers* are, from the
meer love of novelty and change. He goes on to say, that they
are even less constant in their judgements than in their dress:
        —— *their constancies*
Expire before their fashions. TYRWHITT.

The reading of the old copy—*fathers*, is supported by a similar
passage in *Cymbeline:*
        " —— some jay of Italy
        " Whose *mother* was her *painting*—."
Again, by another in the same play:
        " ——No, nor thy tailor, rascal,
        " Who is thy *grandfather*; he made those *cloaths*,
        " Which, as it seems, *make* thee."
There the garment is said to be the father of the man:—in the text,
the judgement, being employed solely in forming or giving *birth*
to new dresses, is called *the father of the garment.* So, in *King*
Henry IV. P. II:
        " ——every minute now
        " Should be the *father* of some stratagem." MALONE.

KING. If he were living, I would try him yet;—
Lend me an arm;—the reft have worn me out
With feveral applications:—nature and ficknefs
Debate it' at their leifure. Welcome, count;
My fon's no dearer.

BER.   Thank your majefty.
                          [Exeunt. Flourifh.

SCENE III.

Roufillon. *A Room in the* Countefs's *Palace.*

Enter Countefs, Steward, *and* Clown.[6]

COUNT. I will now hear: what fay you of this gentlewoman?

---

[5] *——nature and ficknefs*
Debate *it*—] So, in *Macbeth* :
   " Death and nature do *contend* about them."
                          STEEVENS,

[6] *——Steward, and* Clown.] A *Clown* in Shakfpeare is commonly taken for a *licenfed jefter*, or domeftick fool. We are not to wonder that we find this character often in his plays, fince fools were at that time maintained in all great families, to keep up merriment in the houfe. In the picture of Sir Thomas More's family, by Hans Holbein, the only fervant reprefented is Patifon the *fool*. This is a proof of the familiarity to which they were admitted, not by the great only, but the wife.
   In fome plays, a fervant, or a ruftic, of a remarkable petulance and freedom of fpeech, is likewife called a *clown.* JOHNSON.

   Cardinal Wolfey, after his difgrace, wifhing to fhow King Henry VIII. a mark of his refpect, fent him his fool *Patch*, as a prefent; whom, fays Stowe, " the King received very gladly."
                          MALONE.

   This dialogue, or that in *Twelfth Night*, between Olivia and the *Clown*, feems to have been particularly cenfured by Cartwright, in one of the copies of verfes prefixed to the works of Beaumont and Fletcher:

Stew. Madam, the care I have had to even your content,[7] I wish might be found in the calendar of my past endeavours; for then we wound our modesty, and make foul the clearness of our deservings, when of ourselves we publish them.[8]

Count. What does this knave here? Get you gone, sirrah: The complaints, I have heard of you, I do not all believe; 'tis my slowness, that I do not: for, I know, you lack not folly to commit

---

" *Shakspeare* to thee was dull, whose best jest lies
" I' th' *lady's* questions, and the *fool's* replies;
" Old fashion'd wit, which walk'd from town to town
" In trunk-hose, which our fathers call'd the *Clown.*"

In the MS. register of Lord Stanhope of Harrington, treasurer of the chamber to King james I. from 1613 to 1616, are the following entries: " Tom Derry, his majesty's *fool*, at 2s. per diem,—1615: Paid John Mawe for the diet and lodging of Thomas Derrie, her majesty's *jester*, for 13 weeks, 10l. 18s. 6d.—1616."

STEEVENS.

The following lines in *The Careless Shepherdess,* a comedy, 1656, exhibit probably a faithful portrait of this once admired character:

" Why, I would have *the fool* in every act,
" Be it comedy or tragedy. I have laugh'd
" Untill I cry'd again, to see what faces
" The rogue will make.—O, it does me good
" *To see him bold out his chin, hang down his hands,*
" *And twirl his bauble.* There is ne'er a part
" About him but breaks jests.—
" I'd rather hear him leap, or laugh, or cry,
" Than hear the gravest speech in all the play.
" I never saw READE peeping through the curtain,
" But ravishing joy enter'd into my heart." MALONE.

[7] ——— *to even your content,*] To act up to your desires.

JOHNSON.

[8] ——— *when of ourselves we publish them.*] So, in *Troilus and Cressida:*

" The worthiness of praise distains his worth,
" If he that's prais'd, himself brings the praise forth."

MALONE.

P 3

,them, and have ability enough ,to ' make ,fuch
knaveries yours.⁹   ad'

Clo. 'Tis not unknown to·you, madam, I am a
poor fellow.   !   ·   ·   ͻ

Count. Well,·fir.   ı   ·   ·   ıv   ⌐

, ,*Clo.* ·No, madam, 'tis not fo well, that I am
poor; though many of the rich·are damn'd:ᵃ But,
if, I may have your ladyſhip's good will to' go to
the world,³ Iſbel the woman and I⁴·will do as we
may.   ·

Count. Wilt thou needs be a beggar?

Clo. I do beg your good-will in this cafe.

Count. In what cafe?

Clo. In' Iſbel's cafe, and mine own. Service is
no heritage:⁵ and, I think, I ſhall never have the

. ⁹ ——*you lack not folly to commit* them, *and have ability enough
to make fuch knaveries* yours.]   After premiſing that the accufative,
them, refers to the precedent word, *complaints,* and that this by a
metonymy of the effect for the caufe, ſtands for the freaks which
occaſioned thofe complaints, the fenfe will be extremely clear.
" You are fool enough to commit thofe irregularities you are
charged with, and yet not fo much fool neither, as to difcredit the
accufation by any defect in your ability." HEATH.

It appears to me that the accufative *them* refers to *knaveries,* and
the natural fenfe of the paſſage feems to be this: " You have folly
enough to defire to commit thefe knaveries, and ability enough to
accomplish them." M. MASON.

ᵃ ——*are damn'd:*] See *S. Mark,* x. 25; *S. Luke,* xviii. 25.
                                                    GREY.

³ —— *to go to the world,*] This phrafe has already occurred in
Much ado about nothing, and fignifies to be *married:* and thus, in
As you Like it, Audrey fays: " —— it is no difhoneſt defire, to
defire to be *a woman of the world.*" STEEVENS.

⁴ —— *and I—*] *I,* which was inadvertently omitted in the firſt
copy, was fupplied by the editor of the fecond folio. MALONE.

⁵ *Service is no heritage:*] This is a proverbial expreffion. *Needs
muſt when the devil drives,* is another. RITSON.

bleffing of God, till I have iffue of my body; for, they fay, bearns are bleffings.

Count. Tell me thy reafon why thou wilt marry.

Clo. My poor body, madam, requires it: I am driven on by the flefh; and he muft needs go, that the devil drives.

Count. Is this all your worfhip's reafon?

Clo. Faith madam, I have other holy reafons, fuch as they are.

Count. May the world know them?

Clo. I have been, madam, a wicked creature, as you and all flefh and blood are; and, indeed, I do marry, that I may repent.

Count. Thy marriage, fooner than thy wicked-nefs.

Clo. I am out of friends, madam; and I hope to have friends for my wife's fake.

Count. Such friends are thine enemies, knave.

Clo. You are fhallow, madam; e'en great friends;[6]

---

[6] Clo. *You are fhallow, madam*; e'en *great friends*;] The mean-ing [i. e. of the ancient reading mentioned in the fubfequent note] feems to be, you are not deeply fkilled in the character or offices of great friends. JOHNSON.

The old copy reads—*in* great friends; evidently a miftake for *e'en*, which was formerly written *e'n*. The two words are fo near in found, that they might eafily have been confounded by an in-attentive hearer.

The fame miftake has happened in many other places in our author's plays. So, in the prefent comedy, Act III. fc. ii. folio, 1623:

"*Lady.* What have we here?

"*Clown. In* that you have there."

Again, in *Antony and Cleopatra*:

"No more but *in* a woman."

Again, in *Twelfth Night*:

"'Tis with him *in* ftanding water, between boy and man."

The corruption of this paffage was pointed out by Mr. Tyrwhitt. For the emendation now made, I am anfwerable. MALONE.

for the knaves come to do that for me, which I am
a-weary of. He, that ears my land, spares my team,
and gives me leave to inn the crop: if I be his
cuckold, he's my drudge: He, that comforts my
wife, is the cherisher of my flesh and blood; he,
that cherishes my flesh and blood, loves my flesh
and blood; he, that loves my flesh and blood, is
my friend: *ergo*, he that kisses my wife, is my
friend. If men could be contented to be what
they are, there were no fear in marriage; for young
Charbon the puritan, and old Poysam the papist,

6 ——*the knaves come to do that for me, which I am a-weary of.*] The same thought is more dilated in an old MS. play, entitled, *The Second Maid's Tragedy:*

" *Soph.* I have a wife, would she were so preferr'd!.
" I could but be her subject; so I am now.
" I allow her her owne frend to stop her mowth,
" And keep her quiet; give him his table free,
" And the huge feeding of his great stone-horse,
" On which he rides in pompe about the cittie
" Only to speake to gallants in bay-windowes.
" Marry, his lodging he paies deerly for;
" He getts me all my children, there I save by't;
" Beside, I drawe my life owte by the bargaine
" Some twelve yeres longer than the tymes appointed;
" When my young prodigal gallant kicks up's heels
" At one and thirtie, and lies dead and rotten
" Some five and fortie yeares before I'm coffin'd.
" 'Tis the right waie to keep a woman honest:
" One friend is baracadoe to a hundred,
" And keepes 'em owte; nay more, a husband's sure
" To have his children all of one man's gettinge;
" And he that performes best, can have no better:
" I'm e'en as happie then that save a labour."
STEEVENS.

7 ——*that ears my land,*] To ear is to plough. So, in *Antony and Cleopatra:*
" Make the sea serve them, which they ear and wound
" With keels of every kind." STEEVENS.

See 1 *Sam.* viii. 12. *Isaiah,* xxx. 24. *Deut.* xxi. 4. *Gen.* xlv. 6. *Exod.* xxxiv. 21. for the use of this verb. HENLEY.

howfoe'er their hearts are fever'd in religion, their
heads are both one, they may joll horns together,
like any deer i' the herd.

Coun. Wilt thou ever be a foul-mouth'd and
calumnious knave?

Clo. A prophet I, madam; and I fpeak the
truth the next way :[8]

> *For I the ballad will repeat,*
> *Which men full true fhall find;*
> *Your marriage comes by deftiny,*
> *Your cuckoo fings by kind.*[9]

Coun. Get you gone, fir; I'll talk with you
more anon.

[8] *A prophet I, madam; and I fpeak the truth the next way:*] It
is a fuperftition, which has run through all ages and people, that
natural fools have fomething in them of divinity. On which account they were efteemed facred : Travellers tell us in what efteem
the Turks now hold them; nor had they lefs honour paid them
heretofore in France, as appears from the old word *bénet*, for a
natural fool. Hence it was that Pantagruel, in *Rabelais*, advifed
Panurge to go and confult the fool Triboulet as an oracle; which
gives occafion to a fatirical ftroke upon the privy council of
Francis the Firft—*Par l'avis, confeil,* prediction *des fols vos fcavez
quants princes, &c. ont efté confervez,* &c.—The phrafe—*fpeak the
truth the next way,* means *directly*; as they do who are only the
inftruments or *canals* of others; fuch as infpired perfons were fuppofed to be. WARBURTON.

See the popular ftory of *Nixon the Idiot's Chefhire Prophecy.*
DOUCE.

Next way, is *neareft way.* So, in *K. Henry IV.* Part I:
" "Tis the *next way* to turn tailor," &c. STEEVENS.

Next way is a phrafe ftill ufed in Warwickfhire, and fignifies
without circumlocution, or *going about.* HENLEY.

[9] ——*fings by kind.*] I find fomething like two of the lines of
this ballad in *John Grange's Garden,* 1577:
" Content yourfelf as well as I, let reafon rule your minde,
" As cuckoldes come by deftinie, fo cuckowes fing by kinde."
STEEVENS.

Stew. May it please you, madam, that he bid Helen come to you; of her I am to speak.

Count. Sirrah, tell my gentlewoman, I would speak with her; Helen I mean.

Clo. Was this fair face the cause,[2] *quoth she,*
        [Singing.
 Why the Grecians sacked Troy?
 Fond done,[3] *done fond,*
 Was this king Priam's joy.

[2] *Was this fair face the cause,* &c.] The name of *Helen*, whom the Countess has just called for, brings an old ballad on the sacking of Troy to the Clown's mind. MALONE.

This is a stanza of an old ballad, out of which a word or two are dropt, equally necessary to make the sense and alternate rhyme. For it was not Helen, who was King Priam's joy, but Paris. The third line therefore should be read thus:

 Fond done, fond done, for Paris, he——. WARBURTON.

If this be a stanza taken from any ancient ballad, it will probably in time be found entire, and then the restoration may be made with authority. STEEVENS.

In confirmation of Dr. Warburton's conjecture, Mr. Theobald has quoted from Fletcher's *Maid in the Mill,* the following stanza of another old ballad:

 " And here fair *Paris* comes,
  " The hopeful youth of *Troy,*
 " Queen Hecuba's darling son,
  " King *Priam's* only *joy.*"

This renders it extremely probable, that Paris was the person described as " king Priam's joy" in the ballad quoted by our author; but Mr. Heath has justly observed, that Dr. Warburton, though he has supplied the words supposed to be lost, has not explained them; nor indeed do they seem, as they are connected, to afford any meaning. In 1585 was entered on the Stationers' books by Edward White, " *The lamentation of Hecuba, and the ladyes of Troye;*" which probably contained the stanza here quoted."

           MALONE.

[3] *Fond done,*] Is foolishly done. So, in *King Richard III.* Act III. sc. iii:

 " —— Sorrow and grief of heart,
 " Makes him speak *fondly.*" STEEVENS.

With that she sighed as she stood,
With that she sighed as she stood,[4]
And gave this sentence then;
Among nine bad if one be good,
Among nine bad if one be good,
There's yet one good in ten.[5]

COUNT. What, one good in ten? you corrupt the song, sirrah.

CLO. One good woman in ten, madam; which is a purifying o' the song: 'Would God would serve the world so all the year! we'd find no fault with the tythe-woman, if I were the parson: One in ten, quoth a'! an we might have a good woman born but every blazing star,[6] or at an earthquake, 'twould mend the lottery well;[7] a man may draw his heart out, ere he pluck one.

---

[4] *With that she sighed as she stood,*] At the end of the line of which this is a repetition, we find added in Italick characters the word *bis,* denoting, I suppose, the necessity of its being repeated. The corresponding line was twice printed, as it is here inserted, from the oldest copy. STEEVENS.

[5] *Among nine bad if one be good,*
There's yet one good in ten.] This second stanza of the ballad is turned to a joke upon the women: a confession, that there was one good in ten. Whereon the Countess observed, that he corrupted the song; which shows the song said—*nine good in ten.*
If one be bad amongst nine good,
There's but one bad in ten.
This relates to the ten sons of Priam, who all behaved themselves well but Paris. For though he once had fifty, yet at this unfortunate period of his reign he had but ten; *Agathon, Antiphon, Deiphobus, Dius, Hector, Helenus, Hippothous, Pammon, Paris,* and *Polites.* WARBURTON.

[6] —— *but every blazing star,*] The old copy reads—*but ore every blazing star.* STEEVENS.

I suppose *o'er* was a misprint for *or,* which was used by our old writers for *before.* MALONE.

[7] —— *'twould* mend *the lottery* well;] This surely is a strange

Count. You'll be gone, fir' knave, and do as I command you?

Clo. That man fhould be at woman's command, and yet no hurt done!—Though honefty be no puritan, yet it will do no hurt; it will wear the furplice of humility over the black gown of a big heart.[8]—I am going, forfooth: the bufinefs is for Helen to come hither.   [*Exit* Clown.

---

kind of phrafeology. I have never met with any example of it in any of the contemporary writers; and if there were any proof that in the lotteries of Queen Elizabeth's time *wheels* were employed, I fhould be inclined to read—lottery *wheel.* MALONE.

[8] *Clo. That man, &c.*] The Clown's anfwer is obfcure. His lady bids him do as he is *commanded.* He anfwers with the licentious petulance of his character, that *if a man does as a woman commands, it is likely he will do amifs*; that he does not amifs being at the command of a woman, he makes the effect, not of his lady's goodnefs, but of his own *honefty*, which, though not very nice or *puritanical*, will *do no hurt*; and will not only do no hurt, but, unlike the *puritans*, will comply with the injunctions of fuperiors, and wear the *furplice of humility over the black gown of a big heart*; will obey commands, though not much pleafed with a ftate of fubjection.

Here is an allufion, violently enough forced in, to fatirize the obftinacy with which the *puritans* refufed the ufe of the ecclefiaftical habits, which was, at that time, one principal caufe of the breach of the union, and, perhaps, to infinuate, that the modeft purity of the furplice was fometimes a cover for pride.
                                                                       JOHNSON.

The averfion of the *puritans* to a *furplice* is alluded to in many of the old comedies. So, in *Cupid's Whirligig*, 1607:

—— " She loves to act in as clean linen as any gentlewoman of her function about the town; and truly that's the reafon that your fincere *puritans* cannot abide a *furplice*, becaufe they fay 'tis made of the fame thing that your villainous fin is committed in, of your prophane holland."

Again, in *The Match at Midnight*, 1633:

" He has turn'd my ftomach for all the world like a *puritan's* at the fight of a *furplice.*"

Again, in *The Hollander*, 1640:

—— " A *puritan*, who, becaufe he faw a *furplice* in the church, would needs hang himfelf in the bell-ropes." STEEVENS.

Count. Well, now.

Stew. I know, madam, you love your gentle-woman entirely.

Count. Faith, I do : her father bequeath'd her to me ; and she herself, without other advantage, may lawfully make title to as much love as she finds : there is more owing her, than is paid ; and more shall be paid her, than she'll demand.

Stew. Madam, I was very late more near her than, I think, she wish'd me : alone she was, and did communicate to herself, her own words to her own ears ; she thought, I dare vow for her, they touch'd not any stranger sense. Her matter was, she loved your son : Fortune, she said, was no god-dess, that had put such difference betwixt their two estates ; Love, no god, that would not extend his might, only where qualities were level ; [9] Diana,

---

I cannot help thinking we should read—*Though honefty be a puritan*—. TYRWHITT.

Surely Mr. Tyrwhitt's correction is right. If our author had meant to say—though *honefty be* no *puritan*,—why should he add—*that it would wear the furplice,* &c. or, in other words, that it would be content to assume a covering that puritans in general re-probated ? What would there be extraordinary in this ? Is it matter of wonder, that he who is no puritan, should be free from the scruples and prejudices of one ?

The Clown, I think, means to say, " Though honefty be rigid and confcientious as *a* puritan, yet it will not be obftinate, but humbly comply with the lawful commands of its fuperiors, while at the fame time its proud fpirit inwardly revolts against them." I fufpect however a ftill farther corruption ; and that the compofitor caught the words " *no hurt* " from the preceding line. Our author perhaps wrote—" Though honefty be *a* puritan, yet it will do *what is enjoined* ; it will wear the furplice of humility, over the black gown of a big heart." I will therefore obey my miftrefs, however reluctantly, and go for Helena. MALONE.

[9] —— *only where qualities were level* ;] The meaning may be, where qualities only, *and not fortunes* or *conditions,* were level. Or perhaps *only* is ufed for *except.* " —that would not extend his might, *except* where two perfons were of equal rank." MALONE.

no queen of virgins, that would suffer her. poor
knight to be surprised, without rescue, in the first
assault, or ransom afterward:⁹ This she deliver'd
in the most bitter touch of sorrow, that e'er I
heard virgin exclaim in: which I held my duty,
speedily to acquaint you withal; sithence,² in the
loss that may happen, it concerns you something
to know it.

Count. You have discharged this honestly; keep
it to yourself: many likelihoods inform'd me of
this before, which hung so tottering in the balance,
that I could neither believe, nor misdoubt: Pray
you, leave me: stall this in your bosom, and I
thank you for your honest care: I will speak with
you further anon.   [*Exit* Steward.

Enter HELENA.

Count. Even so it was with me, when I was
                young:
    If we are nature's,¹ these are ours; this thorn
Doth to our rose of youth rightly belong;
    Our blood to us, this to our blood is born;

---

⁹ —— *Love, no god,* &c. Diana, no *queen of virgins,* &c.] This
passage stands thus in the old copies:

*Love, no god, that would not extend his might only where qualities
were level; queen of virgins, that would suffer her poor knight,* &c.

'Tis evident to every sensible reader that something must have
slipt out here, by which the meaning of the context is rendered
defective. The steward is speaking in the very words he over-
heard of the young lady; fortune was no goddess, she said, for
one reason; love, no god, for another;—what could she then more
naturally subjoin, than as I have amended in the text.

Diana, no *queen of virgins, that would suffer her poor knight to be
surprised without rescue,* &c.

For in poetical history Diana was as well known to preside over
chastity, as Cupid over *love,* or *Fortune* over the *change* or *regulation*
of our *circumstances.* THEOBALD.

² ——*sithence,*] i. e. since. So, in *Spenser's State of Ireland:*
∧ —— the beginning of all other evils which *sithence* have af-

It is the show and seal of nature's truth,
Where love's strong passion is imprefs'd in youth:
By our remembrances [4] of days foregone,
Such were our faults;—or then we thought them
   none.[5]
Her eye is sick on't; I observe her now.

Hel. What is your pleafure, madam?

Count.   You know, Helen,
I am a mother to you.

Hel. Mine honourable miftrefs.

Count.   Nay, a mother;
Why not a mother? When I faid, a mother,
Methought you faw a ferpent: What's in mother,
That you ftart at it? I fay, I am your mother;
And put you in the catalogue of thofe
That were enwombed mine: 'Tis often feen,
Adoption ftrives with nature; and choice breeds
A native flip to us from foreign feeds:[6]

flicted that land." Chaucer frequently ufes *fith*, and *fithen*, in the fame fenfe. STEEVENS.

 [5] *If we are nature's,*] The old copy reads—*If ever we are nature's.* STEEVENS.

The emendation was made by Mr. Pope. MALONE.

 [4] *By our remembrances—*] That is, *according to* our recollection. So we fay, he is old *by* my reckoning. JOHNSON.

 [5] *Such were our faults;—or then we thought them none.*] We fhould read: ———*O! then we thought them none.* A motive for pity and pardon, agreeable to fact, and the indulgent character of the fpeaker. This was fent to the Oxford *editor,* and he altered O, to *though.* WARBURTON.

Such were the faulty weakneffes of which I was guilty in my youth, or fuch at leaft were then my *feelings,* though perhaps at that period of my life I did not think they deferved the name of *faults.* Dr. Warburton, without neceffity, as it feems to me, reads—" *O!* then we thought them none;"—and the fubfequent editors adopted the alteration. MALONE.

 [6] ———— *and choice breeds*
 A native flip to us from foreign feeds:] And our choice furnifhes

5

You ne'er oppress'd me with a mother's groan,
Yet I express to you a mother's care:—
God's mercy, maiden! does it curd thy blood,
To say, I am thy mother? What's the matter,
That this distemper'd messenger of wet,
The many-colour'd Iris, rounds thine eye?'
Why?——that you are my daughter?

   Hel.   That I am not.

   Count. I say, I am your mother.

   Hel.   Pardon, madam;
The count Rousillon cannot be my brother:
I am from humble, he from honour'd name;
No note upon my parents, his all noble:
My master, my dear lord he is; and I
His servant live, and will his vassal die:
He must not be my brother.

   Count.   Nor I your mother?

   Hel. You are my mother, madam; 'Would you
         were
(So that my lord, your son, were not my brother,)
Indeed, my mother!—or were you both our mo-
         thers,
I care no more for, than I do for heaven,

---

us with a slip propagated to us from foreign seeds, which we educate and treat, as if it were native to us, and sprung from ourselves.

                                    HEATH.

7 ————— *What's the matter,*
   That this distemper'd messenger of wet,
   The many-colour'd Iris, rounds thine eye?] There is something exquisitely beautiful in this representation of that suffusion of colours which glimmers around the sight when the eye-lashes are wet with tears. The poet hath described the same appearance in his *Rape of Lucrece:*

    " And round about her tear-distained eye
    " Blue circles stream'd like rainbows in the sky."

                                      HANLEY.

So I were not his fifter:[8] Can't no other,
But, I your daughter, he muft be my brother?[9]

   Count. Yes, Helen, you might be my daughter-
            in-law;
God fhield, you mean it not! daughter, and mother,
So ftrive[2] upon your pulfe: What, pale again?
My fear hath catch'd your fondnefs: Now I fee
The myftery of your lonelinefs, and find
Your falt tears' head.[3]   Now to all fenfe 'tis grofs,

---

[8] ———— *or were you both our mothers,*
   I care no more for, *than I do for heaven,*
   So I were not his fifter :] There is a defigned ambiguity: *I
care no more for,* is, I care *as much for.*—I wifh it equally.
                              FARMER.

   In *Troilus and Creffida* we find—" I care *not* to be the loufe of
a lazar, *fo I were not* Menelaus." There the words certainly
mean, I fhould not be forry or unwilling to be, &c. According
to this, then, the meaning of the paffage before us fhould be, " If
you were mother to us both, it would not give me more folicitude
than heaven gives me,—fo I were not his fifter." But Helena
certainly would not confefs an indifference about her future ftate.
However, fhe may mean, as Dr. Farmer has fuggefted, " I fhould
not care *more* than, but *equally as,* I care for future happinefs; I
fhould be as content, and folicit it as much, as I pray for the
blifs of heaven." MALONE.

[9] ——*Can't no other,*
   But, I your daughter, he muft be my brother?] The meaning is
obfcured by the elliptical diction. *Can it* be *no other* way, *but* if
I be *your daughter, he muft be my brother?* JOHNSON.

[2] ——*ftrive* —] To *ftrive* is to contend. So, in *Cymbeline:*
   " That it did *ftrive* in workmanfhip and value."
                              STEEVENS.

[3] ————*Now I fee*
   The ery *of your* lonelinefs, *and find*
   Your falt tears' head.] The old copy reads—*lovelinefs.*
                              STEEVENS.
   The myftery of her *lovelinefs* is beyond my comprehenfion: the
old Countefs is faying nothing ironical, nothing taunting, or in
reproach, that this word fhould find a place here; which it could
not, unlefs farcaftically employed, and with fome fpleen. I dare

You love my fon; invention is afham'd,
Againft the proclamation of thy paffion,
To fay, thou doft not: therefore tell me true;
But tell me then, 'tis fo:—for, look, thy cheeks
Confefs it, one to the other; and thine eyes
See it fo grofsly fhown in thy behaviours,
That in their kind⁴ they fpeak it; only fin
And hellifh obftinacy tie thy tongue,
That truth fhould be fufpected: Speak, is't fo?
If it be fo, you have wound a goodly clue;
If it be not, forfwear't: howe'er, I charge thee,
As heaven fhall work in me for thine avail,
To tell me truly.

HEL.   Good madam, pardon me!

COUNT. Do you love my fon?

HEL.   Your pardon, noble miftrefs!

COUNT. Love you my fon?

HEL.   Do not you love him, madam?

COUNT. Go not about; my love hath in't a bond,
Whereof the world takes note: come, come, dif-
      clofe

warrant the poet meant his old lady fhould fay no more than this:
" I now find the myftery of your creeping into corners, and weeping, and pining in fecret." For this reafon I have amended the
text, *lonelinefs.* The Steward, in the foregoing fcene, where he gives
the Countefs intelligence of Helena's behaviour, fays—
  " *Alone fhe* was, and did communicate to herfelf, her own words
to her own ears." THEOBALD.

  The late Mr. Hall had corrected this, I believe, rightly,—your
lowlinefs. TYRWHITT.

  I think Theobald's correction as plaufible. To choofe folitude
is a mark of love. STEEVENS.

  Your falt tears' head.] The fource, the fountain of your tears,
the caufe of your grief. JOHNSON.

  ⁴ —— *in their* kind—] i. e. in their language, according to their
nature. STEEVENS.

The ſtate of your affection; for your paſſions
Have to the full appeach'd.

    Hel.   Then, I confeſs,
Here on my knee, before high heaven and you,
That before you, and next unto high heaven,
I love your ſon :—
My friends were poor, but honeſt; ſo's my love:
Be not offended; for it hurts not him,
That he is lov'd of me: I follow him not
By any token of preſumptuous ſuit;
Nor would I have him, till I do deſerve him;
Yet never know how that deſert ſhould be.
I know I love in vain, ſtrive againſt hope;
Yet, in this captious and intenible ſieve,[5]
I ſtill pour in the waters of my love,
And lack not to loſe ſtill:[6] thus, Indian-like,

---

[5] ——captious *and* intenible *ſieve*,] The word *captious* I never found in this ſenſe; yet I cannot tell what to ſubſtitute, unleſs *carious* for *rotten*, which yet is a word more likely to have been miſtaken by the copiers than uſed by the author. JOHNSON.

    Dr. Farmer ſuppoſes *captious* to be a contraction of *capacious*. As violent ones are to be found among our ancient writers, and eſpecially in Churchyard's Poems, with which Shakſpeare was not unacquainted. STEEVENS.

    By *captious*, I believe Shakſpeare only meant *recipient*, capable of *receiving* what is put into it; and by *intenible*, incapable of holding or retaining it. How frequently he and the other writers of his age confounded the active and paſſive adjectives, has been already more than once obſerved.

    The original copy reads—*intemible*. The correction was made in the ſecond folio. MALONE.

[6] *And lack not to loſe ſtill:*] Perhaps we ſhould read—
    And lack not to love ſtill. TYRWHITT.

    I believe *loſe* is right. So afterwards, in this ſpeech:
    " ——whoſe ſtate is ſuch, that cannot chooſe
    " But lend and give, where ſhe is ſure to *loſe*."
Helena means, I think, to ſay that, like a perſon who pours water into a veſſel full of holes, and ſtill continues his employment though he finds the water all loſt, and the veſſel empty, ſo, though

Religious in mine error, I adore
The fun, that looks upon his worfhipper,
But knows of him no more. My deareft madam,
Let not your hate encounter with my love,
For loving where you do: but, if yourfelf,
Whofe aged honour cites a virtuous youth,[1]
Did ever, in fo true a flame of liking,
Wifh chaftly, and love dearly; that your Dian
Was both herfelf and Love;[8] O then, give pity
To her, whofe ftate is fuch, that cannot choofe
But lend and give, where fhe is fure to lofe;
That feeks not to find that her fearch implies,
But, riddle-like, lives fweetly where fhe dies.

COUNT. Had you not lately an intent, fpeak truly,
To go to Paris?

HEL.   Madam, I had.

COUNT.   Wherefore? tell true.[9]

---

fhe finds that *the waters of her love* are ftill *loft*, that her affection
is thrown away on an object whom fhe thinks fhe never can deferve,
fhe yet is not difcouraged, but perfeveres in her hopelefs endeavour
to accomplifh her wifhes.   The poet evidently alludes to the trite
ftory of the daughters of Danaus. MALONE.

[1] *Whofe aged honour cites a virtuous youth*,] i. e. whofe re-
fpectable conduct in age *fhows*, or *proves*, that you were no lefs
virtuous when young. As a fact is *proved* by *citing* witnefles, or
examples from books, our author with his ufual licenfe ufes to *cite*,
in the fenfe of *to prove*. MALONE.

[8] *Wifh chaftly, and love dearly, that your Dian*
   Was both herfelf and Love;] i. e. Venus. Helena means to
fay—"If ever you wifhed that the deity who prefides over chaftity,
and the queen of amorous rites, were one and the fame perfon;
or, in other words, if ever you wifhed for the honeft and lawful
completion of your chafte defires."   I believe, however, the words
were accidentally tranfpofed at the prefs, and would read—
   Love dearly, and wifh chaftly, that your Dian, &c.
                                                    MALONE.

[9] —— *tell true*.] This is an evident interpolation. It is
needlefs, becaufe it repeats what the Countefs had already faid:
it is injurious, becaufe it fpoils the meafure. STEEVENS.

I

Hel. I will tell truth; by grace itself, I swear.
You know, my father left me some prescriptions
Of rare and prov'd effects, such as his reading,
And manifest experience, had collected
For general sovereignty; and that he will'd me
In heedfullest reservation to bestow them,
As notes, whose faculties inclusive[2] were,
More than they were in note: amongst the rest,
There is a remedy, approv'd, set down,
To cure the desperate languishings, whereof
The king is render'd lost.

Count.   This was your motive
For Paris, was it? speak.

Hel. My lord your son made me to think of this;
Else Paris, and the medicine, and the king,
Had, from the conversation of my thoughts,
Haply, been absent then.

Count.   But think you, Helen,
If you should tender your supposed aid,
He would receive it? He and his physicians
Are of a mind; he, that they cannot help him,
They, that they cannot help: How shall they credit
A poor unlearned virgin, when the schools,
Embowell'd of their doctrine,[3] have left off
The danger to itself?

Hel. There's something hints,
More than my father's skill, which was the greatest

---

² —— *notes, whose faculties* inclusive—] Receipts in which greater *virtues* were inclosed than appeared to observation.
                                                    JOHNSON.

³ Embowell'd *of their doctrine,*] i. e. exhausted of their skill. So, in the old spurious play of *K. John:*
    " Back war-men, back; *embowel* not the clime."
                                                    STEEVENS.

Q 3

Of his profeffion, that his good receipt [4]
Shall, for my legacy, be fanctified
By the luckieft ftars in heaven: and, would your
    honour
But give me leave to try fuccefs, I'd venture
The well-loft life of mine on his grace's cure,
By fuch a day, and hour.

    Count.   Doft thou believe't?

    Hel. Ay, madam, knowingly.

    Count. Why, Helen, thou fhalt have my leave,
    and love,
Means, and attendants, and my loving greetings
To thofe of mine in court; I'll ftay at home,
And pray God's bleffing into thy attempt: [5]
Be gone to-morrow; and be fure of this,
What I can help thee to, thou fhalt not mifs.

                           [Exeunt.

---

  [4] *There's fomething* hints
    More than my father's ſkill, ——
    —— that *his good receipt,* &c.] The old copy reads—*fomething*
in't. Steevens.

    Here is an inference, [*that*] without any thing preceding, to
which it refers, which makes the fentence vicious, and fhows that
we fhould read—
    There's fomething hints
    More than my father's ſkill, ——
    —— *that his good receipt* ——
i. e. I have a fecret premonition, or prefage. Warburton.

    This neceffary correction was made by Sir Thomas Hanmer.
                                Malone.

  [5] —— into *thy attempt :*] So in the old copy. We might more
intelligibly read, according to the third folio,—unto *thy attempt.*
                                Steevens.

ACT II. SCENE I.

Paris. *A Room in the King's Palace.*

Flourish. **Enter** King, *with young Lords taking leave for the* Florentine *war;* BERTRAM, PAROLLES, *and Attendants.*

KING. Farewell,[6] young lord, these warlike prin-
    ciples
Do not throw from you :—and you, my lord, fare-
    - well :[7]—
Share the advice betwixt you; if both gain all,
The gift doth stretch itself as 'tis receiv'd,
And is enough for both.

[6] *Farewell,* &c.] In all the latter copies these lines stood thus:
    Farewell, young lords; *these warlike principles*
    Do not throw from you. You, my lords, *farewell;*
    Share the advice betwixt you; if both again,
    The gift doth stretch itself as 'tis receiv'd.
The third line in that state was unintelligible. Sir Thomas Hanmer
reads thus:
    Farewell, young lord : *these warlike principles*
    Do not throw from you; you, my lord, *farewell;*
    Share the advice betwixt you: If both gain, well!
    The gift doth stretch itself as 'tis receiv'd,
    And is enough for both.
    The first edition, from which the passage is restored, was suffi-
ciently clear; yet it is plain, that the latter editors preferred a
reading which they did not understand. JOHNSON.

[7] —— *and you, my* lord, *farewell:*] The old copy, both in
this and the following instance, reads—*lords,* STEEVENS.
    It does not any where appear that more than two French lords
(besides Bertram) went to serve in Italy; and therefore I think the
King's speech should be corrected thus:
    Farewell, young lord; *these warlike principles*
    Do not throw from you; and you, my lord, *farewell;*

1 LORD.   It is our hope, fir,
After well-enter'd foldiers, to return
And find your grace in health.

    KING. No, no, it cannot be; and yet my heart
Will not confefs he owes the malady
That doth my life befiege.[8] Farewell, young lords;
Whether I live or die, be you the fons
Of worthy Frenchmen: let higher Italy
(Thofe 'bated, that inherit but the fall
Of the laft monarchy,) fee, that you come
Not to woo honour, but to wed it;[9] when

what follows, fhows this correction to be neceffary:
     " Share the advice betwixt you; if both gain all," &c.
                           TYRWHITT.
    Tyrwhitt's amendment is clearly right. Advice is the only
thing that may be fhared between two, and yet both gain all.
                                M. MASON.

   [8] *—— and yet my heart*
     Will not confefs he owes the malady
     That doth my life befiege.] i. e. as the common phrafe runs,
I am ftill heart-whole; my fpirits, by not finking under my diftemper, do not acknowledge its influence. STEEVENS.

   [9] *—————— let higher Italy*
     (Thofe 'bated, that inherit but the fall
     Of the laft monarchy,) fee, &c.] The ancient geographers have
divided Italy into the higher and the lower, the Apennine hills
being a kind of natural line of partition; the fide next the
Adriatick was denominated the higher Italy, and the other fide
the lower: and the two feas followed the fame terms of diftinction,
the Adriatick being called the upper Sea and the Tyrrhene or
Tufcan the lower. Now the Sennones, or Senois, with whom the
Florentines are here fuppofed to be at war, inhabited the higher
Italy, their chief town being Arminium, now called Rimini, upon
the Adriatick. HANMER.

    Italy, at the time of this fcene, was under three very different
tenures. The emperor, as fucceffor of the Roman emperors, had
one part; the pope, by a pretended donation from Conftantine,
another; and the third was compofed of free ftates. Now by the
laft monarchy is meant the *Roman*, the laft of the four general monarchies. Upon the fall of this monarchy, in the fcramble, feveral
cities fet up for themfelves, and became free ftates: now thefe

The braveſt queſtant ſhrinks, find what you ſeek,

might be ſaid properly to *inherit* the *fall* of the monarchy. This being premiſed, let us now conſider ſenſe. The King ſays *higher* Italy;—giving it the rank of preference to France; but he corrects himſelf and ſays, I except thoſe from that precedency, who only inherit the fall of the laſt monarchy; as all the little petty ſtates; for inſtance, Florence, to whom theſe volunteers were going. As if he had ſaid, I give the place of honour to the emperor and the pope, but not to the free ſtates. WARBURTON.

Sir T. Hanmer reads:

Thoſe baſtards *that inherit*, &c.

with this note:

" Reflecting upon the abject and degenerate condition of the cities and ſtates which aroſe out of the ruins of the Roman empire, the laſt of the four great monarchies of the world."

Dr. Warburton's obſervation is learned, but rather too ſubtle; Sir Thomas Hanmer's alteration is merely arbitrary. The paſſage is confeſſedly obſcure, and therefore I may offer another explanation. I am of opinion that the epithet *higher* is to be underſtood of ſituation rather than of dignity. The ſenſe may then be this, *Let upper Italy*, where you are to exerciſe your valour, *ſee that you come to gain honour, to the* abatement, *that is, to the diſgrace and depreſſion of thoſe* that have now loſt their ancient military fame, and *inherit but the fall of the laſt monarchy.* To *abate* is uſed by Shakſpeare in the original ſenſe of *abatre,* to *depreſs,* to *ſink,* to *deject,* to *ſubdue.* So, in *Coriolanus :*

" —— till ignorance deliver you,
" As moſt *abated* captives to ſome nation
" That won you without blows."

And *bated* is uſed in a kindred ſenſe in *The Merchant of Venice :*

" —— in a bondman's key,
" With *bated* breath, and whiſp'ring humbleneſs."

The word has ſtill the ſame meaning in the language of the law. JOHNSON.

In confirmation of Johnſon's opinion, that *higher* relates to ſituation, not to dignity, we find in the third ſcene of the fourth Act, that one of the Lords ſays,—" What will Count Rouſillon do then? will he travel *higher,* or return again to France?"

M. MASON.

Thoſe 'bated may here ſignify " thoſe being *taken away* or *excepted.*" *Bate,* thus contracted, is in colloquial language ſtill uſed with this meaning. This parenthetical ſentence implies no more than *they excepted who poſſeſs modern Italy, the remains of the Roman empire.* HOLT WHITE.

That fame may cry you loud:[2] I say, farewell.

2 LORD. Health, at your bidding, serve your
  majesty!

KING. Those girls of Italy, take heed of them;
They say, our French lack language to deny,
If they demand: beware of being captives,
Before you serve.[3]

BOTH.   Our hearts receive your warnings.

KING. Farewell.—Come hither to me.
     [*The* King *retires to a couch.*

1 LORD. O my sweet lord, that you will stay behind us!

PAR. 'Tis not his fault; the spark——

2 LORD.   O, 'tis brave wars!

PAR. Most admirable: I have seen those wars.

BER. I am commanded here, and kept a coil
  with;
Too young, and *the next year,* and *'tis too early.*

PAR. An thy mind stand to it, boy, steal away
  bravely.

BER. I shall stay here the forehorse to a smock,
Creaking my shoes on the plain masonry,
Till honour be bought up, and no sword worn,
But one to dance with![4] By heaven, I'll steal
  away.

---

[2] *That fame may cry you loud:*] So, in *Troilus and Cressida:*
  " ——*fame* with her *loud'st* O yes,
  " *Cries,* This is he." STEEVENS.

[3] —— *beware of being captives,*
  Before you serve.] The word *serve* is equivocal; the sense is,
Be not captives before you serve in the war. *Be not captives before
you are soldiers.* JOHNSON.

[4] ———— *and no sword worn,*
  But one to dance *with!*] It should be remembered that in
Shakspeare's time it was usual for gentlemen to dance with swords

1 Lord. There's honour in the theft.[5]

Par.   Commit it, count.[3]

2 Lord. I am your acceffary; and fo farewell.

Ber. I grow to you, and our parting is a tortured body.[6]

1 Lord. Farewell, captain.

2 Lord. Sweet monfieur Parolles!

Par. Noble heroes, my fword and yours are kin. Good fparks and luftrous, a word, good metals:—You fhall find in the regiment of the Spinii, one captain Spurio, with his cicatrice,[7] an emblem of

---

on.—Our author, who gave to all countries the manners of his own, has again alluded to this ancient cuftom in *Antony and Cleopatra:* Act III. fc. ix:

"———— He, at Philippi kept

" His fword, even like a *dancer.*"

See Mr. Steevens's note there. MALONE.

[5] ———— I'll *fteal* away.————

There's honour *in the theft.*] So, in *Macbeth:*

" There's *warrant* in that theft,

" Which *fteals* itfelf————." STEEVENS.

[6] *I grow to you, and our parting is a tortured body.*] I read thus—*Our parting is* the parting of *a tortured body.* Our parting is as the difruption of limbs torn from each other. Repetition of a word is often the caufe of miftakes: the eye glances on the wrong word, and the intermediate part of the fentence is omitted. JOHNSON.

So, in *K. Henry VIII.* Act II. fc. iii:

" ———— it is a fufferance, panging

" As foul and body's fevering." STEEVENS.

As they grow together, the tearing them afunder was torturing a body. Johnfon's amendment is unneceffary, M. MASON.

We two growing together, and having, as it were, but one body, (" like to a double cherry, feeming parted,") our parting is a tortured body; i. e. cannot be effected but by a difruption of limbs which are now common to both. MALONE.

[7] ———— with *his cicatrice,*] The old copy reads,—*his cicatrice with.* STEEVENS.

war, here on his finister cheek; it was this very
fword entrench'd it: fay to him, I live; and obferve
his reports for me.

2 *Lord.* We fhall, noble captain.

Par. Mars dote on you for his novices! [*Exeunt
Lords.*] What will you do?

Ber. Stay; the king—— [*Seeing him rife.*

Par. Ufe a more fpacious ceremony to the noble
lords; you have reftrain'd yourfelf within the lift
of too cold an adjeu: be more expreffive to them;
for they wear themfelves in the cap of the time,
there do mufter true gait, eat, fpeak, and move under the influence of the moft received ftar;[1] and

It is furprifing, none of the editors could fee that a flight
tranfpofition was abfolutely neceffary here, when there is not common fenfe in the paffage, as it ftands without fuch tranfpofition.
Parolles only means, " You fhall find one captain Spurio in the
camp, with a fcar on his left cheek, a mark of war that my fword
gave him." THEOBALD.

[1] ——*they wear themfelves in the cap of the time, there* do
mufter true gait, &c.] The main obfcurity of this paffage arifes
from the miftake of a fingle letter. We fhould read, inftead of, *do
mufter,* to *mufter.*—*To wear themfelves in the cap of the time,* fignifies
to be the foremoft in the fafhion: the figurative allufion is to the
gallantry then in vogue, of wearing jewels, flowers, and their
miftrefs's favours in their caps.—*There to mufter true gait,* fignifies
to affemble together in the high road of the fafhion. All the reft
is intelligible and eafy. WARBURTON.

I think this emendation cannot be faid to give much light to
the obfcurity of the paffage. Perhaps it might be read thus:——
They *do mufter* with the *true gait,* that is, they have the true military ftep. Every man has obferved fomething peculiar in the
ftrut of a foldier. JOHNSON.

Perhaps we fhould read—*mafter* true gait. To *mafter* any thing,
is to learn it perfectly. So, in *King Henry IV.* P. I:
     " As if he *mafter'd* there a double fpirit
     " Of teaching and of learning——."
Again, in *King Henry V:*
     " Between the promife of his greener days,
     " And thofe he *mafters* now."

though the devil lead the meafure,[9] fuch are to be
follow'd: after them, and take a more dilated farewell.

Ber. And I will do fo.

Par. Worthy fellows; and like to prove moft
finewy fword-men.

     [Exeunt BERTRAM *and* PAROLLES.

    Enter LAFEU.

Laf. Pardon, my lord, *[Kneeling.]* for me and
   for my tidings.

King. I'll fee thee to ftand up.

Laf.   Then here's a man
Stands, that has brought[2] his pardon. I would, you
Had kneel'd, my lord, to afk me mercy; and
That, at my bidding, you could fo ftand up.

King. I would I had; fo I had broke thy pate,
And afk'd thee mercy for't.

In this laft inftance, however, both the quartos, viz. 1600, and
1608, read *mufters.* STEEVENS.

The obfcurity of the paffage arifes only from the fantaftical
language of a character like Parolles, whofe affectation of wit
urges his imagination from one allufion to another, without
allowing time for his judgement to determine their congruity.
The *cap of time* being the firft image that occurs, *true gait,* manner
of *eating, fpeaking,* &c. are the feveral ornaments which they
mufter, place, or arrange in *time's cap.* This is done *under the
influence of the moft received ftar*; that is, the perfon in the higheft
repute for fetting the fafhions:—and though the devil were to lead
the meafure or *dance* of fafhion, fuch is their implicit fubmiffion,
that even he muft be followed. HENLEY.

9 —— *lead the* meafure,] i. e. the dance. So, in *Much ado
about Nothing,* Beatrice fays: " Tell him there is *meafure* in every
thing, and fo dance out the anfwer." STEEVENS.

2 —— *brought* —] Some modern editions read—*bought.*
              MALONE.

Laf.   Goodfaith, acrofs:[1]
But, my **good** lord, 'tis thus; Will you be cur'd
Of your infirmity?

King.   No.

Laf.   O, will you eat
No grapes, my royal fox? yes, but you will,
My noble grapes, an if my royal fox
Could reach them:[4] I have feen a medicine,[5]
That's able to breathe life into a ftone;
Quicken a rock, and make you dance canary,[6]
With fpritely fire and motion; whofe fimple touch[7]
Is powerful to araife king Pepin, nay,

[3] ——*acrofs:*] This word, as has been already obferved, is ufed when any pafs of wit mifcarries. JOHNSON.

While chivalry was in vogue, breaking fpears againft a quintain was a favourite exercife. He who fhivered the greateft number was efteemed the moft adroit; but then it was to be performed exactly with the point, for if atchieved by a fide-ftroke or *acrofs*, it fhowed unfkilfulnefs, and difgraced the practifer. Here, therefore, Lafeu reflects on the King's wit as aukward and ineffectual, and, in the terms of play, good for nothing. HOLT WHITE.

See *As you Like it*, Act III. fc. iv. p. 113. STEEVENS.

[4] ——*yes, but you will,*
My noble grapes, &c.] The words—*My noble grapes,* feem to Dr. Warburton and Sir T. Hanmer to ftand fo much in the way, that they have filently omitted them. They may be indeed rejected without great lofs, but I believe they are Shakfpeare's words. *You will eat,* fays Lafeu, *no grapes. Yes, but you will eat fuch noble grapes,* as I bring you, *if you could reach them.* JOHNSON.

[5] ——*medicine,*] is here put for a *fhe-phyfician.* HANMER.

[6] ——*and make you dance* canary,] Mr. Rich. Broome, in his comedy entitled, *The City Wit, or the Woman wears the Breeches,* Act IV. fc. i. mentions this among other dances: "As for corantoes, lavoltos, jigs, meafures, pavins, brawls, galliards or canaries; I fpeak it not fwellingly, but I fubfcribe to no man." Dr. GREY.

[7] ——*whofe fimple* touch, &c.] Thus, *Ovid,* Amor. III. vii. 41:
Illius ad tactum *Pylius juvenefcere poffit,*
Tithonofque annis fortior effe fuis. STEEVENS.

To give great Charlemain a pen in his hand,
And write [8] to her a love-line.

King.   What her is this?

Laf. Why, doctor she: My lord, there's one ar-
riv'd,
If you will see her,—now, by my faith and honour,
If seriously I may convey my thoughts
In this my light deliverance, I have spoke
With one, that, in her sex, her years, profession, [9]
Wisdom, and constancy, hath amaz'd me more
Than I dare blame my weakness: [2] Will you see her,
(For that is her demand,) and know her business?
That done, laugh well at me.

King.   Now, good Lafeu,
Bring in the admiration; that we with thee
May spend our wonder too, or take off thine,
By wond'ring how thou took'st it.

Laf.   Nay, I'll fit you,
And not be all day neither.   [*Exit* Lafeu.

King. Thus he his special nothing ever prologues.

---

[8] *And write —*] I believe a line preceding this has been lost.
                                        Malone.

[9] *—— her years,* profession,] By *profession* is meant her de-
claration of the end and purpose of her coming.
                                        Warburton.

[2] *Than I dare blame my weakness:*] This is one of Shakspeare's
perplexed expressions. " To acknowledge how much she has
astonished me, would be to acknowledge a weakness; and this I am
unwilling to do." Steevens.

Lafeu's meaning appears to me to be this:—" That the amaze-
ment she excited in him was so great, that he could not impute it
merely to his own weakness, but to the wonderful qualities of the
object that occasioned it." M. Mason.

Re-enter LAFEU, *with* HELENA.

LAF. Nay, come your ways.

KING.   This hafte hath wings indeed.

LAF. Nay, come your ways;
This is his majefty, fay your mind to him:
A traitor you do look like; but fuch traitors
His majefty feldom fears: I am Creffid's uncle,
That dare leave two together; fare you well.

                       [*Exit.*

KING. Now, fair one, does your bufinefs fol-
     low us?

HEL. Ay, my good lord. Gerard de Narbon was
My father; in what he did profefs, well found.[5]

KING. I knew him.

HEL. The rather will I fpare my praifes towards
     him;
Knowing him, is enough. On his bed of death
Many receipts he gave me; chiefly one,
Which, as the deareft iffue of his practice,
And of his old experience the only darling,
He bad me ftore up, as a triple eye,[6]
Safer than mine own two, more dear; I have fo:
And, hearing your high majefty is touch'd

---

[3] *——come your ways;*] This vulgarifm is alfo put into the mouth of *Polonius.* See *Hamlet*, Act I. fc. iii.
                    STEEVENS.

[4] *—— Creffid's uncle,*] I am like Pandarus. See *Troilus and Creffida.* JOHNSON.

[5] *—— well found.*] i. e. of known, acknowledged, excellence.
                    STEEVENS.

[6] *—— a* triple eye,] i. e. a *third* eye. STEEVENS.

With that malignant caufe wherein the honour
Of my dear father's gift ftands chief in power,[7]
I come to tender it, and my appliance,
With all bound humblenefs.

 KING.   We thank you, maiden;
But may not be fo credulous of cure,—
When our moft learned doctors leave us; and
The congregated college have concluded
That labouring art can never ranfom nature
From her inaidable eftate,—I fay we muft not
So ftain our judgement, or corrupt our hope,
To proftitute our paft-cure malady
To émpiricks; or to diffever fo
Our great felf and our credit, to efteem
A fenfelefs help, when help paft fenfe we deem.

 HEL. My duty then fhall pay me for my pains:
I will no more enforce mine office on you;
Humbly entreating from your royal thoughts
A modeft one, to bear me back again.

 KING. I cannot give thee lefs, to be call'd grateful:
Thou thought'ft to help me; and fuch thanks I give,
As one near death to thofe that wifh him live:
But, what at full I know, thou know'ft no part;
I knowing all my peril, thou no art.

 HEL. What I can do, can do no hurt to try,
Since you fet up your reft 'gainft remedy:
He that of greateft works is finifher,
Oft does them by the weakeft minifter:

---

[7] ———— wherein the honour
 Of my dear father's gift ftands chief in power,] Perhaps we may
better read:
   ———— wherein the power
 Of my dear father's gift ftands chief in honour.
              JOHNSON.

So holy writ in babes hath judgement fhown,
When judges have been babes.[6] Great floods have
    flown
From fimple fources; and great feas have dried,
When miracles have by the greateft been denied.[7]
Oft expectation fails, and moft oft there
Where moft it promifes; and oft it hits,
Where hope is coldeft, and defpair moft fits.[8]

[6] *So holy writ in babes hath judgement fhown,*
When judges have been babes.] The allufion is to St. Matthew's Gofpel, xi. 25. " O father, lord of heaven and earth, I thank thee, becaufe *thou haft hid thefe things from the wife and prudent, and revealed them unto babes.*" See alfo 1 Cor. i. 27. " But GOD hath chofen the foolifh things of the world to confound the wife; and GOD hath chofen the weak things of the world, to confound the things which are mighty." MALONE.

[7] *When miracles have by the greateft been denied.*] I do not fee the import or connection of this line. As the next line ftands without a correfpondent rhyme, I fufpect that fomething has been loft. JOHNSON.

I point the paffage thus; and then I fee no reafon to complain of want of connection:
When judges have been babes. Great floods, &c.
When miracles have by the greateft been denied.
Shakfpeare, after alluding to *the production of water from a rock,* and *the drying up of the Red Sea,* fays, that *miracles had been denied by the* GREATEST; or in other words, that the ELDERS of ISRAEL (who juft before, in reference to another text, were ftyled *judges*) had notwithftanding thefe miracles, wrought for their own prefervation, refufed that compliance they ought to have yielded. See the Book of Exodus, and particularly Ch. xvii. 5, 6, &c.
HENLEY.

So holy writ, &c. alludes to Daniel's judging, when " a young youth," the two Elders in the ftory of *Sufannah. Great floods,* i. e. when Mofes fmote the rock in Horeb, Exod. xvii.
———— *great feas have dry'd*
When miracles have by the greateft been deny'd.
Dr. Johnfon did *not fee the import or connection of this line.* It certainly refers to the children of Ifrael paffing the Red Sea, when miracles had been denied, or *not hearkened to,* by Pharaoh.
HOLT WHITE.

[8] ———— *and defpair moft* fits.] The old copy reads—*fhifts.* The correction was made by Mr. Pope. MALONE.

I

KING. I muſt not hear thee; fare thee well, kind
   maid;
Thy pains, not us'd, muſt by thyſelf be paid:
Proffers, not took, reap thanks for their reward.

HEL. Inſpired merit ſo by breath is barr'd:
It is not ſo with him that all things knows,
As 'tis with us that ſquare our gueſs by ſhows:
But moſt it is preſumption in us, when
The help of heaven we count the act of men.
Dear ſir, to my endeavours give conſent;
Of heaven, not me, make an experiment.
I am not an impoſtor, that proclaim
Myſelf againſt the level of mine aim; [9]
But know I think, and think I know moſt ſure,
My art is not paſt power, nor you paſt cure.

KING. Art thou ſo confident? Within what ſpace
Hop'ſt thou my cure?

HEL.   The greateſt grace lending grace, [1]
Ere twice the horſes of the ſun ſhall bring
Their fiery torcher his diurnal ring;
Ere twice in murk and occidental damp
Moiſt Heſperus hath quench'd his ſleepy lamp; [2]

---

 [9] *Myſelf againſt the level of mine aim;*] i. e. pretend to greater
things than befits the mediocrity of my condition.
             WARBURTON.

 I rather think that ſhe means ſo ſay,—*I am not an impoſtor that
proclaim* one thing and deſign another, *that proclaim* a cure and *aim*
at a fraud; I think what I ſpeak. JOHNSON.

 [1] *The greateſt* grace *lending* grace,] I ſhould have thought the
repetition of *grace* to have been ſuperfluous, if the *grace of grace*
had not occurred in the ſpeech with which the tragedy of *Macbeth*
concludes. STEEVENS.

 The former *grace* in this paſſage, and the latter in *Macbeth*,
evidently ſignify *divine grace*. HENLEY.

 [2] —— his *ſleepy lamp*;] Old copy—her *ſleepy lamp*. Corrected
by Mr. Rowe. MALONE.

       R 2

Or four and twenty times the pilot's glaſs
Hath told the thieviſh minutes how they paſs;
What is infirm from your ſound parts ſhall fly,
Health ſhall live free, and ſickneſs freely die.

King. Upon thy certainty and confidence,
What dar'ſt thou venture?

Hel.　　　　　　　　　　　　Tax of impudence,——
A ſtrumpet's boldneſs, a divulged ſhame,——
Traduc'd by odious ballads; my maiden's name
Sear'd otherwiſe; no worſe of worſt extended,
With vileſt torture let my life be ended.[4]

[4] —————— *a divulged ſhame,——*
Traduc'd by odious ballads; my maiden's name
Sear'd otherwiſe; no worſe of worſt extended,
　With vileſt torture let my life be endrd.] *I would bear* (ſays ſhe)
the tax of impudence, which is the denotement of a ſtrumpet; would
endure a ſhame reſulting from my failure in what I have undertaken,
and thence become the ſubject of odious ballads; let my maiden reputa
tion be otherwiſe branded; and, *no worſe of worſt* extended, i. e.
provided nothing worſe is offered to me, (meaning violation,) *let my life*
be ended with the worſt of tortures. The poet for the ſake of rhyme
has obſcured the ſenſe of the paſſage. *The worſt that can befal a*
woman, being extended to me, ſeems to be the meaning of the laſt
line. STEEVENS.

Tax of impudence, that is, to be charged with having the boldneſs
of a ſtrumpet:—*a divulged ſhame;* i. e. to be traduced by odious
ballads:—*my maiden name's ſeared otherwiſe;* i. e. to be ſtigmatized
as a proſtitute:—*no worſe of worſt extended;* i. e. to be ſo defamed
that nothing ſeverer can be ſaid againſt thoſe who are moſt publickly reported to be infamous. Shakſpeare has uſed the word
ſear and *extended* in *The Winter's Tale,* both in the ſame ſenſe as
above:
　　　　" —————— for calumny will *ſear*
　　　　" Virtue itſelf!"——
And " The report of her is *extended* more than can be thought."
　　　　　　　　　　　　　　　　　　　　　　HENLEY.

The old copy reads, not *no,* but *ne,* probably an error for *nay,*
or *the.* I would wiſh to read and point the latter part of the
paſſage thus:
　　　—————— *my maiden's name*
Sear'd otherwiſe; nay, worſt of worſt, extended
With vileſt torture, let my life be ended.

KING. Methinks, in thee fome bleffed fpirit doth
    fpeak;
His powerful found, within an organ weak: [5]
And what impoffibility would flay
In common fenfe, fenfe faves another way.[6]
Thy life is dear; for all, that life can rate
Worth name of life, in thee hath eftimate; [7]
Youth, beauty, wifdom, courage, virtue, all [8]
That happinefs and prime [9] can happy call:

i. e. Let me be otherwife branded;—and (what is *the worſt of
worſt*, the confummation of mifery,) my body being extended on
the rack by the moft cruel torture, let my life pay. the forfeit of
my prefumption.
  So, in Daniel's *Cleopatra*, 1594:
    " —— the *worſt of worſt* of ills."
No was introduced by the editor of the fecond folio.
Again, in *The Remedie of Love*, 4to. 1600:
    " If fhe be fat, then fhe is fwollen, fay,
    " If browne, then tawny as the Africk Moore;
    " If flender, leane, meagre and worne away,
    " If courtly, wanton, *worſt of worſt* before." MALONE.

  [5] *Methinks, in thee fome bleffed fpirit doth fpeak;
  His* powerful found, *within an organ weak:*] The verb, *doth
fpeak*, in the firft line, fhould be underſtood to be repeated in the
conftruction of the fecond, thus:

    His powerful found fpeaks *within a weak organ.* HEATH.

  This, in my opinion, is a very juft and happy explanation.
                     STEEVENS.

  [6] *And what impoffibility would flay
  In common fenfe, fenfe faves another way.*] i. e. and that which,
if I trufted to my reafon, I fhould think impoffible, I yet, perceiving
thee to be actuated by fome bleffed fpirit, think thee capable of
effecting, MALONE.

  [7] —— *in thee hath* eftimate;] May be *counted* among the gifts
enjoyed by thee. JOHNSON.

  [8] *Youth, beauty, wifdom, courage*, virtue, *all*—] The old copy
omits *virtue*. It was fupplied by Dr. Warburton, to remedy a
defect in the meafure. STEEVENS.

  [9] —*prime*—] Youth; the fpring or morning of life. JOHNSON.
  Should we not read—*pride?* Dr. Johnfon explains *prime* to
mean *youth*; and indeed I do not fee any other plaufible interpre-

Thou this to hazard, needs muſt intimate
Skill infinite, or monſtrous deſperate.
Sweet practiſer, thy phyſick I will try;
That miniſters thine own death, if I die.

   HEL. If I break time, or flinch in property[a]
Of what I ſpoke, unpitied let me die;
And well-deſerv'd: Not helping, death's my fee;
But, if I help, what do you promiſe me?

   KING. Make thy demand.

   HEL.   But will you make it even?

   KING. Ay, by my ſceptre, and my hopes of heaven.[b]

---

tation that can be given of it. But how does that ſuit with the context? " You have all that is worth the name of life; *youth*, beauty, &c. all. That happineſs and *youth* can happy call."— *Happineſs and pride* may ſignify, I think, *the pride of happineſs*; the proudeſt ſtate of happineſs. So, in *The Second Part of Henry IV.* Act III. ſc. i. *the voice and echo*, is put for *the voice of echo*, or, *the echoing voice.* TYRWHITT.

I think, with Dr. Johnſon, that *prime* is here uſed as a ſubſtantive, but that it means, that *ſprightly vigour* which uſually accompanies us in the prime of life. So, in Montaigne's *Eſſaies*, tranſlated by Florio, 1603, B. II. c. 6: " Many things ſeeme greater by imagination, than by effect. I have paſſed over a good part of my age in ſound and perfect health. I ſay, not only ſound, but blithe and wantonly-luſtful. That ſtate, full of luſt, of *prime* and mirth, made me deeme the conſideration of ſickneſſes ſo yrkſome, that when I came to the experience of them, I have found their fits but weak." MALONE.

   [a] —— *in* property —] In *property* ſeems to be here uſed, with much laxity, for—*in the due performance.* In a ſubſequent paſſage it ſeems to mean either a thing poſſeſſed, or a ſubject diſcriminated by peculiar qualities:

   " The *property* by what it is ſhould go,
   " Not by the title." MALONE.

   [b] *Ay, by my ſceptre, and my hopes of* heaven.] The old copy reads:

   —————— *my hopes of* help. STEEVENS.

 The King could have but a very ſlight hope of *help* from her, ſcarce enough to ſwear by: and therefore Helen might ſuſpect he

Hel. Then fhalt thou give me, with thy kingly
    hand,
What bufband in thy power I will command:
Exempted be from me the arrogance
To choofe from forth the royal blood of France;
My low and humble name to propagate
With any branch or image of thy ftate:[4]
But fuch a one, thy vaffal, whom I know
Is free for me to afk, thee to beftow.

King. Here is my hand; the premifes obferv'd,
Thy will by my performance fhall be ferv'd:
So make the choice of thy own time; for I,
Thy refolv'd patient, on thee ftill rely.
More fhould I queftion thee, and more I muft;
Though, more to know, could not be more to truft;
From whence thou cam'ft, how tended on,—But
    reft
Unqueftion'd welcome, and undoubted bleft.—

meant to equivocate with her. Befides, obferve, the greateft part
of the fcene is ftrictly in rhyme: and there is no fhadow of reafon
why it fhould be interrupted here. I rather imagine the poet
wrote:
    Ay, by my fceptre, and my hopes of heaven. THIRLBY.

[4] *With any* branch *or* image *of thy ftate:*] Shakfpeare unquef-
tionably wrote *impage,* grafting. *Impe,* a graff, or flip, or fucker:
by which fhe means one of the fons of France, Caxton calls our
Prince Arthur, *that noble* impe *of fame.* WARBURTON.

Image is furely the true reading, and may mean any reprefenta-
tive of thine; i. e. any one who refembles you as being related to
your family, or as a prince reflects any part of your ftate and
majefty. There is no fuch word as *impage*; and, as Mr. M. Mafon
obferves, were fuch a one coined, it would mean nothing but the
art of grafting. Mr. Henley adds, that *branch* refers to the collateral defcendants of the royal blood, and *image* to the direct and
immediate line. STEEVENS.

    Our author again ufes the word *image* in the fame fenfe as here,
in his *Rape of Lucrece:*
    " O, from thy cheeks my *image* thou haft torn."
                                 MALONE.

Give me fome help here, ho!—If thou proceed
As high as word, my deed fhall match thy deed.

[*Flourifh. Exeunt.*

S C E N E II.

Roufillon.　*A Room in the Countefs's Palace.*

Enter Countefs *and* Clown.

Count. Come on, fir; I fhall now put you to the
height of your breeding.

Clo. I will fhow myfelf highly fed, and lowly
taught: I know my bufinefs is but to the court.

Count. To the court! why, what place make
you fpecial, when you put off that with fuch contempt? But to the court!

Clo. Truly, madam, if God have lent a man any
manners, he may eafily put it off at court: he that
cannot make a leg, put off's cap, kifs his hand,
and fay nothing, has neither leg, hands, lip, nor
cap; and, indeed, fuch a fellow, to fay precifely,
were not for the court: but, for me, I have an anfwer will ferve all men.

Count. Marry, that's a bountiful anfwer, that
fits all queftions.

Clo. It is like a barber's chair, that fits all but-
tocks; the pin-buttock, the quatch-buttock, the
brawn-buttock, or any buttock.

---

⁵ *It is like a* barber's chair, &c.] This expreffion is proverbial.
See Ray's *Proverbs.*
So, in *More Fooles Yet,* by R. S. a collection of Epigrams. 4to.
1610:

Count. Will your answer serve fit to all queftions?

Clo. As fit as ten groats is for the hand of an
attorney, as your French crown for your taffata
punk, as Tib's rush for Tom's fore-finger,[6] as

> " Moreover fattin futes he doth compare
> " Unto the fervice of a *barber's chayre*;
> " As fit for every Jacke and journeyman,
> " As for a knight or worthy gentleman." STEEVENS.

[6] ——Tib's rush *for* Tom's fore-finger,] *Tom* is the man, and by
Tib we are to underftand the woman, and therefore, more properly
we might read—Tom's *rush for*, &c. The allufion is to an ancient
practice of marrying with a rush ring, as well in other countries as
in England. Breval, in his *Antiquities of Paris*, mentions it as a
kind of efpoufal ufed in France, by fuch perfons as meant to live
together in a ftate of concubinage: but in England it was fcarce
ever practifed except by defigning men, for the purpofe of cor-
rupting thofe young women to whom they pretended love.
    Richard Poore, bifhop of Salifbury, in his *Conftitutions, anni*,
1217, forbids the putting of *rush rings*, or any the like matter, on
women's fingers, in order to the debauching them more readily:
and he infinuates as the reafon of the prohibition, that there were
fome people weak enough to believe, that what was thus done in
jeft. was a real marriage.
    But notwithftanding this cenfure on it, the practice was not abo-
lifhed; for it is alluded to in a fong in a play written by fir William
D'Avenant, called *The Rivals :*
> " I'll crown thee with a garland of ftraw then,
> " And I'll marry thee with a *rush ring."*
which fong, by the way, was firft fung by Mifs Davis; fhe acted
the part of Celania in the play; and King Charles II. upon hearing it, was fo pleafed with her voice and action, that he took her
from the ftage, and made her his miftrefs.
    Again, in the fong called *The Winchefter Wedding*, in D'Urfey's
Pills to purge Melancholy, Vol. I. p. 276:
> " Pert Strephon was kind to Betty,
>   " And blithe as a bird in the fpring;
> " And Tommy was fo to Katy,
>   " And wedded her with a *rush ring."* SIR J. HAWKINS.

    Tib and *Tom*, in plain Englifh, I believe, ftand for *wanton*
and *rogue*. So, in *Churchyard's Choife :*
> " Tufhe, that's a toye; let *Tomkin* talke of *Tibb.*"

a pancake for Shrove-tuefday, a morris for May-day, as the nail to his hole, the cuckold to his horn, as a fcolding quean to a wrangling knave, as the nun's lip to the friar's mouth; nay, as the pudding to his fkin.

Again, in the *Queenes Majeflies Entertainment in Suffolk and Nor-folk*, &c. by Tho. Churchyard, 4to. no date:

Cupid.
" And doth not *Jove* and *Mars* bear fway? Tufh, that is true."
Philofopher.
" Then put in *Tom* and *Tibbe*, and all beares fway as much as you." STEEVENS.

An anonymous writer, [Mr. Ritfon,] with fome probability, fuppofes that this is one of thofe covert allufions in which Shakfpeare frequently indulges himfelf. The following lines of Cleiveland on an *Hermaphrodite* feem to countenance the fuppofition:
" Nay, thofe which modefty can mean,
" But dare not fpeak, are Epicene.
" That gamefter needs muft overcome,
" That can play both with *Tib* and *Tom*."
Sir John Hawkins would read—" as *Tom's* rufh for *Tib's* fore-finger." But if this were the author's meaning, it would be necef-fary to alter ftill farther, and to read—As *Tom's* rufh for Tib's *fourth* finger. MALONE.

At the game of Gleek, the ace was called *Tib*, and the knave *Tom*; and this is the proper explanation of the lines cited from Cleiveland. The practice of marrying with a *rufh ring* mentioned by Sir john Hawkins is very queftionable, and it might be difficult to find any authority in fupport of this opinion. DOUCE.

Sir John Hawkins's alteration is unneceffary. It was the practice in former times for the woman to give the man a ring as well as for the man to give her one. So, in the laft fcene of *Twelfth Night*, the prieft giving an account of Olivia's marriage, fays, it was
" Attefted by the holy clofe of lips,
" Strengthen'd by *enterchangement of your rings*."
M. MASON.

I believe what many of us have afferted refpecting the exchange of rings in the *marriage ceremony*, is only true of the *marriage contract*, in which fuch a practice undoubtedly prevailed.
STEEVENS.

Count. Have you, I fay, an anfwer of fuch fit-
nefs for all queftions?

Clo. From below your duke, to beneath your
conftable, it will fit any queftion.

Count. It muft be an anfwer of moft monftrous
fize, that muft fit all demands.

Clo. But a trifle neither, in good faith, if the
learned fhould fpeak truth of it: here it is, and all
that belongs to't: Afk me, if I am a courtier; it
fhall do you no harm to learn.

Count. To be young again,' if we could:—I will
be a fool in queftion, hoping to be the wifer by
your anfwer. I pray you, fir, are you a courtier?

Clo. O Lord, fir,'——There's a fimple putting
off;—more, more, a hundred of them.

Count. Sir, I am a poor friend of yours, that
loves you.

Clo. O Lord, fir,—Thick, thick, fpare not me.

Count. I think, fir, you can eat none of this
homely meat.

Clo. O Lord, fir,—Nay, put me to't, I warrant
you.

Count. You were lately whipp'd, fir, I think.

Clo. O Lord, fir,—Spare not me.

---

⁷ *To be young again,*] The lady cenfures her own levity in
trifling with her jefter, as a ridiculous attempt to return back to
youth. JOHNSON.

⁸ *O Lord, fir,*] A ridicule on that foolifh expletive of fpeech
then in vogue at court. WARBURTON.

Thus Clove and Orange, in *Every Man out of his Humour:*
    " You conceive me, fir?——O Lord, fir!"
Cleiveland, in one of his fongs, makes his Gentleman—
    " Anfwer, O Lord, fir! and talk *play-book* oaths."
                             FARMER.

Count. Do you cry, *O Lord, fir*, at your whipping, and *spare not me?* Indeed, your *O Lord, fir,* is very fequent to your whipping; you would anfwer very well to a whipping, if you were but bound to't.

Clo. I ne'er had worfe luck in my life, in my— *O Lord, fir:* I fee, things may ferve long, but not ferve ever.

Count. I play the noble houfewife with the time, to entertain it fo merrily with a fool.

Clo. O Lord, fir,—Why, there't ferves well again.

Count. An end, fir, to your bufinefs: Give Helen
          this,
And urge her to a prefent anfwer back:
Commend me to my kinfmen, and my fon;
This is not much.

Clo. Not much commendation to them.

Count. Not much employment for you: You underftand me?

Clo. Moft fruitfully; I am there before my legs.

Count. Hafte you again.   [*Exeunt feverally.*

SCENE III.

Paris.   *A Room in the King's Palace.*

Enter BERTRAM, LAFEU, *and* PAROLLES.

Laf. They fay, miracles are paft; and we have our philofophical perfons, to make modern [9] and

---

[9] —— *modern*—] i. e. common, ordinary. So, in *As you Like it:*
      " Full of wife faws, and *modern* inftances."
Again, in another play: [*All's well*, &c. Act V. fc. iii.] " —with her *modern* grace—." MALONE.

familiar things, supernatural and causeless. Hence is it, that we make trifles of terrors; ensconcing ourselves into seeming knowledge,[9] when we should submit ourselves to an unknown fear.[2]

PAR. Why, 'tis the rarest argument of wonder, that hath shot out in our latter times.

BER. And so 'tis.

LAF. To be relinquish'd of the artists,——

PAR. So I say; both of Galen and Paracelsus.

LAF. Of all the learned and authentick fellows,[3]——

---

[9] ——ensconcing *ourselves* into *seeming knowledge*,] To *ensconce* literally signifies to secure as in a fort. So, in *The Merry Wives of Windsor:* " I will *ensconce* me behind the arras." *Into* (a frequent practice with old writers) is used for *in*. STEEVENS.

[2] ——*unknown* fear.] *Fear* is here an object of fear. JOHNSON.

[3] Par. *So I say; both of Galen and Paracelsus.*

Laf. *Of all the* learned *and* authentick *fellows*,] Shakspeare, as I have often observed, never throws out his words at random. Paracelsus, though no better than an ignorant and knavish enthusiast, was at this time in such vogue, even amongst the learned, that he had almost justled Galen and the ancients out of credit. On this account *learned* is applied to Galen, and *authentick* or fashionable to Paracelsus. Sancy, in his *Confession Catholique*, p. 301. Ed. Col. 1720, is made to say: " *Je trouve la Riviere premier medecin, de meilleure humeur que ces gens-la. Il est bon* Galeniste, *& tres bon* Paracelsiste. *Il dit que la doctrine de* Galien *est honorable, & non mesprisable pour la pathologie, & profitable pour les boutiques. L'autre, pourveu que ce soit de vrais preceptes de* Paracelse, *est* bonne à suivre pour la verité, pour la subtilité, pour l'espargne; en somme pour la Therapeutique." WARBURTON.

As the whole merriment of this scene consists in the pretensions of Parolles to knowledge and sentiments which he has not, I believe here are two passages in which the words and sense are bestowed upon him by the copies, which the author gave to Lafeu. I read this passage thus:
Laf. *To be relinquished of the artists*——
Par. *So I say.*
Laf. *Both of Galen and Paracelsus, of all the learned and authentick fellows*——
Par. *Right, so I say.* JOHNSON.

Par. Right, so I say.

Laf. That gave him out incurable,—

Par. Why, there 'tis; so say I too.

Laf. Not to be help'd,—

Par. Right; as 'twere, a man assur'd of an—

Laf. Uncertain life, and sure death.

Par. Just, you say well; so would I have said.

Laf. I may truly say, it is a novelty to the world.

Par. It is, indeed: if you will have it in showing, you shall read it in,——What do you call there?⁴—

Laf. A sbowing of a heavenly effect in an earthly actor.⁵

Par. That's it I would have said; the very same.

Laf. Why, your dolphin is not lustier:⁶ 'fore me I speak in respect——

——authentick *fellows*,] The phrase of the diploma is, *authentice* licentiatus. Musgrave.

The epithet *authentick* was in our author's time particularly applied to the learned. So, in Drayton's *Owle*, 4to. 1604:

" For which those grave and still *authentick* sages,
" Which sought for knowledge in those golden ages,
" From whom we hold the science that we have," &c.
                                                        Malone.

⁴ Par. *It is, indeed: if you will have it in sbowing,* &c.] We should read, I think: *It is, indeed, if you will have it a sbowing—you shall read it in what do you call there.*— Tyrwhitt.

Does not, *if you will have it* IN *sbowing,* signify IN a demonstration or statement of the case? Henley.

⁵ *A sbowing of a heavenly effect,* &c.] The title of some pamphlet here ridiculed. Warburton.

⁶ *Why, your* dolphin *is not lustier:*] By *dolphin* is meant the *dauphin*, the heir apparent, and the hope of the crown of France. His title is so translated in all the old books. Steevens.

Par. Nay, 'tis ſtrange, 'tis very ſtrange, that is the brief and the tedious of it; and he is of a moſt facinorous ſpirit,[7] that will not acknowledge it to be the——

Laf. Very hand of heaven.

Par. Ay, ſo I ſay.

Laf. In a moſt weak——

Par. And debile miniſter, great power, great tranſcendence: which ſhould, indeed, give us a further uſe to be made, than alone the recovery of the king,[8] as to be——

Laf. Generally thankful.

What Mr. Steevens obſerves is certainly true; and yet the additional word *your* induces me to think that by *dolphin* in the paſſage before us the fiſh ſo called was meant. Thus in *Antony and Cleopatra:*

"——————His delights
" Were *dolphin*-like; they ſhow'd his back above
" The element he liv'd in."

Lafeu, who is an old courtier, if he had meant the king's ſon, would ſurely have ſaid—" *the* dolphin." I uſe the old ſpelling.

MALONE.·

In the colloquial language of Shakſpeare's time *your* was frequently employed as it is in this paſſage: So, in *Hamlet*, the Gravedigger obſerves, that " *your* water is a ſore decayer of *your* whorſon dead body." Again, in *As you Like it:* " *Your* if is the only peacemaker." STEEVENS.

[7] ——facinorous *ſpirit*,] This word is uſed in Heywood's *Engliſh Traveller,* 1633:

" And magnified for high *facinorous* deeds."

Facinorous is wicked. The old copy ſpells the word *facinerious*; but as Parolles is not deſigned for a verbal blunderer, I have adhered to the common ſpelling. STEEVENS.

[8] —— *which ſhould, indeed, give us a further uſe to be made,* &c.] I believe Parolles has again uſurped words and ſenſe to which he has no right; and I read this paſſage thus:

Laf. *In a moſt weak and debile miniſter, great power, great tranſcendence; which ſhould, indeed, give us a further uſe to be made than the mere recovery of the king.*

Par. *As to be——*

Laf. *Generally thankful.* JOHNSON.

Enter King, HELENA, and Attendants.

PAR. I would have faid it; you fay well: Here
comes the king.

LAF. Luftick, as the Dutchman fays:[9] I'll like
a maid the better, whilft I have a tooth in my head:
Why, he's able to lead her a coranto.

PAR. Mort du Vinaigre! Is not this Helen?

LAF. 'Fore God, I think fo.

KING. Go, call before me all the lords in court.——
　　　　　　　　　　　　[Exit an Attendant.
Sit, my preferver, by thy patient's fide;
And with this healthful hand, whofe banifh'd fenfe
Thou haft repeal'd, a fecond time receive
The confirmation of my promis'd gift,
Which but attends thy naming.

When the parts are written out for players, the names of the
characters which they are to reprefent are never fet down; but only
the laft words of the preceding fpeech which belongs to their
partner in the fcene. If the plays of Shakfpeare were printed (as
there is good reafon to fufpect) from thefe piece-meal tranfcripts,
how eafily may the miftake be accounted for, which Dr. Johnfon
has judicioufly ftrove to remedy? STEEVENS.

[9] Luftick, *as the Dutchman fays:*] *Luftigh* is the Dutch word for
lufty, chearful, pleafant. It is ufed in *Hans Beer-pot's Invifible
Comedy*, 1618:
　　　"————can walk a mile or two
　　"As *luftique* as a hoor————."
Again, in *The Witches of Lancafhire*, by Heywood and Broome,
1634:
　　　"What all *luftick*, all frolickfome!"
The burden alfo of one of our ancient *Medleys* is
　　　"Hey *Lufticke*." STEEVENS.

In the narrative of the cruelties committed by the Dutch at
Amboyna, in 1622, it is faid, that after a night fpent in prayer, &c.
by fome of the prifoners, "the Dutch that guarded them offered
them wine, bidding them drink *luftick*, and drive away the forrow,
according to the cuftom of their own nation." REED.

Enter several Lords.

Fair maid, fend forth thine eye: this youthful parcel
Of noble bachelors ftand at my beftowing,
O'er whom both fovereign power and father's voice [2]
I have to ufe: thy frank election make;
Thou haft power to choofe, and they none to for-
    fake.

HEL. To each of you one fair and virtuous mif-
    trefs
Fall, when love pleafe!—marry, to each, but one! [3]

LAF. I'd give bay Curtal, [4] and his furniture,
My mouth no more were broken [5] than thefe boys',
And writ as little beard.

KING.   Perufe them well:
Not one of thofe, but had a noble father.

---

[2] *O'er whom both fovereign power and* father's *voice*—] They
were his *wards* as well as his fubjects. HENLEY.

[3] ——*marry, to each,* but one!] I cannot underftand this paffage
in any other fenfe, than as a ludicrous exclamation, in confequence
of Helena's wifh of *one* fair and virtuous miftrefs *to each* of the
lords. If that be fo, it cannot belong to Helena; and might
properly enough be given to Parolles. TYRWHITT.

Tyrwhitt's obfervations on this paffage are not conceived with
his ufual fagacity. He miftakes the import of the words *but one,*
which does not mean *one only,* but *except one.*
Helena wifhes a fair and virtuous miftrefs to each of the young
lords who were prefent, one only excepted; and the perfon excepted is Bertram, whofe miftrefs fhe hoped fhe herfelf fhould be;
and fhe makes the exception out of modefty: for otherwife the
defcription of a fair and virtuous miftrefs would have extended to
herfelf. M. MASON.

[4] ——*bay Curtal,*] i. e. a bay, dock'd horfe. STEEVENS.

[5] *My mouth no more were* broken—] A *broken mouth* is a mouth
which has loft part of its teeth. JOHNSON.

VOL. VI.   S

Hel. Gentlemen,
Heaven hath, through me, reftor'd the king to
    health.

All. We underftand it, and thank heaven for
    you.

Hel. I am a fimple maid ; and therein wealthieft,
That, I proteft, I fimply am a maid :——
Pleafe it your majefty, I have done already :
The blufhes in my cheeks thus whifper me,
We blufh, that thou fhould'ft choofe; but, be refus'd,
Let the white death fit on thy cheek for ever ;
We'll ne'er come there again.[6]

King.   Make choice; and, fee,
Who fhuns thy love, fhuns all his love in me.

Hel. Now, Dian, from thy altar do I fly;
And to imperial Love, that god moft high,
Do my fighs ftream.—Sir, will you hear my fuit ?

1 Lord. And grant it.

Hel.   Thanks, fir; all the reft is mute.[7]

---

[6] *We blufh, that thou fhould'ft choofe; but, be refus'd,*
    Let the white death, &c.] In the original copy, thefe lines are
pointed thus :
    We blufh that thou fhould'ft choofe, but be refus'd;
    Let the white death fit on thy cheek for ever; &c.
This punctuation has been adopted in all the fubfequent editions.
The prefent regulation of the text appears to me to afford a much
clearer fenfe. " My blufhes, (fays Helen,) thus whifper me. We
blufh that thou fhould'ft have the nomination of thy hufband.
However, choofe him at thy peril. But, if thou be refufed, let
thy cheeks be for ever pale ; we will never revifit them again."
    The blufhes, which are here perfonified, could not be fuppofed
to know that Helena would be refufed, as, according to the former
punctuation, they appear to do ; and, even if the poet had meant
this, he would furely have written " —and be refufed," not
" — but be refufed."
    Be refus'd means the fame as—" thou being refufed,"—or, " be
thou refufed." MALONE.
   [7] *The* white death *is the* chlorofis. JOHNSON.

Laf. I had rather be in this choice, than throw ames-ace[8] for my life.

Hel. The honour, fir, that flames in your fair
eyes,
Before I fpeak, too threatningly replies:
Love make your fortunes twenty times above
Her that fo wifhes, and her humble love!

2 *Lord.* No better, if you pleafe.

Hel.   My wifh receive,
Which great love grant! and fo I take my leave.

Laf. Do all they deny her[9]? An they were fons
of mine, I'd have them whipp'd; or I would fend
them to the Turk, to make eunuchs of.

Hel. Be not afraid [*To a* Lord.] that I your hand
fhould take;
I'll never do you wrong for your own fake:
Bleffing upon your vows! and in your bed
Find fairer fortune, if you ever wed!

Laf. Thefe boys are boys of ice, they'll none
have her: fure, they are baftards to the Englifh;
the French ne'er got them.

Hel. You are too young, too happy, and too good,
To make yourfelf a fon out of my blood.

4 *Lord.* Fair one, I think not fo.

---

[7] ——*all* the reft is mute.] i. e. I have no more to fay to you. So, Hamlet: " ——*the reft is filence.*" STEEVENS.

[8] ——*ames-ace*—] i. e. the loweft chance of the dice. So, in *The Ordinary*, by Cartwright: " ——may I at my laft ftake, &c. throw *ames-aces* thrice together." STEEVENS.

[9] Laf. *Do all they deny her?*] None of them have yet denied her, or deny her afterwards but Bertram. The fcene muft be fo regulated that Lafeu and Parolles talk at a diftance, where they may fee what paffes between Helena and the lords, but not hear it, fo that they know not by whom the refufal is made.
                                                            ·JOHNSON.

LAF. There's one grape yet,[1]—I am sure, thy fa‑
ther drank wine.—But if thou be'st not an aſs, I
am a youth of fourteen; I have known thee already.

HEL. I dare not say, I take you; [*To* BERTRAM.]
        but I give
Me, and my ſervice, ever whilſt I live,
Into your guiding power.—This is the man.

KING. Why then, young Bertram, take her, ſhe's
        thy wife.

BER. My wife, my liege? I ſhall beſeech your
        highneſs,
In ſuch a buſineſs give me leave to uſe
The help of mine own eyes.

KING.   •   Know'ſt thou not, Bertram,
What ſhe has done for me?

BER.   Yes, my good lord;
But never hope to know why I ſhould marry her.

KING. Thou know'ſt, ſhe has rais'd me from my
        ſickly bed.

BER. But follows it, my lord, to bring me down
Muſt anſwer for your raiſing? I know her well;
She had her breeding at my father's charge:
A poor phyſician's daughter my wife!—Diſdain
Rather corrupt me ever!

---

[1] *There's one grape yet,*] This ſpeech the three laſt editors
[Theobald, Hanmer, and Warburton,] have perplexed themſelves
by dividing between Lafeu and Parolles, without any authority
of copies, or any improvement of ſenſe. I have reſtored the old
reading, and ſhould have thought no explanation neceſſary, but
that Mr. Theobald apparently miſunderſtood it.

Old Lafeu having, upon the ſuppoſition that the lady was refuſed,
reproached the young lords as *boys of ice*, throwing his eyes on
Bertram who remained, cries out, *There is one yet into whom his
father put good blood——but I have known thee long enough to know
thee for an aſs.* JOHNSON.

KING. 'Tis only title³ thou difdain'ft in her, the
 ' which
I can build up. Strange is it, that our bloods,
Of colour, weight, and heat,⁴ pour'd all together,
Would quite confound diftinction, yet ftand off
In differences fo mighty : If fhe be
All that is virtuous, (fave what thou diflik'ft,
A poor phyfician's daughter,) thou diflik'ft
Of virtue for the name : but do not fo :
From loweft place when virtuous things proceed,⁵
The place is dignified by the doer's deed :
Where great additions fwell,⁶ and virtue none,
It is a dropfied honour : good alone
Is good, without a name ; vilenefs is fo :⁷
The property by what it is fhould go,

---

³ *'Tis only title*—] i. e. the want of title. MALONE.

⁴ *Of colour, weight, and heat,*] That is, which are of *the fame*
colour, weight, &c. MALONE.

⁵ *From loweft place* when *virtuous things proceed,*] The old copy
has—*whence.* This eafy correction [*when*] was prefcribed by
Dr. Thirlby. THEOBALD.

⁶ *Where great* additions *fwell,*] *Additions* are the titles and de-
fcriptions by which men are diftinguifhed from each other.
              MALONE.

⁷ ———*good alone*
Is good, without a name ; vilenefs is fo :] Shakfpeare may mean,
that external circumftances have no power over the real nature of
things. *Good alone* (i. e. by itfelf) *without a name* (i. e. without
the addition of titles) *is good. Vilenefs is fo* (i. e. is itfelf.) Either
of them is what its name implies :
  " The property by what it is fhould go,
  " Not by the title———."
  " Let's write good angel on the devil's horn,
  " 'Tis not the devil's creft." *Meafure for Meafure.*
              STEEVENS.
Steevens's laft interpretation of this paffage is very near being
right ; but I think it fhould be pointed thus :
  ———*good alone*
  Is good ;—without a name, vilenefs is fo.
Meaning that good is good without any addition, and vilenefs

Not by the title. She is young, wife, fair;
In these to nature she's immediate heir;[8]
And these breed honour: that is honour's scorn,
Which challenges itself as honour's born,
And is not like the fire:[9] Honours best thrive,[2]
When rather from our acts we them derive
Than our fore-goers: the mere word's a slave,
Debauch'd on every tomb; on every grave,
A lying trophy; and as oft is dumb,
Where dust, and damn'd oblivion, is the tomb

would still be vileness, though we had no such name to distinguish
it by. A similar expression occurs in *Macbeth*:
  " Though all things foul would wear the brows of grace,
  " Yet grace must still look *so*."
That is, grace would still be grace, as vileness would still be
vileness. M. MASON.

The meaning is,—Good is good, independent on any worldly
distinction or title: so vileness is vile, in whatever state it may
appear. MALONE.

[8] *In these to nature she's* immediate heir;] To be *immediate heir*
is to inherit without any intervening transmitter: thus she inherits
beauty *immediately* from *nature*, but honour is transmitted by an-
cestors. JOHNSON.

[9] ———— *that is honour's scorn,*
Which challenges itself as honour's born,
And is not like the fire:] Perhaps we might read more elegantly—
as *honour-born,*—honourably descended: the child of honour.
                                    MALONE.
Honour's born, is the *child* of honour. *Born* is here used, as
bairn still is in the North. HENLEY.

[2] *And is not like the fire: Honours* best *thrive, &c.*] The first
folio omits—*best*; but the second folio supplies it, as it is necessary
to enforce the sense of the passage, and complete its measure.
                                    STEEVENS.

The modern editors read—*Honours* best *thrive*; in which they
have followed the editor of the second folio, who introduced the
word *best* unnecessarily; not observing that *fire* was used by our
author, like *fire*, *hour*, &c. as a dissyllable. MALONE.

Where is an example of *fire*, used as a dissyllable, to be found?
Fire and *hour* were anciently written *fier* and *bower*; and conse-
quently the concurring vowels could be separated in pronunciation.
                                    STEEVENS.

Of honour'd bones indeed. What fhould be faid?
If thou canft like this creature as a maid,
I can create the reft : virtue, and fhe,
Is her own dower; honour, and wealth, from me.

Ber. I cannot love her, nor will ftrive to do't.

King. Thou wrong'ft thyfelf, if thou fhould'ft
    ftrive to choofe.

Hel. That you are well reftor'd, my lord, I am glad;
Let the reft go.

King. My honour's at the ftake ; which to defeat,
I muft produce my power:[3] Here, take her hand,
Proud fcornful boy, unworthy this good gift ;
That doft in vile mifprifion fhackle up
My love, and her defert ; that canft not dream,
We, poizing us in her defective fcale,
Shall weigh thee to the beam;[4] that wilt not know,

---

[3] *My honour's at the ftake ; which to* defeat,
    I muft produce my power :] The poor King of France is again
made a man of Gotham, by our unmerciful editors. For he is
not to make ufe of his authority to *defeat*, but to *defend*, his
honour. THEOBALD.

Had Mr. Theobald been aware that the *implication* or *claufe* of
the fentence (as the grammarians fay) ferved for the antecedent
" Which *danger* to *defeat*," there had been no need of his wit or
his alteration. FARMER.

Notwithftanding Mr. Theobald's pert cenfure of former editors
for retaining the word *defeat*, I fhould be glad to fee it reftored
again, as I am perfuaded it is the true reading. The French
verb *defaire* (from whence our *defeat*) fignifies *to free, to difem-
barrafs*, as well as *to deftroy*. *Defaire un nœud*, is *to untie a knot* ;
and in this fenfe, I apprehend, *defeat* is here ufed. It may be
obferved, that our verb *undo* has the fame varieties of fignification;
and I fuppofe even Mr. Theobald would not have been much
puzzled to find the fenfe of this paffage, if it had been written;—
My honour's at the ftake, which to undo *I muft produce my power.*
                                  TYRWHITT.

[4] ———— *that canft not dream,*
  We, poizing us in her defective fcale,
  Shall weigh thee to the beam;] That canft not underftand, that

It is in us to plant thine honour, where
We pleafe to have it grow : Check thy contempt:
Obey our will, which travails in thy good :
Believe not thy difdain, but prefently
Do thine own fortunes that obedient right,
Which both thy duty owes, and our power claims ;
Or I will throw thee from my care for ever,
Into the ftaggers,⁵ and the carelefs lapfe
Of youth and ignorance ; both my revenge and hate,
Loofing upon thee in the name of juftice,
Without all terms of pity : Speak ; thine anfwer.

Ber. Pardon, my gracious lord ; for I fubmit
My fancy to your eyes : When I confider,
What great creation, and what dole of honour,
Flies where you bid it, I find, that fhe, which late
Was in my nobler thoughts moft bafe, is now
The praifed of the king ; who, fo ennobled,
Is, as 'twere, born fo.

King.   Take her by the hand,
And tell her, fhe is thine : to whom I promife
A counterpoize ; if not to thy eftate,
A balance more replete.

Ber.   I take her hand.

King. Good fortune, and the favour of the king,

---

if you and this maiden fhould be weighed together, and our royal
favours fhould be thrown into her fcale, (which you efteem fo
light,) we fhould make that in which you fhould be placed, to
ftrike the beam. MALONE.

⁵ *Into the* ftaggers,] One fpecies of the *ftaggers,* or the *horfe's
apoplexy,* is a raging impatience which makes the animal dafh
himfelf with deftructive violence againft pofts or walls. To this
the allufion, I fuppofe, is made. JOHNSON.

Shakfpeare has the fame expreffion in *Cymbeline,* where Poft-
humus fays :

    " Whence come thefe *ftaggers* on me?" STEEVENS.

Smile upon this contráct; whoſe ceremony
Shall ſeem expedient on the now-born brief,
And be perform'd to-night:[6] the ſolemn feaſt

---

[6] —— *whoſe ceremony*
Shall ſeem expedient *on the* now-born brief,
And be perform'd to-night:] Several of the modern editors
read—new-born brief. STEEVENS.

This, if it be at all intelligible, is at leaſt obſcure and inaccurate.
Perhaps it was written thus:
—————— what *ceremony*
Shall ſeem expedient on the now-born brief,
Shall *be perform'd to-night*; *the ſolemn feaſt*
Shall more attend ——.
The *brief* is the *contract of eſpouſal*, or the *licence* of the church.
The King means, What *ceremony* is neceſſary to make this *contract*
a *marriage*, ſhall be immediately *performed*; the reſt may be de-
layed. JOHNSON.

The only authentick ancient copy reads—*now*-born. I do not
perceive that any change is neceſſary. MALONE.

The whole ſpeech is unnaturally expreſſed; yet I think it intelligible as it ſtands, and ſhould therefore reject Johnſon's amendment and explanation.

The word *brief* does not here denote either a contract or a
licence, but is an adjective, and means *ſhort* or *contracted*: and the
words *on the now-born*, ſignify *for the preſent*, in oppoſition to *upon
the coming ſpace*, which means *hereafter*. The ſenſe of the whole
paſſage ſeems to be this:—" The king and fortune ſmile on this
contract; the ceremony of which it ſeems expedient to abridge for
the preſent; the ſolemn feaſt ſhall be performed at a future time,
when we ſhall be able to aſſemble friends." M. MASON.

Though I have inſerted the foregoing note, I do not profeſs to
comprehend its meaning fully. Shakſpeare uſes the words *expedience, expedient*, and *expediently*, in the ſenſe of *haſte, quick, ex-
peditiouſly*. A *brief*, in ancient language, means any ſhort and
ſummary writing or proceeding. The *now-born brief* is only
another phraſe for *the contract recently and ſuddenly made. The
ceremony of it* (ſays the king) *ſhall ſeem to haſten after its ſhort pre-
liminary, and be performed to-night*, &c. STEEVENS.

Now-*born*, the epithet in the old copy, prefixed to *brief*, un-
queſtionably ought to be reſtored. The NOW-*born brief*, is the
breve originale of the feudal times, which, in this inſtance, formally
notified the king's conſent to the marriage of Bertram, his ward.
HENLEY.

Shall more attend upon the coming space,
Expecting abfent friends.   As thou lov'ft her,
Thy love's to me religious; elfe, does err.

> [*Exeunt* King, BERTRAM, HELENA, Lords, *and*
> *Attendants.*[7]

LAF. Do you hear, monfieur? a word with you.

PAR. Your pleafure, fir?

LAF. Your lord and mafter did well to make his recantation.

PAR. Recantation?—My lord? my mafter?

LAF. Ay; Is it not a language, I fpeak?

PAR. A moft harfh one; and not to be underftood without bloody fucceeding.   My mafter?

LAF. Are you companion to the count Roufillon?

PAR. To any count; to all counts; to what is man.

LAF. To what is count's man; count's mafter is of another ftyle.

PAR. You are too old, fir; let it fatisfy you, you are too old.

Our author often ufes *brief* in the fenfe of a fhort note, or intimation concerning any bufinefs; and fometimes without the idea of writing.   So, in the laft Act of this play:

" —— fhe told me
" In a fweet verbal *brief,*" &c.

Again, in the Prologue to *Sir John Oldcaftle,* 1600:

" To ftop which fcruple, let this *brief* fuffice:—
" It is no pamper'd glutton we prefent," &c.

The meaning therefore of the prefent paffage, I believe, is;—Good fortune, and the king's favour fmile on this fhort contract; the ceremonial part of which fhall *immediately* pafs,—*fhall follow clofe on the troth now plighted* between the parties, and be performed this night; the folemn feaft fhall be delayed to a future time. MALONE.

[7] The old copy has the following fingular continuation: *Parolles and Lafeu ftay behind, commenting of this wedding.* This could have been only the marginal note of a prompter, and was never defigned to appear in print. STEEVENS.

To *comment* means, I believe, to affume the appearance of perfons deeply engaged in thought. MALONE.

Laf. I muſt tell thee, ſirrah, I write man; to which title age cannot bring thee.

Par. What I dare too well do, I dare not do.

Laf. I did think thee, for two ordinaries,[1] to be a pretty wiſe fellow; thou didſt make tolerable vent of thy travel; it might paſs: yet the ſcarfs, and the bannerets, about thee, did manifoldly diſſuade me from believing thee a veſſel of too great a burden. I have now found thee; when I loſe thee again, I care not: yet art thou good for nothing but taking up;[9] and that thou art ſcarce worth.

Par. Hadſt thou not the privilege of antiquity upon thee,——

Laf. Do not plunge thyſelf too far in anger, leſt thou haſten thy trial; which if—Lord have mercy on thee for a hen! So, my good window of lattice, fare thee well; thy caſement I need not open, for I look through thee. Give me thy hand.

Par. My lord, you give me moſt egregious indignity.

Laf. Ay, with all my heart; and thou art worthy of it.

Par. I have not, my lord, deſerv'd it.

Laf. Yes, good faith, every dram of it; and I will not bate thee a ſcruple.

Par. Well, I ſhall be wiſer.

Laf. E'en as ſoon as thou canſt, for thou haſt to pull at a ſmack o'the contrary. If ever thou be'ſt bound in thy ſcarf, and beaten, thou ſhalt find what it is to be proud of thy bondage. I have a deſire to hold my acquaintance with thee, or rather my

---

[1] *——for two ordinaries—*] While I ſat twice with thee at table. JOHNSON.

[9] *——taking up;*] To *take up* is to *contradict*, to *call to account*; as well as to *pick off the ground.* JOHNSON.

knowledge; that I may fay, in the default,[2] he is a man I know.

PAR. My lord, you do me moft infupportable vexation.

LAF. I would it were hell-pains for thy fake, and my poor doing eternal: for doing I am paft; as I will by thee, in what motion age will give me leave.[3]   [*Exit.*

PAR. Well, thou haft a fon fhall take this difgrace off me;[4] fcurvy, old, filthy, fcurvy lord!—Well, I muft be patient; there is no fettering of authority. I'll beat him, by my life, if I can meet him with any convenience, an he were double and double a lord. I'll have no more pity of his age, than I would have of—I'll beat him, an if I could but meet him again.

---

[2] —— *in the default,*] That is, *at a need.* JOHNSON.

[3] —— *for doing I am paft; as I will by thee, in what motion age will give me leave.*] The conceit, which is fo thin that it might well efcape a hafty reader, is in the word *paft—I am paft, as I will be* paft *by thee.* JOHNSON.

Lafeu means to fay, "for doing I am paft, as I will *pafs* by thee in what motion age will permit." Lafeu fays, that he will *pafs* by Parolles, not that he will be *paffed* by him; and Lafeu is actually the perfon who goes out. M. MASON.

Dr. Johnfon is, I believe, miftaken. Mr. Edwards has, I think, given the true meaning of Lafeu's words. "*I cannot do much,* fays Lafeu; *doing I am* paft, as I will by thee *in what motion age will give me leave*; i. e. *as I will* pafs *by thee as faft as I am able*:—and he immediately goes out. It is a play on the word *paft*: the conceit indeed is poor, but Shakfpeare plainly meant it." MALONE.

Doing is here ufed obfcenely. So, in Ben Jonfon's tranflation of a paffage in an *Epigram* of Petronius:

    Brevis eft, &c. et fæda voluptas.

    " *Doing* a filthy pleafure is, and fhort." COLLINS.

[4] *Well, thou haft a fon fhall take this difgrace off me;*] This the poet makes Parolles fpeak alone; and this is nature. A coward fhould try to hide his poltroonery even from himfelf. An ordinary writer would have been glad of fuch an opportunity to bring him to confeffion. WARBURTON.

Re-enter LAFEU.

Laf. Sirrah, your lord and mafter's married, there's news for you; you have a new miftrefs.

Par. I moft unfeignedly befeech your lordfhip to make fome refervation of your wrongs: He is my good lord: whom I ferve above, is my mafter.

Laf. Who? God?

Par. Ay, fir.

Laf. The devil it is, that's thy mafter. Why doft thou garter up thy arms o' this fafhion? doft make hofe of thy fleeves? do other fervants fo? Thou wert beft fet thy lower part where thy nofe ftands. By mine honour, if I were but two hours younger, I'd beat thee: methinks, thou art a general offence, and every man fhould beat thee. I think, thou waft created for men to breathe themfelves upon thee.

Par. This is hard and undeferved meafure, my lord.

Laf. Go to, fir; you were beaten in Italy for picking a kernel out of a pomegranate; you are a vagabond, and no true traveller: you are more faucy with lords, and honourable perfonages, than the heraldry of your birth and virtue gives you commiffion.⁵ You are not worth another word, elfe I'd call you knave. I leave you. [*Exit.*

Enter BERTRAM.

Par. Good, very good; it is fo then.—Good, very good; let it be conceal'd a while.

---

⁵ ——*than the heraldry of your birth,* &c.] In former copies:— *than the commiffion of your birth and virtue gives you heraldry.* Sir Thomas Hanmer reftored it. JOHNSON.

Ber. Undone, and forfeited to cares for ever!

Par. What is the matter, sweet heart?

Ber. Although before the solemn priest I have
   sworn,
I will not bed her.

Par. What? what, sweet heart?

Ber. O my Parolles, they have married me :——
I'll to the Tuscan wars, and never bed her.

Par. France is a dog-hole, and it no more merits
The tread of a man's foot : to the wars!

Ber. There's letters from my mother; what the
   import is,
I know not yet.

Par. Ay, that would be known : To the wars,
   my boy, to the wars!
He wears his honour in a box unseen,
That hugs his kicksy-wicksy here at home;[6]
Spending his manly marrow in her arms,
Which should sustain the bound and high curvet
Of Mars's fiery steed : To other regions!
France is a stable; we that dwell in't, jades;
Therefore, to the war!

Ber. It shall be so; I'll send her to my house,
Acquaint my mother with my hate to her,
And wherefore I am fled; write to the king
That which I durst not speak : His present gift
Shall furnish me to those Italian fields,
Where noble fellows strike : War is no strife
To the dark house, and the detested wife.[7]

---

[6] *That hugs his* kicksy-wicksy, &c.] Sir T. Hanmer, in his
Glossary, observes that *kicksy-wicksy* is a made word in ridicule and
disdain of a wife. Taylor, the water-poet, has a *poem* in disdain
of his *debtors*, entitled, *A kicksy-winsy*, or a *Lerry come-twang.*
             Grey.

[7] *To the* dark house, &c.] The *dark house* is a house made gloomy

Par. Will this capricio hold in thee, art fure?

Ber. Go with me to my chamber, and advife me.
I'll fend her ftraight away: To-morrow [8]
I'll to the wars, fhe to her fingle forrow.

Par. Why, thefe balls bound; there's noife in
      it.—'Tis hard;
A young man, married, is a man that's marr'd:
Therefore away, and leave her bravely; go:
The king has done you wrong; but, hufh! 'tis fo.
                            [*Exeunt.*

---

by difcontent. Milton fays of *death* and the *king* of hell preparing
to combat:

    " So frown'd the mighty combatants, that hell
    " Grew *darker* at their frown." Johnson.

Perhaps this is the fame thought we meet with in *K. Henry IV.*
only more folemnly expreffed:

    " —— he's as tedious
    " As is a tired horfe, a *railing wife,*
    " Worfe than a *fmoaky houfe.*"

The proverb originated before chimneys were in general ufe,
which was not till the middle of Elizabeth's reign. See *Piers
Plowman,* paffus 17:

    " Thre thinges there be that doe a man by ftrength
    " For to flye his owne houfe, as holy wryte fheweth:
    " That one is a wycked wife, that wyll not be chaftyfed;
    " Her fere flyeth from her, for feare of her tonge:—
    " And when *fmolke* and *fmoulder fmight in his fyghte,*
    " It doth him worfe than his *wyfe,* or wete to flepe;
    " For *fmolke* or *fmoulder, fmiteth in his eyen*
    " 'Til he be blear'd or blind," &c.

The old copy reads—*detected* wife. Mr. Rowe made the correction. Steevens.

The emendation is fully fupported by a fubfequent paffage:

    " 'Tis a hard bondage to become the wife
    " Of a *detefting* lord." Malone.

[8] *I'll fend her ftraight away: To-morrow —*] As this line wants a
foot, I fuppofe our author wrote—" *Betimes* to-morrow." So, in
Macbeth:

    " ———— I will to-morrow,
    " *Betimes* I will," &c. Steevens.

SCENE IV.

The same. Another Room in the same.

Enter HELENA *and* Clown.

HEL. My mother greets me kindly: Is she well?

CLO. She is not well; but yet she has her health: she's very merry; but yet she is not well: but thanks be given, she's very well, and wants nothing i'the world; but yet she is not well.

HEL. If she be very well, what does she ail, that she's not very well?

CLO. Truly, she's very well, indeed, but for two things.

HEL. What two things?

CLO. One, that she's not in heaven, whither God send her quickly! the other, that she's in earth, from whence God send her quickly!

Enter PAROLLES.

PAR. Bless you, my fortunate lady!

HEL. I hope, sir, I have your good will to have mine own good fortunes.[*]

PAR. You had my prayers to lead them on; and to keep them on, have them still.—O, my knave! How does my old lady?

CLO. So that you had her wrinkles, and I her money, I would she did as you say.

[*] ——*fortunes.*] Old copy—*fortune.* Corrected by Mr. Steevens.
MALONE.

Par. Why, I fay nothing.

Clo. Marry, you are the wifer man; for many a man's tongue fhakes out his mafter's undoing: To fay nothing, to do nothing, to know nothing, and to have nothing, is to be a great part of your title; which is within a very little of nothing.

Par. Away, thou'rt a knave.

Clo. You fhould have faid, fir, before a knave thou art a knave; that is, before me thou art a knave: this had been truth, fir.

Par. Go to, thou art a witty fool, I have found thee.

Clo. Did you find me in yourfelf, fir? or were you taught to find me? The fearch, fir, was profitable; and much fool may you find in you, even to the world's pleafure, and the increafe of laughter.

Par. A good knave, i'faith, and well fed.[9]—
Madam, my lord will go away to-night;
A very ferious bufinefs calls on him.
The great prerogative and rite of love,
Which, as your due, time claims, he does acknow
       ledge;
But puts it off by a compell'd reftraint;[2]

---

[9] —— *and* well fed.] An allufion, perhaps, to the old faying— " Better fed than taught;" to which the Clown has himfelf alluded in a preceding fcene:—" I will fhow myfelf *highly fed* and lowly taught." STEEVENS.

[2] *But puts it off* by *a compell'd reftraint*;] The old copy reads— *to* a compell'd reftraint. STEEVENS.

The editor of the third folio reads—*by* a compell'd reftraint; and the alteration has been adopted by the modern editors; perhaps without neceffity. Our poet might have meant, in his ufual licentious manner, that Bertram puts off the completion of his wifhes *to* a future day, *till* which he is *compelled* to *reftrain* his defires. This, it muft be confeffed, is very harfh; but our author is often fo licentious in his

Whofe want, and whofe delay, is ftrew'd with fweets,
Which they diftil now in the curbed time,[2]
To make the coming hour o'erflow with joy,
And pleafure drown the brim.

HEL.   What's his will elfe?

PAR. That you will take your inftant leave o'the
         king,
And make this hafte as your own good proceeding,
Strengthen'd with what apology you think
May make it probable need.[3]

HEL.   What more commands he?

phrafeology, that change on that ground alone is very dangerous. In *K. Henry VIII.* we have a phrafeology not very different:

    " —— All-fouls day
    " Is the *determin'd refpite* of my wrongs."

i. e. the day to which my wrongs are refpited. MALONE.

[2] *Whofe want, and whofe delay,* &c.] The *fweets* with which that *want* are *ftrewed,* I fuppofe, are compliments and profeffions of kindnefs. JOHNSON.

Johnfon feems not to have underftood this paffage; the meaning of which is merely this:—" That the delay of the joys, and the ex- pectation of them, would make them more delightful when they come." The *curbed time,* means the time of reftraint. *Whofe want,* means *the want of which.* So, in *The Two Noble Kinfmen,* Thefeus fays:

    " —— A day or two
    " Let us look fadly,—*in whofe end,*
    " The vifages of bridegrooms we'll put on." M. MASON.

The *fweets* which are diftilled, by the reftraint faid to be impofed on Bertram, from " the want and delay of the great prerogative of love," are the fweets of *expectation.* Parolles is here fpeaking of Bertram's feelings during this " curbed time," not, as Dr. Johnfon feems to have thought, of thofe of Helena. The following lines in *Troilus and Creffida* may prove the beft comment on the prefent paffage:

    " I am giddy; *expectation* whirls me round.
    " The *imaginary* relifh is fo *fweet*
    " That it enchants my fenfe. What will it be,
    " When that the watery palate *taftes indeed*
    " Love's thrice-reputed nectar? Death, I fear me,
    " Swooning deftruction;" &c. MALONE.

[3] ——*probable need.*] A fpecious appearance of neceffity.
                                        JOHNSON.

PAR. That, having this obtain'd, you prefently
Attend his further pleafure.

HEL. In every thing I wait upon his will.

PAR. I fhall report it fo.

HEL.   I pray you.—Come, firrah. [*Exeunt.*

SCENE V.

Another Room in the fame.

Enter LAPEU *and* BERTRAM.

LAF. But, I hope, your lordfhip thinks not him
a foldier.

BER. Yes, my lord, and of very valiant approof.

LAF. You have it from his own deliverance.

BER. And by other warranted teftimony.

LAF. Then my dial goes not true; I took this
lark for a bunting.[4]

BER. I do affure you, my lord, he is very great
in knowledge, and accordingly valiant.

LAF. I have then finned againft his experience,
and tranfgrefs'd againft his valour; and my ftate
that way is dangerous, fince I cannot yet find in my
heart to repent. Here he comes; I pray you, make
us friends, I will purfue the amity.

Enter PAROLLES.

PAR. Thefe things fhall be done, fir. [*To* BERTRAM.

---

[4] —— *a bunting.*] This bird is mentioned in Lyly's *Love's Metamorphofis*, 1601: " —— but forefters think all birds to be *bunt-
ings.*" Barrett's *Alvearie, or Quadruple Dictionary*, 1580, gives
this account of it: " Terraneola et rubetra, avis alaudæ fimilis, &c.
Dicta terraneola quod non in arboribus, fed in terra verfetur et
nidificet." The following proverb is in Ray's Collection: " A
gofshawk beats not a *bunting.*" STEEVENS.

Laf. 'Pray you, fir, who's his tailor?

Par. Sir?

Laf. O, I know him well: Ay, fir; he, fir, is a good workman, a very good tailor.

Ber. Is fhe gone to the king?

[*Afide to* PAROLLES.

Par. She is.

Ber. Will fhe away to-night?

Par. As you'll have her.

Ber. I have writ my letters, cafketed my treafure, Given order for our horfes; and to-night, When I fhould take poffeffion of the bride,— And, ere I do begin,——

Laf. A good traveller is fomething at the latter end of a dinner; but one that lies three thirds,' and ufes a known truth to pafs a thoufand nothings with, fhould be once heard, and thrice beaten.—God fave you, captain.

Ber. Is there any unkindnefs between my lord and you, monfieur?

Par. I know not how I have deferv'd to run into my lord's difpleafure.

Laf. You have made fhift to run into't, boots and fpurs and all, like him that leap'd into the cuftard;⁶ and out of it you'll run again, rather than fuffer queftion for your refidence.

---

⁵ *A good traveller is fomething at the latter end of a dinner; but one that lies three thirds,* &c.] So, in Marlowe's *King Edward II.* 1598:

"*Gav.* What art thou?
" 2 *Poor Man.* A *traveller.*
"*Gav.* Let me fee; thou would'ft well
" To wait on my trencher, and *tell me lies at dinner-time.*"

MALONE.

⁶ *You have made fhift to run into't,* boots and fpurs and all, like him that leap'd into the cuftard;] This odd allufion is not introduced

Ber. It may be, you have miftaken him, my lord.

Laf. And fhall do fo ever, though I took him at his prayers. Fare you well, my lord: and believe this of me, There can be no kernel in this light nut; the foul of this man is his clothes: truft him not in matter of heavy confequence; I have kept of them tame, and know their natures.—Farewell, monfieur: I have fpoken better of you, than you have or will deferve [7] at my hand; but we muft do good againft evil.   [*Exit.*

Par. An idle lord, I fwear,

Ber. I think fo.

Par. Why, do you not know him?

Ber. Yes, I do know him well; and common fpeech Gives him a worthy pafs.   Here comes my clog.

Enter Helena.

Hel. I have, fir, as I was commanded from you, Spoke with the king, and have procur'd his leave

---

without a view to fatire. It was a foolery practifed at city enter-tainments, whilft the jefter or zany was in vogue, for him to jump into a large deep cuftard, fet for the purpofe, *to fet on a quantity of barren fpectators to laugh,* as our poet fays in his *Hamlet.* I do not advance this without fome authority; and a quotation from Ben Jonfon will very well explain it:

  " He may perchance, in tail of a fheriff's dinner,
  " Skip with a rhime o' th' table, from New-nothing,
  " And take his *Almain-leap* into a *cuftard,*
  " Shall make my lady mayorefs, and her fifters,
  " Laugh all their hoods over their fhoulders."
                  Devil's an afs, Act I. fc. i.   Theobald.

  [7] ———*than you have or will deferve*—]   The oldeft copy erro-neoufly reads—have or will *to* deferve.   Steevens.

  Something feems to have been omitted; but I know not how to rectify the paffage.   Perhaps we fhould read—than you have quali-ties or will *to* deferve.   The editor of the fecond folio reads—than you have or will deferve———.   Malone.

For prefent parting; only, he defires
Some private fpeech with you.

BER. I fhall obey his will.
You muft not marvel, Helen, at my courfe,
Which holds not colour with the time, nor does
The miniftration and required office
On my particular: prepar'd I was not
For fuch a bufinefs; therefore am I found
So much unfettled: This drives me to entreat you,
That prefently you take your way for home;
And· rather mufe, than afk, why I entreat you:⁸
For my refpects are better than they feem;
And my appointments have in them a need,
Greater than fhows itfelf, at the firft view,
To you that know them not. This to my mother:
[*Giving a letter.*
'Twill be two days ere I fhall fee you; fo
I leave you to your wifdom.

HEL. Sir, I can nothing fay,
But that I am your moft obedient fervant.

BER. Come, come, no more of that.

HEL. And ever fhall
With true obfervance feek to eke out that,
Wherein toward me my homely ftars have fail'd
To equal my great fortune.

BER. Let that go:
My hafte is very great: Farewell; hie home.

HEL. Pray, fir, your pardon.

BER. Well, what would you fay?

HEL. I am not worthy of the wealth I owe;⁹
Nor dare I fay, 'tis mine; and yet it is;

⁸ *And rather* mufe, &c.] To *mufe* is to *wonder*. So, in *Macbeth:*
"Do not *mufe* at me my moft noble friends." STEEVENS.

⁹ —— *the wealth I* owe;] i. e. *I own, poffefs.* STEEVENS.

But, like a timorous thief, moſt fain would ſteal
What law does vouch mine own.

    Ber.   What would you have?

    Hel. Something; and ſcarce ſo much :—nothing,
             indeed.—
I would not tell you what I would; my lord—'faith,
          yes ;—
Strangers, and foes, do ſunder, and not kiſs.

    Ber. I pray you, ſtay not, but in haſte to horſe.

    Hel. I ſhall not break your bidding, good my
        lord.

    Ber. Where are my other men, monſieur?—
        Farewell.[2]   [*Exit* HELENA.
Go thou toward home; where I will never come,
Whilſt I can ſhake my ſword, or hear the drum:—
Away, and for our flight.

    Par.   Bravely, coragio!
                      [*Exeunt.*

---

    [2] *Where are my other men*, monſieur ?—Farewell.] In former
copies:
       Hel. Where are my other men ? *Monſieur, farewell.*
What other men is Helen here enquiring after? Or who is ſhe
ſuppoſed to aſk for them? The old Counteſs, 'tis certain, did not
ſend her to the court without ſome attendants: but neither the
Clown, nor any of her retinue, are now upon the ſtage: Bertram,
obſerving Helen to linger fondly, and wanting to ſhift her off, puts
on a ſhow of haſte, aſks Parolles for his ſervants, and then gives
his wife an abrupt diſmiſſion. THEOBALD.

ACT III.   SCENE I.

Florence.   A Room in the Duke's *Palace.*

Flourish.   Enter the Duke of Florence, *attended;
two* French *Lords, and Others.*

DUKE. So that, from point to point, now have
         you heard
The fundamental reason of this war;
Whose great decision hath much blood let forth,
And more thirsts after.   ·

1 LORD.   Holy seems the quarrel
Upon your grace's part; black and fearful
On the opposer.

DUKE. Therefore we marvel much, our cousin
         France
Would, in so just a business, sbut his bosom
Against our borrowing prayers.

2 LORD.   Good my lord,
The reasons of our state I cannot yield,[3]
But like a common and an outward man,[4]
That the great figure of a council frames
By self-unable motion:[5] therefore dare not

---

[3] —— *I cannot* yield,] I cannot inform you of the reasons.
                                       JOHNSON.

Thus, in *Antony and Cleopatra:*
    " If thou say so, villain, thou kill'st thy mistress:
    " But well and free,
    " If thou so *yield* him, there is gold——." STEEVENS.

[4] —— *an* outward *man,*] i. e. one not in the secret of affairs.
                                     WARBURTON.

So, *inward* is familiar, admitted to secrets.   " I was an *inward*
of his." *Measure for Measure.* JOHNSON.

[5] *By self-unable* motion:] We should read *notion.* WARBURTON.
This emendation has also been recommended by Mr. Upton.
                                       STEEVENS.

Say what I think of it; since I have found
Myself in my uncertain grounds to fail
As often as I guess'd.

Duke.   Be it his pleasure.

2 *Lord.* But I am sure, the younger of our na-
ture,[6]
That surfeit on their ease, will, day by day,
Come here for physick.

Duke.   Welcome shall they be;
And all the honours, that can fly from us,
Shall on them settle. You know your places well;
When better fall, for your avails they fell:
To-morrow to the field.   [*Flourish. Exeunt.*

SCENE II.

Roussillon. *A Room in the* Countess's *Palace.*

Enter Countess *and* Clown.

Count. It hath happened all as I would have had
it, save, that he comes not along with her.

Clo. By my troth, I take my young lord to be a
very melancholy man.

Count. By what observance, I pray you?

Clo. Why, he will look upon his boot, and sing;
mend the ruff, and sing;[7] ask questions, and sing;

---

[6] —— *the younger of our* nature,] i. e. as we say at present, *our
young fellows.* The modern editors read—*nation.* I have restored
the old reading. STEEVENS.

[7] Clo. *Why, he will look upon his boot, and sing; mend the* ruff,
and sing;] The tops of the boots in our author's time turned down,
and hung loosely over the leg. The folding is what the Clown
means by the *ruff.* Ben Jonson calls it *ruffle;* and perhaps it
should be so here. " Not having leisure to put off my silver
spurs, one of the rowels catch'd hold of the *ruffle* of my boot."
Every Man out of his Humour, Act IV. sc. vi. WHALLEY.

pick his teeth, and sing: I know a man that had
this trick of melancholy, sold a goodly manor for
a song.[7]

COUNT. Let me see what he writes, and when he
means to come. [*Opening a Letter.*]

CLO. I have no mind to Isbel, since I was at court:
our old lings and our Isbels o'the country are nothing like your old ling and your Isbels o'the court:
the brains of my Cupid's knock'd out; and I begin to love, as an old man loves money, with no
stomach.

COUNT. What have we here?

CLO. E'en that[8] you have there. [*Exit.*]

COUNT. [Reads.] *I have sent you a daughter-in-*
law: she hath recovered the king, and undone me. I
have wedded her, not bedded her; and sworn to make
the not eternal. You shall hear, I am run away; know
it, before the report come. If there be breadth enough
in the world, I will hold a long distance. My duty
to you.

Your unfortunate son,

BERTRAM.

This is not well, rash and unbridled boy,
To fly the favours of so good a king;
To pluck his indignation on thy head,
By the misprizing of a maid too virtuous
For the contempt of empire.

To this fashion Bishop Earle alludes in his *Characters*, 1638,
Signat. E. 10. " He has learnt to ruffle his face from his boots;
and takes great delight in his walk to heare his spurs gingle."

MALONE.

[7] —— sold *a goodly manor for a song.*] Thus the modern editors.
The old copy reads—hold *a goodly*, &c. The emendation, however,
which was made in the third folio, seems necessary. STEEVENS.

[8] *Clo.* E'en *that*—] Old copy—*In* that. Corrected by Mr.
Theobald. MALONE.

Re-enter Clown.

Clo. O madam, yonder is heavy news within, between two foldiers and my young lady.

Count. What is the matter?

Clo. Nay, there is fome comfort in the news, fome comfort; your fon will not be kill'd fo foon as I thought he would.

Count. Why fhould he be kill'd?

Clo. So fay I, madam, if he run away, as I hear he does: the danger is in ftanding to't; that's the lofs of men, though it be the getting of children. Here they come, will tell you more: for my part, I only hear, your fon was run away. [*Exit* Clown.

Enter HELENA *and two Gentlemen.*

1 *Gen.* Save you, good madam.

Hel. Madam, my lord is gone, for ever gone.

2 *Gen.* Do not fay fo.

Count. Think upon patience.—'Pray you, gentle-
　　　men,—
I have felt fo many quirks of joy, and grief,
That the firft face of neither, on the ftart,
Can woman me[9] unto't:—Where is my fon, I pray
　　　you?

2 *Gen.* Madam, he's gone to ferve the duke of
　　　Florence:
We met him thitherward; for thence we came,
And, after fome defpatch in hand at court,
Thither we bend again.

Hel. Look on his letter, madam; here's my
　　　paffport.

─────────

[9] *Can* woman *me*—] i. e. affect me fuddenly and deeply, as my fex are ufually affected. STEEVENS.

[*Reads.*] *When thou canft get the ring upon my finger,*[9] *which never fhall come off, and fhow me a child begotten of thy body, that I am father to, then call me hufband: but in fuch a then I write a never.*
This is a dreadful fentence.

COUNT. Brought you this letter, gentlemen?

1 GEN. Ay, madam;
And, for the contents' fake, are forry for our pains.

COUNT. I pr'ythee, lady, have a better cheer;
If thou engroffeft all the griefs are thine,
Thou robb'ft me of a moiety:[2] He was my fon;
But I do wafh his name out of my blood,
And thou art all my child.—Towards Florence is he?

2 GEN. Ay, madam.

COUNT. And to be a foldier?

2 GEN. Such is his noble purpofe: and, believe't,
The duke will lay upon him all the honour
That good convenience claims.

9 *When thou canft get the ring* upon my *finger,*] i. e. When thou canft get the ring, which is on my finger, into thy poffeffion. The Oxford editor, who took it the other way, to fignify, when thou canft get it on upon my finger, very fagacioufly alters it to—*When thou canft get the ring* from *my finger.* WARBURTON.

I think Dr. Warburton's explanation fufficient; but I once read it thus: *When thou canft get the ring upon* thy *finger, which never fhall come off* mine. JOHNSON.

Dr. Warburton's explanation is confirmed inconteftably by thefe lines in the fifth act, in which Helena again repeats the fubftance of this letter:

" —— there is your ring;
" And, look you, here's your letter; this it fays:
" *When from my finger you can get this ring,*" &c. MALONE.

2 *If thou engroffeft all the griefs* are *thine,*
Thou robb'ft me of a moiety:] We fhould certainly read:
—— *all the griefs* as *thine,*
inftead of—are *thine.* M. MASON.

This fentiment is elliptically expreffed, but, I believe, means no more than—*If thou keepeft all thy forrows to thyfelf,* i. e. " all the griefs *that* are thine," &c. STEEVENS.

Count.   Return you thither?

1 *Gen.* Ay, madam, with the fwifteft wing of fpeed.

Hel. [*Reads.*] *'Till I have no wife, I have nothing*
            in France.

'Tis bitter.

Count.   Find you that there?

Hel.   Ay, madam.

1 *Gen.* 'Tis but the boldnefs of his hand, haply,
        which
His heart was not confenting to.

Count. Nothing in France, until he have no wife!
There's nothing here, that is too good for him,
But only fhe; and fhe deferves a lord,
That twenty fuch rude boys might tend upon,
And call her hourly, miftrefs. Who was with him?

1 *Gen.* A fervant only, and a gentleman
Which I have fome time known.

Count.   Parolles, was't not?

1 *Gen.* Ay, my good lady, he.

Count. A very tainted fellow, and full of wick-
       ednefs.
My fon corrupts a well-derived nature
With his inducement.

1 *Gen.*   Indeed, good lady,
The fellow has a deal of that, too much,
Which holds him much to have.[3]

---

[3] *——a deal of that, too much,*
    Which holds him much to have.] That is, his vices ftand him in
ftead. Helen had before delivered this thought in all the beauty
of expreffion :
       " ——I know him a notorious liar;
       " Think him a great way fool, folely a coward;
       " Yet thefe fix'd evils fit fo fit in him,
       " That they take place, while virtue's fteely bones
       " Look bleak in the cold wind——." WARBURTON.

Count. You are welcome, gentlemen,
I will entreat you, when you see my son,
To tell him, that his sword can never win
The honour that he loses : more I'll entreat you
Written to bear along.

2 *Gen.*   We serve you, madam,
In that and all your worthiest affairs.

Count. Not so, but as we change our courtesies.[4]
Will you draw near?

              [*Exeunt* Countess *and Gentlemen.*

Hel. Till I have no wife, I have nothing in France.
Nothing in France, until he has no wife !
Thou shalt have none, Rousillon, none in France,
Then hast thou all again. Poor lord ! is't I
That chase thee from thy country, and expose
Those tender limbs of thine to the event
Of the none-sparing war? and is it I
That drive thee from the sportive court, where thou
Wast shot at with fair eyes, to be the mark
Of smoky muskets? O you leaden messengers,
That ride upon the violent speed of fire,
Fly with false aim; move the still-piecing air,
That sings with piercing,[5] do not touch my lord !

Mr. Heath thinks that the meaning is, this fellow hath a deal
too much of *that* which alone can hold or judge that he has much
in him; i. e. folly and ignorance. MALONE.

[4] *Not so,* &c.] The gentlemen declare that they are servants to
the Countess; she replies,—No otherwise than as she returns the
same offices of civility. JOHNSON.

[5] ——move *the* still-piecing *air,*
    That sings with piercing,] The words are here oddly shuffled
into nonsense. We should read:
    —— pierce *the* still-moving *air,*
    That sings with piercing,
i. e. pierce the air, which is in perpetual motion, and suffers no
injury by piercing. WARBURTON.

The old copy reads—*the* still-*peering* air.
Perhaps we might better read:
    —— *the* still-piecing *air.*

Whoever fhoots at him, I fet him there;
Whoever charges on his forward breaft,
I am the caitiff, that do hold him to it;
And, though I kill him not, I am the caufe
His death was fo effected: better 'twere,
I met the ravin lion[6] when he roar'd
With fharp conftraint of hunger; better 'twere
That all the miferies, which nature owes,
Were mine at once: No, come thou home, Rou-
 fillon,
Whence honour but of danger wins a fcar,[7]
As oft it lofes all; I will be gone:
My being here it is, that holds thee hence:
Shall I ftay here to do't? no, no, although
The air of paradife did fan the houfe,
And angels offic'd all: I will be gone;
That pitiful rumour may report my flight,

---

i. e. the air that clofes immediately. This has been propofed already, but I forget by whom. STEEVENS.

 Piece was formerly fpelt—*peece*: fo that there is but the change
of one letter. See *Twelfth Night*, firft folio, p. 262:
  " Now, good Cefario, but that *peece* of fong—." MALONE.

 I have no doubt that *ftill-piecing* was Shakfpeare's word. But
the paffage is not yet quite found. We fhould read, I believe,
  ——*rove the ftill-piecing air.*
i. e. *fly at random through.* The allufion is to *fhooting at rovers* in
archery, which was fhooting without any particular aim.
              TYRWHITT.

 Mr. Tyrwhitt's reading deftroys the defigned antithefis between
move and *ftill*; nor is he correct in his definition of roving, which
is not fhooting without a *particular aim*, but at *marks* of *uncertain*
lengths. DOUCE.

 [6] ——*the* ravin *lion*—] i. e. the *ravenous* or ravening lion. To
ravin is to fwallow voracioufly. MALONE.

 [7] *Whence honour but of danger*, &c.] The fenfe is, from that
abode, where all the advantages that honour ufually reaps from the
danger it rufhes upon, is only a fcar in teftimony of its bravery,
as on the other hand, it often is the caufe of lofing all, even life
itfelf. HEATH.

To confolate thine ear.   Come, night; end, day!
For, with the dark, poor thief, I'll fteal away.

                       [*Exit.*

S C E N E   III.

Florence.   *Before the* Duke's *Palace.*

Flourifh.   *Enter the Duke of* Florence, BERTRAM,
    Lords, *Officers, Soldiers, and Others.*

    Duke. The general of our horfe thou art; and we,
Great in our hope, lay our beft love and credence,
Upon thy promifing fortune.

    Ber.   Sir, it is
A charge too heavy for my ftrength; but yet
We'll ftrive to bear it for your worthy fake,
To the extreme edge of hazard.'

    Duke.   Then go thou forth;
And fortune play upon thy profperous helm,'
As thy aufpicious miftrefs!

    Ber.   This very day,
Great Mars, I put myfelf into thy file:
Make me but like my thoughts; and I fhall prove
A lover of thy drum, hater of love.   [*Exeunt.*

    ' *We'll ftrive to* bear *it for your worthy fake,*
      To the extreme edge *of hazard.*] So, in our author's 116th
Sonnet:
       " But *bears* it out even to the *edge* of doom." MALONE.
Milton has borrowed this expreffion; *Par. Reg.* B. 1:
      " You fee our danger on the utmoft *edge*
      " Of hazard." STEEVENS.
    ' *And* fortune play *upon thy profperous* helm,]   So, in *King
Richard III:*
      " *Fortune* and victory fit on thy *helm!*"
Again, in *King John:*
      " And victory with little lofs doth *play*
      " Upon the dancing banners of the French." STEEVENS.

SCENE IV.

Rouſillon. *A Room in the* Counteſs's *Palace.*

Enter Counteſs *and* Steward.

Count. Alas! and would you take the letter of
 her?
Might you not know, ſhe would do as ſhe has done,
By ſending me a letter? Read it again.

 Stew. I am Saint Jaques' pilgrim,[9] *thither gone;*
Ambitious love hath ſo in me offended,
That bare-foot plod I the cold ground upon,
With ſainted vow my faults to have amended.
Write, write, that, from the bloody courſe of war,
My deareſt maſter, your dear ſon may hie;
Bleſs him at home in peace, whilſt I from far,
His name with zealous fervour ſanĉtify:
His taken labours bid him me forgive;
I, his deſpiteful Juno,[2] *ſent him forth*
From courtly friends, with camping foes to live,
Where death and danger dog the heels of worth:
He is too good and fair for death and me;
Whom I myſelf embrace, to ſet him free.

---

[9] —*Saint* Jaques' *pilgrim,*] I do not remember any place famous
for pilgrimages confecrated in Italy to St. james, but it is common
to viſit St. James of Compoſtella, in Spain. Another ſaint might
eaſily have been found, Florence being ſomewhat out of the road
from Rouſillon to Compoſtella. JOHNSON.

 From Dr. Heylin's *France painted to the Life,* 8vo. 1656,
p. 270, 276, we learn that at Orleans was a church dedicated to
St. Jacques, to which Pilgrims formerly uſed to reſort, to adore a
part of the croſs pretended to be found there. REED.

[2] ——*Juno,*] Alluding to the ſtory of Hercules. JOHNSON.

Count. Ah, what sharp stings are in her mildest
      words!——
Rinaldo, you did never lack advice so much,[3]
As letting her pass so; had I spoke with her,
I could have well diverted her intents,
Which thus she hath prevented.

Stew.   Pardon me, madam:
If I had given you this at over-night,
She might have been o'erta'en; and yet she writes,
Pursuit would be but vain.

Count.   What angel shall
Bless this unworthy husband? he cannot thrive,
Unless her prayers, whom heaven delights to hear,
And loves to grant, reprieve him from the wrath
Of greatest justice.—Write, write, Rinaldo,
To this unworthy husband of his wife;
Let every word weigh heavy of her worth,
That he does weigh too light:[4] my greatest grief,
Though little he do feel it, set down sharply.
Despatch the most convenient messenger:——
When, haply, he shall hear that she is gone,
He will return; and hope I may, that she,
Hearing so much, will speed her foot again,
Led hither by pure love: which of them both
Is dearest to me, I have no skill in sense
To make distinction:—Provide this messenger:——
My heart is heavy, and mine age is weak;
Grief would have tears, and sorrow bids me speak.
                            [*Exeunt.*

---

[3] ——*lack advice so much,*] *Advice*, is *discretion* or *thought.*
                             JOHNSON.

So in *King Henry V:*
    " And, on his more *advice* we pardon him.". STEEVENS.

[4] *That he does* weigh *too light:*] To *weigh* here means to *value,*
or *esteem.* So, in *Love's Labour's Lost:*
    " You *weigh* me not, O, that's you care not for me."
                               MALONE.

SCENE V.

Without the Walls of Florence.

A tucket afar off. Enter an old Widow *of* Florence, DIANA, VIOLENTA, MARIANA, *and other Citizens.*

WID. Nay, come; for if they do approach the city, we fhall lofe all the fight.

DIA. They fay, the French count has done moft honourable fervice.

WID. It is reported that he has taken their greateft commander; and that with his own hand he flew the duke's brother. We have loft our labour; they are gone a contrary way: hark! you may know by their trumpets.

MAR. Come, let's return again, and fuffice our-felves with the report of it. Well, Diana, take heed of this French earl: the honour of a maid is her name; and no legacy is fo rich as honefty.

WID. I have told my neighbour, how you have been folicited by a gentleman his companion.

MAR. I know that knave; hang him! one Pa-rolles: a filthy officer he is in thofe fuggeftions for the young earl.⁵—Beware of them, Diana; their promifes, enticements, oaths, tokens, and all thefe engines of luft, are not the things they go under:⁶

---

⁵ —— *thofe* fuggeftions *for the young earl.*] *Suggeftions* are temptations. So, in *Love's Labour's Loft*:

"*Suggeftions* are to others as to me." STEEVENS.

⁶ —— *are* not *the things they go under*:] They are not really fo true and fincere, as in appearance they feem to be. THEOBALD.

To go under the name of any thing is a known expreffion. The meaning is, they are not the things for which their names would make them pafs. JOHNSON.

many a maid hath been feduced by them; and the mifery is, example, that fo terrible fhows in the wreck of maidenhood, cannot for all that diffuade fucceffion, but that they are limed with the twigs that threaten them. I hope, I need not to advife you further; but, I hope, your own grace will keep you where you are, though there were no further danger known, but the modefty which is fo loft.

Dia. You fhall not need to fear me.

Enter Helena, *in the drefs of a Pilgrim.*

Wid. I hope fo.——Look, here comes a pilgrim: I know fhe will lie at my houfe: thither they fend one another: I'll queftion her.—
God fave you pilgrim! Whither are you bound?

Hel. To Saint Jaques le grand.
Where do the palmers [7] lodge, I do befeech you?

Wid. At the Saint Francis here, befide the port.

Hel. Is this the way?

Wid.　　　　　　Ay, marry, is it.—Hark you!
　　　　　　　　　　[*A march afar off.*
They come this way:—If you will tarry, holy pilgrim, [8]
But till the troops come by,

---

[7] ——*palmers*—] Pilgrims that vifited holy places; fo called from a ftaff, or bough of palm they were wont to carry, efpecially fuch as had vifited the holy places at Jerufalem. " A pilgrim and a palmer differed thus: a *pilgrim* had fome dwelling-place, a *palmer* had none; the *pilgrim* travelled to fome certain place, the *palmer* to all, and not to any one in particular; the *pilgrim* muft go at his own charge, the *palmer* muft profefs wilful poverty; the *pilgrim* might give over his profeffion, the *palmer* muft be conftant." See Blount's *Gloffography*. Anonymous.

[8] ——holy *pilgrim*,] The interpolated epithet *holy*, which adds nothing to our author's fenfe, and is injurious to his metre, may be fafely omitted. Steevens.

I will conduct you where you shall be lodg'd;
The rather, for, I think, I know your hostess
As ample as myself.

HEL.   Is it yourself?

WID. If you shall please so, pilgrim.

HEL. I thank you, and will stay upon your leisure.

WID. You came, I think, from France?

HEL.   I did so.

WID. Here you shall see a countryman of yours,
That has done worthy service.

HEL.   His name, I pray you.

DIA. The count Roufillon: Know you such a
one?

HEL. But by the ear, that hears most nobly of
him:
His face I know not.

DIA.   Whatsoe'er he is,
He's bravely taken here. He stole from France,
As 'tis reported, for the king [8] had married him
Against his liking: Think you it is so?

HEL. Ay, surely, mere the truth; [9] I know his lady.

DIA. There is a gentleman, that serves the count,
Reports but coarsely of her.

HEL.   What's his name?

DIA. Monsieur Parolles.

HEL.   O, I believe with him,
In argument of praise, or to the worth
Of the great count himself, she is too mean

---

[8] —— for *the king*, &c.] *For*, in the present instance, signifies *because*. So, in *Othello*:
" —— and great business scant,
" *For* she is with me." STEEVENS.
[9] —— mere *the truth*;] The exact, the *entire* truth. MALONE.

To have her name repeated; all her deserving
Is a reserved honesty, and that
I have not heard examin'd.[9]

DIA.　　　　　　　　　Alas, poor lady!
'Tis a hard bondage, to become the wife
Of a detesting lord.

WID. A right good creature:[2] wheresoe'er she is,
Her heart weighs sadly: this young maid might do
　　　　　her
A shrewd turn, if she pleas'd.

HEL.　　　　　　　　　How do you mean?
May be, the amorous count solicits her
In the unlawful purpose.

WID.　　　　　　　　He does, indeed;
And brokes[3] with all that can in such a suit
Corrupt the tender honour of a maid:
But she is arm'd for him, and keeps her guard
In honestest defence.

---

[9] ——*examin'd.*] That is, *questioned, doubted.* JOHNSON.

[2] *A* right *good creature:*] There is great reason to believe, that when these plays were copied for the press, the transcriber trusted to the ear, and not to the eye; one person dictating, and another transcribing. Hence probably the error of the old copy, which reads——*I write* good creature. For the emendation now made I am answerable. The same expression is found in *The Two Noble Kinsmen,* 1634:
　　"A *right good creature* more to me deserving," &c.
　　　　　　　　　　　　　　　　MALONE.

Perhaps, Shakspeare wrote—
　I weet, *good creature, wheresoe'er she is,*—
i. e. I know, I am well assured. He uses the word in *Antony and Cleopatra.* Thus also, Prior:
　　" But well I *weet,* thy cruel wrong
　　" Adorns a nobler poet's song." STEEVENS.

[3] ——*brokes*—] Deals as a *broker.* JOHNSON.

To *broke* is to deal with panders. A *broker* in our author's time meant a bawd or pimp. See a note on *Hamlet,* Act I. sc. iii.
　　　　　　　　　　　　　　　　MALONE.

Enter with drum and colours, a party of the Florentine
army, BERTRAM, *and* PAROLLES.

MAR. The gods forbid elfe!

WID.   So, now they come:—
That is Antonio, the duke's eldeſt ſon;
That, Eſcalus.

HEL.   Which is the Frenchman?

DIA.   He;
That with the plume: 'tis a moſt gallant fellow;
I would, he lov'd his wife: if he were honeſter,
He were much goodlier:—Is't not a handſome gen-
          tleman?

HEL. I like him well.

DIA. 'Tis pity, he is not honeſt: Yond's that
          faᵏe knave,
That leads him to theſe places;⁴ were I his lady,
I'd poiſon that vile raſcal.

HEL.   Which is he?

DIA. That jack-an-apes with ſcarfs: Why is he
melancholy?

HEL. Perchance he's hurt i'the battle.

PAR. Loſe our drum! well.

---

4 ——*Yond's that ſame knave,*
    That leads him to theſe places;] What *places?* Have they been
talking of brothels; or, indeed, of any particular locality? I make
no queſtion but our author wrote:
    That leads him to theſe paces.
i. e. ſuch irregular ſteps, to courſes of debauchery, to not loving
his wife. THEOBALD.

  The *places* are, apparently, where he
        " ——*brokes* with all, that can in ſuch a ſuit
        " Corrupt the tender honour of a maid." STEEVENS.

Mar. He’s shrewdly vex’d at something: Look, he has spied us.

Wid. Marry, hang you!

Mar. And your courtesy, for a ring-carrier!

[*Exeunt* Bertram, Parolles, *Officers, and Soldiers.*

Wid. The troop is past: Come, pilgrim, I will
       bring you
Where you shall host: of enjoin’d penitents
There’s four or five, to great Saint Jaques bound,
Already at my house.

Hel. I humbly thank you:
Please it this matron, and this gentle maid,
To eat with us to-night, the charge, and thanking,
Shall be for me; and, to requite you further,
I will bestow some precepts on this’ virgin,
Worthy the note.

Both.   We’ll take your offer kindly.

[*Exeunt.*

SCENE VI.

Camp before Florence.

Enter Bertram, *and the two* French *Lords.*

1 *Lord.* Nay, good my lord, put him to’t; let him have his way.

2 *Lord.* If your lordship find him not a hilding,[6] hold me no more in your respect.

---

5 ——on *this*—] Old copy—*of* this. Corrected in the second folio. Malone.

6 ——*a* hilding.] A *hilding* is a paltry cowardly fellow. So, in *King Henry V:*
    “ To purge the field from such a *hilding* foe.” Steevens.
See note on the Second Part of *K. Henry IV.* Act I. sc. i. Reed.

1 Lord. On my life, my lord, a bubble.

Ber. Do you think, I am so far deceived in him?

1 Lord. Believe it, my lord, in mine own direct knowledge, without any malice, but to speak of him as my kinsman, he's a most notable coward, an infinite and endless liar, an hourly promise-breaker, the owner of no one good quality worthy your lordship's entertainment.

2 Lord. It were fit you knew him; lest, reposing too far in his virtue, which he hath not, he might, at some great and trusty business, in a main danger, fail you.

Ber. I would, I knew in what particular action to try him.

2 Lord. None better than to let him fetch off his drum, which you hear him so confidently undertake to do.

1 Lord. I, with a troop of Florentines, will suddenly surprize him; such I will have, whom, I am sure, he knows not from the enemy: we will bind and hood-wink him so, that he shall suppose no other but that he is carried into the leaguer of the adversaries,[7] when we bring him to our tents: Be but your lordship present at his examination; if he do not, for the promise of his life, and in the highest compulsion of base fear, offer to betray you, and deliver all the intelligence in his power against you, and that with the divine forfeit of his

---

[7] ——*he's carried into the* leaguer *of the adversaries,*] i. e. *camp.* " They will not vouchsafe in their speaches or writings to use our ancient termes belonging to matters of warre, but doo call a campe by the Dutch name of *Legar*; nor will not affoord to say, that such a towne or such a fort is besieged, but that it is *belegard.*" *Sir John Smythe's Discourses,* &c. 1590. fo. 2, Douce.

foul upon oath, never truft my judgement in any thing.

2 LORD. O for the love of laughter, let him fetch his drum; he fays, he has a ftratagem for't: when your lordſhip fees the bottom of his fuccefs in't, and to what metal this counterfeit lump of ore⁹ will be melted, if you give him not John Drum's entertainment,¹ your inclining cannot be removed. Here he comes.

---

⁸ —— *of his*—] Old copy—*of this*. Corrected by Mr. Rowe.
MALONE.

⁹ —— *of ore*—] Old copy—*of ours*. MALONE.

Lump *of ours* has been the reading of all the editions. *Ore*, according to my emendation, bears a confonancy with the other terms accompanying, (viz. *metal*, *lump*, and *melted*,) and helps the propriety of the poet's thought: for fo one metaphor is kept up, and all the words are proper and fuitable to it.
THEOBALD.

¹ —— *if you give him not* John Drum's entertainment,] But, what is the meaning of *John Drum's entertainment?* Lafeu feveral times afterwards calls Parolles, Tom Drum. But the difference of the Chriftian name will make none in the explanation. There is an old motley interlude, (printed in 1601,) called *Jack Drum's Entertainment: Or, The Comedy of Pafquil and Catharine*. In this, Jack Drum is a fervant of intrigue, who is ever aiming at projects, and always foiled, and given the drop. And there is another old piece (publiſhed in 1627) called, *Apollo ſhroving*, in which I find thefe expreffions :

 " *Thuriger*. Thou lozel, hath Slug infected you?

 " Why do you give fuch kind *entertainment* to that cobweb?

 " *Scopas*. It ſhall have *Tom Drum's entertainment*: a flap with a fox-tail."

But both thefe pieces are, perhaps too late in time, to come to the affiftance of our author: fo we muft look a little higher. What is faid here to Bertram is to this effect: " My lord, as you have taken this fellow [Parolles] into fo near a confidence, if, upon his being found a counterfeit, you don't caſhier him from your favour, then your attachment is not to be removed." I will now fubjoin a quotation from Holinſhed, (of whofe books Shakfpeare was a moft diligent reader) which will pretty well afcertain Drum's

Enter PAROLLES.

1 LORD. O, for the love of laughter, hinder not the humour of his defign; let him fetch off his drum in any hand.[3]

BER. How now, monfieur? this drum fticks forely in your difpofition.

2 LORD. A pox on't let it go; 'tis but a drum.

PAR. But a drum! Is't but a drum? A drum fo

---

hiftory. This chronologer, in his defcription of Ireland, fpeaking of Patrick Sarsefield, (mayor of Dublin in the year 1551,) and of his extravagant hofpitality, fubjoins, that no gueft had ever a cold or forbidding look from any part of his family: fo that *his porter or any other officer, durft not, for both his eares, give the fimpleft man that reforted to his houfe, Tom Drum his entertaynement, which is,* to hale a man in by the heade, and thruft him out by both the fhoulders. THEOBALD.

A contemporary writer has ufed this expreffion in the fame manner that our author has done; fo that there is no reafon to fufpect the word *John* in the text to be a mifprint: " In faith good gentlemen, I think we fhall be forced to give you right *John* Drum's entertainment, [i. e. to treat you very ill,] for he that compofed the book we fhould prefent, hath—fnatched it from us at the very inftant of entrance." Introduction to *Jack Drum's Entertainment*, a comedy, 1601. MALONE.

Again, in Taylor's *Laugh and be fat*, 78:
" And whither now is Mons' Odcome come
" Who on his owne backe-fide receiv'd his pay?
" Not like the *Entertainm' of Jacke Drum*,
" Who was beft welcome when he went away."

Again, in *Manners and Cuftoms of all Nations*, by Ed. Afton, 1611, 4to. p. 280: " —— fome others on the contrarie part, give them *John Drum's intertainm'* reviling and beating them away from their houfes," &c. REED.

[3] —— *in any hand.*] The ufual phrafe is—*at any hand*, but *in any hand* will do. It is ufed in Holland's *Pliny*, p. 456.—" he muft be a free citizen of Rome *in any hand.*" Again, p. 508, 553, 546. STEEVENS.

loft!—There was an excellent command! to charge in with our horfe upon our own wings, and to rend our own foldiers.

2 LORD. That was not to be blamed in the command of the feryice; it was a difafter of war, that Cæfar himfelf could not have prevented, if he had been there to command.

BER. Well, we cannot greatly condemn our fuc-cefs: fome difhonour we had in the lofs of that drum; but it is not to be recover'd.

PAR. It might have been recover'd.

BER. It might; but it is not now.

PAR. It is to be recover'd: but that the merit of fervice is feldom attributed to the true and exact performer, I would have that drum or another, or *bic jacet.*[4]

BER. Why, if you have a ftomach to't, mon-fieur, if you think your myftery in ftratagem can bring this inftrument of honour again into his na-tive quarter, be magnanimous in the enterprize; and go on; I will grace the attempt for a worthy exploit: if you fpeed well in it, the duke fhall both fpeak of it, and extend to you what further becomes his greatnefs, even to the utmoft fyllable of your worthinefs.

PAR. By the hand of a foldier, I will under-take it.

BER. But you muft not now flumber in it.

PAR. I'll about it this evening: and I will pre-

---

4 —— *I would have that drum or another, or* hic jacet.] i. e. *Here lies;*—the ufual beginning of epitaphs. I would (fays Parolles) recover either the drum I have loft, or another belonging to the enemy; or *die in the attempt.* MALONE.

fently-pen down my dilemmas,[5] encourage myfelf in my certainty, put myfelf into my mortal prepara- tion, and, by midnight, look to hear further from me.

Ber. May I be bold to acquaint his grace, you are gone about it?

Par. I know not what the fuccefs will be, my lord; but the attempt I vow.

Ber. I know, thou art valiant; and, to the pof- fibility of thy foldierfhip,[6] will fubfcribe for thee. Farewell.

Par. I love not many words. [*Exit.*

1 *Lord.* No more than a fifh loves water.[7]—Is not this a ftrange fellow, my lord? that fo con- fidently feems to undertake this bufinefs, which he

---

[5] *—— I will prefently pen down my dilemmas,*] By this word, Parolles is made to infinuate that he had feveral ways, all equally certain of recovering his drum. For a *dilemma* is an argument that concludes both ways. WARBURTON.

Shakfpeare might have found the word thus ufed in Holinfhed. STEEVENS.

I think, that by penning down his *dilemmas*, Parolles means, that he will pen down his plans on the one fide, and the probable obftructions he was to meet with, on the other. M. MASON.

[6] *—— poffibility of thy foldierfhip,*] *I will fubfcribe* (fays Bertram) *to the poffibility of your foldierfhip.* His doubts being now raifed, he fupprefses that he fhould not be fo willing to vouch for its *pro- bability.* STEEVENS.

I believe, Bertram means no more than that he is confident Pa- rolles will do all that foldierfhip can effect. He was not yet certain that he was " a hilding." MALONE.

[7] *Par. I love not many words.*
1 *Lord. No more than a fifh loves water.*] Here we have the origin of this boafter's name; which, without doubt, (as Mr. Steevens has obferved) ought in ftrict propriety to be written— *Paroles.* But our author certainly intended it otherwife, having made it a trifyllable:
" Ruft fword, cool blufhes, and *Parolles* live."
He probably did not know the true pronunciation. MALONE.

knows is not to be done; damns himself to do, and dares better be damn'd than to do't.

2 Lord. You do not know him, my lord, as we do: certain it is, that he will steal himself into a man's favour, and, for a week, escape a great deal of discoveries; but when you find him out, you have him ever after.

Ber. Why, do you think, he will make no deed at all of this, that so seriously he does address him-self unto?

1 Lord. None in the world; but return with an invention, and clap upon you two or three probable lies: but we have almost embofs'd him,[8] you shall see his fall to-night; for, indeed, he is not for your lordship's respect.

2 Lord. We'll make you some sport with the fox, ere we case him.[9] He was first smoked by the old lord Lafeu: when his disguise and he is parted, tell me what a sprat you shall find him; which you shall see this very night.

1 Lord. I must go look my twigs; he shall be caught.

---

[8] —— *we have almost* embofs'd *him,*] To *embofs* a deer is to inclose him in a wood. Milton uses the same word:

" Like that self-begotten bird
" In the Arabian woods *imboft,*
" Which no second knows or third." Johnson.

It is probable that Shakspeare was unacquainted with this word in the sense which Milton affixes to it, viz. from *embofcare,* Ital. to enclose in a thicket.

When a deer is run hard and foams at the mouth, in the language of the field, he is said to be *embofi'd.* Steevens.

" To know when a stag is *weary* (as Markham's *Country Con-tentments* say) you shall see him *imboft,* that is, *foaming* and *flouer-ing* about the mouth with a thick white froth," &c. Tollet.

[9] —— *ere we* case *him.*] That is, before we strip him naked.
Johnson.

Ber. Your brother, he fhall go along with me.

1 *Lord.* As't pleafe your lordfhip: I'll leave
you.[2] [*Exit.*

Ber. Now will I lead you to the houfe, and fhow
you
The lafs I fpoke of.

2 *Lord.* But, you fay, fhe's honeft.

Ber. That's all the fault: I fpoke with her but
once,
And found her wondrous cold; but I fent to her,
By this fame coxcomb that we have i'the wind,[3]
Tokens and letters which fhe did re-fend;
And this is all I have done: She's a fair creature;
Will you go fee her?

2 *Lord.* With all my heart, my lord.
[*Exeunt.*

SCENE VII.

Florence. *A Room in the* Widow's *Houfe.*

Enter HELENA, *and* Widow.

Hel. If you mifdoubt me that I am not fhe,
I know not how I fhall affure you further,
But I fhall lofe the grounds I work upon.[4]

---

[2] —— *I'll leave you.*] This line is given in the old copy to the
fecond lord, there called Captain G, who goes out; and the *firft*
lord, there called Captain E, remains with Bertram. The whole
courfe of the dialogue fhows this to have been a miftake. See p. 297.
" 1. Lord. [i. e. Captain E.] I, with a troop of Florentines" &c.
MALONE.

[3] —— *we have i'the wind,*] To have *one in the wind,* is enumerated as a proverbial faying by Ray, p. 261. REED.

[4] *But I fhall lofe the grounds I work upon.*] i. e. by difcovering
herfelf to the count. WARBURTON.

I

WID. Though my eſtate be·fallen, I was well
      born,
Nothing acquainted with theſe buſineſſes;
And would not put my reputation now
In any ſtaining act.

HEL.   Nor would I wiſh you.
Firſt, give me truſt, the count he is my huſband;
And, what to your ſworn counſel ⁵ I have ſpoken,
Is ſo, from word to word; and then you·cannot,
By the good aid that I of you ſhall borrow,
Err in beſtowing it.

WID.   I ſhould believe you;
For you have ſhow'd me that, which well approves
You are great in fortune.

HEL.   Take this purſe of gold,
And let me buy your friendly help thus far,
Which I will over-pay, and pay again,
When I have found it.   The count he wooes your
      daughter,
Lays down his wanton ſiege before her beauty,
Reſolves to carry her; let her, in fine, conſent,
As we'll direct her how 'tis beſt to bear it,
Now his important blood will nought deny ⁶
That ſhe'll demand: A ring the county wears,⁷
That downward hath ſucceeded in his houſe,
From ſon to ſon, ſome four or five deſcents
Since the firſt father wore it: this ring he holds

---

⁵ —— *to your* ſworn counſel—] To your private knowledge,
after having required from you an oath of ſecreſy.   JOHNSON.

⁶ *Now bis* important *blood will nought deny* —] *Important* here,
and elſewhere, is *importunate.*   JOHNSON.

So, Spenſer in *The Fairy Queen,* B. II. c. vi. ſt. 29:
    " And with *important* outrage him aſſailed."
Important, from the Fr. *Emportant.*   TYRWHITT.

⁷ —— *the* county *wears,*] i. e. the count.   So, in *Romeo and
Juliet,* we have " the *county* Paris."   STEEVENS.

In moft rich choice; yet, in his idle fire,
To buy his will, it would not feem too dear,
Howe'er repented after.

WID.   Now I fee
The bottom of your purpofe.

HEL. You fee it lawful then: It is no more,
But that your daughter, ere fhe feems as won,
Defires this ring; appoints him an encounter;
In fine, delivers me to fill the time,
Herfelf moft chaftely abfent: after this,[8]
To marry her, I'll add three thoufand crowns
To what is paft already.

WID.   I have yielded:
Inftruct my daughter how fhe fhall perféver,
That time and place, with this deceit fo lawful,
May prove coherent. Every night he comes
With muficks of all forts, and fongs compos'd
To her unworthinefs: it nothing fteads us,
To chide him from our eaves; for he perfifts,
As if his life lay on't.

HEL.   Why then, to-night
Let us affay our plot; which, if it fpeed,
Is wicked meaning in a lawful deed,
And lawful meaning in a lawful act;[9]
Where both not fin, and yet a finful fact:
But let's about it.   [*Exeunt.*

[8] ——*after* this,] The latter word was added to complete the
metre, by the editor of the fecond folio. MALONE.

[9] *Is wicked meaning in a lawful deed,*
    And lawful meaning in a lawful *act;*] To make this gingling
riddle complete in all its parts, we fhould read the fecond line
thus:
    And lawful meaning in a wicked *act;*
The fenfe of the two lines is this: It is a *wicked meaning* becaufe
the woman's intent is to deceive; but a *lawful deed*, becaufe the

ACT IV. SCENE I.

Without the Florentine *Camp.*

Enter first Lord, *with five or six Soldiers in ambush.*

1 LORD. He can come no other way but by this hedge' corner: When you sally upon him, speak what terrible language you will; though you under-stand it not yourselves, no matter: for we must not seem to understand him; unless some one among us, whom we must produce for an interpreter.

1 SOLD. Good captain, let me be the interpreter.

1 LORD. Art not acquainted with him? knows he not thy voice?

man enjoys his own wife. Again, it is a *lawful meaning* because done by her to gain her husband's estranged affection, but it is a *wicked act* because he goes intentionally to commit adultery. The riddle concludes thus: *Where both not sin, and yet a sinful fact,* i. e. Where neither of them sin, and yet it is a sinful fact on both sides; which conclusion, we see, requires the emendation here made. WARBURTON.

Sir Thomas Hanmer reads in the same sense:
    Unlawful *meaning in a lawful act.* JOHNSON.

Bertram's meaning is wicked in a lawful deed, and Helen's meaning is lawful in a lawful act; and neither of them sin: yet on his part it was a sinful act, for his meaning was to commit adultery, of which he was innocent, as the lady was his wife. TOLLET.

The first line relates to Bertram. The *deed* was *lawful,* as being the duty of marriage, owed by the husband to the wife; but his *meaning* was *wicked,* because he intended to commit adultery. The second line relates to Helena; whose *meaning was lawful,* in as much as she intended to reclaim her husband, and demanded only the rights of a wife. The *act* or *deed* was *lawful* for the reason already given. The subsequent line relates to them both. The *fact* was *sinful,* as far as Bertram was concerned, because he intended to commit adultery; yet neither he nor Helena actually sinned: not the wife, because both her intention and action were innocent; not the husband, because he did not accomplish his intention; he did not commit adultery.—This note is partly Mr. Heath's. MALONE.

1 *Sold.* No, fir, I warrant you.

1 *Lord.* But what linfy-woolfy haft thou to fpeak to us again?

1 *Sol.* Even fuch as you fpeak to me.

1 *Lord.* He muft think us fome band of ftrangers i'the adverfary's entertainment.[2] Now he hath a fmack of all neighbouring languages; therefore we muft every one be a man of his own fancy, not to know what we fpeak one to another; fo we feem to know, is to know ftraight our purpofe:[3] chough's language,[4] gabble enough, and good enough. As for you, interpreter, you muft feem very politick. But couch, ho! here he comes; to beguile two hours in a fleep, and then to return and fwear the lies he forges.

Enter PAROLLES.

Par. Ten o'clock: within thefe three hours 'twill be time enough to go home. What fhall I fay I have done? It muft be a very plaufive invention that carries it: They begin to fmoke me; and difgraces have of late knock'd too often at my door.

---

[2] —*fome band of ftrangers i'the adverfary's entertainment.*] That is, *foreign troops in the enemy's pay.* JOHNSON.

[3] —*fo we feem to know, is to know,* &c.] I think the meaning is,—Our feeming to know what we fpeak one to another, is *to make him* to know our purpofe immediately; to difcover our defign to him. *To know,* in the laft inftance, fignifies *to make known.* Sir Thomas Hanmer very plaufibly reads—to *fhow* ftraight our purpofe. MALONE.

The fenfe of this paffage with the context I take to be this.—We muft each fancy a jargon for himfelf, without aiming to be underftood by one another, for provided we appear to underftand, that will be fufficient for the fuccefs of our project. HENLEY.

[4] —*chough's language,*] So, in *The Tempeft:*

" ——I myfelf could make

" A chough of as deep chat." STEEVENS.

X 2

I find, my tongue is too fool-hardy; but my heart hath the fear of Mars before it, and of his creatures, not daring the reports of my tongue.

1 LORD. This is the first truth that e'er thine own tongue was guilty of.   [*Aside.*

PAR. What the devil should move me to undertake the recovery of this drum; being not ignorant of the impossibility, and knowing I had no such purpose? I must give myself some hurts, and say, I got them in exploit: Yet flight ones will not carry it: They will say, Came you off with so little? and great ones I dare not give. Wherefore? what's the instance?⁴ Tongue, I must put you into a butter-woman's mouth, and buy another of Bajazet's mule,⁵ if you prattle me into these perils.

1 LORD. Is it possible, he should know what he is, and be that he is?   [*Aside.*

PAR. I would the cutting of my garments would serve the turn; or the breaking of my Spanish sword.

1 LORD. We cannot afford you so.   [*Aside.*

---

⁴ —— *the* instance?] The *proof.* JOHNSON.

⁵ —— *of Bajazet's* mule,] Dr. Warburton would read—*mute.*
                MALONE.

As a *mule* is as dumb by nature, as the mute is by art, the reading may stand. In one of our old Turkish histories, there is a pompous description of Bajazet riding on a *mule* to the Divan.
                STEEVENS.

Perhaps there may be here a reference to the following apologue mentioned by Maitland, in one of his despatches to Secretary Cecil: " I think yow have hard the apologue off the Philosopher who for th' emperor's plesure tooke upon him to make a *Moyle* speak: In many yeares the lyke may yet be, eyther that the *Moyle,* the Philosopher, or Eamperor may dye before the tyme be fully ronne out." *Haynes's Collection,* 369. Parolles probably means, he must buy a tongue which has still to learn the use of speech, that he may run himself into no more difficulties by his loquacity.
                REED.

Par. Or the baring of my beard; and to fay, it was in ftratagem.

1 *Lord.* 'Twould not do. [*Afide.*

Par. Or to drown my clothes, and fay, I was ftripp'd.

1 *Lord.* Hardly ferve. [*Afide.*

Par. Though I fwore I leap'd from the window of the citadel———

1 *Lord.* How deep? [*Afide.*

Par. Thirty fathom.

1 *Lord.* Three great oaths would fcarce make that be believed. [*Afide.*

Par. I would, I had any drum of the enemy's; I would fwear, I recover'd it.

1 *Lord.* You fhall hear one anon. [*Afide.*

Par. A drum now of the enemy's! [*Alarum within.*

1 *Lord. Throca movoufus, cargo, cargo, cargo.*

All. Cargo, cargo, villianda par corbo, cargo.

Par. O! ranfom, ranfom:—Do not hide mine eyes.
[*They feize him and blindfold him.*

1 *Sold. Bofkos thromuldo bofkos.*

Par. I know you are the Mufkos' regiment.
And I fhall lofe my life for want of language:
If there be here German, or Dane, low Dutch,
Italian, or French, let him fpeak to me,
I will difcover that which fhall undo
The Florentine.

1 *Sold.* *Bofkos vauvado:*———
I underftand thee, and can fpeak thy tongue:———
Kerelybonto:———Sir,
Betake thee to thy faith, for feventeen poniards
Are at thy bofom.

Par. Oh!

X 3

1 *Sold.*   O, pray, pray, pray.———
Manka revania dulcbe.

1 LORD.   *Ofcorbi dulcbos volivorco.*

1 *Sold.* The general is content to fpare thee yet;
And, hood-wink'd as thou art, will lead thee on
To gather from thee: haply, thou may'ft inform
Something to fave thy life.

Par.   O, let me live,
And all the fecrets of our camp I'll fhow,
Their force, their purpofes: nay, I'll fpeak that
Which you will wonder at.

1 *Sold.*   But wilt thou faithfully?

Par. If I do not, damn me.

1 *Sold.*   *Acordo linta.*———
Come on, thou art granted fpace.
         [*Exit, with* PAROLLES *guarded.*

1 *Lord.* Go, tell the count Roufillon and my
         brother,
We have caught the woodcock, and will keep him
         muffled,
Till we do hear from them.

2 *Sold.*   Captain, I will.

1 *Lord.* He will betray us all unto ourfelves;—
Inform 'em[6] that.

2 *Sold.*   So I will, fir.

1 *Lord.* Till then, I'll keep him dark, and fafely
         lock'd.   [*Exeunt.*

---

[6] *Inform* 'em—] Old copy—Inform *on.* Corrected by Mr. Rowe.
         MALONE.

SCENE II.

Florence.   A Room in the Widow's *House.*

Enter BERTRAM *and* DIANA.

BER. They told me, that your name was Fontibell.

DIA. No, my good lord, Diana.

BER.   Titled goddefs;
And worth it, with addition! But, fair foul,
In your fine frame hath love no quality?
If the quick fire of youth light not your mind,
You are no maiden, but a monument:
When you are dead, you fhould be fuch a one
As you are now, for you are cold and ftern;[7]
And now you fhould be as your mother was,
When your fweet felf was got.

DIA. She then was honeft.

BER.   So fhould you be.

DIA.   No:
My mother did but duty; fuch, my lord,
As you owe to your wife.

BER.   No more of that!
I pr'ythee, do not ftrive againft my vows:
I was compell'd to her;[8] but I love thee

---

[7] *You are no maiden, but a* monument:
——*for you are* cold *and* ftern;] Our author had here probably
in his thoughts fome of the *ftern* monumental figures with which
many churches in England were furnifhed by the rude fculptors of
his own time. He has again the fame allufion in *Cymbeline:*
　　" And be her fenfe but as a *monument,*
　　" Thus *in a chapel lying.*" MALONE.

　I believe, the epithet *ftern,* refers only to the feverity often im-
preffed by death on features which, in their animated ftate, were
of a placid turn. STEEVENS.

[8] *No more of that!*
　I pr'ythee, do not ftrive againft my vows:
　I was compell'd to her;] Againft his vows, I believe, means——

X 4

By love's own fweet conftraint, and will for ever
Do thee all rights of fervice.

DIA.   Ay, fo you ferve us,
Till we ferve you: but when you have our rofes,
You barely leave our thorns to prick ourfelves,
And mock us with our barenefs.

BER.   How have I fworn?

DIA. 'Tis not the many oaths, that make the truth;
But the plain fingle vow, that is vow'd true.
What is not holy, that we fwear not by,[9]
But take the Higheft to witnefs: Then, pray you,
     tell me,
If I fhould fwear by Jove's great attributes,[2]
I lov'd you dearly, would you believe my oaths,
When I did love you ill? this has no holding,

---

againft his determined refolution never to cohabit with Helena; and
this *vow*, or *refolution*, he had very ftrongly expreffed in his letter
to the countefs. STEEVENS.

So, in *Vittoria Corombona*, a tragedy by Webfter, 1612:
  " Henceforth *I'll never lie with thee*,—
  " My *vow* is fix'd." MALONE.

[9] *What is not holy, that we fwear not by*,] The fenfe is,—We
never fwear by what is not holy, but fwear by, or take to witnefs,
the Higheft, the Divinity. The tenor of the reafoning contained
in the following lines perfectly correfponds with this: If I fhould
fwear by Jove's great attributes, that I lov'd you dearly, would
you believe my oaths, when you found by experience that I loved
you ill, and was endeavouring to gain credit with you in order to
feduce you to your ruin? No, furely; but you would conclude
that I had no faith either in Jove or his attributes, and that my
oaths were mere words of courfe. For that oath can certainly
have no tie upon us, which we fwear by him we profefs to love
and honour, when at the fame time we give the ftrongeft proof of
our difbelief in him, by purfuing a courfe which we know will
offend and difhonour him. HEATH.

[2] *If I fhould fwear by Jove's great attributes*,] In the print of
the old folio, it is doubtful whether it be *Jove's* or *Love's*, the
characters being not diftinguifhable. If it is read *Love's*, perhaps
it may be fomething lefs difficult. I am ftill at a lofs.
                                        JOHNSON.

To fwear by him whom I proteft to love,
That I will work againft him:³ Therefore, your oaths
Are words, and poor conditions; but unfeal'd;
At leaft, in my opinion.

BER.   Change it, change it;
Be not fo holy-cruel: love is holy;
And my integrity ne'er knew the crafts,
That you do charge men with: Stand no more off,
But give thyfelf unto my fick defires,
Who then recover: fay, thou art mine, and ever
My love, as it begins, fhall fo perféver.

DIA. I fee, that men make hopes, in fuch affairs,⁴
That we'll forfake ourfelves.   Give me that ring.

---

³ *To fwear by him whom I proteft to love*, &c.] This paffage like-
wife appears to me corrupt. She fwears not *by* him whom fhe
loves, but by Jupiter. I believe we may read—*To fwear to him.*
There is, fays fhe, no *holding*, no confiftency, in fwearing to one
that *I love him*, when I fwear it only to *injure* him.
                                        JOHNSON.

This appears to me a very probable conjecture. Mr. Heath's
explanation, which refers the words—" whom I proteft to love"—
to *Jove*, can hardly be right. Let the reader judge.
                                        MALONE.

⁴ *I fee, that men* make hopes *in fuch* affairs,] The four folio
editions read:
            ——make rope's *in fuch a* fcarre.
The emendation was introduced by Mr. Rowe. I find the word
fcarre in *The Tragedy of Hoffman*, 1631; but do not readily
perceive how it can fuit the purpofe of the prefent fpeaker:
        " I know a cave, wherein the bright day's eye,
        " Look'd never but afcance, through a fmall creeke,
        " Or little cranny of the fretted *fcarre:*
        " There have I fometimes liv'd," &c.
Again:
        " Where is the villain's body ?——
        " Marry, even heaved over the *fcarr*, and fent a fwimming," &c.
Again:
        " Run up to the top of the dreadful *fcarre.*"
Again:
        " I ftood upon the top of the high *fcarre.*"

Ber. I'll lend it thee, my dear, but have no power
To give it from me.

Dia.   Will you not, my lord?

Ray says, that a *fcarre* is a cliff of a rock, or a naked rock on the dry land, from the Saxon *carre*, cautes. He adds, that this word gave denomination to the town of *Scarborough*.

STEEVENS.

I fee, that men make hopes, in fuch a fcene,
That we'll forfake ourfelves.] i. e. I perceive that while our lovers are making profeffions of love, and acting their affumed parts in this kind of amorous *interlude*, they entertain hopes that we fhall be betrayed by our paffions to yield to their defires. So, in *Much ado about Nothing*: " The fport will be, when they hold an opinion of one another's dotage, and no fuch matter,—that's the *fcene* that I would fee," &c. Again, in *The Winter's Tale*:

" ——It fhall be fo my care
" To have you royally appointed, as if
" The *fcene* you play, were mine."

The old copy reads:

I fee, that men make ropes *in fuch a* fcarre, &c.

which Mr. Rowe altered to—*make hopes in fuch* affairs; and all the fubfequent editors adopted his correction. It being entirely arbitrary, any emendation that is nearer to the traces of the unintelligible word in the old copy, and affords at the fame time an eafy fenfe, is better entitled to a place in the text.

A corrupted paffage in the firft fketch of *The Merry Wives of Windfor*, fuggefted to me [fcene,] the emendation now introduced. In the fifth Act Fenton defcribes to the hoft his fcheme for marrying Anne Page:

" And in a robe of white this night difguifed
" Wherein fat Falftaff had [r. hath] a mighty *fcarre*,
" Muft Slender take her," &c.

It is manifeft from the correfponding lines in the folio, that *fcarre* was printed by miftake for *fcene*; for in the folio the paffage runs—

" ——fat Falftaff
" Hath a great *fcene*." MALONE.

Mr. Rowe's emendation is not only liable to objection from its diffimilarity to the reading of the four folios, but alfo from the awkwardnefs of his language, where the *literal* refemblance is moft, like the words, rejected. *In fuch affairs*, is a phrafe too vague for Shakfpeare, when a determined point, to which the preceding converfation had been gradually narrowing, was in queftion; and to MAKE *hopes*, is as uncouth an expreffion as can well be imagined.

Ber. It is an honour 'longing to our houſe,
Bequeathed down from many anceſtors;
Which were the greateſt obloquy i'the world
In me to loſe.

Dia.   Mine honour's ſuch a ring:
My chaſtity's the jewel of our houſe,
Bequeathed down from many anceſtors;
Which were the greateſt obloquy i'the world
In me to loſe: Thus your own proper wiſdom
Brings in the champion honour on my part,
Againſt your vain aſſault.

Ber.   Here, take my ring:
Mine houſe, mine honour, yea, my life be thine,
And I'll be bid by thee.

Dia. When midnight comes, knock at my cham-
            ber window;
I'll order take, my mother ſhall not hear.
Now will I charge you in the band of truth,
When you have conquer'd my yet maiden bed,
Remain there but an hour, nor ſpeak to me:
My reaſons are moſt ſtrong; and you ſhall know
            them,   .
When back again this ring ſhall be deliver'd:
And on your finger, in the night, I'll put
Another ring; that, what in time proceeds,
May token to the future our paſt deeds.

Nor is Mr. Malone's ſuppoſition, of *ſcene* for *ſcarre*, a whit more
in point; for, firſt, *ſcarre*, in every part of England where rocks
abound, is well known to ſignify *the detached protruſion of a large
rock*; whereas *ſcare* is *terror* or *affright*.   Nor was *ſcare*, in the firſt
ſketch of *The Merry Wives of Windſor*, a miſtake for *ſcene*, but an
intentional change of ideas; *ſcare* implying only *Falſtaff's terror*,
but *ſcene* including the ſpectator's entertainment.   On the ſuppoſal
that *make hopes* is the true reading, *in ſuch a ſcarre*, may be taken
figuratively for *in ſuch an extremity*, i. e. in ſo deſperate a ſituation.
HENLEY.

Adieu, till then; then, fail not: You have won
A wife of me, though there my hope be done.

   Ber. A heaven on earth I have won, by wooing
       thee.   [*Exit.*

   Dia. For which live long to thank both heaven
       and me!
You may so in the end.——
My mother told me just how he would woo,
As if she sat in his heart; she says, all men
Have the like oaths: he had sworn to marry me,
When his wife's dead; therefore I'll lie with him,
When I am buried. Since Frenchmen are so braid,
Marry that will, I'll live and die a maid: [5]
Only, in this disguise, I think't no sin
To cozen him, that would unjustly win.   [*Exit.*

---

[5] —— *Since Frenchmen are so* braid,
   Marry that will, I'll live and die a maid:] Braid signifies
crafty or *deceitful.* So, in Greene's *Never too Late,* 1616:
    " Dian rose with all her maids,
    " Blushing thus at love his *braids.*"
Chaucer uses the word in the same sense; but as the passage where
it occurs in his *Troilus and Cressida* is contested, it may be necessary
to observe, that Bneð is an Anglo-Saxon word, signifying *fraus,*
astus. Again, in Tho. Drant's *Translation of Horace's Epistles,*
where its import is not very clear:
    " Professing thee a friend, to plaie the ribbalde at a *brade.*"
In *The Romaunt of the Rose,* v. 1336, *Braid* seems to mean *forthwith,*
or, *at a jerk.* There is nothing to answer it in the French, except
tantost. STEEVENS.

SCENE III.

The Florentine *Camp.*

Enter the two French Lords, *and two or three* Soldiers.

1 LORD. You have not given him his mother's letter?

2 LORD. I have deliver'd it an hour since: there is something in't that stings his nature; for, on the reading it, he changed almost into another man.

1 LORD.[6] He has much worthy blame laid upon him, for shaking off so good a wife, and so sweet a lady.

---

[6] 1 *Lord.*] The latter editors have with great liberality bestowed lordship upon these interlocutors, who, in the original edition, are called, with more propriety, *capt.* E. and *capt.* G. It is true that *captain* E. in a former scene is called *lord* E. but the subordination in which they seem to act, and the timorous manner in which they converse, determines them to be only captains. Yet as the latter readers of Shakspeare have been used to find them lords, I have not thought it worth while to degrade them in the margin.

JOHNSON.

These two personages may be supposed to be two young French Lords serving in the Florentine camp, where they now appear in their military capacity. In the first scene where the two French Lords are introduced, taking leave of the king, they are called in the original edition, Lord E. and Lord G.

G. and E. were, I believe, only put to denote the players who performed these characters. In the list of actors prefixed to the first folio, I find the names of Gilburne and Eccleston, to whom these insignificant parts probably fell. Perhaps, however, these performers first represented the French lords, and afterwards two captains in the Florentine army; and hence the confusion of the old copy. In the first scene of this act, one of these captains is called throughout, 1. *Lord* E. The matter is of no great importance. MALONE.

2 *Lord.* Efpecially he hath incurred the ever-
lafting difpleafure of the king, who had even tuneα
his bounty to fing happinefs to him. I will tell
you a thing, but you fhall let it dwell darkly with
you.

1 *Lord.* When you have fpoken it, 'tis dead, and
I am the grave of it.

2 *Lord.* He hath perverted a young gentlewoman here in Florence, of a moft chafte renown;
and this night he flefhes his will in the fpoil of her
honour: he hath given her his monumental ring,
and thinks himfelf made in the unchafte compofition.

1 *Lord.* Now, God delay our rebellion; as we
are ourfelves, what things are we!

2 *Lord.* Merely our own traitors. And as in the
common courfe of all treafons, we ftill fee them
reveal themfelves, till they attain to their abhorr'd
ends;[7] fo he, that in this action contrives againft
his own nobility, in his proper ftream o'erflows
himfelf.[8]

1 *Lord.* Is it not meant damnable in us,[9] to be

---

[7] —— till *they attain to their abhorr'd ends;*] This may mean——
they are perpetually talking about the mifchief they intend to do,
till they have obtained an opportunity of doing it. Steevens.

[8] —— *in his proper ftream o'erflows himfelf.*] That is, *betrays his
own fecrets in his own talk.* The reply fhows that this is the
meaning. Johnson.

[9] *Is it not* meant damnable *in us,*] I once thought that we ought
to read——*Is it not* moft *damnable*; but no change is neceffary.
Adjectives are often ufed as adverbs by our author and his contem-
poraries. So, in *The Winter's Tale:*
  " That did but fhow thee, of a fool, inconftant,
  " And *damnable* ungrateful."
Again, in *Twelfth Night:* " ——and as thou draweft, fwear *hor-
rible*——."

trumpeters of our unlawful intents? We fhall not then have his company to-night?

2 LORD. Not till after midnight; for he is dieted to his hour.

1 LORD. That approaches apace: I would gladly have him fee his company ² anatomiz'd; that he might take a meafure of his own judgements,³ wherein fo curioufly he had fet this counterfeit.⁴

2 LORD. We will not meddle with him till he come; for his prefence muft be the whip of the other.

1 LORD. In the mean time, what hear you of thefe wars?

2 LORD. I hear, there is an overture of peace.

1 LORD. Nay, I affure you, a peace concluded.

2 LORD. What will count Roufillon do then? will he travel higher, or return again into France?

1 LORD. I perceive, by this demand, you are not altogether of his council.

Again, in *The Merry Wives of Windfor:*
" Let the fuppofed fairies pinch him *found.*"
Again, in Maffinger's *Very Woman:*
" I'll beat thee *damnable.*" MALONE.
Mr. M. Mafon wifhes to read—*mean* and damnable.
STEEVENS.

² —— his *company*—] i. e. his *companion.* It is fo ufed in *King Henry V.* MALONE.

³ —— *be might take a meafure of bis own judgements,*] This is a very juft and moral reafon. Bertram, by finding how erroneoufly he has judged, will be lefs confident, and more eafily moved by admonition. JOHNSON.

⁴ —— *wherein fo curioufly be had fet this* counterfeit.] Parolles is the perfon whom they are going to anatomize. *Counterfeit,* befides its ordinary fignification,—[a perfon pretending to be what be is not,] fignified alfo in our author's time a falfe coin, and a picture. The word *fet* fhows that it is here ufed in the firft and the laft of thefe fenfes. MALONE.

2 *Lord.* Let it be forbid, fir! fo fhould I be a great deal of his act.

1 *Lord.* Sir, his wife, fome two months fince, fled from his houfe; her pretence is a pilgrimage to Saint Jaques le grand; which holy undertaking, with moft auftere fanctimony, fhe accomplifh'd: and, there refiding, the tendernefs of her nature became as a prey to her grief; in fine, made a groan of her laft breath, and now fhe fings in heaven.

2 *Lord.* How is this juftified?

1 *Lord.* The ftronger part of it by her own letters; which makes her ftory true, even to the point of her death: her death itfelf, which could not be her office to fay, is come, was faithfully confirm'd by the rector of the place.

2 *Lord.* Hath the count all this intelligence?

1 *Lord.* Ay, and the particular confirmations, point from point, to the full arming of the verity.

2 *Lord.* I am heartily forry, that he'll be glad of this.

1 *Lord.* How mightily, fometimes, we make us comforts of our loffes!

2 *Lord.* And how mightily, fome other times, we drown our gain in tears! The great dignity, that his valour hath here acquired for him, fhall at home be encounter'd with a fhame as ample.

1 *Lord.* The web of our life is of a mingled yarn, good and ill together: our virtues would be proud, if our faults whipp'd them not; and our crimes would defpair, if they were not cherifh'd by our virtues.—

Enter a Servant.

How now? where's your mafter?

Serv. He met the duke in the ſtreet, ſir, of whom he hath taken a ſolemn leave; his lordſhip will next morning for France. The duke hath offered him letters of commendations to the king.

2 *Lord.* They ſhall be no more than needful there, if they were more than they can commend.

Enter BERTRAM.

1 *Lord.* They cannot be too ſweet for the king's tartneſs. Here's his lordſhip now. How now, my lord, is't not after midnight?

Ber. I have to-night deſpatched ſixteen buſi-neſſes, a month's length a-piece, by an abſtract of ſucceſs: I have conge'd with the duke, done my adieu with his neareſt; buried a wife, mourn'd for her; writ to my lady mother, I am returning; en-tertain'd my convoy; and, between theſe main parcels of deſpatch, effected many nicer needs; the laſt was the greateſt, but that I have not ended yet.

2 *Lord.* If the buſineſs be of any difficulty, and this morning your departure hence, it requires haſte of your lordſhip.

Ber. I mean, the buſineſs is not ended, as fear-ing to hear of it hereafter: But ſhall we have this dialogue between the fool and the ſoldier?—— Come, bring forth this counterfeit module;⁵ he

---

⁵ ——*bring forth this counterfeit* module;] *Module* being the *pattern* of any thing, may be here uſed in that ſenſe. Bring-forth this fellow, who by *counterfeit* virtue pretended to make himſelf a *pattern.* JOHNSON.

It appears from Minſheu that *module* and *model* were ſynony-mous.

has deceived me, like a double-meaning prophefier.[6]

2 LORD. Bring him forth: [*Exeunt Soldiers.*] he
has fat in the ftocks all night, poor gallant knave.

BER. No matter; his heels have deferved it, in
ufurping his fpurs fo long.[7] How does he carry
himfelf?

1 LORD. I have told your lordfhip already; the
ftocks carry him. But, to anfwer you as you would
be underftood; he weeps, like a wench that had
fhed her milk: he hath confefs'd himfelf to Mor-
gan, whom he fuppofes to be a friar, from the time
of his remembrance, to this very inftant difafter of
his fetting i'the ftocks: And what think you he
hath confeffed?

BER. Nothing of me, has he?

2 LORD. His confeffion is taken, and it fhall be
read to his face: if your lordfhip be in't, as, I believe you are, you muft have the patience to hear
it.

In *K. Richard II. model* fignifies a thing fafhioned after an
archetype:
"Who was the *model* of thy father's life."
Again, in *K. Henry VIII:*
"The *model* of our chafte loves, his young daughter."
Our author, I believe, ufes the word here in the fame fenfe:—
Bring forth this counterfeit *reprefentation* of a foldier. MALONE.

6 ——— *a double-meaning prophefier.*] So, in *Macbeth:*
"That palter with us in a *double fenfe,*
"And keep the word of promife to our ear,
"But break it to our hope." STEEVENS.

7 ——— *in ufurping his fpurs fo long.*] The punifhment of a *recreant,*
or coward, was to have his fpurs hacked off. MALONE.

I believe thefe words allude only to the ceremonial degradation
of a *knight.* I am yet to learn, that the fame mode was practifed
in difgracing daftards of inferior rank. STEEVENS.

Re-enter Soldiers, with PAROLLES.[2]

BER. A plague upon him! muffled! he can fay nothing of me; hufh! hufh!

1 LORD. Hoodman comes!—*Porto tartaroffa.*

1 SOLD. He calls for the tortures; What will you fay without 'em?

PAR. I will confefs what I know without conftraint; if ye pinch me like a pafty, I can fay no more.

1 SOLD. *Bofko chimurcho.*

2 LORD. *Boblibindo chicurmurco.*

1 SOLD. You are a merciful general:—Our general bids you anfwer to what I fhall afk you out of a note.

PAR. And truly, as I hope to live.

1 SOLD. *Firft demand of him how many horfe the duke is ftrong.* What fay you to that?

PAR. Five or fix thoufand; but very weak and unferviceable: the troops are all fcatter'd, and the commanders very poor rogues, upon my reputation and credit, and as I hope to live.

1 SOLD. Shall I fet down your anfwer fo?

PAR. Do; I'll take the facrament on't, how and which way you will.

BER. All's one to him.[9] What a paft-faving flave is this!

---

[2] *Re-enter Soldiers, with* Parolles.] See an account of the examination of one of Henry the Eighth's captains, who had gone over to the enemy (which may poffibly have fuggefted this of Parolles) in *The Life of Iacke Wilton,* 1594. fig. C. iii. RITSON.

[9] *All's one to him.*] In the old copy thefe words are given by

1 *Lord.* You are deceived, my lord; this is monſieur Parolles, the gallant militariſt, (that was his own phraſe,) that had the whole theorick⁸ of war in the knot of his ſcarf, and the practice in the chape of his dagger.

2 *Lord.* I will never truſt a man again, for keeping his ſword clean; nor believe he can have every thing in him, by wearing his apparel neatly.

1 *Sold.* Well, that's ſet down.

Par. Five or ſix thouſand horſe, I ſaid,—I will ſay true,—or thereabouts, ſet down,—for I'll ſpeak truth.

1 *Lord.* He's very near the truth in this.

Ber. But I con him no thanks for't,⁹ in the nature he delivers it.²

---

miſtake to Parolles. The preſent regulation, which is clearly right, was ſuggeſted by Mr. Steevens. MALONE.

It will be better to give theſe words to one of the Dumains, than to Bertram. RITSON.

⁸ —— *that had the whole* theorick—] i. e. *theory.* So, in Montaigne's Eſſaies, tranſlated by J. Florio, 1603: "They know the *theorique* of all things, but you muſt ſeek who ſhall put it in practice." MALONE.

In 1597 was publiſhed "*Theorique* and Practiſe of Warre, written by Don Philip Prince of Caſtil, by Don Bernardino de Mendoza. Tranſlated out of the Caſtilian tonge in Engliſhe, by Sir Edward Hoby, Knight." 4to. REED.

⁹ —— I con *him no thanks for't,*] To con *thanks* exactly anſwers the French *ſcavoir grè.* To con is to know. I meet with the ſame expreſſion in *Pierce Pennileſſe his Supplication,* &c.

"—— I believe he will con *thee little thanks for it.*"
Again, in *Wily Beguiled,* 1606:
"*I con* maſter Churms *thanks* for this."
Again, in *Any Thing for a Quiet Life:* "He would not truſt you with it, I con him *thanks* for it." STEEVENS.

² —— *in the nature be delivers it.*] He has ſaid truly that our numbers are about five or ſix thouſand; but having deſcribed them as "weak and unſerviceable," &c. I am not much obliged to him. MALONE.

Par. Poor rogues, I pray you, fay.

1 *Sold.* Well, that's fet down.

Par. I humbly thank you, fir: a truth's a truth, the rogues are marvellous poor.

1 Sold. *Demand of him, of what ftrength they are a-foot.* What fay you to that?

Par. By my troth, fir, if I were to live this pre-fent hour,[3] I will tell true. Let me fee: Spurio a hundred and fifty, Sebaftian fo many, Corambus fo many, Jaques fo many; Guiltian, Cofmo, Lo-dowick, and Gratii, two hundred fifty each: mine own company, Chitopher, Vaumond, Bentii, two hundred and fifty each: fo that the mufter-file, rotten and found, upon my life, amounts not to fifteen thoufand poll; half of the which dare not fhake the fnow from off their caffocks,[4] left they fhake themfelves to pieces.

Rather, perhaps, becaufe his narrative, however near the truth, was uttered for a treacherous purpofe. STEEVENS.

[3] —— *if I were to* live *this prefent hour,* &c.] I do not under-ftand this paffage. Perhaps (as an anonymous correfpondent ob-ferves) we fhould read:—if I were to live *but* this prefent hour.
STEEVENS.

Perhaps he meant to fay—if I were to *die* this prefent hour. But fear may be fuppofed to occafion the miftake, as poor frighted Scrub cries: " Spare all I have, and take my *life*." TOLLET.

[4] —— *off their* caffocks,] *Caffock* fignifies a horfeman's loofe coat, and is ufed in that fenfe by the writers of the age of Shak-fpeare. So, in *Every Man in his Humour,* Brainworm fays:—
" He will never come within the fight of a *caffock* or a mufquet-reft again." Something of the fame kind likewife appears to have been part of the drefs of rufticks, in *Mucedorus,* an anonymous comedy, 1598, erroneoufly attributed to Shakfpeare:
" Within my clofet there does hang a *caffock,*
" Though bafe the weed is, 'twas a fhepherd's."
Again, in Whetftone's *Promos and Caffandra,* 1578:
" ———— I will not ftick to wear
" A blue *caffock*."
On this occafion a woman is the fpeaker.

Ber. What shall be done to him?

1 *Lord.* Nothing, but let him have thanks. Demand of him my conditions,⁵ and what credit I have with the duke.

1 *Sold.* Well, that's set down. *You shall demand of him, whether one Captain Dumain be i'the camp, a Frenchman; what his reputation is with the duke, what his valour, honesty, and expertness in wars; or whether he thinks, it were not possible, with well-weighing sums of gold, to corrupt him to a revolt.* What say you to this? what do you know of it?

Par. I beseech you, let me answer to the particular of the intergatories:⁶ Demand them singly.

1 *Sold.* Do you know this captain Dumain?

Par. I know him: he was a botcher's 'prentice in Paris, from whence he was whipp'd for getting the sheriff's fool⁷ with child; a dumb innocent, that could not say him, nay.⁸

[Dumain *lifts up his hand in anger.*

So again, Puttenham, in his *Art of Poetry,* 1589:—" Who would not think it a ridiculous thing to see a lady in her milk-house with a velvet gown, and at a bridal in her *cassock of moccado?*"

In *The Hollander,* a comedy by Glapthorne, 1640, it is again spoken of as part of a soldier's dress:

" Here, sir, receive this military *cassock,* it has seen service."

" ——This military *cassock* has, I fear, some military hangbys." Steevens.

⁵ —— *my* conditions,] i. e. my disposition and character. See Vol. VI. p. 29, n. 8. Malone.

⁶ —— *Intergatories:*] i. e. *interrogatories.* Reed.

⁷ —— *the* sheriff's fool——] We are not to suppose that this was a *fool* kept by the *sheriff* for his diversion. The custody of all *ideots,* &c. possessed of landed property, belonged to the King, who was intitled to the income of their lands, but obliged to find them with necessaries. This prerogative, when there was a large estate in the case, was generally granted to some court-favourite, or other person who made suit for and had interest enough to obtain it,

Ber. Nay, by your leave, hold your hands; though I know, his brains are forfeit to the next tile that falls.[9]

1 *Sold.* Well, is this captain in the duke of Florence's camp?

Par. Upon my knowledge, he is, and lousy.

---

which was called *begging a fool.* But where the land was of inconfiderable value, the *natural* was maintained out of the profits, by the *fheriff,* who accounted for them to the crown. As for thofe unhappy creatures who had neither poffeffions nor relations, they feem to have been confidered as a fpecies of property, being fold or given with as little ceremony, treated as capricioufly, and very often, it is to be feared, left to perifh as miferably, as dogs or cats. RITSON.

[8] —— *a dumb* innocent, *that could not fay him, nay.*] *Innocent* does not here fignify a perfon without guilt or blame; but means, in the good-natured language of our anceftors, an *ideot* or *natural* fool. Agreeably to this fenfe of the word is the following entry of a burial in the parifh regifter of Charlewood in Surrey :—— " Thomas Sole, an *innocent* about the age of fifty years and upwards, buried 19th September, 1605." WHALLEY.

Doll Common, in *The Alchemiff,* being afked for her opinion of the *Widow Pliant,* obferves that fhe is—" a good dull *innocent.*" Again, in *I Would and I Would Not,* a poem, by B. N. 1614:

" I would I were an *innocent,* a foole,
    " That can do nothing elfe but laugh or crie,
" And eate fat meate, and never go to fchoole,
    " And be in love, but with an apple-pie;
" Weare a pide coate, a cockes combe, and a bell,
" And think it did become me paffing well."

Mr. Douce obferves to me, that the term—*innocent,* was originally French.

See alfo note on Ford's *'Tis Pity fhe's a Whore,* new edition of Dodfley's Collection of Old Plays, Vol. VIII. p. 24.
                                                    STEEVENS.

[9] —— *though I know, his brains are forfeit to the next tile that falls.*] In Lucian's *Contemplantes,* Mercury makes Charon remark a man that was killed by the falling of a tile upon his head, whilft he was in the act of putting off an engagement to the next day :—— ϰỳ μϵίαξὺ λίϵϊϊος, ἀπὸ τῦ τϵϒϵς ϰϵϱαμϵίς ἰϰϵτϵϊῦϵϊα, ϵϰ ϊϵϗ ὅτϵ ϰϵϒϵαϊϵς, ἀϵϵϰϵϵϵ ἀϵϵϗ. See the life of Pyrrhus in Plutarch. Pyrrhus was killed by a tile. S. W.

Y 4

1 *Lord.* Nay, look not ſo upon me; we ſhall hear of your lordſhip [9] anon.

1 *Sold.* What is his reputation with the duke?

Par. The duke knows him for no other but a poor officer of mine; and writ to me this other day, to turn him out o'the band: I think, I have his letter in my pocket.

1 *Sold.* Marry, we'll ſearch.

Par. In good ſadneſs, I do not know; either it is there, or it is upon a file, with the duke's other letters, in my tent.

1 *Sold.* Here 'tis; here's a paper; Shall I read it to you?

Par. I do not know, if it be it, or no.

Ber. Our interpreter does it well.

1 *Lord.* Excellently.

1 *Sold.* Dian. *The count's a fool, and full of gold,* [2]—

Par. That is not the duke's letter, ſir; that is an advertiſement to a proper maid in Florence, one Diana, to take heed of the allurement of one

---

[9] ——*your* lordſhip—] The old copy has *Lord.* In the Mſs. of our author's age they ſcarcely ever wrote *Lordſhip* at full length.　Malone.

[2] Dian. *The count's a fool, and full of gold.*] After this line there is apparently a line loſt, there being no rhyme that correſponds to *gold.* Johnson.

I believe this line is incomplete. The poet might have written:
Dian.
 The count's a fool, and full of golden ſtore—*or* ore;
and this addition rhymes with the following alternate verſes.　Steevens.

May we not ſuppoſe the former part of the letter to have been proſe, as the concluding words are? The ſonnet intervenes.

The feigned letter from Olivia to Malvolio, is partly proſe, partly verſe.　Malone.

count Roufillon, a foolifh idle boy, but, for all
that, very ruttifh: I pray you, fir, put it up again.

1 SOLD. Nay, I'll read it firft, by your favour.

PAR. My meaning in't, I proteft, was very honeft in the behalf of the maid: for I knew the
young count to be a dangerous and lafcivious boy;
who is a whale to virginity, and devours up all the
fry it finds.

BER. Damnable, both fides rogue!

1 SOLD. *When he fwears oaths, bid him drop gold,*
and take it;
After he fcores, be never pays the fcore:
Half won, is match well made; match, and well make
it; [3]
He ne'er pays after debts, take it before;

---

[3] *Half won, is match well made; match, and well make it;*]
This line has no meaning that I can find. I read, with a very
flight alteration: *Half won is match well made; watch, and well*
make it. That is, *a match well made is half won; watch, and*
make it well.

This is, in my opinion, not all the error. The lines are mifplaced, and fhould be read thus:

Half won is match well made; watch, and well make it;
When he fwears oaths, bid him drop gold, and take it.
After he fcores, he never pays the fcore:
He ne'er pays after-debts, take it before,
And fay——

That is, take his money, and leave him to himfelf. When the
players had loft the fecond line, they tried to make a connection
out of the reft. Part is apparently in couplets, and the whole was
probably uniform. JOHNSON.

Perhaps we fhould read:

Half won is match well made, match an' we'll make it.
i. e. if we mean to make any match of it at all. STEEVENS.

There is no need of change. The meaning is, " A match well
made, is half won; make your match therefore, but make it well."
M. MASON.

The verfes having been defigned by Parolles as a caution to
Diana, after informing her that Bertram is both *rich* and *faithlefs,*

And say, a soldier, Dian, *told thee this,*
Men are to mell with, boys are not to kiss : [4]
For count of this, the count's a fool, I know it
Who pays before, but not when he does owe it.

Thine, as he vow'd to thee in thine ear,

PAROLLES

he admonishes her not to yield up her virtue to his ~~oaths~~, but his
gold; and having enforced this advice by an adage, recommends her
to comply with his importunity, provided half the sum for which
she shall stipulate be previously paid her :—*Half won is match well
made; match, and well make it.* HENLEY.

Gain half of what he offers, and you are well off; if you yield
to him, make your bargain secure. MALONE.

4 *Men are to mell with, boys are not to kiss :*] The meaning of
the word *mell*, from *meler*, French, is obvious.
So, in *Ane very Excellent and Delectabill Treatise, intitulit* PHILOTUS,
&c. 1603 :
    " But he na husband is to mee;
    " Then how could we twa disagree
      " That never had na *melling*."

    " Na *melling*, mistress? will you then
    " Deny the mariage of that man?"
Again in *The Corpus Christi Play*, acted at Coventry. MSS. Cott.
Vesp. VIII. p. 122 :
    " A fayr yonge qwene herby doth dwelle,
    " Both frech and gay upon to loke,
    " And a tall man with her doth *melle*,
    " The way into hyr chawmer ryght evyn he toke."
The argument of this piece is *The Woman taken in Adultery.*
                        STEEVENS.

Men are to mell with, boys are not to kiss :] Mr. Theobald and
the subsequent editors read—*boys are but to kiss.* I do not see any
need of change, nor do I believe that any opposition was intended
between the words *mell* and *kiss.* Parolles wishes to recommend
himself to Diana, and for that purpose advises her to grant her
favours to *men*, and not to *boys.* He himself calls his letter " An
advertisement to Diana to take heed of the allurement of one
count Roussillon, a foolish idle *boy*."
To *mell* is used by our author's contemporaries in the sense of
meddling, without the indecent idea which Mr. Theobald supposed

Ber. He shall be whipp'd through the army, with this rhyme in his forehead.

2 *Lord.* This is your devoted friend, sir, the manifold linguist, and the armipotent soldier.

Ber. I could endure any thing before but a cat, and now he's a cat to me.

1 *Sold.* I perceive, sir, by the general's looks,[5] we shall be fain to hang you.

Par. My life, sir, in any case: not that I am afraid to die; but that, my offences being many, I would repent out the remainder of nature: let me live, sir, in a dungeon, i'the stocks, or any where, so I may live.[6]

1 *Sold.* We'll see what may be done, so you confess freely; therefore, once more to this captain Dumain: You have answer'd to his reputation with the duke, and to his valour: What is his honesty?

Par. He will steal, sir, an egg out of a cloister;[7]

---

to be couched under the word in this place. So, in Hall's *Satires,* 1597:

"Hence, ye profane; *mell* not with holy things."
Again, in Spenser's *Faery Queen,* B. IV. c. 1:
"With holy father fits not with such things to *mell.*"
MALONE.

[5] *——by the general's looks,*] The old copy has—*by your.* The emendation was made by the editor of the second folio, and the misprint probably arose from yᵉ in the MS. being taken for yʳ.
MALONE.

[6] *——let me live, sir, in a dungeon, i'the stocks, or any where, so I may live.*] Smith might have had this abject sentiment of Parolles in his memory, when he put the following words into the mouth of Lycon, in *Phædra and Hippolytus:*
"O, chain me, whip me, let me be the scorn
"Of sordid rabbles, and insulting crowds;
"Give me but life, and make that life most wretched!"
STEEVENS.

[7] *——an egg out of a cloister;*] I know not that *cloister,* though it may etymologically signify *any thing shut,* is used by our author

I

for rapes and ravifhments he parallels Neffus. He profeffes not keeping of oaths; in breaking them, he is ftronger than Hercules. He will lie, fir, with fuch volubility, that you would think truth were a fool: drunkennefs is his beft virtue; for he will be fwine-drunk; and in his fleep he does little harm, fave to his bed-clothes about him; but they know his conditions, and lay him in ftraw. I have but little more to fay, fir, of his honefty: he has every thing that an honeft man fhould not have; what an honeft man fhould have, he has nothing.

1 *Lord.* I begin to love him for this.

Ber. For this defcription of thine honefty? A pox upon him for me, he is more and more a cat.

1 *Sold.* What fay you to his expertnefs in war?

Par. Faith, fir, he has led the drum before the Englifh tragedians,—to belie him, I will not,—and more of his foldierfhip I know not; except, in that country, he had the honour to be the officer at a place there call'd Mile-end,[7] to inftruct for the doubling of files: I would do the man what honour I can, but of this I am not certain.

1 *Lord.* He hath out-villain'd villainy fo far, that the rarity redeems him.

Ber. A pox on him! he's a cat ftill.[8]

otherwife than for a *monaftery*, and therefore I cannot guefs whence this hyperbole could take its original: perhaps it means only this: *He will fteal any thing, however trifling, from any place, however holy.* Johnson.

Robbing the fpital, is a common phrafe, of the like import. M. Mason.

[7] ——*as a place there call'd Mile-end*,] See a note on *King Henry IV.* P. II. Act III. fc. ii. Malone.

[8] ——*he's a cat ftill.*] That is, throw him how you will, he lights upon his legs. Johnson.

1 Sold. His qualities being at this poor price, I need not afk you, if gold will corrupt him to revolt.

Par. Sir, for a *quart d'ecu*[9] he will fell the fee-fimple of his falvation, the inheritance of it; and cut the entail from all remainders, and a perpetual fucceffion for it perpetually.

1 Sold. What's his brother, the other captain Dumain?

2 Lord. Why does he afk him of me?[2]

1 Sold. What's he?

Par. E'en a crow of the fame neft; not altogether

Bertram has no fuch meaning. In a fpeech or two before, he declares his averfion to a cat, and now only continues in the fame opinion, and fays he hates Parolles as much as he hates a cat. The other explanation will not do, as Parolles could not be meant by the *cat*, which always lights on its legs, for Parolles is now in a fair way to be totally difconcerted. STEEVENS.

I am ftill of my former opinion. The fpeech was applied by King James to Coke, with refpect to his fubtilties of law, that throw him which way we would, he could ftill, like a cat, light upon his legs. JOHNSON.

The count had faid, that formerly a cat was the only thing in the world which he could not endure; but that now Parolles was as much the object of his averfion as that animal. After Parolles has gone through his next lift of falfhoods, the count adds, " he's more and more a cat,"—ftill more and more the object of my averfion than he was. As Parolles proceeds ftill further, one of the Frenchmen obferves, that the fingularity of his impudence and villainy redeems his character.—Not at all, replies the count; " he's a cat ftill;" he is as hateful to me as ever. There cannot therefore, I think, be any doubt that Dr. Johnfon's interpretation, " throw him how you will, he lights upon his legs,"—is founded on a mifapprehenfion. MALONE.

[9] ——*for a* quart d'ecu—] The fourth part of the fmaller French crown; about eight-pence of our money. MALONE.

[2] *Why does he afk him of me?*] This is nature. Every man is on fuch occafions more willing to hear his neighbour's character than his own. JOHNSON.

so great as the first in goodness, but greater a great deal in evil. He excels his brother for a coward, yet his brother is reputed one of the best that is: In a retreat he out-runs any lackey; marry, in coming on he has the cramp.

1 *Sold.* If your life be saved, will you undertake to betray the Florentine?

Par. Ay, and the captain of his horse, count Rousillon.

1 *Sold.* I'll whisper with the general, and know his pleasure.

Par. I'll no more drumming; a plague of all drums! Only to seem to deserve well, and to beguile the supposition³ of that lascivious young boy the count, have I run into this danger: Yet, who would have suspected an ambush where I was taken?

[*Aside.*

1 *Sold.* There is no remedy, sir, but you must die: the general says, you, that have so traiterously discovered the secrets of your army, and made such pestiferous reports of men very nobly held, can serve the world for no honest use; therefore you must die. Come, headsman, off with his head.

Par. O Lord, sir; let me live, or let me see my death!

1 *Sold.* That shall you, and take your leave of all your friends.   [*Unmuffling him.*
So, look about you; Know you any here?

Ber. Good morrow, noble captain.

2 *Lord.* God bless you, captain Parolles.

1 *Lord.* God save you, noble captain.

---

³ —— *to beguile the supposition*—] That is, *to deceive the opinion,* to make the count think me a man that *deserves well.*
                                                  JOHNSON.

2 Lord. Captain, what greeting will you to my lord Lafeu? I am for France.

1 Lord. Good captain, will you give me a copy of the fonnet you writ to Diana in behalf of the count Roufillon? an I were not a very coward, I'd compel it of you; but fare you well.

[*Exeunt* BERTRAM, Lords, &c.

1 Sold. You are undone, captain; all but your fcarf, that has a knot on't yet.

Par. Who cannot be crufh'd with a plot?

1 Sold. If you could find out a country where but women were that had received fo much fhame, you might begin an impudent nation. Fare you well, fir; I am for France too; we fhall fpeak of you there. [*Exit.*

Par. Yet am I thankful: if my heart were great,
'Twould burft at this: Captain I'll be no more;
But I will eat and drink, and fleep as foft
As captain fhall: fimply the thing I am
Shall make me live. Who knows himfelf a braggart,
Let him fear this; for it will come to pafs,
That every braggart fhall be found an afs.
Ruft, fword! cool, blufhes! and, Parolles, live
Safeft in fhame! being fool'd, by foolery thrive!
There's place, and means, for every man alive.
I'll after them. [*Exit.*

SCENE IV.

Florence. *A Room in the* Widow's *House.*

Enter HELENA, Widow, *and* DIANA.

HEL. That you may well perceive I have not
    wrong'd you,
One of the greateft in the chriftian world
Shall be my furety; 'fore whofe throne, 'tis needful,
Ere I can perfect mine intents, to kneel:
Time was, I did him a defired office,
Dear almoft as his life; which gratitude
Through flinty Tartar's bofom would peep forth,
And anfwer, thanks: I duly am inform'd,
His grace is at Marfeilles;[4] to which place
We have convenient convoy. You muft know,
I am fuppofed dead: the army breaking,
My hufband hies him home; where, heaven aiding,
And by the leave of my good lord the king,
We'll be, before our welcome.

WID.   Gentle madam,
You never had a fervant, to whofe truft
Your bufinefs was more welcome.

HEL.   Nor you,[5] miftrefs,
Ever a friend, whofe thoughts more truly labour
To recompence your love; doubt not, but heaven
Hath brought me up to be your daughter's dower,

---

[4] *His grace is at* Marfeilles; &c.] From this line, and others, it appears that *Marfeilles* was pronounced by our author as a word of three fyllables. The old copy has here *Marcellæ*, and in the laft fcene of this Act *Marcellus*. MALONE.

[5] *Nor you,*] Old copy—Nor *your*. Corrected by Mr. Rowe.
MALONE.

As it hath fated her to be my motive[5]
And helper to a husband.   But O strange men!
That can such sweet use make of what they hate,
When saucy trusting of the cozen'd thoughts
Defiles the pitchy night![6] so lust doth play
With what it loaths, for that which is away:
But more of this hereafter:——You, Diana,
Under my poor instructions yet must suffer
Something in my behalf.

DIA.   Let death and honesty[7]
Go with your impositions,[8] I am yours
Upon your will to suffer.

HEL.   Yet, I pray you,——
But with the word, the time will bring on summer,
When briars shall have leaves as well as thorns,
And be as sweet as sharp.[9]   We must away;

---

[5] ——*my* motive—] *Motive* for assistant. WARBURTON.

Rather for *mover*. So, in the last Act of this play:
    " ——all impediments in fancy's course
    " Are *motives* of more fancy." MALONE.

[6] *When* saucy *trusting of the cozen'd thoughts*
Defiles the pitchy night!] Saucy may very properly signify
luxurious, and by consequence *lascivious*. JOHNSON.

So, in *Measure for Measure*:
    " ——as to remit
    " Their *saucy* sweetness, that do coin heaven's image
    " In stamps that are forbid." MALONE.

[7] ——*death and honesty*—] i. e. an honest death. So in another
of our author's plays, we have " death and honour" for *honourable death*. STEEVENS.

[8] ——*your* impositions,] i. e. your commands. MALONE.

An *imposition* is a task imposed. The term is still current in
Universities. STEEVENS.

[9] *But* with the word, *the time will bring on summer*, &c.] *With the
word*, i. e. in an instant of time. WARBURTON.

The meaning of this observation is, that as *briars* have *sweetness* with their *prickles*, so shall these *troubles* be recompensed with
joy. JOHNSON.

Our waggon is prepar'd, and time revives us : [9]

I would read:
> *Yet I 'fray you*
> *But with the word: the time will bring,* &c.

And then the sense will be, " I only frighten you by mentioning the word *suffer*; for a short time will bring on the season of happiness and delight." BLACKSTONE.

As the beginning of Helen's reply is evidently a designed aposiopesis, a break ought to follow it, thus:

> Hel. *Yet, I pray you:*——

The sense appears to be this:—Do not think that I would engage you in any service that should expose you to such an alternative, or indeed, to any lasting inconvenience; *But with the word,* i. e. But on the contrary, you shall no sooner have delivered what you will have to testify on my account, than the irksomeness of the service will be over, and every pleasant circumstance to result from it, will instantaneously appear. HENLEY.

[9] *Our waggon is prepar'd, and time* revives us:] The word *revives* conveys so little sense, that it seems very liable to suspicion.

——*and time* revyes us:

i. e. looks us in the face, calls upon us to hasten.

WARBURTON.

The present reading is corrupt, and I am afraid the emendation none of the soundest. I never remember to have seen the word *revye.* One may as well leave blunders as make them. Why may we not read for a shift, without much effort, *the time* invites us? JOHNSON.

To *vye* and *revye* were terms at several ancient games at cards, but particularly at *Gleek.* So, in *Greene's Art of Coney-catching,* 1592: " I'll either win something or lose something, therefore I'll *vie* and *revie* every card at my pleasure, till either yours or mine come out; therefore 12d. upon this card, my card comes first." Again: " —— so they *vie* and *revie* till some ten shillings be on the stake," &c. Again: " This flesh oth the Conie, and the sweetness of gain makes him frolick, and none more ready to *vie* and *revie* than he." Again: " So they *vie* and *revie*, and for once that the Barnacle wins, the Conie gets five." Perhaps, however, *revyes* is not the true reading. Shakspeare might have written—*time* reviles *us,* i. e. reproaches us for wasting it. Yet, —*time* revives *us* may mean, it *rouses* us. So, in another play of our author:

> " —— I would *revive* the soldiers' hearts,
> " Because I found them ever as myself." STEEVENS.

I

All's well that ends well:[2] ftill the fine's[3] the crown;
Whate'er the courfe, the end is the renown.

[*Exeunt.*

SCENE V.

Roufillon. *A Room in the* Countefs's *Palace.*

Enter Countefs, LAFEU, *and* Clown.

LAF. No, no, no, your fon was mifled with a
fnipt-taffata fellow there; whofe villainous faffron
would have made all the unbaked and doughy youth
of a nation in his colour:[4] your daughter-in-law

Time *revives* us, feems to refer to the happy and fpeedy ter-
mination of their embarraffments. She had juft before faid:
"With the word, the time will bring on fummer."

HENLEY.

[2] *All's well that ends well:*] So, in *The Spanifh Tragedy:*
"The *end is crown* of every work well done."
All's well that ends well, is one of Camden's proverbial fentence,

MALONE.

[3] —— *the fine's* —] i. e. the end. So, in *The London Prodigal,*
1605:
"Nature hath done the laft for me, and there's the *fine.*"

MALONE.

[3] —— *whofe villainous faffron would have made all the unbaked
and doughy youth of a nation in his colour:*] Parolles is reprefented
as an affected follower of the fafhion, and an encourager of his
mafter to run into all the follies of it; where he fays, "Ufe a
more fpacious ceremony to the noble lords—they wear themfelves
in the cap of time—and though the devil lead the meafure, fuch
are to be followed." Here fome particularities of fafhionable
drefs are ridiculed. *Snipt-taffata* needs no explanation; but *villainous faffron* is more obfcure. This alludes to a fantaftic fafhion,
then much followed, of ufing *yellow ftarch* for their bands and
ruffs. So, Fletcher, in his *Queen of Corinth:*
"—— Has he familiarly
"Diflik'd your yellow ftarch; or faid your doublet
"Was not exactly frenchified?——"

Z 2

had been alive at this hour; and your ſon here at
home, more advanced by the king, than by that
red-tail'd humble-bee I ſpeak of.

And Jonſon's *Devil's an Aſs:*
"Carmen and chimney-ſweepers are got into the *yellow ſtarch.*"
This was invented by one Turner, a tire-woman, a court-bawd;
and, in all reſpects, of ſo infamous a character, that her invention
deſerved the name of *villainous ſaffron.* This woman was, afterwards, amongſt the miſcreants concerned in the murder of Sir
Thomas Overbury, for which ſhe was hanged at Tyburn, and
would die in a *yellow ruff* of her own invention: which made yellow ſtarch ſo odious, that it immediately went out of faſhion. 'Tis
this, then, to which Shakſpeare alludes: but uſing the word *ſaffron*
for *yellow*, a new idea preſented itſelf, and he purſues his thought
under a quite different alluſion—*Whoſe villainous ſaffron would
have made all the unbaked and doughy youths of a nation in his colour,*
i. e. of his temper and diſpoſition. Here the general cuſtom of
that time, of colouring *paſte* with ſaffron, is alluded to. So, in
The Winter's Tale:
"I muſt have *ſaffron* to colour the warden pyes."
WARBURTON.

This play was probably written ſeveral years before the death of Sir
Thomas Overbury.—The plain meaning of the paſſage ſeems to
be:—"Whoſe evil qualities are of ſo deep a dye, as to be ſufficient to corrupt the moſt innocent, and to render them of the ſame
diſpoſition with himſelf." MALONE.

Stubbs, in his *Anatomie of Abuſes*, publiſhed in 1595, ſpeaks of
ſtarch of various colours:
"——The one arch or piller wherewith the devil's kingdome
of great ruffes is underpropped, is a certain kind of liquid matter
which they call *ſtarch*, wherein the devill hath learned them to
waſh and die their ruffes, which, being drie, will ſtand ſtiff and
inflexible about their neckes. And this ſtartch they make of divers ſubſtances, ſometimes of wheate flower, of branne, and other
graines: ſometimes of rootes, and ſometimes of other thinges;
of all collours and hues, as white, redde, blewe, purple, and the
like."
In *The World toſs'd at Tennis*, a maſque by Middleton, *the five
ſtarches* are perſonified, and introduced conteſting for ſuperiority.
Again, in *Albumazar*, 1615:
"What price bears wheat and *ſaffron*, that your band's ſo
ſtiff and *yellow?*"
Again, in Heywood's *If you know not Me, you know Nobody,*

Count. I would, I had not known him![4] it was the death of the moſt virtuous gentlewoman, that ever nature had praiſe for creating: if ſhe had partaken of my fleſb, and coſt me the deareſt groans of a mother, I could not have owed her a more rooted love.

Laf. 'Twas a good lady, 'twas a good lady: we may pick a thouſand ſallads, ere we light on ſuch another herb.

Clo. Indeed, ſir, ſhe was the ſweet-marjoram of the ſallad, or, rather the herb of grace.[5] .

Laf. They are not ſallad-herbs, you knave, they are noſe-herbs.

Clo. I am no great Nebuchadnezzar, ſir, I have not much ſkill in graſs.[6]

Laf. Whether doſt thou profeſs thyſelf; a knave, or a fool?

Clo. A fool, ſir, at a woman's ſervice, and a knave at a man's.

Laf. Your diſtinction?

Clo. I would cozen the man of his wife, and do his ſervice.

1606: " —— have taken an order to wear *yellow* garters, points, and ſhoe-tyings, and 'tis thought *yellow* will grow a cuſtom."

" It has been long uſed at London."

It may be added, that in the year 1446, a parliament was held at Trim in Ireland, by which the natives were directed, among other things, not to wear ſhirts ſtained with *ſaffron*. STEEVENS.

See a note on *Albumazar*. Dodſley's *Collection of Old Plays*, Vol. VII. p. 156, edit. 1780. REED.

[4] *I would, I had not known him!*] This dialogue ſerves to connect the incidents of Parolles with the main plan of the play, JOHNSON.

[5] —— *herb of grace*.] i. e. rue. So, in *Hamlet:* "there's rue for you—we may call it *herb of grace* o' Sundays." STEEVENS.

[6] —— *in graſs*.] The old copy, by an evident error of the preſs, reads—*grace*. The correction was made by Mr. Rowe. The word *ſallad* in the preceding ſpeech was alſo ſupplied by him. MALONE.

LAF. So you were a knave at his service, indeed.

CLO. And I would give his wife my bauble, fir, to do her service.[6]

LAF. I will subscribe for thee; thou art both knave and fool.

CLO. At your service.

LAF. No, no, no.

CLO. Why, fir, if I cannot serve you, I can serve as great a prince as you are.

---

[6] —— *I would give his wife my* bauble, *fir, to do her service.*] Part of the furniture of a *fool* was a *bauble*, which, though it be generally taken to fignify any thing of fmall value, has a precife and determinable meaning. It is, in fhort, a kind of truncheon with a head carved on it, which the *fool* anciently carried in his hand. There is a reprefentation of it in a picture of Watteau, formerly in the collection of Dr. Mead, which is engraved by Baron, and called *Comediens Italiens*. A faint refemblance of it may be found in the frontifpiece of L. de Guernier to *King Lear*, in Mr. Pope's edition in duodecimo. SIR J. HAWKINS.

So, in Marfton's *Dutch Courtefan*, 1604:
" ——if a *fool*, we muft bear his *bauble*."
Again, in *The Two Angry Women of Abingdon*, 1599: " The *fool* will not leave his *bauble* for the Tower of London:"
Again, in *Jack Drum's Entertainment*, 1601:
" She is enamoured of the *fool's bauble*."
In the STULTIFERA NAVIS, 1497, are feveral reprefentations of this inftrument, as well as in *Cocke's Lorel's Bote*, printed by Wynkyn de Worde. Again, in Lyte's *Herbal*: " In the hollownefs of the faid flower (the great blue wolfe's-bane) grow two fmall crooked hayres, fomewhat great at the end, fafhioned like a *fool's bauble*." An ancient proverb, in Ray's collection, points out the materials of which thefe *baubles* were made: " If every fool fhould wear a *bable*, fewel would be dear." See figure 12, in the plate at the end of *The Firft Part of King Henry IV.* with Mr. Tollet's explanation. STEEVENS.

The word *bauble* is here ufed in two fenfes. The Clown had another *bauble* befides that which the editor alludes to. M. MASON.

When Cromwell, 1653, forcibly turned out the rump-parliament, he bid the foldiers " take away that *fool's bauble*," pointing to the fpeaker's mace. BLACKSTONE.

Laf. Who's that? a Frenchman?

Clo. Faith, fir, he has an Englifh name;[7] but his phifnomy is more hotter in France, than there.[8]

Laf. What prince is that?

Clo. The black prince,[9] fir, *alias*, the prince of darknefs; *alias*, the devil.

Laf. Hold thee, there's my purfe: I give thee not this to fuggeft thee from thy mafter[2] thou talk'ft of; ferve him ftill.

Clo. I am a woodland fellow, fir, that always loved a great fire;[3] and the mafter I fpeak of, ever keeps a good fire. But, fure, he is the prince of the

---

[7] —— *an Englifh* name;] The old copy reads *maine*.

STEEVENS.

Correƈted by Mr. Rowe. MALONE.

Maine, or *head of hair*, agrees better with the context than *name*. His hair was *thick*. HENLEY.

[8] —— *his phifnomy is more* hotter *in France, than there.*] This is intolerable nonfenfe. The ftupid editors, becaufe the devil was talked of, thought no quality would fuit him but *hotter*. We fhould read, more *honour'd*. A joke upon the French people, as if they held a dark complexion, which is natural to them, in more eftimation than the Englifh do, who are generally white and fair.

WARBURTON,

The allufion is, in all probability, to the *Morbus Gallicus*.

STEEVENS.

[9] *The* black prince,] Bifhop Hall, in his *Satires*, B. V. Sat. ii. has given the fame name to Pluto: " So the *black prince* is broken loofe againe," &c. HOLT WHITE.

[2] —— *to* fuggeft *thee from thy mafter*—] Thus the old copy. The modern editors read—*feduce*, but without authority. To *fuggeft* had anciently the fame meaning. So, in *The Two Gentlemen of Verona*:

" Knowing that tender youth is foon *fuggefted*,

" I nightly lodge her in an upper tower." STEEVENS.

[3] *I am a woodland fellow, fir*, &c.] Shakfpeare is but rarely guilty of fuch impious trafh. And it is obfervable, that then he always puts that into the mouth of his *fools*, which is now grown the characterittic of the *fine gentleman*. WARBURTON.

world,' let his nobility remain in his court. I am for the house with the narrow gate, which I take to be too little for pomp to enter: some, that humble themselves, may; but the many will be too chill and tender; and they'll be for the flowery way, that leads to the broad gate, and the great fire.⁴

LAF. Go thy ways, I begin to be a-weary of thee; and I tell thee so before, because I would not fall out with thee. Go thy ways; let my horses be well look'd to, without any tricks.

CLO. If I put any tricks upon 'em, sir, they shall be jades' tricks; which are their own right by the law of nature. [*Exit.*

LAF. A shrewd knave, and an unhappy.⁵

COUNT. So he is. My lord, that's gone, made himself much sport out of him: by his authority he remains here, which he thinks is a patent for his sauciness; and, indeed, he has no pace, but runs where he will.⁶

LAF. I like him well; 'tis not amiss: and I was about to tell you, Since I heard of the good lady's

---

³ —— *But, sure, be is the prince of the world,*] I think we should read—*But since be is,* &c. and thus Sir T. Hanmer. STEEVENS.

⁴ —— *the* flowery way,——*and the* great fire.] The same impious stuff occurs again in *Macbeth:* " ——the *primrose way* to the *everlasting bonfire.*" STEEVENS.

⁵ —— *unhappy.*] i. e. *mischievously waggish, unlucky.* JOHNSON. So, in *King Henry VIII:*
   " You are a churchman, or, I'll tell you, cardinal,
   " I should judge now *unhappily.*" STEEVENS.

⁶ *So be is. My lord, that's gone, made himself much sport out of him: by his authority he remains here, which he thinks is a patent for his sauciness; and, indeed, he has no pace, but runs where he will.*] Should not we read—no *place,* that is, no *station,* or *office* in the family? TYRWHITT.

A *pace* is a certain or prescribed walk; so we say of a man meanly obsequious, that he has learned his *paces,* and of a horse who moves irregularly, that he has *no paces.* JOHNSON.

death, and that my lord your fon was upon his return home, I moved the king my mafter, to fpeak
in the behalf of my daughter; which, in the mi-
nority of them both, his majefty, out of a felf-gra-
cious remembrance, did firft propofe: his highnefs
hath promifed me to do it: and, to ftop up the difpleafure he hath conceived againft your fon, there
is no fitter matter. How does your ladyfhip like it?

Count. With very much content, my lord, and
I wifh it happily effected.

Laf. His highnefs comes poft from Marfeilles,
of as able body as when he number'd thirty; he
will be here to-morrow, or I am deceived by him
that in fuch intelligence hath feldom fail'd.

Count. It rejoices me, that I hope I fhall fee him
ere I die. I have letters, that my fon will be here
to-night: I fhall befeech your lordfhip, to remain
with me till they meet together.

Laf. Madam, I was thinking, with what manners
I might fafely be admitted.

Count. You need but plead your honourable privilege.

Laf. Lady, of that I have made a bold charter;
but, I thank my God, it holds yet.

Re-enter Clown.

Clo. O madam, yonder's my lord your fon with
a patch of velvet on's face: whether there be a fcar
under it, or no, the velvet knows; but 'tis a goodly ·
patch of velvet: his left cheek is a cheek of two
pile and a half, but his right cheek is worn bare.

Laf. A fcar nobly got, or a noble fcar, is a good
livery of honour: [6] fo, belike, is that.

---

⁷ Laf. *A fcar nobly got*, &c.] This fpeech in the fecond folio
and the modern editions is given to the countefs, and perhaps

Clo. But it is your carbonado'd[1] face.

Laf. Let us go see your son, I pray you; I long to talk with the young noble soldier.

Clo. 'Faith, there's a dozen of 'em, with delicate fine hats, and most courteous feathers, which bow the head, and nod at every man.[8]   [*Exeunt.*

ACT V.   SCENE I.

Marseilles.   *A Street.*

Enter HELENA, Widow, *and* DIANA, *with two Attendants.*

Hel. But this exceeding posting, day and night,
Must wear your spirits low: we cannot help it;
But, since you have made the days and nights as one,
To wear your gentle limbs in my affairs,
Be bold, you do so grow in my requital,
As nothing can unroot you.   In happy time;———

rightly. It is more probable that she should have spoken thus favourably of Bertram, than Lafeu. In the original copy, to each of the speeches of the countess *Lad.* or *La.* [i. e. *Lady*] is prefixed; so that the mistake was very easy. MALONE.

I do not discover the improbability of this commendation from Lafeu, who is at present anxious to marry his own daughter to Bertram. STEEVENS.

[1] ——*carbonado'd*] i. e. scotched like a piece of meat for the gridiron. STEEVENS.

The word is again used in *King Lear.* Kent says to the Steward—
    "I'll *carbonado* your shanks for you." MALONE.

[8] ——*feathers, which——nod at every man.*] So, in *Antony and Cleopatra*:
    "——— a blue promontory,
    "With trees upon't, that nod unto the world——." STEEVENS.

Enter a gentle Aftringer.[9]

This man may help me to his majefty's ear,
If he would fpend his power.—God fave you, fir.

GENT. And you.

HEL. Sir, I have feen you in the court of France.

GENT. I have been fometimes there.

HEL. I do prefume fir, that you are not fallen
From the report that goes upon your goodnefs;
And therefore, goaded with moft fharp occafions,
Which lay nice manners by, I put you to
The ufe of your own virtues, for the which
I fhall continue thankful.

GENT.   What's your will?

HEL. That it will pleafe you
To give this poor petition to the king;
And aid me with that ftore of power you have,
To come into his prefence.

---

[9] *Enter a gentle* Aftringer.] Perhaps *a gentle ftranger*, i. e. a
'ftranger of gentle condition, a gentleman. The error of this conjecture, (which I have learned, fince our firft edition made its appearance, from an old book of Falconry, 1633,) fhould teach
diffidence to thofe who conceive the words which they do not
underftand, to be corruptions. An *oftringer* or *aftringer* is a falconer, and fuch a character was probable to be met with about a
court which was famous for the love of that diverfion. So, in
Hamlet:
    " We'll e'en to it like French *Falconers*."
A *gentle aftringer* is a *gentleman falconer*. The word is derived
from *eftercus* or *auftercus*, a gofhawk; and thus, fays Cowell in his
Law Dictionary: " We ufually call a falconer, who keeps that
kind of hawk, an *auftringer*." Again, in *The Book of Hawking*,
&c. bl. l. no date: " Now bicaufe I fpoke of *oftregiers*, ye fhall
underftand that they ben called *oftregiers* that keep gofhauks or
tercels," &c. I learn from Blount's *Antient Tenures*, that a " gofshawk is in our records termed by the feveral names *Oftercum*,
Hoftricum, *Eftricum*, *Afturcum*, and *Aufturcum*," and all from the
French *Auftour*. STEEVENS.

Gent. The king's not here.

Hel.   Not here, fir?

Gent.   Not, indeed:
He hence remov'd laft night, and with more hafte
Than is his ufe.

Wid.   Lord, how we lofe our pains!

Hel. *All's well that ends well,* yet;
Though time feem fo advérfe, and means unfit.—
I do befeech you, whither is he gone?

Gent. Marry, as I take it, to Roufillon;
Whither I am going.

Hel.   I do befeech you, fir,
Since you are like to fee the king before me,
Commend the paper to his gracious hand;
Which, I prefume, fhall render you no blame,
But rather make you thank your pains for it:
I will come after you, with what good fpeed
Our means will make us means.[9]

Gent.   This I'll do for you.

Hel. And you fhall find yourfelf to be well
            thank'd,
Whate'er falls more.—We muft to horfe again;—
Go, go, provide.   [*Exeunt.*

---

[9] *Our means will make us means.*] Shakfpeare delights much in
this kind of reduplication, fometimes fo as to obfcure his meaning.
Helena fays, *they will follow with fuch fpeed as the means which
they have will give them ability to exert.* JOHNSON.

SCENE II.

Roufillon. *The inner Court of the* Countefs's *Palace.*

Enter Clown *and* PAROLLES.

PAR. Good monfieur Lavatch,[1] give my lord Lafeu this letter: I have ere now, fir, been better known to you, when I have held familiarity with frefher clothes; but I am now, fir, muddied in fortune's moat, and fmell fomewhat ftrong of her ftrong difpleafure.[3]

---

[1] —— *Lavatch,*] This is an undoubted and perhaps irremediable corruption of fome French word. STEEVENS.

[3] —— *but I am now, fir, muddied in fortune's* moat, &c.] In former editions:—*but I am now, fir, muddied in fortune's* mood, *and fmell fomewhat ftrong of her ftrong difpleafure.* I believe the poet wrote—*in fortune's* moat; becaufe the Clown in the very next fpeech replies—"I will henceforth eat no *fifh* of fortune's buttering;" and again, when he comes to repeat Parolles's petition to Lafeu, "That hath fallen into the unclean *fifhpond* of her difpleafure, and, as he fays, is *muddied* withal." And again—"Pray you, fir, ufe the *carp* as you may," &c. In all which places, it is obvious a moat or a pond is the allufion. Befides, Parolles fmelling ftrong, as he fays, of fortune's ftrong difpleafure, carries on the fame image; for as the *moats* round old feats were always replenifhed with fifh, fo the Clown's joke of holding his nofe, we may prefume, proceeded from this, that the privy was always over the moat; and therefore the Clown humouroufly fays, when Parolles is preffing him to deliver his letter to Lord Lafeu, "Foh! pr'ythee ftand away; a paper from fortune's *clofeftool,* to give to a nobleman!" WARBURTON.

Dr. Warburton's correction may be fupported by a paffage in *The Alchemift:*

"*Subtle.* ——Come along fir,
" I muft now fhew you *Fortune's privy lodgings.*
"*Face.* Are they perfum'd, and his bath ready?
"*Sub.* All.
" Only the fumigation fomewhat ftrong." FARMER.

Clo. Truly, fortune's difpleafure is but fluttifh, if it fmell fo ftrong as thou fpeak'ft of: I will henceforth eat no fifh of fortune's buttering. Pr'ythee, allow the wind.[4]

Par. Nay, you need not to ftop your nofe, fir; I fpake but by a metaphor.

Clo. Indeed, fir, if your metaphor ftink, I will ftop my nofe; or againft any man's metaphor.[5] Pr'ythee, get thee further.

By the whimfical *caprice* of Fortune, I am fallen into the mud, and fmell fomewhat ftrong of her difpleafure. In *Pericles, Prince of Tyre*, 1609, we meet with the fame phrafe:

" —— but *Fortune's mood*
" Varies again."

Again, in *Timon of Athens:*

" When *fortune*, in her fhift and change of *mood*,
" Spurns down her late belov'd."

Again, in *Julius Cæfar:*

" *Fortune* is merry,
" And in this *mood* will give us any thing."

Mood is again ufed for *refentment* or *caprice*, in *Othello:* " You are but now caft in his *mood*, a punifhment more in policy than in malice."

Again, for *anger*, in the old *Taming of a Shrew*, 1607:

" —— This brain-fick man,
" That in his *mood* cares not to murder me."

Dr. Warburton in his edition changed *mood* into *moat*, and his emendation was adopted, I think, without neceffity, by the fubfequent editors. All the expreffions enumerated by him,—" I will eat no *fifh*,"—" he hath fallen into the unclean *fifhpond* of her difpleafure," &c.—agree fufficiently well with the text, without any change. Parolles having talked metaphorically of being *muddy'd* by the difpleafure of fortune, the clown to render him ridiculous, fuppofes him to have actually fallen into a *fifhpond.*

MALONE.

Though Mr. Malone defends the old reading, I have retained Dr. Warburton's emendation, which, in my opinion, is one of the luckieft ever produced. STEEVENS.

4 —— *allow the wind.*] i. e. ftand to the leeward of me.

STEEVENS.

5 *Indeed, fir, if your metaphor ftink, I will ftop my nofe; or againft any man's metaphor.*] Nothing could be conceived with greater

Par. Pray you, fir, deliver me this paper.

Clo. Foh, pr'ythee, ftand away; A paper from fortune's clofe-ftool to give to a nobleman! Look, here he comes himfelf.

Enter LAFEU.

Here is a pur of fortune's, fir, or of fortune's cat,[6] (but not a mufk-cat,) that has fallen into the unclean fifhpond of her difpleafure, and, as he fays, is muddied withal: Pray you, fir, ufe the carp as you may; for he looks like a poor, decay'd, ingenious, foolifh, rafcally knave. I do pity his diftrefs

humour or juftnefs of fatire, than this fpeech. The ufe of the *ftinking metaphor* is an odious fault, which grave writers often commit. It is not uncommon to fee moral declaimers againft vice, defcribe her as Hefiod did the fury Triftitia:

Τῆς ἐκ ῥῖνων μύξαις ῥέον.

Upon which Longinus juftly obferves, that, inftead of giving a *terrible* image, he has given a very nafty one. Cicero cautions well againft it, in his book *de Orat.* " *Quoniam hæc,* fays he, *vel fumma laus eft in verbis transferendis ut fenfum feriat id, quod tranflatum fit, fugienda eft omnis turpitudo earum rerum, ad quas eorum animos qui audiunt trahet fimilitudo. Nolo morte dici Africani caftratam effe rempublicam. Nolo fturcus curiæ dici Glauciam.* Our poet himfelf is extremely delicate in this refpect; who, throughout his large writings, if you except a paffage in *Hamlet,* has fcarce a metaphor that can offend the moft fqueamifh reader.

WARBURTON.

Dr. Warburton's recollection muft have been weak, or his zeal for his author extravagant. Otherwife, he could not have ventured to countenance him on the fcore of delicacy; his offenfive metaphors and allufions being undoubtedly more frequent than thofe of all his dramatick predeceffors or contemporaries. STEEVENS.

[6] *Here is a* pur *of fortune's, fir, or of fortune's cat,*] We fhould read—*or fortune's cat*; and indeed I believe there is an error in the former part of the fentence, and that we ought to read—*Here is a* pufs *of fortune's,* inftead of *pur.* M. MASON.

in my fmiles of comfort,⁵ and leave him to your lordfhip. [*Exit* Clown.

Par. My lord, I am a man whom fortune hath cruelly fcratch'd.

Laf. And what would you have me to do? 'tis too late to pare her nails now. Wherein have you play'd the knave with fortune, that fhe fhould fcratch you, who of herfelf is a good lady, and would not have knaves thrive long under her?⁶ There's a quart d'ecu for you: Let the juftices make you and fortune friends; I am for other bufinefs.

Par. I befeech your honour, to hear me one fingle word.

Laf. You beg a fingle penny more: come, you fhall ha't; fave your word.⁷

Par. My name, my good lord, is Parolles.

Laf. You beg more than one word then.⁸—Cox' my paffion! give me your hand:—How does your drum?

---

⁵ —— *I do pity his diftrefs in my* fmiles *of comfort,*] We fhould read,—*fimilies* of comfort, fuch as the calling him *fortune's cat, carp,* &c. WARBURTON.

The meaning is, I teftify my pity for his diftrefs, by encouraging him with a gracious fmile. The old reading may ftand.
HEATH.

Dr. Warburton's propofed emendation may be countenanced by an entry on the books of the Stationers' Company, 1595: " —— A booke of verie pythie *fimilies, comfortable* and profitable for all men to reade." STEEVENS.

⁶ —— *under* her?] *Her,* which is not in the firft copy, was fupplied by the editor of the fecond folio. MALONE.

⁷ —— *fave your word.*] i. e. you need not afk;—here it is.
MALONE.

⁸ *You beg more than* one word *then.*] A quibble is intended on the word *Parolles,* which in French is plural, and fignifies *words. One,* which is not found in the old copy, was added, perhaps unneceffarily, by the editor of the third folio. MALONE.

P<small>AR</small>. O my good lord, you were the firſt that found me.

L<small>AF</small>. Was I, in ſooth? and I was the firſt that loſt thee.

P<small>AR</small>. It lies in you, my lord, to bring me in ſome grace, for you did bring me out.

L<small>AF</small>. Out upon thee, knave! doſt thou put upon me at once both the office of God and the devil? one brings thee in grace, and the other brings thee out. [*Trumpets ſound.*] The king's coming, I know by his trumpets.—Sirrah, inquire further after me; I had talk of you laſt night: thqugh you are a fool and a knave, you ſhall eat;[9] go to, follow.

P<small>AR</small>. I praiſe God for you. [*Exeunt.*

SCENE III.

The ſame. A Room in the Counteſs's *Palace.*

Flouriſh. Enter King, Counteſs, L<small>AFEU</small>, Lords, Gentlemen, *Guards, &c.*

K<small>ING</small>. We loſt a jewel of her; and our eſteem [a] Was made much poorer by it: but your ſon,

---

[9] *——you ſhall eat;*] Parolles has many of the lineamerits of Falſtaff, and ſeems to be the character which Shakſpeare delighted to draw, a fellow that had more wit than virtue. Though juſtice required that he ſhould be detected and expoſed, yet his *vices ſit ſo fit in him* that he is not at laſt ſuffered to ſtarve.

J<small>OHNSON</small>.

[a] *——eſteem——*] Dr. Warburton, in Theobald's edition, altered this word to *eſtate*; in his own he lets it ſtand and explains it by *worth* or *eſtate*. But *eſteem* is here *reckoning* or *eſtimate*. Since the loſs of *Helen* with her *virtues* and *qualifications*, our *account* is *ſunk*; what we have to *reckon* ourſelves king of, is much *poorer* than before. J<small>OHNSON</small>.

As mad in folly, lack'd the sense to know
Her estimation home.[3]

COUNT.   'Tis past, my liege:
And I beseech your majesty to make it
Natural rebellion, done i'the blaze of youth;[4]
When oil and fire, too strong for reason's force,
O'erbears it, and burns on.

KING.   My honour'd lady,
I have forgiven and forgotten all;
Though my revenges were high bent upon him,
And watch'd the time to shoot.

LAF.   This I must say,——
But first I beg my pardon,—The young lord
Did to his majesty, his mother, and his lady,
Offence of mighty note; but to himself
The greatest wrong of all: he lost a wife,
Whose beauty did astonish the survey

Meaning that his esteem was lessened in its value by Bertram's
misconduct; since a person who was honoured with it could be so
ill treated as Helena had been, and that with impunity. M. MASON.

[3] ——home.] That is, completely, in its full extent. JOHNSON.
So, in Macbeth: "That thrusted home," &c. MALONE.

[4] ——blaze of youth;] The old copy reads—blade.
                                        STEEVENS.
"Blade of youth" is the spring of early life, when the man is
yet green. Oil and fire suit but ill with blade, and therefore Dr.
Warburton reads, blaze of youth. JOHNSON.

This very probable emendation was first proposed by Mr.
Theobald, who has produced these two passages in support of it:
    "——I do know
    "When the blood burns, how prodigal the soul
    "Lends the tongue vows. These blazes," &c. Hamlet.
Again, in Troilus and Cressida:
    "For Hector, in his blaze of wrath," &c. MALONE.

In Hamlet we have also "flaming youth," and in the present
comedy "the quick fire of youth." I read, therefore, without
hesitation,—blaze. STEEVENS.

I

Of richeſt eyes;[5] whoſe words all ears took cap-
  tive;
Whoſe dear perfection, hearts that ſcorn'd to ſerve,
Humbly call'd miſtreſs.

KING.   Praiſing what is loſt,
Makes the remembrance dear.——Well, call him
      hither;——
We are reconcil'd, and the firſt view ſhall kill
All repetition:[6]—Let him not aſk our pardon;
The nature of his great offence is dead,
And deeper than oblivion we do bury
The incenſing relicks of it: let him approach,
A ſtranger, no offender; and inform him,
So 'tis our will he ſhould.

GENT.   I ſhall, my liege.
                            [Exit Gentleman.

KING. What ſays he to your daughter? have you
      ſpoke?

LAF. All that he is hath reference to your high-
      neſs.

---

[5] Of richeſt eyes;] Shakſpeare means that her beauty had
aſtoniſhed thoſe, who, having ſeen the greateſt number of fair
women, might be ſaid to be the richeſt in ideas of beauty. So, in
As you Like it: "——to have ſeen much and to have nothing, is
to have rich eyes and poor hands." STEEVENS.

  [6] ——the firſt view ſhall kill
    All repetition:] The firſt interview ſhall put an end to all re-
collection of the paſt. Shakſpeare is now haſtening to the end of the
play, finds his matter ſufficient to fill up his remaining ſcenes, and
therefore, as on other ſuch occaſions, contracts his dialogue and
precipitates his action. Decency required that Bertram's double
crime of cruelty and diſobedience, joined likewiſe with ſome hy-
pocriſy, ſhould raiſe more reſentment; and that though his mother
might eaſily forgive him, his king ſhould more pertinaciouſly vindicate his own authority and Helen's merit. Of all this Shakſpeare
could not be ignorant, but Shakſpeare wanted to conclude his play.
                                        JOHNSON.

KING. Then ſhall we have a match. I have letters
      ſent me,
That ſet him high in fame.

Enter BERTRAM.

LAF.   He looks well on't.

KING. I am not a day of ſeaſon,[7]
For thou may'ſt ſee a ſun-ſhine and a hail
In me at once: But to the brighteſt beams
Diſtracted clouds give way; ſo ſtand thou forth,
The time is fair again.

BER.   My high-repented blames,[8]
Dear ſovereign pardon to me.

KING.   All is whole;
Not one word more of the conſumed time.
Let's take the inſtant by the forward top;
For we are old, and on our quick'ſt decrees
The inaudible and noiſeleſs foot of time
Steals ere we can effect them:[9] You remember
The daughter of this lord?

---

[7] *I am not a day of ſeaſon.*] That is, of *uninterrupted rain:* one
of thoſe *wet days* that uſually happen about the vernal equinox.
A ſimilar expreſſion occurs in *The Rape of Lucrece:*
    " But I alone, alone muſt ſit and pine,
    " *Seaſoning* the earth with ſhowers."
The word is ſtill uſed in the ſame ſenſe in Virginia, in which
government, and eſpecially on the eaſtern ſhore of it, where the
deſcendants of the firſt ſettlers have been leſs mixed with later
emigrants, many expreſſions of Shakſpeare's time are ſtill current.
                                 HENLEY.

[8] *My high-repented blames.*] *High-repented blames,* are faults repented of to the height, to the utmoſt. Shakſpeare has *high-fan-
taſtical* in *Twelfth Night.* STEEVENS.

[9] *The inaudible and noiſeleſs foot of time,* &c.] This idea ſeems to
have been caught from the third Book of Sidney's *Arcadia:*
" The ſummons of *Time* had ſo creepingly ſtolne upon him, that
hee had heard ſcarcely the *noiſe of his feet.*" STEEVENS.

Ber.   Admiringly,

My liege: At first
I stuck my choice upon her, ere my heart
Durst make too bold a herald of my tongue:
Where the impression of mine eye infixing,
Contempt his scornful perspective did lend me,
Which warp'd the line of every other favour;
Scorn'd a fair colour, or express'd it stol'n;
Extended or contracted all proportions,
To a most hideous object: Thence it came,
That she, whom all men prais'd, and whom my-
        self,
Since I have lost, have lov'd, was in mine eye
The dust that did offend it.

    King.   Well excus'd:
That thou didst love her, strikes some scores away
From the great compt: But love, that comes too
        late,
Like a remorseful pardon slowly carried,
To the great sender turns a sour offence,
Crying, That's good that's gone: our rash faults
Make trivial price of serious things we have,
Not knowing them, until we know their grave:
Oft our displeasures, to ourselves unjust,
Destroy our friends, and after weep their dust:
Our own love waking cries to see what's done,
While shameful hate sleeps out the afternoon.[2]

---

[2] *Our own love waking, &c.]* These two lines I should be glad
to call *an interpolation of a player.* They are ill connected with
the former, and not very clear or proper in themselves. I believe
the author made two couplets to the same purpose; wrote them
both down that he might take his choice; and so they happened to
be both preserved.

    For *sleep* I think we should read *slept. Love cries* to see what was
done while hatred *slept,* and suffered mischief to be done. Or the
meaning may be, that *hatred* still *continues* to *sleep* at ease, while
love is weeping; and so the present reading may stand. JOHNSON.

Be this fweet Helen's knell, and now forget her.
Send forth your amorous token for fair Maudlin:
The main confents are had; and here we'll ftay
To fee our widower's fecond marriage-day.

    COUNT. Which better than the firft, O dear hea-
        ven, blefs!
Or, ere they meet, in me, O nature, ceafe![3]

    LAF. Come on, my fon, in whom my houfe's
        name
Muft be digefted, give a favour from you,
To fparkle in the fpirits of my daughter,
That fhe may quickly come.—By my old beard,
And every hair that's on't, Helen, that's dead,
Was a fweet creature; fuch a ring as this,

    I cannot comprehend this paffage as it ftands, and have no doubt
but we fhould read—
    Our old *love waking*, &c.
    Extinctus amabitur idem.
Our own love, can mean nothing but our *felf-love*, which would not
be fenfe in this place; but *our old love waking*, means our former
affection being revived. M. MASON.

    This conjecture appears to me extremely probable; but *waking*
will not, I think, here admit of Mr. M. Mafon's interpretation,
being revived; nor indeed is it neceffary to his emendation. It is
clear from the fubfequent line that *waking* is here ufed in its ordinary fenfe. Hate *fleeps* at eafe, unmolefted by any remembrance
of the dead, while old love, reproaching itfelf for not having been
fufficiently kind to a departed friend, " *wakes* and weeps;" crying,
" that's good that's gone." MALONE.

    [3] *Which better than the firft, O dear heaven, blefs!*
    Or, ere they meet, in me, O nature, ceafe!] I have ventured
againft the authorities of the printed copies, to prefix the Countefs's
name to thefe two lines. The king appears, indeed, to be a fa-
vourer of Bertram: but if Bertram fhould make a bad hufband the
fecond time, why fhould it give the king fuch mortal pangs? A
fond and difappointed mother might reafonably not defire to live
to fee fuch a day: and from her the wifh of dying, rather than to
behold it, comes with propriety. THEOBALD.

The laſt that e'er I took her leave [4] at court,
I ſaw upon her finger.

Ber.   Hers it was not.

King. Now, pray you, let me ſee it; for mine eye,
While I was ſpeaking, oft was faſten'd to't.—
This ring was mine; and, when I gave it Helen,
I bade her, if her fortunes ever ſtood
Neceſſitied to help, that [5] by this token
I would relieve her: Had you that craft, to reave her
Of what ſhould ſtead her moſt?

Ber.   My gracious ſovereign,
Howe'er it pleaſes you to take it ſo,
The ring was never her's.

Count.   Son, on my life,
I have ſeen her wear it; and ſhe reckon'd it
At her life's rate.

Laf.   I am ſure, I ſaw her wear it.

Ber. You are deceiv'd, my lord, ſhe never ſaw it:
In Florence was it from a caſement thrown me, [6]
Wrapp'd in a paper, which contain'd the name
Of her that threw it: noble ſhe was, and thought
I ſtood ingag'd: [7] but when I had ſubſcrib'd

---

[4] *The laſt that e'er I took her leave —*] The laſt time that I ſaw her, when ſhe was leaving the court. Mr. Rowe and the ſubſequent editors read—*that e'er ſhe took*, &c. MALONE.

[5] *I bade her, if her fortunes ever ſtood*
  Neceſſitied to help, that—] Our author here, as in many other places, ſeems to have forgotten in the cloſe of the ſentence how he began to conſtruct it. See p. 189, n. 9. The meaning however is clear, and I do not ſuſpect any corruption. MALONE.

[6] *In Florence was it from a caſement thrown me,*] Bertram ſtill continues to have too little virtue to deſerve Helen. He did not know indeed that it was Helen's ring, but he knew that he had it not from a window. JOHNSON.

[7] —— *noble ſhe was, and thought*
  I ſtood ingag'd:] Thus the old copy. Dr. Johnſon reads—*engaged.* STEEVENS.

To mine own fortune, and inform'd her fully,
I could not anfwer in that courfe of honour
As fhe had made the overture, fhe ceas'd,
In heavy fatisfaction, and would never
Receive the ring again.

KING.   Plutus himfelf,
That knows the tinct and multiplying medicine,[8]
Hath not in nature's myftery more fcience,
Than I have in this ring: 'twas mine, 'twas Helen's,
Whoever gave it you: Then, if you know
That you are well acquainted with yourfelf,
Confefs 'twas hers,[9] and by what rough enforcement

The plain meaning is, when fhe faw me receive the ring, fhe
thought me *engaged* to her. JOHNSON.

Ingag'd, may be intended in the fame fenfe with the reading
propofed by Mr. Theobald, [*ungag'd*] i. e. *not engaged*; as Shakfpeare in another place ufes *gag'd* for *engaged. Merchant of Venice*,
Act I. fc. i. TYRWHITT.

I have no doubt that *ingaged* (the reading of the folio) is right.
Gaged is ufed by other writers, as well as by Shakfpeare, for
engaged. So, in a *Pafloral*, by Daniel, 1605:
    " Not that the earth did *gage*
    " Unto the hufbandman
    " Her voluntary fruits, free without fees."
Ingaged, in the fenfe of *unengaged*, is a word of exactly the
fame formation as *inhabitable*, which is ufed by Shakfpeare and the
contemporary writers for *uninhabitable*. MALONE.

[8] *Plutus himfelf,*
    That knows the tinct *and* multiplying *medicine*,] Plutus, the
grand alchemift, who knows the *tincture* which confers the properties of gold upon bafe metals, and the *matter* by which *gold* is
multiplied, by which a fmall quantity of gold is made to communicate its qualities to a large mafs of bafe metal.
    In the reign of Henry the Fourth a law was made to forbid *all men
thenceforth to* multiply *gold, or ufe any craft of* multiplication. Of
which law, Mr. Boyle, when he was warm with the hope of
tranfmutation, procured a repeal. JOHNSON.

[9] —— *Then*, if you know
    That you are well acquainted with yourfelf,
    Confefs 'twas hers,] i. e. confefs the ring was hers, for you
know it as well as you know that you are yourfelf. EDWARDS.

You got it from her: she call'd the saints to surety,
That she would never put it from her finger,
Unless she gave it to yourself in bed,
(Where you have never come,) or sent it us
Upon her great disaster.

BER.   She never saw it.

KING. Thou speak'st it falsely, as I love mine ho-
    nour;
And mak'st conjectural fears to come into me,
Which I would fain shut out: If it should prove
That thou art so inhuman,—'twill not prove so;—
And yet I know not:—thou didst hate her deadly,
And she is dead; which nothing, but to close
Her eyes myself, could win me to believe,
More than to see this ring.—Take him away.—

                [Guards seize BERTRAM.
My fore-past proofs, howe'er the matter fall,
Shall tax my fears of little vanity,
Having vainly fear'd too little.'—Away with him;—
We'll sift this matter further.

BER.   If ou shall prove
This ring was ever hers, you shall as easy
Prove that I husbanded her bed in Florence,
Where yet she never was.

                [Exit BERTRAM, guarded.

The true meaning of this expression is, *If you know that your faculties are so sound, as that you have the proper consciousness of your own actions*, and are able to recollect and relate what you have done, *tell me*, &c. JOHNSON.

' *My fore-past proofs, howe'er the matter fall,*
  Shall tax my fears of little vanity,
  Having vainly fear'd too little.] The proofs which I have already had are sufficient to show that my fears were not *vain* and irrational. I have rather been hitherto more easy than I ought, and have *unreasonably* had *too little fear*. JOHNSON.

Enter a Gentleman.

King. I am wrapp'd in difmal thinkings.

Gent. Gracious fovereign,
Whether I have been to blame, or no, I know not;
Here's a petition from a Florentine,
Who hath, for four or five removes, come fhort
To tender it herfelf.[3]   I undertook it,
Vanquifh'd thereto by the fair grace and fpeech
Of the poor fuppliant, who by this, I know,
Is here attending: her bufinefs looks in her
With an importing vifage; and fhe told me,
In a fweet verbal brief, it did concern
Your highnefs with herfelf.

King. [Reads.]—*Upon his many proteflations to
marry me, when his wife was dead, I blufh to fay it, he
won me.   Now is the count Roufillon a widower; his
vows are forfeited to me, and my honour's paid to him.
He ftole from Florence, taking no leave, and I follow
him to his country for juftice: Grant it me, O king; in
you it beft lies; otherwife a feducer flourifhes, and a
poor maid is undone.*

DIANA CAPULET.

Laf. I will buy me a fon-in-law in a fair, and
toll him: for this, I'll none of him.[4]

---

[3] *Who hath, for four or five removes, come fhort, &c.*] Who hath
miffed the opportunity of prefenting it in perfon to your majefty,
either at Marfeilles, or on the road from thence to Roufillon, in
confequence of having been four or five removes behind you.

MALONE.

Removes are journies or poft-ftages. JOHNSON.

[4] *I will buy me a fon-in-law in a fair, and toll* him: *for this,
I'll none of him.*] Thus the fecond folio. The firft omits—him.
Either reading is capable of explanation.

The meaning of the earlieft copy feems to be this: I'll buy me a
new fon-in-law, &c. and *toll* the bell for this; i. e. look upon him

KING. The heavens have thought well on thee,
 Lafeu,

as a dead man.—The fecond reading, as Dr. Percy fuggefts, may
imply: I'll buy me a fon-in-law as they buy a horfe in a fair;
toul him, i. e. enter him on the *toul* or *toll-book,* to prove I came
honeftly by him, and afcertain my title to him. In a play called
The famous Hiftory of Tho. Stukely, 1605, is an allufion to this
cuftom :

 " *Gov.* I will be anfwerable to thee for thy *horfes.*
 " *Stuk.* Doft thou keep a *tole-booth?* zounds, doft thou make a
horfe-courfer of me !"

 Again, in *Hudibras,* p. II. C. I :

  " —— a roan gelding
  " Where, when, by whom, and what y'were fold for
  " And in the open market fell'd for."

 Alluding (as Dr. Grey obferves) to the two ftatutes relating to
the fale of horfes, 2 and 3 *Phil. and Mary,* and 31 *Eliz.* c. 12.
and publickly *tolling* them in fairs, to prevent the fale of fuch as
were ftolen, and to preferve the property to the right owner.

 The previous mention of a *Fair,* feems to juftify the reading I
have adopted from the fecond folio. STEEVENS.

 The paffage fhould be pointed thus:

I will buy me a fon-in-law in a fair, and toll;
For this, I'll none of him.

That is, " I'll buy me a fon-in-law in a fair, and pay toll; as for
this, I will have none of him." M. MASON.

 The meaning, I think, is, " I will purchafe a fon-in-law at a
fair, and get rid of this worthlefs fellow, by *tolling* him *out of it.*"
To *toll* a perfon *out of a fair* was a phrafe of the time. So, in
Camden's *Remaines,* 1605: " At a Bartholomew Faire at London
there was an efcheator of the fame city, that had arrefted a clothier
that was outlawed, and had feized his goods, which he had brought
into the faire, *tolling him out of the fairs,* by a traine."

 And *toll for this* may however mean—and I will fell this fellow
in a fair, as I would a horfe, publickly entering in the *toll-book* the
particulars of the fale. For the hint of this latter interpretation
I am indebted to Dr. Percy. I incline, however, to the former
expofition.

 The following paffage in *King Henry IV.* P. II. may be adduced
in fupport of Mr. Steevens's interpretation of this paffage: " Come,
thou fhalt go to the wars in a gown,—and I will take fuch order
that thy friends fhall *ring for thee.*"

 Here Falftaff certainly means to fpeak equivocally; and one of
his fenfes is, " I will take care to have thee knocked in the head,
and thy friends fhall ring thy funeral knell." MALONE.

To bring forth this difcovery.—Seek thefe fuitors :—
Go, fpeedily, and bring again the count.

   [*Exeunt* Gentleman, *and fome Attendants.*

I am afeard, the life of Helen, lady,
Was foully fnatch'd.

COUNT.   Now, juftice on the doers!

Enter BERTRAM, *guarded.*

KING. I wonder, fir, fince wives are monfters to
    you,[4]
And that you fly them as you fwear them lordfhip,
Yet you defire to marry.—What woman's that?

Re-enter Gentleman, *with* Widow, *and* DIANA.

DIA. I am, my lord, a wretched Florentine,
Derived from the ancient Capulet;
My fuit, as I do underftand, you know,
And therefore know how far I may be pitied.

---

[4] *I wonder, fir, fince wives,* &c.] This paffage is thus read in
the firft folio :

  I wonder, fir, fir, wives are monfters to you,
  And that you fly them, as you fwear them lordfhip,
  Yet you defire to marry.——

Which may be corrected thus :

  I wonder, fir, fince *wives are monfters,* &c.

  The editors have made it—*wives are* fo monftrous *to you,* and
in the next line—*fwear to them,* inftead of—*fwear them lordfhip.*
Though the latter phrafe be a little obfcure, it fhould not have
been turned out of the text without notice. I fuppofe *lordfhip* is
put for that *protection* which the hufband in the marriage ceremony
promifes to the wife. TYRWHITT.

  As, I believe, here fignifies *as foon as.* MALONE.

  I read with Mr. Tyrwhitt, whofe emendation I have placed in
the text. It may be obferved, however, that the fecond folio
reads :

  I wonder, fir, wives are fuch *monfters to you——.*

            STEEVENS.

Wid. I am her mother, fir, whofe age and honour
Both fuffer under this complaint we bring,
And both fhall ceafe,⁵ without your remedy.

 King. Come hither, count; Do you know thefe
   women?

 Ber. My lord, I neither can, nor will deny
But that I know them: Do they charge me further?

 Dia. Why do you look fo ftrange upon your
   wife?

 Ber. She's none of mine, my lord.

 Dia   If you fhall marry,
You give away this hand, and that is mine;
You give away heaven's vows, and thofe are mine;
You give away myfelf, which is known mine;
For I by vow am fo embodied yours,
That fhe, which marries you, muft marry me,
Either both, or none.

 Laf. Your reputation [*To* Bertram.] comes
too fhort for my daughter, you are no hufband for
her.

 Ber. My lord, this is a fond and defperate crea-
   ture,
Whom fometime I have laugh'd with: let your
   highnefs
Lay a more noble thought upon mine honour,
Than for to think that I would fink it here.

 King. Sir, for my thoughts, you have them ill to
   friend,
Till your deeds gain them: Fairer prove your honour,
Than in my thought it lies!

---

 ⁵ ——*fhall* ceafe,] i. e. deceafe, die. So, in *King Lear:*
" Fall and *ceafe.*" The word is ufed in the fame fenfe in p. 358
of the prefent comedy. Steevens.

DIA.   Good my lord,
Aſk him upon his oath, if he does think
He had not my virginity.

KING. What ſay'ſt thou to her?

BER.   She's impudent, my lord;
And was a common gameſter to the camp.[6]

DIA. He does me wrong, my lord; if I were ſo,
He might have bought me at a common price:
Do not believe him: O, behold this ring,
Whoſe high reſpect, and rich validity,[7]
Did lack a parallel; yet, for all that,
He gave it to a commoner o'the camp,
If I be one.

COUNT.   He bluſhes, and 'tis it:[8]
Of ſix preceding anceſtors, that gem
Conferr'd by teſtament to the ſequent iſſue,

---

[6] *—— a common gameſter to the camp.*] The following paſſage, in an ancient MS. tragedy, entitled *The Second Maiden's Tragedy*, will ſufficiently elucidate the idea once affixed to the term *gameſter*, when applied to a female:

> "'Tis to me wondrous how you ſhould ſpare the day
> "From amorous clips, much leſs the general ſeaſon
> "When all the world's a *gameſter*."

Again, in *Pericles*, Lyſimachus aſks Marina—
> "Were you a *gameſter* at five or at ſeven?"

Again, in *Troilus and Creſſida*:
> "—— daughters of the *game*." STEEVENS.

[7] *Whoſe high reſpect, and rich* validity,] *Validity* means *value*. So, in *K. Lear*:
> "No leſs in ſpace, *validity*, and pleaſure."

Again in *Twelfth-Night*:
> "Of what *validity* and pitch ſoever." STEEVENS.

[8] *—— 'tis it:*] The old copy has—'tis *bit*. The emendation was made by Mr. Steevens. In many of our old chronicles I have found *bit* printed inſtead of *it*. Hence probably the miſtake here. Mr. Pope reads—and 'tis *bis*. MALONE.

Or, *be bluſhes, and 'tis ſit.* HENLEY.

Hath it been ow'd, and worn.   This is his wife;
That ring's a thousand proofs.

King.   Methought, you said,[9]
You saw one here in court could witness it.

Dia. I did, my lord, but loth am to produce
So bad an instrument; his name's Parolles.

Laf. I saw the man to-day, if man he be.

King. Find him, and bring him hither.

Ber.   What of him?
He's quoted for a most perfidious slave,[2]
With all the spots o'the world tax'd and debosh'd;[3]
Whose nature sickens, but to speak a truth:[4]
Am I or that, or this, for what he'll utter,
That will speak any thing?

King.   She hath that ring of yours.

Ber. I think, she has: certain it is, I lik'd her,
And boarded her i'the wanton way of youth:
She knew her distance, and did angle for me,
Madding my eagerness with her restraint,

---

[9] *Methought, you said,*] The poet has here forgot himself. Diana has said no such thing. BLACKSTONE.

[2] *He's* quoted *for a most perfidious slave,*] *Quoted* has the same sense as *noted,* or *observed.*

So, in *Hamlet:*
        " I'm sorry that with better heed and judgement
        " I had not *quoted* him." STEEVENS.

[3] —— *debosh'd;*] See a note on *The Tempest,* Act III. sc. ii. Vol. III. p. 95. STEEVENS.

[4] *Whose nature sickens, but to speak a truth:*] Here the modern editors read:
        Which nature sickens with:——
a most licentious corruption of the old reading, in which the punctuation only wants to be corrected. We should read, as here printed:
        Whose nature sickens, but *to speak a truth:*
i. e. *only* to speak a truth. TYRWHITT.

As all impediments in fancy's course
Are motives of more fancy;[5] and, in fine,
Her infuit coming with her modern grace,
Subdued me to her rate: fhe got the ring;
And I had that, which any inferior might
At market-price have bought.

　　DIAN.　　　　　　　　I muft be patient:
You, that turn'd off a firft fo noble wife,
May juftly diet me.[6]　I pray you yet,

　　⁵ ——*all impediments in fancy's courfe*
　　Are motives of more fancy; &c.] *Every thing that obftructs love is
an occafion by which love is heightened. And, to conclude, her folicitation
concurring with her fafhionable appearance,* fhe got the ring.
　　I am not certain that I have attained the true meaning of the
word *modern,* which, perhaps, fignifies rather *meanly pretty.*
　　　　　　　　　　　　　　　　　　　　Johnson.

　　I believe *modern* means *common.* The fenfe will then be this—
Her folicitation concurring with her appearance of being common, i. e.
with the appearance of her *being to be had* as we fay at prefent.
Shakfpeare ufes the word *modern* frequently, and always in this
fenfe. So, in *King John:*
　　" ——fcorns a *modern* invocation."
Again, in *As you Like it:*
　　" Full of wife faws and *modern* inftances.
　　" Trifles, fuch as we prefent *modern* friends with."
Again, in the prefent comedy, p. 252: " ——to make *modern*
and familiar things fupernatural and caufelefs."
　　Mr. M. Mafon fays, that *modern grace* means, *with a tolerable
degree of beauty.* He queftions alfo the infufficiency of the inftances
brought in fupport of my explanation, but adduces none in defence
of his own. Steevens.

　　Dr. Johnfon's laft interpretation is certainly the true one. See
p. 68, n. 9; and p. 252, n. 9. I think with Mr. Steevens, that
modern here, as almoft every where in Shakfpeare, means *common,
ordinary;* but do not fuppofe that Bertram here means to call Diana
a common gamefter, though he has ftyled her fo in a former paffage.
　　　　　　　　　　　　　　　　　　　　Malone.

　　⁶ *May juftly diet me.*] *May juftly loath* or *be weary of me,* as
people generally are of a regimen or, prefcribed *diet.* Such, I
imagine, is the meaning. Mr. Collins thinks, fhe means, " May
juftly make me faft, by depriving me (as Defdemona fays) of the
rites for which I love you." Malone.

(Since you lack virtue, I will lofe a hufband,)
Send for your ring, I will return it home,
And give me mine again.

Ber. I have it not.

King. What ring was yours, I pray you?

Dia. Sir, much like
The fame upon your finger.

King. Know you this ring? this ring was his of
late.

Dia. And this was it I gave him, being a-bed.

King. The ftory then goes falfe, you threw it him
Out of a cafement.

Dia. I have fpoke the truth.

Enter PAROLLES.

Ber. My lord, I do confefs, the ring was hers.

King. You boggle fhrewdly, every feather ftarts
you.——
Is this the man you fpeak of?

Dia. Ay, my lord.

King. Tell me, but, firrah, tell me true, I charge
you,
Not fearing the difpleafure of your mafter,
(Which, on your juft proceeding, I'll keep off,)
By him, and by this woman here, what know you?

Par. So pleafe your majefty, my mafter hath

Mr. Collins's interpretation is juft. The allufion may be to the
management of hawks, who were half *ftarved* till they became
tractable. Thus, in *Coriolanus:*

"——I'll watch him,
"Till he be *dieted* to my requeft."
"To *faft*, like one who takes *diet*," is a comparifon that occurs in
The Two Gentlemen of Verona. STEEVENS.

been an honourable gentleman; tricks he hath had in him, which gentlemen have.

KING. Come, come, to the purpofe: Did he love this woman?

PAR. 'Faith, fir, he did love her; But how?⁶

KING. How, I pray you?

PAR. He did love her, fir, as a gentleman loves a woman.

KING. How is that?

PAR. He loved her, fir, and loved her not.

KING. As thou art a knave, and no knave:— What an equivocal companion⁷ is this?

PAR. I am a poor man, and at your majefty's command.

LAF. He's a good drum, my lord, but a naughty orator.

DIA. Do you know, he promifed me marriage?

PAR. 'Faith, I know more than I'll fpeak.

KING. But wilt thou not fpeak all thou know'ft?

PAR. Yes, fo pleafe your majefty; I did go between them, as I faid; but more than that, he loved her,—for, indeed, he was mad for her, and talk'd of Satan, and of limbo, and of furies, and I

---

⁶ —*be did love her;* But how?] *But how* perhaps belongs to the King's next fpeech:

But how, how, I pray you?

This fuits better with the King's apparent impatience and follicitude for Helena. MALONE.

Surely, all transfer of thefe words is needlefs. *Hamlet* addreffes fuch another flippant interrogatory to himfelf: "The moufe-trap. *Marry, how?* Tropically." STEEVENS.

⁷ — *companion*—] i. e. fellow. So, in *K. Henry VI. P. II:*

"Why, rude *companion*, whatfoe'er thou be,

"I know thee not." STEEVENS.

I

know not what: yet I was in that credit with them at that time, that I knew of their going to bed; and of other motions, as promising her marriage, and things that would derive me ill will to speak of, therefore I will not speak what I know.

King. Thou hast spoken all already, unless thou canst say they are married: But thou art too fine in thy evidence;[8] therefore stand aside.—
This ring, you say was yours?

Dia. Ay, my good lord.

King. Where did you buy it? or who gave it you?

Dia. It was not given me, nor I did not buy it.

King. Who lent it you?

Dia. It was not lent me neither.

King. Where did you find it then?

Dia. I found it not.

King. If it were yours by none of all these ways, How could you give it him?

Dia. I never gave it him.

Laf. This woman's an easy glove, my lord; she goes off and on at pleasure.

King. This ring was mine, I gave it his first wife.

Dia. It might be yours, or hers, for aught I know.

King. Take her away, I do not like her now;
To prison with her: and away with him.—
Unless thou tell'st me where thou had'st this ring,
Thou diest within this hour.

Dia. I'll never tell you.

---

[8] —— *But thou art* too fine *in thy evidence*;] *Too fine*, too full of finesse; too artful. A French expression—*trop fine*.
So, in Sir Henry Wotton's celebrated Parallel: " We may rate this one secret, as it was *finely* carried, at 4000l. in present money."
MALONE.

King. Take her away.

Dia.   I'll put in bail, my liege.

King. I think thee now some common customer.[9]

Dia. By Jove, if ever I knew man, 'twas you.

King: Wherefore hast thou accus'd him all this
   while?

Dia. Because he's guilty, and he is not guilty:
He knows, I am no maid, and he'll swear to't:
I'll swear, I am a maid, and he knows not.
Great king, I am no strumpet, by my life;
I am either maid, or else this old man's wife.
     [*Pointing to* LAFEU.

King. She does abuse our ears; to prison with her.

Dia. Good mother, fetch my bail.—Stay, royal sir;
       [*Exit* Widow.
The jeweller, that owes the ring, is sent for,
And he shall surety me.   But for this lord,
Who hath abus'd me, as he knows himself,
Though yet he never harm'd me, here I quit him:
He knows himself, my bed he hath defil'd;[1]
And at that time he got his wife with child:
Dead though she be, she feels her young one kick;
So there's my riddle, One, that's dead, is quick:
And now behold the meaning.

---

9 ——*customer.*] i. e. a common woman. So, in *Othello*:
 " I marry her!—what?—a *customer!*" STEEVENS.

1 *He knows himself,* &c.] The dialogue is too long, since the
audience already knew the whole transaction; nor is there any
reason for puzzling the King and playing with his passions; but it
was much easier than to make a pathetical interview between
Helen and her husband, her mother, and the King. JOHNSON.

Re-enter Widow, *with* HELENA.

KING.   Is there no exorcist
Beguiles the truer office of mine eyes?
Is't real, that I see?

HEL.   No, my good lord;
'Tis but the shadow of a wife you see,
The name, and not the thing.

BER.   . Both, both; O, pardon!

HEL. O, my good lord, when I was like this maid,
I found you wond'rous kind.   There is your ring;
And, look you, here's your letter; This it says,
When from my finger you can get this ring,

——exorcist—] This word is used, not very properly, for *enchanter.* JOHNSON.

Shakspeare invariably uses the word *exorcist*, to imply a person who can raise spirits, not in the usual sense of one that can lay them. So, Ligarius, in *Julius Cæsar* says—

" Thou, like an *exorcist*, hast conjur'd up
" My mortified spirit."

And in the Second Part of *Henry VI.* where Bolingbroke is about to raise a spirit, he asks of Eleanor,

" Will her ladyship behold and hear our *exorcisms?*"
M. MASON.

Such was the common acceptation of the word in our author's time. So, Minsheu in his DICT. 1617: " An *Exorcist*, or *Conjurer*."—So also, " To *conjure* or *exorcise* a spirit."

The difference between a *Conjurer*, a *Witch*, and an *Inchanter*, according to that writer, is as follows:

" The *Conjurer* seemeth by praiers and invocations of God's powerfull names, to compell the Divell to say or doe what he commandeth him.' The *Witch* dealeth rather by a friendly and voluntarie conference or agreement between him or her and the Divell or Familiar, to have his or her turne served, in lieu or stead of blood or other gift offered unto him, especially of his or her soule:—And both these differ from *Inchanters* or *Sorcerers*, because the former two have personal conference with the Divell, and the other meddles but with medicines and ceremonial formes of words called *charmes*, without apparition." MALONE.

B b 3

And are' *by me with child,* &c.—This is done:
Will you be mine, now you are doubly won?

BER. If fhe, my liege, can make me know this
      clearly,
I'll love her dearly, ever, ever dearly.

HEL. If it appear not plain, and prove untrue,
Deadly divorce ftep between me and you!—
O, my dear mother, do I fee you living?

LAF. Mine eyes fmell onions, I fhall weep anon:—
Good Tom Drum, [*To* PAROLLES.] lend me a handkerchief: So, I thank thee; wait on me home, I'll
make fport with thee: Let thy courtefies alone, they
are fcurvy ones.

KING. Let us from point to point this ftory **know,**
To make the even truth in pleafure flow:—
If thou be'ft yet a frefh uncropped flower,
                                    [*To* DIANA.
Choofe thou thy hufband, and I'll pay thy dower;
For I can guefs, that, by thy honeft aid,
Thou kept'ft a wife herfelf, thyfelf a maid.—
Of that, and all the progrefs, more and lefs,
Refolvedly more leifure fhall exprefs:
All yet feems well; and, if it end fo meet,
The bitter paft, more welcome is the fweet.
                                    [*Flourifh.*

Advancing.

The king's a beggar, now the play is done: [4]
All is well ended, *if this fuit be won,*

   [3] *And* are—] The old copy reads—And *is.* Mr. Rowe made
the emendation. MALONE.

   [4] *The* king's a beggar, *now the play is done:*] Though thefe
lines are fufficiently intelligible in their obvious fenfe, yet perhaps
there is fome allufion to the old tale of *The King and the Beggar,*
which was the fubject of a ballad, and, as it fhould feem from

That you exprefs content ; which we will pay,
With ftrife to pleafe you, day exceeding day :
Ours be your patience then, and yours our parts ; [5]
Your gentle hands lend us, and take our hearts.

[*Exeunt.*

the following lines in *King Richard II.* of fome popular interlude
alfo :

    " Our *fcene* is altered from a ferious thing,
    " And now chang'd to *the beggar and the king.*"

MALONE.

[5] *Ours be your patience then, and yours our parts ;*] The meaning
is: Grant *us then your patience* ; hear us without interruption. *And*
take *our parts* ; that is, fupport and defend us. JOHNSON.

This play has many delightful fcenes, though not fufficiently
probable, and fome happy characters, though not new, nor produced by any deep knowledge of human nature. Parolles is a
boafter and a coward, fuch as has always been the fport of the
ftage, but perhaps never raifed more laughter or contempt than in
the hands of Shakfpeare.

I cannot reconcile my heart to Bertram; a man noble without
generofity, and young without truth; who marries Helen as a
coward, and leaves her as a profligate: when fhe is dead by his
unkindnefs, fneaks home to a fecond marriage, is accufed by a
woman whom he has wronged, defends himfelf by falfehood, and
is difmiffed to happinefs.

The ftory of Bertram and Diana had been told before of Mariana and Angelo, and, to confefs the truth, fcarcely merited to be
heard a fecond time. JOHNSON.

TAMING

OF THE

S HREW.*

* TAMING OF THE SHREW.] We have hitherto supposed Shakspeare the authour of *The Taming of the Shrew*, but his property in it is extremely disputable. I will give my opinion, and the reasons on which it is founded. I suppose then the present play not *originally* the work of Shakspeare, but restored by him to the stage, with the whole Induction of the Tinker; and some other occasional improvements; especially in the character of Petruchio. It is very obvious that the Induction and the Play were either the works of different hands, or written at a great interval of time. The former is in our author's *best* manner, and a great part of the *latter* in his *worst*, or even below it. Dr. Warburton declares it to be certainly spurious; and without doubt, *supposing* it to have been written by Shakspeare, it must have been one of his earliest productions. Yet it is not mentioned in the list of his works by Meres in 1598.

I have met with a facetious piece of Sir John Harrington, printed in 1596, (and possibly there may be an earlier edition,) called *The Metamorphosis of Ajax*, where I suspect an allusion to the old play: "Read the *Booke* of *Taming a Shrew*, which hath made a number of us so perfect, that *now* every one can rule a shrew in our countrey, save he that hath hir."——I am aware a *modern* linguist may object that the word *book* does not at present seem *dramatick*, but it was once *technically* so: Gosson, in his *Schoole of Abuse, containing a pleasaunt Invective against Poets, Pipers, Players, Jesters, and such like Caterpillars of a Commonwealth,* 1579, mentions " twoo prose *bookes* played at the Bell-Sauage:" and Hearne tells us, in a note at the end of William of Worcester, that he had seen a MS. in the nature of a *Play* or *Interlude*, intitled *The Booke of Sir Thomas Moore.*

And in fact there is such an old *anonymous* play in Mr. Pope's list: " A pleasant conceited history, called, *The Taming of a Shrew*—sundry times acted by the earl of Pembroke his servants." Which seems to have been republished by the remains of that company in 1607, when Shakspeare's copy appeared at the Black-Friars or the Globe.——Nor let this seem derogatory from the character of our poet. There is no reason to believe that he wanted to claim the play as his own; for it was not even printed till some years after his death; but he merely revived it on his stage as a *manager.*

In support of what I have said relative to this play, let me only observe further at present, that the author of *Hamlet* speaks of Gonzago, and his wife Baptista; but the author of *The Taming of the Shrew* knew Baptista to be the name of a man. Mr. Capell indeed made me doubt, by declaring the authenticity of it to be confirmed by the testimony of Sir Aston Cockayn. I knew Sir Aston was much acquainted with the writers immediately subsequent to Shakspeare; and I was not inclined to dispute his authosity; but how was I surprised, when I found that Cockayn ascribes nothing more to Shakspeare, than the *Induction-Wincot-Ale and the Beggar!* I hope this was only a slip of Mr. Capell's memory.

FARMER.

The following is Sir Aston's Epigram:

To Mr. Clement Fisher, of Wincot.

" Shakspeare your Wincot-ale hath much renown'd,
" That fox'd a beggar so (by chance was found
" Sleeping) that there needed not many a word
" To make him to believe he was a lord:
" But you affirm (and in it seem most eager)
" 'Twill make a lord as drunk as any beggar.
" Bid Norton brew such ale as Shakspeare fancies
" Did put *Kit Sly* into such lordly trances:
" And let us meet there (for a fit of gladness)
" And drink ourselves merry in sober sadness."

Sir A. Cockayn's Poems, 1659, p. 124.

In spite of the great deference which is due from every commentator to Dr. Farmer's judgement, I own I cannot concur with him on the present occasion. I know not to whom I could impute this comedy, if Shakspeare was not its author. I think his hand is visible in almost every scene, though perhaps not so evidently as in those which pass between Katharine and Petruchio.

I once thought that the name of this play might have been taken from an old story, entitled, *The Wyf lapped in Morells Skin,* or *The Taming of a Shrew*; but I have since discovered among the entries in the books of the Stationers' Company the following: " Peter Shorte] May 2, 1594, a pleasaunt conceyted hystorie, called, *The Tayminge of a Shrowe.*" It is likewise entered to Nich. Ling, Jan. 22, 1606; and to John Smythwicke, Nov. 19, 1607.

It was no uncommon practice among the authors of the age of Shakspeare, to avail themselves of the titles of ancient performances. Thus, as Mr. Warton has observed, Spenser sent out his *Pastorals* under the title of *The Shepherd's Kalendar,* a work which had been printed by Wynken de Worde, and reprinted about twenty years before these poems of Spenser appeared, viz. 1559.

Dr. Percy, in the first volume of his *Reliques of Ancient English Poetry,* is of opinion, that *The Frolicksome Duke,* or *the Tinker's Good Fortune,* an ancient ballad in the Pepys' Collection, might have suggested to Shakspeare the Induction for this comedy.

Chance, however, has at last furnished me with the original to which Shakspeare was indebted for his fable; nor does this discovery at all dispose me to retract my former opinion, which the reader may find at the conclusion of the play. Such parts of the dialogue as our author had immediately imitated, I have occafionally pointed out at the bottom of the page; but muſt refer the reader, who is deſirous to examine the whole ſtructure of the piece, to *Six old Plays on which Shakſpeare founded*, &c. publiſhed by S. Leacroft, at Charing-croſs, as a Supplement to our commentaries on Shakſpeare.

Beaumont and Fletcher wrote what may be called a ſequel to this comedy, viz. *The Woman's Prize, or the Tamer Tam'd*; in which Petruchio is ſubdued by a ſecond wife. STEEVENS.

Among the books of my friend the late Mr. William Collins of Chicheſter, now diſperſed, was a collection of ſhort comick ſtories in proſe, printed in the black letter under the year 1570, " ſett forth by maiſter Richard Edwards, mayſter of her Majeſties revels." Among theſe tales was that of the INDUCTION OF THE TINKER in Shakſpeare's *Taming of the Shrew*; and perhaps Edwards's ſtory-book was the immediate ſource from which Shakſpeare, or rather the author of the old *Taming of a Shrew*, drew that diverting apologue. If I recollect right, the circumſtances almoſt tallied with an incident which Heuterus relates from an epiſtle of Ludovicus Vives to have actually happened at the marriage of Duke Philip the Good of Burgundy, about the year 1440. That perſpicuous annaliſt, who flouriſhed about the year 1580, ſays, this ſtory was told to Vives by an old officer of the Duke's court. T. WARTON.

See the earlieſt Engliſh original of this ſtory, &c. at the concluſion of the play. STEEVENS.

Our author's *Taming of the Shrew* was written, I imagine, in 1594. See *An Attempt to aſcertain the Order of Shakſpeare's Plays*, Vol. I. MALONE.

PERSONS reprefented.

A Lord.
Chriftopher Sly, *a drunken tinker.* ⎤ *Perfons in the*
Hoftefs, *Page, Players, Huntfmen, and* ⎱ *Induction.*
   other fervants attending on the Lord. ⎦

Baptifta, *a rich gentleman of* Padua.
Vincentio, *an old gentleman of* Pifa.
Lucentio, *fon to* Vincentio, *in love with* Bianca.
Petruchio, *a gentleman of* Verona, *a fuitor to* Katha-
   rina.
Gremio, ⎱ *Suitors to* Bianca.
Hortenfio, ⎰
Tranio, ⎱ *Servants to* Lucentio.
Biondello, ⎰
Grumio, ⎱ *Servants to* Petruchio.
Curtis, ⎰
Pedant, *an old fellow fet up to perfonate* Vincentio.

Katharina, *the Shrew;* ⎱ *Daughters to* Baptifta.
Bianca, *her fifter,* ⎰
Widow.

Tailor, Haberdafher, *and Servants attending on* Baptifta *and* Petruchio.

SCENE, *fometimes in* Padua; *and fometimes in* Petruchio's *Houfe in the Country.*

Characters in the Induction

to the Original Play of *The Taming of a Shrew*, entered on the Stationers' books in 1594, and printed in quarto in 1607.

A Lord, &c.
Sly.
A Tapster.
Page, Players, Huntsmen, &c.

Persons represented.

Alphonsus, *a merchant of* Athens.
Jerobel, *Duke of* Cestus.
Aurelius, *his son,* ⎫
Ferando, ⎬ *Suitors to the daughters of* Alphonsus.
Polidor, ⎭
Valeria, *servant to* Aurelius.
Sander, *servant to* Ferando.
Phylotus, *a merchant who personates the* Duke.

Kate, ⎫
Emelia, ⎬ *Daughters to* Alphonsus.
Phylema, ⎭

Tailor, Haberdasher, and Servants to Ferando *and* Alphonsus.

SCENE, Athens; *and sometimes* Ferando's *Country House.*

TAMING

OF THE

SHREW.*

* TAMING OF THE SHREW.] We have hitherto supposed Shakspeare the authour of *The Taming of the Shrew*, but his property in it is extremely disputable. I will give my opinion, and the reasons on which it is founded. I suppose then the present play not *originally* the work of Shakspeare, but restored by him to the stage, with the whole Induction of the Tinker; and some other occasional improvements; especially in the character of Petruchio. It is very obvious that the Induction and the Play were either the works of different hands, or written at a great interval of time. The former is in our author's *best* manner, and a great part of the *latter* in his *worst*, or even below it. Dr. Warburton declares it to be certainly spurious; and without doubt, *supposing* it to have been written by Shakspeare, it must have been one of his earliest productions. Yet it is not mentioned in the list of his works by Meres in 1598.

I have met with a facetious piece of Sir John Harrington, printed in 1596, (and possibly there may be an earlier edition,) called *The Metamorphosis of Ajax*, where I suspect an allusion to the old play: "Read the *Booke* of *Taming a Shrew*, which hath made a number of us so perfect, that *now* every one can rule a shrew in our countrey, save he that hath hir."——I am aware a *modern* linguist may object that the word *book* does not at present seem *dramatick*, but it was once *technically* so: Gosson, in his *Schoole of Abuse, containing a pleasaunt Invective against Poets, Pipers, Players, Jesters, and such like Caterpillars of a Commonwealth*, 1579, mentions "twoo prose *bookes* played at the Bell-Sauage:" and Hearne tells us, in a note at the end of William of Worcester, that he had seen a MS. in the nature of a *Play* or *Interlude*, intitled *The Booke of Sir Thomas Moore*.

And in fact there is such an old *anonymous* play in Mr. Pope's list: "A pleasant conceited history, called, *The Taming of a Shrew*—sundry times acted by the earl of Pembroke his servants." Which seems to have been republished by the remains of that company in 1607, when Shakspeare's copy appeared at the Black-Friars or the Globe.——Nor let this seem derogatory from the character of our poet. There is no reason to believe that he wanted to claim the play as his own; for it was not even printed till some years after his death; but he merely revived it on his stage as a *manager*.

In support of what I have said relative to this play, let me only observe further at present, that the author of *Hamlet* speaks of Gonzago, and his wife Baptista; but the author of *The Taming of the Shrew* knew Baptista to be the name of a man. Mr. Capell indeed made me doubt, by declaring the authenticity of it to be confirmed by the testimony of Sir Afton Cockayn. I knew Sir Afton was much acquainted with the writers immediately subsequent to Shakspeare; and I was not inclined to dispute his authosity; but how was I surprised, when I found that Cockayn ascribes nothing more to Shakspeare, than the *Induction Wincot-Ale and the Beggar?* I hope this was only a slip of Mr. Capell's memory.

FARMER.

The following is Sir Aston's Epigram:

TO MR. CLEMENT FISHER, OF WINCOT.

" Shakspeare your Wincot-ale hath much renown'd,
" That fox'd a beggar so (by chance was found
" Sleeping) that there needed not many a word
" To make him to believe he was a lord:
" But you affirm (and in it seem most eager)
" 'Twill make a lord as drunk as any beggar.
" Bid Norton brew such ale, as Shakspeare fancies
" Did put *Kit Sly* into such lordly trances:
" And let us meet there (for a fit of gladness)
" And drink ourselves merry in sober sadness."

Sir A. Cockayn's Poems, 1659, p. 124.

In spite of the great deference which is due from every commentator to Dr. Farmer's judgement, I own I cannot concur with him on the present occasion. I know not to whom I could impute this comedy, if Shakspeare was not its author. I think his hand is visible in almost every scene, though perhaps not so evidently as in those which pass between Katharine and Petruchio.

I once thought that the name of this play might have been taken from an old story, entitled, *The Wyf lapped in Morells Skin,* or *The Taming of a Shrew*; but I have since discovered among the entries in the books of the Stationers' Company the following: " Peter Shorte] May 2, 1594, a pleasaunt conceyted hystorie, called, *The Tayminge of a Shrowe."* It is likewise entered to Nich. Ling, Jan. 22, 1606; and to John Smythwicke, Nov. 19, 1607.

It was no uncommon practice among the authors of the age of Shakspeare, to avail themselves of the titles of ancient performances. Thus, as Mr. Warton has observed, Spenser sent out his *Pastorals* under the title of *The Shepherd's Kalendar,* a work which had been printed by Wynken de Worde, and reprinted about twenty years before these poems of Spenser appeared, viz. 1559.

Dr. Percy, in the first volume of his *Reliques of Ancient English Poetry,* is of opinion, that *The Frolicksome Duke, or the Tinker's Good Fortune,* an ancient ballad in the Pepys' Collection, might have suggested to Shakspeare the Induction for this comedy.

Chance, however, has at last furnished me with the original to which Shakspeare was indebted for his fable; nor does this discovery at all dispose me to retract my former opinion, which the reader may find at the conclusion of the play. Such parts of the dialogue as our author had immediately imitated, I have occafionally pointed out at the bottom of the page; but muſt refer the reader, who is deſirous to examine the whole ſtructure of the piece, to *Six old Plays on which Shakſpeare founded*, &c. publiſhed by S. Leacroft, at Charing-croſs, as a Supplement to our commentaries on Shakſpeare.

Beaumont and Fletcher wrote what may be called a ſequel to this comedy, viz. *The Woman's Prize, or the Tamer Tam'd*; in which Petruchio is ſubdued by a ſecond wife. STEEVENS.

Among the books of my friend the late Mr. William Collins of Chicheſter, now diſperſed, was a collection of ſhort comick ſtories in proſe, printed in the black letter under the year 1570, " ſett forth by maiſter Richard Edwards, mayſter of her Majeſties revels." Among theſe tales was that of the INDUCTION OF THE TINKER in Shakſpeare's *Taming of the Shrew*; and perhaps Edwards's ſtory-book was the immediate ſource from which Shakſpeare, or rather the author of the old *Taming of a Shrew*, drew that diverting apo-logue. If I recollect right, the circumſtances almoſt tallied with an incident which Heuterus relates from an epiſtle of Ludovicus Vives to have actually happened at the marriage of Duke Philip the Good of Burgundy, about the year 1440. That perſpicuous annaliſt, who flouriſhed about the year 1580, ſays, this ſtory was told to Vives by an old officer of the Duke's court. T. WARTON.

See the earlieſt Engliſh original of this ſtory, &c. at the conclu-ſion of the play. STEEVENS.

Our author's *Taming of the Shrew* was written, I imagine, in 1594. See *An Attempt to aſcertain the Order of Shakſpeare's Plays*, Vol. I. MALONE.

And couple Clowder with the deep-mouth'd brach.

That the latter of these criticks is right, will appear
use of the word *brach*, in Sir T. More's *Comfort against*
tion, Book III. ch. xxiv:—" Here it must be known of some men
that can skill of hunting, whether that we mistake not our terms,
for then are we utterly ashamed as ye wott well.—And I am so
cunning, that I cannot tell, whether among them a bitche be a
bitche or no; but as I remember she is no bitch but a
The meaning of the latter part of the paragraph seems to be, " I
am so little skilled in hunting, that I can hardly tell whether a
bitch be a bitch or not; my judgement goes no further,
to direct me to call either dog or bitch by their general
Hound." I am aware that Spelman acquaints his reader, that
brache was used in his days for a *lurcher*, and that Shakspeare himself has made it a dog of a particular species:

" Mastiff, greyhound, mungrill grim,
" Hound or spaniel, *brach* or lym."

King Lear, Act III. sc. v.

But it is manifest from the passage of *More* just cited, that it was
sometimes applied in a general sense, and may therefore be so un-
derstood in the passage before us; and it may be added, that
brach appears to be used in the same sense by Beaumont and
Fletcher:

" *A*. Is that your brother?
" *E*. Yes, have you lost your memory?
" *A*. As I live he is a pretty fellow.
" *Y*. O this is a sweet *brach*."

Scornful Lady, Act I. sc. i.   T. WARTON.

I believe *brach Merriman* means only *Merriman the brach*. So in
the old song:

" *Cow Crumbock* is a very good cow."

Brach however appears to have been a particular sort of hound.
In an old metrical charter, granted by Edward the Confessor to the
hundred of Cholmer and Dancing, in Essex, there are the two following lines:

" Four greyhounds & six *Bratches*,
" For hare, fox, and wild-cattes."

Merriman surely could not be designed for the name of a female
of the canine species. STEEVENS.

It seems from the commentary of Ulitius upon *Gratius*, from
Caius de Canibus Britannicis, from *brocco*, in Spelman's *Glossary*,
and from Markham's *Country Contentments*, that *brache* originally
meant a bitch. Ulitius, p. 163, observes, that bitches have a su-
perior sagacity of nose:—" fœminis [canibus] sagacitatis plari-

Saw'ſt thou not, boy, how Silver made it good⁹

mum ineſſe, uſus docuit;" and hence, perhaps, any hound with eminent quickneſs of ſcent, whether dog or bitch, was called *brache*, for the term *brache* is ſometimes applied to males. Our anceſtors hunted much with the large ſouthern hounds, and had in every pack a couple of dogs peculiarly good and cunning to find game, or recover the ſcent, as *Markham* informs us. To this cuſtom Shakſpeare ſeems here to allude, by naming *two braches*, which, in my opinion, are beagles; and this diſcriminates *brach*, from the *lym*, a blood-hound mentioned together with it, in the tragedy of *King Lear*. In the following quotation offered by Mr. Steevens on another occaſion, the *brache* hunts truly by the ſcent, behind the doe, while the hounds are on every ſide:

" For as the dogs purſue the ſilly doe,
" The *brache* behind, the hounds on every ſide;
" So trac'd they me among the mountains wide."

Phaer's Legend of Owen Glendower. TOLLET.

The word is certainly uſed by Chapman in his *Gentleman Uſher*, a comedy, 1606, as ſynonymous to *bitch*: " *Venus*, your *brach* there, runs ſo proud, &c." So alſo our author in *K. Henry IV.* P. I: " I'd rather hear *Lady*, my *brach*, howl in Iriſh." The ſtructure of the paſſage before us, and the manner in which the next line is connected with this, [*And* couple, &c.] added to the circumſtance of the word *brach* occurring in the end of that line, incline me to think that *Brach* is here a corruption, and that the line before us began with a verb, not a noun. MALONE.

Sir Thomas Hanmer reads—*Leech* Merriman; that is, *apply ſome remedies* to Merriman, the poor cur has his *joints ſwell'd*.— Perhaps we might read—*bathe* Merriman, which is, I believe, the common practice of huntſmen; but the preſent reading may ſtand. JOHNSON.

Emboſs'd is a hunting term. When a deer is hard run, and foams at the mouth, he is ſaid to be *emboſs'd*. A dog alſo when he is ſtrained with hard running (eſpecially upon hard ground) will have his knees ſwelled, and then he is ſaid to be *emboſs'd*: from the French word *boſſe*, which ſignifies a tumour. This explanation of the word will receive illuſtration from the following paſſage in the old comedy, intitled, *The Shoemakers Holiday, or the gentle Craft*, acted at court, and printed in the year 1600, ſignat. C:

" —— Beate every brake, the game's not farre,
" This way with winged feet he fled from death:
" Beſides, the miller's boy told me even now,
" He ſaw him take ſoyle, and he hallowed him,
" Affirming him ſo *emboſs'd*." T. WARTON.

At the hedge' corner, in the coldeſt fault?
I would not loſe the dog for twenty pound.

   1 HUN. Why, Belman is as good as he, my lord;
He cried upon it at the mereſt loſs,
And twice to-day pick'd out the dulleſt ſcent:
Truſt me, I take him for the better dog.

   LORD. Thou art a fool; if Echo were as fleet,
I would eſteem him worth a dozen ſuch.
But ſup them well, and look unto them all;
To-morrow I intend to hunt again.

   1 HUN. I will, my lord.

   LORD. What's here? one dead, or drunk? See,
        doth he breathe?

   2 HUN. He breathes, my lord: Were he not
        warm'd with ale,
This were a bed but cold to ſleep ſo ſoundly.

   Mr. T. Warton's firſt explanation may be juſt. Lyly, in his *Midas*,
1592, has not only given us the term, but the explanation of it:
  "*Pet.* There was a boy leaſh'd on the ſingle, becauſe when he
was *imboſs'd* he took ſoyle.
  "*Li.* What's that?
  "*Pet.* Why a boy was beaten on the tayle with a leathern thong,
becauſe, when he *ſom'de at the mouth* with running, he went into
the water." STEEVENS.

   From the Spaniſh, *des embocar*, to caſt out of the mouth. We
have again the ſame expreſſion in *Antony and Cleopatra*:
    "————— the boar of Theſſaly
    "Was never ſo *emboſs'd*." MALONE.

   Can any thing be more evident than that *imboſs'd* means *ſwelled*
in the knees, and that we ought to read *bathe?* What has the *im-
boſſing* of a *deer* to do with that of a *hound?* "Imboſſed ſores"
occur in *As you Like it*; and in the Firſt Part of *King Henry IV.*
the Prince calls Falſtaff " *imboſs'd* raſcal." RITSON.

   3 ——— *bow Silver* made it good—] This, I ſuppoſe, is a
technical term. It occurs likewiſe in the 23d ſong of Drayton's
Polyolbion:
    " What's offer'd by the firſt, the other *good doth make.*"
                     STEEVENS.

Lord. O monftrous beaft! how like a fwine he
   lies!
Grim death, how foul and loathfome is thine image!
Sirs, I will practife on this drunken man.——
What think you, if he were convey'd to bed,
Wrap'd in fweet clothes, rings put upon his fingers,
A moft delicious banquet by his bed,
And brave attendants near him when he wakes,
Would not the beggar then forget himfelf?

 1 *Hun.* Believe me, lord, I think he cannot
   choofe.

 2 *Hun.* It would feem ftrange unto him when he
   wak'd.

 Lord. Even as a flattering dream, or worthlefs
   fancy.
Then take him up, and manage well the jeft:—
Carry him gently to my faireft chamber,
And hang it round with all my wanton pictures:
Balm his foul head with warm diftilled waters,
And burn fweet wood to make the lodging fweet:
Procure me mufick ready when he wakes,
To make a dulcet and a heavenly found;
And if he chance to fpeak, be ready ftraight,
And, with a low fubmiffive reverence,
Say,—What is it your honour will command?
Let one attend him with a filver bafon,
Full of rofe-water, and beftrew'd with flowers;
Another bear the ewer, the third a diaper,
And fay,—Will't pleafe your lordfhip cool your
   hands?
Some one be ready with a coftly fuit,
And afk him what apparel he will wear;
Another tell him of his hounds and horfe,
And that his lady mourns at his difeafe:
Perfuade him, that he hath been lunatick;

And, when he fays he is —, fay, that he dreams,
For he is nothing but a mighty lord.[4]
This do, and do it kindly,[5] gentle firs;
It will be paftime paffing excellent,
If it be hufbanded with modefty.[6]

   1 HUN. My lord, I warrant you, we'll play our
           part,
As he fhall think, by our true diligence,
He is no lefs than what we fay he is.

   LORD. Take him up gently, and to bed with him;
And each one to his office, when he wakes.—
          [*Some bear out* SLY. *A trumpet founds.*
Sirrah, go fee what trumpet 'tis that founds:—
                 [*Exit* Servant.

---

[4] *And, when he fays he is ——, fay, that he dreams,*
  For he is nothing but a mighty lord.] I rather think (with Sir
Thomas Hanmer) that Shakfpeare wrote :
  And when he fays he's poor, fay that he dreams.
The dignity of a lord is then fignificantly oppofed to the poverty
which it would be natural for Sly to acknowledge. STEEVENS.

  If any thing fhould be inferted, it may be done thus :
  And when he fays he's Sly, *fay that he dreams.*
The likenefs in writing of *Sly* and *fay* produced the omiffion.
                     JOHNSON.

  This is hardly right; for how fhould the Lord know the beggar's
name to be *Sly?* STEEVENS.

  Perhaps the fentence is left imperfect, becaufe he did not know
by what name to call him. BLACKSTONE.

  I have no doubt that the blank was intended by the author. It
is obfervable that the metre of the line is perfect, without any fupplemental word. In *The Tempeft* a fimilar blank is found, which
Shakfpeare there alfo certainly intended :—" I fhould know that
voice; it fhould be ——; but he is drown'd, and thefe are devils."
                     MALONE.

[5] *This do, and do it* kindly,] *Kindly,* means naturally.
                     M. MASON.

[6] —— *modefty.*] By *modefty* is meant *moderation*, without fuffering our merriment to break into an excefs. JOHNSON.

Belike, fome noble gentleman; that means,
Travelling fome journey, to repofe him here.——

Re-enter a Servant.

How now? who is it?

Ser.   An it pleafe your honour,
Players that offer fervice to your lordfhip.

Lord. Bid them come near:

Enter Players.[7]

                    Now, fellows, you are welcome.

1 *Play.* We thank your honour.

Lord. Do you intend to ftay with me to-night?

2 *Play.* So pleafe your lordfhip to accept our duty.[8]

---

[7] *Enter Players.*] The old play already quoted reads:
" *Enter two of the plaïers with packs at their backs, and a boy.*
" Now, firs, what ftore of plaies have you?
" *San.* Marry my lord you may have a tragicall,
" Or a commoditie, or what you will.
" *The other.* A comedie thou fhouldft fay, founs thou'lt fhame
            us all.
" *Lord.* And what's the name of your comedie?
" *San.* Marrie my lord, 'tis calde *The Taming of a Shrew:*
" 'Tis a good leffon for us my L. for us that are maried men, &c."
                                        Steevens.

[8] ——*to accept our duty.*] It was in thofe times the cuftom of
players to travel in companies, and offer their fervice at great
houfes. Johnson.

In the fifth *Earl of Northumberland's Houfehold Book,* (with a
copy of which I was honoured by the late duchefs,) the following
article occurs. The book was begun in the year 1512.
            " Rewards to Playars.
" Item, to be payd to the faid Richard Gowge and Thomas
Percy for rewards to players for playes playd in Chryftinmas by
ftranegers in my houfe after xxd. every play by eftimacion fomme
xxxiijs. iiijd. Which ys apoynted to be paid to the faid Richard
Gowge and Thomas Percy at the faid Chriftynmas in full contenta-
cion of the faid rewardys xxxiijs. iiijd." Steevens.

Lord. With all my heart.—This fellow I remember,
Since once he play'd a farmer's eldeſt ſon;—
'Twas where you woo'd the gentlewoman ſo well:
I have forgot your name; but, ſure, that part
Was aptly fitted, and naturally perform'd.

  1 *Play.* I think, 'twas Soto⁹ that your honour
      means.

  Lord. 'Tis very true;—thou didſt it excellent.—
Well, you are come to me in happy time;
The rather for I have ſome ſport in hand,
Wherein your cunning can aſſiſt me much.

⁹ *I think, 'twas* Soto—] I take our author here to be paying
a compliment to Beaumont and Fletcher's *Women Pleaſed,* in
which comedy there is the character of *Soto,* who is a farmer's ſon,
and a very facetious ſerving-man. Mr. Rowe and Mr. Pope prefix the name of *Sim* to the line here ſpoken; but the firſt folio has
it *Sincklo;* which, no doubt, was the name of one of the players
here introduced, and who had played the part of *Soto* with applauſe.
                                                  Theobald.

  As the old copy prefixes the name of *Sincklo* to this line, why
ſhould we diſplace it? *Sincklo* is a name elſewhere uſed by Shakſpeare. In one of the parts of *King Henry VI. Humphrey* and
Sincklo enter with their bows, as foreſters.

  With this obſervation I was favoured by a learned lady, and
have replaced the old reading. Steevens.

  It is true that *Soto,* in the play of *Women Pleaſed,* is a *farmer's
eldeſt ſon,* but *he does not wooe any gentlewoman;* ſo that it may be
doubted, whether that be the character alluded to. There can be
little doubt that *Sincklo* was the name of one of the players, which
has crept in, both here and in the Third Part of *Henry VI.* inſtead
of the name of the perſon repreſented.

  Again, at the concluſion of the Second Part of *King Henry IV:*
" Enter *Sincklo* and three or four officers." See the quarto 1600.
                                                Tyrwhitt.

If *Soto* were the character alluded to, the compliment would be
to the perſon who played the part, not to the author. M. Mason.

  Sincklo or *Sinkler,* was certainly an actor in the ſame company
with Shakſpeare, &c.—He is introduced together with Burbage,
Condell, Lowin, &c. in the Induction to Marſton's *Malcontent,*
1604, and was alſo a performer in the entertainment entitled *The
Seven Deadlie Sinns.* Malone.

There is a lord will hear you play to-night:
But I am doubtful of your modesties;
Lest, over-eying of his odd behaviour,
(For yet his honour never heard a play,)
You break into some merry passion,
And so offend him; for I tell you, sirs,
If you should smile, he grows impatient.

   1 *PLAY.* Fear not, my lord; we can contain our-
         selves,
Were he the veriest antick in the world.[2]

---

   [2] —— *in the world.*] Here follows another insertion made by
Mr. Pope from the old play. These words are not in the folio, 1623.
I have therefore degraded them, as we have no proof that the first
sketch of the piece was written by Shakspeare:

   " *San.* [*to the other.*] Go, get a dishclout to make cleane
your shooes, and Ile speak for the properties.*   [*Exit Player.*

   " My lord, we must have a shoulder of mutton for a propertie,
and a little vinegre to make our diuell rore.† "

   The *shoulder of mutton* might indeed be necessary afterwards for
the dinner of Petruchio, but there is no devil in this piece, or in
the original on which Shakspeare form'd it; neither was it yet determined what comedy should be represented. STEEVENS.

   * *Property*] in the language of a playhouse, is every implement necessary to
the exhibition. JOHNSON.

   † —— *a little* vinegre *to make our* diuell rore.] When the acting the mysteries
of the Old and New Testament was in vogue, at the representation of the mys-
tery of the Passion, Judas and the devil made a part. And the devil, wherever
he came, was always to suffer some disgrace, to make the people laugh: as here,
the buffoonery was to apply the gall and vinegar to make him roar. And the
Passion being that, of all the mysteries, which was most frequently represented,
vinegar became at length the standing implement to torment the devil; and was
used for this purpose even after the mysteries ceased, and the moralities came in
vogue; where the devil continued to have a considerable part.—The mention of
it here, was to ridicule so absurd a circumstance in these old farces.
                                        WARBURTON.

   All that Dr. Warburton has said relative to *Judas* and the *vinegar,* wants confirmation. I have met with no such circumstances in any mysteries, whether
in MS. or in print; and yet both the *Chester* and *Coventry* collections are preserved in the British Museum. See MS. Harl. 2013, and Cotton MS. Vespa-
sian D. viii.

   Perhaps, however, some entertainments of a farcical kind might have been
introduced between the acts. Between the divisions of one of the *Chester Mysteries,* I met with this marginal direction: *Here the Boy and Pig;* and perhaps the
devil in the intervals of this first comedy of *The Taming of the Shrew,* might

Lord. **Go, firrah, take them to the buttery,[2]**
And give them friendly welcome every one;
Let them want nothing that my houfe affords.——
　　　　　　　[Exeunt Servant *and Players.*

be tormented for the entertainment of the audience; or, according to a cuftom obferved in fome of our ancient puppet-fhews, might beat his wife with a fhoulder of mutton. In the Preface to Marlowe's *Tamburlaine,* 1590, the Printer fays:

"I have (purpofelie) omitted and left out fome fond and frivolous jeftures, digreffing (and in my poore opinion) farre unmeete for the matter, which I thought might feeme more tedious unto the wife, than any way els to be re-garded, though (happly) they have bene of fome vaine conceited fondlings greatly gaped at, what time they were fhowed upon the ftage in their graced de-formities: neverthelefse now to be mixtured in print with fuch matter of worth, it would prove a great difgrace," &c.

The *bladder of vinegar* was, however, ufed for other purpofes. I meet with the following ftage direction in the old play of *Cambyfes,* (by T. Prefton,) where one of the characters is fuppofed to die from the wounds he had juft received:—*Here let a fmall bladder of vinegar be prick'd.* I fuppofe to counterfeit blood; red-wine vinegar was chiefly ufed, as appears from the ancient books of cookery.

In the ancient Tragedy, or rather Morality, called *All for Money,* by T. Lupton, 1578, *Sin* fays:

　　"I knew I would make him foon change his note,
　　"I will make him fing the Black Sanctus, I hold him a groat."
　　　　　"Here *Satan* fhall cry and roar."

Again, a little after.
　　　　　"Here he *roareth and crieth.*"

Of the kind of wit current through thefe productions, a better fpecimen can hardly be found than the following:

　　"*Satan.* Whatever thou wilt have, I will not thee denie.
　　"*Sinne.* Then give me a piece of thy tayle to make a flappe for a flie.
　　"For if I had a piece thereof, I do verely believe
　　"The humble bees ftinging fhould never me grieve.
　　"*Satan.* No, my friend, no, my tayle I cannot fpare,
　　"But afke what thou wilt befides, and I will it prepare.
　　"*Sinne.* Then your nofe I would have to ftop my tayle behind,
　　"For I am combred with collike and letting out of winde:
　　"And if it be too little to make thereof a cafe,
　　"Then I would be fo bold to borrowe your face."

Such were the entertainments, of which our maiden queen fat a fpectrefs in the earlier part of her reign. STEEVENS.

[2] —— *take them to the* buttery,] Mr. Pope had probably thefe words in his thoughts, when he wrote the following paffage of his preface: "—the top of the profeffion were then mere players, not gentlemen of the ftage; they were led into the *buttery* by the ftew-ard, not placed at the lord's table, or the lady's toilette." But he feems not to have obferved, that the players here introduced are *ftrollers;* and there is no reafon to fuppofe that our author, Heminge, Burbage, Condell, &c. who were licenfed by King James, were treated in this manner. MALONE.

Sirrah, go you to Bartholomew my page,

        . [*To a* Servant.

And fee him drefs'd in all fuits like a lady:

That done, conduct him to the drunkard's chamber,

And call him—madam, do him obeifance.

Tell him from me, (as he will win my love,)

He bear himfelf with honourable action,

Such as he hath obferv'd in noble ladies

Unto their lords, by them accomplifhed:

Such duty to the drunkard let him do,

With foft low tongue,[3] and lowly courtefy;

And fay,—What is't your honour will command,

Wherein your lady, and your humble wife,

May fhow her duty, and make known her love?

And then—with kind embracements, tempting

   kiffes,

And with declining head into his bofom,—

Bid him fhed tears, as being overjoy'd

To fee her noble lord reftor'd to health,

Who, for twice feven years, hath efteemed him

No better than a poor and loathfome beggar:[4]

---

[3] *With* foft low *tongue,*] So, in *King Lear:*

 " —————— Her voice was ever *foft,*

 " Gentle and *low*; an excellent thing in woman."

           MALONE.

[4] *Who, for* twice *feven years,* &c.] In former editions:

  Who for this feven years hath efteemed him

  No better than a poor and loathfome beggar.

I have ventured to alter a word here, againft the authority of the printed copies; and hope, I fhall be juftified in it by two fubfequent paffages. That the poet defigned the tinker's fuppofed lunacy fhould be of fourteen years ftanding at leaft, is evident upon two parallel paffages in the play to that purpofe. THEOBALD.

 The remark is juft, but perhaps the alteration may be thought unneceffary by thofe who recollect that our author rarely reckons time with any great correctnefs. Both Falftaff and Orlando forget the true hour of their appointments. STEEVENS.

 In both thefe paffages the term mentioned is *fifteen,* not *fourteen,* years. The fervants may well be fuppofed to forget the precife

And if the boy have not a woman's gift,
To rain a fhower of commanded tears,
An onion⁵ will do well for fuch a fhift;
Which in a napkin being clofe convey'd,
Shall in defpite enforce a watry eye.
See this defpatch'd with all the hafte thou canft;
Anon I'll give thee more inftructions.——

                    [*Exit* Servant.

I know, the boy will well ufurp the grace,
Voice, gait, and action of a gentlewoman:
I long to hear him call the drunkard, hufband;
And how my men will ftay themfelves from laughter,
When they do homage to this fimple peafant.
I'll in to counfel them: haply, my prefence
May well abate the over-merry fpleen,
Which otherwife would grow into extremes.

                    [*Exeunt.*

---

period dictated to them by their mafter, or, as is the cuftom of fuch perfons, to aggravate what they have heard. There is therefore, in my opinion, no need of change. MALONE.

——*hath efteemed* him —] This is an error of the prefs.—We fhould read *himfelf,* inftead of *him.* M. MASON.

Him is ufed inftead of *himfelf,* as *you* is ufed for *yourfelves* in *Macbeth:*
    " Acquaint *you* with the perfect fpy o'the time—."
i. e. acquaint *yourfelves.*
    Again, in *Ovid's Banquet of Sence,* by Chapman, 1595:
    " Sweet touch, the engine that love's bow doth bend,
    " The fence wherewith he feeles *him* deified."
                    STEEVENS.

⁵ *An* onion—] It is not unlikely that the *onion* was an expedient ufed by the actors of interludes. JOHNSON.

So, in *Antony and Cleopatra:*
    " The tears live in an *onion* that fhould water this forrow."
                    STEEVENS.

SCENE II.

A Bedchamber in the Lord's Houſe.[6]

Sᴌʏ *is diſcovered*[7] *in a rich night gown, with Attendants; ſome with apparel, others with baſon,
ewer, and other appurtenances. Enter* Lord, *dreſs'd
like a Servant.*

Sᴌʏ. For God's ſake, a pot of ſmall ale.[8]

ɪ Sᴇʀᴠ. Will't pleaſe your lordſhip drink a cup
of ſack?

---

[6] *A Bedchamber,* &c.] From the original ſtage-direction in the
firſt folio it appears that Sly and the other perſons mentioned in the
Induction, were intended to be exhibited here, and during the repreſentation of the comedy, in a balcony above the ſtage. The
direction here is—" *Enter* aloft the *drunkard with attendants,* &c."
So afterwards at the end of this ſcene—" *The Preſenters* above
ſpeak." See the Account of our old Theatres, Vol. II.

Mᴀʟᴏɴᴇ.

[7] *Sly is diſcovered,* &c.] Thus in the original play:
" *Enter two with a table and a banquet on it, and two other, with*
Slie *aſleepe in a chaire, richlie apparelled, and the muſick plaieng.*
" *One.* So, ſirha, now go call my lord;
" And tell him all things are ready as he will'd it.
" *Another.* Set thou ſome wine upon the boord,
" And then Ile go fetch my lord preſently.   [*Exit.*
" *Enter the Lord and his men.*
" *Lord.* How now, what is all things readie?
" *One.* Yea, my lord.
" *Lord.* Then ſound the muſicke, and Ile wake him ſtrait,
" And ſee you doe as earſt I gave in charge.
" My lord, my lord, (he ſleeps ſoundly,) my lord.
" *Slie.* Tapſter, give's a little ſmall ale: heigh ho.
" *Lord.* Heere's wine, my lord, the pureſt of the grape.
" *Slie.* For which lord?
" *Lord.* For your honor, my lord.
" *Slie.* Who I, am I a lord?—Ieſus, what fine apparell have I got!
" *Lord.* More richer far your honour hath to weare,
" And if it pleaſe you, I will fetch them ſtraight.

Vᴏʟ. VI.   D d

2 *Serv.* Will't pleafe your honour tafte of thefe conferves?

3 *Serv.* What raiment will your honour wear to-day?

Sly. I am Chriftophero Sly; call not me—honour, nor lordfhip: I ne'er drank fack in my life; and if you give me any conferves, give me conferves of beef: Ne'er afk me what raiment I'll wear; for I have no more doublets than backs, no more ftockings than legs, nor no more fhoes than feet; nay, fometimes, more feet than fhoes, or fuch fhoes as my toes look through the overleather.

Lord. Heaven ceafe this idle humour in your honour!

O, that a mighty man, of fuch defcent,
Of fuch poffeffions, and fo high efteem,
Should be infufed with fo foul a fpirit!

Sly. What, would you make me mad? Am not I Chriftopher Sly, old Sly's fon of Burton-heath; [9]

" *Wil.* And if your honour pleafe to ride abroad,
" Ile fetch your luftie fteedes more fwift of pace
" Then winged Pegafus in all his pride,
" That ran fo fwiftlie over Perfian plaines.
" *Tom.* And if your honour pleafe to hunt the deere,
" Your hounds ftands readie cuppled at the doore,
" Who in running will oretake the row,
" And make the long-breathde tygre broken-winded." STEEVENS.

[8] ——*fmall ale.*] This beverage is mentioned in the accounts of the Stationers' Company in the year 1558: " For a ftande of *fmall ale;*" I fuppofe it was what we now call *fmall beer,* no mention of that liquor being made on the fame books, though *duble bere,* and *duble duble ale,* are frequently recorded. STEEVENS.

It appears from *The Captain,* by Beaumont and Fletcher, Act IV. fc. ii. that *fingle beer* and *fmall beer* were fynonymous terms.
                                                                MALONE.

[9] —— *of* Burton-heath; ——*Marian Hacket, the fat ale-wife of Wincot,*] I fufpect we fhould read—*Barton-heath.* *Barton* and *Woodmancot,* or, as it is vulgarly pronounced, *Wancot,* are both of them in Gloucefterfhire, near the refidence of Shakfpeare's old

by birth a pedler, by education a card-maker, by
tranfmutation a bear-herd, and now by prefent profeffion a tinker? Afk Marian Hacket, the fat ale-
wife of Wincot, if fhe know me not: if fhe fay I
am not fourteen pence on the fcore for fheer ale,
fcore me up for the lying'ft knave in Chriftendom.
What, I am not beftraught:[3] Here's———

enemy, Juftice Shallow. Very probably too, this fat ale-wife
might be a real character. STEEVENS.

Wilnecotte is a village in Warwickfhire, with which Shakfpeare
was well acquainted, near Stratford. The houfe kept by our ge-
nial hoftefs, ftill remains, but is at prefent a mill. The meaneft
hovel to which Shakfpeare has an allufion, interefts curiofity, and
acquires an importance: at leaft, it becomes the object of a poetical
antiquarian's inquiries. T. WARTON.

Burton Dorfet is a village in Warwickfhire. RITSON.

There is likewife a village in Warwickfhire called *Burton* Haftings.
Among Sir A. Cockayn's poems (as Dr. Farmer and Mr. Steevens
have obferved) there is an epigram on Sly and his ale, addreffed to
Mr. Clement Fifher of *Wincot*.
The text is undoubtedly right.
There is a village in Warwickfhire called *Barton on the Heath*,
where Mr. Dover, the founder of the Cotfwold games, lived.
MALONE.

[3] ——— *I am not* beftraught:] I once thought that if our poet
did not defign to put a corrupted word into the mouth of the
Tinker, we ought to read—*diftraught*, i. e. *diftracted*. So, in
Romeo and Juliet :
  " O, if I wake, fhall I not be *diftraught*," &c.
For there is no verb extant from which the participle *beftraught* can
be formed. In *Albion's England*, however, by Warner, 1602, I
meet with the word as fpelt by Shakfpeare:
  " Now teares had drowned further fpeech, till fhe as one
    beftrought
  " Did crie," &c.
Again, in the old Song, beginning, " When griping grief," &c.
No. 53. *Paradyfe of dainty Devifes*, edit. 1576:
  " *Be-ftraughted* heads relyef hath founde."
Again, in Lord Surrey's tranflation of the 4th Book of Virgil's
Æneid :
  " 'Well near *beftraught*, upftart his heare for dread."
STEEVENS.

1 *Serv.* O, this it is that makes your lady mourn.

2 *Serv.* O, this it is that makes your fervants
        droop.

Lord. Hence comes it that your kindred fhun
        your houfe,
As beaten hence by your ftrange lunacy.
O, noble lord, bethink thee of thy birth;
Call home thy ancient thoughts from banifhment,
And banifh hence thefe abject lowly dreams:
Look, how thy fervants do attend on thee,
Each in his office ready at thy beck.
Wilt thou have mufick? hark! Apollo plays,
                                    [*Mufick.*

And twenty caged nightingales do fing:
Or wilt thou fleep? we'll have thee to a couch,
Softer and fweeter than the luftful bed
On purpofe trimm'd up for Semiramis.
Say, thou wilt walk; we will beftrew the ground:
Or wilt thou ride? thy horfes fhall be trapp'd,
Their harnefs ftudded all with gold and pearl.
Doft thou love hawking? thou haft hawks will
        foar
Above the morning lark: Or wilt thou hunt?
Thy hounds fhall make the welkin anfwer them,
And fetch fhrill echoes from the hollow earth.

    1 *Serv.* Say, thou wilt courfe; thy greyhounds
        are as fwift
As breathed ftags, ay, fleeter than the roe.

    2 *Serv.* Doft thou love pictures? we will fetch
        thee ftraight
Adonis, painted by a running brook;
And Cytherea all in fedges hid;

Beftraught feems to have been fynonymous to *diftraught* or diftracted. See Minfheu's Dict. 1617: "*Beftract*, a Lat. diftractus
mente. Vi. *Mad* and Bedlam." Malone.

Which feem to move and wanton with her breath,
Even as the waving fedges play with wind.

Lord. We'll fhow thee Io, as fhe was a maid;
And how fhe was beguiled and furpris'd,
As lively painted as the deed was done.

3 *Serv.* Or Daphne, roaming through a thorny
wood;
Scratching her legs, that one fhall fwear fhe bleeds:
And at that fight fhall fad Apollo weep,
So workmanly the blood and tears are drawn.

Lord. Thou art a lord, and nothing but a lord:
Thou haft a lady far more beautiful
Than any woman in this waning age.

1 *Serv.* And, till the tears, that fhe hath fhed
for thee,
Like envious floods, o'er-ran her lovely face,
She was the faireft creature in the world;
And yet fhe is inferior to none.

Sly. Am I a lord? and have I fuch a lady?
Or do I dream? or have I dream'd till now?
I do not fleep: I fee, I hear, I fpeak;
I fmell fweet favours, and I feel foft things:—
Upon my life, I am a lord, indeed;
And not a tinker, nor Chriftophero Sly.—
Well, bring our lady hither to our fight;
And once again, a pot o' the fmalleft ale.

2 *Serv.* Will't pleafe your mightinefs to wafh
your hands?

[Servants *prefent an ewer, bafon, and napkin.*
O, how we joy to fee your wit reftor'd!
O, that once more you knew but what you are!
Thefe fifteen years you have been in a dream;
Or, when you wak'd, fo wak'd as if you flept.

Sly. Thefe fifteen years! by my fay, a goodly nap.
But did I never fpeak of all that time?

1 Serv. O, yes, my lord; but very idle words:—
For though you lay here in this goodly chamber,
Yet would you say, ye were beaten out of door;
And rail upon the hostess of the house;
And say, you would present her at the leet,[1]
Because she brought stone jugs, and no seal'd quarts:
Sometimes, you would call out for Cicely Hacket.

Sly. Ay, the woman's maid of the house.

3 Serv. Why, sir, you know no house, nor no
        such maid;
Nor no such men, as you have reckon'd up,—
As Stephen Sly, and old John Naps of Greece,[4]

---

[1] —— *leet,*] At the *Court-leet,* or courts of the manor.
                        JOHNSON.

And say, you would present her at the leet,
  Because she brought stone jugs, and no seal'd quarts:] The *leet* is
the *Court-leet,* or *View of frank pledge,* held anciently once a year,
within a particular hundred, manor, or lordship, before the steward
of the leet. See Kitchen *On Courts,* 4th edit. 1663. " The resi-
due of the matters of the charge which ensue," says that writer,
on Court Leets, p. 21, " are enquirable and *presentable,* and are
also punishable in a leet." He then enumerates the various articles,
of which the following is the twenty-seventh : " Also if tiplers sell
by CUPS *and dishes, or measures sealed,* or not sealed, *is inquirable.*"
See also *Characterismi, or Lenton's Leasures,* 12mo. 1631 : " He
[an informer] transforms himselfe into several shapes, to avoid
suspicion of *inne-holders,* and inwardly joyes at the sight of a blacke
pot or *jugge,* knowing that their sale by *sealed quarts,* spoyles his
market." MALONE.
   [4] —— *John Naps of* Greece,] A *hart of Greece,* was a *fat
hart. Graisse,* Fr. So, in the old ballad of *Adam Bell,* &c.
   " Eche of them slew a hart of *graece,*"
Again, in *Ives's Select Papers,* at the coronation feast of Elizabeth
of York, queen of King Henry VII. among other dishes were
" capons *of high Greece.*"
   Perhaps this expression was used to imply that *John Naps* (who
might have been a real character) was *a fat man:* or as Poins calls
the associates of Falstaff *Trojans,* John Naps might be called a
Grecian for such another reason. STEEVENS.
   For *old John Naps* of Greece, read—*old John Naps* o' th'
Green. BLACKSTONE.

And Peter Turf, and Henry Pimpernell;
And twenty more such names and men as these,
Which never were, nor no man ever saw.

Sly. Now, Lord be thanked for my good amends!

All. Amen.[5]

Sly. I thank thee; thou shalt not lose by it.

Enter the Page, *as a lady, with Attendants.*[6]

Page. How fares my noble lord?

Sly. Marry, I fare well; for here is cheer enough.
Where is my wife?

The addition seems to have been a common one. So, in our
author's *King Henry IV.* P. II:
  " Who is next?—Peter Bullcalf *of the Green.*"
  In *The London Chanticleers*, a comedy, 1659, a ballad entitled
" George *o' the Green*" is mentioned. Again, in our author's
King Henry IV. P. II: " I beseech you, sir, to countenance
William Visor of Woncot, against Clement Perkes *o' the hill.*"—
The emendation proposed by Sir W. Blackstone was also suggested
in Theobald's edition, and adopted by Sir T. Hanmer.

Malone.

  [5] In this place, Mr. Pope, and after him other editors, had in-
troduced the three following speeches, from the old play, 1607.
I have already observed that it is by no means probable, that this
former comedy of *The Taming of the Shrew* was written by Shak-
speare, and have therefore removed them from the text:
  " *Sly.* By the mass, I think I am a lord indeed:
" What is thy name?
  " *Man. Sim*, an it please your honour.
  " *Sly. Sim?* that's as much as to say, *Simeon*, or *Simon*. Put
forth thy hand, and fill the pot." Steevens.

  [6] *Enter the* Page, *&c.*] Thus in the original play:
      " *Enter the Boy in woman's attire.*
  " Slie. *Sim*, is this she?
  " Lord. I, my lord.
  " Slie. Masse 'tis a pretty wench; what's her name?
  " Boy. Oh that my lovelie lord would once vouchsafe

PAGE. Here, noble lord; What is thy will with her?

SLY. Are you my wife, and will not call me— husband?

My men should call me—lord; I am your good- man.

PAGE. My husband and my lord, my lord and husband;

I am your wife in all obedience.

SLY. I know it well:—What must I call her?

LORD. Madam.

SLY. Al'ce madam, or Joan madam?

LORD. Madam, and nothing else; so lords call ladies.

" To looke on me, and leave these frantike fits!
" Or were I now but halfe so eloquent
" To paint in words what Ile performe in deedes,
" I know your honour then would pittie me.
" *Slie.* Harke you, mistresse; will you eat a peece of bread?
" Come, sit downe on my knee: *Sim,* drinke to her, *Sim*;
" For she and I will go to bed anon.
" *Lord.* May it please you, your honour's plaiers be come
" To offer your honour a plaie.
" *Slie.* A plaie, *Sim,* O brave! be they my plaiers?
" *Lord.* I my lord.
" *Slie.* Is there not a foole in the plaie?
" *Lord.* Yes, my lord.
" *Slie.* When will they plaie, *Sim?*
" *Lord.* Even when it please your honour; they be readie.
" *Boy.* My lord, Ile go bid them begin their plaie.
" *Slie.* Doo, but looke that you come againe.
" *Boy.* I warrant you, my lord; I will not leave you thus.
　　　　　　　　　　　　　　　　[*Exit Boy.*
" *Slie.* Come, *Sim,* where be the plaiers? *Sim,* stand by me,
" And we'll flowt the plaiers out of their coates.
" *Lord.* Ile cal them my lord. Ho, where are you there?
" *Sound trumpets.*
" *Enter two young gentlemen, and a man, and a boy.*" STEEVENS.

Sly. Madam wife,[1] they fay, that I have dream'd,
and flept
Above fome fifteen year and more.

Page. Ay, and the time feems thirty unto me;
Being all this time abandon'd from your bed.

Sly. 'Tis much;——Servants, leave me and her
alone.——
Madam, undrefs you, and come now to bed.[8]

Page. Thrice noble lord, let me entreat of you,
To pardon me yet for a night or two;
Or, if not fo, until the fun be fet:
For your phyficians have exprefsly charg'd,
In peril to incur your former malady,
That I fhould yet abfent me from your bed:
I hope, this reafon ftands for my excufe.

Sly. Ay, it ftands fo, that I may hardly tarry fo
long. But I would be loth to fall into my dreams
again; I will therefore tarry, in defpite of the flefh
and the blood.

Enter a Servant.

Serv. Your honour's players, hearing your
amendment,
Are come to play a pleafant comedy,
For fo your doctors hold it very meet;
Seeing too much fadnefs hath congeal'd your blood,
And melancholy is the nurfe of frenzy,

---

[1] *Madam wife,*] Mr. Pope gives likewife the following prefix
to this fpeech from the elder play:
" *Sly.* Come, fit down on my knee. *Sim,* drink to her." Madam, &c. STEEVENS.

[8] —— *come now to bed.*] Here Mr. Pope adds again,—*Sim, drink
to her.* STEEVENS.

Therefore, they thought it good you hear a play,
And frame your mind to mirth and merriment,
Which bars a thoufand harms, and lengthens life.

Sly. Marry, I will; let them play it: Is not a commonty a Chriftmas gambol, or a tumbling trick? [9]

Page. No, my good lord; it is more pleafing ftuff.

Sly. What, houfhold ftuff?

Page. It is a kind of hiftory.

Sly. Well, we'll fee't: Come, madam wife, fit by my fide, and let the world flip; we fhall ne'er be younger. *[They fit down.*

---

[9] *Is not a* commonty *a Chriftmas gambol, or a tumbling trick* ?] Thus the old copies; the modern ones read—*It* is not a *commodity,* &c. *Commonty* for comedy, &c. STEEVENS.

In the old play the players themfelves ufe the word *commodity* corruptly for a *comedy.* BLACKSTONE.

ACT I. SCENE I.

Padua. *A public Place.*

Enter LUCENTIO *and* TRANIO.

Luc. Tranio, fince—for the great defire I had
To fee fair Padua, nurfery of arts,—
I am arriv'd for fruitful Lombardy,[1]
The pleafant garden of great Italy;
And, by my father's love and leave, am arm'd
With his good will, and thy good company,
Moft trufty fervant, well approv'd in all;
Here let'us breathe, and happily inftitute
A courfe of learning, and ingenious [3] ftudies.
Pifa, renowned for grave citizens,
Gave me my being, and my father firft,
A merchant of great traffick through the world,
Vincentio, come of the Bentivolii.[4]

---

[1] —— for *fruitful Lombardy,*] Mr. Theobald reads *from.* The former editions, inftead of *from* had *for.* JOHNSON.

Padua is a city of Lombardy, therefore Mr. Theobald's emendation is unneceffary. STEEVENS.

[3] —— *ingenious*—] I rather think it was written—*ingenuous* ftudies, but of this and a thoufand fuch obfervations there is little certainty. JOHNSON.

In Cole's Dictionary, 1677, it is remarked——"*ingenuous* and *ingenious* are too often confounded."

Thus, in *The Match at Midnight*, by Rowley, 1633:—"Me-thinks he dwells in my opinion: a right *ingenious* fpirit, veil'd merely with the variety of youth, and wildnefs."

Again, in *The Bird in a Cage*, 1633:

" —— deal *ingenioufly*, fweet lady." REED.

[4] *Pifa, renowned for grave citizens,* &c.] This paffage, I think, fhould be read and pointed thus:

I

Vincentio his fon,' brought up in Florence,
It fhall become, to ferve all hopes conceiv'd,⁶
To deck his fortune with his virtuous deeds:
And therefore, Tranio, for the time I ftudy,
Virtue, and that part of philofophy⁷

> *Pifa, renowned for grave citizens,*
> *Gave me my being, and my father firft,*
> *A merchant of great traffick through the world,*
> *Vincentio, come of the Bentivolii.*

In the next line, which fhould begin a new fentence, *Vincentio his fon,* is the fame as *Vincentio's fon,* which Mr. Heath not apprehending, has propofed to alter Vincentio into Lucentio. It may be added, that Shakfpeare in other places expreffes the genitive cafe in the fame improper manner. See *Troilus and Creffida,* Act II. fc. i: " *Mars his idiot.*" And *Twelfth Night,* Act III. fc. iii: " *The Count his gallies.*" TYRWHITT.

Vincentio, *come of the Bentivolii.*] The old copy reads—*Vincentio's.* The emendation was made by Sir T. Hanmer. I am not fure that it is right. Our author might have written:
Vincentio's fon, come of the Bentivolii.
If that be the true reading, this line fhould be connected with the following, and a colon placed after *world* in the preceding line; as is the cafe in the original copy, which adds fome fupport to the emendation now propofed:
Vincentio's fon, come of the Bentivolii,
Vincentio's fon brought up in Florence,
It fhall become, &c. MALONE.

⁵ *Vincentio his fon,*] The old copy reads—*Vincentio's.* STEEVENS.
Vincentio's is here ufed as a quadrifyllable. Mr. Pope, I fuppofe, not perceiving this, unneceffarily reads—Vincentio his fon, which has been too haftily adopted by the fubfequent editors. MALONE.

Could I have read the line, as a verfe, without Mr. Pope's emendation, I would not have admitted it. STEEVENS.

⁶ —— *to ferve all hopes conceiv'd,*] To fulfil the expectations of his friends. MALONE.

⁷ *Virtue, and that part of philofophy*—] Sir Thomas Hanmer, and after him Dr. Warburton, read—*to virtue;* but formerly *ply* and *apply* were indifferently ufed, as to *ply* or *apply* his ftudies.
JOHNSON.

The word *ply* is afterwards ufed in this fcene, and in the fame manner, by Tranio:
" For who fhall bear your part, &c.
" Keep houfe and *ply* his book?" M. MASON.

Will I apply, that treats of happinefs
By virtue 'fpecially to be achiev'd.
Tell me thy mind: for I have Pifa left,
And am to Padua come; as he that leaves
A fhallow plafh, to plunge him in the deep,
And with fatiety feeks to quench his thirft.

 TRA. *Mi perdonate*,[8] gentle mafter mine,
I am in all affected as yourfelf;
Glad that you thus continue your refolve,
To fuck the fweets of fweet philofophy.
Only, good mafter, while we do admire
This virtue, and this moral difcipline,
Let's be no ftoicks, nor no ftocks, I pray; .
Or fo devote to Ariftotle's checks,[9]
As Ovid be an outcaft quite abjur'd:.
Talk logick[2] with acquaintance that you have,
And practice rhetorick in your common talk;
Mufick and poefy ufe, to quicken you;[3]
·The mathematicks, and the metaphyficks,

So, in *The Nice Wanton*, an ancient interlude, 1560:
  " O ye children, let your time be well fpent,
  " *Applye* your learning, and your elders obey."
 Again, in Gafcoigne's *Suppofes*, 1566: " I feare he *applyes* his
ftudy fo, that he will not leave the minute of an houre from his
booke." MALONE.

 [8] *Mi perdonate*,] Old copy—*Me pardonato.* The emendation
was fuggefted by Mr. Steevens. MALONE.

 [9] ——— *Ariftotle's* checks,] are, I fuppofe, the harfh rules of
Ariftotle. STEEVENS.

 Such as tend to *check* and reftrain the indulgence of the paffions.
              MALONE.

 Tranio is here defcanting on academical learning, and mentions
by name fix of the feven liberal fciences. I fufpect this to be a
mif-print, made by fome copyift or compofitor, for *ethicks.* The
fenfe confirms it. BLACKSTONE.

 [2] Talk *logick*—] Old copy—*Balk.* Corrected by Mr. Rowe.
              MALONE.

 [3] ——— *to* quicken *you;*] i. e. *animate.* So, in *All's well that
ends well*:
  " *Quicken* a rock, and make you dance canary." STEEVENS.

Fall to them, as you find your ſtomach ſerves you:
No profit grows, where is no pleaſure ta'en;—
In brief, ſir, ſtudy what you moſt affect.

Luc. Gramercies, Tranio, well doſt thou adviſe.
If, Biondello, thou wert come aſhore,
We could at once put us in readineſs;
And take a lodging, fit to entertain
Such friends as time in Padua ſhall beget.
But ſtay awhile: What company is this?

Tra. Maſter, ſome ſhow, to welcome us to town.

Enter BAPTISTA, KATHARINA, BIANCA, GREMIO, *and*
HORTENSIO. LUCENTIO *and* TRANIO *ſtand aſide.*

Bap. Gentlemen, impórtune me no further,
For how I firmly am reſolv'd you know;
That is,—not to beſtow my youngeſt daughter,
Before I have a huſband for the elder:
If either of you both love Katharina,
Becauſe I know you well, and love you well,
Leave ſhall you have to court her at your pleaſure.

Gre. To cart her rather: She's too rough for me :—
There, there Hortenſio, will you any wife?

Kath. I pray you, ſir, [*To* Bap.] is it your will
To make a ſtale of me amongſt theſe mates?

Hor. Mates, maid! how mean you that? no
  mates for you,
Unleſs you were of gentler, milder mould.

Kath. I'faith, ſir, you ſhall never need to fear;
I wis, it is not half way to her heart:
But, if it were, doubt not, her care ſhould be
To comb your noddle with a three-legg'd ſtool,
And paint your face, and uſe you like a fool.

Hor. From all ſuch devils, good Lord, deliver us!

Gre. And me too, good Lord!

T̄ʀᴀ. Huſh, maſter! here is ſome good paſtime
       toward;
That wench is ſtark mad, or wonderful froward.

Lᴜᴄ. But in the other's ſilence I do ſee
Maids' mild behaviour and ſobriety.
Peace, Tranio.

T̄ʀᴀ. Well ſaid, maſter; mum! and gaze your fill.

Bᴀᴘ. Gentlemen, that I may ſoon make good
What I have ſaid,—Bianca, get you in:
And let it not diſpleaſe thee, good Bianca;
For I will love thee ne'er the leſs, my girl.

Kᴀᴛʜ. A pretty peat![3] 'tis beſt
Put finger in the eye,—an ſhe knew why.

Bɪᴀɴ. Siſter, content you in my diſcontent.—
Sir, to your pleaſure humbly I ſubſcribe:
My books, and inſtruments, ſhall be my company;
On them to look, and practiſe by myſelf.

Lᴜᴄ. Hark, Tranio! thou may'ſt hear Minerva
      ſpeak.   *[Aſide.*

Hᴏʀ. Signior Baptiſta, will you be ſo ſtrange?[4]
Sorry am I, that our good will effects
Bianca's grief.

---

[3] *A pretty* peat!] *Peat* or *pet* is a word of endearment from *petit,
little,* as if it meant pretty little thing. Jᴏʜɴsᴏɴ.

  This word is uſed in the old play of *King Leir* (not Shakſpeare's :)
      " *Gon.* I marvel, Ragan, how you can endure
      " To ſee that proud, pert *peat,* our youngeſt ſiſter," &c.
Again, in *Coridon's Song,* by Tho. Lodge; publiſhed in *England's
Helicon,* 1600:
      " And God ſend every *pretty peate,*
      " Heigh hoe the *pretty peate,*" &c.
and is, I believe, of Scotch extraction. I find it in one of the
proverbs of that country, where it ſignifies *darling.*
  " He has fault of a wife, that marries mam's *pet.*" i. e. He is
in great want of a wife who marries one that is her mother's
darling. Sᴛᴇᴇᴠᴇɴs.

  [4] ——*ſo ſtrange?*] That is, ſo odd, ſo different from others in
your conduct. Jᴏʜɴsᴏɴ.

GRE. Why, will you mew her up,
Signior Baptista, for this fiend of hell,
And make her bear the penance of her tongue?

BAP. Gentlemen, content ye; I am refolv'd:—
Go in, Bianca.   *[Exit* BIANCA.
And for I know, fhe taketh moft delight
In mufick, inftruments, and poetry,
Schoolmafters will I keep within my houfe,
Fit to inftruct her youth.—If you, Hortenfio,
Or fignior Gremio, you,—know any fuch,
Prefer them hither; for to cunning men [5]
I will be very kind, and liberal
To mine own children in good bringing-up;
And fo farewell.   Katharina you may ftay;
For I have more to commune with Bianca. *[Exit.*

KATH. Why, and I truft, I may go too, May I not?
What, fhall I be appointed hours; as though, belike,
I knew not what to take, and what to leave? Ha!
[Exit.

GRE. You may go to the devil's dam; your gifts [6]
are fo good, here is none will hold you.   Their love
is not fo great, Hortenfio, but we may blow our
nails together, and faft it fairly out; [7] our cake's

---

5 ——*cunning men,*] *Cunning* had not yet loft its original fignification of *knowing, learned,* as may be obferved in the tranflation
of the Bible. JOHNSON.

6 ——*your* gifts —] *Gifts* for *endowments.* MALONE.

So, before in this comedy :
  " —— a woman's *gift,*
  " To rain a fhower of commanded tears." STEEVENS.

7 —— Their *love is not fo great, Hortenfio, but we may blow our
nails together, and faft it fairly out ;*] I cannot conceive whofe love
Gremio can mean by the words *their love,* as they had been talking
of no love but that which they themfelves felt for Bianca. We
muft therefore read, *our* love, inftead of *their.* M. MASON.

Perhaps we fhould read—*Your* love. In the old manner of
writing y[e] ftood for either *their* or *your.* The editor of the third

dough on both fides. Farewell:—Yet, for the love I bear my fweet Bianca, if I can by any means light on a fit man, to teach her that wherein fhe delights, I will wifh him to her father.[8]

Hor. So will I, fignior Gremio: But a word, I pray. Though the nature of our quarrel yet never brook'd parle, know now, upon advice,[9] it toucheth us both,—that we may yet again have accefs to our fair miftrefs, and be happy rivals in Bianca's love,— to labour and effect one thing 'fpecially.

Gre. What's that, I pray?

Hor. Marry, fir, to get a hufband for her fifter.

Gre. A hufband! a devil.

Hor. I fay, a hufband.

Gre. I fay, a devil: Think'ft thou, Hortenfio, though her father be very rich, any man is fo very a fool to be married to hell?

Hor. Tufh, Gremio! though it pafs your patience, and mine, to endure her loud alarums, why, man, there be good fellows in the world, an a man could light on them, would take her with all faults, and money enough.

Gre. I cannot tell: but I had as lief take her dowry with this condition,—to be whipp'd at the high-crofs every morning.

---

folio and fome modern editors, with, I think, lefs probability, read *our*. If *their* love be right, it muft mean—the good will of Baptifta and Bianca towards us. MALONE.

[8] —— *I will wifh him to her father.*] i. e. I will *recommend* him. So, in *Much ado about Nothing*:

"To *wifh* him wreftle with affection." REED.

[9] —— *upon advice*,] i. e. on confideration, or reflection. So, in *The Two Gentlemen of Verona*:

"How fhall I dote on her, with more *advice*,
"That thus, without *advice*, begin to love her!" STEEVENS.

Hor. 'Faith, as you say, there's small choice in rotten apples. But, come; since this bar in law makes us friends, it shall be so far forth friendly maintain'd,—till by helping Baptista's eldest daughter to a husband, we set his youngest free for a husband, and then have to't afresh.—Sweet Bianca!— Happy man be his dole! [9] He that runs fastest, gets the ring. [1] How say you, signior Gremio?

Gre. I am agreed: and 'would I had given him the best horse in Padua to begin his wooing, that would thoroughly woo her, wed her, and bed her, and rid the house of her. Come on.

            [*Exeunt* GREMIO *and* HORTENSIO.

Tra. [*Advancing.*] I pray, sir, tell me,—Is it possible
That love should of a sudden take such hold?

Luc. O, Tranio, till I found it to be true,
I never thought it possible, or likely;
But see! while idly I stood looking on,
I found the effect of love in idleness:
And now in plainness do confess to thee,—
That art to me as secret, and as dear,
As Anna to the queen of Carthage was,—
Tranio, I burn, I pine, I perish, Tranio,
If I achieve not this young modest girl:
Counsel me Tranio, for I know thou canst;
Assist me, Tranio, for I know thou wilt.

<hr>

   [9] *Happy man be his* dole!] A proverbial expression. It is used in *Damon and Pithias,* 1571. *Dole* is any thing dealt out or distributed, though its original meaning was the provision given away at the doors of great men's houses. STEEVENS.

   In *Cupid's Revenge,* by Beaumont and Fletcher, we meet with a similar expression, which may serve to explain that before us: " Then *happy man* be his *fortune!*" i. e. May his fortune be that of a happy man! MALONE.

   [1] —— *He that runs fastest, gets the* ring.] An allusion to the sport of running at the ring. DOUCE.

TRA. Mafter, it is no time to chide you now;
Affection is not rated [3] from the heart:
If love have touch'd you, nought remains but fo,[4]—
Redime te captum quam queas minimo.[5]

Luc. Gramercies, lad; go forward: this contents;
The reft will comfort, for thy counfel's found.

TRA. Mafter, you look'd fo longly [6] on the maid,
Perhaps you mark'd not what's the pith of all.

Luc. O yes, I faw fweet beauty in her face,
Such as the daughter of Agenor [7] had,
That made great Jove to humble him to her hand,
When with his knees he kifs'd the Cretan ftrand.

---

[3] —— *is not* rated —] Is not driven out by chiding. MALONE.
So, in *Antony and Cleopatra:*
 " —— 'tis to be chid,
 " As we *rate* boys." STEEVENS.

[4] *If love have* touch'd *you, nought remains but fo,*] The next line
from Terence fhows that we fhould read:
 If Love hath toyl'd *you,* ——
i. e. taken you in his toils, his nets. Alluding to the *captus eft,
habet,* of the fame author. WARBURTON.

It is a common expreffion at this day to fay, when a bailiff has
arrefted a man, that he has *touched* him on the fhoulder. Therefore
touch'd is as good a tranflation of *captus,* as *toyl'd* would be. Thus,
in *As you Like it,* Rofalind fays to Orlando: " Cupid hath *clapt*
him on the fhoulder, but I warrant him heart-whole." M. MASON.

[5] *Redime,* &c.] Our author had this line from *Lilly,* which I
mention, that it may not be brought as an argument for his learning.
 JOHNSON.
Dr. Farmer's pamphlet affords an additional proof that this line
was taken from *Lilly,* and not from *Terence;* becaufe it is quoted,
as it appears in the *grammarian,* and not as it appears in the *poet.*
It is introduced alfo in Decker's *Bellman's Night-Walk,* &c. It
may be added, that *captus eft, habet,* is not in the fame play which
furnifhed the quotation. STEEVENS.

[6] —— *longly* —] i. e. longingly. I have met with no example
of this adverb. STEEVENS.

[7] —— *daughter of Agenor* —] Europa, for whofe fake Jupiter
transformed himfelf into a bull. STEEVENS.

Tra. Saw you no more? mark'd you not, how
   her sister
Began to scold; and raise up such a storm,
That mortal ears might hardly endure the din?

Luc. Tranio, I saw her coral lips to move,
And with her breath she did perfume the air;
Sacred, and sweet, was all I saw in her.

Tra. Nay, then, 'tis time to stir him from his trance.
I pray, awake, sir; If you love the maid,
Bend thoughts and wits to achieve her. Thus it
   stands :—
Her elder sister is so curst and shrewd,
That, till the father rid his hands of her,
Master, your love must live a maid at home;
And therefore has he closely mew'd her up,
Because she shall not be annoy'd [7] with suitors.

Luc. Ah, Tranio, what a cruel father's he!
But art thou not advis'd, he took some care
To get her cunning schoolmasters to instruct her?

Tra. Ay, marry, am I, sir; and now 'tis plotted.

Luc. I have it, Tranio.

Tra.   Master, for my hand,
Both our inventions meet and jump in one.

Luc. Tell me thine first.

Tra.   You will be schoolmaster,
And undertake the teaching of the maid:
That's your device.

Luc.   It is: May it be done?

Tra. Not possible; For who shall bear your part,
And be in Padua here Vincentio's son?
Keep house, and ply his book; welcome his friends;
Visit his countrymen, and banquet them?

---

[7] ——*she* shall *not be annoy'd*—] Old copy—*she will not.*
Corrected by Mr. Rowe. MALONE.

Luc. Baſta;[8] content thee; for I have it full.[9]
We have not yet been ſeen in any houſe;
Nor can we be diſtinguiſh'd by our faces,
.For man, or maſter: then it follows thus;——
Thou ſhalt be maſter, Tranio, in my ſtead,
Keep houſe, and port,[2] and ſervants, as I ſhould:
I will ſome other be; ſome Florentine,
Some Neapolitan, or mean man of Piſa.[3]——
'Tis hatch'd, and ſhall be ſo:——Tranio, at once
Uncaſe thee; take my colour'd hat and cloak:
When Biondello comes, he waits on thee;
But I will charm him firſt to keep his tongue.

Tra. So had you need.   [*They exchange habits.*
In brief, ſir, ſith it your pleaſure is,
And I am tied to be obedient;
(For ſo your father charg'd me at our parting;
Be ſerviceable to my ſon, quoth he,
Although, I think, 'twas in another ſenſe,)
I am content to be Lucentio.
Becauſe ſo well I love Lucentio.

Luc. Tranio, be ſo, becauſe Lucentio loves:
And let me be a ſlave, to achieve that maid
Whoſe ſudden ſight hath thrall'd my wounded eye.

---

[8] *Baſta;*] i. e, *'tis enough*; Italian and Spaniſh. This expreſſion occurs in *The Mad Lover,* and *The Little French Lawyer,* of Beaumont and Fletcher. STEEVENS.

[9] —— *I have it full.*] i. e. conceive our ſtratagem in its full extent, I have already planned the whole of it. So, in *Othello:*
     " I have it, *'tis engender'd*——." STEEVENS.

[2] ——*port,*] Port, is figure, ſhow, appearance. JOHNSON.
So, in *The Merchant of Venice:*
     " 'Tis not unknown to you, Antonio,
     " How much I have diſabled mine eſtate
     " By ſomething ſhowing a more ſwelling *port*
     " Than my faint means would grant continuance." REED.

[3] —— *or mean man of Piſa.*] The old copy, regardleſs of metre, reads—*meaner.* STEEVENS.

Enter BIONDELLO.

Here comes the rogue.—Sirrah, where have you
    been?

BION. Where have I been? Nay, how now, where
    are you?
Mafter, has my fellow Tranio ftol'n your clothes?
Or you ftol'n his? or both? pray, what's the news?

LUC. Sirrah, come hither; 'tis no time to jeft,
And therefore frame your manners to the time.
Your fellow Tranio here, to fave my life,
Puts my apparel and my countenance on,
And I for my efcape have put on his;
For in a quarrel, fince I came afhore,
I kill'd a man, and fear I was defcried: [2]
Wait you on him, I charge you, as becomes,
While I make way from hence to fave my life:
You underftand me?

BION.   I, fir? ne'er a whit.

LUC. And not a jot of Tranio in your mouth;
Tranio is chang'd into Lucentio.

BION. The better for him; 'Would, I were fo
    too!

TRA. So would I,[3] 'faith, boy, to have the next
    wifh after,—
That Lucentio indeed had Baptifta's youngeft
    daughter.

---

[2] —— *and fear I was defcried:*] i. e. I fear I was obferv'd in
the act of killing him. The editor of the third folio reads—*I am
defcried*; which has been adopted by the modern editors.
                       MALONE.

[3] *So* would *I,*] The old copy has—*could.* Corrected by Mr.
Rowe. MALONE.

But, firrah,—not for my fake, but your mafter's,—
 I advife
You ufe your manners difcreetly in all kind of com‑
 panies :
When I am alone, why, then I am Tranio;
But in all places elfe, your mafter [4] Lucentio.

 Luc. Tranio, let's go :—
One thing more refts, that thyfelf execute;—
To make one among thefe wooers : If thou afk me
 why,—
Sufficeth, my reafons are both good and weighty.[5]
         [Exeunt.[6]

 I Serv. *My lord, you nod; you do not mind the play.*

 Sly. *Yes, by faint Anne, do I. A good matter, furely; Comes there any more of it ?*

 Page. *My lord, 'tis but begun.*

 Sly. *'Tis a very excellent piece of work, madam lady; 'Would't were done !*

---

 [4] —— your *mafter* —] Old copy—*you* mafter. Corrected by the editor of the fecond folio. Malone.

 [5] —— *good and weighty.*] The divifion for the fecond act of this play is neither marked in the folio nor quarto editions. Shakfpeare feems to have meant the firft act to conclude here, where the fpeeches of the Tinker are introduced; though they have been hitherto thrown to the end of the firft act, according to a modern and arbitrary regulation. Steevens.

 [6] *Exeunt.*] Here in the old copy we have—" The Prefenters above fpeak."—meaning Sly, &c. who were placed in a balcony raifed at the back of the ftage. After the words—" Would it were done," the marginal direction is—*They fit and mark.*
             Malone.

SCENE II.

The same. Before Hortenfio's *House.*

Enter PETRUCHIO *and* GRUMIO.

PET. Verona, for a while I take my leave,
To fee my friends in Padua; but, of all,
My beſt beloved and approved friend,
Hortenſio; and, I trow, this is his houſe :—
Here, ſirrah Grumio; knock, I ſay.

GRU. Knock, ſir! whom ſhould I knock? is
there any man has rebus'd your worſhip? [6]

PET. Villain, I ſay, knock me here ſoundly.

GRU. Knock you here,[7] ſir? why, ſir, what am I,
ſir, that I ſhould knock you here, ſir?

PET. Villain, I ſay, knock me at this gate,
And rap me well, or I'll knock your knave's pate.

GRU. My maſter is grown quarrelſome: I ſhould
   knock you firſt,
And then I know after who comes by the worſt.

PET. Will it not be?
'Faith, ſirrah, an you'll not knock, I'll wring it;[8]
I'll try how you can *ſol, fa,* and ſing it.
    [*He wrings* GRUMIO *by the ears.*

---

[6] —— *has* rebus'd *your worſhip?*] What is the meaning of *rebus'd?* or is it a falſe print for *abus'd?* TYRWHITT.

[7] *Knock you here,*] Grumio's pretenſions to wit have a ſtrong reſemblance to thoſe of Dromio in *The Comedy of Errors;* and this circumſtance makes it the more probable that theſe two plays were written at no great diſtance of time from each other.
            MALONE.

[8] —— wring *it;*] Here ſeems to be a quibble between *ringing* at a door, and *wringing* a man's ears. STEEVENS.

Gru. Help, mafters,[9] help! my mafter is mad.

Pet. Now knock when I bid you: firrah! villain!

Enter HORTENSIO.

Hor. How now? what's the matter?—My old friend Grumio! and my good friend Petruchio!—How do you all at Verona?

Pet. Signior Hortenfio, come you to part the fray?
Con tutto il core bene trovato, may I fay.

Hor. *Alla noftra cafa bene venuto,*
Molto honorato fignor mio Petruchio.
Rife, Grumio, rife; we will compound this quarrel.

Gru. Nay, 'tis no matter, what he 'leges in Latin.[2]—If this be not a lawful caufe for me to

---

9 *Help,* mafters,] The old copy reads—*here*; and in feveral other places in this play *miftrefs*, inftead of *mafters.* Corrected by Mr. Theobald. In the Mfs. of our author's age *M* was the common abbreviation of *Mafter* and *Miftrefs.* Hence the miftake. See *The Merchant of Venice,* Act V. 1600, and 1623:

" What ho, M. [Mafter] Lorenzo, and M. [Miftrefs] Lorenzo."
MALONE.

2 —— *what he 'leges in Latin.*] i. e. I fuppofe, what he *alleges* in Latin. Petruchio has been juft fpeaking Italian to Hortenfio, which Grumio miftakes for the other language. STEEVENS.

I cannot help fufpecting that we fhould read—*Nay, 'tis no matter what he leges in Latin, if this be not a lawful caufe for me to leave his fervice. Look you, fir.*—That is, " 'Tis no matter what is *law,* if this be not a lawful caufe," &c. TYRWHITT.

Tyrwhitt's amendment and explanation of this paffage is evidently right. Mr. Steevens appears to have been a little abfent when he wrote his note on it. He forgot that Italian was Grumio's native language, and that therefore he could not poffibly miftake it for Latin. M. MASON.

I am grateful to Mr. M. Mafon for his hint, which may prove beneficial to me on fome future occafion, though at the prefent

leave his service,—Look you, sir,—he bid me knock
him, and rap him soundly, sir: Well, was it fit for
a servant to use his master so; being, perhaps, (for
aught I see,) two and thirty,—a pip out?[1]
Whom, 'would to God, I had well knock'd at first,
Then had not Grumio come by the worst.

Pet. A senseless villain!—Good Hortensio,
I bade the rascal knock upon your gate,
And could not get him for my heart to do it.

Gru. Knock at the gate?—O heavens!—
Spake you not these words plain,—*Sirrah, knock me
    here,*
Rap me here, knock me well, and knock me soundly?[4]
And come you now with—knocking at the gate?

Pet. Sirrah, be gone, or talk not, I advise you.

Hor. Petruchio, patience; I am Grumio's pledge:
Why, this a heavy chance 'twixt him and you;
Your ancient, trusty, pleasant servant Grumio.

---

moment it will not operate so forcibly as to change my opinion.
I was well aware that Italian was Grumio's native language, but
was not, nor am now, certain of our author's attention to
this circumstance, because his Italians necessarily speak English
throughout the play, with the exception of a few colloquial sentences. So little regard does our author pay to petty proprieties,
that as often as *Signior*, the Italian appellation, does not occur to
him, or suit the measure of his verse, he gives us in its room,
" *Sir* Vincentio," and " *Sir* Lucentio." Steevens.

[1] ——*a pip out?*] The old copy has—*peepe.* Corrected by
Mr. Pope, Malone.

[4] —— knock me *soundly?*] Shakspeare seems to design a ridicule on this clipped and ungrammatical phraseology; which yet he
has introduced in *Othello:*
    " I pray *talk me* of Cassio."
It occurs again, and more improperly, in heroic translation:
    " —— upon advantage *spide,*
    " Did wound *me* Molphey on the leg," &c.
                    Arthur Golding's *Ovid,* B. V. p. 66. b.
                            Steevens.

And tell me now, fweet friend,—what happy gale
Blows you to Padua here, from old Verona?

Pet. Such wind as fcatters young men through
the world,
To feek their fortunes further than at home,
Where fmall experience grows. But, in a few,[5]
Signior Hortenfio, thus it ftands with me:—
Antonio, my father, is deceas'd;
And I have thruft myfelf into this maze,
Haply to wive, and thrive, as beft I may:
Crowns in my purfe I have, and goods at home,
And fo am come abroad to fee the world.

Hor. Petruchio, fhall I then come roundly to
thee,
And wifh thee to a fhrewd ill-favour'd wife?
Thou'dft thank me but a little for my counfel:
And yet I'll promife thee fhe fhall be rich,
And very rich:—but thou'rt too much my friend,
And I'll not wifh thee to her.

Pet. Signior Hortenfio, 'twixt fuch friends as
we,
Few words fuffice: and, therefore, if thou know
One rich enough to be Petruchio's wife,
(As wealth is burthen of my wooing dance,[6])
Be fhe as foul as was Florentius' love,[7]

---

[5] *Where fmall experience grows. But, in a few,*] *In a few,*
means the fame as *in fhort, in few* words. JOHNSON.

So, in *K. Henry IV.* Part II:
"In *few*;—his death, whofe fpirit lent a fire," &c.
STEEVENS.

[6] (*As wealth is* burthen *of my wooing* dance,)] The *burthen* of a
dance is an expreffion which I have never heard; the *burthen of
his wooing fong* had been more proper. JOHNSON.

[7] *Be fhe as foul as was Florentius' love,*] I fuppofe this alludes
to the ftory of a Florentine, which is met with in the eleventh Book
of Thomas Lupton's *Thoufand Notable Things,* and perhaps in other
Collections.

As old as Sibyl, and as curſt and ſhrewd
As Socrates' Xantippe, or a worſe,
She moves me not, or not removes, at leaſt,

" 39. A *Florentine* young gentleman was ſo deceived by the luſtre and orientneſs of her jewels, pearls, rings, lawns, ſcarfes, laces, gold ſpangles, and other gaudy devices, that he was raviſhed overnight, and was mad till the marriage was ſolemnized. But next morning by light viewing of her before ſhe was ſo gorgeouſly trim'd up, ſhe was ſuch a leane, yellow, riveled, deformed creature, that he never lay with her, nor lived with her afterwards; and would ſay that he had married himſelf to a ſtinking houſe of office, painted over, and ſet out with fine garments: and ſo for grief conſumed away in melancholy, and at laſt poyſoned himſelf. *Gomeſius, lib. 3. de Sal. Gen. cap. 22.*" FARMER.

The alluſion is to a ſtory told by Gower in the firſt book *De Confeſſione Amantis.* *Florent* is the name of a knight who had bound himſelf to marry a deformed hag, provided ſhe taught him the ſolution of a riddle on which his life depended. The following is the deſcription of her:

" *Florent* his wofull heed up lifte,
" And ſaw this vecke, where that ſhe fit,
" Which was the lotheſt wighte
" That ever man caſte on his eye:
" Hir noſe baas, hir browes hie,
" Hir eyes ſmall, and depe ſette,
" Hir chekes ben with teres wette,
" And rivelyn as an empty ſkyn,
" Hangyng downe unto the chyn;
" Hir lippes ſhronken ben for age,
" There was no grace in hir viſage.
" Hir front was narowe, hir lockes hore,
" She loketh foorth as doth a more:
" Hir necke is ſhorte, hir ſhulders courbe,
" That might a mans luſte diſtourbe:
" Hir bodie great, and no thyng ſmall,
" And ſhortly to deſcrive hir all,
" She hath no lith without a lacke,
" But like unto the woll ſacke:" &c.——
" Though ſhe be the *fouleſte* of all," &c.

This ſtory might have been borrowed by Gower from an older narrative in the *Geſta Romanorum.* See the Introductory Diſcourſe to *The Canterbury Tales of Chaucer,* Mr. Tyrwhitt's edition, Vol. IV. p. 153. STEEVENS.

Affection's edge in me; were she as rough [8]
As are the swelling Adriatick seas:
I come to wive it wealthily in Padua;
If wealthily, then happily in Padua.

GRU. Nay, look you, sir, he tells you flatly what
his mind is: Why, give him gold enough, and marry
him to a puppet, or an aglet-baby; [9] or an old trot
with ne'er a tooth in her head, though she have as
many diseases as two and fifty horses: [2] why, nothing
comes amiss, so money comes withal.

HOR. Petruchio, since we have stepp'd thus far in,
I will continue that I broach'd in jest.
I can, Petruchio, help thee to a wife
With wealth enough, and young, and beauteous;
Brought up, as best becomes a gentlewoman:
Her only fault (and that is faults enough,) [3]

---

[8] —— *were she as rough*—] The old copy reads—*were she is
as rough.* Corrected by the editor of the second folio.
MALONE.

[9] —— *aglet-baby*;] i. e. a diminutive being, not exceeding in
size the tag of a point.
So, in *Jeronimo*, 1605:
"And all those stars that gaze upon her face,
"Are *aglets* on her sleeve-pins and her train."
STEEVENS.

An *aglet-baby* was a small image or head cut on the tag of a
point, or lace. That such figures were sometimes appended to
them, Dr. Warburton has proved, by a passage in Mezeray, the
French historian:—" portant meme sur les *aiguillettes* [points] des
petites *tetes* de mort." MALONE.

[2] —— *as many diseases as two and fifty horses :*] I suspect this
passage to be corrupt, though I know not how to rectify it.—*The
fifty diseases of a horse* seem to have been proverbial. So, in *The
Yorkshire Tragedy,* 1608: "O stumbling jade! the spavin o'ertake
thee! the *fifty diseases* stop thee!" MALONE.

[3] —— *(and that is* faults *enough,)*] And that one is itself a host
of faults. The editor of the second folio, who has been copied by
all the subsequent editors, unnecessarily reads—*and that is* fault.
enough. MALONE.

Is,—that she is intolerably curst,
And shrewd,[4] and froward; so beyond all measure,
That, were my state far worser than it is,
I would not wed her for a mine of gold.

Pet. Hortensio, peace; thou know'st not gold's
   effect:—
Tell me her father's name, and 'tis enough;
For I will board her, though she chide as loud
As thunder, when the clouds in autumn crack.

Hor. Her father is Baptista Minola,
An affable and courteous gentleman:
Her name is, Katharina Minola,
Renown'd in Padua for her scolding tongue.

Pet. I know her father, though I know not her;
And he knew my deceased father well:—
I will not sleep, Hortensio, till I see her;
And therefore let me be thus bold with you,
To give you over at this first encounter,
Unless you will accompany me thither.

Gru. I pray you, sir, let him go while the humour
lasts. O' my word, an she knew him as well as I
do, she would think scolding would do little good
upon him: She may, perhaps, call him half a score
knaves, or so: why, that's nothing; an he begin
once, he'll rail in his rope-tricks.[5] I'll tell you

---

4 ——*shrewd,*] here means, having the qualities of a *shrew.*
The adjective is now used only in the sense of *acute, intelligent.*
           M<small>ALONE</small>.

 I believe *shrewd* only signifies *bitter, severe.* So, in *As you Like it,*
sc. ult:
  " That have endur'd *shrewd* days and nights with us."
           S<small>TEEVENS</small>.

 5 ——*an he begin once, he'll rail in his* rope-tricks.] This is obscure. Sir Thomas Hanmer reads—*he'll rail in his* rhetorick; *I'll
tell you,* &c. Rhetorick agrees very well with *figure* in the suc-
ceeding part of the speech, yet I am inclined to believe that *rope-
tricks* is the true word. J<small>OHNSON</small>.

I

what, fir,—an fhe ftand him [6] but a little, he will throw a figure in her face, and fo disfigure her with it, that fhe fhall have no more eyes to fee withal than a cat: [7] You know him not, fir.

In *Romeo and Juliet*, Shakfpeare ufes *ropery* for *roguery*, and therefore certainly wrote *rope-tricks*.

Rope-tricks we may fuppofe to mean tricks of which the contriver would deferve the *rope*.   STEEVENS.

Rope-tricks is certainly right.—*Ropery* or *rope-tricks* originally fignified abufive language, without any determinate idea; fuch language as parrots are taught to fpeak.   So, in *Hudibras:*

" Could tell what fubt'left parrots mean,
" That fpeak, and think contrary clean;
" What member 'tis of whom they talk,
" When they cry *rope*, and walk, knave, walk."

The following paffage in Wilfon's *Arte of Rhetorique*, 1553, fhews that this was the meaning of the term: " Another good fellow in the countrey, being an officer and maiour of a toune, and defirous to fpeak like a fine learned man, having juft occafion to rebuke a runnegate fellow, faid after this wife in great heate: Thou yngram and vacation knave, if I take thee any more within the circumcifion of my damnacion, I will fo corrupte thee that all vacation knaves fhall take ill fample by thee." This the author in the margin calls " *rope-ripe* chiding." So, in *May-day*, a comedy by Chapman, 1611: " Lord! how you roll in your *rope-ripe* terms."   MALONE.

[6] ——ftand *him*—] i. e. withftand, refift him.

STEEVENS.

[7] ——*that fhe fhall have no more eyes to fee withal than a cat:*] The humour of this paffage I do not underftand. This animal is remarkable for the keennefs of its fight.   In the *Caftell of Laboure*, however, printed by Wynkyn de Worde, 1506, is the following line: " That was as *blereyed* as a cat."

There are two proverbs which any reader who can, may apply to this allufion of Grumio:

" Well might the *cat* wink when both her eyes were out."
" A *muffled* cat was never a good hunter."

The firft is in *Ray's Collection*, the fecond in *Kelly's*.

STEEVENS.

It may mean, that he fhall fwell up her eyes with blows, till fhe fhall feem to peep with a contracted pupil, like a cat in the light.   JOHNSON.

Hor. Tarry, Petruchio, I muſt go with thee;
For in Baptiſta's keep[6] my treaſure is:
He hath the jewel of my life in hold,
His youngeſt daughter, beautiful Bianca;
And her withholds from me, and other more
Suitors to her, and rivals in my love:[7]
Suppoſing it a thing impoſſible,
(For thoſe defects I have before rehears'd,)
That ever Katharina will be woo'd,
Therefore this order hath Baptiſta ta'en;[8]——
That none ſhall have acceſs unto Bianca,
Till Katharine the curſt have got a huſband

Gru. Katharine the curſt!
A title for a maid, of all titles the worſt.

Hor. Now ſhall my friend Petruchio do me grace;
And offer me, diſguis'd in ſober robes,
To old Baptiſta as a ſchool-maſter
Well ſeen in muſick,[9] to inſtruct Bianca:
That ſo I may by this device, at leaſt,

---

[7] ——*in Baptiſta's* keep——] *Keep* is cuſtody. The ſtrongeſt part of an ancient caſtle was called the *keep*. STEEVENS.

[8] *And her withholds,* &c.] It ſtood thus:
    And her withholds from me.
    Other more ſuitors to her, and rivals in my love, &c.
The regulation which I have given to the text, was dictated to me by the ingenious Dr. Thirlby. THEOBALD.

[9] *Therefore this* order *hath Baptiſta* ta'en;] To *take order* is, to take *meaſures.* So, in *Othello:*
    " Honeſt Iago hath *ta'en order* for it." STEEVENS.

[9] *Well* ſeen *in muſick,*] *Seen* is verſed, practiſed. So, in a very ancient comedy called *The longer thou Liveſt the more Fool thou art:*
    " Sum would have you ſeen in ſtories,
    " Sum to feates of arms will you allure, &c.
    " Sum will move you to reade Scripture.
    " Marry, I would have you ſeene in cardes and diſe."
Again, in Spenſer's *Faery Queen,* B. IV. c. ii:
    " Well ſeene in every ſcience that mote bee."
                   · STEEVENS.

Have leave and leifure to make love to her,
And, unfufpected, court her by herfelf.

Enter GREMIO; *with him* LUCENTIO *difguifed, with*
books under his arm.

GRU. Here's no knavery! See; to beguile the
old folks, how the young folks lay their heads to_
gether! Mafter, mafter, look about you: Who goes
there? ha!

HOR. Peace, Grumio; 'tis the rival of my love:—
Petruchio, ftand by a while.

GRU. A proper ftripling, and an amorous!

[*They retire.*

GRE. O, very well; I have perus'd the note.
Hark you, fir; I'll have them very fairly bound:
All books of love, fee that at any hand;[2]
And fee you read no other lectures to her:
You underftand me:—Over and befide
Signior Baptifta's liberality,
I'll mend it with a largefs:—Take your papers too,
And let me have them very well perfum'd;
For fhe is fweeter than perfume itfelf,
To whom they go.[3] What will you read to her?

LUC. Whate'er I read to her, I'll plead for you,
As for my patron, (ftand you fo affur'd,)
As firmly as yourfelf were ftill in place:
Yea, and (perhaps) with more fuccefsful words
Than you, unlefs you were a fcholar, fir.

GRE. O this learning! what a thing it is!

---

[2] ——*at any hand*;] i. e. at all events. So, in *All's well that*
ends well:
   " ——let him fetch off his drum, *in any hand.*"
                                        STEEVENS.
[3] *To whom they go.*] The old copy reads—*To whom they go to.*
                                        STEEVENS.

Gru. O this woodcock! what an afs it is!

Pet. Peace, firrah.

Hor. Grumio, mum!—God fave you, fignior
    Gremio!

Gre. And you're well met, fignior Hortenfio.
    Trow you,
Whither I am going?—To Baptifta Minola.
I promis'd to enquire carefully
About a fchoolmafter for fair Bianca: [2]
And, by good fortune, I have lighted well
On this young man; for learning, and behaviour,
Fit for her turn; well read in poetry,
And other books,—good ones, I warrant you.

Hor. 'Tis well: and I have met a gentleman,
Hath promis'd me to help me [3] to another,
A fine mufician to inftruct our miftrefs;
So fhall I no whit be behind in duty
To fair Bianca, fo belov'd of me.

Gre. Belov'd of me,—and that my deeds fhall
    prove.

Gru. And that his bags fhall prove.   [*Afide.*

Hor. Gremio, 'tis now no time to vent our love:
Liften to me, and if you fpeak me fair,
I'll tell you news indifferent good for either.
Here is a gentleman, whom by chance I met,
Upon agreement from us to his liking,
Will undertake to woo curft Katharine;
Yea, and to marry her, if her dowry pleafe.

Gre. So faid, fo done, is well:—
Hortenfio, have you told him all her faults?

***

[2] *—for fair Bianca :*] The old copy redundantly reads—
" for *the* fair Bianca." STEEVENS.

[3] *—help me—*] The old copy reads—help *me.* STEEVENS.
Corrected by Mr. Rowe. MALONE.

Pet. I know, she is an irkſome brawling ſcold;
If that be all, maſters, I hear no harm.

Gre. No, ſay'ſt me ſo, friend? What countryman?

Pet. Born in Verona, old Antonio's ſon: [4]
My father dead, my fortune lives for me;
And I do hope good days, and long, to ſee.

Gre. O, ſir, ſuch a life, with ſuch a wife, were
ſtrange:
But, if you have a ſtomach, to't o'God's name;
You ſhall have me aſſiſting you in all.
But will you woo this wild cat?

Pet. Will I live?

Gru. Will he woo her? ay, or I'll hang her.
[Aſide.

Pet. Why came I hither, but to that intent?
Think you, a little din can daunt mine ears?
Have I not in my time heard lions roar?
Have I not heard the ſea, puff'd up with winds,
Rage like an angry boar, chafed with ſweat?
Have I not heard great ordnance in the field,
And heaven's artillery thunder in the ſkies?
Have I not in a pitched battle heard
Loud 'larums, neighing ſteeds, and trumpets'
clang? [5]

[4] —— *old* Antonio's *ſon:*] The old copy reads——*Batonio's* ſon.
STEEVENS.
Corrected by Mr. Rowe. MALONE.

[5] —— *and trumpets'* clang?] Probably the word *clang* is here
uſed adjectively, as in the *Paradiſe Loſt,* B. XI. v. 834, and not
as a verb:
" —— an iſland ſalt and bare,
" The haunt of ſeals, and orcs, and ſea-mews *clang.*"
T. WARTON.

I believe Mr. Warton is miſtaken. *Clang,* as a ſubſtantive, is
uſed in *The Noble Gentleman* of Beaumont and Fletcher:
" I hear the *clang* of trumpets in this houſe."[6]

And do you tell me of a woman's tongue;
That gives not half fo great a blow to the ear,[6]
As will a chefnut in a farmer's fire?
Tufh! tufh! fear boys with bugs.[7]

GRU.   For he fears none.
                                        [*Afide.*

GRE. Hortenfio, hark!
This gentleman is happily arriv'd,
My mind prefumes, for. his own good, and yours.

HOR. I promis'd, we would be contributors,
And bear his charge of wooing, whatfoe'er.

GRE. And fo we will; provided, that he win her.

GRU. I would, I were as fure of a good dinner.
                                        [*Afide.*

Again, in *Tamburlaine*, &c. 1590:
  " —— hear you the *clang*
  " Of Scythian trumpets?" ——
Again, in *The Cobler's Prophecy*, 1594:
  " The trumpets *clang*, and roaring noife of drums."
Again, in *Claudius Tiberius Nero*, 1607:
  " Hath not the *clang* of harfh Armenian troops," &c.
Again, in Drant's tranflation of Horace's *Art of Poetry*, 1567:
  " Fit for a chorus, and as yet the boyftus founde and fhryll
  " Of trumpetes *clang* the ftalles was not accuftomed to fill."
The Trumpet's clang is certainly the *clang of trumpets*, and not an
epithet beftowed on thofe inftruments. STEEVENS.

  [6] —— *fo great a blow to* the ear,] The old copy reads—to
bear. STEEVENS.

  This aukward phrafe could never come from Shakfpeare. He
wrote, without queftion,
          —— *fo great a blow to* th' ear. WARBURTON.

  The emendation is Sir T. Hanmer's. MALONE.

  So, in *K. John:*
  " Our *ears* are *cudgell'd*; not a word of his
  " But *buffets* better than a fift of France." STEEVENS.

  [7] —— *with* bugs.] i. e. with *bug-bears.*
So, in *Cymbeline:*
  " —— are become
  " The mortal *bugs* o' the field." STEEVENS.

Enter TRANIO, *bravely apparell'd; and* BIONDELLO.

TRA. Gentlemen, God fave you! If I may be
    bold,
Tell me, I befeech you, which is the readieft way
To the houfe of fignior Baptifta Minola?

GRE. He that has the two fair daughters :—is't
[*Afide to* TRANIO.] he you mean? [8]

TRA. Even he. Biondello!

GRE. Hark you, fir; You mean not her to——

TRA. Perhaps, him and her, fir; What have
    you to do?

PET. Not her that chides, fir, at any hand, I
    pray.

TRA. I love no chiders, fir:—Biondello, let's away.

LUC. Well begun, Tranio.   [*Afide.*

---

[8] *He that has the two fair daughters : &c.*] In the old copy, this
fpeech is given to *Biondello.* STEEVENS.

It fhould rather be given to Gremio; to whom, with the others,
Tranio has addreffed himfelf. The following paffages might be
written thus:
    Tra. *Even he, Biondello!*
    Gre. *Hark you, fir; you mean not her* too. TYRWHITT,
I think the old copy, both here and in the preceding fpeech is
right. Biondello adds to what his mafter had faid, the words—
" He that has the two fair daughters," to afcertain more precifely
the perfon for whom he had enquired; and then addreffes Tranio;
" is't he you mean?"

——*You mean not her to* —] I believe, an abrupt fentence was
intended; or perhaps Shakfpeare might have written—*her to woo.*
Tranio in his anfwer might mean, that he would *woo* the father,
to obtain his confent, and the daughter for herfelf. This, however, will not complete the metre. I incline therefore to my firft
fuppofition. MALONE.

I have followed Mr. Tyrwhitt's regulation. STEEVENS,

Hor. Sir, a word ere you go;—
Are you a fuitor to the maid you talk of, yea, or no?

Tra. An if I be, fir, is it any offence?

Gre. No; if, without more words, you will get
        you hence.

Tra. Why, fir, I pray, are not the ftreets as free
For me, as for you?

Gre.   But fo is not fhe.

Tra. For what reafon, I befeech you?

Gre. For this reafon, if you'll know,——
That fhe's the choice love of fignior Gremio.

Hor. That fhe's the chofen of fignior **Hor-**
        tenfio.

Tra. Softly, my mafters! if you be gentlemen,
Do me this right,—hear me with patience.
Baptifta is a noble gentleman,
To whom my father is not all unknown;
And, were his daughter fairer than fhe is,
She may more fuitors have, and me for one.
Fair Leda's daughter had a thoufand wooers;
Then well one more may fair Bianca have:
And fo fhe fhall; Lucentio fhall make one,
Though Paris came, in hope to fpeed alone.

Gre. What! this gentleman will out-talk us all.

Luc. Sir, give him head; I know, he'll prove
        a jade.

Pet. Hortenfio, to what end are all thefe words?

Hor. Sir, let me be fo bold as to afk you,
Did you yet ever fee Baptifta's daughter?

Tra. No, fir; but hear I do, that he hath two;
The one as famous for a fcolding tongue,
As is the other for beauteous modefty.

Pet. Sir, fir, the firft's for me; let her go by.

Gre. Yea, leave that labour to great Hercules;
And let it be more than Alcides' twelve.

Pet. Sir, underſtand you this of me, infooth;—
The youngeſt daughter, whom you hearken for,
Her father keeps from all acceſs of ſuitors;
And will not promiſe her to any man,
Until the elder ſiſter firſt be wed:
The younger then is free, and not before.

Tra. If it be ſo, ſir, that you are the man
Muſt ſtead us all, and me among the reſt;
An if you break the ice, and do this feat,[9]—
Achieve the elder, ſet the younger free
For our acceſs,—whoſe hap ſhall be to have her,
Will not ſo graceleſs be, to be ingrate.

Hor. Sir, you ſay well, and well you do conceive;
And ſince you do profeſs to be a ſuitor,
You muſt, as we do, gratify this gentleman,
To whom we all reſt generally beholden.

Tra. Sir, I ſhall not be ſlack: in ſign whereof,
Pleaſe ye we may contrive this afternoon,[2]

---

[9] ——*this* feat,] The old copy reads—this *ſeek.* The emendation was made by Mr. Rowe.

[2] *Pleaſe ye we may* contrive *this afternoon,*] Mr. Theobald aſks *what they were to contrive?* and then ſays, *a fooliſh corruption poſſeſſes the place,* and ſo alters it to *convive;* in which he is followed as he pretty conſtantly is, when wrong, by the Oxford editor. But the common reading is right, and the critic was only ignorant of the meaning of it. *Contrive* does not ſignify here to *project* but to *ſpend,* and *wear out.* As in this paſſage of Spenſer:

" Three ages ſuch as mortal men *contrive.*"

Fairy Queen, B. XI. ch. ix. WARBURTON.

The word is uſed in the ſame ſenſe of *ſpending* or *wearing out,* in Painter's *Palace of Pleaſure.* JOHNSON.

So, in *Damon and Pithias,* 1571:

" In travelling countries, we three have *contrived*
" Full many a year," &c.

F f 4

And quaff carouſes to our miſtreſs' health;
And do as adverſaries do in law,[2]—
Strive mightily, but eat and drink as friends.

GRU. BION. O excellent motion! Fellows, let's
begone.[3]

HOR. The motion's good indeed, and be it
ſo;—
Petruchio, I ſhall be your *ben venuto*.   [*Exeunt.*

Contrive, I ſuppoſe, is from *contero*. So, in the *Hecyra* of Terence.
" Totum hunc *contrivi* diem." STEEVENS.

[2] —— *as* adverſaries *do* in law,] By *adverſaries in law*, I believe,
our author means not ſuitors, but *barriſters*, who,
in their oppoſition to each other in the courts of law, live in greater
harmony and friendſhip in private, than perhaps thoſe of
of the liberal profeſſions. Their *clients* ſeldom " eat
with their adverſaries as friends." MALONE.

[3] —— Fellows, *let's begone.*] *Fellows* means *fellow-ſervants*.
Grumio and Biondello addreſs each other, and alſo the diſguiſed
Lucentio. MALONE.

ACT II.   SCENE I.

The same.   A Room in Baptista's *House.*

Enter KATHARINA *and* BIANCA.

BIAN. Good fifter, wrong me not, nor wrong
    yourfelf,[4]
To make a bondmaid and a flave of me;
That I difdain: but for thefe other gawds,[5]—
Unbind my hands, I'll pull them off myfelf,
Yea, all my raiment, to my petticoat;
Or, what you will command me, will I do,
So well I know my duty to my elders.

KATH. Of all thy fuitors, here I charge thee,[6] tell
Whom thou lov'ft beft: fee thou diffemble not.

BIAN. Believe me, fifter, of all the men alive,
I never yet beheld that fpecial face
Which I could fancy more than any other.

KATH. Minion, thou lieft; Is't not Hortenfio?

BIAN. If you affect him, fifter, here I fwear,
I'll plead for you myfelf, but you fhall have him.

KATH. O then, belike, you fancy riches more;
You will have Gremio to keep you fair.[7]

---

[4] —— *nor* wrong *yourfelf,*] Do not act in a manner unbecoming
a woman and a fifter. So, in *The Merry Wives of Windfor:*
" Mafter Ford, this *wrongs* you." MALONE.

[5] —— *but for thefe other* gawds,] The old copy reads—*thefe
other* goods. STEEVENS.

This is fo trifling and unexpreffive a word, that I am fatisfied
our author wrote *gawds,* (i. e. toys, trifling ornaments;) a term
that he frequently ufes and feems fond of. THEOBALD.

[6] —— *I charge* thee,] *Thee,* which was accidentally omitted in
the old copy, was fupplied by the editor of the fecond folio. MALONE.

[7] —— *to keep you* fair.] I wifh to read—*to keep you* fine. But
either word may ferve. JOHNSON.

Bian. Is it for him you do envy me fo?
Nay, then you jeft; and now I well perceive,
You have but jefted with me all this while:
I pr'ythee, fifter Kate, untie my hands.

Kath. If that be jeft, then all the reft was fo.
[*Strikes her.*

Enter BAPTISTA.

Bap. Why, how now, dame! whence grows this
            infolence?——
Bianca, ftand afide;—poor girl! fhe weeps:—
Go ply thy needle; meddle not with her.——
For fhame, thou hilding[8] of a devilifh fpirit,
Why doft thou wrong her that did ne'er wrong
            thee?
When did fhe crofs thee with a bitter word?

Kath. Her filence flouts me, and I'll be reveng'd.
[*Flies after* BIANCA.

Bap. What, in my fight?—Bianca, get thee in.
[*Exit* BIANCA.

Kath. Will you not fuffer me?[9] Nay, now I fee,
She is your treafure, fhe muft have a hufband;
I muft dance bare-foot on her wedding-day,
And, for your love to her, lead apes in hell.[1]

---

8 ——*hilding*—] The word *hilding* or *hinderling*, is a *low
wretch*; it is applied to Katharine for the coarfenefs of her behaviour. JOHNSON.

9 *Will you not fuffer me?*] The old copy reads—*What*, will, &c.
The compofitor probably caught the former word from the preceding line. Corrected by Mr. Pope. MALONE.

1 *And, for your love to her, lead apes in hell.*] " To lead apes"
was in our author's time, as at prefent, one of the employments of
a bear-herd, who often carries about one of thofe animals along
with his bear: but I know not how this phrafe came to be applied

Talk not to me; I will go fit and weep,
Till I can find occafion of revenge.

                    [*Exit* KATHARINA.

    BAP. Was ever gentleman thus griev'd as I?
But who comes here?

Enter GREMIO, *with* LUCENTIO *in the habit of a
mean man;* PETRUCHIO, *with* HORTENSIO *as a
mufician; and* TRANIO, *with* BIONDELLO *bearing
a lute and books.*

    GRE. Good-morrow, neighbour Baptifta.

    BAP. Good-morrow, neighbour Gremio: God
fave you, gentlemen!

    PET. And you, good fir! Pray, have you not a
            daughter
Call'd Katharina, fair, and virtuous?

    BAP. I have a daughter, fir, call'd Katharina.

    GRE. You are too blunt, go to it orderly.

    PET. You wrong me, fignior Gremio; give me
            leave.—
I am a gentleman of Verona, fir,
That,—hearing of her beauty, and her wit,
Her affability, and bafhful modefty,
Her wondrous qualities, and mild behaviour,—
Am bold to fhow myfelf a forward gueft
Within your houfe, to make mine eye the witnefs
Of that report which I fo oft have heard.
And, for an entrance to my entertainment,

to old maids. We meet with it again in *Much ado about Nothing:*
" Therefore (fays Beatrice,) I will even take fix-pence in earneft of
the *bear-herd,* and lead his *apes* to hell." MALONE.

    That women who refufed to bear children, fhould, after death,
be condemned to the care of apes in leading-ftrings, might have
been confidered as an act of pofthumous retribution. STEEVENS.

I

I do prefent you with a man of mine,
           [*Prefenting* HORTENSIO.
Cunning in mufick, and the mathematicks,
To inftruct her fully in thofe fciences,
Whereof, I know, fhe is not ignorant:
Accept of him, or elfe you do me wrong;
His name is Licio, born in Mantua.

    BAP. You're welcome, fir; and he, for your good
        fake:
But for my daughter Katharine,—this I know,
She is not for your turn, the more my grief.

    PET. I fee, you do not mean to part with her;
Or elfe you like not of my company.

    BAP. Miftake me not, I fpeak but as I find.
Whence are you, fir? what may I call your name?

    PET. Petruchio is my name; Antonio's fon,
A man well known throughout all Italy.

    BAP. I know him well: you are welcome for his
        fake.

    GRE. Saving your tale, Petruchio, I pray,
Let us, that are poor petitioners, fpeak too:
Baccare! you are marvellous forward.[3]

---

  [3] Baccare! *you are marvellous forward.*] We muft read, *Baccalare*; by which the Italians mean, thou arrogant, prefumptuous man! the word is ufed fcornfully upon any one that would affume a port of grandeur. WARBURTON.

  The word is neither wrong nor Italian: it was an old proverbial one, ufed by John Heywood; who hath made, what he pleafes to call, *Epigrams* upon it. Take two of them, fuch as they are:
    " *Backare*, quoth Mortimer to his fow,
    " Went that fow *backe* at that bidding, trow you?"

    " *Backare*, quoth Mortimer to his fow: fe,
    " Mortimer's fow fpeaketh as good Latin as he."
Howel takes this from Heywood, in his *Old Sawes and Adages:*
and Philpot introduces it into the proverbs collected by Camden.
                       FARMER.

Pet. O, pardon me, fignior Gremio; I would fain be doing.

Gre. I doubt it not, fir; but you will curfe your wooing.——

Neighbour,[4] this is a gift[5] very grateful, I am fure of it. To exprefs the like kindnefs myfelf, that have been more kindly beholden to you than any, I freely give unto you this young fcholar,[6] [*Prefenting* Lucentio,] that hath been long ftudying at Rheims; as cunning in Greek, Latin, and other languages, as the other in mufick and mathematicks : his name is Cambio; pray, accept his fervice.

Again, in the ancient Enterlude of *The Repentance of Mary Magdalene*, 1567:

    " Nay, hoa there, *Backare*, you muft ftand apart:
    " You love me beft, I trow, myftreffe Mary."

Again, in John *Lyly's Midas*, 1592: " The mafculine gender is more worthy than the feminine, and therefore, Licio, *Backare*."

Again, in John Grange's *Golden Aphroditis*, 1577: "——yet wrefted he fo his effeminate bande to the fiege of *backwarde* affection, that both trumpe and drumme founded nothing for their larum, but *Baccare, Baccare.*" Steevens.

4 *Neighbour,*] The old copy has—*neighbours.* Corrected by Mr. Theobald. Malone.

5 *I doubt it not, fir; but you will curfe your wooing.——*
    Neighbour, this is a gift—] The old copy gives the paffage as follows :
      I doubt it not, fir. But you will curfe
      Your wooing neighbors : this is a guift—. Steevens.

This nonfenfe may be rectified by only pointing it thus: *I doubt it not, fir, but you will curfe your wooing. Neighbour, this is a gift,* &c. addreffing himfelf to Baptifta. Warburton.

6 *I freely give unto you this young fcholar,*] Our modern editors had been long content with the following fophifticated reading: ——*free leave give to this young fcholar,*——. Steevens.

This is an injudicious correction of the firft folio, which reads— *freely give unto this young fcholar.* We fhould read, I believe—
    I freely give unto you this young fcholar,
    That hath been long ftudying at Rheims ; as cunning
    In Greek, &c. Tyrwhitt.

If this emendation wanted any fupport, it might be had in the

Bap. A thousand thanks, signior Gremio: welcome, good Cambio.—But, gentle sir, [*To* Tranio.] methinks, you walk like a stranger; May I be so bold to know the cause of your coming?

Tra. Pardon me, sir, the boldness is mine own;
That, being a stranger in this city here,
Do make myself a suitor to your daughter,
Unto Bianca, fair, and virtuous.
Nor is your firm resolve unknown to me,
In the preferment of the eldest sister:
This liberty is all that I request,—
That, upon knowledge of my parentage,
I may have welcome 'mongst the rest that woo,
And free access and favour as the rest.
And, toward the education of your daughters,
I here bestow a simple instrument,
And this small packet of Greek and Latin books:
If you accept them, then their worth is great.

Bap. Lucentio is your name?[1] of whence, I pray?

Tra. Of Pisa, sir; son to Vincentio.

preceding part of this scene, where Petruchio, presenting Hortensio to Baptista, uses almost the same form of words:

 " And, for an entrance to my entertainment,
 " *I do present you* with a man of mine,
 " Cunning in musick," &c.

Free leave give, &c. was the absurd correction of the editor of the third folio. Malone.

 [6] —— *this small packet of Greek and Latin books:*] In Queen Elizabeth's time the young ladies of quality were usually instructed in the learned languages, if any pains were bestowed on their minds at all. Lady Jane Grey and her sisters, Queen Elizabeth, &c. are trite instances. Percy.

 [7] *Lucentio is your name?*] How should Baptista know this? Perhaps a line is lost, or perhaps our author was negligent. Mr. Theobald supposes they converse privately, and that thus the name is learned; but then the action must stand still; for there is no speech interposed between that of Tranio and this of Baptista. Another editor imagines that Lucentio's name was written on the packet of books. Malone.

BAP. A mighty man of Pifa; by report
I know him well:[8] you are very welcome, fir.——
Take you [*To* HOR.] the lute, and you [*To* LUC.]
    the fet of books,
You fhall go fee your pupils prefently.
Holla, within!——

       Enter a Servant.

Sirrah, lead
Thefe gentlemen to my daughters; and tell them
    both,
Thefe are their tutors; bid them ufe them well.
    [*Exit* Servant, *with* HORTENSIO, LUCENTIO,
    and BIONDELLO.
We will go walk a little in the orchard,
And then to dinner: You are paffing welcome,
And fo I pray you all to think yourfelves.

    PET. Signior Baptifta, my bufinefs afketh hafte,

---

[8] *I know him well:*] It appears in a fubfequent part of this
play, that Baptifta was not *perfonally* acquainted with Vincentio.
The pedant indeed talks of Vincentio and Baptifta having lodged
together twenty years before at an inn in Genoa; but this appears
to have been a fiction for the *nonce*; for when the pretended Vincentio is introduced, Baptifta expreffes no furprife at his not being
the fame man with whom he had formerly been acquainted; and,
when the real Vincentio appears, he fuppofes him an impoftor.
The words therefore, *I know him well,* muft mean, " I know
well who he is." Baptifta ufes the fame words before, fpeaking
of Petruchio's father: " I know him well; you are welcome for
his fake"—where they muft have the fame meaning; viz. *I know
who he was*; for Petruchio's father is fuppofed to have died before
the commencement of this play.
    Some of the modern editors point the paffage before us thus:
      A mighty man of Pifa; by report
      I know him well.——
but it is not fo pointed in the old copy, and the regulation feems
unneceffary, the very fame words having been before ufed with
equal licence concerning the father of Petruchio.
    Again, in *Timon of Athens:* " We *know him* for no lefs, though
we are but ftrangers to him." MALONE,

And every day I cannot come to woo.'
You knew my father well; and in him, me,
Left folely heir to all his lands and goods,
Which I have better'd rather than decreas'd:
Then tell me,—if I get your daughter's love,
What dowry fhall I have with her to wife?

Bap. After my death, the one half of my lands:
And, in poffeffion, twenty thoufand crowns.

Pet. And, for that dowry, I'll affure her of
Her widowhood,'—be it that fhe furvive me,—
In all my lands and leafes whatfoever:
Let fpecialties be therefore drawn between us,
That covenants may be kept on either hand.

Bap. Ay, when the fpecial thing is well obtain'd,
This is,—her love; for that is all in all.

Pet. Why, that is nothing; for I tell you, father,
I am as peremptory as fhe proud-minded;
And where two raging fires meet together,
They do confume the thing that feeds their fury:
Though little fire grows great with little wind,
Yet extreme gufts will blow out fire and all:
So I to her, and fo fhe yields to me;
For I am rough, and woo not like a babe.

---

9 *And every day I cannot come to woo.*] This is the burthen of
part of an old ballad entitled *The Ingenious Braggadocio:*
  " And I cannot come every day to wooe."
It appears alfo from a quotation in Puttenham's *Arte of English
Poefie,* 1589, that it was a line in his Interlude, entitled *The Wars:*
  " Iche pray you good mother tell our young dame
  " Whence I am come, and what is my name;
  " *I cannot come a wooing every day.*" STEEVENS.

2 ——*Ill affure her of
   Her widowhood,*] Sir T. Hanmer reads—*for* her widowhood.
The reading of the old copy is harfh to our ears, but it might have
been the phrafeology of the time. MALONE.

Perhaps we fhould read—*on* her widowhood. In the old copies
on and *of* are not unfrequently confounded, through the printers'
inattention. STEEVENS.

Bap. Well may'ft thou woo, and happy be thy
  fpeed!
But be thou arm'd for fome unhappy words.

Pet. Ay, to the proof; as mountains are for
  winds,
That fhake not, though they blow perpetually.

Re-enter HORTENSIO, *with his head broken.*

Bap. How now, my friend? why doft thou look
  fo pale?

Hor. For fear, I promife you, if I look pale.

Bap. What, will my daughter prove a good mufician?

Hor. I think, fhe'll fooner prove a foldier;
Iron may hold with her, but never lutes.

Bap. Why, then thou canft not break her to the
  lute?

Hor. Why, no; for fhe hath broke the lute to
  me.
I did but tell her, fhe miftook her frets,[3]
And bow'd her hand to teach her fingering;
When, with a moft impatient devilifh fpirit,
Frets, call you thefe? quoth fhe: *I'll fume with them:*
And, with that word, fhe ftruck me on the head,
And through the inftrument my pate made way;
And there I ftood amazed for a while,
As on a pillory, looking through the lute:
While fhe did call me,—rafcal fiddler,

---

[3] *——her* frets,] A fret is that ftop of a mufical inftrument
which caufes or regulates the vibration of the ftring. JOHNSON.

And—twangling Jack;[3] with twenty fuch vile terms,
As fhe had[4] ftudied to mifufe me fo.

Pet. Now, by the world, it is a lufty wench;
I love her ten times more than e'er I did:
O, how I long to have fome chat with her!

Bap. Well, go with me, and be not fo difcom-
fited:
Proceed in practice with my younger daughter;
She's apt to learn, and thankful for good turns.—
Signior Petruchio, will you go with us;
Or fhall I fend my daughter Kate to you?

Pet. I pray you do; I will attend her here,—
[*Exeunt* BAPTISTA, GREMIO, TRANIO, *and*
HORTENSIO.
And woo her with fome fpirit when fhe comes.
Say, that fhe rail; Why, then I'll tell her plain,
She fings as fweetly as a nightingale:
Say, that fhe frown; I'll fay, fhe looks as clear
As morning rofes newly wafh'd with dew:[5]

---

[3] *And—twangling* Jack;] Of this contemptuous appellation
I know not the precife meaning. Something like it, however,
occurs in *Magnificence*, an ancient folio interlude by Skelton, printed
by Raftell:

 " ——ye wene I were fome hafter,
 " Or ellys fome *jangelynge jacke* of the vale." STEEVENS.

 To *twangle* is a provincial expreffion, and fignifies to flourifh
capricioufly on an inftrument, as performers often do after having
tuned it, previous to their beginning a regular compofition.
HENLEY.

Twangling Jack is, *mean, paltry* lutanift. MALONE.

 I do not fee with Mr. Malone, that *twangling Jack* means
" paltry *lutanift*," though it may " paltry *mufician*." DOUCE.

[4] *——fhe had—*] In the old copy thefe words are accidentally
tranfpofed. Corrected by Mr. Rowe. MALONE.

[5] *As morning rofes newly* wafh'd with dew:] Milton has honoured
this image by adopting it in his *Allegro:*
 " And frefh-blown rofes *wafh'd in dew*." STEEVENS.

Say, she be mute, and will not speak a word;
Then I'll commend her volubility,
And say—she uttereth piercing eloquence:
If she do bid me pack, I'll give her thanks,
As though she bid me stay by her a week;
If she deny to wed, I'll crave the day
When I shall ask the banns, and when be married :—
But here she comes; and now, Petruchio, speak.

Enter KATHARINA.

Good morrow, Kate;[6] for that's your name, I
    hear.

[6] *Good-morrow, Kate*; &c.] Thus in the original play:
"*Feran.* Twenty good-morrows to my lovely *Kate*.
" *Kate.* You jest I am sure; is she yours already?
" *Feran.* I tel thee *Kate*, I know thou lov'st me wel.
" *Kate.* The divel you do; who told you so?
" *Feran.* My mind, sweet *Kate*, doth say I am the man,
" Must wed, and bed, and marrie bonnie *Kate*.
" *Kate.* Was ever seene so grosse an asse as this?
" *Feran.* I, to stand so long and never get a kisse.
" *Kate.* Hands off, I say, and get you from this place;
" Or I will set my ten commandements in your face.
" *Feran.* I prithy do, *Kate*; they say thou art a shrew,
" And I like thee better, for I would have thee so.
" *Kate.* Let go my hand, for feare it reach your eare.
" *Feran.* No, *Kate*, this hand is mine, and I thy love.
" *Kate.* Yfaith, sir, no; the woodcoke wants his taile.
" *Feran.* But yet his bil will serve, if the other faile.
" *Alfon.* How now, *Ferando?* what [says] my daughter?
" *Feran.* Shee's willing, sir, and loves me as her life.
" *Kate.* 'Tis for your skin then, but not to be your wife.
" *Alfon.* Come hither, *Kate*, and let me give thy hand,
" To him that I have chosen for thy love;
" And thou to-morrow shalt be wed to him.
" *Kate.* Why, father, what do you mean to do with me,
" To give me thus unto this brainsicke man,
" That in his mood cares not to murder me?
                                  She turnes aside and speaks.
" But yet I will consent and marry him,

G g 2

Kath. Well have you heard, but fomething hard
　　　of hearing;[7]
They call me—Katharine, that do talk of me..

Pet. You lie, in faith; for you are call'd plain
　　　Kate,
And bonny Kate, and fometimes Kate the curft;
But Kate, the prettieft Kate in Chriftendom,
Kate of Kate-Hall, my fuper-dainty Kate,　　.
For dainties are all cates: and therefore, Kate,
Take this of me, Kate of my confolation;—
Hearing thy mildnefs prais'd in every town,
Thy virtues fpoke of, and thy beauty founded,
(Yet not fo deeply as to thee belongs,)
Myfelf am mov'd to woo thee for my wife.

Kath. Mov'd! in good time: let him that mov'd
　　　you hither,
Remove you hence: I knew you at the firft,
You were a moveable.

Pet.　　　　　　Why, what's a moveable?

Kath. A joint-ftool.[8]

<hr />

" (For I methinkes have liv'd too long a maide,)
" And match him too, or elfe his manhood's good.
　" *Alfon.* Give me thy hand: *Ferando* loves thee well,
" And will with wealth and eafe maintaine thy ftate.
" Here *Ferando*, take her for thy wife,
" And Sunday next fhall be our wedding-day.
　" *Feran.* Why fo, did I not tel thee I fhould be the man?
" Father, I leave my lovely *Kate* with you.
" Provide yourfelves againft our marriage day,
" For I muft hie me to my country houfe
" In hafte, to fee provifion may be made
" To entertaine my *Kate* when fhe doth come," &c. STEEVENS.

　[7] *Well have you* heard, *but fomething hard of hearing;*] A poor
quibble was here intended. It appears from many old Englifh
books that *heard* was pronounced in our author's time, as if it were
written *hard.* MALONE.

　[8] *A joint-ftool.*] This is a proverbial expreffion:
　　" Cry you mercy, I took you for a join'd ftool."

PET.   Thou haſt hit it: come, ſit on me.

KATH. Aſſes are made to bear, and ſo are you.

PET. Women are made to bear, and ſo are you.

KATH. No ſuch jade, ſir,[9] as you, if me you mean.

PET. Alas, good Kate! I will not burden thee:
For, knowing thee to be but young and light,—

KATH. Too light for ſuch a ſwain as you to catch;
And yet as heavy as my weight ſhould be.

PET. Should be? ſhould buz.

KATH.   Well ta'en, and like a buzzard.

PET. O, ſlow-wing'd turtle! ſhall a buzzard take thee?

KATH. Ay, for a turtle; as he takes a buzzard.[a]

PET. Come, come, you waſp; i'faith, you are too angry.

See Ray's *Collection.* It is likewiſe repeated as a proverb in *Mother Bombie,* a comedy by Lyly, 1594, and by the Fool in *King Lear.* STEEVENS.

[9] *No ſuch* jade, ſir,] The latter word, which is not in the old copy, was ſupplied by the editor of the ſecond folio.
MALONE.

Perhaps we ſhould read—no ſuch *jack.* However there is authority for *jade* in a male ſenſe. So, in *Soliman and Perſeda, Piſton* ſays of *Baſiliſco,* " He juſt like a *knight!* He'll *juſt* like a *jade.*"
FARMER.

So, before, p. 438: " I know *he'll* prove a *jade.*" MALONE.

[a] *Ay, for a turtle;* as *he takes a buzzard.*] Perhaps we may read better—
Ay, for a turtle, and *he takes a buzzard.*
That is, he may take me for a *turtle,* and he ſhall find me a *hawk.*
JOHNSON.

This kind of expreſſion likewiſe ſeems to have been proverbial. So, in *The Three Lords of London,* 1590:
" —— haſt no more ſkill,
" Than *take a faulcon for a buzzard?*" STEEVENS.

KATH. If I be wafpifh, beft beware my fting.

PET. My remedy is then, to pluck it out.

KATH. Ay, if the fool could find it where it lies.

PET. Who knows not where a wafp doth wear
      his fting?
In his tail.

KATH.   In his tongue.

PET.   Whofe tongue?

KATH. Yours, if you talk of tails;[3] and fo fare-
      well.

PET. What, with my tongue in your tail? nay,
      come again,
Good Kate; I am a gentleman.

KATH.   That I'll try.
                   [*Striking him.*

PET. I fwear I'll cuff you, if you ftrike again.

KATH. So may you lofe your arms:
If you ftrike me, you are no gentleman;
And if no gentleman, why, then no arms.

PET. A herald, Kate? O, put me in thy books.

KATH. What is your creft? a coxcomb?

PET. A comblefs cock, fo Kate will be my hen.

KATH. No cock of mine, you crow too like a
      craven.[4]

---

[3] *Yours, if you talk of* tails;] The old copy reads—*tales*, and it
may perhaps be right.—" Yours, if your talk be no better than
an *idle tale.*" Our author is very fond of ufing words of fimilar
founds in different fenfes.—I have, however, followed the emendation made by Mr. Pope, which all the modern editors have adopted.
                     MALONE.

[4] ——*a* craven.] A *craven* is a degenerate, difpirited cock.
So, in *Rhodon and Iris*, 1631:
    " That he will pull the *craven* from his neft."
                     STEEVENS.

Pet. Nay, come, Kate, come; you muſt not look
  ſo four.

Kath. It is my faſhion, when I ſee a crab.

Pet. Why, here's no crab; and therefore look
  not four,

Kath. There is, there is.

Pet. Then ſhow it me.

Kath.   Had I a glaſs, I would.

Pet. What, you mean my face?

Kath.   Well aim'd of ſuch a young one.

Pet. Now, by ſaint George, I am too young for
  you.

Kath. Yet you are wither'd.

Pet.   'Tis with cares.

Kath.   I care not.

Pet. Nay, hear you, Kate: in ſooth, you 'ſcape
  not ſo.

Kath. I chaſe you, if I tarry; let me go.

Pet. No, not a whit; I find you paſſing gentle.
'Twas told me, you were rough, and coy, and ſul-
  len,
And now I find report a very liar;
For thou art pleaſant, gameſome, paſſing courteous;
But ſlow in ſpeech, yet ſweet as ſpring-time flowers:
Thou canſt not frown, thou canſt not look aſkance,
Nor bite the lip, as angry wenches will;

Craven was a term alſo applied to thoſe who in appeals of
battle became recreant, and by pronouncing this word, called for
quarter from their opponents; the conſequence of which was, that
they for ever after were deemed infamous.
 See note on *'Tis Pity ſhe's a Whore.* Dodſley's *Collection of Old
Plays*, Vol. VIII. p. 10. edit. 1780. REED.

Nor haſt thou pleaſure to be croſs in talk;
But thou with mildneſs entertain'ſt thy wooers,
With gentle conference, ſoft and affable.
Why does the world report, that Kate doth limp?
O ſlanderous world! Kate, like the hazle-twig,
Is ſtraight, and ſlender; and as brown in hue
As hazle nuts, and ſweeter than the kernels.
O, let me ſee thee walk: thou doſt not halt.

 KATH. Go, fool, and whom thou keep'ſt command.[5]

 PET. Did ever Dian ſo become a grove,
As Kate this chamber with her princely gait?
O, be thou Dian, and let her be Kate;
And then let Kate be chaſte, and Dian ſportful!

 KATH. Where did you ſtudy all this goodly ſpeech?

 PET. It is extempore, from my mother-wit.

 KATH. A witty mother! witleſs elſe her ſon.

 PET. Am I not wiſe?

 KATH.   Yes; keep you warm.[6]

 PET. Marry, ſo I mean, ſweet Katharine, in thy
  bed:
And therefore, ſetting all this chat aſide,
Thus in plain terms:—Your father hath conſented
That you ſhall be my wife; your dowry 'greed on;

 [5] *Go, fool, and whom thou keep'ſt command.*] This is exactly the
Παϲϲάμιϖ ἰϰίταϲϲι of Theocritus, Eid. xv. v. 90. and yet I
would not be poſitive that Shakſpeare had ever read even a tranſlation of Theocritus. TYRWHITT.

 [6] Pet. *Am I not wiſe?*
  Kath. *Yes; keep you warm.*] So, in Beaumont and Fletcher's
Scornful Lady:
   " ——your houſe has been kept *warm*, ſir.
   " I am glad to hear it; pray God, you are *wiſe* too."
Again, in our poet's *Much Ado about Nothing:*
   " —— that if he has *wit* enough to keep himſelf *warm*."
             STEEVENS.

And, will you, nill you,[7] I will marry you.
Now, Kate, I am a husband for your turn;
For, by this light, whereby I see thy beauty,
(Thy beauty, that doth make me like thee well,)
Thou must be married to no man but me:
For I am he am born to tame you, Kate;
And bring you from a wild Cat to a Kate[8]
Conformable, as other houshold Kates.
Here comes your father; never make denial,
I must and will have Katharine to my wife.

Re-enter BAPTISTA, GREMIO, *and* TRANIO.

BAP. Now,
Signior Petruchio: How speed you with
My daughter?

PET.   How but well, sir? how but well?
It were impossible, I should speed amiss.

BAP. Why, how now, daughter Katharine? in
           your dumps?

KATH. Call you me, daughter? now, I promise
           you,
You have show'd a tender fatherly regard,
To wish me wed to one half lunatick;

---

[7] —— nill *you*,] So, in *The Death of Robert Earl of Huntington*, 1601:
      " *Will* you or *nill* you, you must yet go in."
Again, in *Damon and Pithias*, 1571:
      " Neede hath no law; *will I, or nill I*, it must be done."
                                             STEEVENS.

[8] —— *a wild* cat *to a Kate* —] The first folio reads——
      —— *a wild* Kate *to a Kate*, &c.
The second folio——
      —— *a wild* Kat *to a Kate*, &c.   STEEVENS.

   The editor of the second folio with some probability reads—
from a wild Kat (meaning certainly *cat*.) So before: " But will
you woo this *wild cat?*" MALONE.

A mad-cap ruffian, and a fwearing Jack,
That thinks with oaths to face the matter out.

Pet. Father, 'tis thus,—yourfelf and all the
      world,
That talk'd of her, have talk'd amifs of her;
If fhe be curft, it is for policy:
For fhe's not froward, but modeft as the dove;
She is not hot, but temperate as the morn;
For patience fhe will prove a fecond Griffel;[9]
And Roman Lucrece for her chaftity:
And to conclude,—we have 'greed fo well to-
      gether,
That upon funday is the wedding-day.

Kath. I'll fee thee hang'd on funday firft.

Gre. Hark, Petruchio! fhe fays, fhe'll fee thee
      hang'd firft.

Tra. Is this your fpeeding? nay, then, good night
      our part!

Pet. Be patient, gentlemen; I choofe her for
      myfelf;
If fhe and I be pleas'd, what's that to you?
'Tis bargain'd 'twixt us twain, being alone,
That fhe fhall ftill be curft in company.
I tell you, 'tis incredible to believe
How much fhe loves me: O, the kindeft Kate!—

---

    9 ——*a fecond* Griffel; &c.] So, in *The Fair Maid of Briftow,*
1605, bl. l:
      " I will become as mild and dutiful
      " As ever *Griffel* was unto her lord,
      " And for my conftancy as *Lucrece* was."
There is a play entered at Stationers' Hall, May 28, 1599, called
" The plaie of *Patient Griffil.*" Bocaccio was the firft known
writer of the ftory, and Chaucer copied it in his *Clerke of Oxen-
forde's Tale.* STEEVENS.

    The ftory of *Grifel* is older than Bocaccio, and is to be found
among the compofitions of the French Fabliers. DOUCE.

She hung about my neck; and kiſs on kiſs
She vied ſo faſt,[2] proteſting oath on oath,
That in a twink ſhe won me to her love.
O, you are novices! 'tis a world to ſee,[3]
How tame, when men and women are alone,
A meacock wretch[4] can make the curſteſt ſhrew.—
Give me thy hand, Kate: I will unto Venice,

---

[2] —— *kiſs on kiſs*

She vied *ſo faſt*,] *Vye and revye* were terms at cards, now ſuperſeded by the more modern word, *brag.* Our author has in another place, " time *revyes* us," which has been unneceſſarily altered. The words were frequently uſed in a ſenſe ſomewhat remote from their original one. In the famous trial of the ſeven biſhops, the chief juſtice ſays, " We muſt not permit *vying and revying* upon one another." FARMER.

It appears from a paſſage in Green's *Tu Quoque,* that to *vie* was one of the terms uſed at the game of *Gleek*—" I *vie* it."—" I'll none of it;"—" nor I."

The ſame expreſſion occurs in Randolph's *Jealous Lovers,* 1632:
" All that I have is thine, though I could *vie,*
" For every ſilver hair upon my head,
" A piece of gold." STEEVENS.

Vie and *Revie* were terms at *Primero,* the faſhionable game in our author's time. See Florio's *Second Frutes,* quarto, 1591: S. " Let us play at Primero then. A. What ſhall we play for? S. One ſhilling ſtake and three reſt.—I *vye* it; will you hould it? A. Yea, ſir, I hould it, and *revye* it."

To *out-vie* Howel explains in his Dictionary, 1660, thus: " Faire peur ou intimider avec un vray ou feint *envy,* et faire quitter le jeu a la partie contraire." MALONE.

[3] —— *'tis a world to ſee,*] i. e. it is wonderful to ſee. This expreſſion is often met with in old hiſtorians as well as dramatic writers. So, in *Holinſhed,* Vol. I. p. 209: " *It is a world to ſee how many ſtrange heartes,*" &c. STEEVENS.

[4] *A* meacock *wretch*—] i. e. a timorous daſtardly creature. So, in Decker's *Honeſt Whore,* 1604:
" A woman's well holp up with ſuch a *meacock.*"
Again, in Glapthorne's *Hollander,* 1640:
" They are like my huſband; mere *meacocks* verily."
Again, in *Apius and Virginia,* 1575:
" As ſtout as a ſtockfiſh, as meek as a *meacock.*"
STEEVENS.

To buy apparel 'gainſt the wedding-day :—
Provide the feaſt, father, and bid the gueſts;
I will be ſure, my Katharine ſhall be fine.

 Bap. I know not what to ſay : but give me your
    hands;
God ſend you joy, Petruchio! 'tis a match.

 Gre. Tra. Amen, ſay we; we will be witneſſes.

 Pet. Father, and wife, and gentlemen, adieu;
I will to Venice, ſunday comes apace :——
We will have rings, and things, and fine array;
And kiſs me, Kate, we will be married o'ſunday.
 [*Exeunt* PETRUCHIO *and* KATHARINE, *ſeverally.*

 Gre. Was ever match clap'd up ſo ſuddenly?

 Bap. Faith, gentlemen, now I play a merchant's
    part,
And venture madly on a deſperate mart.

 Tra. 'Twas a commodity lay fretting by you :
'Twill bring you gain, or periſh on the ſeas.

 Bap. The gain I ſeek is—quiet in the match.[5]

 Gre. No doubt, but he hath got a quiet catch.
But now, Baptiſta, to your younger daughter ;—
Now is the day we long have looked for;
I am your neighbour, and was ſuitor firſt.

 Tra. And I am one, that love Bianca more
Than words can witneſs, or your thoughts can
    gueſs.

 Gre. Youngling! thou canſt not love ſo dear as I.

 Tra. Grey-beard! thy love doth freeze.

 Gre.   But thine doth fry.[6]

---

 [5] —— in *the match.*] Old copy—*me* the match. Corrected by
Mr. Pope. MALONE.

 [6] *But thine doth fry.*] Old Gremio's notions are confirmed by
Shadwell :

Skipper, ftand back; 'tis age, that nourifheth.

TRA. But youth, in ladies' eyes that flourifheth.

BAP. Content you, gentlemen; I'll compound
   this ftrife:
'Tis deeds, muft win the prize; and he, of both,
That can affure my daughter greateft dower,
Shall have Bianca's love.—
Say, fignior Gremio, what can you affure her?

GRE. Firft, as you know, my houfe within the
   city
Is richly furnifhed with plate and gold;
Bafons, and ewers, to lave her dainty hands;
My hangings all of Tyrian tapeftry:
In ivory coffers I have ftuff'd my crowns;
In cyprefs chefts my arras, counterpoints,[7]

  " The fire of love in youthful blood,
  " Like what is kindled in brufh-wood,
   " But for the moment burns: ——
  " But when crept into aged veins,
  " It flowly burns, and long remains;
  " It glows, and with a fullen heat,
  " Like fire in logs, it burns, and warms us long;
  " And though the flame be not fo great,
  " Yet is the heat as ftrong." JOHNSON.

So alfo, in *A Wonder, a Woman never Vex'd,* a comedy by
Rowley, 1632:
" My old dry wood fhall make a lufty bonfire, when thy green
chips lie hiffing in the chimney-corner."
The thought, however, might originate from Sidney's *Arcadia,*
Book II:
  " Let not old age difgrace my high defire,
   " O heavenly foule, in humane fhape contain'd!
  " Old wood inflam'd doth yeeld the braveft fire,
   " When yonger doth in fmoke his vertue fpend."
           STEEVENS.

[7] ——*counterpoints,*] So, in *A Knack to know a Knave,* 1594:
  " Then I will have rich *counterpoints* and mufk."
Thefe coverings for beds are at prefent called *counterpanes*; but
either mode of fpelling is proper.

Coftly apparel, tents, and canopies,[8]
Fine linen, Turky cufhions bofs'd with pearl,
Valance of Venice gold in needle-work,
Pewter[9] and brafs, and all things that belong
To houfe, or houfekeeping: then, at my farm,
I have a hundred milch-kine to the pail,
Sixfcore fat oxen ftanding in my ftalls,
And all things anfwerable to this portion.
Myfelf am ftruck in years, I muft confefs;
And, if I die to-morrow, this is hers,
If, whilft I live, fhe will be only mine.

    Tra. That, only, came well in——Sir, lift to me,
I am my father's heir, and only fon:

Counterpoint is the monkifh term for a particular fpecies of
mufick, in which notes of equal duration, but of different harmony,
are fet in oppofition to each other.

    In like manner *counterpanes* were anciently compofed of patch-
work, and fo contrived that every *pane* or partition in them, was
contrafted with one of a different colour, though of the fame di-
menfions. STEEVENS.

    Counterpoints were in ancient times extremely coftly. In Wat
Tyler's rebellion, Stowe informs us, when the infurgents broke into
the wardrobe in the Savoy, they deftroyed a coverlet, worth a
thoufand marks. MALONE.

    [8] ——tents, *and canopies,*] I fuppofe by *tents* old Gremio means
work of that kind which the ladies call *tent-ftitch.* He would
hardly enumerate *tents* (in their common acceptation) among his
domeftick riches. STEEVENS.

    I fufpect, the furniture of fome kind of bed, in the form of a
pavillion, was known by this name in our author's time.
                              MALONE.

    I conceive, the *pavillon,* or tent-bed, to have been an article of
furniture unknown in the age of Shakfpeare. STEEVENS.

    [9] *Pewter*—] We may fuppofe that *pewter* was, even in the
time of Queen Elizabeth, too coftly to be ufed in common. It
appears from " The regulations and eftablifhment of the houfehold of Henry Algernon Percy, the fifth earl of Northumberland," &c. that veffels of *pewter* were hired by the year. *This
houfehold-book* was begun in the year 1512. See Holinfhed's
Defcription of England, p. 188, and 189. STEEVENS.

I

If I may have your daughter to my wife,
I'll leave her houfes three or four as good,
Within rich Pifa walls, as any one
Old fignior Gremio has in Padua;
Befides two thoufand ducats by the year,
Of fruitful land, all which fhall be her jointure.—
What, have I pinch'd you, fignior Gremio?

GRE. Two thoufand ducats by the year, of land!
My land amounts not to fo much in all:
That fhe fhall have; befides ² an argofy,³
That now is lying in Marfeilles' road:———
What, have I chok'd you with an argofy?

TRA. Gremio, 'tis known, my father hath no lefs
Than three great argofies; befides two galliaffes,⁴

---

² Gre. *Two thoufand ducats by the year, of land!*
My land amounts not *to fo much in all:*
That fhe fhall have; befides—] Though all copies concur in this reading, furely, if we examine the reafoning, fomething will be found wrong. Gremio is ftartled at the high fettlement Tranio propofes: fays, his whole eftate in land can't match it, yet he'll fettle fo much a year upon her, &c. This is playing at crofs purpofes. The change of the *negative* in the fecond line falves the abfurdity, and fets the paffage right. Gremio and Tranio vying in their offers to carry Bianca, the latter boldly propofes to fettle land to the amount of two thoufand ducats per annum. My whole eftate, fays the other, in land, amounts *but* to that value; yet fhe fhall have *that:* I'll endow her with the *whole*; and confign a rich veffel to her ufe over and above. Thus all is intelligible, and he goes on to out-bid his rival. WARBURTON.

Gremio only fays, his whole eftate in land doth not indeed amount to two thoufand ducats a year, but fhe fhall have that, whatever be its value, and an argofy over and above; which argofy muft be underftood to be of very great value from his fub-joining:
What, have I chok'd you with an argofy? HEATH.

³ *That fhe fhall have; befides an argofy,*] She fhall have that, whatever be its value, and an argofy over and above. HEATH.

⁴ ——*two* galliaffes,] A *galeas* or *galliafs*, is a heavy low-built veffel of burthen, with both fails and oars, partaking at once of

And twelve tight gallies: thefe I will affure her,
And twice as much, whate'er thou offer'ft next.

Gre. Nay, I have offer'd all, I have no more;
And fhe can have no more than all I have;—
If you like me, fhe fhall have me and mine.

Tra. Why, then the maid is mine from all the
world,
By your firm promife; Gremio is out-vied.[5]

Bap. I muft confefs, your offer is the beft;
And, let your father make her the affurance,
She is your own; elfe, you muft pardon me:
If you fhould die before him, where's her dower?

Tra. That's but a cavil; he is old, I young.

Gre. And may not young men die, as well as
old?

Bap. Well, gentlemen,
I am thus refolv'd:—On funday next you know,
My daughter Katharine is to be married:
Now, on the funday following, fhall Bianca
Be bride to you, if you make this affurance;
If not, to fignior Gremio:
And fo I take my leave, and thank you both.
[*Exit.*

Gre. Adieu, good neighbour.—Now I fear thee
not;

the nature of a fhip and a galley. So, in *The Noble Soldier,*
1634:
" —— to have rich gulls come aboard their pinnaces, for then
they are fure to build *galliaffes.*" STEEVENS.

5 ——*out-vied.*] This is a term at the old game of *gleek.* When
one man was *vied* upon another, he was faid to be *out-vied.* So,
in Greene's *Art of Coneycatching,* 1592: " They draw a card, and
the barnacle *vies,* and the countryman *vies* upon him," &c.
Again, in *The Jealous Lovers,* by Randolph, 1632:
" Thou canft not finde out wayes enow to fpend it;
" They will *out-vie* thy pleafures." STEEVENS.

Sirrah, young gamefter,[6] your father were a fool
To give thee all, and, in his waning age,
Set.foot under thy table: Tut! a toy!
An old Italian fox is not fo kind, my boy. [*Exit.*

TRA. A vengeance on your crafty wither'd hide!
Yet I have faced it with a card of ten.[7]

---

[6] *Sirrah, young* gamefter,] Perhaps alluding to the pretended
Lucentio's having before talk'd of *out-vying* him. See the laft note.
MALONE.

Gamefter, in the prefent inftance, has no reference to gaming,
and only fignifies—a wag, a frolickfome character. So, in *King
Henry VIII*:
  " You are a merry *gamefter*, my lord Sands." STEEVENS.

[7] *Yet I have faced it with a* card of ten.] That is, with the
higheft card, in the old fimple games of our anceftors. So that
this became a proverbial expreffion. So, Skelton:
  " Fyrfte pycke a quarrel, and fall out with him then,
  " And fo outface him with *a card of ten.*
And, Ben Jonfon, in his *Sad Shepherd*:
  " —— a Hart of ten
  " I trow he be."
i. e. an extraordinary good one. WARBURTON.

A hart of ten has no reference to *cards*, but is an expreffion taken
from *The Laws of the Foreft*, and relates to the age of the deer.
When a hart is paft fix years old, he is generally called *a hart of
ten*. See *Foreft Laws*, 4to. 1598.
Again, in the fixth fcene of *The Sad Shepherd*:
  " —— a great large deer!
  " *Rob.* What head?
  " *John.* Forked. *A hart of ten.*"
The former expreffion is very common. So, in *Law-Tricks*, &c. 1608:
  " I may be out-fac'd with a *card of ten.*"
  Mr. Malone is of opinion that the phrafe was " applied to thofe
perfons who gained their ends by impudence, and bold confident
affertion."
  As we are on the fubject of cards, it may not be amifs to take
notice of a common blunder relative to their names. We call the
king, queen, and *knave, court-cards*, whereas they were anciently
denominated *coats*, or *coat-cards*, from their *coats* or dreffes. So,
Ben Jonfon, in his *New Inn*:
  " When fhe is pleas'd to trick or trump mankind,
  " Some may be *coats*, as in the cards."

'Tis in my head to do my mafter good :—
I fee no reafon, but fuppos'd Lucentio
Muft get a father, call'd—fuppos'd Vincentio;
And that's a wonder : fathers, commonly,
Do get their children ; but, in this cafe of wooing,
A child fhall get a fire, if I fail not of my cunning.'

[*Exit.*

Again, in *May-day*, a comedy by Chapman, 1611:
" She had in her hand the ace of harts and a *coat-card.* She
led the board with her *coat*; I plaid the varlet, and took up her
coat; and meaning to lay my finger on her ace of hearts, up ftarted
a quite contrary card."

Again, in Rowley's *When you fee me you know me,* 1621 :
" You have been at *noddy*, I fee.
" Ay, and the firft *card* comes to my hand is a *knave.*
" I am a *coat-card*, indeed.
" Then thou muft needs be a *knave,* for thou art neither
queen nor *king*." STEEVENS.

⁷ —— *if I fail not of my* cunning.] As this is the conclufion of
an act, I fufpect that the poet defign'd a rhyming couplet. Inftead
of *cunning* we might read—*doing,* which is often ufed by Shakfpeare in the fenfe here wanted, and agrees perfectly well with the
beginning of the line—" a child fhall *get* a fire."

After this, the former editors add,

" *Sly*. Sim, when will the fool come again?*
" *Sim.* Anon, my lord.
" *Sly*. Give us fome more drink here; where's the tapfter?
" Here, Sim, eat fome of thefe things.
" *Sim.* I do, my lord.
" *Sly*. Here, Sim, I drink to thee."

Thefe fpeeches of the prefenters, (as they are called,) are not in
the folio. Mr. Pope, as in fome former inftances, introduced them
from the old fpurious play of the fame name ; and therefore we
may eafily account for their want of connection with the prefent comedy. I have degraded them as ufual into the note. By
the *fool* in the original piece, might be meant *Sander* the fervant
to *Ferando* (who is the *Petruchio* of Shakfpeare) or *Ferando* himfelf.

* —— *when will the fool come again?*] The character of the *fool* has not been
introduced in this drama, therefore I believe that the word *again* fhould be
omitted, and that Sly afks, *When will the fool come?* the fool being the favourite
of the vulgar, or, as we now phrafe it, of the upper gallery, was naturally
expected in every interlude. JOHNSON.

ACT III. SCENE I.

A Room in Baptifta's *Houfe.*

Enter LUCENTIO, HORTENSIO, *and* BIANCA.

Luc. Fidler, forbear; you grow too forward, fir:
Have you fo foon forgot the entertainment
Her fifter Katharine welcom'd you withal?

Hor. But, wrangling pedant, this is[8]
The patronefs of heavenly harmony:
Then give me leave to have prerogative;
And when in mufick we have fpent an hour,
Your lecture fhall have leifure for as much.

Luc. Prepofterous afs! that never read fo far
To know the caufe why mufick was ordain'd!
Was it not, to refrefh the mind of man,
After his ftudies, or his ufual pain?
Then give me leave to read philofophy,
And, while I paufe, ferve in your harmony.

It appears however from the following paffage in the eleventh
Book of Thomas Lupton's *Notable Things,* edit. 1660, that it was the
conftant office of the Fool to preferve the ftage from vacancy:
" 79. When Stage-plays were in ufe, there was in every place
one that was called the *Foole;* as the Proverb faies, *like a Fool in a
Play.* At the Red Bull Play-houfe it did chance that the *Clown* or
the *Fool,* being in the attireing houfe, was fuddenly called upon
the ftage, for it was empty. He fuddenly going, forgot his Fooles-
cap. One of the players bad his boy take it, and put it on his
head as he was fpeaking. No fuch matter (faies the Boy) there's
no manners nor wit in that, nor wifdom neither; and my mafter
needs no cap, for he is known to be a Fool without it, as well as
with it." STEEVENS.

[8] —— *this is —*] Probably our author wrote—this *lady* is,
which completes the metre, *wrangling* being ufed as a trifyllable.
MALONE.

We fhould read, with Sir T. Hanmer:
 But, wrangling pedant, know this lady *is.* RITSON.

Hor. Sirrah, I will not bear thefe braves of thine.

Bian. Why, gentlemen, you do me double wrong,
To ftrive for that which refteth in my choice:
I am no breeching fcholar⁹ in the fchools;
I'll not be tied to hours, nor 'pointed times,
But learn my leffons as I pleafe myfelf.
And, to cut off all ftrife, here fit we down:——
Take you your inftrument, play you the whiles;
His lecture will be done, ere you have tun'd.

Hor. You'll leave his lecture when I am in tune?
[*To* BIANCA.—HORTENSIO *retires.*

Luc. That will be never;—tune your inftrument.

Bian. Where left we laft?

Luc. Here, madam:——
Hac ibat Simois; hic eft Sigeia tellus;
Hic fteterat Priami regia celfa fenis.

Bian. Conftrue them.

Luc. Hac ibat, as I told you before,—*Simois,* I
am Lucentio,—*hic eft,* fon unto Vincentio of Pifa,—
Sigeia tellus, difguifed thus to get your love;—*Hic
fteterat,* and that Lucentio that comes a wooing,—
Priami, is my man Tranio,—*regia,* bearing my
port,—*celfa fenis,* that we might beguile the old
pantaloon.²

Hor. Madam, my inftrument's in tune.
[*Returning.*

⁹ —— *no* breeching *fcholar*—] i. e. no fchool-boy liable to
corporal correction. So, in *King Edward the Second,* by Marlow,
1598:
" Whofe looks were as a *breeching* to a boy."
Again, in *The Hog has loft his Pearl,* 1614:
" —— he went to fetch whips, I think, and, not refpecting my
honour, he would have *breech'd* me."
Again, in *Amends for Ladies,* 1618:
" If I had had a fon of fourteen that had ferved me fo, I would
have *breech'd* him." STEEVENS.

² ——*pantaloon.*] The old cully in Italian farces. JOHNSON.

Bian. Let's hear:— [Hortensio *plays.*
O fie! the treble jars.

Luc. Spit in the hole, man, and tune again.

Bian. Now let me fee if I can conftrue it: *Hac ibat Simois,* I know you not; *hic eft Sigeia tellus,* I truft you not;—*Hic fteterat Priami,* take heed he hear us not;—*regia,* prefume not;—*celfa fenis,* defpair not.

Hor. Madam, 'tis now in tune.

Luc. All but the bafe.

Hor. The bafe is right; 'tis the bafe knave that jars.
How fiery and forward our pedant is!
Now, for my life, the knave doth court my love:
Pedafcule,[3] I'll watch you better yet.

Bian. In time I may believe, yet I miftruft.[4]

Luc. Miftruft it not; for, fure, Æacides
Was Ajax,[5]—call'd fo from his grandfather.

Bian. I muft believe my mafter; elfe, I promife you,

---

[3] *Pedafcule,*] He fhould have faid, *Didafcale,* but thinking this too honourable, he coins the word *Pedafcule,* in imitation of it, from *pedant.* WARBURTON.

I believe it is no coinage of Shakfpeare's, it is more probable that *it lay in his way, and he found it.* STEEVENS.

[4] *In time I may believe, yet I miftruft.*] This and the feven verfes that follow, have in all the editions been ftupidly fhuffled and mifplaced to wrong fpeakers; fo that every word faid was glaringly out of character. THEOBALD.

[5] —*for, fure, Æacides,* &c.] This is only faid to deceive Hortenfio who is fuppofed to liften. The pedigree of *Ajax,* however, is properly made out, and might have been taken from Golding's Verfion of Ovid's *Metamorphofis,* Book XIII:
" —— The higheft Jove of all
" Acknowledgeth this *Æacus,* and dooth his fonne him call.
" Thus am I *Ajax* third from Jove." STEEVENS.

I ſhould be arguing ſtill upon that doubt:
But let it reſt.—Now, Licio, to you :—
Good maſters,⁵ take it not unkindly, pray,
That I have been thus pleaſant with you both.

   Hor. You may go walk, [*To* Lucentio.] and
          give me leave awhile;
My leſſons make no muſick in three parts.

   Luc. Are you ſo formal, ſir? well, I muſt wait,
And watch withal; for, but I be deceiv'd,⁶
Our fine muſician groweth amorous.   [*Aſide.*

   Hor. Madam, before you touch the inſtrument,
To learn the order of my fingering,
I muſt begin with rudiments of art;
To teach you gamut in a briefer ſort,
More pleaſant, pithy, and effectual,
Than hath been taught by any of my trade:
And there it is in writing, fairly drawn.

   Bian. Why, I am paſt my gamut long ago.

   Hor. Yet read the gamut of Hortenſio.

   Bian. [*Reads.*] Gamut *I am, the ground of all*
       accord,
   A re, *to plead Hortenſio's paſſion;*
  B mi, *Bianca, take him for thy lord,*
    C faut, *that loves with all affection:*
  D ſol re, *one cliff, two notes have I;*
  E la mi, *ſhow pity, or I die.*
Call you this—gamut? tut! I like it not:
Old faſhions pleaſe me beſt; I am not ſo nice,
To change true rules for odd inventions.⁷

---

⁵ *Good* maſters,] Old copy—*maſter.* Corrected by Mr. Pope.
                                 Malone.

⁶ —— but *I be deceiv'd,*] *But* has here the ſignification of *unleſs.*
                                 Malone.

⁷ *To* change *true rules for* odd *inventions.*] The old copy reads—
To charge *true rules for* old *inventions:* The former emendation was

Enter a Servant.[8]

Serv. Miftrefs, your father prays you leave your
books,
And help to drefs your fifter's chamber up;
You know, to-morrow is the wedding-day.

Bian. Farewell, fweet mafters, both; I muft be
gone.   [*Exeunt* Bianca *and* Servant.

Luc. 'Faith, miftrefs, then I have no caufe to
ftay.   [*Exit.*

Hor. But I have caufe to pry into this pedant;
Methinks, he looks as though he were in love:—
Yet if thy thoughts, Bianca, be fo humble,
To caft thy wand'ring eyes on every ftale,
Seize thee, that lift: If once I find thee ranging,
Hortenfio will be quit with thee by changing.
                                        [*Exit.*

made by the editor of the fecond folio; the latter by Mr.
Theobald. *Old,* however may be right. I believe, an oppofition
was intended. As *change* was corrupted into *charge,* why might
not *true* have been put inftead of *new?* Perhaps the author wrote
        To change new *rules for old inventions.*
i. e. to accept of new rules in exchange for old inventions.
                                        Malone.

[8] *Enter a* Servant.] The old copy reads—*Enter a* Meffenger—
who, at the beginning of his fpeech is called—*Nicke.* Ritson.

Meaning, I fuppofe, *Nicholas Tooley.* See Mr. Malone's *Hifto-
rical Account of the Englifh Stage.* Steevens.

SCENE II.

The fame.   Before Baptifta's *Houfe.*

Enter Baptista, Gremio, Tranio, Katharina, Bianca, Lucentio, *and Attendants.*

Bap. Signior Lucentio, [*To* Tranio.] this is the
          'pointed day
That Katharine and Petruchio fhould be married,
And yet we hear not of our fon-in-law:
What will be faid? what mockery will it be,
To want the bridegroom, when the prieft attends
To fpeak the ceremonial rites of marriage?
What fays Lucentio to this fhame of ours?

Kath. No fhame but mine: I muft, forfooth,
          be forc'd
To give my hand, oppos'd againft my heart,
Unto a mad-brain rudefby, full of fpleen;[8]
Who woo'd in hafte, and means to wed at leifure.
I told you, I, he was a frantick fool,
Hiding his bitter jefts in blunt behaviour:
And, to be noted for a merry man,
He'll woo a thoufand, 'point the day of marriage,
Make friends, invite, yes, and proclaim the banns;[9]

[8] ——*full of* fpleen;] That is, *full of* humour, caprice, and
inconftancy.   Johnson.

So, in the Firft Part of *Henry IV:*
    " A hare-brain'd Hotfpur, govern'd by a *fpleen.*"
                                                M. Mason.

[9] *Make friends, invite, yes, and proclaim the banns;*] Mr. Malone
reads:
    Make friends, invite them, *&c.*   Steevens.

Them is not in the old copy. For this emendation I am anfwerable.   The editor of the fecond folio, to fupply the defect in the
metre, reads, with lefs probability in my opinion—
    Make friends, invite, yes, and proclaim, &c.   Malone.

Yet never means to wed where he hath woo'd.
Now muſt the world point at poor Katharine,
And ſay,—*Lo, there is mad Petruchio's wife,*
If it would pleaſe him come and marry her.

TRA. Patience, good Katharine, and Baptiſta
too;
Upon my life, Petruchio means but well,
Whatever fortune ſtays him from his word:
Though he be blunt, I know him paſſing wiſe;
Though he be merry, yet withal he's honeſt.

KATH. 'Would, Katharine had never ſeen him
though!
[*Exit, weeping, followed by* BIANCA, *and Others.*

BAP. Go, girl; I cannot blame thee now to weep;
For ſuch an injury would vex a ſaint,[2]
Much more a ſhrew of thy impatient humour.[3]

Enter BIONDELLO.

BION. Maſter, maſter! news, old news,[4] and ſuch
news as you never heard of!

BAP. Is it new and old too? how may that be?

BION. Why, is it not news, to hear of Petruchio's
coming?

BAP. Is he come?

BION. Why, no, ſir.

---

[2] —— *vex a ſaint,*] The old copy redundantly reads—vex a
very faint. STEEVENS.

[3] —— *of* thy *impatient humour.*] *Thy,* which is not in the old
copy, was inſerted by the editor of the ſecond folio. MALONE.

[4] —— *old news,*] Theſe words were added by Mr. Rowe, and
neceſſarily, for the reply of Baptiſta ſuppoſes them to have been
already ſpoken, *old laughing—old utis,* &c. are expreſſions of that
time merely hyperbolical, and have been more than once uſed by
Shakſpeare. See note on *Henry IV.* Part II. Act II. ſc. iv.
STEEVENS.

Bap. What then?

Bion. He is coming.

Bap. When will he be here?

Bion. When he ftands where I am, and fees you
there.

Tra. But, fay, what :—To thine old news.

Bion. Why, Petruchio is coming, in a new hat,
and an old jerkin; a pair of old breeches, thrice
turn'd; a pair of boots that have been candle-
cafes, one buckled, another laced; an old rufty
fword ta'en out of the town armory, with a broken
hilt, and chapelefs; with two broken points:[4] His
horfe hip'd with an old mothy faddle, the ftirrups
of no kindred: befides, poffefs'd with the glanders,
and like to mofe in the chine; troubled with the

---

4 ——*a pair of boots—one buckled, another laced; an old rufty
fword ta'en out of the town-armory, with a broken hilt, and chapelefs;
with two broken points:*] How a fword fhould have *two broken points,*
I cannot tell. There is, I think, a tranfpofition caufed by the
feeming relation of *point* to *fword.* I read, *a pair of boots, one
buckled, another laced* with two broken points; *an old rufty fword—
with a broken hilt, and chapelefs.* JOHNSON.

I fufpect that feveral words giving an account of Petruchio's
belt are wanting. The belt was then broad and rich, and worn
on the outfide of the doublet.—*Two broken points* might therefore
have concluded the defcription of its oftentatious meannefs.
                                          STEEVENS.

The *broken points* might be the two broken tags to the laces.
                                          TOLLET.

——*that have been* candle-cafes,] That is, I fuppofe, boots
long left off, and after having been converted into cafes to hold
the ends of candles, returning to their firft office. I do not know
that I have ever met with the word *candle-cafe* in any other places,
except the following preface to a dramatic dialogue, 1604, entitled,
The Cafe is Alter'd, How?—" I write upon cafes, neither knife-
cafes, pin-cafes, nor *candle-cafes.*"

And again, in *How to choofe a Good Wife from a Bad,* 1602:

" A bow-cafe, a cap-cafe, a comb-cafe, a lute-cafe, a fiddle-
cafe, and a randle-cafe." STEEVENS.

lampafs, infected with the fafhions, full of wind-
galls, fped with fpavins, raied with the yellows, paft
cure of the fives,[6] ftark fpoiled with the ftaggers,
begnawn with the bots; fway'd in the back,[7] and
fhoulder-fhotten; ne'er-legg'd before,[8] and with a
half-check'd bit, and a head-ftall of fheep's leather; which, being reftrain'd to keep him from
ftumbling, hath been often burft, and now repair'd
with knots: one girt fix times pieced, and a woman's
crupper of velure,[9] which hath two letters for her
name, fairly fet down in ftuds, and here and there
pieced with packthread.

[6] —— *infected with the* fafhions,——*paft cure of the* **fives,**]
Fafhions. So called in the Weft of England, but by the beft writers
on farriery, *farcens,* or *farcy.*

Fives. So called in the Weft: *vives* elfewhere, and *avives* by
the French; a diftemper in horfes, little differing from the ftrangles.
GREY.

Shakfpeare is not the only ·writer who ufes *fafhions* for *farcy.*
So, in Decker's comedy of *Old Fortunatus,* 1600:

" *Shad.* What fhall we learn by travel?

" *Andel.* Fafhions.

" *Shad.* That's a *beaftly difeafe.*"

Again, in *The New Ordinary,* by Brome:

" My old beaft is infected with the *fafhions,* fafhion-fick."

Again, in Decker's *Guls Hornbook,* 1609: " *Fafhions* was then
counted a difeafe, and *horfes* died of it." STEEVENS.

[7] —— fway'd *in the back,*] The old copy has—*waid.* Corrected by Sir T. Hanmer. MALONE.

[8] —— ne'er *legg'd before,*] i. e. founder'd in his fore-feet;
having, as the jockies term it, *never a fore leg* to ftand on. The
fubfequent words—" which, being reftrain'd, to keep him from
ftumbling,"—feem to countenance this interpretation. The modern
editors read—*near-legg'd* before; but to go near before is not
reckoned a defect, but a perfection, in a horfe. MALONE.

[9] —— *crupper of* velure,] *Velure* is velvet. *Velours,* Fr. So,
in *The World toffed at Tennis,* by Middleton and Rowley:

" Come, my well-lined foldier (with valour,

" Not *velure*) keep me warm."

Again, in *The Noble Gentleman,* by Beaumont and Fletcher:

" —— an old hat,

" Lin'd with *velure.*" STEEVENS.

BAP. Who comes with him?

BION. O, fir, his lackey, for all the world ca-parifon'd like the horfe; with a linen ftock[9] on one leg, and a kerfey boot-hofe on the other, gar-ter'd with a red and blue lift; an old hat, and *The bumour of forty fancies* prick'd in't for a feather:[2]

[9] —*ftock* —] i.e. ftocking. So, in *Twelfth Night*: " —it [his leg] does indifferent well in a flame-coloured *ftock*."
STEEVENS.

[2] —*an old bat, and* The humour of forty fancies *prick'd in't for a feather*:] This was fome ballad or drollery at that time, which the poet here ridicules, by making Petruchio prick it up in his foot-boy's hat for a feather. His fpeakers are perpetually quoting fcraps and ftanzas of old ballads; and often very obfcurely; for, fo well are they adapted to the occafion, that they feem of a piece with the reft. In Shakfpeare's time, the kingdom was over-run with thefe doggrel compofitions, and he feems to have borne them a very particular grudge. He frequently ridicules both them and their makers, with excellent humour. In *Much ado about Nothing*, he makes Benedick fay, " Prove that ever I lofe more blood with love than I get again with drinking, prick out my eyes with a ballad-maker's pen." As the bluntnefs of it would make the execution of it extremely painful. And again, in *Troilus and Creffida*, Pandarus in his diftrefs having repeated a very ftupid ftanza from an old ballad, fays, with the higheft humour, " There never was a truer rhyme; let's caft away nothing, for we may live to have need of fuch a verfe. We fee it, we fee it."
WARBURTON.

I have fome doubts concerning this interpretation. A *fancy* appears to have been fome ornament worn formerly in the hat. So Peacham, in his *Worth of a Penny*, defcribing " an indigent and difcontented foldat," fays, " he walks with his arms folded, his belt without a fword or rapier, that perhaps being fomewhere in trouble; a *bat* without a band, hanging over his eyes; only it wears a weather-beaten *fancy* for fafhion-fake." This lackey therefore did not wear a common *fancy* in his hat, but fome fan-taftical ornament, comprizing the humour of forty different fancies. Such, I believe is the meaning. A couplet in one of Sir John Davies's Epigrams, 1598, may alfo add fupport to my interpretation:
" Nor for thy love will I once gnafh a bricke,
" Or fome *pied colours* in my bonnet *fticke*."

A *fancy*, however, meant alfo a love-fong or fonnet, or other poem. So, in *Sapho and Phao*, 1591: " I muft now fall from

monster, a very monster in apparel; and not like a christian footboy, or a gentleman's lackey.

Tra. 'Tis some odd humour pricks him to this
        fashion;—
Yet often times he goes but mean apparell'd.

 . *Bap.* I am glad he is come, howsoe'er he comes.

Bion. Why, sir, he comes not.

Bap. Didst thou not say, he comes?

Bion. Who? that Petruchio came?

Bap. Ay, that Petruchio came.

Bion. No, sir; I say, his horse comes with him on his back.

Bap. Why, that's all one.

Bion. Nay, by saint Jamy, I hold you a penny,
A horse and a man is more than one, and yet not
        many.

---

love to labour, and endeavour with mine oar to get a fare, not with my pen to write a *fancy.*" If the word was used here in this sense, the meaning is, that the lackey had stuck forty ballads together, and made something like a feather out of them.

                                    MALONE.

Dr. Warburton might have strengthened his supposition by observing, that the *Humour of Forty Fancies* was probably a collection of those short poems which are called *Fancies*, by Falstaff, in the Second Part of *K. Henry IV:* " —— sung those tunes which he heard the carmen whistle, and swore they were his *Fancies*, his good-nights." Nor is the *Humour of Forty Fancies* a more extraordinary title to a collection of poems, than the well-known *Hundred sundrie Flowers bounde up in one small Poesie.—A Paradise of dainty Devises.—The Arbor of amorous Conceits.—The Gorgeous Gallery of gallant Inventions.—The Forest of Histories.—The Ordinary of Humors,* &c. Chance, at some future period, may establish as a certainty what is now offered as a conjecture. A penny book, containing forty short poems, would, properly managed, furnish no unapt imitation of a plume of feathers for the hat of a humourist's servant. STEEVENS.

Enter PETRUCHIO *and* GRUMIO.[3]

PET. Come, where be thefe gallants ? who is at home ?

BAP. You are welcome, fir.

PET.   And yet I come not well.

BAP. And yet you halt not.

TRA.   Not fo well apparell'd
As I wifh you were.

PET. Were it better I fhould rufh in thus.

---

[3] *Enter Petruchio and Grumio.*] Thus, in the original play:
  " *Enter* Ferando, *bafely attired, and a red cap on his head,*
  " *Feran.* Good morrow, father: *Polidor* well met,
  " You wonder, I know, that I have ftaide fo long.
  " *Alfon.* Yea, marry fonne : we were almoft perfuaded
  " That we fhould fcarce have had our bridegroome heere :
  " But fay, why art thou thus bafely attired ?
  " *Feran.* Thus richly, father, you fhould have faide ;
  " For when my wife and I are married once,
  " Shee's fuch a fhrew, if we fhould once fall out,
  " Sheele pull my coftly futes over mine ears,
  " And therefore I am thus attir'd a while :
  " For many things I tell you's in my head,
  " And none muft know thereof but *Kate* and I ;
  " For we fhall live like lambes and lions fure :
  " Nor lambes to lions never were fo tame,
  " If once they lie within the lions pawes,
  " As *Kate* to me, if we were married once :
  " And therefore, come, let's to church prefently.
  " *Pol.* Fie, *Ferando!* not thus attired : for fhame,
  " Come to my chamber, and there fuite thyfelfe,
  " Of twenty futes that I did never weare.
  " *Feran.* Tufh, *Polidor*, I have as many futes
  " Fantaftike made to fit my humour fo,
  " As any in *Athens*; and as richly wrought
  " As was the maffie robe that late adorn'd
  " The ftately legat of the *Perfian* king,
  " And this from them I have made choife to weare.
  " *Alfon.* I prethee, *Ferando*, let me intreat,
  " Before thou go'ft unto the church with us,
  " To put fome other fute upon thy backe.
  " *Feran.* Not for the world," &c. STEEVENS.

But where is Kate? where is my lovely bride?—
How does my father?—Gentles, methinks you
    frown:
And wherefore gaze this goodly company;
As if they faw fome wondrous monument,
Some comet, or unufual prodigy?

    Bap. Why, fir, you know, this is your wedding-
    day:
Firft were we fad, fearing you would not come;
Now fadder, that you come fo unprovided.
Fie! doff this habit, fhame to your eftate,
An eyefore to our folemn feftival.

    Tra. And tell us, what occafion of import
Hath all fo long detain'd you from your wife,
And fent you hither fo unlike yourfelf?

    Pet. Tedious it were to tell, and harfh to hear:
Sufficeth, I am come to keep my word,
Though in fome part enforced to digrefs;[4]
Which, at more leifure, I will fo excufe
As you fhall well be fatisfied withal.
But, where is Kate? I ftay too long from her;
The morning wears, 'tis time we were at church.

    Tra. See not your bride in thefe unreverent robes;
Go to my chamber, put on clothes of mine.

    Pet. Not I, believe me; thus I'll vifit her.

    Bap. But thus, I truft, you will not marry her.

    Pet. Good footh, even thus; therefore have done
    with words;
To me fhe's married, not unto my clothes:
Could I repair what fhe will wear in me,
As I can change thefe poor accoutrements,
'Twere well for Kate, and better for myfelf.
But what a fool am I, to chat with you,

---

4 ——*to digrefs;*] To deviate from my promife.
                              Johnson.

When I ſhould bid good-morrow to my bride,
And ſeal the title with a lovely kiſs?

[*Exeunt* PETRUCHIO, GRUMIO, *and* BIONDELLO.

TRA. He hath ſome meaning in his mad attire:
We will perſuade him, be it poſſible,
To put on better ere he go to church.

BAP. I'll after him, and ſee the event of this. [*Exit.*

TRA. But, ſir, to her love⁵ concerneth us to add
Her father's liking: Which to bring to paſs,
As I before imparted⁶ to your worſhip,
I am to get a man,—whate'er he be,
It ſkills not much; we'll fit him to our turn,—

---

⁵ *Tra. But, ſir, to her love*—] Mr. Theobald reads—*our love.*
                                                    STEEVENS.

Our is an injudicious interpolation. The firſt folio reads—*But,
ſir, love concerneth us to add, Her father's liking—which,* I think,
ſhould be thus corrected:

　　But ſir, to her love concerneth us to add
　　Her father's liking.—

We muſt ſuppoſe, that Lucentio had before informed Tranio in
private of his having obtained Bianca's love; and Tranio here
reſumes the converſation, by obſerving, that *to her love* it concerns
them to add *her father's conſent,* and then goes on to propoſe a
ſcheme for obtaining the latter. TYRWHITT.

The nominative caſe to the verb *concerneth* is here underſtood.
A ſimilar licence may be found in *Coriolanus:*
　　" *Remains* that in the official marks inveſted,
　　" You anon do meet the ſenate."
Again, in *Troilus and Creſſida:*
　　" The beauty that is borne here in the face
　　" The bearer knows not, but *commends* itſelf
　　" To others' eyes." MALONE.

⁶ *As I before imparted*—] *I,* which was inadvertently omitted
in the old copy, was added by the editor of the ſecond folio; but
with his uſual inaccuracy was inſerted in the wrong place.
                                                    MALONE.

The ſecond folio reads:
　　As before I imparted, &c.
As this paſſage is now pointed, where is the inaccuracy of it? or,
if there be any, might it not have happened through the care-
leſſneſs of the compoſitor? STEEVENS.

And he fhall be Vincentio of Pifa;
And make affurance, here in Padua,
Of greater fums than I have promifed.
So fhall you quietly enjoy your hope,
And marry fweet Bianca with confent.

Luc. Were it not that my fellow fchoolmafter
Doth watch Bianca's fteps fo narrowly,
'Twere good, methinks, to fteal our marriage;
Which once perform'd, let all the world fay—no,
I'll keep mine own, defpite of all the world.

Tra. That by degrees we mean to look into,
And watch our vantage in this bufinefs:
We'll overreach the greybeard, Gremio,
The narrow-prying father, Minola;
The quaint mufician, amorous Licio;
All for my mafter's fake, Lucentio.—

Re-enter GREMIO.

Signior Gremio! came you from the church?

Gre. As willingly as e'er I came from fchool.[7]

Tra. And is the bride and bridegroom coming
    home?

Gre. A bridegroom, fay you? 'tis a groom, in-
    deed,
A grumbling groom, and that the girl fhall find.

Tra. Curfter than fhe? why, 'tis impoffible.

Gre. Why, he's a devil, a devil, a very fiend.

Tra. Why, fhe's a devil, a devil, the devil's
    dam.

---

[7] *As willingly,* &c.] This is a proverbial faying. See Ray's
Collection. STEEVENS.

Gre. Tut! she's a lamb, a dove, a fool to him.
I'll tell you, sir Lucentio; When the priest
Should ask—if Katharine should be his wife,
Ay, by gogs-wouns, quoth he; and swore so loud,
That, all amaz'd, the priest let fall the book:
And, as he stoop'd again to take it up,
The mad-brain'd bridegroom took him such a cuff,
That down fell priest and book, and book and
      priest;
Now take them up, quoth he, *if any list.*

Tra. What said the wench, when he arose again?

Gre. Trembled and shook; for why, he stamp'd,
     and swore,
As if the vicar meant to cozen him.
But after many ceremonies done,
He calls for wine:—*A health,* quoth he; as if
He had been aboard, carousing to his mates
After a storm:—Quaff'd off the muscadel,[8]

---

[8] —— *Quaff'd off the* muscadel,] It appears from this passage,
and the following one in *The History of the two Maids of More-
clacke,* a comedy by Robert Armin, 1609, that it was the custom
to drink wine immediately after the marriage ceremony. Armin's
play begins thus:

  " *Enter a Maid strewing flowers, and a serving-man perfuming the door.*
  " *Maid.* Strew, strew.
  " *Man.* The *muscadine* stays for the bride at church.
  " The priest and Hymen's ceremonies 'tend
  " To make them man and wife."
  Again, in Decker's *Satiromastix,* 1602:
  " ——and when we are at church, bring the *wine* and cakes."
In Ben Jonson's *Magnetic Lady,* the wine drank on this occasion
is called a " *knitting cup.*"
  Again, in *No Wit like a Woman's,* by Middleton:
  " Even when my lip touch'd the *contracting cup.*"
There was likewise a flower that borrowed its name from this ce-
remony:
  " Bring sweet carnations, and *sops in wine,*
  " Worne of paramours."
                 Hobbinol's Dittie, &c. by Spenser.

And threw the fops all in the fexton's face;
Having no other reafon,—

Again, in Beaumont and Fletcher's *Scornful Lady:*
 " Were the rofemary branches dipp'd, and all
 " The *hippocras* and *cakes* eat and drunk off;
 " Were thefe two arms encompafs'd with the hands
 " Of bachelors to lead me to the church," &c.
Again, in the *Articles ordained by K. Henry VII. for the Regulation of his Houfehold:* Article—" For the Marriage of a Princefs."—
" Then pottes of *Ipocrice* to bee ready, and to bee putt into the cupps with *foppe,* and to bee borne to the eftates; and to take a *foppe* and drinke," &c. STEEVENS.

So, in an old canzonet on a wedding, fet to mufick by Morley, 1606:
 " *Sops in wine,* fpice-cakes are a dealing." FARMER.

The fafhion of introducing a bowl of wine into the church at a wedding to be drank by the bride and bridegroom and perfons prefent, was very anciently a conftant ceremony; and, as appears from this paffage, not abolifhed in our author's age. We find it practifed at the magnificent marriage of Queen Mary and Philip, in Winchefter cathedral, 1554: " The trumpetts founded, and they both returned to their traverfes in the quire, and there re-mayned untill maffe was done: at which tyme, *wyne* and *fopes* were hallowed and delyvered to them both." *Collect. Append.* Vol. IV. p. 400, edit. 1770. T. WARTON.

I infert the following quotation merely to fhow that the cuftom remained in Shakfpeare's time. At the marriage of the Elector Palatine to King James's daughter, the   day of February, 1612, we are told by one who affifted at the ceremonial: " —In conclufion, a joy pronounced by the king and queen, and feconded with congratulation of the lords there prefent, which crowned with draughts of *Ippocras* out of a great golden bowle, as an health to the profperity of the marriage, (began by the prince Pa-latine and anfwered by the princefs) After which were ferved up by fix or feven barons fo many bowles filled with wafers, fo much of that work was confummate." *Finet's Philoxenis,* 1656, p. 11.
                REED.

This cuftom is of very high antiquity; for it fubfifted among our Gothick anceftors.—" *Ingreffus domum convivalem fponfus cum pronubo fuo, fumpto poculo, quod maritale vocant, ac paucis a pronubo de mutato vitæ genere prefatis, in fignum conftantiæ, virtutis, de-fenfionis et tutelæ,* propinat *fponfæ & fimul morgennaticam* [dotalitium

But that his beard grew thin and hungerly,
And feem'd to afk him fops as he was drinking.
This done, he took the bride about the neck;
And kifs'd her lips with fuch a clamorous fmack,
That, at the parting, all the church did echo.⁹
I, feeing this,² came thence for very fhame;
And after me, I know, the rout is coming:
Such a mad marriage never was before:
Hark, hark! I hear the minftrels play.   [*Mufick.*

Enter PETRUCHIO, KATHARINA, BIANCA, BAP-
TISTA, HORTENSIO, GRUMIO, *and Train.*

PET. Gentlemen and friends, I thank you for your
          pains:
I know, you think to dine with me to-day,
And have prepar'd great ftore of wedding cheer;
But fo it is, my hafte doth call me hence,
And therefore here I mean to take my leave.

ob virginitatem] *promittit, quod ipfa grato animo recolens, pari ratione & modo, paulo poft mutato in uxorium habitum operculo capitis, ingreffa, poculum, uti noftrates vocant,* uxorium leviter delibans, *amorem, fidem, diligentiam, & fubjectionem promittit.*" Stiernhook *de Jure Sueonum & Gothorum vetufto,* p. 163, quarto, 1672. MALONE.

⁹ *And* kifs'd *her lips with fuch a clamorous fmack,*
    That, at the parting, all the church *did* echo.] It appears from
the following paffage in Marfton's *Infatiate Countefs,* that this was
alfo part of the marriage ceremonial:
    " The *kiffe thou gav'ft me in the church,* here take."
                                        STEEVENS.

This alfo is a very ancient cuftom, as appears from the following
rubrick, with which I was furnifhed by the late Reverend Mr.
Bowle. " Surgant ambo, fponfus et fponfa, et accipiat fponfus
pacem a facerdote, et ferat fponfæ, *ofculans eam,* et neminem alium,
nec ipfe, nec ipfa." *Manuale Sarum,* Paris, 1533, 4to. fol. 69.
                                        MALONE.

² I, *feeing this,*] The old copy has,—*And* I *feeing*—. *And* was
probably caught from the beginning of the next line. The
emendation is Sir T. Hanmer's. MALONE.

Bap. Is't poffible, you will away to-night?

Pet. I muft away to-day, before night come :—
Make it no wonder; if you knew my bufinefs,
You would entreat me rather go than ftay.
And, honeft company, I thank you all,
That have beheld me give away myfelf
To this moft patient, fweet, and virtuous wife:
Dine with my father, drink a health to me;
For I muft hence, and farewell to you all.

Tra. Let us entreat you ftay 'till after dinner.

Pet. It may not be.

Gre.   Let me entreat you.[3]

Pet. It cannot be.

Kath.   Let me entreat you.

Pet. I am content.

Kath.   Are you content to ftay?

Pet. I am content you fhall entreat me ftay;
But yet not ftay, entreat me how you can.

Kath. Now, if you love me, ftay.

Pet.   Grumio, my horfes.[4]

Gru. Ay, fir, they be ready; the oats have eaten
the horfes.[5]

---

[3] *Let me entreat you.*] At the end of this fpeech, as well as of the next but one, a fyllable is wanting to complete the meafure. I have no doubt of our poet's having written—in both inftances—
Let me entreat you ftay. STEEVENS.

[4] —— *my horfes.*] Old copy—*horfe.* STEEVENS.

[5] —— *the oats have eaten the horfes.*] There is ftill a ludicrous expreffion ufed when horfes have ftaid fo long in a place as to have eaten more than they are worth—viz. that *that their heads are too big for the ftable-door.* I fuppofe Grumio has fome fuch meaning, though it is more openly expreffed, as follows, in the original play:

" *Enter* Ferando *and* Kate, *and* Alfonfo *and* Polidor, *and* Emilia,
and Aurelius *and* Phylema.

" *Feran.* Father, farewel; my *Kate* and I muft home:

KATH. Nay, then,
Do what thou canſt, I will not go to-day;
No, nor to-morrow, nor till⁴ I pleaſe myſelf.
The door is open, ſir, there lies your way,

" Sirrha, go make ready my horſe preſently.
" *Alfon.* Your horſe! what ſon, I hope you do but jeſt;
" I am ſure you wil not go ſo ſuddainely.
" *Kate.* Let him go or tarry, I am reſolv'd to ſtay;
" And not to travel on my wedding day.
" *Feran.* Tut, *Kate*, I tel thee we muſt needes go home:
" Vilaine, haſt thou ſadled my horſe?
" *San.* Which horſe? your curtall?
" *Feran.* Souns you ſlave, ſtand you prating here?
" Saddle the bay gelding for your miſtris.
" *Kate.* Not for me, for I wil not go.
" *San. The oſtler will not let me have him: you owe ten pence*
" *For his meate, and 6 pence for ſtuffing my miſtris ſaddle.*
" *Feran.* Here, villaine; goe pay him ſtrait.
" *San.* Shall I give them another pecke of lavender?
" *Feran.* Out ſlave, and bring them preſently to the dore.
" *Alfon.* Why ſon, I hope at leaſt youle dine with us.
" *San.* I pray you, maſter, lets ſtay til dinner be done.
" *Feran.* Sounes vilaine, art thou here yet?   [*Exit* Sander.
" Come, *Kate*, our dinner is provided at home.
" *Kate.* But not for me, for here I meane to dine:
" Ile have my wil in this as wel as you;
" Though you in madding mood would leave your frinds,
" Deſpite of you Ile tarry with them ſtill.
" *Feran.* I *Kate* ſo thou ſhalt, but at ſome other time:
" When as thy ſiſters here ſhall be eſpousd,
" Then thou and I wil keepe our wedding-day,
" In better ſort then now we can provide;
" For heere I promiſe thee before them all,
" We will ere longe returne to them againe:
" Come, *Kate*, ſtand not on termes; we will away;
" This is my day, to-morrow thou ſhalt rule,
" And I will doe whatever thou commandes.
" Gentlemen, farewell, wee'l take our leaves;
" It will be late before that we come home.
                              [*Exeunt* Ferando *and* Kate.
" *Pol.* Farewell *Ferando*, ſince you will be gone.
" *Alfon.* So mad a couple did I never ſee," &c.   STEEVENS.

⁴ —— nor *till* —] Old copy—*not* till. Correcſted by Mr. Rowe.
                                              MALONE.

You may be jogging, whiles your boots are green;
For me, I'll not be gone, 'till I pleafe myfelf:—
'Tis like, you'll prove a jolly furly groom,
That take it on you at the firft fo roundly.

 Per. O, Kate, content thee; pr'ythee, be not
    angry.

 Kath. I will be angry; What haft thou to do?—
Father, be quiet; he fhall ftay my leifure.

 Gre. Ay, marry, fir: now it begins to work.

 Kath. Gentlemen, forward to the bridal dinner:—
I fee, a woman may be made a fool,
If fhe had not a fpirit to refift.

 Per. They fhall go forward, Kate, at thy com-
    mand:——
Obey the bride, you that attend on her:
Go to the feaft, revel and domineer,
Caroufe full meafure to her maidenhead,
Be mad and merry,——or go hang yourfelves;
But for my bonny Kate, fhe muft with me.
Nay, look not big, nor ftamp, nor ftare, nor fret;
I will be mafter of what is mine own:
She is my goods, my chattels; fhe is my houfe,
My houfhold-ftuff, my field, my barn,[5]
My horfe, my ox, my afs,[6] my any thing;
And here fhe ftands, touch her whoever dare;
I'll bring mine action on the proudeft he
That ftops my way in Padua.——Grumio,
Draw forth thy weapon, we're befet with thieves;

---

 [5] *My houfhold-ftuff, my field, my barn,*] This defective verfe
might be completed by reading, with Hanmer—
  She is *my houfhold-ftuff, my field, my barn*;
or,
   My houfhold-ftuff, my field, my barn, my ftable—. Steevens.

 [6] —— *my houfe,*——*my ox, my afs,*] Alluding to the tenth
commandment: "—thou fhalt not covet thy neighbour's *houfe,*——
nor his *ox,* nor his *afs,*—" Ritson.

Rescue thy mistress, if thou be a man :—
Fear not, sweet wench, they shall not touch thee, Kate;
I'll buckler thee against a million.

    [*Exeunt* PETRUCHIO, KATHARINE, *and* GRUMIO.

BAP. Nay, let them go, a couple of quiet ones.

GRE. Went they not quickly, I should die with
        laughing.

TRA. Of all mad matches, never was the like!

LUC. Mistress, what's your opinion of your sister?

BIAN. That, being mad herself, she's madly
        mated.

GRE. I warrant him, Petruchio is Kated.

BAP. Neighbours and friends, though bride and
        bridegroom wants
For to supply the places at the table,
You know, there wants no junkets at the feast;—
Lucentio, you shall supply the bridegroom's place;
And let Bianca take her sister's room.

TRA. Shall sweet Bianca practise how to bride it?

BAP. She shall, Lucentio.—Come, gentlemen
        let's go.   [*Exeunt.*

ACT IV. SCENE I.

A Hall in Petruchio's *Country House.*

Enter GRUMIO.

GRU. Fie, fie, on all tired jades! on all mad
masters! and all foul ways! Was ever man so
beaten? was ever man so ray'd?[5] was ever man so

---

    [5] *——was ever man so* ray'd?] That is, was ever man so mark'd
with lashes. JOHNSON.

weary? I am fent before to make a fire, and they are coming after to warm them. Now, were not I a little pot, and foon hot,[6] my very lips might freeze to my teeth, my tongue to the roof of my mouth, my heart in my belly, ere I fhould come by a fire to thaw me:—But, I, with blowing the fire, fhall warm myfelf; for, confidering the wea_ther, a taller man than I will take cold. Holla, hoa! Curtis!

Enter CURTIS.

CURT. Who is that, calls fo coldly?

GRU. A piece of ice: If thou doubt it, thou may'ft flide from my fhoulder to my heel, with no greater a run but my head and my neck. A fire, good Curtis.

CURT. Is my mafter and his wife coming, Grumio?

GRU. O, ay, Curtis, ay: and therefore fire, fire; caft on no water.[7]

It rather means *bewray'd*, i. e. made dirty. So, Spenfer fpeaking of a fountain:

"Which fhe increafed with her bleeding heart,
"And the clean waves with purple gore did *ray*."

Again, B. III. c. viii. ft. 32:

"Who whiles the piteous lady up did rife,
"Ruffled and foully *ray'd* with filthy foil." TOLLET.

So, in *Summer's laft Will and Teftament*, 1600: "Let there be a few rufhes laid in the place where Backwinter fhall tumble, for fear of *raying* his clothes." STEEVENS.

[6] —— *a little pot, and foon hot*,] This is a proverbial expreffion. It is introduced in *The Ifle of Gulls*, 1606:

"—— Though I be but a *little pot*, I fhall be as *foon hot* as another." STEEVENS.

[7] —— *fire, fire; caft on no water.*] There is an old popular catch of three parts in thefe words:

"Scotland burneth, Scotland burneth.
"Fire, fire;——Fire, fire;
"Caft on fome more water." BLACKSTONE.

CURT. Is she so hot a shrew as she's reported?

GRU. She was, good Curtis, before this frost: but, thou know'st, winter tames man, woman, and beast; for it hath tam'd my old master, and my new mistress, and myself, fellow Curtis.[8]

CURT. Away, you three-inch fool![9] I am no beast.

GRU. Am I but three inches? why, thy horn is

---

[8] —— *winter tames man, woman, and beast; for it hath tam'd my old master, and my new mistress, and* myself, *fellow Curtis.* &c.] " *Winter,* says Grumio, tames *man, woman, and beast*; for it has tamed my old master, my new mistress, and *myself,* fellow *Curtis.*——*Away, you three-inch fool, replies Curtis, I am no beast.*" Why, asks Dr. Warburton, had Grumio called him one? he alters therefore *myself* to *thyself,* and all the editors follow him. But there is no necessity; if Grumio calls *himself* a *beast,* and *Curtis, fellow;* surely he calls *Curtis a beast* likewise. Malvolio takes this sense of the word, " let this *fellow* be look'd to!——*Fellow!* not *Malvolio,* after my degree, but *fellow!*"

In Ben Jonson's *Case is Altered,* " What says my *Fellow Onion?*" quoth *Christophero.*—" All of a house, replies *Onion,* but not *fellows.*"

In the old play, called *The Return from Parnassus,* we have a curious passage, which shows the opinion of contemporaries concerning the *learning* of Shakspeare; this use of the word *fellow* brings it to my remembrance. Burbage and Kempe are introduced to teach the university-men the art of acting, and are represented (particularly Kempe) as *leaden spouts—very illiterate.* " Few of the university (says Kempe) pen plays well; *they* smell too much of that writer *Ovid,* and that writer *Metamorphosis:*—why here's our *Fellow Shakspeare* puts them all down." FARMER.

The sentence delivered by Grumio, is proverbial:
" Wedding, and ill-wintering, tame both man and beast."
See Ray's *Collection.* STEEVENS.

[9] *Away, you* three-inch *fool!*] i. e. with a skull three inches thick; a phrase taken from the thicker sort of planks. WARBURTON.

This contemptuous expression alludes to Grumio's diminutive size. He has already mentioned it himself:—" Now, were not I a *little pot*—." His answer likewise, " —and so *long* am I, at the least,"—shows that this is the meaning, and that Dr. Warburton was mistaken in supposing that these words allude to the *thickness* of Grumio's *skull.* MALONE.

a foot; and fo long am I, at the leaſt.[2] But wilt thou make a fire, or ſhall I complain on thee to our miſtreſs, whoſe hand (ſhe being now at hand,) thou ſhalt ſoon feel, to thy cold comfort, for being ſlow in thy hot office.

Curt. I pr'ythee, good Grumio, tell me, How goes the world?

Gru. A cold world, Curtis, in every office but thine; and, therefore, fire: Do thy duty, and have thy duty; for my maſter and miſtreſs are almoſt frozen to death.

Curt. There's fire ready; And therefore, good Grumio, the news?

Gru. Why, *Jack boy! ho boy!*[3] and as much news as thou wilt.[4]

---

[2] —*why, thy horn is a foot; and ſo long am I, at the leaſt.*] Though all the copies agree in this reading, Mr. Theobald ſays, yet he cannot find what horn Curtis had; therefore he alters it to *my horn.* But the common reading is right, and the meaning is, that he had made Curtis a cuckold. WARBURTON.

[3] ——*Jack boy! ho boy!*] is the beginning of an old round in three parts.

SIR J. HAWKINS.

[4] ——*as* thou wilt.] Old copy—*wilt thou.* Corrected by the editor of the ſecond folio. MALONE.

Cur. Come, you are so full of conycatching:—

Gru. Why therefore, fire; for I have caught extreme cold. Where's the cook? is supper ready, the house trimm'd, rushes strew'd, cobwebs swept; the servingmen in their new fustian, their white stockings,[5] and every officer his wedding-garment on? Be the jacks fair within, the jills fair without,[6] the carpets laid,[7] and every thing in order?

Cur. All ready; And therefore, I pray thee, news?[8]

[5] —— their *white stockings.*] The old copy reads—*the white*—. Corrected by the editor of the third folio. MALONE.

[6] —— *Be the Jacks fair within, the Jills fair without,*] i. e. are the drinking vessels clean, and the maid servants dress'd? But the Oxford editor alters it thus:
Are the Jacks fair without, the Jills fair within?
What his conceit is in this, I confess I know not. WARBURTON.

Sir T. Hanmer's meaning seems to be this: " Are the men who are waiting without the house to receive my master, dress'd; and the maids, who are waiting within, dress'd too?"

I believe the poet meant to play upon the words *Jack* and *Jill*, which signify *two drinking measures*, as well as *men* and *maid servants.* The distinction made in the questions concerning them, was owing to this: The *Jacks* being of leather, could not be made to appear beautiful on the outside, but were very apt to contract foulness within; whereas, the *Jills*, being of metal, were expected to be kept bright externally, and were not liable to dirt on the inside, like the leather.

The quibble on the former of these words I find in *The Atheist's Tragedy*, by C. Tourner, 1611:
" ——have you drunk yourselves mad?
" 1 *Ser.* My lord, the *Jacks* abus'd me.
" *D'Am.* I think they are *Jacks* indeed that have abus'd thee."
Again, in *The Puritan*, 1607: " I owe money to several hostesses, and you know such *jills* will quickly be upon a man's *jack.*"
In this last instance, the allusion to drinking measures is evident.
STEEVENS.

[7] —— *the carpets laid.*] In our author's time it was customary to cover tables with carpets. Floors, as appears from the present passage and others, were strewed with rushes. MALONE.

[8] —— *I pray* thee, *news?*] I believe the author wrote—*I pray, thy news.* MALONE.

Gru. Firſt, know, my horſe is tired; my maſter and miſtreſs fallen out.

Curt. How?

Gru. Out of their ſaddles into the dirt; And thereby hangs a tale.

Curt. Let's ha't, good Grumio.

Gru. Lend thine ear.

Curt. Here.

Gru. There.   [*Striking him.*

Curt. This is⁹ to feel a tale, not to hear a tale.

Gru. And therefore 'tis called, a ſenſible tale: and this cuff was but to knock at your ear, and be-ſeech liſtening. Now I begin: *Imprimis*, we came down a foul hill, my maſter riding behind my miſ-treſs :—

Curt. Both on one horſe?ᵃ

Gru. What's that to thee?

Curt. Why, a horſe.

Gru. Tell thou the tale :——But hadſt thou not croſs'd me, thou ſhould'ſt have heard how her horſe fell, and ſhe under her horſe; thou ſhould'ſt have heard, in how miry a place: how ſhe was bemoil'd;³ how he left her with the horſe upon her; how he beat me becauſe her horſe ſtumbled; how ſhe waded through the dirt to pluck him off me; how he ſwore; how ſhe pray'd—that never pray'd before;⁴

---

⁹ *This is*—] Old copy—*This 'tis*—. Correfted by Mr. Pope.
                                                    MALONE.

ᵃ ——on *one horſe?*] The old copy reads—*of* one horſe?
                                                    STEEVENS.

³ ——*bemoil'd*;] i. e. be-draggled; bemired. STEEVENS.

⁴ ——*how he ſwore; how ſhe pray'd—that never pray'd before*;] Theſe lines, with little variation, are found in the old copy of *King Leir*, publiſhed before that of Shakſpeare. STEEVENS.

how I cried; how the horfes ran away; how her bridle was burft;[4] how I loft my crupper;—with many things of worthy memory; which now fhall die in oblivion, and thou return unexperienced to thy grave.

Curt. By this reckoning, he is more fhrew than fhe.

Gru. Ay; and that thou and the proudeft of you all fhall find, when he comes home. But what talk I of this?—call forth Nathaniel, Jofeph, Nicholas, Philip, Walter, Sugarfop, and the reft : let their heads be fleekly combed, their blue coats brufhed,[5] and their garters of an indifferent knit :[6]

---

[4] —*was* burft;] i. e. broken. So, in the firft fcene of this play : " You will not pay for the glaffes you have *burft ?*"
STEEVENS.

[5] —*their* blue coats *brufh'd,*] The drefs of fervants at the time. So, in Decker's *Belman's Night Walkes,* fig. E. 3 : " —the other act their parts in *blew coates,* as they were their *ferving men,* though indeed they be all fellowes." Again, in *The Curtain Drawer of the World,* 1612, p. 2 : " Not a *ferving man* dare appeare in a *blew coat,* not becaufe it is the livery of charity, but left he fhould be thought a retainer to their enemy." REED.

[6] —*garters of an* indifferent *knit :*] What is the fenfe of this I know not, unlefs it means, that their *garters* fhould be *fellows : indifferent,* or *not different,* one from the other. JOHNSON.

This is rightly explained. So, in *Hamlet :*
" As the *indifferent* children of the earth."
Again, in *King Richard II :*
" Look on my wrongs with an *indifferent* eye."
i. e. an impartial one. STEEVENS.

Perhaps by " garters of an *indifferent* knit," the author meant *parti-coloured* garters ; garters of a *different* knit. In Shakfpeare's time *indifferent* was fometimes ufed for *different.* Thus Speed, (*Hift. of Gr. Brit.* p. 770,) defcribing the French and Englifh armies at the battle of Agincourt, fays, " — the face of thefe hoafts were diverfe and *indifferent.*"

That garters of a *different knit* were formerly worn, appears from TEXNOΓAMIA, *or the Marriages of the Arts,* by Barton Holyday, 1630, where the following ftage direction occurs. " Phantaftes in let them curt'fy with their left legs; and not prefume to touch a hair of my mafter's horfe-tail, till they kifs their hands. Are they all ready?

CURT. They are.

GRU. Call them forth.

CURT. Do you hear, ho? you muft meet my maf-ter, to countenance my miftrefs.

GRU. Why, fhe hath a face of her own.

CURT. Who knows not that?

GRU. Thou, it feems; that call'ft for company to countenance her.

CURT. I call them forth to credit her.

GRU. Why, fhe comes to borrow nothing of them.

Enter feveral Servants.

NATH. Welcome home, Grumio.

PHIL. How now, Grumio?

Jos. What, Grumio!

NICH. Fellow Grumio!

NATH. How now, old lad?

GRU. Welcome, you;—how now, you;—what, you;—fellow, you;—and thus much for greeting. Now, my fpruce companions, is all ready, and all things neat?

NATH. All things is ready:[7] How near is our mafter?

a branched velvet jerkin,—red filk ftockings, and *parti-coloured garters.*" MALONE.

[7] *All things is ready:*] Though in general it is proper to correct the falfe concords that are found in almoft every page of the old copy, here it would be improper; becaufe the language fuits the character. MALONE.

GRU. E'en at hand, alighted by this; and therefore be not,——Cock's paffion, filence!——I hear my mafter.

Enter PETRUCHIO *and* KATHARINA.[8]

PET. Where be thefe knaves? What, no man at door,[9]

---

[8] *Enter* Petruchio, &c.] Thus the original play:

    " *Enter* Ferando *and* Kate.

" *Ferand.* Now welcome *Kate.* Wheres thefe villaines,
" Heere? what, not fupper yet upon the boord!
" Nor table fpread, nor nothing done at all!
" Where's that villaine that I fent before?
    " *San.* Now, adfum, fir.
    " *Feran.* Come hither you villaine; Ile cut your nofe
" You rogue: help me off with my bootes: wil't pleafe
" You to lay the cloth? Sowns the villaine
" Hurts my foote: pull eafily I fay: yet againe?
    [*He beats them all. They cover the boord, and fetch in the meate.*
" Sowns, burnt and fcorch't! who dreft this meate?
    " *Will.* Forfooth, *John Cooke.*
    [*He throwes downe the table and meate, and all, and beates them all.*
    " *Feran.* Goe, you villaines; bring me fuch meate?
" Out of my fight, I fay, and bear it hence.
" Come, *Kate,* wee'l have other meate provided:
" Is there a fire in my chamber, fir?
    " *San.* I, forfooth.   [*Exeunt* Ferando *and* Kate.
    " *Manent ferving men, and eate up all the meate.*
    " *Tom.* Sownes, I thinke of my confcience my mafter's madde
fince he was married.
    " *Will.* I faft what a box he gave *Sander*
" For pulling off his bootes.
        " *Enter* Ferando *again.*
    " *San.* I hurt his foot for the nonce, man.
    " *Feran.* Did you fo, you damned villaine?
        [*He beates them all out againe.*
" This humour muft I hold me to a while,
" To bridle and holde back my head-ftrong wife,
" With curbes of hunger, eafe, and want of fleepe:
" Nor fleep nor meate fhall fhe enjoy to-night;
" Ile mew her up as men do mew their hawkes,
" And make her gently come unto the lewre:

To hold my ſtirrup, nor to take my horſe!
Where is Nathaniel, Gregory, Philip?——

ALL SERV. Here, here, ſir; here ſir.

PET. Here, ſir! here, ſir! here, ſir! here, ſir!—
You loggerheaded and unpoliſh'd grooms!
What, no attendance? no regard? no duty?—
Where is the fooliſh knave I ſent before?

GRU. Here, ſir; as fooliſh as I was before.

PET. You peaſant ſwain! you whoreſon malt-
  horſe drudge!
Did I not bid thee meet me in the park,
And bring along theſe raſcal knaves with thee?

GRU. Nathaniel's coat, ſir, was not fully made,
And Gabriel's pumps were all unpink'd i' the heel;
There was no link to colour Peter's hat,[2]
And Walter's dagger was not come from ſheath-
  ing:
There were none fine, but Adam, Ralph, and Gre-
  gory;
The reſt were ragged, old, and beggarly;
Yet, as they are, here are they come to meet you.

PET. Go, raſcals, go, and fetch my ſupper in.—
       [*Exeunt ſome of the* Servants.

 " Were ſhe as ſtubborne, or as full of ſtrength
 " As was the Thracian horſe Alcides tamde,
 " That king *Egeus* fed with fleſh of men,
 " Yet would I pull her downe and make her come,
 " As hungry hawkes do flie unto their lewre."
           [*Exit.*
        STEEVENS.

  9 ——*at* door,] *Door* is here, and in other places, uſed as a
diſſyllable. MALONE.

  2 ——*no* link *to colour Peter's hat,*] A *link* is a torch of pitch.
Greene, in his *Mihil Mumchance,* ſays—" This cozenage is uſed
likewiſe in ſelling old hats found upon dung-hills, inſtead of newe,
blackt over with the *ſmoake of an old linke.*" STEEVENS.

VOL. VI.   K k

Where is the life that late I led[3]——   [Sings.
Where are thofe——Sit down, Kate, and wel-
    come.
Soud, foud, foud, foud![4]

Re-enter Servants, *with fupper.*

Why, when, I fay?—Nay, good fweet Kate, be
    merry.
Off with my boots, you rogues, you villains; When?

    It was the friar of orders grey,[5]   [Sings.
    As he forth walked on his way :——

[3] *Where,* &c.] A fcrap of fome old ballad. Ancient Piftol elfewhere quotes the fame line. In an old black letter book intituled,
" *A gorgious Gallery of Gallant Inventions,* London, 1578, 4to. is a
fong to the tune of *Where is the life that late I led.*" RITSON.

This ballad was peculiarly fuited to Petruchio's prefent fituation:
for it appears to have been defcriptive of the ftate of a lover who
had newly refigned his freedom. In an old collection of Sonnets,
entitled *A handeful of pleafant delites, containing fundrie new fonts,*
&c. by Clement Robinfon, 1584, is " Dame Beautie's replie to
the *lover late at libertie,* and now complaineth himfelfe to be her
captive, intituled, *Where is the life that late I led:*
    " The life that erft thou led'ft, my friend,
    " Was pleafant to thine eyes," &c. MALONE.

[4] *Soud, foud,* &c.] That is, *fweet, fweet.* *Soot,* and fometimes
footh, is *fweet.* So, in Milton, *to fing foothly,* is to fing fweetly.
    JOHNSON.

  So, in *Promos and Caffandra,* 1578:
    " He'll hang handfome young men for the *foote* finne of love."
    STEEVENS.

These words feem merely intended to denote the humming of a
tune, or fome kind of ejaculation, for which it is not neceffary to
find out a meaning. M. MASON.

This, I believe, is a word coined by our poet, to exprefs the
noife made by a perfon heated and fatigued. MALONE.

[5] *It was the friar of orders grey,*] Difperfed through Shakfpeare's
plays are many little fragments of ancient ballads, the entire copies
of which cannot now be recovered. Many of thefe being of the

7

Out, out, you rogue![6] you pluck my foot awry:
Take that, and mend the plucking off the other.—
[Strikes him.

Be merry, Kate:—Some water, here; what ho!—
Where's my fpaniel Troilus?—Sirrah, get you
    hence,
And bid my coufin Ferdinand come hither:[7]—
[Exit Servant.

One, Kate, that you muft kifs, and be acquainted
    with.—
Where are my flippers?—Shall I have fome
    water?   [A bafon is prefented to him.
Come, Kate, and wafh,[8] and welcome heartily:—
[Servant lets the ewer fall.

moft beautiful and pathetic fimplicity, Dr. Percy has felected fome
of them, and connected them together with a few fupplemental
ftanzas; a work, which at once demonftrates his own poetical abilities, as well as his refpect to the truely venerable remains of our
moft ancient bards. STEEVENS.

[6] *Out, out, you rogue!*] The fecond word was inferted by Mr.
Pope, to complete the metre. When a word occurs twice in the
fame line, the compofitor very frequently omits one of them.
MALONE.

[7] *And bid my coufin Ferdinand come hither:*] This coufin Ferdinand, who does not make his perfonal appearance on the fcene,
is mentioned, I fuppofe, for no other reafon than to give Katharine
a hint, that he could keep even his own relations in order, and
make them obedient as his fpaniel Troilus. STEEVENS.

[8] *Come, Kate, and* wafh,] It was the cuftom in our author's time,
(and long before,) to wafh the hands immediately before dinner and
fupper, as well as afterwards. So, in Ives's *Select Papers*, p. 139:
" And after that the Queen [Elizabeth, the wife of K. Henry VII.]
was retourned and *wafhed*, the Archbifhop faid grace." Again,
in Florio's *Second Frutes*, 1591: C. " The meate is coming, let
us fit downe. S. I would wafh firft—. What ho, bring us fome
water to wafh our hands.—Give me a faire, cleane and white
towel." From the fame dialogue it appears that it was cuftomary
to wafh after meals likewife, and that fetting the water on the
table was then (as at prefent) peculiar to Great Britain and Ireland.
" Bring fome water (fays one of the company) when dinner is

K k 2

You whoreſon villain! will you let it fall?

[*Strikes him.*

KATH. Patience, I pray you; 'twas a fault unwilling.

PET. A whoreſon, beetleheaded, flapear'd knave!
Come, Kate, ſit down; I know you have a ſto-
mach.
Will you give thanks, ſweet Kate; or elſe ſhall I?—
What is this? mutton?

1 *SERV.* Ay.

PET. Who brought it?

1 *SERV.* I.

PET. 'Tis burnt; and ſo is all the meat:
What dogs are theſe?—Where is the raſcal cook?
How durſt you, villains, bring it from the dreſſer,
And ſerve it thus to me that love it not?
There, take it to you, trenchers, cups, and all:

[*Throws the meat, &c. about the ſtage.*

You heedleſs joltheads, and unmanner'd ſlaves!
What, do you grumble? I'll be with you ſtraight.

KATH. I pray you, huſband, be not ſo diſquiet;
The meat was well, if you were ſo contented.

ended,) to waſh our hands, and ſet the bacin upon the board, *after
the Engliſh faſhion*, that all may waſh."
    That it was the practice to waſh the hands immediately before
ſupper, as well as before dinner, is aſcertained by the following
paſſage in *The Fountayne of Fame, erected in an Orcharde of amorous
adventures*, by Anthony Munday, 1580: "Then was our *ſupper*
brought up very orderly, and ſhe brought me *water to waſhe my
handes*. And after I had waſhed, I ſat downe, and ſhe alſo; but
concerning what good cheere we had, I need not make good
report." MALONE.

    As our anceſtors eat with their fingers, which might not be over-
clean before meals, and after them muſt be greaſy, we cannot
wonder at ſuch repeated ablutions. STEEVENS.

Pet. I tell thee, Kate, 'twas burnt, and dried
    away;
And I exprefsly am forbid to touch it,
For it engenders choler, planteth anger;
And better 'twere, that both of us did faft,—
Since, of ourfelves, ourfelves are cholerick,—
Than feed it with fuch over-roafted flefh.
Be patient; to-morrow it fhall be mended,
And, for this night, we'll faft for company:—
Come, I will bring thee to thy bridal chamber.

    [*Exeunt* PETRUCHIO, KATHARINA, *and* CURTIS.

Nath. [*Advancing.*] Peter, didft ever fee the like?

Peter. He kills her in her own humour.

Re-enter CURTIS.

Gru. Where is he?

Curt. In her chamber,
Making a fermon of continency to her:
And rails, and fwears, and rates; that fhe, poor foul,
Knows not which way to ftand, to look, to fpeak;
And fits as one new-rifen from a dream.
Away, away! for he is coming hither.   [*Exeunt.*

Re-enter PETRUCHIO.

Pet. Thus have I politickly begun my reign,
And 'tis my hope to end fuccefsfully:
My faulcon now is fharp, and paffing empty;
And, till fhe ftoop, fhe muft not be full-gorg'd,[9]

---

[9] ——*full-gorg'd*, &c.] A hawk too much fed was never tractable. So, in the *Tragedie of Cræfus*, 1604:
    " And like a hooded hawk, *gorg'd* with vain pleafures,
    " At random flies, and wots not where he is."

For then fhe never looks upon her lure.
Another way I have to man my haggard,[2]
To make her come, and know her keeper's call;
That is,—to watch her, as we watch thefe kites,[3]
That bate,[4] and beat, and will not be obedient.
She eat no meat to-day, nor none fhall eat;
Laft night fhe flept not, nor to night fhe fhall not;
As with the meat, fome undeferved fault
I'll find about the making of the bed;
And here I'll fling the pillow, there the bolfter,
This way the coverlet, another way the fheets:—
Ay, and amid this hurly, I intend,[5]
That all is done in reverend care of her;
And, in conclufion, fhe fhall watch all night:
And, if fhe chance to nod, I'll rail, and brawl,

Again, in *The Booke of Haukyng*, bl. l. no date:
" —ye fhall fay your hauke is *full-gorg'd*, and not cropped."
The *lure* was only a thing ftuffed like that kind of bird which
the hawk was defigned to purfue. The ufe of the *lure* was to tempt
him back after he had flown. STEEVENS.

[2] — *to* man *my* haggard,] A *baggard* is a *wild bawk*; to *man*
a hawk is to *tame* her. JOHNSON.

[3] — watch *ber, as we* watch *thefe kites,*] Thus in the fame
book of *Haukyng*, &c. bl. l. commonly called, *The Book of St.
Albans:* " And then the fame night after the teding, *wake* her all
night, and on the morrowe all day."
Again, in *The Lady Errant*, by Cartwright: " We'll keep you
as they do *bawks*; *watching* you until you leave your wildnefs."
STEEVENS.

[4] *That* bate,] i. e. flutter. So, in *K. Henry IV.* P. I:
" *Bated* like eagles having lately bath'd." STEEVENS.

To *bate* is to flutter as a hawk does when it fwoops upon its
prey. Minfheu fuppofes it to be derived either from *batre*, Fr.
to beat, or from *s'abatre*, to defcend. MALONE.

[5] — *amid this hurly, I* intend,] *Intend* is fometimes ufed by
our author for *pretend*, and is, I believe, fo ufed here. So, in *King
Richard III:*
" Tremble and ftart at wagging of a ftraw,
" *Intending* deep fufpicion." MALONE.

And with the clamour keep her ſtill awake.
This is a way to kill a wife with kindneſs;
And thus I'll curb her mad and headſtrong hu-
  mour:——
He that knows better how to tame a ſhrew,
Now let him ſpeak; 'tis charity, to ſhow. [*Exit.*

S C E N E II.[6]

Padua. *Before* Baptiſta's *Houſe.*

Enter TRANIO *and* HORTENSIO.

TRA. Is't poſſible, friend Licio, that Bianca[7]
Doth fancy any other but Lucentio?
I tell you, ſir, ſhe bears me fair in hand.

[6] *Scene II. Padua, &c.*] This ſcene, Mr. Pope, upon what authority I cannot pretend to gueſs, has in his editions made the *firſt* of the *fifth* act: in doing which, he has ſhown the very power and force of criticiſm. The conſequence of this judicious regu-lation is, that two unpardonable abſurdities are fixed upon the author, which he could not poſſibly have committed. For, in the firſt place, by this ſhuffling the ſcenes out of their true poſition, we find Hortenſio, in the fourth Act, already gone from Baptiſta's to Petruchio's country-houſe; and afterwards in the beginning of the fifth Act we find him firſt forming the reſolution of quitting Bianca; and Tranio immediately informs us, he is gone to the Taming-ſchool to Petruchio. There is a figure, indeed, in rhe-torick, called ὕϛϵρον πρότϵρον; but this is an abuſe of it, which the rhetoricians will never adopt upon Mr. Pope's authority. Again, by this miſ-placing, the Pedant makes his firſt entrance, and quits the ſtage with Tranio in order to go and dreſs himſelf like Vincentio, whom he was to perſonate: but his ſecond *entrance* is upon the very heels of his *exit*; and without any interval of an *act*, or one word intervening, he comes out again equipped like Vincentio. If ſuch a critic be fit to publiſh a ſtage-writer, I ſhall not envy Mr. Pope's admirers, if they ſhould think fit to applaud his ſa-gacity. I have replaced the ſcenes in that order, in which I found them in the old books. THEOBALD.

[7] ——*that Bianca*——] The old copy redundantly reads—that *miſtreſs* Bianca. STEEVENS.

Hor. Sir, to fatisfy you in what I have faid,
Stand by, and mark the manner of his teaching.
[*They ſtand aſide.*

Enter BIANCA *and* LUCENTIO.

Luc. Now, miftrefs, profit you in what you read?

Bian. What, mafter, read you? firft, refolve me
that.

Luc. I read that I profefs, the art to love.

Bian. And may you prove, fir, mafter of your
art!

Luc. While you, fweet dear, prove miftrefs of
my heart. [*They retire.*

Hor. Quick proceeders, marry![7] Now, tell me,
I pray,
You that durft fwear that your miftrefs Bianca
Lov'd none[8] in the world fo well as Lucentio.

Tra. O defpiteful love! unconftant woman-
kind!—
I tell thee, Licio, this is wonderful.

Hor. Miftake no more: I am not Licio,
Nor a mufician, as I feem to be;
But one that fcorn to live in this difguife,
For fuch a one as leaves a gentleman,
And makes a god of fuch a cullion:
Know, fir, that I am call'd—Hortenfio.

Tra. Signior Hortenfio, I have often heard
Of your entire affection to Bianca;

---

[7] *Quick* proceeders, *marry!*] Perhaps here an equivoque was
intended. To *proceed* Mafter of Arts, &c. is the academical term.
MALONE.

[8] *Lov'd none—*] Old copy—Lov'd *me—.* Mr. Rowe made
this neceffary correction. MALONE.

And fince mine eyes are witnefs of her lightnefs,
I will with you,—if you be fo contented,—
Forfwear Bianca and her love for ever.

Hor. See, how they kifs and court!——Signior
    Lucentio,
Here is my hand, and here I firmly vow—
Never to woo her more; but do forfwear her,
As one unworthy all the former favours
That I have fondly flatter'd her withal.[9]

Tra. And here I take the like unfeigned oath,—
Ne'er to marry with her though fhe would entreat:
Fie on her! fee, how beaftly fhe doth court him.

Hor. 'Would, all the world, but he, had quite
    forfworn!
For me,—that I may furely keep mine oath,
I will be married to a wealthy widow,
Ere three days pafs; which hath as long lov'd me,
As I have lov'd this proud difdainful haggard:
And fo farewell, fignior Lucentio.—
Kindnefs in women, not their beauteous looks,
Shall win my love:—and fo I take my leave,
In refolution as I fwore before.

    [*Exit* Hortensio.—Lucentio *and* Bianca
        advance.

Tra. Miftrefs Bianca, blefs you with fuch grace
As 'longeth to a lover's blefled cafe!
Nay, I have ta'en you napping, gentle love;
And have forfworn you, with Hortenfio.

Bian. Tranio, you jeft; But have you both for-
    fworn me?

Tra. Miftrefs, we have.

Luc.   Then we are rid of Licio.

---

[9] *That I have fondly flatter'd her withal.*] The old copy reads—
them withal. The emendation was made by the editor of the
third folio. MALONE.

Tra. I'faith, he'll have a lufty widow now,
That fhall be woo'd and wedded in a day.

Bian. God give him joy!

Tra. Ay, and he'll tame her.[9]

Bian.   He fays fo, Tranio.

Tra. 'Faith, he is gone unto the taming-fchool.

Bian. The taming-fchool! what, is there fuch a
place?

Tra. Ay, miftrefs, and Petruchio is the mafter;
That teacheth tricks eleven and twenty long,—
To tame a fhrew, and charm her chattering tongue.[2]

Enter BIONDELLO, *running.*

Bion. O mafter, mafter, I have watch'd fo long
That I'm dog-weary; but at laft I fpied
An ancient angel[3] coming down the hill,
Will ferve the turn.

[9] *Ay, and he'll tame her,* &c.] Thus in the original play:
" ——he means to tame his wife ere long.
" *Val.* Hee faies fo.
" *Aurel.* Faith he's gon unto the taming-fchoole.
" *Val.* The taming-fchoole! why is there fuch a place?
" *Aurel.* I; and *Ferando* is the maifter of the fchoole."
                                        STEEVENS.

[2] ——charm *her chattering tongue.*] So, in *King Henry VI.*
P. III:
" Peace, wilful boy, or I will *charm* your tongue."
                                        STEEVENS.

[3] *An ancient* angel—] For *angel* Mr. Theobald, and after him
Sir T. Hanmer and Dr. Warburton, read *engle.* JOHNSON.

It is true that the word *enghle,* which Sir T. Hanmer calls a
gull, (deriving it from *engluer,* Fr. to catch with bird-lime,) is
fometimes ufed by Ben Jonfon. It cannot, however, bear that
meaning at prefent, as Biondello confeffes his ignorance of the
quality of the perfon who is afterwards perfuaded to reprefent the
father of Lucentio. The precife meaning of it is not afcertained
in Jonfon, neither is the word to be found in any of the original

TRA.   What is he, Biondello?

BION. Mafter, a mercatantè, or a pedant,[4]
I know not what; but formal in apparel,
In gait and countenance furely like a father.[5]

copies of Shakfpeare. I have alfo reafon to fuppofe that the true
import of the word *engble* is fuch as can have no connection with
this paffage, and will not bear explanation.

Angel primitively fignifies a *meffenger*, but perhaps this fenfe is
inapplicable to the paffage before us. So, Ben Jonfon, in *The
Sad Shepherd :*

" ——the dear good *angel* of the fpring,
" The nightingale——."

And Chapman, in his tranflation of *Homer*, always calls a meffenger an *angel*. See particularly B. xxiv.

In *The Scornful Lady* of Beaumont and Fletcher, an old ufurer is
indeed called

" —— old *angel* of gold."

It is poffible, however, that inftead of *ancient angel*, our author
might have written—*angel-merchant*, one whofe bufinefs it was to
negociate money. He is afterwards called a *mercatantè*, and profeffes himfelf to be one who has bills of exchange about him.

            STEEVENS.

[4] *Mafter, a* mercatantè, *or a* pedant,] The old editions read
marcantant. The Italian word *mercatantè* is frequently ufed in the
old plays for a merchant, and therefore I have made no fcruple of
placing it here. The modern editors, who printed the word as
they found it fpelt in the folio, were obliged to fupply a fyllable
to make out the verfe, which the Italian pronunciation renders unneceffary. A *pedant* was the common name for a teacher of languages.
So, in *Cynthia's Revels*, by Ben Jonfon: " He loves to have a
fencer, a *pedant*, and a mufician, feen in his lodgings."

            STEEVENS.

Mercatantè,] So, Spenfer, in the third Book of his *Fairy Queen :*
" Sleeves dependant Albanefè wife."
And our author has *Veronesè* in his *Othello*.   FARMER.

——*pedant*,] *Charon*, the fage *Charon*, as Pope calls him,
defcribes a *peaunt*, as fynonymous to a *houfehold fchoolmafter*, and
adds a general character of the fraternity by no means to their
advantage. See *Charon on Wifdom*, 4to. 1640. Lennard's *Tranflation*, p. 158.   REED.

[5] ——*furely* like *a father*.] I know not what he is, fays the
fpeaker, however this is certain, he has the gait and countenance
of a fatherly man.   WARBURTON.

Luc. And what of him, Tranio?

Tra. If he be credulous, and truſt my tale,
I'll make him glad to ſeem Vincentio;
And give aſſurance to Baptiſta Minola,
As if he were the right Vincentio.
Take in your love, and then let me alone.[6]

[*Exeunt* LUCENTIO *and* BIANCA.

Enter a Pedant.

Ped. God ſave you, ſir!

Tra.　　　　And you, ſir! you are welcome.
Travel you far on, or are you at the furtheſt?

Ped. Sir, at the furtheſt for a week or two:
But then up further; and as far as Rome;
And ſo to Tripoly, if God lend me life.

Tra. What countryman, I pray?

Ped.　　　　　　　　Of Mantua.

Tra. Of Mantua, ſir?—marry, God forbid!
And come to Padua, careleſs of your life?

Ped. My life, ſir! how I pray? for that goes hard.

Tra. 'Tis death for any one in Mantua
To come to Padua;[7] Know you not the cauſe?
Your ſhips are ſtaid at Venice; and the duke

The editor of the ſecond folio reads—*ſurly,* which Mr. Theobald
adopted, and has quoted the following lines, addreſſed by Tranio to
the pedant, in ſupport of the emendation:

　　" 'Tis well; and hold your own in any caſe,
　　" With ſuch *auſterity* as *longeth* to a *father*." MALONE.

[6] *Take* in *your love, and then let me alone.*] The old copies
exhibit this line as follows, disjoining it from its predeceſſors.

　　Par. *Take* me *your love, and then let me alone.* STEEVENS.
Corrected by Mr. Theobald. MALONE.

[7] *'Tis death for any one in Mantua,* &c.] So, in *The Comedy of
Errors:*

　　" —— if any Syracuſan born
　　" Come to the bay of Epheſus, he dies." STEEVENS.

(For private quarrel 'twixt your duke and him,)
Hath publifh'd and proclaim'd it openly:
'Tis marvel; but that you're but newly come,
You might have heard it elfe proclaim'd about.

Ped. Alas, fir, it is worfe for me than fo;
For I have bills for money by exchange
From Florence, and muft here deliver them.

Tra. Well, fir, to do you courtefy,
This will I do, and this will I advife you;—
Firft, tell me, have you ever been at Pifa?

Ped. Ay, fir, in Pifa have I often been;
Pifa, renowned for grave citizens.[8]

Tra. Among them, know you one Vincentio?

Ped. I know him not, but I have heard of him;
A merchant of incomparable wealth.

Tra. He is my father, fir; and, footh to fay,
In countenance fomewhat doth refemble you.

Bion. As much as an apple doth an oyfter, and
all one.   [*Afide.*

Tra. To fave your life in this extremity,
This favour will I do you for his fake;
And think it not the worft of all your fortunes,
That you are like to fir Vincentio.
His name and credit fhall you undertake,
And in my houfe you fhall be friendly lodg'd;—
Look, that you take upon you as you fhould;
You underftand me, fir;—fo fhall you ftay
Till you have done your bufinefs in the city:
If this be courtefy, fir, accept of it.

Ped. O, fir, I do; and will repute you ever
The patron of my life and liberty.

Tra. Then go with me, to make the matter good.
This, by the way, I let you underftand;—

---

[8] *Pifa, renowned for grave citizens.*] This line has been already
ufed by Lucentio. See Aɛt I. fc. i. RITSON.

My father is here look'd for every day,
To pafs affurance [8] of a dower in marriage
'Twixt me and one Baptifta's daughter here:
In all thefe circumftances I'll inftruct you:
Go with me, fir, to clothe you as becomes you.[9]

[*Exeunt.*

SCENE III.

A Room in Petruchio's *Houfe.*

Enter KATHARINA *and* GRUMIO.[2]

GRU. No, no, forfooth; I dare not, for my life.

KATH. The more my wrong, the more his fpite
appears:

[8] *To pafs* affurance—] *To pafs affurance* means to make a con-
veyance or deed. Deeds are by law-writers called, " The common *affurances* of the realm," becaufe thereby each man's property
is *affured* to him. So, in a fubfequent fcene of this act, " they
are bufied about a counterfeit *affurance.*" MALONE.

[9] *Go with me,* fir, *&c.*] Thus the fecond folio. The firft
omits the word—*fir.* STEEVENS.

Go with me, &c.] There is an old comedy called *Suppofes,*
tranflated from Ariofto, by George Gafcoigne. Thence Shakfpeare borrowed this part of the plot, (as well as fome of the
phrafeology) though Theobald pronounces it his own invention.
There likewife he found the quaint name of Petruchio. My young
mafter and his man exchange habits, and perfuade a *Scenæfe,* as he
is called, to perfonate *the father,* exactly as in this play, by the
pretended danger of his coming from *Sienna* to *Ferrara,* contrary
to the order of the government. FARMER.

In the fame play our author likewife found the name of *Licio.*
MALONE.

[2] *Enter* Katharina *and* Grumio.] Thus the original play:
" *Enter* Sander *and his miftris.*
" *San.* Come, miftris.
" *Kate.* Sander, I prethee helpe me to fome meat;
" I am fo faint that I can fcarcely ftand.
" *San.* I marry miftris: but you know my maifter
" Has given me a charge that you muft eat nothing,
" But that which he himfelf giveth you.

What, did he marry me to famifh me?
Beggars, that come unto my father's door,

" *Kate.* Why man, thy mafter needs never know it.

" *San.* You fay true, indeed. Why looke you, miftris;

" What fay you to a pece of bieffe and muftard now?

" *Kate.* Why, I fay, 'tis excellent meat; canft thou helpe me to fome?

" *San.* I, I could helpe you to fome, but that I doubt

" The muftard is too chollerick for you.

" But what fay you to a fheepes head and garlicke?

" *Kate.* Why any thing; I care not what it be.

" *San.* I, but the garlicke I doubt will make your breath ftincke; and then my mafter will courfe me for letting you eate it. But what fay you to a fat capon?

" *Kate.* That's meat for a king; fweete *Sander* help me to fome of it.

" *San.* Nay, berlady, then 'tis too deere for us; we muft not meddle with the king's meate.

" *Kate.* Out villaine! doft thou mocke me?

" Take that for thy fawfineffe.   [*She beates him.*

" *San.* Sounes are you fo light-fingred, with a murrin;

" Ile keepe you fafting for it thefe two daies.

" *Kate.* I tell thee villaine, Ile tear the flefh off

" Thy face and eate it, and thou prate to me thus.

" *San.* Here comes my mafter now: heele courfe you.

" *Enter* Ferando *with a piece of meate upon his dagger point, and* Polidor *with him.*

" *Feran.* See here, *Kate*, I have provided meat for thee:

" Here, take it: what, is't not worthy thanks?

" Go, firha, take it away againe, you fhall be

" Thankful for the next you have.

" *Kate.* Why, I thanke you for it.

" *Feran.* Nay, now 'tis not worth a pin: go, firha, and take it hence, I fay.

" *San.* Yes, fir, Ile carrie it hence: Mafter, let hir

" Have none; for fhe can fight, as hungry as fhe is.

" *Pol.* I pray you, fir, let it ftand; for ile eat

" Some with her myfelfe.

" *Feran.* Wel, firha, fet it downe againe.

" *Kate.* Nay, nay, I pray you, let him take it hence,

" And keepe it for your own diet, for ile none;

" Ile nere be beholding to you for your meat:

" I tel thee flatly here unto thy teeth,

" Thou fhalt not keepe me nor feed me as thou lift,

" For I will home againe unto my father's houfe.

" *Feran.* I, when y'are meeke and gentle, but not before:

Upon entreaty, have a prefent alms;
If not, elfewhere they meet with charity:
But I,—who never knew how to entreat,
Nor never needed that I fhould entreat,—
Am ftarv'd for meat, giddy for lack of fleep;
With oaths kept waking, and with brawling fed:
And that which fpites me more than all thefe wants,
He does it under name of perfect love;
As who fhould fay,—if I fhould fleep, or eat,
'Twere deadly ficknefs, or elfe prefent death.—
I pr'ythee go, and get me fome repaft;
I care not what, fo it be wholefome food.

Gru. What fay you to a neat's foot?

Kath. 'Tis paffing good; I pr'ythee let me have it.

Gre. I fear, it is too cholerick a meat: [3]—
How fay you to a fat tripe, finely broil'd?

Kath. I like it well; good Grumio, fetch it me.

Gru. I cannot tell; I fear, 'tis cholerick.
What fay you to a piece of beef, and muftard?

" I know your ftomacke is not yet come downe,
" Therefore no marvel thou canft not eat:
" And I will go unto your father's houfe.
" Come *Polidor,* let us go in againe;
" And *Kate* come in with us: I know, ere long,
" That thou and I fhall lovingly agree."
The circumftance of *Ferundo* bringing meat to *Katharine* on the point of his dagger, is a ridicule on Marlowe's *Tamburlaine,* who treats *Bajazet* in the fame manner. STEEVENS.

[3] *I fear, it is too* cholerick *a meat:*] So before:
" And I exprefsly am forbid to touch it;
" For it engenders *choler.*"
The editor of the fecond folio arbitrarily reads—too *phlegmatick* a meat; which has been adopted by all the fubfequent editors. MALONE.

Though I have not difplaced the oldeft reading, that of the fecond folio may be right. It prevents the repetition of *cholerick,* and preferves its meaning; for *phlegmatick,* irregularly derived from φλεγμονὴ, might anciently have been a word in phyfical ufe, fignifying *inflammatory,* as *phlegmonous* is at prefent. STEEVENS.

Kath. A diſh that I do love to feed upon.

Gru. Ay, but the muſtard is too hot a little.[4]

Kath. Why, then the beef, and let the muſtard reſt.

Gru. Nay, then I will not; you ſhall have the muſtard,

Or elſe you get no beef of Grumio.

Kath. Then both, or one, or any thing thou wilt.

Gru. Why, then the muſtard without the beef.

Kath. Go, get thee gone, thou falſe deluding ſlave,   [*Beats him.*

That feed'ſt me with the very name of meat:

Sorrow on thee, and all the pack of you,

That triumph thus upon my miſery!

Go, get thee gone, I ſay.

Enter PETRUCHIO, *with a diſh of meat; and* HORTENSIO.

Pet. How fares my Kate? What, ſweeting, all amort?[5]

Hor. Miſtreſs, what cheer?

Kath.   'Faith, as cold as can be.

[4] *Ay, but the muſtard is too hot a little.*] This is agreeable to the doctrine of the times. In *The Glaſs of Humors*, no date, p. 60, it is ſaid, " But note here, that the firſt diet is not only in avoiding ſuperfluity of meats, and ſurfeits of drinks, but alſo in eſchewing ſuch as are moſt obnoxious, and leaſt agreeable with our happy temperate ſtate; as for a cholerick man to abſtain from all ſalt, *ſcorched, dry meats*, from *muſtard*, and ſuch like things as will aggravate his malignant humours," &c.

So Petruchio before objects to the over-roaſted mutton. REED.

[5] ——*What, ſweeting, all* amort?] This Galliciſm is common to many of the old plays. So, in *Wily Beguiled:*

   " Why how now, Sophos, all *amort?*"

Again, in *Ram Alley, or Merry Tricks,* 1611:

   " What all *amort!* What's the matter?" STEEVENS.

That is, all ſunk and diſpirited. MALONE.

Pet. Pluck up thy spirits, look cheerfully upon
    me.
Here, love; thou fee'ft how diligent I am,
To drefs thy meat myfelf, and bring it thee:
                    [Sets the difh on a table.
I am fure, fweet Kate, this kindnefs merits thanks.
What, not a word? Nay then, thou lov'ft it not;
And all my pains is forted to no proof: [6]——
Here, take away this difh.

    Kath.   'Pray you, let it ftand.

    Pet. The pooreft fervice is repaid with thanks;
And fo fhall mine, before you touch the meat.

    Kath. I thank you, fir.

    Hor. Signior Petruchio, fie! you are to blame:
Come, miftrefs Kate, I'll bear you company.

    Pet. Eat it up all, Hortenfio, if thou lov'ft me.——
                           [Afide.

Much good do it unto thy gentle heart!
Kate, eat apace:——And now, my honey love,
Will we return unto thy father's houfe;
And revel it as bravely as the beft,
With filken coats, and caps, and golden rings,
With ruffs, and cuffs, and farthingales, and things; [7]

---

[6] *And all my pains is forted to no proof:*] And all my labour has
ended in nothing, or *proved* nothing. "We tried an experiment,
but it *forted* not." *Bacon.* JOHNSON.

[7] ——*farthingales, and* things;] Though *things* is a poor word,
yet I have no better, and perhaps the author had not another that
would rhyme. I once thought to tranfpofe the words *rings* and
things, but it would make little improvement. JOHNSON.

However poor the word, the poet muft be anfwerable for it,
as he had ufed it before, Act II. fc. v. when the rhyme did not
force it upon him:

We will have rings and things, *and fine array.*
Again, in *The Tragedy of Hoffman,* 1632:

    " 'Tis true that I am poor, and yet have *things,*
    " And golden rings," &c.

With ſcarfs, and fans, and double change of bravery,
With amber bracelets, beads, and all this knavery.
What, haſt thou din'd? The tailor ſtays thy lei-
    ſure,
To deck thy body with his ruffling treaſure.[8]—

A *thing* is a trifle too inconſiderable to deſerve particular diſ-
crimination. STEEVENS.

[8] ——*with his* ruffling *treaſure.*] This is the reading of the
old copy, which Mr. Pope changed to *ruſtling,* I think, without
neceſſity. Our author has indeed in another play,—" *Prouder* than
ruſtling in unpaid for ſilk;" but *ruffling* is ſometimes uſed in *nearly*
the ſame ſenſe. Thus, in *K. Lear:*

" —— the high winds
" Do ſorely *ruffle.*"

There clearly the idea of noiſe as well as turbulence is annexed to
the word. A *ruffler* in our author's time ſignified a *noiſy* and tur-
bulent ſwaggerer; and the word *ruffling* may here be applied in
a kindred ſenſe to dreſs. So, in *K. Henry VI. P. II:*

" And his proud wife, high-minded Eleanor,
" That *ruffles* it with ſuch a troop of ladies,
" As ſtrangers in the court take her for queen."

Again, more appoſitely, in Camden's *Remaines,* 1605: " There
was a nobleman merry conceited and riotouſly given, that having
lately ſold a manor of a hundred tenements, came *ruffling* into the
court in a *new ſute,* ſaying, Am not I a mightie man that beare an
hundred houſes on my backe?"

Boyle ſpeaks of the *ruffling* of ſilk, and *ruffled* is uſed by ſo late
an author as Addiſon in the ſenſe of *plaited;* in which laſt ſignification perhaps the word *ruffling* ſhould be underſtood here. Petruchio
has juſt before told Catharine that ſhe " ſhould revel it with *ruffs*
and cuffs;" from the former of which words, *ruffled,* in the ſenſe
of plaited, ſeems to be derived. As *ruffling* therefore may be
underſtood either in this ſenſe, or that firſt ſuggeſted, (which I
incline to think the true one,) I have adhered to the reading of the
old copy.

To the examples already given in ſupport of the reading of the
old copy, may be added this very appoſite one from Lyly's *Euphues,*
and his England, 1580: " Shall I *ruffle* in new devices, with
chains, with *bracelets,* with *rings,* with roabes?"

Again, in Drayton's *Battaile of Agincourt,* 1627:
" With *ruffling* banners, that do brave the ſky."

MALONE.

Enter Tailor.

Come, tailor, let us fee thefe ornaments; [2]

Enter Haberdafher. [3]

Lay forth the gown.—What news with you, fir?

Hab. Here is the cap your worfhip did befpeak.

---

[2] *Come, tailor, let us fee thefe ornaments;*] In our poet's time, women's gowns were ufually made by men. So, in the Epiftle to the Ladies, prefixed to *Euphues and his England*, by John Lyly, 1580: "If a *taylor make your gown* too little, you cover his fault with a broad ftomacher; if too great, with a number of pleights; if too fhort, with a fair guard; if too long, with a falfe gathering." MALONE.

[3] *Enter Haberdafher.*] Thus in the original play:

" *San.* Mafter, the haberdafher has brought my miftris home hir cap here.

" *Feran.* Come hither, firha: what have you there?

" *Haber.* A velvet cap, fir, and it pleafe you.

" *Feran.* Who fpoke for it? Didft thou, *Kate?*

" *Kate.* What if I did? Come hither, firha, give me the cap; ile fee if it will fit me. [*She fets it on her head.*

" *Feran.* O monftrous! why it becomes thee not.

" Let me fee it, *Kate:* here, firha, take it hence;

" This cap is out of fafhion quite.

" *Kate,* The fafhion is good inough: belike you mean to make a fool of me.

" *Feran.* Why true, he means to make a foole of thee,

" To have thee put on fuch a curtald cap:

" Sirha, begone with it.

" *Enter the* Taylor, *with a gowne.*

" *San.* Here is the Taylor too with my miftris gowne.

" *Feran.* Let me fee it, Taylor: What, with cuts and jags?

" Sounes, thou vilaine, thou haft fpoil'd the gowne.

" *Taylor.* Why, fir, I made it as your man gave me direction;

" You may read the note here.

" *Feran.* Come hither, firha: Taylor, read the note.

" *Taylor.* Item, a faire round compafs'd cape.

" *San.* I, that's true.

" *Taylor.* And a large truncke fleeve.

" *San.* That's a lie maifter; I faid two truncke fleeves.

" *Feran.* Well, fir, go forward.

" *Taylor.* Item, a loofe-bodied gowne.

" *San.* Maifter, if ever I faid loofe bodies gowne,

Pet. Why, this was moulded on a porringer; [4]

" Sew me in a feame, and beat me to death
" With a bottom of browne thred.
" *Taylor.* I made it as the note bade me.
" *San.* I fay the note lies in his throate, and thou too, an thou fayeft it.
" *Tay.* Nay, nay, ne'er be fo hot, firha, for I feare you not.
" *San.* Dooft thou heare, Tailor? thou haft braved many men:
" Brave not me. Th'aft fac'd many men.
" *Taylor.* Wel, fir.
" *San.* Face not me: I'le neither be fac'd, nor braved, at thy hands, I can tell thee.
" *Kate.* Come, come, I like the fashion of it wel inough;
" Heere's more adoe than needes; I'le have it, I;
" And if you doe not like it, hide your eies:
" I thinke I fhall have nothing, by your will.
" *Feran.* Go, I fay, and take it up for your maifter's ufe!
" *San.* Souns villaine, not for thy life; touch it not:
" Souns, take up my miftris gowne to his maifter's ufe!
" *Feran.* Well, fir, what's your conceit of it?
" *San.* I have a deeper conceit in it than you think for. Take up my miftris gowne to his maifter's ufe!
" *Feran.* Taylor, come hither; for this time make it:
" Hence againe, and Ile content thee for thy paines.
" *Taylor.* I thanke you, fir.   [*Exit* Tailer.
" *Feran.* Come, *Kate,* wee now will go fee thy father's houfe,
" Even in thefe honeft meane abiliments;
" Our purfes fhall be rich, our garments plaine,
" To fhrowd our bodies from the winter rage;
" And that's inough, what fhould we care for more?
" Thy fifters, *Kate,* to-morrow muft be wed,
" And I have promifed them thou fhould'ft be there:
" The morning is well up; let's hafte away;
" It wil be nine a clocke ere we come there.
" *Kate.* Nine a clocke! why 'tis already paft two in the afternoon, by al the clockes in the towne.
" *Feran.* I fay 'tis but nine a clocke in the morning.
" *Kate.* I fay 'tis two a clocke in the afternoone.
" *Feran.* It fhall be nine then ere you go to your fathers:
" Come backe againe; we will not goe to day:
" Nothing but croffing me ftil?
" Ile have you fay as I doe, ere I goe. [*Exeunt omnes.*" STEEVENS.

[4] —— *on a* porringer;] The fame thought occurs in *King Henry VIII:* " —— rail'd upon me till her pink'd *porringer* fell off her head." STEEVENS.

A velvet difh ;—fie, fie! 'tis lewd and filthy :
Why, 'tis a cockle, or a walnutfhell,
A knack, a toy, a trick, a baby's cap;
Away with it, come, let me have a bigger.

KATH. I'll have no bigger; this doth fit the time,
And gentlewomen wear fuch caps as thefe.

PET. When you are gentle, you fhall have one too,
And not till then.

HOR.   That will not be in hafte. [Afide.

KATH. Why, fir, I truft, I may have leave tofpeak;[5]
And fpeak I will; I am no child, no babe :
Your betters have endur'd me fay my mind;
And, if you cannot, beft you ftop your ears.
My tongue will tell the anger of my heart;
Or elfe my heart, concealing it, will break :
And, rather than it fhall, I will be free
Even to the uttermoft, as I pleafe, in words.

PET. Why, thou fay'ft true; it is a paltry cap,
A cuftard-coffin,[6] a bauble, a filken pie :
I love thee well, in that thou lik'ft it not.

---

[5] *Why, fir, I truft, I may have leave to fpeak*, &c.] Shakfpeare
has here copied nature with great fkill. Petruchio, by frightening,
ftarving, and overwatching his wife, had tamed her into gentlenefs
and fubmiffion. And the audience expects to hear no more of the
fhrew : when on her being croffed, in the article of fafhion and
finery, the moft inveterate folly of the fex, fhe flies out again,
though for the laft time, into all the intemperate rage of her
nature. WARBURTON.

[6] *A cuftard*-coffin,] A *coffin* was the ancient culinary term for the
raifed cruft of a pie or cuftard. So, in Ben Jonfon's *Staple of News :*
 " —— if you fpend
 " The red-deer pies in your houfe, or fell them forth, fir,
 " Caft fo, that I may have their *coffins* all
 " Return'd," &c.
Again, in Ben Jonfon's Mafque of *Gypfies Metamorphofed :*
 " And *coffin'd in cruft* 'till now fhe was hoary."
        STEEVENS.

Kath. Love me, or love me not, I like the cap;
And it I will have, or I will have none.

Pet. Thy gown? why, ay:—Come, tailor, let
us fee't.
O mercy, God! what mafking ftuff is here?
What's this? a fleeve? 'tis like a demicannon:
What! up and down, carv'd like an appletart?
Here's fnip, and nip, and cut, and flifh, and flafh,
Like to a cenfer[6] in a barber's fhop:—
Why, what, o'devil's name, tailor, call'ft thou
this?

Hor. I fee, fhe's like to have neither cap nor
gown.   [*Afide.*

Tai. You bid me make it orderly and well,
According to the fafhion, and the time.

Pet. Marry, and did; but if you be remember'd
I did not bid you mar it to the time.
Go, hop me over every kennel home,
For you fhall hop without my cuftom, fir:
I'll none of it; hence, make your beft of it.

Again, in a receipt to bake lampreys. *MS. Book of Cookery.*
Temp. Hen. 6:
" —— and then cover the *coffyn*, but fave a litell hole to blow
into the *coffyn*, with thy mouth, a gode blaft; and fodenly ftoppe,
that the wynde abyde withynne to ryfe up the *coffyn* that it falle nott
down." Douce.

[7] ——*cenfer*—] *Cenfers* in barber's fhops are now difufed, but
they may eafily be imagined to have been veffels which, for the
emiffion of the fmoke, were cut with great number and varieties of
interftices. Johnson.

In *K. Henry VI.* Part II. Doll calls the beadle " thou thin man
in a *cenfer.*" Malone.

I learn from an ancient print, that thefe *cenfers* refembled in fhape
our modern *brafieres.* They had pierced convex covers, and ftood
on feet. They not only ferved to fweeten a barber's fhop, but
to keep his water warm, and dry his cloths on. See note on *King
Henry IV.* Part II. Act V. fc. iv. Steevens.

KATH. I never faw a better-fafhion'd gown,
More quaint, more pleafing, nor more commendable:
Belike, you mean to make a puppet of me.

PET. Why, true; he means to make a puppet of
thee.

TAI. She fays, your worfhip means to make a
puppet of her.

PET. O monftrous arrogance! Thou lieft, thou
thread,
Thou thimble,[8]
Thou yard, three-quarters, half-yard, quarter, nail,
Thou flea, thou nit, thou winter cricket thou:——
Brav'd in mine own houfe with a fkein of thread!
Away, thou rag, thou quantity, thou remnant;
Or I fhall fo be-mete[9] thee with thy yard,
As thou fhalt think on prating whilft thou liv'ft!
I tell thee, I, that thou haft marr'd her gown.

TAI. Your worfhip is deceiv'd; the gown is made
Juft as my mafter had direction:
Grumio gave order how it fhould be done.

GRU. I gave him no order, I gave him the ftuff.

TAI. But how did you defire it fhould be made?

GRU. Marry, fir, with needle and thread.

TAI. But did you not requeft to have it cut?

GRU. Thou haft faced many things.[2]

---

[8] ———— *thou* thread,
  Thou thimble,] We fhould only read:
    O monftrous arrogance! thou lieft, thou thimble.
He calls him afterwards—a fkein of *thread.* RITSON.

The tailor's trade, having an appearance of effeminacy, has always
been, among the rugged Englifh, liable to farcafms and contempt.
                                    JOHNSON.

[9] ——*be*-mete—] i. e. be-meafure thee. STEEVENS.

[2] ——faced *many things.*] i. e. turned up many gowns, &c. with
facings, &c.] So, in *K. Henry IV:*
    " To *face* the garment of rebellion
    " With fome fine colour." STEEVENS.

TAI. I have.

GRU. Face not me: thou haft braved many men;[3] brave not me; I will neither be faced nor braved. I fay unto thee,—I bid thy mafter cut out the gown; but I did not bid him cut it to pieces:[4] *ergo*, thou lieft.

TAI. Why, here is the note of the fafhion to tef-tify.

PET. Read it.

GRU. The note lies in his throat, if he fay I faid fo.

TAI. *Imprimis, a loofe-bodied gown:*

GRU. Mafter, if ever I faid loofe-bodied gown,[5] few me in the fkirts of it, and beat me to death with a bottom of brown thread: I faid, a gown.

PET. Proceed.

TAI. *With a fmall compafs'd cape;*[6]

---

[3] ——braved *many men*;] i. e. made many men *fine*. *Bravery* was the ancient term for elegance of drefs. STEEVENS.

[4] ——*but I did not bid him cut it to pieces:*] This fcene appears to have been borrowed from a ftory of Sir Philip Caulthrop, and John Drakes, a filly fhoemaker of Norwich, which is related in Leigh's *Accidence of Armorie*, and in Camden's *Remaines.* DOUCE.

[5] ——loofe-bodied *gown*,] I think the joke is impair'd, unlefs we read with the original play already quoted—a *loofe body's* gown. It appears, however, that *loofe-bodied* gowns were the drefs of *harlots.* Thus, in *The Michaelmas Term*, by Middleton, 1607: " Doft dream of virginity now? remember a *loofe-bodied* gown, wench, and let it go." STEEVENS.

See Dodfley's *Old Plays*, Vol. III. p. 479, edit. 1780. REED.

[6] ——*a fmall* compafs'd *cape*;] A *compafs'd cape* is a round cape. To *compafs* is *to come round.* JOHNSON.

Thus, in *Troilus and Creffida*, a circular bow window is called a—*compaffed* window.

Stubbs, in his *Anatomy of Abufes*, 1565, gives a moft elaborate defcription of the gowns of women; and adds, " Some have *capes* reaching down to the midft of their backs, faced with velvet, or

Gru. I confefs the cape.

Tai. With a trunk fleeve;——

Gru. I confefs two fleeves.

Tai. The fleeves curioufly cut.

Pet. Ay, there's the villainy.

Gru. Error i'the bill, fir; error i'the bill. I commanded the fleeves fhould be cut out, and fewed up again; and that I'll prove upon thee, though thy little finger be armed in a thimble.

Tai. This is true, that I fay; an I had thee in place where, thou fhoud'ft know it.

Gru. I am for thee ftraight: take thou the bill,[7] give me thy mete-yard,[8] and fpare not me.

Hor. God-a-mercy, Grumio! then he fhall have no odds.

Pet. Well, fir, in brief, the gown is not for me.

Gru. You are i'the right, fir; 'tis for my miftrefs.

Pet. Go, take it up unto thy mafter's ufe.

Gru. Villain, not for thy life: Take up my miftrefs' gown for thy mafter's ufe!

Pet. Why, fir, what's your conceit in that?

elfe with fome fine wrought taffata, at the leaft, fringed about, very bravely." STEEVENS.

So, in the Regifter of Mr. Henflowe, proprietor of the Rofe theatre, (a manufcript of which an account has been given in Vol. II: " 3 of June 1594. Lent, upon a womanes gowne of villet in grayne, with a velvet *cape* imbroidered with bugelles, for xxxvi s." MALONE.

[7] —— *take thou the* bill,] The fame quibble between the written *bill,* and *bill* the ancient weapon carried by foot-foldiers, is to be met with in *Timon of Athens.* STEEVENS.

[8] —— *thy* mete-*yard,*] i. e. thy meafuring-yard. So, in *The Miferies of Inforc'd Marriage,* 1607:

 " Be not a bar between us, or my fword

 " Shall *mete* thy grave out." STEEVENS.

Gru. O, fir, the conceit is deeper than you think
    for :
Take up my miftrefs' gown to his mafter's ufe!
O, fie, fie, fie!

Pet. Hortenfio, fay thou wilt fee the tailor
    paid :—   [*Afide.*
Go take it hence; be gone, and fay no more.

Hor. Tailor, I'll pay thee for thy gown to-morrow.
Take no unkindnefs of his hafty words :
Away, I fay; commend me to thy mafter.

                       [*Exit* Tailor.

Pet. Well, come, my Kate; we will unto your
    father's,
Even in thefe honeft mean habiliments;
Our purfes fhall be proud, our garments poor:
For 'tis the mind that makes the body rich;
And as the fun breaks through the darkeft clouds,
So honour peereth in the meaneft habit.
What, is the jay more precious than the lark,
Becaufe his feathers are more beautiful?
Or is the adder better than the eel,
Becaufe his painted fkin contents the eye?
O, no, good Kate; neither art thou the worfe
For this poor furniture, and mean array.
If thou account'ft it fhame, lay it on me:
And therefore, frolick; we will hence forthwith,
To feaft and fport us at thy father's houfe.—
Go, call my men, and let us ftraight to him;
And bring our horfes unto Long-lane end,
There will we mount, and thither walk on foot.—
Let's fee; I think, 'tis now fome feven o'clock,
And well we may come there by dinner time.

Kath. I dare affure you, fir, 'tis almoft two;
And 'twill be fupper time, ere you come there.

Pet. It fhall be feven, ere I go to horfe:

Look, what I fpeak, or do, or think to do,
You are ftill croffing it.—Sirs, let't alone:
I will not go to-day; and ere I do,
It fhall be what o'clock I fay it is.

    Hor. Why, fo! this gallant will command the fun.
                              [*Exeunt.*⁸

S C E N E IV.⁹

Padua. *Before* Baptifta's *Houfe.*

Enter TRANIO, *and the* Pedant *dreffed like* VINCENTIO.

    Tra. Sir, this is the houfe;² Pleafe it you, that I call?

    Ped. Ay, what elfe? and, but I be deceived,³
Signior Baptifta may remember me,
Near twenty years ago, in Genoa, where
We were lodgers at the Pegafus.⁴

---

⁸ *Exeunt.*] After this exeunt, the characters before whom the play is fuppofed to be exhibited, have been hitherto introduced from the original fo often mentioned in the former notes.
    " *Lord.* Who's within there?
              " *Enter Servants.*
    " Afleep again! go take him eafily up, and put him in his own apparel again. But fee you wake him not in any cafe.
    " *Serv.* It fhall be done, my lord; come help to bear him hence."   [*They bear off* Sly. STEEVENS.

⁹ I cannot but think that the direction about the Tinker, who is always introduced at the end of the acts, together with the change of the fcene, and the proportion of each act to the reft, make it probable that the fifth act begins here. JOHNSON.

² Sir, *this is the houfe*;] The old copy has—*Sirs.* Corrected by Mr. Theobald. MALONE.

³ ——but *I be deceived,*] *But,* in the prefent inftance, fignifies, *without, unlefs.* So, in *Antony and Cleopatra:*
    " *But* being charg'd, we will be ftill by land." STEEVENS.

⁴ *We were lodgers at the Pegafus.*] This line has in all the editions hitherto been given to Tranio. But Tranio could with no pro-

Tra. . 'Tis well;
And hold your own, in any cafe, with fuch
Aufterity as 'longeth to a father.

Enter BIONDELLO.

Ped. I warrant you : But, fir, here comes your boy;
'Twere good, he were fchool'd.

Tra. Fear you not him. Sirrah, Biondello,
Now do your duty throughly, I advife you;
Imagine 'twere the right Vincentio.

Bion. Tut! fear not me.

Tra. But haft thou done thy errand to Baptifta?

Bion. I told him, that your father was at Venice;
And that you look'd for him this day in Padua.

Tra. Thou'rt a tall fellow; hold thee that to drink.
Here comes Baptifta :—fet your countenance, fir.—

Enter BAPTISTA and LUCENTIO.[5]

Signior Baptifta, you are happily met :—
Sir, [*To the* Pedant.]
This is the gentleman I told you of;

priety fpeak this, either in his affumed or real character. Lucentio
was too young to know any thing of lodging with his father, twenty
years before at Genoa: and Tranio muft be as much too young, or
very unfit to reprefent and perfonate Lucentio. I have ventured to
place the line to the Pedant, to whom it muft certainly belong,
and is a fequel of what he was before faying. THEOBALD.

Shakfpeare has taken a fign out of *London*, and hung it up in
Padua :
    " Meet me an hour hence at the fign of the *Pegafus* in Cheap-
fide." *Return from Parnaffus,* 1606.
    Again, in *The Jealous Lovers,* by Randolph, 1632 :
        " A pottle of elixir at the *Pegafus,*
        " Bravely carous'd, is more reftorative."
    The *Pegafus* is the arms of the Middle-Temple; and, from that
circumftance, became a popular fign. STEEVENS.

    5 *Enter* Baptifta *and* Lucentio.] and (according to the old copy)
Pedant, booted and bareheaded. RITSON.

I pray you, ftand good father to me now,
Give me Bianca for my patrimony.

   Ped. Soft, fon!—
Sir, by your leave; having come to Padua
To gather in fome debts, my fon Lucentio·
Made me acquainted with a weighty caufe
Of love between your daughter and himfelf:
And,—for the good report I hear of you;
And for the love he beareth to your daughter,
And fhe to him,—to ftay him not too long,
I am content, in a good father's care,
To have him match'd; and,—if you pleafe to like
No worfe than I, fir,—upon fome agreement,
Me fhall you find moft ready and moft willing⁴
With one confent to have her fo beftow'd:
For curious I cannot be with you,⁵
Signior Baptifta, of whom I hear fo well.

   Bap. Sir, pardon me in what I have to fay;—
Your plainnefs, and your fhortnefs, pleafe me well.
Right true it is, your fon Lucentio here
Doth love my daughter, and fhe loveth him,
Or both diffemble deeply their affections:
And, therefore, if you fay no more than this,—
That like a father you will deal with him,
And pafs my daughter a fufficient dower,⁶

---

⁴ *Me fhall you find* moft *ready and* moft *willing*—] The repeated word *moft*, is not in the old copy, but was fupplied by Sir T. Hanmer, to complete the meafure. Steevens.

⁵ *For* curious *I cannot be with you.*] Curious is fcrupulous. So, in Holinfhed, p. 888: "The emperor obeying more compaffion than the reafon of things, was not curious to condefcend to performe fo good an office." Again, p. 890: "—and was not curious to call him to eat with him at his table." Steevens.

⁶ *And* pafs *my daughter a fufficient dower,*] To pafs is, in this place, fynonymous to affure or convey; as it fometimes occurs in the covenant of a purchafe deed, that the granter has power to bargain, fell, &c. "and thereby to pafs and convey" the premifes to the grantee. Ritson.

The match is fully made, and all is done:[8]
Your son shall have my daughter with consent.

TRA. I thank you, sir. Where then do you know
best,
We be affied;[9] and such assurance ta'en,
As shall with either part's agreement stand?

BAP. Not in my house, Lucentio; for, you know,
Pitchers have ears, and I have many servants:
Besides, old Gremio is heark'ning still;
And, happily, we might be interrupted.[2]

TRA. Then at my lodging, an it like you, sir:[3]
There doth my father lie; and there, this night,
We'll pass the business privately and well:
Send for your daughter by your servant here,
My boy shall fetch the scrivener presently.
The worst is this,—that, at so slender warning,
You're like to have a thin and slender pittance.

BAP. It likes me well:—Cambio, hie you home,
And bid Bianca make her ready straight:
And, if you will, tell what hath happened:—

---

[8] *The match is* **fully** *made, and all is done:*] The word—*fully*
(to complete the verse) was inserted by Sir Thomas Hanmer, who
might have justified his emendation by a foregoing passage in this
comedy:
"Nathaniel's coat, sir, was not *fully made.*" STEEVENS.

[9] *We be* affied;] i. e. betrothed. So, in *K. Henry VI.* P. II:
"For daring to *affy* a mighty lord
"Unto the daughter of a worthless king." STEEVENS.

[2] *And,* happily, *we might be interrupted.*] Thus the old copy.
Mr. Pope reads:
And haply then *we might be interrupted.* STEEVENS.

Happily, in Shakspeare's time, signified *accidentally*, as well as
fortunately. It is rather surprising, that an editor should be guilty
of so gross a corruption of his author's language, for the sake of
modernizing his orthography. TYRWHITT.

[3] ——*an it like you,* sir:] The latter word, which is not in the
old copy, was added by the editor of the second folio.
MALONE.

Lucentio's father is arriv'd in Padua,
And how fhe's like to be Lucentio's wife.

Luc. I pray the gods fhe may, with all my heart![9]

Tra. Dally not with the gods, but get thee gone.[1]
Signior Baptista, fhall I lead the way?
Welcome! one mefs is like to be your cheer:
Come, fir; we'll better it in Pifa.

Bap.   I follow you.
    [*Exeunt* Tranio, Pedant, *and* Baptista.

Bion. Cambio.—

Luc.   What fay'ft thou, Biondello?

Bion. You faw my mafter wink and laugh upon you?

Luc. Biondello, what of that?

Bion. 'Faith nothing; but he has left me here
behind, to expound the meaning or moral[1] of his
figns and tokens.

Luc. I pray thee, moralize them.

Bion. Then thus. Baptista is fafe, talking with
the deceiving father of a deceitful fon.

Luc. And what of him?

Bion. His daughter is to be brought by you to
the fupper.

Luc. And then?—

---

[9] *Luc. I pray, &c.*] In the old copy this line is by miftake
given to Biondello. Corrected by Mr. Rowe. MALONE.

[1] *Dally not with the gods, but get thee gone.*] Here the old copy
adds—*Enter Peter.* RITSON.

——get thee gone.] It feems odd management to make Lucentio go out here for nothing that appears, but that he may return
again five lines lower. It would be better, I think, to fuppofe
that he lingers upon the ftage, till the reft are gone, in order to
talk with Biondello in private. TYRWHITT.

I have availed myfelf of the regulation propofed by Mr. Tyrwhitt.
                                        STEEVENS.

[1] *——or moral—*] i. e. the fecret purpofe. See Vol. IV. p. 491.
                                        MALONE.

Bion. The old prieſt at ſaint Luke's church is at your command at all hours.

Luc. And what of all this?

Bion. I cannot tell; except⁴ they are buſied about a counterfeit aſſurance: Take you aſſurance of her, *cum privilegio ad imprimendum ſolùm:*⁵ to the church;⁶—take the prieſt, clerk, and ſome ſufficient honeſt witneſſes:

If this be not that you look for, I have no more to
    ſay,
But, bid Bianca farewell for ever and a day.
                             [*Going.*

Luc. Hear'ſt thou, Biondello?

Bion. I cannot tarry: I knew a wench married in an afternoon as ſhe went to the garden for par-ſley to ſtuff a rabbit; and ſo may you, ſir; and ſo adieu, ſir. My maſter hath appointed me to go to ſaint Luke's, to bid the prieſt be ready to come againſt you come with your appendix.   [*Exit.*

Luc. I may, and will, if ſhe be ſo contented:
She will be pleaſ'd, then wherefore ſhould I doubt?
Hap what hap may, I'll roundly go about her;
It ſhall go hard, if Cambio go without her.
                             [*Exit.*⁷

---

⁴ *I cannot tell;* except —] The firſt folio reads *expeƈ.*
                              MALONE.

Except is the reading of the ſecond folio. *Expeƈ,* ſays Mr. Malone, means—wait the event. STEEVENS.

⁵ —— *cum privilegio ad imprimendum ſolùm:*] It is ſcarce ne-ceſſary to obſerve that theſe are the words which commonly were put on books where an excluſive right had been granted for printing them. REED.

⁶ —— *to the church;*] i. e. go to the church, &c.
                              TYRWHITT.

⁷ *Exit.*] Here, in the original play, the *Tinker* ſpeaks again, and the ſcene continues thus:

SCENE V.

A publick Road.

Enter PETRUCHIO, KATHARINA, *and* HORTENSIO.

PET. Come on, o'God's name; once more toward
our father's.

" *Slie.* Sim, muſt they be married now?
" *Lord.* I, my lord.
     " *Enter* Ferando, *and* Kate, *and* Sander.
" *Slie.* Looke, *Sim,* the foole is come againe now.
" *Feran.* Sirha, go fetch our horſes forth, and bring them to
the backe-gate preſently.
" *San.* I wil, ſir, I warrant you.   [*Exit* Sander.
" *Feran.* Come, *Kate:* the moone ſhines cleere to-night, me-
thinkes.
" *Kate.* The moone; why huſband you are deceiv'd; it is the
ſun.
" *Feran.* Yet againe? come backe againe; it ſhal be the moone
ere we come at your fathers.
" *Kate.* Why Ile ſay as you ſay; it is the moone.
" *Feran. Ieſus,* ſave the glorious moone!
" *Kate. Ieſus,* ſave the glorious moone!
" *Feran.* I am glad, *Kate,* your ſtomacke is come downe;
" I know it well thou knowſt it is the ſun,
" But I did trie to ſee if thou wouldſt ſpeake,
" And croſſe me now as thou haſt done before:
" And truſt me, *Kate,* hadſt thou not namde the moone,
" We had gone backe againe as ſure as death.
" But ſoft, who's this that's comming here?
     " *Enter the Duke of* Ceſtus *alone.*
" *Duke.* Thus al alone from Ceſtus am I come,
" And left my princely court, and noble traine,
" To come to *Athens,* and in this diſguiſe
" To ſee what courſe my ſon *Aurelius* takes.
" But ſtay; here's ſome it may be travels thither:
" Good ſir, can you direct me the way to *Athens?*
     [Ferando *ſpeaks to the old man.*
  His ſpeech is very partially and incorrectly quoted by Mr. Pope
in page 532. STEEVENS.

Good Lord, how bright and goodly fhines the
    moon!

KATH. The moon! the fun; it is not moonlight
    now.

PET. I fay, it is the moon that fhines fo bright.

KATH. I know, it is the fun that fhines fo bright.

PET. Now, by my mother's fon, and that's my-
    felf,

It fhall be moon, or ftar, or what I lift,
Or ere I journey to your father's houfe :—
Go on, and fetch our horfes back again.—
Evermore croft, and croft; nothing but croft!

HOR. Say as he fays, or we fhall never go.

KATH. Forward, I pray, fince we have come fo
    far,

And be it moon, or fun, or what you pleafe:
And if you pleafe to call it a rufh candle,
Henceforth I vow it fhall be fo for me.

PET. I fay, it is the moon.

KATH.   I know it is.[8]

PET. Nay, then you lie; it is the bleffed fun.[9]

KATH. Then, God be blefs'd, it is the bleffed
    fun:—

But fun it is not, when you fay it is not;
And the moon changes, even as your mind.

---

[8] *I know it is.*] The old copy redundantly reads—I know it is
the moon. STEEVENS.

The humour of this fcene bears a very ftriking refemblance to
what Monf. Bernier tells us of the Mogul Omrahs, who continually bear in mind the Perfian proverb, " If the King faith at noon-
day it is night, you are to behold the moon and the ftars." *Hiftory
of the Mogul Empire*, Vol. IV. p. 45. DOUCE.

[9] —— *it is the bleffed fun:*] For *is* the old copy has *in.* Gorrected
in the fecond folio. MALONE.

What you will have it nam'd, even that it is;
And ſo it ſhall be ſo,[9] for Katharine.

Hor. Petruchio, go thy ways; the field is won.

Pet. Well, forward, forward: thus the bowl
     ſhould run,
And not unluckily againſt the bias.—
But ſoft; what company is coming here?[2]

Enter VINCENTIO, *in a travelling dreſs.*

Good-morrow, gentle miſtreſs: Where away?—
                    [*To* VINCENTIO.
Tell me, ſweet Kate,[3] and tell me truly too,

---

   [9] *And ſo it ſhall be ſo,*] A modern editor very plauſibly reads—
And ſo it ſhall be, Sir. MALONE.

   Read:
     And ſo it ſhall be ſtill, *for Katharine.* RITSON.

   [2] *But ſoft; what* company *is coming here?*] The pronoun—*what,*
which is wanting in the old copy, I have inſerted by the advice of
Mr. Ritſon, whoſe punctuation and ſupplement are countenanced
by the correſponding paſſage in the elder play:
    " But ſoft; who's this that's coming here?"
See p. 530. STEEVENS.

   [3] *Tell me, ſweet Kate,*] In the firſt ſketch of this play, printed
in 1607, we find two ſpeeches in this place worth preſerving, and
ſeeming to be of the hand of Shakſpeare, though the reſt of that
play is far inferior:
    " Fair lovely maiden, young and affable,
    " More clear of hue, and far more beautiful
    " Than precious ſardonyx, or purple rocks
    " Of amethiſts, or gliſtering hyacinth ——
    " —— Sweet Katharine, this lovely woman——
    " *Kath.* Fair lovely lady, bright and chryſtalline,
    " Beauteous and ſtately as the eye-train'd bird;
    " As glorious as the morning waſh'd with dew,
    " Within whoſe eyes ſhe takes her dawning beams,
    " And golden ſummer ſleeps upon thy cheeks.
    " Wrap up thy radiations in ſome cloud,
    " Leſt that thy beauty make this ſtately town
    " Unhabitable as the burning zone,
    " With ſweet reflections of thy lovely face." POPE.

Haft thou beheld a frefher gentlewoman?
Such war of white and red within her cheeks!
What ftars do fpangle heaven with fuch beauty,
As thofe two eyes become that heavenly face?—
Fair lovely maid, once more good day to thee:—
Sweet Kate, embrace her for her beauty's fake.

> Hor. 'A will make the man mad, to make a wo_
> man [4] of him.

> Kath. Young budding virgin, fair, and frefh,
> and fweet,

Whither away; or where is thy abode? [5]
Happy the parents of fo fair a child;
Happier the man, whom favourable ftars
Allot thee for his lovely bed-fellow! [6]

•

An attentive reader will perceive in this fpeech feveral words
which are employed in none of the legitimate plays of Shakfpeare.
Such, I believe, are, *fardonyx, hyacinth, eye-train'd, radiations,* and
efpecially *unhabitable*; our poet generally ufing *inhabitable* in its
room, as in *Richard II*: •
    " Or any other ground *inhabitable.*"
Thefe inftances may ferve as fome flight proofs, that the former
piece was not the work of Shakfpeare: but I have fince obferved
that Mr. Pope had changed *inhabitable* into *unhabitable.*
                                                        Steevens.

[4] —— *to make* a *woman*—] The old copy reads—*the* woman.
Corrected by the editor of the fecond folio. Malone.

[5] —— *where is thy abode?*] Inftead of *where*, the printer of
the old copy inadvertently repeated *whither*. Corrected in the
fecond folio. Malone.

[6] *Happy the parents of fo fair a child;*
    Happier the man, whom favourable ftars
    Allot thee for his lovely bed-fellow!] This is borrowed from
Golding's Tranflation of *Ovid's Metamorphofis*, Book IV. edit.
1587, p. 56:
        " —— right happie folke are they
        " By whome thou camft into this world; right happie is
            (I fay)

PET. Why, how now, Kate! I hope, thou art not
      mad:
This is a man, old, wrinkled, faded, wither'd;
And not a maiden, as thou fay'ft he is.

KATH. Pardon, old father, my miftaking eyes,
That have been fo bedazzled with the fun,
That every thing I look on feemeth green:[6]
Now I perceive, thou art a reverend father;
Pardon, I pray thee, for my mad miftaking.

PET. Do, good old grandfire; and, withal, make
      known
Which way thou travelleft: if along with us,
We fhall be joyful of thy company.

VIN. Fair fir,—and you my merry miftrefs,[7]—
That with your ftrange encounter much amaz'd
      me;
My name is call'd—Vincentio; my dwelling—Pifa;
And bound I am to Padua; there to vifit
A fon of mine, which long I have not feen.

    " Thy mother and thy fifter too (if anie be :) good hap
    " That woman had that was thy nurfe, and gave thy mouth
       hir pap.
    " But far above all other far, more bliffe than thefe is
       fhee
    " Whome thou thy wife and bed-fellow vouchfafeft for to
       bee."
I fhould add, however, that Ovid borrowed his ideas from the
fixth Book of the *Odyffey*, 154, &c.

Τρισμάκαρες μὲν σοί γε πατὴρ καὶ πότνια μήτηρ,
Τρισμάκαρες δὲ κασίγνητοι· μαλα πύ &c.
Κεῖνος δ' αὖ περι κῆρι μακάρτατος ἔξοχον ἄλλων,
Ὅς κέ σ'εεδνοισι βρίσας οἰκόνδ' ἀγάγηται. STEEVENS.

[6] *That every thing I look on feemeth green:*] Shakfpeare's obfervations on the phænomena of nature are very accurate. When
one has fat long in the funfhine, the furrounding objects will
often appear tinged with *green*. The reafon is affigned by many
of the writers on opticks. BLACKSTONE.

[7] —*miftrefs,*] is here ufed as a trifyllable. STEEVENS.

Pet. What is his name?

Vin.   Lucentio, gentle fir.

Pet. Happily met; the happier for thy fon.
And now by law, as well as reverend age,
I may entitle thee—my loving father;
The fifter to my wife, this gentlewoman,
Thy fon by this hath married: Wonder not,
Nor be not griev'd; fhe is of good efteem,
Her dowry wealthy, and of worthy birth;
Befide, fo qualified as may befeem
The fpoufe of any noble gentleman.
Let me embrace with old Vincentio:
And wander we to fee thy honeft fon,
Who will of thy arrival be full joyous.

Vin. But is this true? or is it elfe your pleafure,
Like pleafant travellers, to break a jeft
Upon the company you overtake?

Hor. I do affure thee, father, fo it is.

Pet. Come, go along, and fee the truth hereof;
For our firft merriment hath made thee jealous.
[*Exeunt* PETRUCHIO, KATHARINA, *and* VINCENTIO.

Hor. Well, Petruchio, this hath put me in heart.
Have to my widow; and if fhe be froward,
Then haft thou taught Hortenfio to be untoward.
[*Exit.*

ACT V. SCENE I.

Padua. Before Lucentio's *House.*

Enter on one side BIONDELLO, LUCENTIO, *and* BIANCA; GREMIO *walking on the other side.*

BION. Softly and fwiftly, fir; for the prieft is ready.

LUC. I fly, Biondello: but they may chance to need thee at home, therefore leave us.

BION. Nay, faith, I'll fee the church o' your back; and then come back to my mafter as foon as I can.[8]
[*Exeunt* LUCENTIO, BIANCA, *and* BIONDELLO.

GRE. I marvel, Cambio comes not all this while.

Enter PETRUCHIO, KATHARINA, VINCENTIO, *and Attendants.*

PET. Sir, here's the door, this is Lucentio's houfe, My father's bears more toward the marketplace; Thither muft I, and here I leave you, fir.

VIN. You fhall not choofe but drink before you go; I think, I fhall command your welcome here, And, by all likelihood, fome cheer is toward. [*Knocks.*

---

[8] ——*and then come back to my* mafter *as foon as I can.*] The editions all agree in reading *miftrefs*; but what miftrefs was Biondello to come back to? he muft certainly mean—" Nay, faith, fir, I muft fee you in the church; and then for fear I fhould be wanted, I'll run back to wait on Tranio, who at prefent perfonates you, and whom therefore I at prefent acknowledge for my *mafter.*"
THEOBALD.

Probably an M was only written in the MS. See p. 425.

The fame miftake has happened again in this fcene: " Didft thou never fee thy *miftrefs'* father, Vincentio?" The prefent emendation was made by Mr. Theobald, who obferves rightly, that by " mafter" Biondello means his pretended mafter, Tranio. MALONE.

Gre. They're bufy within, you were beft knock louder.

Enter Pedant *above, at a window.*

Ped. What's he, that knocks as he would beat down the gate?

Vin. Is fignior Lúcentio within, fir?

Ped. He's within, fir, but not to be fpoken withal.

Vin. What if a man bring him a hundred pound or two, to make merry withal.

Ped. Keep your hundred pounds to yourfelf; he fhall need none, fo long as I live.

Pet. Nay, I told you, your fon was belov'd in Padua.—Do you hear, fir?—to leave frivolous cir-cumftances,—I pray you, tell fignior Lucentio, that his father is come from Pifa, and is here at the door to fpeak with him.

Ped. Thou lieft; his father is come from Pifa,[9] and here looking out at the window.

Vin. Art thou his father?

Ped. Ay, fir; fo his mother fays, if I may believe her.

Pet. Why, how now, gentleman! [*To* Vincen.] why, this is flat knavery, to take upon you another man's name.

---

[9] ——*from* Pifa,] The reading of the old copies is *from Padua,* which is certainly wrong. The editors have made it *to Pádua;* but it fhould rather be *from Pifa.* Both parties agree that Lu-centio's father is *come from Pifa,* as indeed they neceffarily muft; the point in difpute is, whether he be *at the door,* or *looking out of the window.* TYRWHITT.

I fufpect we fhould read—from *Mantua,* from whence the Pedant himfelf came, and which he would naturally name, fuppofing he forgot, as might well happen, that the real Vincentio was of Pifa. In *The Two Gentlemen of Verona, Padua* and *Verona* occur in two different fcenes, inftead of *Milan.* MALONE.

Ped. Lay hands on the villain; I believe, 'a means to cozen fomebody in this city under my countenance.

Re-enter BIONDELLO.

Bion. I have feen them in the church together; God fend 'em good fhipping!—But who is here? mine old mafter, Vincentio? now we are undone and brought to nothing.

Vin. Come hither, crack-hemp.
[*Seeing* BIONDELLO.

Bion. I hope, I may choofe, fir.

Vin. Come hither, you rogue; What, have you forgot me?

Bion. Forgot you? no, fir: I could not forget you, for I never faw you before in all my life.

Vin. What, you notorious villain, didft thou never fee thy mafter's father, Vincentio?[2]

Bion. What, my old, worfhipful old mafter? yes, marry, fir; fee where he looks out of the window.

Vin. Is't fo, indeed?   [*Beats* BIONDELLO.

Bion. Help, help, help! here's a madman will murder me.   [*Exit.*

Ped. Help, fon! help, fignior Baptifta!
[*Exit, from the window.*

Pet. Pr'ythee, Kate, let's ftand afide, and fee the end of this controverfy.   [*They retire.*

---

[2] ——*thy* mafter's *father, Vincentio?*] Old copy—thy *miftrefs'* father. Correfted by the editor of the fecond folio. MALONE.

Re-enter Pedant *below*; BAPTISTA, TRANIO, *and Servants.*

TRA. Sir, what are you, that offer to beat my servant?

VIN. What am I, sir? nay, what are you, sir?—O immortal gods! O fine villain! A silken doublet! a velvet hose! a scarlet cloak! and a copatain hat![3]—O, I am undone! I am undone! while I play the good husband at home, my son and my servant spend all at the university.

TRA. How now! what's the matter?

BAP. What, is the man lunatick?

TRA. Sir, you seem a sober ancient gentleman by your habit, but your words show you a madman: Why, sir, what concerns it you, if I wear pearl and gold? I thank my good father, I am able to maintain it.

VIN. Thy father? O, villain! he is a sailmaker in Bergamo.[4]

---

[3] —— *a copatain-hat!*] is, I believe, a hat with a conical crown, such as was anciently worn by well-dressed men. JOHNSON.

This kind of hat is twice mentioned by Gascoigne. See *Hearbes,* p. 154:

 " A *coptankt* hat made on a Flemish block."

And again, in his *Epilogue,* p. 216:

 " With high *copt* hats, and feathers flaunt a flaunt."

In Stubbs's *Anatomie of Abuses,* printed 1595, there is an entire chapter " on the hattes of England," beginning thus:

 " Sometimes they use them sharpe on the crowne, pearking up like the speare or shaft of a steeple, standing a quarter of a yard above the crowne of their heads, &c. STEEVENS.

[4] —— *a sailmaker in Bergamo.*] Chapman has a parallel passage in his *Widow's Tears,* a comedy, 1612:

 " —— he draws the thread of his descent from Leda's distaff, when 'tis well known his grandsire cried coney-skins in Sparta."

 STEEVENS.

Bap. You, miſtake, ſir; you miſtake, ſir: Pray, what do you think is his name?

Vin. His name? as if I knew not his name: I have brought him up ever ſince he was three years old, and his name is—Tranio.

Ped. Away, away, mad aſs! his name is Lucentio; and he is mine only ſon, and heir to the lands of me ſignior Vincentio.

Vin. Lucentio! O, he hath murdered his maſter!—Lay hold on him, I charge you, in the duke's name:—O, my ſon, my ſon!—tell me, thou villain, where is my ſon Lucentio?

Tra. Call forth an officer: [5] [*Enter one with an Officer.*] carry this mad knave to the gaol:—Father Baptiſta, I charge you, ſee, that he be forthcoming.

Vin. Carry me to the gaol!

Gre. Stay, officer; he ſhall not go to priſon.

Bap. Talk not, ſignior Gremio; I ſay, he ſhall go to priſon.

Gre. Take heed, ſignior Baptiſta, leſt you be concy-catch'd [6] in this buſineſs; I dare ſwear, this is the right Vincentio.

Ped. Swear, if thou dar'ſt.

<hr />

[5] *Call forth an officer:* &c.] Here, in the original play, the *Tinker* ſpeaks again:

" *Slie.* I ſay weele have no ſending to priſon.
" *Lord.* Mv lord, this is but the play; they're but in jeſt.
" *Slie.* I tell thee *Sim*, weele have no ſending
" To priſon, that's flat: why *Sim*, am not I don *Chriſto Vari?*
" Therefore, I ſay, they ſhall not goe to priſon.
" *Lord.* No more they ſhall not, my lord:
" They be runne away.
" *Slie.* Are they ron away, *Sim?* that's well:
" Then gis ſome more drinke, and let them play againe.
" *Lord.* Here, my lord." STEEVENS.

[6] —— *concy-catch'd* —] i. e. deceived, cheated. STEEVENS.

Gre. Nay, I dare not fwear it.

Tra. Then thou wert beft fay, that I am not Lucentio.

Gre. Yes, I know thee to be fignior Lucentio.

Bap. Away with the dotard; to the gaol with him.

Vin. Thus ftrangers may be haled and abus'd:—O monftrous villain!

Re-enter BIONDELLO, *with* LUCENTIO *and* BIANCA.

Bion. O, we are fpoiled, and—Yonder he is; deny him, forfwear him, or elfe we are all undone.

Luc. Pardon, fweet father.   *[Kneeling.*

Vin.   Lives my fweeteft fon?
    *[*BIONDELLO, TRANIO, *and* Pedant *run out.*[7]

Bian. Pardon, dear father.   *[Kneeling.*

Bap.   How haft thou offended?—Where is Lucentio?

Luc.   Here's Lucentio,
Right fon unto the right Vincentio;
That have by marriage made thy daughter mine,
While counterfeit fuppofes blear'd thine cyne.[8]

---

[7] —— *run out.*] The old copy fays—*as faft as may be.* RITSON.

[8] *While counterfeit* fuppofes *blear'd thine eyne.*] The modern editors read *fuppofers,* but wrongly. This is a plain allufion to Gafcoigne's comedy entitled *Suppofes,* from which feveral of the incidents in this play are borrowed. TYRWHITT.

This is highly probable; but yet *fuppofes* is a word often ufed in its common fenfe, which, on the prefent occafion is fufficiently commodious. So, in Greene's *Farewell to Folly,* 1617: " —with Plato to build a commonwealth on *fuppofes.*" Shakfpeare ufes the word in *Troilus and Creffida:* " That we come fhort of our *fuppofe* fo far," &c. It appears likewife from the Preface to Greene's *Metamorphofis,* that *fuppofes* was a game of fome kind. " After *fuppofes,* and fuch ordinary fports, were paft, they fell to

Gre. Here's packing,[8] with a witnefs, to deceive us all!

Vin. Where is that damned villain, Tranio, That fac'd and brav'd me in this matter fo?

Bap. Why, tell me, is not this my Cambio?

Bian. Cambio is chang'd into Lucentio.

Luc. Love wrought thefe miracles. Bianca's love Made me exchange my ftate with Tranio, While he did bear my countenance in the town; And happily I have arriv'd at laft Unto the wifhed haven of my blifs:— What Tranio did, myfelf enforc'd him to; Then pardon him, fweet father, for my fake.

Vin. I'll flit the villain's nofe, that would have fent me to the gaol.

Bap. But do you hear fir? [*To* Lucentio.] Have you married my daughter without afking my good-will?

---

prattle," &c. Again, in Drayton's Epiftle from *K. John* to *Matilda:*

" And tells me thofe are fhadows and *fuppofes.*"

To blear the eye, was an ancient phrafe fignifying *to deceive.* So, in Chaucer's *Manciple's Tale,* v. 17202, Mr. Tyrwhitt's edit:

" For all thy waiting, *blered is thin eye.*"

Again, in the 10th pageant of *The Coventry Plays,* in the Britifh Mufeum, MS. Cott. Vefp. D. VIII:

" Shuld I now in age begynne to dote,

" If I chyde, fhe wolde clowte my cote,

" *Blere mine ey,* and pyke out a mote." Steevens.

The ingenious editor's explanation of *blear the eye,* is ftrongly fupported by Milton, *Comus,* v. 155:

" Spells————

" Of power to *cheat the eye* with *blear* illufion."

Holt White.

[8] *Here's* packing,] i. e. plotting, underhand contrivance. So, in *K. Lear:*

" Snuffs and *packings* of the dukes." Steevens.

Vin. Fear not, Baptifta; we will content you, go to:
But I will in, to be reveng'd for this villainy. [*Exit.*

Bap. And I, to found the depth of this knavery.
[*Exit.*

Luc. Look not pale, Bianca; thy father will not
frown. [*Exeunt* LUCENTIO *and* BIANCA.

Gre. My cake is dough:⁹ But I'll in among the
reft;
Out of hope of all,—but my fhare of the feaft. [*Exit.*

PETRUCHIO *and* KATHARINA *advance.*

Kath. Hufband, let's follow, to fee the end of
this ado.

Pet. Firft kifs me, Kate, and we will.

Kath. What, in the midft of the ftreet?

Pet. What, art thou afham'd of me?

Kath. No, fir; God forbid: but afham'd to kifs.

Pet. Why, then let's home again:—Come, firrah,
let's away.

Kath. Nay, I will give thee a kifs: now pray thee,
love, ftay.

Pet. Is not this well?—Come, my fweet Kate;
Better once than never, for never too late.
[*Exeunt.*

---

⁹ *My cake is dough:*] This is a proverbial expreffion which
alfo occurs in the old interlude of *Tom Tyler and his Wife:*
  " Alas poor Tom, *his cake is dough.*"
Again, in *The Cafe is Alter'd*, 1609:
  " Steward, *your cake is dough*, as well as mine." STEEVENS.
  It was generally ufed when any projeft mifcarried. MALONE.

  Rather when any difappointment was fuftained, contrary to every
appearance or expeftation. Howell in one of his letters, mentioning the birth of Lewis the Fourteenth, fays—" The Queen is
delivered of a Dauphin, the wonderfulleft thing of this kind that
any ftory can parallel, for this is the three-and-twentieth year fince
fhe was married, and hath continued childlefs all this while. So
that now Monfieur's *cake is dough.*" REED.

SCENE II.

A Room in Lucentio's *Houfe.*

A Banquet fet out. Enter BAPTISTA, VINCENTIO, GREMIO, *the* Pedant, LUCENTIO, BIANCA, PETRUCHIO, KATHARINA, HORTENSIO, *and* Widow. TRANIO, BIONDELLO, GRUMIO, *and Others, attending.* . . .

Luc. At laft, though long, our jarring notes agree:
And time it is, when raging war is done,[9]
To fmile at 'fcapes and perils over-blown.—
My fair Bianca, bid my father welcome,
While I with felf-fame kindnefs welcome thine:—
Brother Petruchio,—fifter Katharina,—
And thou, Hortenfio, with thy loving widow,—
Feaft with the beft, and welcome to my houfe;
My banquet [2] is to clofe our ftomachs up,
After our great good cheer: Pray you, fit down;
For now we fit to chat, as well as eat.
                          [*They fit at table.*

Pet. Nothing but fit and fit, and eat and eat!

Bap. Padua affords this kindnefs, fon Petruchio.

Pet. Padua affords nothing but what is kind.

---

9 ——*when raging war is* done,] This is Mr. Rowe's emendation. The old copy has—*when raging war is* come, which cannot be right. Perhaps the author wrote—*when raging war is* calm formerly fpelt *calme.* So, in *Othello:*
  " If after every tempeft come fuch *calms—.*"
The word " overblown," in the next line, adds fome little fupport to this conjecture. MALONE.

Mr. Rowe's conjecture is juftified by a paffage in *Othello:*
  " News, lords! our *wars are done.*" STEEVENS.

2 *My* banquet—] A *banquet,* or (as it is called in fome of our old books) an *afterpaft,* was a flight refection, like our modern defert, confifting of cakes, fweetmeats, and fruit. See note on *Romeo and Juliet,* Act I. fc. v. STEEVENS.

Hor. For both our fakes, I would that word were
true.

Pet. Now, for my life, Hortenfio fears his widow.[3]

Wid. Then never truft me if I be afeard.

Pet. You are fenfible, and yet you mifs my fenfe;[4]
I mean, Hortenfio is afeard of you.

Wid. He that is giddy, thinks the world turns
round.

Pet. Roundly replied.

Kath.   Miftrefs, how mean you that?

Wid. Thus I conceive by him.

Pet. Conceives by me!—How likes Hortenfio
that?

Hor. My widow fays, thus fhe conceives her tale.

Pet. Very well mended: Kifs him for that, good
widow.

Kath. He that is giddy, thinks the world turns
round:——
I pray you, tell me what you meant by that.

Wid. Your hufband, being troubled with a fhrew,
Meafures my hufband's forrow by his woe:[5]
And now you know my meaning.

Kath. A very mean meaning.

Wid.   Right, I mean you.

---

[3] —— fears *his widow.*] To *fear,* as has been already obferved,
meant in our author's time both to dread, and to intimidate. The
widow underftands the word in the latter fenfe; and Petruchio tells
her, he ufed it in the former. MALONE.

[4] *You are fenfible, and yet you mifs my fenfe*;] The old copy redundantly reads—You are *very* fenfible. STEEVENS.

[5] ——*fhrew,*——*woe :*] As this was meant for a rhyming
couplet, it fhould be obferved that anciently the word—fhrew was
pronounced as if it had been written—fhrow. See the *finale* of the
play, p. 557. STEEVENS.

Kath. And I am mean, indeed, refpecting you.

Pet. To her, Kate!

Hor. To her, widow!

Pet. A hundred marks, my Kate does put her down.

Hor. That's my office.[3]

Pet. Spoke like an officer:—Ha' to thee, lad.[4]
      [*Drinks to* Hortensio.

Bap. How likes Gremio thefe quick-witted folks?

Gre. Believe me, fir, they butt together well.

Bian. Head, and butt? an hafty-witted body
Would fay, your head and butt were head and horn.

Vin. Ay, miftrefs bride, hath that awaken'd you?

Bian. Ay, but not frighted me; therefore I'll
   fleep again.

Pet. Nay, that you fhall not; fince you have begun,
Have at you for a bitter jeft or two.[5]

---

[3] ——*put her down.*

 That's my office.] This paffage will be beft explained by another, in *Much ado about Nothing* : " Lady, you have *put him down.*—So I would not *be fhould do me,* my lord, left I fhould prove *the mother of fools.*" Steevens.

 [4] —— *Ha to* thee, *lad.*] The old copy has—to *the.* Corrected by the editor of the fecond folio. Malone.

 [5] *Have at you for a* bitter *jeft or two.*] The old copy reads—a *better* jeft. The emendation, (of the propriety of which there cannot, I conceive, be the fmalleft doubt,) is one of the very few corrections of any value made by Mr. Capell. So before in the prefent play:
  " Hiding his *bitter jefts* in blunt behaviour."
Again, in *Love's Labour's Loft* :
  " Too *bitter* is thy *jeft.*"
Again, in Baftard's *Epigrams,* 1598 :
  " He fhut up the matter with this *bitter jeft.*" Malone.

 I have received this emendation; and yet " a *better* jeft" may mean no more than a *good* one. Shakfpeare often ufes the *compa-rative* for the *pofitive* degree. So, in *K. Lear* :
  " ——her fmiles and tears
  " Were like a *better* day."

Bian. Am I your bird? I mean to fhift my bufh,
And then purfue me as you draw your bow :—
You are welcome all.

      [*Exeunt* BIANCA, KATHARINA, *and* Widow.

Pet. She hath prevented me.—Here, fignior
      Tranio,
This bird you aim'd at, though you hit her not;
Therefore, a health to all that fhot and mifs'd.

Tra. O, fir, Lucentio flipp'd me like his grey-
      hound,
Which runs himfelf, and catches for his mafter.

Pet. A good fwift[6] fimile, but fomething currifh.

Tra. 'Tis well, fir, that you hunted for yourfelf;
'Tis thought, your deer does hold you at a bay.

Bap. O ho, Petruchio, Tranio hits you now.

Luc. I thank thee for that gird, good Tranio.[7]

Hor. Confefs, confefs; hath he not hit you here?

Pet. 'A has a little gall'd me, I confefs;
And, as the jeft did glance away from me,
'Tis ten to one it maim'd you two outright.[8]

Bap. Now, in good fadnefs, fon Petruchio,
I think thou haft the verieft fhrew of all.

Again, in *Macbeth*:
    " ——go not my horfe the *better*——."
i. e. if he does not go *well*. STEEVENS.

  [6] ——*fwift*—] befides the original fenfe of *fpeedy in motion*,
fignified *witty, quick-witted*. So, in *As you Like it*, the Duke fays
of the Clown, " He is very *fwift* and fententious." *Quick* is
now ufed in almoft the fame fenfe as *nimble* was in the age after
that of our author. Heylin fays of Hales, that *he had known
Laud for a* nimble *difputant*. JOHNSON.

  [7] ——*that* gird, *good Tranio*.] A *gird* is a *farcafm*, a gibe. So,
in Stephen Goffon's *School of Abufe*, 1579: " Curculio may chatte
till his heart ake, ere any be offended with his *gyrdes*."
                                STEEVENS.

  [8] ——*you* two *outright*.] Old copy—you *too*. Corrected by
Mr. Rowe. MALONE.

Pet. Well, I fay—no: and therefore, for affu_
  rance,[9]
Let's each one fend unto his wife;[2]

9 ——for *affurance,*] Inftead of *for* the original copy has *fir.*
Corrected by the editor of the fecond folio. MALONE.

2 *Let's each one fend unto his wife;*] Thus in the original play:
" *Feran.* Come, gentlemen; nowe that fupper's done,
" How fhall we fpend the time til we go to bed?
" *Aurel.* Faith, if you wil, in trial of our wives,
" Who wil come fooneft at their hufbands cal.
" *Pol.* Nay, then, *Ferando,* he muft needes fit out;
" For he may cal, I thinke, til he be weary,
" Before his wife wil come before fhe lift.
" *Feran.* 'Tis wel for you that have fuch gentle wives:
" Yet in this trial wil I not fit out;
" It may be *Kate* wil come as foone as I do fend.
" *Aurel.* My wife comes fooneft, for a hundred pound.
" *Pol.* I take it. Ile lay as much to yours,
" That my wife comes as foone as I do fend.
" *Aurel.* How now, *Ferando!* you dare not lay, belike.
" *Feran.* Why true, I dare not lay indeed:
" But how? So little mony on fo fure a thing.
" A hundred pound! Why I have laid as much
" Upon my dog in running at a deere.
" She fhall not come fo far for fuch a trifle:
" But wil you lay five hundred markes with me?
" And whofe wife fooneft comes, when he doth cal,
" And fhewes herfelfe moft loving unto him,
" Let him injoy the wager I have laid:
" Now what fay you? Dare you adventure thus?
" *Pol.* I, were it a thoufand pounds, I durft prefume
" On my wife's love: and I wil lay with thee,
                 Enter Alfonfo.
" *Alfon.* How now fons! What in conference fo hard?
" May I, without offence, know where about?
" *Aurel.* Faith, father, a waighty caufe, about our wives:
" Five hundred markes already we have laid;
" And he whofe wife doth fhew moft love to him,
" He muft injoy the wager to himfelfe.
" *Alfn.* Why then *Ferando,* he is fure to lofe it:
" I promife thee fon, thy wife wil hardly come;
" And therefore I would not wifh thee lay fo much..
" *Feran.* Tufh, father; were it ten times more,

And he, whofe wife is moft obedient
To come at firft when he doth fend for her,
Shall win the wager which we will propofe.

" I durft adventure on my lovely *Kate*:—
" But if I lofe, Ile pay, and fo fhal you.
  " *Aurel.* Upon mine honor, if I lofe, Ile pay.
  " *Pol.* And fo wil I upon my faith, I vow.
  " *Feran.* Then fit we downe, and let us fend for them.
  " *Alfon.* I promife thee *Ferando*, I am afraid thou wilt lofe.
  " *Aurel.* Ile fend for my wife firft : *Valeria*,
" Go bid your miftris come to me.
  " *Val.* I wil, my lord.   [*Exit* Valeria.
  " *Aurel.* Now for my hundred pound:—
" Would any lay ten hundred more with me,
" I know I fhould obtain it by her love.
  " *Feran.* I pray God, you have laid too much already.
  " *Aurel.* Truft me, *Ferando*, I am fure you have;
" For you, I dare prefume, have loft it al.

      " *Enter* Valeria *againe.*
" Now, firha, what faies your miftris?
  " *Val.* She is fomething bufie, but fheele come anone.
  " *Feran.* Why fo: did I not tel you this before?
" She was bufie, and cannot come.
  " *Aurel.* I pray God, your wife fend you fo good an anfwere:
" She may be bufie, yet fhe faies fheele come.
  " *Feran.* Wel, wel: *Polidor*, fend you for your wife.
  " *Pol.* Agreed. Boy, defire your miftris to come hither.
  " *Boy.* I wil, fir.   [*Exit.*
  " *Feran.* I, fo, fo; he defires hir to come.
  " *Alfon. Polidor*, I dare prefume for thee,
" I thinke thy wife wil not denie to come;
" And I do marvel much, *Aurelius*,
" That your wife came not when you fent for her.

      " *Enter the Boy againe.*
  " *Pol.* Now, wher's your miftris?
  " *Boy.* She bade me tell you that fhee will not come:
" And you have any bufineffe, you muft come to her.
  " *Feran.* O monftrous intollerable prefumption,
" Worfe then a blafing ftar, or fnow at midfummer,
" Earthquakes, or any thing unfeafonable!
" She will not come; but he muft come to hir.
  " *Pol.* Wel, fir, I pray you, let's heare what
" Anfwere your wife will make.
  " *Feran.* Sirha, command your miftris to come
" To me prefently.   [*Exit* Sander.

Hor. Content;——What is the wager?

Luc.   Twenty crowns,

" *Aurel.* I thinke, my wife, for all fhe did not come,
" Wil prove moft kind; for now I have no feare,
" For I am fure *Ferando's* wife, fhe will not come.
" *Feran.* The more's the pitty; then I muft lofe.
                " *Enter* Kate *and* Sander.
" But I have won, for fee where *Kate* doth come.
" *Kate.* Sweete hufband, did you fend for me?
" *Feran.* I did, my love, I fent for thee to come:
" Come hither, *Kate:* What's that upon thy head?
" *Kate.* Nothing, hufband, but my cap, I thinke.
" *Feran.* Pul it off and tread it under thy feet;
" 'Tis foolifh; I wil not have thee weare it.
                    [*She takes off her cap, and treads on it.*
" *Pol.* Oh wonderful metamorphofis!
" *Aurel.* This is a wonder, almoft paft beleefe.
" *Feran.* This is a token of her true love to me;
" And yet Ile try her further you fhall fee.
" Come hither, *Kate:* Where are thy fifters?
" *Kate.* They be fitting in the bridal chamber.
" *Feran.* Fetch them hither; and if they will not come,
" Bring them perforce, and make them come with thee.
" *Kate.* I will.
" *Alfon.* I promife thee, *Ferando,* I would have fworne
" Thy wife would ne'er have done fo much for thee.
" *Feran.* But you fhal fee fhe wil do more then this;
" For fee where fhe brings her fifters forth by force.
" *Enter* Kate, *thrufting* Phylema *and* Emelia *before her, and makes*
                them come unto their hufbands cal.
" *Kate.* See hufband, I have brought them both.
" *Feran.* 'Tis wel done, *Kate,*
" *Emel.* I fure; and like a loving peece, you're worthy
" To have great praife for this attempt.
" *Phyle.* I, for making a foole of herfelfe and us.
" *Aurel.* Befhrew thee, *Phylema,* thou haft
" Loft me a hundred pound to night;
" For I did lay that thou wouldft firft have come,
" *Pol.* But, thou, *Emelia,* haft loft me a great deal more,
" *Emel.* You might have kept it better then?
" Who bade you lay?
" *Feran.* Now, lovely *Kate,* before their hufbands here,
" I prethee tel unto thefe head-ftrong women
" What dewty wives do owe unto their hufbands.

Pet. Twenty crowns!
I'll venture so much on my hawk, or hound,
But twenty times so much upon my wife.

" *Kate.* Then, you that live thus by your pampered wils,
" Now list to me, and marke what I shall say.—
" Th' eternal power, that with his only breath,
" Shall cause this end, and this beginning frame,
" Not in time, nor before time, but with time confus'd,
" For al the course of yeares, of ages, months,
" Of seasons temperate, of dayes and houres,
" Are tun'd and stopt by measure of his hand.
" The first world was a forme without a forme,
" A heape confus'd, a mixture al deform'd,
" A gulfe of gulfes, a body bodilesse,
" Where al the elements were orderlesse,
" Before the great commander of the world,
" The king of kings, the glorious God of heaven,
" Who in six daies did frame his heavenly worke,
" And made al things to stand in perfect course.
" Then to his image he did make a man,
" Olde *Adam*, and from his side asleepe,
" A rib was taken; of which the Lord did make
" The woe of man, so term'd by *Adam* then,
" Woman, for that by her came sinne to us,
" And for her sinne was *Adam* doom'd to die.
" As *Sara* to her husband, so should we
" Obey them, love them, keepe and nourish them,
" If they by any meanes do want our helpes:
" Laying our hands under their feet to tread,
" If that by that we might procure their ease;
" And, for a president, Ile first begin,
" And lay my hand under my husband's feet.
　　　　　　　[*She laies her hand under her husband's feet.*
" *Feran.* Inough sweet; the wager thou hast won;
" And they, I am sure, cannot deny the same.
" *Alfon.* I, *Ferando*, the wager thou hast won;
" And for to shew thee how I am pleas'd in this,
" A hundred pounds I freely give thee more,
" Another dowry for another daughter,
" For she is not the same she was before.
" *Feran.* Thanks, sweet father; gentlemen, good night;
" For *Kate* and I will leave you for to-night:

Luc. A hundred then.

Hor.   Content.

Pet.   A match; 'tis done.

Hor. Who fhall begin?

Luc.   That will I.   Go,
Biondello, bid your miftrefs come to me.

Bion. I go.   [*Exit.*

Bap. Son, I will be your half, Bianca comes.

Luc. I'll have no halves; I'll bear it all myfelf.

Re-enter BIONDELLO.

How now! what news?

Bion.   Sir, my miftrefs fends you word
That fhe is bufy, and fhe cannot come.

" 'Tis *Kate* and I am wed, and you are fped :
" And fo farewell, for we will to our bed.
                    [*Exeunt* Ferando, Kate, *and* Sander.
   " *Alfon.* Now *Aurelius*, what fay you to this?
   " *Aurel.* Beleeve me, father I rejoyce to fee
" *Ferando* and his wife fo lovingly agree.
          [*Exeunt* Aurelius *and* Phylema, *and* Alfonfo *and* Valeria.
   " *Emel.* How now, *Polidor?* in a dumpe! What faift thou
man ?
   " *Pol.* I fay, thou art a fhrew.
   " *Emel.* That's better than a fheepe.
   " *Pol.* Well, fince 'tis done, come, let's goe.
                    [*Exeunt* Polidor *and* Emilia.
" *Then enter two, bearing of* Slie *in his own apparell againe, and
leaves him where they found him, and then goes out: then enters the*
Tapfter.
   " *Tapfter.* Now that the darkefome night is overpaft,
" And dawning day appeares in chriftall fkie,
" Now muft I hafte abroade: but foft! who's this?
" What *Slie?* o wondrous! hath he laine heere all night?
" Ile wake him; I thinke hee's ftarved by this,
" But that his belly was fo ftufft with ale:
" What now *Slie!* awake for fhame."—&c. STEEVENS.

Pet. How! fhe is bufy, and fhe cannot come!
Is that an anfwer?

Gre.   Ay, and a kind one too:
Pray God, fir, your wife fend you not a worfe.

Pet. I hope, better.

Hor. Sirrah, Biondello, go, and entreat my wife
To come to me forthwith.   [*Exit* Biondello.

Pet.   O, ho! entreat her!
Nay, then fhe needs muft come.

Hor.   I am afraid, fir,
Do what you can, yours will not be entreated.

Re-enter Biondello.

Now, where's my wife?

Bion. She fays, you have fome goodly jeft in hand;
She will not come; fhe bids you come to her.

Pet. Worfe and worfe; fhe will not come! O vile,
Intolerable, not to be endur'd!
Sirrah, Grumio, go to your miftrefs;
Say, I command her come to me.   [*Exit* Grumio.

Hor. I know her anfwer.

Pet.   What?

Hor.   She will not come.[3]

Pet. The fouler fortune mine, and there an end.

Enter Katharina.

Bap. Now, by my holidame, here comes Katha-
        rina!

Kath. What is your will, fir, that you fend for me?

---

[3] *She will not* come.] I have added the word—*come*, to complete the meafure, which was here defective; as indeed it is, almoft
irremediably, in feveral parts of the prefent fcene.   Steevens.

Pet. Where is your fifter, and Hortenfio's wife?

Kath. They fit conferring by the parlour fire.

Pet. Go, fetch them hither; if they deny to
  come,
Swinge me them foundly forth unto their hufbands:
Away, I fay, and bring them hither ftraight.
       [Exit KATHARINA.

Luc. Here is a wonder, if you talk of a wonder.

Hor. And fo it is; I wonder, what it bodes.

Pet. Marry, peace it bodes, and love, and quiet
  life,
And awful rule, and right fupremacy;
And, to be fhort, what not, that's fweet and happy.

Bap. Now fair befal thee, good Petruchio!
The wager thou haft won; and I will add
Unto their loffes twenty thoufand crowns;
Another dowry to another daughter,
For fhe is chang'd, as fhe had never been.

Pet. Nay, I will win my wager better yet;
And fhow more fign of her obedience,
Her new-built virtue and obedience.

Re-enter KATHARINA, *with* BIANCA *and* Widow.

See, where fhe comes; and brings your froward
  wives
As prifoners to her womanly perfuafion.—
Katharine, that cap of yours becomes you not;
Off with that bauble, throw it under foot.
  *[*KATHARINA *pulls off her cap, and throws it
  down.*

Wid. Lord, let me never have a caufe to figh,
Till I be brought to fuch a filly pafs!

Bian. Fie! what a foolifh duty call you this?

Luc. I would, your duty were as foolifh too:
The wifdom of your duty, fair Bianca,
Hath coft me an hundred crowns² fince fupper-
 time.

Bian. The more fool you, for laying on my duty.

Pet. Katharine, I charge thee, tell thefe head-
 ftrong women
What duty they do owe their lords and hufbands.

Wid. Come, come, you're mocking; we will
 have no telling.

Pet. Come on, I fay; and firft begin with her.

Wid. She fhall not.

Pet. I fay, fhe fhall;—and firft begin with her.

Kath. Fie, fie! unknit that threat'ning unkind
 brow;
And dart not fcornful glances from thofe eyes,
To wound thy lord, thy king, thy governor:
It blots thy beauty, as frofts bite the meads;³
Confounds thy fame, as whirlwinds fhake fair buds;
And in no fenfe is meet, or amiable.
A woman mov'd, is like a fountain troubled,
Muddy, ill-feeming, thick, bereft of beauty;
And, while it is fo, none fo dry or thirfty
Will deign to fip, or touch one drop of it.
Thy hufband is thy lord, thy life, thy keeper,
Thy head, thy fovereign; one that cares for thee,
And for thy maintenance: commits his body

---

² —— an *hundred crowns*—] Old copy—*five* hundred. Corrected by Mr. Pope. In the MS. from which our author's plays
were printed, probably numbers were always expreffed in figures,
which has been the occafion of many miftakes in the early editions.
 Malone.

³ —— as *frofts bite the meads*;] The old copy reads—frofts *do*
bite. The correction was made by the editor of the fecond folio.
 Malone.

To painful labour, both by fea and land;
To watch the night in ftorms, the day in cold,
While thou lieft warm at home, fecure and fafe,
And craves no other tribute at thy hands,
But love, fair looks, and true obedience;—
Too little payment for fo great a debt.
Such duty as the fubject owes the prince,
Even fuch, a woman oweth to her hufband :
And, when fhe's froward, peevifh, fullen, four,
And, not obedient to his honeft will,
What is fhe, but a foul contending rebel,
And gracelefs traitor to her loving lord ?—
I am afham'd, that women are fo fimple
To offer war where they fhould kneel for peace;
Or feek for rule, fupremacy, and fway,
When they are bound to ferve, love, and obey.
Why are our bodies foft, and weak, and fmooth,
Unapt to toil and trouble in the world;
But that our foft conditions,' and our hearts,
Should well agree with our external parts?
Come, come, you froward and unable worms!
My mind hath been as big as one of yours,
My heart as great; my reafon, haply, more,
To bandy word for word, and frown for frown:
But now, I fee our lances are but ftraws;
Our ftrength as weak, our weaknefs paft compare,—
That feeming to be moft, which we leaft are.⁴
Then vail your ftomachs,' for it is no boot;
And place your hands below your hufband's foot:

' ——our foft conditions,] The gentle qualities of our minds.
MALONE.

So, in King Henry V: " my tongue is rough coz, and my condition is not fmooth." STEEVENS.

⁴ ——which we leaft are.] The old copy erroneoufly prolongs this line by reading—which we indeed leaft are. STEEVENS.

' Then vail your ftomachs,] i. e. abate your pride, your fpirit.

In token of which duty, if he pleafe,
My hand is ready, may it do him eafe.

Pet. Why, there's a wench!—Come on, and
kifs me, Kate.

Luc. Well, go thy ways, old lad; for thou fhalt.
ha't.

Vin. 'Tis a good hearing, when children are
toward.

Luc. But a harfh hearing, when women are froward.

Pet. Come, Kate, we'll to-bed:——
We three are married, but you two are fped.[6]
'Twas I won the wager, though you hit the white;[7]
                                    [*To* Lucentio.
And, being a winner, God give you good night!

            [*Exeunt* Petruchio *and* Katharina.

Hor. Now go thy ways, thou haft tam'd a curft
fhrew.

Luc. 'Tis a wonder, by your leave, fhe will be
tam'd fo.   [*Exeunt.*[8]

So, in *King Henry IV.* P. I:
      " 'Gan *vail his ftomach*, and did grace the fhame
      " Of thofe that turn'd their backs." Steevens.

[6] —— *you two* are fped.] i. e. the fate of you both is decided;
for you have wives who exhibit early proofs of difobedience.
                                    Steevens.

[7] —— *though you hit the* white;] To hit the *white* is a phrafe
borrowed from archery: the mark was commonly white. Here it
alludes to the name *Bianca*, or *white*. Johnson.

So, in Feltham's *Anfwer* to Ben Jonfon's Ode at the end of his
New Inn:
      " As oft you've wanted brains
      " And art to ftrike the *white*,
      " As you have levell'd right."
Again, in Sir Afton Cokayn's *Poems*, 1658:
      " And as an expert archer *hits the white*." Malone.

[8] *Exeunt.*] At the conclufion of this piece, Mr. Pope continued
his infertions from the old play, as follows:

" *Enter two servants, bearing* Sly *in his own apparel, and leaving him on the stage. Then enter a* Tapster.

" *Sly.* [*awaking.*] Sim, give's some more wine.——What, all the players gone?——Am I not a lord?

" *Tap.* A lord, with a murrain?—Come, art thou drunk still?

" *Sly.* Who's this? Tapster!—Oh, I have had the bravest dream that ever thou heard'st in all thy life.

" *Tap.* Yea, marry, but thou hadst best get thee home, for your wife will curse you for dreaming here all night.

" *Sly.* Will she? I know how to *tame a shrew.* I dreamt upon it all this night, and thou hast wak'd me out of the best dream that ever I had. But I'll to my wife, and tame her too, if she anger me."

These passages, which have been hitherto printed as part of the work of Shakspeare, I have sunk into the notes, that they may be preserved, as they seem to be necessary to the integrity of the piece, though they really compose no part of it, being not published in the folio 1623. Mr. Pope, however, has quoted them with a degree of inaccuracy which would have deserved censure, had they been of greater consequence than they are. The players delivered down this comedy, among the rest, as one of Shakspeare's own; and its intrinsic merit bears sufficient evidence to the propriety of their decision.

May I add a few reasons why I neither believe the former comedy of *The Taming the Shrew*, 1607, nor the old play of *King John*, in two Parts, to have been the work of Shakspeare? He generally followed every novel or history from whence he took his plots, as closely as he could; and is so often indebted to these originals for his very thoughts and expressions, that we may fairly pronounce him not to have been above borrowing, to spare himself the labour of invention. It is therefore probable, that both these plays, (like that of *Henry V.* in which Oldcastle is introduced) were the unsuccessful performances of contemporary players. Shakspeare saw they were meanly written, and yet that their plans were such as would furnish incidents for a better dramatist. He therefore might lazily adopt the order of their scenes, still writing the dialogue anew, and inserting little .more from either piece, than a few lines which he might think worth preserving, or was too much in haste to alter. It is no uncommon thing in the literary world, to see the track of others followed by those who would never have given themselves the trouble to mark out one of their own. STEEVENS.

It is almost unnecessary to vindicate Shakspeare from being the author of the old *Taming of a Shrew.* Mr. Pope in consequence of his being very superficially acquainted with the phraseology of our early writers, first ascribed it to him, and on his authority this ftrange opinion obtained credit for half a century. He might with juft as much propriety have fuppofed that our author wrote the old *King Henry IV.* and *V.* and *The Hiftory of King Leir and his three daughters,* as that he wrote two plays on the fubject of *Taming a Shrew,* and two others on the ftory of *King John.*—The error prevailed for fuch a length of time, from the difficulty of meeting with the piece, which is fo extremely fcarce, that I have never feen or heard of any copy exifting but one in the collection of Mr. Steevens, and another in my own: and one of our author's editors [Mr. Capell] fearched for it for thirty years in vain. Mr. Pope's copy is fuppofed to be irrecoverably loft.

. I fufpect that the anonymous *Taming of a Shrew* was written about the year 1590, either by George Peele or Robert Greene.

MALONE.

The following are the obfervations of Dr. Hurd on the Induction to this comedy. They are taken from his *Notes on the Epiftle to Auguftus:* " The Induction, as Shakfpeare calls it, to *The Taming of the Shrew,* deferves, for the excellence of its moral defign and beauty of execution, throughout, to be fet in a juft light.

" This *Prologue* fets before us the picture of a *poor drunken beggar,* advanced, for a fhort feafon, into the proud rank of *nobility.* And the humour of the fcene is taken to confift in the furprize and aukward deportment of *Sly,* in this his ftrange and unwonted fituation. But the poet had a further defign, and more worthy his genius, than this farcical pleafantry. He would expofe, under cover of this mimic fiction, the truly ridiculous figure of men of rank and quality, when they employ their great advantages of *place and fortune,* to no better purpofes, than the foft and felfifh gratification of their own intemperate paffions: Of *thofe,* who take the mighty privilege of *defcent* and *wealth* to live in the freer indulgence of thofe pleafures, which the beggar as fully enjoys, and with infinitely more propriety and confiftency of character, than their *lordfhips.*

" To give a poignancy to his fatire, the poet makes a *man of quality* himfelf, juft returned from the chace, with all his mind intent upon his pleafures, contrive this metamorphofis of the beggar, in the way of fport and derifion only; not confidering, how feverely the jeft was going to turn upon himfelf. His firft reflections, on feeing this brutal drunkard, are excellent:

' O! monftrous beaft! how like a fwine he lies!
' Grim death! how foul and loathfome is thy image!'

" The *offence* is taken at *human nature,* degraded into *beftiality;* and at a ftate of ftupid *infenfibility, the image of death.* Nothing can be jufter, than this reprefentation. For thefe lordly fenfualifts have a very nice and faftidious abhorrence of fuch ignoble brutality. And what alarms their fears with the profpect of death, cannot choofe but prefent *a foul and loathfome image*. It is, alfo, faid in perfect confiftency with the true Epicurean character, as given by thefe, who underftood it beft, and which is, here, fuftained by this noble difciple. For, though thefe great mafters of wifdom made *pleafure* the *fupreme good*, yet, they were among the firft, as we are told, to cry out againft the *Afotos*; meaning fuch grofs fenfualifts, " qui in menfam vomunt & qui de conviviis auferuntur, crudique poftridie fe rurfus ingurgitant." But as for the " mundos, elegantes, optumis *cocis, piftoribus, pifcatu, aucupio, venatione*, his omnibus exquifitis, vitantes cruditatem," thefe they complimented with the name of *beatos* and *fapientes*. [Cic. *de Fin.* lib. ii. 8.]

" And then, though their philofophy promifed an exemption from the terrors of death, yet the boafted exemption confifted only in a trick of keeping it out of the memory by continual diffipation; fo that when accident forced it upon them, they could not help, on all occafions, expreffing the moft dreadful apprehenfions, of it.

" However, this tranfient gloom is foon fucceeded by gayer profpects. My *lord* bethinks himfelf to raife a little diverfion out of this adventure:

' Sirs, I will practife on this drunken man :'

And, fo, propofes to have him *conveyed to bed*, and bleffed with all thofe regalements of coftly luxury, in which a felfifh opulence is wont to find its fupreme happinefs.

" The project is carried into execution. And now the jeft begins. *Sly*, awakening from his drunken nap, calls out as ufual for a *cup of ale*. On which the *lord*, very characteriftically, and (taking the poet's defign,* as here explained) with infinite fatyr, replies :

' O! that a mighty man of fuch defcent,
' Of fuch poffeffions, and fo high efteem,
' Should be infufed with fo foul a fpirit !'

" And again, afterwards :

' Oh! noble Lord, bethink thee of thy birth,
' Call home thy ancient thoughts from banifhment;
' And banifh hence thefe lowly abject themes.'

For, what is the recollection of this *high defcent* and large *poffeffions* to do for him? And, for the introduction of what better thoughts and nobler purpofes, are thefe *lowly abject themes* to be difcarded? Why the whole inventory of Patrician pleafures is

---

* To apprehend it thoroughly, it may not be amifs to recollect what the fenfible Bruyere obferves on a like occafion. " Un *Grand* aime la *Champagne*, abhorre la *Brie*; il s'enyvre de meilleure vin, que l'homme de peuple : *feule difference*, que la crapule laiffe entre les conditions les plus difproportionées, entre le *Seigneur*, & l'*Eftaffier*. [Tom. ii. p. 12.]

called over; and he hath his choice of whichfoever of them fuits beft with his lordfhip's improved palate. A long train of *fervants ready at his beck:* mufick, fuch as *twenty caged nightingales do fing:* couches, *fofter and fweeter than the luftful bed of Semiramis: burning odours, and diftilled waters: floors beftrewed with carpets:* the diverfions of *hawks, hounds, and horfes:* in fhort, all the objects of exquifite indulgence are prefented to him.

"But among thefe, one fpecies of refined enjoyment, which requires a tafte, above the coarfe breeding of abject commonalty, is chiefly infifted on. We had a hint, of what we were to expect, before:

' Carry him gently to my faireft chamber,
' And hang it round with all my *wanton pictures.*' Sc. ii.
And what lord, in the luxury of his wifhes, could feign to himfelf a more delicious collection, than is here delineated?

' 2 *Man.* Doft thou love *pictures?* We will fetch thee ftraight
' *Adonis* painted by a running brook;
' And *Cytherea* all in fedges hid;
' Which feem to move and wanton with her breath,
' Even as the waving fedges play with wind.

' *Lord.* We'll fhew thee *Io,* as fhe was a maid;
' And how fhe was beguiled and furprized,
' As lively painted, as the deed was done.

' 3 *Man.* Or *Daphne,* roaming through a thorny wood;
' Scratching her legs, that one fhall fwear, fhe bleeds:
' So workmanly the blood and tears are drawn.'

Thefe pictures, it will be owned, are, all of them, well chofen.* But the fervants were not fo deep in the fecret, as their mafter. They dwell entirely on circumftantials. While his lordfhip, who had, probably, been trained in the *chaft* fchool of Titian, is for coming to the point more directly. There is a fine ridicule implied in this.

"After thefe incentives of *picture,* the charms of *beauty itfelf* are prefented, as the crowning privilege of his high ftation:
' Thou haft a lady far more beautiful
' Than any woman in this waning age.'

---

* Sir Epicure Mammon, indeed, would have thought this an infipid collection; for he would have *his rooms,*
"Fill'd with fuch pictures, as Tiberius took
"From Elephantis, and dull Aretine
"But coldly imitated." *Alchemift,* Act II. fc. ii.
But then Sir Epicure was one of the *Afoti,* before mentioned. In general, the fatiric intention of the poet in this collection of pictures may be further gathered from a fimilar ftroke in Randolph's *Mufe's Looking-Glafs,* where, to characterife the *voluptuous,* he makes him fay:
"——— I would delight my fight
"With pictures of Diana and her nymphs
"*Naked and bathing.*"

Here indeed the poet plainly forgets himself. The *ſtate*, if not the *enjoyment*, of nobility, ſurely demanded a *miſtreſs*, inſtead of a *wiſe*. All that can be ſaid in excuſe of this indecorum, is, that he perhaps conceived, a ſimple beggar, all unuſed to the refinements of high life, would be too much ſhocked, at ſetting out, with a propoſal, ſo remote from all his former practices. Be it, as it will, *beauty* even in a *wiſe*, had ſuch an effect on this *mock Lord*, that, quite melted and overcome by it, he yields himſelf at laſt to the inchanting deception:

‘ I ſee, I hear, I ſpeak ;
‘ I ſmell ſweet ſavours, and I feel ſoft things :—
‘ *Upon my life, I am a Lord indeed.*’

The ſatyr is ſo ſtrongly marked in this laſt line, that one can no longer doubt of the writer's intention. If any *ſhould*, let me farther remind him that the poet, in this fiction, but makes his Lord play the ſame game, *in jeſt*, as the Sicilian tyrant acted, long ago, very *ſeriouſly*. The two caſes are ſo ſimilar, that ſome readers may, perhaps, ſuſpect the poet of having taken the whole conceit from Tully. His deſcription of this inſtructive ſcenery is given in the following words:

“ Viſne (inquit Dionyſius) ö Damocle, quoniam te hæc .vita delectat, ipſe eandem deguſtare & fortunam experiri meam? Cum ſe ille cupere dixiſſet, conlocari juſſit hominem in *aureo lecto, ſtrato pulcherrimo, textili ſtragula magnificis operibus picto :* abacoſque complures ornavit *argento auroque caelato :* hinc ad menſam *eximia forma pueros* delectos juſſit conſiſtere, eoſque *nutum illius* Intuentes diligenter miniſtrare: aderant *unguenta, coronæ : incendebantur* odores: *menſæ conquiſitiſſimis epulis extruebantur.*” [Tuſc. Diſp. Lib. V. 21.]

It follows, that *Damocles* fell into the ſweet deluſion of *Chriſtophero Sly.*

‘ *Fortunatus ſibi Damocles videbatur.*’

“ The event in theſe two dramas, was, indeed, different. For the philoſopher took care to make the *flatterer* ſenſible of his miſtake; while the poet did not think fit to diſabuſe the *beggar*. But this was according to the deſign of each. For, the *former* would ſhow the *miſery* of *regal luxury*; the *latter* its *vanity*. The *tyrant*, therefore, is painted *wretched*. And his *Lordſhip* only a *beggar in diſguiſe.*

“ To conclude with our poet. The ſtrong ridicule and decorum of this *Induction* make it appear, how impoſſible it was for Shakſpeare, in his idleſt hours, perhaps, when he was only reviſing the traſh of others, not to leave ſome ſtrokes of the *maſter* behind him. But the morality of its purpoſe ſhould chiefly recommend it to us. For the whole was written with the beſt deſign of expoſing that monſtrous Epicurean poſition, *that the true enjoyment of life conſiſts in a delirium of ſenſual pleaſure.* And this, in a way the

I

moſt likely to work upon the *great*, by ſhowing their pride, that it was fit only to conſtitute the *ſummum bonum* of one

' No better than a poor and loathſome beggar.' Sc. iii.

" Nor let the poet be thought to have dealt too freely with his *betters*, in giving this repreſentation of *nobility*. He had the higheſt authority for what he did. For the great *maſter of life* himſelf gave no other of *Divinity*.

" *Ipſe pater veri Doctus Epicurus in arte*

" *Juſſit & hanc vitam dixit habere Deos.*"

Petron. c. 132. STEEVENS.

The circumſtance on which the *Induction* to the anonymous play, as well as that to the preſent comedy, is founded, is related (as Langbaine has obſerved) by Heuterus, *Rerum, Burgund.* Lib IV. The earlieſt Engliſh original of this ſtory in proſe that I have met with, is the following, which is found in Goulart's ADMIRABLE AND MEMORABLE HISTORIES, tranſlated by E. Grimſtone, quarto, 1607; but this tale (which Goulart tranſlated from Heuterus) had undoubtedly appeared in Engliſh, in ſome other ſhape, before 1594:

" PHILIP called the good Duke of *Bourgundy*, in the memory of our anceſtors, being at Bruxelles with his Court, and walking one night after ſupper through the ſtreets, accompanied with ſome of his favorits, he found lying upon the ſtones a certaine artiſan that was very dronke, and that ſlept ſoundly. It pleaſed the prince in this artiſan to make trial of the vanity of our life, whereof he had before diſcourſed with his familiar friends. He therefore cauſed this ſleeper to be taken up, and carried into his palace: he commands him to be layed in one of the richeſt beds; a riche night-cap to be given him; his foule ſhirt to be taken off, and to have another put on him of fine Holland. When as this dronkard had digeſted his wine, and began to awake, behold there comes about his bed Pages and Groomes of the Dukes chamber, who drawe the curteines, and make many courteſies, and, being bare-headed, aſke him if it pleaſe him to riſe, and what apparell it would pleaſe him to put on that day.——They bring him rich apparell. This new *Monſieur* amazed at ſuch courteſie, and doubting whether he dreampt or waked, ſuffered himſelfe to be dreſt, and led out of the chamber. There came noblemen which ſaluted him with all honour, and conduct him to the Maſſe, where with great ceremonie they gave him the booke of the Goſpell, and the Pixe to kiſſe, as they did uſually to the Duke. From the Maſſe, they bring him backe unto the pallace; he waſhes his hands, and ſittes downe at the table well furniſhed. After dinner, the great Chamberlaine commandes cardes to be brought, with a greate ſumme of money. This Duke in imagination playes with the chiefe of the court. Then they carry him to walke in the gardein, and to hunt the

O o 2

hare, and to hawke. They bring him back unto the pallace, where he fups in ftate. Candles being light, the muſicions begin to play; and, the tables taken away, the gentlemen and gentle-women fell to dancing. *Then they played a pleaſant Comedie, after which followed a Banket,* whereat they had prefently ſtore of Ipocras and pretious wine, with all forts of confitures, to this prince of the new impreſſion; fo as he was dronke, and fell foundlie aſleepe. Hereupon the Duke commanded that he ſhould be difrobed of all his riche attire. He was put into his olde ragges, and carried into the fame place where he had beene found the night before; where he fpent that night. Being awake in the morning, he beganne to remember what had happened before;— he knewe not whether it were true indeede, or a dreame that had troubled his braine. But in the end, after many difcourfes, he concludes that all was but a dreame that had happened unto him; and fo entertained his wife, his children, and his neighbours, with-out any other apprehenfion." MALONE.

The following ſtory, related, as it appears, by an eye-witneſs, may not be thought inapplicable to this *Induction:* " I remember (fays Sir Richard Barckley, in *A Difcourfe of the Felicitie of Man,* 1598, p. 24.) a pretie experiment practifed by the Emperour Charles the Firſt upon a drunkard. As this Emperour on a time entered into Gaunt, there lay a drunken fellow overthwart the ſtreetes, as though he had bene dead; who, leaſt the horfemen ſhould ride ouer him, was drawen out of the way by the legges, and could by no means be wakened; which when the Emperour faw, he cauſed him to be taken vp and carried home to his pallace, and vfed as he had appointed. He was brought into a faire chamber hanged with cofty arras, his clothes taken off, and laid in a ſtately bed meet for the Emperour himfelfe. He continued in a ſleepe vntill the next day almoſt noone. When he awaked and had lyen wondring a while to fee himfelf in fuch a place, and diuers braue gentlemen attending upon him, they took him out of the bed, and apparelled him like a prince, in verie cofty garments, and all this was done with verie great filence on everie fide. When he was ready, there was a table fet and furnifhed with verie daintie meats, and he fet in a chaire to eat, attended vpon with braue courtiers, and ferued as if the Emperour had bin prefent, the cup-boord full of gold plate and diuerfe fortes of wines. When he faw fuch preparation made for him, he left any longer to wonder, and thought it not good to examine the matter any further, but tooke his fortune as it came, and fell to his meate. His waytors with great reuerence and dutie obferued diligently his nods and becks, which were his fignes to call for that he lacked, for words he vfed none. As he thus fate in his majeftie eating and drinking, he tooke in his cups fo freelie, that he fel faft aſleepe againe as

he fate in his cháire. His attendants ftripped him out of his fresh
apparel, and arrayed him with his owne ragges againe, and carried
him to the place where they found him, where he lay fleeping
vntil the next day. After he was awakened, and fell into the
companie of his acquaintance, being afked where he had bene; he
anfwered that he had bene afleepe, and had the pleafanteft dream
that ever he had in his life; and told them all that paffed, thinking
that it had bene nothing but a dreame."

This frolick feems better fuited to the gaiety of the gallant
Francis, or to the revelry of the boifterous Henry, than to the
cold and diftant manners of the referved Charles; of whofe private
character, however, hiftorians have taken but flight notice.

HOLT WHITE.

From this play the *Tatler* formed a ftory, Vol. IV. No. 231.

" THERE are very many ill habits that might with much
eafe have been prevented, which, after we have indulged ourfelves
in them, become incorrigible. We have a fort of proverbial expreffion, of *taking a woman down in her wedding fhoes*, if you
would bring her to reafon. An early behaviour of this fort, had
a very remarkable good effect in a family wherein I was feveral
years an intimate acquaintance.

" A gentleman in Lincolnfhire had four daughters, three of
which were early married very happily; but the fourth, though
no way inferior to any of her fifters, either in perfon or accom-
plifhments, had from her infancy difcovered fo imperious a temper,
(ufually called a high fpirit,) that it continually made great uneafi-
nefs in the family, became her known character in the neighbour-
hood, and deterred all lovers from declaring themfelves. However, in procefs of time, a gentleman of a plentiful fortune and long
acquaintance, having obferved that quicknefs of fpirit to be her
only fault, made his addreffes, and obtained her confent in due
form. The lawyers finifhed the writings, (in which, by the way,
there was no pin-money,) and they were married. After a decent
time fpent in the father's houfe, the bridegroom went to prepare
his feat for her reception. During the whole courfe of his courtfhip, though a man of the moft equal temper, he had artificially
lamented to her, that he was the moft paffionate creature breathing.
By this one intimation, he at once made her to underftand warmth
of temper to be what he ought to pardon in her, as well as that he
alarmed her againft that conftitution in himfelf. She at the fame
time thought herfelf highly obliged by the compofed behaviour
which he maintained in her prefence. Thus far he with great
fuccefs foothed her from being guilty of violences, and ftill refolved
to give her fuch a terrible apprehenfion of his fiery fpirit, that fhe
fhould never dream of giving way to her own. He returned on

the day appointed for carrying her home; but instead of a coach and six horses, together with the gay equipage suitable to the occasion, he appeared without a servant, mounted on a skeleton of a horse, which his huntsman had the day before brought in to send his dogs on the arrival of his new mistress, with a pillion fixed behind, and a case of pistols before him, attended only by a favourite hound. Thus equipped, he in a very obliging (but somewhat positive manner), desired his lady to seat herself on the cushion; which done, away they crawled. The road being obstructed by a gate, the dog was commanded to open it: the poor cur looked up and wagged his tail; but the master, to show the impatience of his temper, drew a pistol and shot him dead. He had no sooner done it, but he fell into a thousand apologies for his unhappy rashness, and begged as many pardons for his excess before one for whom he had so profound a respect. Soon after their steed stumbled, but with some difficulty recovered; however the bridegroom took occasion to swear, if he frightened his wife so again, he would run him through! And alas! the poor animal being now almost tired, made a second trip; immediately on which the careful husband alights, and with great ceremony, first takes off his lady, then the accoutrements, draws his sword, and saves the huntsman the trouble of killing him: then says to his wife, Child, pr'ythee, take up the saddle; which she readily did, and tugged it home, where they found all things in the greatest order, suitable to their fortune and the present occasion. Some time after, the father of the lady gave an entertainment to all his daughters and their husbands, where when the wives were retired, and the gentlemen passing a toast about, our last married man took occasion to observe to the rest of his brethren, how much, to his great satisfaction, he found the world mistaken as to the temper of his lady, for that she was the most meek and humble woman breathing. The applause was received with a loud laugh; but as a trial which of them would appear the most master at home, he proposed they should all by turns send for their wives down to them. A servant was dispatched, and answer made by one, ' Tell him I will come by and by;' and another, ' That she would come when the cards were out of her hand;' and so on. But no sooner was her husband's desire whispered in the ear of our last married lady, but the cards were clapped on the table, and down she comes with, ' My dear, would you speak with me?' He received her in his arms, and, after repeated caresses, tells her the experiment, confesses his good-nature, and assures her, that since she could now command her temper, he would no longer disguise his own."

It cannot but seem strange that Shakspeare should be so little known to the author of the *Tatler*, that he should suffer this story to be obtruded upon him; or so little known to the publick, that he could hope to make it pafs upon his readers as a real narrative of a tranfaction in Lincolnfhire; yet it is apparent, that he was deceived, or intended to deceive, that he knew not himfelf whence the ftory was taken, or hoped that he might rob fo obfcure a writer without detection.

Of this play the two plots are fo well united, that they can hardly be called two without injury to the art with which they are interwoven. The attention is entertained with all the variety of a double plot, yet is not diftracted by unconnected incidents.

The part between Katharine and Petruchio is eminently fpritely and diverting. At the marriage of Bianca the arrival of the real father, perhaps, produces more perplexity than pleafure. The whole play is very popular and diverting. JOHNSON.

THE END OF THE SIXTH VOLUME.

Y

ed on

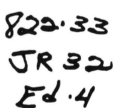

Lightning Source UK Ltd.
Milton Keynes UK
UKHW011520230219
337728UK00007B/483/P